KNIGHTS, RAIDERS, AND TARGETS

KNIGHTS, RAIDERS, AND TARGETS

The Impact of the Hostile Takeover

Edited by

JOHN C. COFFEE, JR.
LOUIS LOWENSTEIN
SUSAN ROSE-ACKERMAN

New York   Oxford
OXFORD UNIVERSITY PRESS
1988

Oxford University Press

Oxford   New York   Toronto
Delhi   Bombay   Calcutta   Madras   Karachi
Petaling Jaya   Singapore   Hong Kong   Tokyo
Nairobi   Dar es Salaam   Cape Town
Melbourne   Auckland

and associated companies in
Beirut   Berlin   Ibadan   Nicosia

Published by Oxford University Press, Inc.,
200 Madison Avenue, New York, New York 10016

Oxford is a registered trademark of Oxford University Press.

Library of Congress Cataloging-in-Publication Data
Knights, raiders, and targets.
Bibliography: p.   Includes index.
1. Consolidation and merger of corporations.
2. Corporate reorganizations.   3. Tender offers (Securities)
I. Coffee, John C., 1944–   .   II. Lowenstein, Louis.
III. Rose-Ackerman, Susan.
HD2746.5.K58   1987   338.8'3   86-33293
ISBN 0-19-504405-3
ISBN 0-19-504404-5 (pbk.)

1 2 3 4 5 6 7 8 9
Printed in the United States of America on acid-free paper

Preface

On November 13–15, 1985 Columbia Law School's Center for Law and Economic Studies hosted the Conference on Takeovers and Contests for Corporate Control that generated the papers for this volume. The conference included a broad range of thinking and research on hostile takeovers, and as a result, the principal papers, comments, and floor discussions collected here will give the reader a lively introduction to current controversies. We hope that the volume will provide a basis for further debate and that it will prove useful both to those on Wall Street and in the business community with direct experience of the phenomenon the book addresses and to students and scholars of law, business, and financial economics who can benefit from a wide-ranging survey of existing research.

The conference was sponsored by the Center for Law and Economic Studies with the assistance of grants from several organizations (listed on page xiii). The center is very grateful to these donors for their support. The conference would not have been possible without their generous contributions. We also wish especially to thank those corporations that have sponsored the center over the years—Exxon, General Electric, General Motors, and Philip Morris. Such assistance is crucial in permitting the center to undertake less visible but no less important activities, such as student fellowships and faculty research grants, and gives us the financial base that permits the planning of conferences such as this one.

Along with the editors of this volume, the conference was organized by a group that included Martin Lipton of Wachtell, Lipton, Rosen & Katz; Ira M. Millstein of Weil, Gotshal & Manges; and Walter A. Schlotterbeck, General Counsel of the General Electric Company. We are grateful for their ideas and encouragement but, of course, absolve them from any responsibility for the result. In addition, we want to thank Walter Schlotterbeck for serving as head of the center's Board of Advisors until his retirement from GE in 1987 and for being so willing to help us in our efforts to further interdisciplinary work at Columbia Law School.

Center Director and Professor of Law and Political Economy   Susan Rose-Ackerman
March 1987

Contents

Contributors

Alan J. Auerbach is Professor of Economics at the University of Pennsylvania and a Research Associate of the National Bureau of Economic Research. He has served as a consultant to the U.S. Treasury on tax reform issues and is Director of the NBER's Project on Mergers and Acquisitions.

Lucian A. Bebchuk is trained as both an economist and a lawyer. He has been a member of the Harvard Society of Fellows since 1983 and is now joining the faculty of the Harvard Law School. His recent research has focused on the legal rules that should govern corporate acquisitions.

Michael Bradley is an Associate Professor of Finance at the Graduate School of Business and Adjunct Associate Professor of Law at the University of Michigan. His research efforts have centered around the economic effects of transactions in the market for corporate control, with particular emphasis on the theory and evidence of takeovers by tender offer.

Victor Brudney is the Weld Professor of Law at Harvard University Law School. He teaches courses in constitutional law, corporations, corporate finance, financial institutions, securities regulation, and theories of the corporation.

Warren E. Buffett is Chairman and Chief Executive Officer of Berkshire Hathaway, Inc., an Omaha-based insurer with major holdings in several other industries including General Foods, Xerox, and Washington Post Company. After graduating from Columbia Business School in 1951, Buffett went to work on Wall Street at Graham-Newman & Company. In 1957 he founded his own partnership, which he ran for ten years.

John C. Coffee, Jr. is the Adolf A. Berle Professor of Law at Columbia University Law School. He also is a Reporter to the American Law Institute's Corporate Governance Project and was Reporter for a chapter of the American Bar Association's Minimum Standards for Criminal Justice. Previously Chairman of the Section on Business Associations of the Association of American Law Schools, he was also a corporate lawyer with Cravath, Swaine & Moore from 1970 to 1976. He is currently writing a book on takeovers that will be published by Oxford University Press.

Hugh A. D'Andrade is Executive Vice President—Administration and a member of the Board of Directors of Schering-Plough Corporation. As head of corporate administration, Mr. D'Andrade has overall responsibility for Schering-Plough's legal and public affairs, investor relations, technical operations, management systems, and acquisition and venture capital activities.

Deborah A. De Mott is a member of the faculty of the Duke University School of Law. She is currently writing a treatise on stockholders' derivative litigation. She is the editor of a 1980 book on corporate governance and of articles dealing with aspects of corporate law and securities regulation, including the regulation of tender offers.

Michael D. Dingman is Chairman and Chief Executive Officer of The Henley Group, Inc. At the time of the Takeovers Conference he was president of Allied-Signal, Inc. In 1964 he joined the Wall Street firm of Burnham & Company (now Drexel Burnham Lambert, Inc.) as an associate in corporate finance, becoming a general partner in 1968. In 1969 he began organizing Wheelabrator Frye, Inc., and in 1983 merged Wheelabrator Frye with the Signal Companies, Inc. In the fall of 1985, the Signal Companies, Inc., merged with Allied Corporation to form the sixteenth largest industrial corporation in the United States.

Franklin R. Edwards is Director of Columbia University's Center for the Study of Futures Markets and a professor at the Graduate School of Business of Columbia University. His primary area of research and expertise is the regulation of financial markets and institutions, including banking, securities, and futures markets. Prior to joining Columbia University, he worked for three years at the Federal Reserve Board and at the Office of the Comptroller of the Currency in Washington, D.C.

Melvin A. Eisenberg is the Koret Professor of Business Law at the University of California at Berkeley. He also is Chief Reporter, American Law Institute, *Principles of Corporate Governance: Analysis and Recommendations,* and is a Fellow in the American Academy of Arts and Sciences. His written work includes *Basic Contract Law* (4th ed., 1981), *Corporations—Cases and Materials* (with W. Cary, 5th ed., 1980), and *The Structure of the Corporation* (1976).

Daniel R. Fischel is Professor of Law and Director of the Law and Economics Program at the University of Chicago Law School. He has written extensively on tender offers.

Peter Frazer has been the Deputy Director General of the Panel on Take-overs and Mergers since 1973. He had originally joined the panel staff from the Bank of England shortly after the panel was set up in the spring of 1968.

Ronald J. Gilson is Professor of Law at Stanford Law School. He has written a number of articles concerning corporate acquisitions and is the author of *The Law and Finance of Corporate Acquisitions* (Foundation Press, in press, 1986). He is a Co-Reporter of the American Law Institute's Corporate Governance Project with special responsibilities for Part VI, Transactions in Control.

Douglas H. Ginsburg, who became Assistant Attorney General for Antitrust in September 1985, was formerly Administrator for Information and Regulatory Affairs, Office of Management and Budget. Prior to that he was a Deputy Assistant Attorney General in the Antitrust Division. Mr. Ginsburg was for ten years a professor at the Harvard Law School, where he specialized in antitrust and economic regulation. He is the author of several books and articles on aspects of antitrust and regulation.

Martin D. Ginsburg is Professor of Law at Georgetown University Law Center in Washington, D.C. His professional corporation is of counsel to the firm of Fried, Frank, Harris, Shriver & Jacobson. From 1974 to 1982, Professor Ginsburg was Consultant to the American law Institute's Federal Income Tax Project on the revision of the corporate and partnership tax laws. Currently, he serves as a member of the ABA Tax Section Council.

Harry J. Gray is Chairman and Chief Executive Officer of United Technologies. Currently, he is also a Director of Citicorp and Citibank, New York City; Union Carbide; The Council for the United States and Italy; and is Chairman of the Board of Directors of the National Science Center for the Communications and Electronics Foundation. Mr. Gray also serves as a member of the President's National Security Telecommunications Advisory Committee.

Edward S. Herman is a Professor of Finance, Wharton School, University of Pennsylvania. He is a specialist in financial institutions, financial regulation, and corporate control and conflict-of-interest issues. He is the author of *Conflicts of Interest: Commercial Bank Trust Departments* (1975) and *Corporate Control, Corporate Power* (1981).

Gregg A. Jarrell has served as Chief Economist of the U.S. Securities and Exchange Commission since April 1984. He has published several articles on the economics of tender offer regulation and was a member of the SEC Advisory Committee on Tender Offer Policy (February through April 1983).

Michael C. Jensen is the LaClare Professor of Finance and Business Administration at the Graduate School of Management, University of Rochester, and Professor of Business Administration at the Harvard Business School. He is also Director of the Managerial Economics Research Center at the University of Rochester. Professor Jensen has written on a wide range of economic, finance, and business-related topics. He is the editor of *The Modern Theory of Corporate Finance* (with Clifford W. Smith, Jr., 1984) and *Studies in the Theory of Capital Markets* (1972).

William Kenneth Jones is Milton Handler Professor of Trade Regulations, Columbia University Law School.

Warren A. Law is the Edmund Cogswell Converse Professor of Finance at the Harvard Business School, where he has been a faculty member since 1958, and at various times has been Chairman of the International Business Area and of the Program for Management Development. He is a director of several firms, in which role he has been on both sides of the takeover game.

Saul Levmore is a professor at the University of Virginia School of Law. His most recent work in the corporate area has included "The Appraisal Remedy and the Goals of Corporate Law" (with H. Kanda), in 32 *U.C.L.A. Law Review* 429 (1985), and "Efficient Markets and Puzzling Intermediaries," in 70 *Virginia Law Review* 645 (1984).

Louis Lowenstein is a Professor of Law, Columbia University, where he teaches corporate finance. Prior to joining the faculty in 1980, he was president of Supermarkets General Corporation, Woodbridge, New Jersey, a diversified retailer. Mr. Lowenstein was a Director and member of the Executive Committee of Supermarkets General for over ten years.

Ellen Magenheim is a graduate student in the economics department of the University of Maryland. She is currently working on her dissertation, which is an analysis of corporate acquisitions.

Ira M. Millstein is a Senior Partner with Weil, Gotshal, & Manges in New York City. He writes and lectures frequently on antitrust and trade regulation matters. He is coauthor of *The Limits of Corporate Power* (1981), coeditor of *The Impact of the Modern Corporation* (1984), and the author of numerous articles on antitrust law, corporate governance, and government regulation, among other topics.

Dennis C. Mueller is Professor of Economics at the University of Maryland. He is the author of *Public Choice, The Determinants and Effects of Mergers: An International Comparison, The Political Economy of Growth*, and *The Determinants of Persistent Profits*. Two additional books are scheduled for publication late this year.

Robert H. Mundheim is Dean and University Professor of Law and Finance at the University of Pennsylvania Law School. He is the general coeditor of the law school's *Journal of Comparative*

Business and Capital Market Law and has authored a number of books and articles.

John Pound is Assistant Professor of Finance and Public Policy at the Kennedy School of Government, Harvard University. He was formerly on the staff of the Securities and Exchange Commission.

David J. Ravenscraft is a research economist for the Federal Trade Commission's Line of Business Program. Current areas of research are mergers, structure-performance, and vertical integration.

David Reishus is currently completing his Ph.D. in economics at Harvard University. He has previously done research looking at the investment incentives due to tax-loss carrying-forwards and is now investigating the tax incentives for mergers.

Richard Roll is currently on leave from the Allstate Professorship of Finance at the UCLA Graduate School of Management, and is Vice President of the Mortgage Securities Department of Goldman, Sachs & Company in New York. He has published two books and about sixty articles in scholarly journals on a wide range of topics in finance.

Susan Rose-Ackerman is Professor of Law and Political Economy at Columbia University and Director of Columbia Law School's Center for Law and Economic Studies. She is the coauthor of *The Uncertain Search for Environmental Policy* (1974) and the author of *Corruption: A Study in Political Economy* (1978), as well as numerous articles in professional journals. Her current work involves the relationship between administrative law and social science.

Richard S. Ruback is an Associate Professor of Finance at the Alfred P. Sloan School of Management, Massachusetts Institute of Technology. His current research deals with a variety of issues in corporate finance, including takeovers, capital budgeting, and the determinants of corporate financial structure.

Michael A. Salinger is Assistant Professor of Economics at Columbia Business School. He is currently on leave from Columbia to work on antitrust enforcement at the Bureau of Economics of the Federal Trade Commission.

Malcolm S. Salter is Faculty Chairman of the International Senior Managers Program. He is also a member of the Faculty of the John F. Kennedy School of Government, where he leads a research seminar on Industrial Governance. Professor Salter is also a consultant in the fields of corporate strategy and organization and a principal of Mars & Co.

F. M. Scherer is Joseph Wharton Professor of Political Economy at Swarthmore College. His research specialties are industrial economics and the economics of technological innovation.

Myron S. Scholes is Frank E. Buck Professor of Finance at the Graduate School of Business and Professor of Law of Stanford University. He has published widely in academic journals.

Joel Seligman is a professor at the George Washington University National Law Center. He is the author of a two-volume study of the Securities and Exchange Commission: *The Transformation of Wall Street: A History of the Securities and Exchange Commission and Modern Corporate Finance* (1982) and *The SEC and the Future of Finance* (1985). Currently, he is writing the third edition of the Loss treatise on securities regulation.

Robert J. Shiller has been a Professor of Economics, Cowles Foundation and School of Management, Yale University, since 1982. His research interests have been in the areas of macroeconomics and financial markets.

Martin Shubik is the Seymour H. Knox Professor of Mathematical Institutional Economics at Yale University. He is the author of *Conservative Investor* (with M. J. Whitman, 1979) and *The Mathematics of Conflict* (1983), and he has written widely on game theory, industrial organization, and behavior of financial markets.

Marshall L. Small is a partner in the law firm of Morrison & Foerster. He is a member of the American Law Institute and currently serves as a Co-Reporter for the American Law Institute's Corporate Governance Project. Mr. Small has lectured and written extensively in the fields of corporate and securities law.

A. A. Sommer, Jr. is a partner of Morgan, Lewis & Bockius in Washington, D.C. From 1973 to 1976 he was a Commissioner of the Securities and Exchange Commission. He has written extensively and lectured frequently on accounting, corporate, and securities matters.

Stanley Sporkin is a Federal Judge of the U.S. District Court, D.C. Circuit. At the time of the Takeovers Conference he was General Counsel of the Central Intelligence Agency (since May 1981) and had had a long career in public service. In 1961 Mr. Sporkin joined the Securities and Exchange Commission, initially to work on the SEC's special study of securities markets. In 1963, at the conclusion of his special assignment, Mr. Sporkin became a staff member of the SEC. In 1974 he was appointed SEC Director of the Division of Enforcement, an appointment he held until May 1981.

John L. Vogelstein is Vice Chairman of E. M. Warburg, Pincus & Co., Inc. He is a Director of Mattel, Inc., SFN Companies, Inc., Orion Pictures Corp., and DeVry, Inc.

Wolf A. Weinhold is President of Wolf Weinhold & Company and has a wide range of experience in mergers and acquisitions, investment banking, general management consulting, and executive education.

Elliott J. Weiss is a Professor of Law at the Benjamin N. Cardozo School of Law, Yeshiva University, New York City. He teaches courses in corporations; securities regulation; accounting, financial information, and law; investment institutions; torts; and various corporate and securities law seminars.

Oliver E. Williamson is the Gordon B. Tweedy Professor of Economics of Law and Organization, Yale University. His books include *Markets and*

Hierarchies: Analysis and Antitrust Implications (1975) and *The Economic Institutions of Capitalism: Firms, Markets, Relational Contracting* (1985). He is editor of and contributor to *Antitrust Law and Economics* (1980).

Mark A. Wolfson is Professor of Accounting at the Graduate School of Business at Stanford University. He currently serves on the editorial boards of the *Journal of Accounting and Economics* and the *Journal of Accounting Research*.

Sponsors of the Center for Law and Economic Studies

Exxon Corporation
General Electric Foundation
General Motors Foundation, Inc.
Philip Morris, Inc.

Major Contributors to the Conference on Takeovers

Alcoa Foundation
Exxon Corporation
General Electric Foundation
Goodyear Tire & Rubber Company
IBM
Owens-Illinois
Procter & Gamble Fund
TRW Foundation
Wachtell, Lipton, Rosen & Katz

Contributors to the Conference on Takeovers

Allied Corporation Foundation
Borg-Warner Corporation
Dart & Kraft Foundation
Deere & Company
David M. Milton Trust
Mobil Oil Corporation
Pfizer Inc.
Schering-Plough Corporation
Textron Charitable Trust
3M
United Technologies

KNIGHTS, RAIDERS, AND TARGETS

Introduction

The ABC Company issues "golden parachutes" to its executives and pursues a "scorched earth" policy by selling its "crown jewels" and issuing a "poison pill" to its shareholders, all in an attempt to foil a takeover bid by Mr. Z, a well-known "shark" and "greenmailer" who floats junk bonds with abandon. When Mr. Z persists, a white knight, otherwise known as Company X, arrives to fend off the hostile attack.[1]

Variations on this scenario have occurred frequently in recent years, are dramatically reported on the nation's business pages, and are followed by at least some members of the public with the intense attention otherwise reserved for contests reported on the sports page. But fascinating as takeovers are, it is far from clear what underlying forces are at work and what their longer-term consequences are. The debate over these questions has taken on a polarized character. Some see takeover threats as a disciplinary mechanism that induces managers to behave efficiently and moves assets to higher-valued uses or into the hands of more effective managers. Others claim that corporate raiders have produced few observable increases in operating efficiency but have, instead, disrupted business planning, enforced a preoccupation with the short run, and tilted the balance sheets of corporate America toward dangerously high debt levels. The sharp conflicts in theory and evidence have produced considerable confusion in Congress and elsewhere in government over the appropriate policy response. A score of bills have been introduced in Congress, but legislators are no more in agreement than scholars. Meanwhile, the stakes keep growing. Mergers and acquisitions have increased in dollar value 15 times in the past ten years,[2] and the circle of those threatened by the possibility of a takeover is wider still.

Yet in spite of the importance of a deeper understanding, partisans have seldom engaged each other in a sustained effort to refine and clarify the issues. To foster such a dialogue, the Columbia Law School's Center for Law and Economic Studies sponsored a symposium in November 1985 that elicited the participation of a broad range of practitioners, investment bankers, business executives, and scholars.

The chapters which follow reproduce the scholarly papers presented at the conference along with the discussants' remarks. On the night before the beginning of the formal proceedings, informal presentations by a panel of chief executive officers served to frame the debate and sound themes that echoed throughout the conference. The three CEOs—Warren Buffett of Berkshire Hathaway; Michael Dingman, then of Allied-Signal and now of The Henley Group; and Harry Gray of United Technologies—reached a high degree of consensus. Their views, however, were sharply challenged by other conference participants.

First, the CEOs were unanimous in their belief that acquirers are paying inflated prices. That, said Dingman, is "where [he] left the takeover party; the prices are . . . just too high, by cash flow, by assets, by earnings, by gross margins or whatever the measure is."[3] But how, the economist asks, can a price ever be too high if a willing buyer and seller agree to it? Debate over this issue turns on whether the managers of bidding firms are doing a good job of representing the interests of their shareholders. Do managers make high bids because they see profitable opportunities not being exploited by present management or because they are motivated by hubris and a will to power? This question was a recurring theme of the conference.

Second, the CEOs asserted that prices in the stock market frequently fail to reflect a firm's long-term prospects under current management. If this is so, then many targets will not be badly managed firms in need of an influx of new ideas and market discipline. According to Buffett, "auction markets . . . periodically . . . price securities at far less than negotiated prices." While most commentators accept the idea that the per-share price for a controlling interest in a firm may exceed the price of an individual share, they differ on how to interpret this evidence. Some claim that the firm which bids for control is willing to pay more because it has a special ability to increase the real value of the firm by improving the efficiency of its operation or by liquidating or converting surplus or underutilized assets. Other commentators, while recognizing this possibility in some situations, argue that the efficiency-enhancement hypothesis applies only to a few cases, in part because the volatility of stock prices makes them poor measures of long-term value even under current management.

In overview, the CEO panel seemed, at first glance, to be articulating two inconsistent ideas: that stock market prices are too low and that takeover prices are too high. One might respond that if stock prices are too low, then maybe takeover prices are just right. In contrast, if takeover prices are too high, then stock prices may be just about right as a reflection of long-term values. However, it is logically possible for both statements about prices to be correct, and many people, not just the CEO panel, hold this view. Since some of the papers presented at the conference found that bidders paid up to 80% over preannouncement market prices, it could be true that stock prices undervalued publicly traded corporations but that competitive bidding raised the cost of the corporation as a whole in the takeover market to an "excessive" level. Possible explanations include such factors as the behavior of the stock

market, conflicts between managers and shareholders over risk levels, empire building or "hubris" by bidders, tax incentives favoring acquisitions, and structural changes in the economy that make partial liquidation the most profitable strategy for some corporations. Each of these factors was explored over the next two days by the conference panels.

The first substantive panel—"Capital Markets, Efficiency, and Corporate Control"—with papers by Robert J. Shiller and Martin Shubik, directly addressed the possibility of stock market undervaluation. Stock market efficiency has always been an important assumption of those who have made the case for the efficiency-enhancing properties of the takeover, because stock price data show that target shareholders profit handsomely from takeovers (while bidders seem to incur either small gains or statistically insignificant losses). Yet if, as Shiller argues, the stock market is characterized by a high degree of volatility, stock market gains do not necessarily imply economic efficiency. The bidder and target could easily reverse roles if, in the market's next permutation, their stock prices were reversed. Moving beyond his earlier work on market volatility, Shiller argued that the historic tendency for markets to experience "bubbles" and "fads" compromises our ability to use the market as a proxy for economic efficiency. Economists need to spend more time understanding and explaining market anomalies, he suggested, before financial economics can be used as a neutral tool by which to resolve questions of public policy.

Next, Shubik frontally attacked the theoretical underpinnings of the claimed economic benefits of takeovers. He emphasized the dynamic nature of financial markets and argued that stock prices will not reflect all the information possessed either by managers or by sophisticated observers. As a consequence, stock prices tend to be biased in favor of short-run performance, and asset conversion through takeovers can be a profitable financial strategy. Accordingly, Shubik argued that "good finance and good industrial policy" could diverge. Conduct that makes good financial sense as a response to low stock prices might not maximize economic efficiency. To correct this disparity, Shubik proposed giving shareholders a more permanent stake in their companies by reducing the liquidity of their shares. Both Shiller and Shubik were disputed by Franklin Edwards and Michael Salinger, who argued that while the available empirical evidence shows some market anomalies, it does not support the more generalized charges of market inefficiency made by Shiller and Shubik and does not suggest that restraints on takeovers would be beneficial.

The second panel, on "Managerial Behavior and Takeovers," addressed issues that virtually every commentator touched upon at some point during the conference. What changes in managerial behavior has the takeover wrought? Two business analysts, Malcolm Salter and Wolf Weinhold, opened this panel with a taxonomy of takeovers. They distinguished between transaction-related asset restructuring (such as an LBO or a bust-up takeover) and more complex operations-coordination restructuring (such as a synergistic merger). In their view, the latter form of combination seldom can be achieved by financial entrepreneurs, because it requires special managerial skills and sensitivities to "the political pressures and social nuances of any large organization." This managerial analysis provides an explanation of why many takeovers do not seem to result in any observable increases in operating efficiency.

John Coffee began from a different starting point and viewed the new wave of "bust-up" takeovers as, at bottom, motivated by a basic conflict between managers and shareholders over the level of risk that a firm should assume. Because shareholders tend to hold diversified portfolios while managers are inherently overinvested in their firm, managers will tend, he predicted, to be more risk-averse than shareholders. This risk aversion differential thesis helps explain behavior which an earlier generation of managerialist theorists attributed simply to strong managerial egos and a desire for empire building. Viewed through the lens of portfolio theory, a policy favoring asset retention, conglomerate acquisitions, low dividend payout, and little use of debt or resort to the capital markets can be seen as symptoms of managerial risk aversion. This thesis also helps explain the "undervaluation" of target companies: The assets of firms that are managed in such a risk-averse fashion will have greater value to shareholders if the firm is broken up in a takeover. Yet because restructuring and higher debt levels expose managers to uncertainty, they resist entering into transactions that maximize value for shareholders. To reduce managerial resistance to takeovers, Coffee proposed alterations in our system of managerial compensation to offset the new level of risk that has been imposed on managers. He concludes that the recent wave of takeovers is forcing management to accept a higher level of risk, and this transition may impose externalities on society generally.

In response, Oliver Williamson suggested that the manager's conflict with shareholders is related less to any difference in their level of risk aversion than to the problem of "firm-specific" capital, which the manager uniquely has at risk. While they disagreed on how to characterize the operating force, both did agree that the manager in the public firm has been subjected to a new level of unbargained-for risk as result of the takeover wave and that this change could justify compensating changes in managerial compensation and other contractual protections. However, Victor Brudney and Melvin Eisenberg strongly disagreed with this latter proposition and, in particular, disputed the "implicit contract" model of the executive/shareholder relationship.

Michael Jensen also postulated a conflict between managers and shareholders. In his view, the core conflict surrounds the payout of free cash flow. To the extent that agency costs are high, managers tend not to pay out this free cash flow to shareholders but, instead, often invest it in relatively unprofitable forms of expansion. As a case study, he examined the oil industry, where he found investment in research and exploration to have been excessive in light of oil prices and the costs of holding these assets. While retrenchment would have been profitable, managers resisted proposals that would have reduced the assets under their control—until they were disciplined by takeovers that in his view understandably focused on the oil companies (e.g., Gulf/Chevron, Getty/Texaco, Dupont/Conoco). In his view, the bust-up takeover has forced desirable retrenchment and ended the wasteful investment of assets in unprofitable exploration and development. He also argued that the increased leverage which may accompany a takeover or be part of an attempt to fight one off can also help to motivate managers by bonding them to pay out a higher proportion of the firm's cash flow. Jensen supported Coffee's view that takeovers have had an important impact on the managerial labor market, which requires the adjustment of managerial compensation, including a greater toleration for *ex post* compensation devices, such as the "golden parachute."

The third panel—"Evidence on the Gains from Mergers and Takeovers"—produced one of the most vigorous debates at the conference and also made the principal empirical contributions to the continuing debate. Each of the papers presented evidence suggesting that a high proportion of acquiring firms suffer losses of wealth from mergers and takeovers—a conclusion that was vigorously contested by some of the discussants on the panel. Ellen Magenheim and Dennis Mueller reported on their longer-term stock price study of 78 acquiring firms that announced mergers or tender offers between 1976 and 1981. Their central finding was that although acquiring firms had experienced abnormal positive returns in the years prior to the acquisition, their postacquisition performance declined significantly, by as much as 42% according to their computation. The inferences that can be drawn from such a finding suggest that the bidder's loss may equal or exceed the target's shareholder's gain. Warren Law, a discussant, interpreted this data to corroborate his own judgment that "social welfare has [not] been increased by any of the acquisition binges of the postwar period." Conversely, Michael Bradley and Gregg Jarrell discounted these find-

ings, arguing that the methodology used to arrive at them was flawed and, when properly interpreted, the postacquisition performance of bidders was statistically insignificant.

Other findings presented at this panel also supported this picture of takeovers as producing wealth transfers from bidder shareholders to target shareholders, rather than real social gains. David Ravenscraft and F. M. Scherer reported on three separate studies they are conducting: (1) Using Federal Trade Commission "line-of-business" data, they studied 27 years of merger history, covering over five thousand acquisitions, to compare premerger and postmerger profitability on the premise that line-of-business data might be more sensitive to changes in acquired business performance than either stock price or published accounting data; (2) they studied sell-offs of businesses using line-of-business data; and (3) they intensively reviewed fifteen specific mergers that resulted in sell-offs in order to understand the factors that led to their disappointing performance. They found that the acquisition game is a search for what they call "gold nuggets, not for dross that could, by some managerial alchemy, be transformed into gold." They also conclude that acquirers did not on average improve the operating results of target firms. Again, there was methodological criticism of the approach taken; Bradley and Jarrell opined that studying sell-offs was like "studying marriage by interviewing only divorced couples." Still, we believe that even a study of a skewed sample can yield new insight into the perplexing topic of whether acquisitions create real value.

Finally, the study by Edward Herman and Louis Lowenstein used reported accounting data to study 9 years (1975–1983) of hostile tender offers, 56 transactions in all. They also sought to compare the profitability of successful bidders before the tender offer with the profitability both of targets and, after the acquisition, of the surviving firm. The principal findings, which were preliminary because a control group was lacking, were that the takeover process seems to have changed over time.

In the earlier, 1970s transactions, bidders were more profitable on average than the companies they acquired. Even though they paid high prices for targets, their performance continued to improve in the years after the acquisitions. In the later, 1980s transactions, the targets enjoyed outstanding results prior to the announcement of the bid and yet the bidders continued to pay enough to yield price-earning ratios that were almost two times the market average. Following these more recent takeovers, however, the bidders suffered sharp declines in profitability, a finding which is consistent with the corporate executives' view that recently there has been a price inflation that is difficult to justify by rational expectations.

Richard Roll's paper provided a framework for interpreting this data about the disappointing postacquisition performance of acquirers. According to his "hubris" hypothesis, the winners in the competitive auctions that result from recent takeover contests are those bidders who most overestimate either the target's value or their capacity for achieving a turnaround. Hence, in an auction environment, successful bidders tend to overpay, and the resulting problem of the winner's curse may at least partially explain both the "overpricing" of target stocks noted initially by our panel of CEOs and the bidder's lackluster postacquisition performance.

Some commentators claim that takeovers are motivated by tax subsidies that bidders exploit without creating real economic value. Again, this hypothesis would partly explain why acquirers will pay more than ordinary shareholders in the trading market, because the latter cannot liquidate or merge the target to realize these benefits. Panel 4—"Mergers and Takeovers: Taxes, Capital Structure, and the Incentives of Managers"—assessed this contention. The papers expressed doubts that this tax subsidy hypothesis could explain more than a marginal amount of takeover activity. The paper by Ronald Gilson, Myron Scholes, and Mark Wolfson is a carefully structured theoretical analysis which argues that the tax calculation must be made on a comprehensive basis, because the gains to the acquiring company are often offset by tax losses to the target company and its shareholders and by transaction costs. These losses are an implicit cost of the transaction to the acquirers. Perhaps more significantly, substitute ways of capturing tax gains are available and thereby reduce the incentive to carry out business acquisitions. The opportunity to increase tax deductions by borrowing money, for example, is also open to corporations that borrow for nonacquisition purposes such as stock repurchases. The authors suggest that in an efficient market the prospective tax gains would in any event be incorporated into the price of the target company shares, thus mitigating the alleged incentive.

In their paper, Alan Auerbach and David Reishus examined a large sample of business acquisitions over the period 1968–1983. An extremely difficult undertaking, theirs is the first empirical attempt to quantify the tax incentives for mergers, and this paper represents only a preliminary report. The authors studied three types of tax benefits—net operating losses, stepped-up basis of acquired assets, and the interest deductions—generated by a more leveraged capital structure. They concluded that there are little if any tax gains from the stepped-up basis or from the increase in interest deductions from long-term debt, but that transfers of net operating losses and tax credits do appear to generate merger tax benefits. As the authors note, however, there is a risk that an aggregated data base such as theirs may conceal significant benefits from some sources, such as a basis step-up.

Discussants were less certain, however, that the tax benefits could be discounted as heavily as both these papers concluded. Martin Ginsburg, one of the discussants, described the acquisition of Electronic Data Systems by General Motors at an aggregate price of about $2.6 billion; he noted that the purchaser wrote up computer software by as much as $2 billion, with little if any recapture. The stepped-up basis could then be written off for tax purposes over a five-year period, producing annual deductions of $400 million, which could not have been achieved in any other way. His conclusion, which seems consistent with that of other tax practitioners, is that net quantifiable tax benefits are "often" available and that "at least some of these would not [otherwise] be achievable."

The remainder of the conference shifted the focus from the causes and consequences of the takeover movement to the legal rules governing takeover contests. Deborah De Mott contrasted the takeover regimes of Australia, Canada, and Britain with that of the United States, noting that these other systems regulate both the bidder and the market more intensively than does the United States. She also contrasted the pattern of shareownership and corporate cross ownership in these countries. Her analysis helps explain why the takeover has not emerged as a significant check on management in Europe but has throughout the Commonwealth. In addition, her analysis points up the much greater emphasis placed by Commonwealth law on equal treatment of shareholders and sharing of the control premium. Peter Frazer, deputy director of the British Panel on Take-Overs and Mergers, provided an in-depth discussion of the British regulatory approach, which in its administrative and informal manner of operation contrasts sharply with the United States' reliance on litigation. Nevertheless, Frazer argues that the panel provides a flexible and effective method of curbing abuses in the British context.

DeMott's emphasis on the equal-treatment rules under Commonwealth legal systems also set the stage for Lucian Bebchuk's analysis of the problem of coercion in takeovers. Bebchuk argued that shareholders' decisions to tender may be distorted by their fear that even if the offer is inadequate, they will be worse off by not tendering. If sufficient shares are tendered to pass control to the bidder, then dissenting shareholders will lose the value of the control premium. Bebchuk offered an elegant but simple solution modeled after the English practice which would require a majority shareholder vote at the time shares are tendered. Unless such an "ap-

proving" vote is secured, the bidder could not accept the offer. This mechanism permits shareholders to tender and yet vote against the offer, thereby protecting themselves from the prospect of being made worse off if the offer succeeds. Douglas Ginsburg argued, however, that Bebchuk's proposal would cost shareholders more than it would help them.

The final panel focused on shareholder voting and a new trend toward "dual-class" capitalization that entitles some shareholders to greater voting rights per share. The impact of this trend is to permit management (or an incumbent control group) to hold majority voting control based on only a much smaller equity ownership. Joel Seligman traced the history of the New York Stock Exchange's "one-share, one-vote" rule and argued that the circumstances that led to its adoption are no less applicable today. In his view, current proposals now pending before the New York Stock Exchange to relax this rule would result in a destructive "race to the bottom" among the stock exchanges and a loss in corporate efficiency and shareholder accountability. His views were vigorously disputed by Daniel Fischel, who found competition among the stock exchanges to be desirable and "dual-class" capitalization to permit flexible governance structures that do not injure shareholder interests. Other discussants took intermediate positions, but all recognized that the nature and structure of shareholder voting rights could be in the process of rapid change.

Where, then, did this conference leave us? As usual, important issues have not been finally resolved, and few conference participants behaved like Saul on the road to Damascus. Yet important data was brought to bear and original new interpretations were offered. That target shareholders receive gains from takeovers was never in doubt, but whether these gains reflect wealth creation, wealth transfers, or even wealth reduction remained very much in dispute. While takeovers may increase wealth by enhancing the efficiency of the economy, it is also possible that even if target shareholders gain, the economy may lose if the new firm operates less efficiently than the old one or if the acquirer can exploit monopoly power. Furthermore, very different kinds of wealth transfers are possible—between bidder shareholders and target shareholders, between creditors and shareholders, between managers and shareholders. The source of takeover gains or losses is, if anything, a deepening mystery, because as this conference showed, there is plausible evidence that many acquirers do poorly in takeovers. Moreover, this conference aired new theories about "hubris," risk aversion "differentials," and "free cash flow" that can explain at least some aspects of takeover activity. The debate will continue, but we believe it will be enriched significantly by the new evidence and new interpretations contained in this volume.

NOTES

1. A rough translation of the first two sentences is: The ABC Company seeks to fend off a hostile takeover by giving its executives generous severance agreements, selling highly profitable divisions, and issuing a security that will permit shareholders other than Mr. Z to exchange their shares for a package of securities at a very favorable exchange ratio that may deter a takeover bid. The aggressive Mr. Z finances his bid by issuing high-risk debt backed by the assets of the firm he is trying to acquire. He is known as a person who sometimes buys a substantial part of a company and then lets himself be bought out at a higher price by a friendly bidder such as Company X.

2. W. T. Grimm and Co.

3. Now that Mr. Dingman has become chief executive of The Henley Group, Inc., and the company has sold $1.3 billion of new shares to finance acquisitions, we asked him whether his earlier comments were still operative. He replied that they were. While he still feels that prices are in general too high, he nevertheless believes that "there are still undervalued stock opportunities in the market which have yet to be recognized." He states that he is "hopeful that Henley will indeed participate in making those investments more valuable to our shareholders." (Private correspondence to Professor Rose-Ackerman.)

1

Hostile Takeovers and Junk Bond Financing: A Panel Discussion

WARREN E. BUFFETT
MICHAEL D. DINGMAN
HARRY J. GRAY
LOUIS LOWENSTEIN, Moderator

For the discussion on November 13, 1985, three CEOs—Warren Buffett of Berkshire Hathaway, Michael Dingman then of Allied Signal now with the Henley Group, and Harry Gray of United Technologies—were asked to comment on the steadily growing level of takeover activity. What did they think was producing it, and as the character of the process changed, did they think that takeovers continued to be useful? The total value of mergers and acquisitions had increased from $12 billion in 1975 to $122 billion in 1984. (It would increase by almost 50% more in 1985, to $180 billion.) The successful bidders, whether the hostile black knights or the friendly white ones, were paying premium prices for target company shares that averaged about 80% over the prebid prices.

While the bidders continued by and large to offer cash to the target company shareholders, many of them lacked the necessary cash or normal borrowing power to finance bids that were by then often for a billion dollars or more. A new class of bidders had entered the picture, and the question was, Where did their money come from? In substantial part it came from junk bond financing, which in turn was largely the creation of a single investment banking firm, Drexel Burnham Lambert Inc.

Traditional bond financing had left the public market for straight, i.e., nonconvertible, debt closed to all but investment-grade issuers, those major companies with strong balance sheets and with pretax incomes that typically exceeded interest and other fixed charges by ratios of 4:1 or more. Junk bonds as such were not new, but until the late 1970s, they were so-called fallen angels—bonds of once strong companies that had fallen on hard times. Weaker, smaller firms borrowed money instead from banks, leasing companies, and other institutional lenders. Except for short "window" periods, they could float public debt only by offering convertible or other hybrid securities.

Drexel Burnham changed these patterns by marketing as new public issues bonds that would have failed the traditional tests by a wide margin. Thus in many junk bond offerings the issuers had total debt well in excess of, sometimes several times larger than, equity capital. And rather than covering fixed charges by a multiple of four or more, the earnings often failed to cover interest charges even once. The shortfall, or the threat of a shortfall, thus helped to produce that new creature of corporate finance, the zero-coupon junk bond, on which "zero" interest was paid until the bond matured six, eight, or more years later. These junk, or "high-yield," bonds, as they were sometimes called, paid interest rates three or four percentage points higher than investment-grade bonds to compensate for their greater riskiness.

Had Drexel Burnham discovered a gap in the public debt market, or was the generally low default rate thus far a function of the fact that most of the bonds had yet to be tested by an economic downturn? While the higher interest rates reflect the fact that junk bond investments are more likely to turn sour than investments in high-grade bonds, are the rates high enough to reflect the risks of this growing source of financing? For the time being, where Drexel Burnham ventured, others feared not to tread. The first-tier, major banking firms soon followed, drawn by the larger underwriting commissions that such issues generated and the more general fear of losing ground. By 1985, the total value of all junk bonds in the marketplace was estimated at about $80 billion, of which about half had been underwritten.

Junk bond financing had a particularly close nexus to takeovers. By 1983, ambitious potential bidders with relatively limited personal resources could turn to Drexel Burnham to finance takeovers of some of American's largest and best-known oil companies, airlines, etc. It seemed as if almost anyone could buy anybody. Where would the process stop? Or should it?

CEO Panelist: Harry J. Gray

Let me start out by postulating that there's nothing wrong with mergers even though no one here has said there is anything wrong with them. I think that mergers also suggest that there may be takeovers involved. I would add that I don't think there is anything wrong with takeovers, either friendly or unfriendly. In fact, I think they are just business. It's all a part of business as we've defined it, and ... I don't think that there's anything to take a moral position on. Many of you are familiar with United Technologies. Let me start off by saying that I think our situation is probably a little bit unique from what a lot of other acquisitors have done. Let me explain and see if I can get your sympathy as I say it. When I first joined the corporation in 1971, I found we had a problem. Ours was a dependence upon two customers which I thought was not a good idea. One was a 99%+ dependence on aerospace,

and the other was a 55% dependence on the U.S. government. Those were really the bases from which we began our diversification and acquisition program. What we did is probably not unique amongst the annals of other corporate structures, but there are takeovers and then there are other takeovers.

I'd like to address my comments to really what I consider the constructive takeover: one where at the end of the road you've built a better business and you've got a better value for your shareholders. In our case we have something in excess of a 10-to-1 multiplier over the time from which we started—I'm talking about net worth or I'm talking about stock value. Cash flow is probably not as good as that, but by most measures, you'll find that it's a pretty solid set of acquisitions and a pretty solid set of businesses. On those things which have not worked out as planned, we've taken the tough medicine and taken the steps to get rid of them.

I submit to you that there's a big difference between our kind of a takeover approach—which was financed out of our own equity, financed off our own balance

This chapter contains the informal remarks of the panelists and the discussion which followed at the opening session of the Conference on Takeovers and Contests for Corporate Control.

sheet, financed from our own performance—and the kind of takeover where junk bonds are involved. It's those that I think we would take exception with. We, as we look at our own future, would not consider junk bond takeovers as a course of action.

Now, we've entered mergers because we felt that it would strengthen our existing businesses and in some cases give us diversification. At the same time we believe that the merger would strengthen the target companies' position in the marketplace. So under that set of equations everybody wins. Our aim has been to mesh our skills and our know-how with the target companies in such a way that the whole becomes stronger than its parts. And I submit to you that so far that has been the case. All this is another way of saying that when we take over another company, we do so because we intend to run it.

Junk bonds being used in takeovers are different, at least as we perceive them. I would say that they add up to an abusive kind of takeover. The junk bond people, I don't believe, are interested in companies as institutions. They don't enter into the merger for the purpose of diversification or expansion or what we would call orderly growth. That's because junk bonds are really used to break apart companies as opposed to putting them together. Frequently, this is even a stated plan of action as the bonds are issued. The bonds themselves are in turn financed largely with borrowed money, and this debt is paid off largely from the target's own cash and assets. And I'm sure you've all read about some of these proposed affairs, where, indeed, the entire junk bond issue is based upon what, in a predetermined manner, will result from selling off pieces. There's no agreement to sell them off, but let's say there's been some awful good "market research" done in order to evaluate the underlying assets.

Those who own shares in the company can make money this way. Certainly, the raiders, if you want to call them that, can make money. Literally, they can come out like bandits. But everyone else, in our opinion—including the company—loses.

The junk bond takeover restricts the ability of the affected business to grow or to provide increased productivity and employment. It encourages management to focus on the short term to avoid becoming a takeover target via the junk bond, which uses your own assets to finance the takeover. It results in defensive measures to ward off actual or anticipated threats. Though these measures are justified when it comes to the junk bonds, they are probably unhealthy in a normal takeover situation.

In our opinion, junk bonds do not add to the national wealth. They merely shift money from those who have an interest in running the company to those who don't. Junk bonds, in my opinion, are not soundly financed. They put the target company in a precarious financial position. In fact, they are so highly leveraged that they are in danger of placing our banks and our credit managers in jeopardy. You can accuse me of having a highly opinionated point there. Junk bonds clearly abuse the takeover process. The market generally corrects itself for abuses. But in the case of the junk bonds, these abuses have become so much a part of the system that, in my opinion, nothing else but legislation will work to stop them.

CEO Panelist: Warren E. Buffett

I took this assignment partly because I thought the commitment would force me to figure out what I thought. I have puzzled over this subject for a long time. And the more I have puzzled and observed, the less satisfactory all the usual answers seem. I didn't always puzzle over how takeover questions should be resolved; but I now bring to it a fair number of perspectives, and those perspectives probably make it a tougher subject for me rather than an easier subject. I have been an investor for 44 years; I've been a CEO for about 20 years; I've been an outside director of a fair number of companies. I know a number of CEOs and directors who, because I won't name names, have been willing to tell me a lot of things about their decision-making process that you won't find in proxy statements. And because my mother isn't here tonight, I'll even confess to you that I have been an arbitrageur.

When I bought my first stock in 1942, I was 11 years old. I bought three shares of Cities Service. Incidentally, it took a long time for that takeover to occur—forty years—and that's probably why my credentials as an arbitrageur are suspect. The position of the stockholder as the unquestioned boss in all corporate matters seemed very simple to me then. I immediately got my three-share certificate ordered out because I didn't want it sitting in street name. I wanted to see that little piece of paper that said I was the owner of Cities Service Company, and I felt that the managers were there to do as I and a few other co-owners said. And I felt that if anybody wanted to buy that company, they should come to me. They didn't for a long time, 40 years after I sold. But I was perfectly willing to have them come directly to me. And I felt that it was essentially like buying an interest in a grocery store—that if somebody came to the manager of a grocery store and said that he wanted to make an offer for it, I should hear about it and make the decision whether or not to sell. The hired hands were to run the operations but not to make ownership decisions.

And I might say that, as chairman of a company that has a number of subsidiaries, if someone came to the manager of one of our subsidiaries, See's Candy or the Buffalo News, and said that he wanted to buy the place, I would feel a little put out if that manager didn't relay that offer to his owner in Omaha. I find interesting the feelings that CEOs have that their subsidiaries should be very subservient to the parent company that owns them, but they sometimes forget that they, too, have an owner, the shareholders of the parent company.

But in any event, I had this idea that some sort of economic Darwinism would work and that if offers were made, it was the invisible hand working and that it would improve the breed of managers. And then over the years I've been troubled by two things I've observed—and I don't know exactly where this leads me—I'll just tell you what bothers me. The first thing is

that over a good many of those 44 years and a good many of the past 10 years, the very best managed companies I know of have very frequently sold in the market at substantial discounts from what they were worth that day on a negotiated basis. It isn't just the weak managements or the companies that are not meeting their potential that are vulnerable to takeovers because of market disparities from negotiated business value.

The best-managed company I know (and I would have said this a year ago when we had no commitment to buy the stock) is Capital Cities Communications. If you'd bought into that 30 years ago—roughly, when it went public—you'd have had a compounded return of 22% per year. And that's been done through management, and it hasn't been done through shenanigans. They've issued very few shares. They've played no games. They've been in a very good business. They've had enough sense to stay in a good business. And they've run the properties very well. It's the best-managed company I know. They treat the people well. They are high class. And in 1974, that company was selling in the market for one-fourth what, that day, you could have had an auction of the properties for and gotten in cash and you would have had a dozen bidders. They happen to own the kind of businesses to which buyers stepped up and stepped up for very fast, and would pay cash for. However, in 1974 the general thinking was you didn't take on anybody that had FCC problems. At the time, they were protected from a hostile offer by the FCC rules, not by ownership. The management owned nothing to speak of: Tom Murphy, the CEO of Cap Cities, owned 1% of the stock and the whole group probably owned 5%. The stock was heavily institutionally owned. That company, if those circumstances existed today, would be gone.

The trouble is, everybody is acting rationally. If you have a very well managed company that is selling in the market at 50% of what it's worth because most companies are selling at 40% of what they are worth, the shareholder who gets an offer for 70% or 80% of what it's worth should make the decision to sell and go into something else that's well managed and selling at the 50% figure. An auction market does not consistently produce negotiated market prices, and the auction market is the one from which owners are forced to make a decision. The owners have their alternatives in the auction market; their alternative is buying into other businesses in the auction market, and if they are offered a price that is well above the auction market comparison, they're going to make the shift. They are going to make the shift whether they own poorly managed companies or whether they own the best-managed companies.

I don't know any way in the world to avoid revolving-door ownership of businesses when there is no cultural or regulatory restriction operating and when you are dealing with auction markets that periodically are going to price securities at far less than negotiated prices. I don't have the answer for that. I don't think it's a good idea that the Tom Murphys of the world are replaced by people whose primary interest is reshuffling the assets. I don't know the answer for it exactly because there is a second problem I'll get to shortly. But I don't think the present situation provides a great environment for managerial stability, and I think today if the Washington Post did not have two classes of voting stock, I think if Capital Cities wasn't perhaps protected by a large owner, whatever it might be, I think those companies would be gone in no time.

The Washington Post in 1974, the whole company sold for 80 million dollars. You could have sold the business that day for 400 million, and only the fact that there was a class A stock with special voting power kept that from happening. Now the bars are down unless a large owner who cannot be tempted by price owns a major portion of the voting stock.

Now the second problem I have is that essentially the people who end up buying businesses in this environment many times do so for very good reasons; this is not a blanket indictment—but it's not a selection inspired by a divine being. In some cases, purchases reflect the megalomania

of people who, through natural selection based upon political skills or hunger for power, move to the top of organizations. And people behave very differently with corporate money frequently than they behave with their own money.

I have a friend who is the chief fundraiser for a philanthropy. Been that for about five years. And he calls on corporate officers and he has a very simple technique when he calls. All he wants to do is take some other big shot with him who will sort of nod affirmatively while he meets with the CEO. He has found that what many big shots love is what I call elephant bumping. I mean they like to go to the places where other elephants are, because it reaffirms the fact when they look around the room and they see all these other elephants that they must be an elephant too, or why would they be there? So when you see the Bohemian Club and the Business Round Table and things like that, it gives you some insight into what moves people. So my friend always takes an elephant with him when he goes to call on another elephant. And the soliciting elephant, as my friend goes through his little pitch, nods and the receiving elephant listens attentively, and as long as the visiting elephant is appropriately large, my friend gets his money. And it's rather interesting, in the last five years he's raised about 8 million dollars. He's raised it from 60 corporations. It almost never fails if he has the right elephant. And in the process of raising this 8 million dollars from 60 corporations from people who nod and say that's a marvelous idea, its prosocial, etc., not one CEO has reached in his pocket and pulled out 10 bucks of his own to give to this marvelous charity. They've given 8 million dollars collectively of other people's money. And so far he's yet to get his first 10-dollar bill. So far, the Salvation Army has done better at Christmas than essentially he's done with all these well-reasoned arguments that lead people to spend other people's money.

You'll find similar behavior with corporate aircraft, where I happen to know what the habits of many CEOs are. They've explained them to me, and they even explain what they get the board of directors to do in order to make sure that it can get by the shareholders and the IRS and so on. I think they probably buy a little different kind of corporate aircraft than they might if they were buying it with their own money. And I think they probably maybe even eat a little differently when they're eating on the company.

And I also notice that when they eat companies, they behave a little differently with the shareholders' money than they would with their own. You see, the equation of the CEO is frequently very different from the shareholders' equation. I might have wanted to own the Redskins when I was a kid. Now if I have to buy the Redskins, that's a lot of money, you know, just to have them look up at me in the Super Bowl with fourth and two with a couple of minutes left and say, "What play do you want to call, Warren?" Of course that would be worth a lot. But it's not worth what the team prices are—at least to me. It was worth it to the guy who bought the Tigers for 50 million because all he wanted to do was put the little cap on that said "Tigers" on it. And he's very honest about it. And he bought it with his own money, which I admire. But my equation might be a little different if I could rationalize some way to buy that with somebody else's money. If I get the ego satisfaction and the check is written on someone else's bank account—say, the shareholders'—the equation can change.

If I owned the *Wall Street Journal,* I would be a more significant guy. I mean, there's no question about it. My personal equation in owning the *Wall Street Journal* at 15 times earnings, 20 times earnings, 30 times earnings—if I own practically 0% of my company stock, it's very clear I become much more significant in life, and the price becomes no object. I'm only going to live once and it doesn't hit my bank account. So I think that you have a major problem in acquisitions in terms of the managers' equation being at odds with the investors' equation.

And the second problem you have is that to be the best in the acquisition game, which is very competitive, and to pay top dollar, there is a great incentive to deal

with phony currency. In the late sixties when the medium of exchange for acquisitions was much more equity-oriented, the operator who could paint the most deceptive mirage for a while in terms of what his company really was worth had the best piece of paper to acquire with. The sillier you could get the price on your own stock, the more you could mislead investors, the better the currency you could use to acquire things. You saw plenty of that in the late sixties. Now it's become much more debt-oriented, and the fellow who is willing to borrow the most money and the fellow who really is the best at selling the junk bonds that Harry talked about has got the edge. I mean, you don't give managerial or ethical tests to these people to determine who should buy businesses. You don't test them by the Boy Scout oath. You simply say who can place the most money on the table. And the fellow who can place the most money on the table these days is the guy who can borrow the most money.

I'm bothered by that; I'm bothered by what the casino society leads to. I went back to Keynes in *The General Theory,* Chapter 12, and he talked at that time, in the midthirties, about the problems of the casino market—believe it or not, in the midthirties. He pointed out the dangers of the American market vs. the English market, because there was this much greater propensity to turn the American market into a casino market. And he had the idea that excessive liquidity in markets essentially was antisocial. In talking about this, he was talking about the question of speculation vs. what he called enterprise and he said, "Speculators may do no harm, as bubbles on a sea of enterprise, but the position is serious when enterprise becomes the bubble on a sea of speculation. When the capital development of a country becomes a by-product of the activities of a casino, the job is likely to be ill done." I think those words have some meaning today.

In the end I'll tell you where I come out. I'm not happy with my conclusion, but there is a narrow range of alternatives. Someone has to have the ability to make the decision on selling a business, and it's going to be the shareholders, it's going to be the management, or it's going to be government or some combination thereof. You notice I don't include the board of directors, because my experience overwhelmingly has been that the boards of directors (there are exceptions) tend to go along with what management wants. So I put them in the management classification. And managements are usually going to resist sale, no matter how attractive the price offered. They will advance all sorts of high-sounding reasons, backed up by legal and investment banking opinions, for rejection. But if you could administer sodium pentathol, you would find that they, like you or me, simply don't want to be dispossessed—no matter how attractive the offer might be for the owner of the property. Their personal equation is simply far different from that of the owners. If they can keep the keys to the store, they usually will.

When I get all through, my heart belongs to the shareholders; I come down with the shareholders, but I would like to figure out ways to attack those problems that I've talked about. Thank you.

Moderator: Louis Lowenstein

I'm reminded, because of the focus on junk bonds, of a conversation that I was having with Stanley Sporkin before the dinner began. Stanley, I wonder if you want to inject your ideas on the junk bond dilemma at this point?

Stanley Sporkin: Yes, I was going to discuss it tomorrow, but I'll do it now. It occurs to me that one way to deal with this problem is through credit regulation. We don't have a model right now, and I don't want to use Regulation T as the model, but it seems to me—and my thinking's confirmed by what you said, Harry—that we do need a restriction of credit. Therefore, it seems to me we know how to do that. We've done it in Regulation T. Again, I haven't figured out all the ramifications, but if you look at the purpose, you could look at the amount raised and you could either do it through a reserve requirement or through credit regulation similar to the

regulations that apply to stocks. I think that might be a way to deal with the problem. It is quite like the model that we know best. It has merit in the sense that if Harry is right, that the problem involves an allocation of credit and there is a need to protect the marketplace, then credit regulation would be the appropriate measure to adopt. I haven't heard this idea before, has someone else written on this?

L. Lowenstein: There was a speech by Gerald Corrigan, the president of the Federal Reserve Bank of New York, in September, suggesting that the level of debt in American industry as a whole was reaching worrisome proportions. Many link that, of course, to the level of public debt. But just looking at American industry, he projected that if we continue to turn equity into debt at the same rate for the balance of the year 1985, we would have, in total, for the years 1984 to 1985, turned 150 billion dollars of shareholders' equity into debt in those two years alone, or roughly the net amount of shareholders' equity that had been created by new issues since the Korean War. Are your concerns about the individual companies, or are you concerned about industry as a whole? Warren? Harry?

H. Gray: I'm worried. I'm worried only if it continues to go at the kind of rate or an accelerated rate that you've indicated. The two worrisome sources—one we've identified, which is the junk bond. It carries too high a premium. As everybody knows, it's not a good-rated security. I'm also worried about the leveraged buy-outs. Should I worry about them right now in 1985? I guess so, but I'd really worry if we had a downturn in the economy. I'm not sure I can tell you exactly where all the junk bonds go, but I'm worried about some places that they go, and that includes savings and loans, because that is a troubled industry as it is. There are a lot of small or medium insurance companies that have bought junk bonds, because they've gone out and sold guaranteed-performance contracts, particularly to pension funds where there is a great deal of pressure for performance. And I'm worried, too, in the leveraged buy-out that some managements have taken a debt structure that they will not be able to service during slower times. Those are the two things that worry me the most; and if that accelerates and you have a downturn, I can see a fundamental collapse in a portion of the credit industry. And if that happens, I think the problem will come to rest on the federal government's doorstep, and that costs the taxpayer money, because I don't think they'll allow all the savings and loans to fail.

W. Buffett: Well, I didn't realize it till tonight, but it's probably our company's New England roots that make me so negative on debt. There's probably a Cotton Mather or something in the background that influences me. I don't view debt as an overwhelming problem in terms of the economy as a whole. And there is a certain rationale, of course, to corporate debt in that the federal government owns a very peculiar kind of what I call class A stock in American industry. This "stock" is entitled to 46% of the earnings and has no share in assets. It's a very unusual stock; it's an income stock. And you can get rid of it. I mean that by substituting debt, you can buy in the government's class A stock for nothing. I've always been intrigued by companies that buy in stock. And when you can get rid of a 46% shareholder by reconstituting the capital structure with debt, that is tempting to people. You might argue that it's surprising it hasn't been done more. It's hard to do with yourself, because you have to have at least 20% change of ownership to satisfy certain IRS rules for favored tax treatment. But maybe if the law didn't read that way and you didn't have to have any change of ownership, everybody would just issue tons and tons of debt to their own shareholders. You might say that if pension funds owned all of American business, they might as well distribute out very large dividends since they are not going to incur any tax on distributions. And they might distribute out very large dividends in the form of debt instruments and get rid of that 46%

shareholder, so that instead of the pension funds owning 54% of the pretax income of the company, they could own 100% of the income of that company.

One problem with debt is that those who like issuing it almost always tend to go too far. Lou mentioned that we own a savings and loan, and he said that it had shrunk a lot. Actually, it hasn't shrunk so much. The deposits are about 280 or 290 million dollars, but now we do it out of one branch instead of 15 or 16, which has certain advantages in cost. We could dress up the earnings of that company incredibly by one of two things. Either we could arrange deals where we get a lot of fees in return for committing debt money, or we could buy junk bonds and show spreads of 400 to 450 basis points over our cost of funds. And if we were desiring to go public or if we were just dumb, that would be a very tempting course of action. We, literally, could raise our reported return on equity to 30% this year by following this policy. And automatically, our earnings growth could be staggering. If somebody were going to shoot me at the end of the year unless I could get the maximum price for our savings and loan, I don't want to think about what I might do in the next few months. Because it's the easy way to do it. It's a nobrainer. And if I lose, FSLIC picks it up. Society is going to mutualize my losses and I get to privatize my gains, and that's a very tempting way to operate. As a matter of fact, it's damn near the only way to operate now. Because if you insist on credit quality and match maturities, there isn't any money in the business. So it tempts people.

I personally think, before it's all over, junk bonds will live up to their name. I went back again to Keynes in a memorandum for the Estates Committee at Kings College, May 8, 1938. He says, "Another important rule is the avoidance of second-class safe investments"—safe means fixed income as he defined it—"none of which can go up and a few of which are sure to go down." And then he goes on and explains why he doesn't believe in what we now call junk bonds. Ben Graham wrote the same thing, stated in all four editions of *Security Analysis,* and I recommend that you read it. When, essentially, you have extreme competition for buying businesses, and then, in effect, the debt holder puts up all of the money for the business, plus all of the vigorish that goes to the investment bankers and so on that Lou was talking about, you're talking about debt of 105% of an extremely competitively derived purchase price. And, believe me, American business is not so stable that you can do that time after time after time without a lot of chickens coming home to roost.

L. Lowenstein: I wonder that someone from Britain might get the impression that the junk bond market is going to dry up, because everyone is against it and there are no dissenting voices. But I know that we have some dissenting voices here. Mike Bradley, for example. Mike, what's wrong with these concerns about junk bonds? I know that you are of the view that the junk bond is only a somewhat different form of equity. There's nothing really all that dramatic happening in the market. Can we engage you on this?

Michael Bradley: Well, you stole my punch line—I am troubled by the use of the pejorative term *junk* to describe these high-yield securities. As you stated, it is my opinion that from this perspective, the "junkiest" bonds in the market are common equity securities. What we are talking about here is the underlying risk of these securities. Now there may be a problem if institutions that are not permitted to hold equity decide to hold these so-called junk bonds, since the latter are indistinguishable from the former. In other words, holding junk bonds may be a way for some institutions to hold essentially equity securities even if they are legally permitted to do so, and this may be troubling to some. But this does not mean that the holders of these junk bonds are naive and do not know the type of instrument that they are holding. If you look at the contracts of these junk bonds, they're pretty much wide open—with very little in the

way of restrictive convenants. So I would just argue that junk bonds lie on the "high end" of the continuum from completely safe, risk-free debt to equity, where there are no promises. But I expect that they are fairly priced to reflect their underlying risk.

L. Lowenstein: Warren, what do you think? It's just equity with a fixed figure on the certificate.

W. Buffett: It may be equity, but if we have a savings and loan with 280 million dollars of deposits and 15 million dollars of equity, I question whether we should have 280 million dollars worth of disguised equities on the asset side. And those junk bonds would be unusually weak equities because the creditors will have a difficult time exercising rights due to the form in which those instruments are put together. Junk bond indentures are not models of tight draftmanship.

I'd like to make one more comment about whether it'll die out. It won't die out without a big bang. There's too much money in it, and Wall Street never voluntarily abandons a highly profitable field. Years ago, there was a story about the fellow down on Wall Street who was standing on a soapbox at noon and giving lectures like they do. He was talking about the evils of drugs. And he ranted on for 15 or 20 minutes to a small crowd, and then finally he finished and he said, "Do you have any questions?" And one very bright investment banking type said to him, "Yeah, who makes the needles?" Well, the needles of the acquisition game are now junk bonds, just as they were phony equity securities in the late sixties, and Wall Street makes the needles.

A. A. Sommer: I want to take issue with what Mike said about the lack of difference between equity and junk bonds. You don't go into default when you don't pay your common stock dividends. You don't have a fixed obligation to pay it off at a given time, and you don't go into receivership and bankruptcy because you didn't pay a dividend. I think there's a hell of a difference between the lowest-rate bond and the highest-rate equity.

M. Bradley: We must keep in mind the practical ramifications of going into default. The real effect of default is to trigger a process to determine whether the firm's assets are worth more in the hands of the current managers (a reorganization) or in the hands of another management team (a liquidation). Just because a firm defaults on its commitment to bondholders does not mean that real assets will be destroyed—they will just be reallocated.

A. Sommer: It's a social phenomenon. That's not something to be lightly taken, I think.

M. Bradley: I don't mean to imply that corporate defaults and bankruptcies are to be taken lightly. I just wanted to point out that in these proceedings, assets will flow to their highest-valued allocation and that they will not be inefficiently destroyed.

L. Lowenstein: Well, I think one response might be that part of the market consists of financial institutions, and they play a role in the economy somewhat different from private investors, whom I think Mike may have been talking about. And the fragility of the banking system is such that we may be aggravating it through the excessive use of the junk bonds. Thus there is the concern that in fiduciary, financial institutions, insurance companies, and banks you have a peculiar class of buyer with potential spillover effects that would be more widespread than if you were selling these bonds to United Technologies.

Unidentified questioner: Let me ask you a question. We seem to be focusing on junk bonds. But isn't that really a symptom rather than the thing itself?

W. Buffett: Well, I think you are right that the junk bond is symptomatic—but the junk bond has emerged as a major tool to pay the top number for a company in a world of competitive sales, just as poor ac-

counting and promotional earnings reports and so on were a tool that people used in order that they could be the winners in the acquisition game of the late sixties. It is an important current tool, and it does have the effect of detaxing earnings. I could make a powerful argument that if all the securities in the United States were owned by pension funds—every single dollar's worth—that they ought to have corporate America capitalized entirely by debt and forgive the interest whenever a company couldn't pay. In this manner they, in effect, would eliminate the government as a partner. I don't think that's a good idea for a lot of other reasons. But it is not an illogical way to attack the question of getting the top dollar for a business, particularly when junk bonds are so easy to merchandise. I get a kick out of the statistical studies that say, Here is the record of owning junk bonds over the last 20 years and isn't it wonderful, because you get an extra couple of hundred basis points after you allow for the defaults. But it's a totally different animal, of course, now. To me that's like looking at the record of deaths from AIDS in the sixties and then going out now and behaving in an inappropriate way.

Michael Jensen: John Coffee presents some data on the makeup of debt in his paper, and it's very interesting. Measured on a book-value basis, debt has a different set of characteristics than if it is measured on a current-value basis. John, what has been the evidence of the last 20 years on the fraction of debt in corporate America? Has it changed?

John C. Coffee, Jr.: If you look at the market value of corporate debt as a percentage of the market value of corporate equity, the picture shows wide swings over the last 15 years, with the current level being very high but not at a record level. If you look at debt as a percentage of replacement cost, the total debt load seems smaller, but the recent increase over the last two years is more dramatic and much closer to the record levels of 1970 to 1971. Finally, if you look at corporate debt as a percentage of book value, the picture looks very ominous and we are at a record level (81%), but this is probably the most misleading comparison to use.

M. Jensen: I just wanted to bring out some facts in the situation. We all know we've been through a period of rapid inflation in the recent past. Asset and stock market values have increased substantially. Those values could support a lot more debt. And if you look at the data, as John Coffee has, the current level of corporate debt doesn't look unreasonable at all.

J. Coffee: Mike, let me add just two words to that, because I'm an agnostic on what will be the future of junk bonds. One difference is who are the purchasers—we are dealing for the first time with creditors who aren't real creditors. If you sell junk bonds to a savings and loan, you are selling them to a company 98% of whose assets are held by depositors who are government-insured. This gives you a classic moral hazard problem. In short, normal analysis does not apply if bidders are selling debt to people who are looking to the federal government to protect them, although this may be a unique and maybe short-term phenomenon—selling debt to someone who doesn't care whether or not the debtor can pay it off.

M. Jensen: I think that's an important point to consider, but let's put it in perspective. Think about the problems of the savings and loan business in this deregulated environment in which we have approximately 3500 S&Ls who are facing, in the next couple of years, the prospect of putting together a commercial lending operation in order to survive. Now, I want you to think about both the organizational cost of this activity and the potential amount of bad paper that's going to be issued while all those new commercial loan officers learn how to handle that job. Now suppose somebody figures out how to do the commercial lending operation on a centralized basis through something called

high-yield bonds. These bonds are, I think, closely comparable to commercial loans. This means the thrifts can avoid the huge investment in commercial lending operations.

I don't know that all is fine in the high-yield bond market, but it isn't nearly as bad as many people on the sidelines would assert. The issue has been blown out of proportion.

The amount of high-yield bonds that have actually gone into S&L portfolios is a tiny fraction of the total. The amount of high-yield bonds that has gone into takeovers is also a tiny fraction of the total. It becomes an issue in the takeover business because these bonds finally break mere size as an effective defense against takeovers—and that makes a lot of managers of very large companies in this country uncomfortable. I understand that and I think we all understand it. What's basically involved in high-yield bond financing of takeovers is the fact that it allows people to buy companies exactly the way you and I buy houses. There are surely going to be defaults. But I'm a little disturbed about some of the things I read in the press. I think people take the "junk bond" label too literally and don't look behind it to see the economic rationale for what's going on.

My own belief is that high-yield bond financing makes capital available to organizations that couldn't get it through the normal markets or could get it only at higher cost through the commercial lending markets. High-yield bonds may well be the most important technical innovation that's taken place in the capital market in the last 20 years. I think it's premature to be talking about legislation that shuts off this innovation.

L. Lowenstein: Let's put to one side for a moment junk bonds, because we had a pretty active takeover market before there were junk bonds. Let's take out the two-tier bids and the greenmail and other tactics. And when you're done, you all refer, in almost the same terms, to the question of the working climate, the environment in which American industry is functioning. As Warren said, he doesn't know what the solution is, but he still likes shareholders. I guess, two questions: First, can you be a little more specific about how you see the takeover process affecting the managers, and I don't mean just the CEOs, the managers of American industry, and second, how would you alter the process?

CEO Panelist: Michael D. Dingman

That's a heavy load. But I'll give a very simple answer. When I first went to Wall Street, I came up with a great idea and presented it to some of my colleagues and they said, "Michael, let us remind you of one issue. The problem isn't buying something, it's selling it." And what prompted this whole discussion was really not a question of how you finance an acquisition but how you get back the money that you put out to pay for the transaction. Somebody ultimately has to make the purchase worth more than the purchase price or it isn't worth it. And I guess that's where I left the takeover party; the prices are too high. They are just too high—in terms of cash flow, assets, earnings, gross margins, or whatever the measure is. And today, the issue is breakup values, and lord knows I've done enough in this business to understand it. And it's difficult. It is completely dependent upon somebody buying you out of your position. Well, it's one thing when you are in an organization like ours where you've got talented managers and people who know how to manage an acquisition. It's another thing when you are just an equity owner sitting back saying, "I'm coming into X company to take it over, to break it up, and to clean it up." That's a tough job. And it is particularly tough when you've paid 125% of what something is potentially worth. Today, the problem is that the prices are just too darn high. Maybe it's the tax considerations that do it, maybe it's the junk bonds. They are here. They are going to be around. I think some of the comments that Mike [Bradley] made about junk bonds are pretty compel-

ling. The fact is they are a form of money. Somebody ultimately has to make the investment worth its price. My concern is that the prices are too high.

L. Lowenstein: Mike, what about the short-term performance pressures on managers, meaning primarily managers of potential targets eager to avoid the trap.

M. Dingman: Well, I think everybody is a target today, perhaps even Columbia Law School. There is no way of avoiding it, and that's a fact of life. Now, I know in the companies that I've been responsible for we have never had antitakeover provisions. I just don't believe in it. I sit in Warren's class: If you've got the money and you want to put it on the table, you are entitled to the company—period. However, to keep good managers and to keep the system running, the people in the company need some incentive. Now, that can be contractual, that can be options, that can be equity in the company. Most people I know who really want to work hard and do a job for a business don't have any money to start with. They are trying to make it. That's why they are there. So you have to devise structures and mechanisms to give people an opportunity to make money. Making money may be buying low and selling high. At the same time, you have to run a business day to day. It has to have managers. There may be too many of them, or maybe there are too few. My concern is that the issue has become a real burden. There's no question that people feel very insecure. How you get around that problem and how people choose to look at their company is something we are just beginning to understand.

And we are also going to find out how well people can run the airlines. They are taking over. It's going to be interesting. Running an airline is a hard business. So is running food stores and chains and some of the other businesses that have been acquired. A lot of it is dependent upon people saying they'll buy a division or an operation at a price that is considerably higher than the cash flows will support.

F. M. Scherer: My question is, when you are under this short-term performance pressure, if at all, do you change the way you actually operate the business? Not finance it, not compensate the managers, but *operate* the business.

M. Dingman: You basically cut back on your long-term development and other things that have a long-range payback, the investments that ultimately produce the big wins.

F. M. Scherer: I'd like to know if the others agree.

H. Gray: Speaking for myself, we try to operate our business based upon a set of objectives that we've laid down. Those objectives get adjusted from year to year, but fundamentally they are based upon growth in the sales volume, a good return to the investor, and all those concepts like dividends, which are based on the old-fashioned point of view of a classical type of an investor. We don't try to run it to be attractive to takeover artists or junk bond takeover types of deals. Now, how does it have an impact on a day-to-day basis? Mike's pointed out you only run organizations with people, and the people don't like short-term kinds of goals. Most of them, if they are over 30, want to get married, they want to raise a family, and they want to have some sort of assured source of income. They are willing to change jobs; they are willing to look for other opportunities. But they'll look within a relatively narrow range of the types of companies. We are speaking now primarily of the major corporations of the United States, which is the only thing I'm answering for. The pressure brought about by these short-term requirements is disruptive. Mike says people are insecure, and indeed they are, if they think that there's a possibility that there's a new set of owners coming in who will change them out of their position. And so they do their daily job with one eye cast over the shoulder. And I don't think we get top productivity out of them, because they are worried about something. Now I happen to think for the time being, I empha-

size for the time being, we at United Technologies don't have the same degree of worry that I see in some other companies where it clearly is counterproductive.

Mike suggested that you trim back some of the investments that you make. In our company we happen to be in businesses that have cycles of investment ranging from seven to ten years. And if you don't make that seven-to-ten-year investment, and in some cases it's a little longer than that, you will not have the product for the marketplace at the right time. Probably the most classic illustration of that is the aircraft engine business where you can be going beyond the ten-year investment cycle. But if you don't put the money in at the time that's necessary, you will not have the profit. That means that you may not have the short-term profit that the kind of investor we are talking about will try to get. The same thing happens to be true in the elevator business and the air-conditioning business. Their cycles are closer to seven than to ten years. But unless you are dealing with a rapid-turnover, short-cycle thing, like a consumer fad or consumer retailing, those are problems you have to face. You have to have a program of balanced R&D investment, and you've got to have something that the people are willing to go along with on a basis beyond the short-term calendar or quarter-to-quarter measurement. That's what the impact is.

W. Buffett: There are basically two impenetrable defenses, and one is to own half or close to half of whatever stock votes in the company. And that's well understood. The other way is to have your stock sell at a price above its negotiated business value. And that negotiated business value available from a sale of the entire company may include not only economic income but psychic income to the potential purchaser. I have probably talked to at least a half-dozen managers who were worried about takeovers. When they express those worries to me and talk about what they should do, they recognize that they are not going to be able to keep the auction market value above the negotiated market value on a perpetual basis. They may achieve that goal during buoyant markets or even normal markets, but they can't achieve it 100% of the time.

These managers and I have seen every fine business in the United States sell well below its negotiated market value at some time. So that is not a perpetual defense, and even trying to goose the short-term earnings or something of the sort can't permanently solve the problem. They don't focus on the short-term earnings "fix"; they really focus on how to strengthen the moat around the corporate castle so that stock valuation is not the only obstacle to crossing it. And they explore with me the idea of personally buying the business, or control of it, preferably without money. They also think about somebody owning a fair amount of stock who will stay put and not try to run the castle, even though he might own a big part of it. They explore various things like that. I've had very few that have ever said to me, "What do I do to get the immediate earnings up, how do I change my managerial techniques?" The interesting question is what would happen if all of a sudden I found out my stock certificates at Berkshire were phony. And instead of thinking that I've 45% of the votes, I find out that I haven't got any of the votes. Now in the 20-year history, even though the stock has gone from maybe 8 or 9 dollars to 2600 dollars, it has probably been sold below its negotiated business value, perhaps 75% of the time. In that valuation environment, Berkshire would be taken away from me. Under those circumstances, I would probably think very hard about how I could stick a few crocodiles and alligators and piranhas in the moat. I just wouldn't want to test myself. It's like being left alone in a bank at two in the morning. I don't want to find out how I'd behave.

L. Lowenstein: There's been a lot of discussion about the difference between auction market prices and negotiated market prices. And thus far it hasn't elicited a response.

Elliott Weiss: I'm glad you brought it up, because it's just what I wanted to ask Warren about. Warren, in your opening remarks, you gave us a characterization of managers and elephants that, to my mind, may explain why the spread exists. You talked about the fact that in many companies—maybe not in the best-managed companies—managers are playing with other people's money and use it in ways, as you described it, quite differently from how they would use it if it were their own money or if they were shareholders. Is that what explains some substantial portion of the spread between stock market prices and takeover bids? And, if so, is there something that can be done about it?

W. Buffett: That's one reason but I would say it's down the list a ways. It doesn't explain Cap Cities in 1974, it doesn't explain the Washington Post, I hope it doesn't explain Berkshire Hathaway. But it enters into it. A dollar you can't get your hands on is not the same as a dollar you can get your hands on. With marketable securities, shareholders felt they were beneficiaries of an irrevocable trust in which they couldn't change trustees; if you got a lemon for a trustee, you lived with him. And people marked down the valuations for trusts run by such trustees. You've also seen it in closed-end investment companies; you can figure out very clearly what the assets are worth, but you don't have your hands on them. In poor hands, those assets are not worth 100 cents on the dollar. But cupidity or stupidity is not the only reason for the existence of market price discounts. There are very many well-managed companies, people that behave with the shareholders' money exactly like they would their own, and those companies still sell at very significant discounts from negotiated values at given times in the auction market existing on the stock exchange. And incidentially, it's a rational price. I mean if poorly run companies are selling at 40% of negotiated value, why should a well-managed company sell for more than 60% or some such number? It's a rational value. That's the dilemma.

L. Lowenstein: Is something about the way the market functions in takeovers that heightens the focus on short-term performance? When you deal with your institutional investors, is their focus also short term?

H. Gray: Yes, I think that's true, but I guess it varies with the institutions. I can tell you some institutions have held our shares, for example, for the last six years and considered them to be a good investment. But they're institutions who have a balanced portfolio. And they wanted a certain part of their portfolio in what are really heavy industrial, not counting steel as one of those, but industrial suppliers to a part of the economy where they felt there would be some growth. Transportation is one part of it; construction is another part of it. And they've been very satisfied with it. They have not been willing to sell out their positions in order to go into something which would give them more short-term performance. I'll say exactly the opposite about some others. And these other institutions are interested only in getting a higher return whether it's 2% or 5% more than we can get. All I can say is, thank God we've got that kind of investors out there.

M. Dingman: I can't resist this one. It's the ultimate irony that the stock market is controlled by the very pension funds that companies give their money to for high yields so they don't have to put in so much. Now we're getting it right back—as the stock goes up, people sell; if it goes down, they buy. And I don't think you are going to change it. That's the way it is. You can court the long-term investor, but there's just no incentive to be a long-term investor. None. Maybe the investor will hold for six months or a year, but certainly not for a period that matches the time frame of a corporate organization. People buy and sell, and that's what's going on. I'm afraid that what's going to continue to happen.

L. Lowenstein: They're buying and selling at a much more rapid rate than they did a few years ago. Since 1960 the rate of turnover, not just absolute number of shares, but the rate of turnover on listed shares has gone up 500%. Whatever Keynes was concerned about was a shadow of the pace of turnover today. Warren, what is there about the market in either its auction or its negotiated aspects that is aggravating this focus on the short term?

W. Buffett: Well, I guess that it's largely in the institutional field. In our own particular company, 4% of the shares turn over in a year; and if I look back two years, 98% of the shares are held by people who held them two years ago. We don't want institutions. We would not get that kind of long-term orientation with institutions. My experience has been that, leaving aside the 10% of individual investors who like to speculate, individual investors tend to be much more sound than institutional investors because institutional investors are being paid to do something that they can't do, namely, outperform the market. They try to solve that problem with activity, and it has not worked.

S. Sporkin: Mike, I'm bothered by something that you're saying here—that you think it's strictly the stock price. You mentioned that the critical thing here is people. You want to get the best people you can to run your company. If you're managing a portfolio, you want to go out and get the Warren Buffetts and the best people to manage that portfolio. And not be worried about whether to buy and sell all the time. Why isn't that a factor? Is that too much?

M. Dingman: Well, there are exceptions. Like Harry, I can name institutions and individuals, big investors, who have followed us for years. By the same token, when you look at their track records, you find that even the best-managed companies go down in value. They go through a period—for whatever reason—of change in multiples. And most of the institutions I'm aware of sell when they anticipate that change coming. Now, the same institutions may come back in at a later date because they have confidence in the management. But they are not really long-term holders who say, "I'm with you from day one." In our own company, it's the same thing. A person who invested in my stock back in

1975 has made more than 500% on his investment, not counting dividends. But people have come and gone. As a manager, I figure there's zero loyalty. Stan, they don't stick around.

S. Sporkin: I don't think it's a loyalty. I think it's betting on a winner.

A. Sommer: To carry what Mike was talking about a step further, every quarter or every 6 months, the companies review the performance of their pension fund managers, and if a manager fails—2 quarters, 3 quarters, 4 quarters—he's out. Now no manager can be right all the time and only have an ascending performance curve. There is a tremendous competition among the managers to make sure there is continuity in their performance, with the result that they have a strong pressure to take their winners on the short term and liquidate them and go into something else so that they can reflect the profits on a short-term basis. That's the answer to your question, Stan.

M. Dingman: That is the tragedy of the market, I think. And it's the fault of the corporations. That's where it starts.

John Pound: I'd just like to comment quickly on the issue of undervaluing long-term activity by the market, which has indeed become a very widely held perception of one of the forces that causes hostile takeovers. A couple of studies have been done recently—one by the SEC—which have tried to generate some data on this issue, because unlike a lot of theories about takeover incentives, the long-term undervaluation argument has straightforward implications. If you believe that firms tend to become undervalued because they focus exceptionally heavily on long-term planning and long-term expenditures, and you believe that those firms therefore become the targets of unwanted takeovers, you can look at the balance sheets of those companies and determine whether they in fact do seem to be spending an excessive amount or larger-than-normal amount on those activities. Several recent studies have tested

this implication by examining expenditures on capital investments. And they've found that, looking at any of these indicators, takeover targets have generally lower, not higher, expenditures than market averages on these measures of long-term planning and long-term investment. So while it's a very appealing argument—it's a very appealing notion of what's causing takeover activity—the facts so far really don't support it. The problem is that it's very easy to test, and you don't see any evidence that it is correct. So I just wonder where else one might look for confirmation of that view, if indeed you have looked at many kinds of expenditures and not found any confirmation for the view.

Unidentified audience member: I don't think there is any evidence that you can make institutional investors more interested in your stock by cutting your investments from long-term projects. It just doesn't demonstrate itself.

M. Dingman: My answer to the question on the long term versus the short term is that it's just today's reality. To sit back and know that you're right, as Harry said, to make an investment of a billion dollars or more today, seven years out, to develop a new engine is a lot of dough. The benefit of that investment is not going to come to today's shareholders; it's going to come to tomorrow's shareholders. Yet if you don't make the investment, you are not going to have a company. It's very difficult to make those kind of arrangements in a volatile environment and to attract people and keep them. Take one of the great companies in America, AT&T and Bell Laboratories. Bell Labs is the finest research institute in America: It can attract people, train them, keep them—it loves them. It's got to be going through tough times right now, although it's a national resource. It's not right, but it's happening. And it's going to affect the Bell System, and it's going to affect a lot of things in our country. This short-term takeover trend is going to affect an awful lot of things that we haven't even looked at. And there are changes in industries that are caused by it. So as we play with the dollars and the junk bonds; there's a whole other game going on, and it's serious.

M. Jensen: Maybe I misunderstood. Warren Buffett was saying that he didn't observe his own or other organizations cutting back investments in long-term projects to concentrate on the short term. Did I hear correctly?

W. Buffett: That's right.

M. Jensen: There also have been studies of what happens when companies announce increases in capital investment—generally the long-term variety. What we observe is systematic and statistically significant positive relationships between stock prices and announcements of increases in long-term—if you want to call them that—expenditures. And the reverse is true for announcements of cuts in capital expenditures. Cuts in capital expenditures are associated with decreases in market prices. Now that doesn't prove that there aren't managers engaging in short-term-oriented behavior. Also, we're all aware that takeovers have been going on at a rapid rate over the last few years. The year 1984, according to a *Business Week* survey, saw R&D expenditures at an all-time record—up 14% in 1984 to a record 2.9% of sales. So the aggregate data is not consistent with the argument that record-high takeover activity is causing cutbacks in R&D. Not only do we have the testimony of several reputable CEOs that they have not observed the asserted short-run behavior, but we also can't find evidence of this phenomenon in the data.

L. Lowenstein: Warren, you started to say before that the pressures to escape from the risks of a takeover are not manifested in terms of reduced R&D but somewhere else.

W. Buffett: Yeah. If I didn't own any Berkshire and I saw somebody out there scribbling away and taking down Drexel's number or whatever it might be, my first call tomorrow would not be to our candymaker

out in L.A. to tell him to quit working on those two new bonbons; it would be to Marty Lipton or somebody at the source, saying, What do I do to build a moat? I agree totally with Mike [Jensen]. I just don't see that as a response at all. For one thing, it would take too long, even if it were effective, which I don't think it would be. If you are worried about a takeover, and a lot of managers are, you're probably going through a time of self-trial when you are trying to remember all those speeches, when you said the company really belonged to its shareholders, whether anybody was taking it down. You don't know quite how you will square those speeches with what you're going to do the next morning.

Let's assume someone told me they were going to throw me out of Berkshire Hathaway, and that the stock was selling at 70% of what it's worth (and it isn't), and furthermore, that I owned very little of it. The only defense I would really have is either to disenfranchise the owners in some way—and to be effective, I should have done this earlier—or to induce the stock to sell above its negotiated business value. But I can't make it sell above its negotiated value all the time.

The investment community leaves me very disappointed most of the time, particularly the institutional investment community. I define an investment as a commitment made where the focus is on the expected results of the enterprise, not the expected price action. In other words, I think that's what investment is all about, trying to figure out what an enterprise is going to do and participate in it, if you've arrived at an affirmative decision. And overwhelmingly, that is not the focus of Wall Street, and I don't think it's likely to be, so I think we ought to deal with the world as it is. Exactly how we deal with that to prevent what I would call revolving-door capitalism, I'm not sure.

F. M. Scherer: Mike Jensen's comment deserves an answer. First of all, the fact that R&D–sales ratios have gone up over the last five years tells you nothing. Productivity growth has been abysmal the past five years, but I don't think you can correlate either one of those divergent trends with takeover action. Second, there is that SEC study of R&D announcements. When do you *announce* that you've got a new R&D project? Over ten years they managed to find 62 announcements. My best estimate is that there are in any given year 20,000 R&D projects going on in U.S. industry. The study managed to pick up 62 of them over ten years. What kinds of unique events are these, out of 20,000, that they selected to analyze? Third, Harry Gray's company, aircraft engines, spends 10% of its sales dollar on company-financed R&D. There are only 2 or 3 out of 250 manufacturing industries that put out that kind of bucks for privately financed R&D. The SEC study has no controls for interindustry differences in R&D, and until you have such controls, you've got *nothing* in the way of analysis.

L. Lowenstein: In closing the evening's proceedings, let me thank our three distinguished panelists and other guests for contributing to an unusually well focused and yet spontaneous discussion. It augurs well for the remainder of the conference at which the various papers will be delivered and then subjected to comment and criticism. Given such a beginning, the proceeding should be lively and well informed.

CAPITAL MARKETS, EFFICIENCY, AND CORPORATE CONTROL

2

Corporate Control, Efficient Markets, and the Public Good

MARTIN SHUBIK

These managements need shaking up—they're horrendous . . . they take money from the peasants [the stockholders] and then hire mercenaries [lawyers] to protect their castle, mainly by browbeating the peasants. So we attack the castle.

Carl Icahn, *Wall Street Journal*, June 20, 1985

DIATRIBE

This chapter has the gall to be divided into three parts. The first, entitled "Diatribe," is devoted to a discussion of the relationship between the law and economic theory and some observations concerning the role of scholarship in an adversarial process.

The second part is entitled "Discourse" and is a discourse on many of the fundamental assumptions and models which underlie efficient-market theory, rational expectations, and much of the microeconomic theory of the efficient, competitive price system. The uses and limitations of these models in furthering our understanding of corporate financial behavior is considered.

The third part is called "Takeovers, Law, and Oligopolistic Competition." It raises questions concerning law, economics, and the fiduciary responsibility of managers and directors to stockholders and vice versa.

Are hostile takeovers, proxy contests, tender offers, leveraged buy-outs (LBOs), and going private good for the public in this best-of-all possible economic worlds? As an economic theorist, I can say with absolutely no equivocation, sometimes yes and sometimes no. Furthermore, as society varies its pantheon of white knights, attackers, defenders, and victims, the accept-

able proportions of how badly whose ox is going to get gored will vary.

As a citizen, investor, and believer in the virtues of competitive markets where they are feasible, my social beliefs modified by professional considerations lead me to view with concern the change in debt structure frequently caused by takeovers and LBOs. The possibilities for late-1980s Insull Empires appear to be growing.

One of the beauties of a competitive price system is that even in a moribund bureaucratic economy such as the Soviet Union, economic forces bubble up and magnify or mollify the factors which the bureaucratic rules were meant to control. In our own system, give a tax break to the small-family farm, and many a lawyer and his brother-in-law, the entrepreneur, are going to become small-family farmers. Allow deductions for interest paid, and Uncle Sam is going to help carry a large part of a debt-financed leveraged buy-out.

Legislators and lawyers are well aware that almost always a new law creates a new group of millionaires. Furthermore, because a society is not static, if the rules concerning finance and accounting are in constant flux, then regardless of the fate of small stockholders or corporate managements, the rule makers, lawyers, accountants, financiers, and even some economic consultants will face full employment.[1]

In spite of the relatively recent interest in the common ground between economics and the law, economic theory and legal thought are far apart. The formal and often simplistic models of microeconomic theory and its stepchild, the academic discipline of finance, are basically not congenial with the subtleties of the law.

The science of a discipline such as economics and the sociology of its application may differ considerably. Thus in a society tribal conversions and religious fervor may overwhelm otherwise staid individuals. Many of us yearn for simple nostrums—cures which are scientific, elegant, authoritative, and simple. Behind many an economist lurks a faith that a Benthamite utilitarian simplicity might pay off as well as Newtonian mechanics. All we need to do is to invoke the magic of marginal disutility of going to jail or the electric chair and the economic theory of crime will spring full blown from Bentham's ear. The marginal utility of the nth child and some approximate indifference curves[2] showing the trade-off between children and other consumer durables should provide an economic theory of marriage and family. We invoke the magic of an institution-free, anonymous, perfect competition complete with delicious phrases such as *efficient markets, perfect foresight, rational expectations,* and *perfect equilibrium* and expect a stern, rational, fair-market-guided theory of finance to show that Widder Brown with her hundred shares of AT&T and Warren Buffett all march to the same drummer.

The law is messy, institutional, historical, and evolutionary. In spite of the joys of an abstract theory of justice, the fuzzy and highly complex processes of society often make it difficult to distinguish the raider from the victim. "It is a thin line that distinguishes a poor defenseless widow from a greedy old lady going for the last eighth of a point." The small stockholder who may or may not be accidentally helped by a Carl Icahn sometimes may feel that he needs at least as much protection from his corporate management contemplating an LBO as he does from an outsider raider offering him a bailout at above-market.

This chapter is a critique of the uses of several of the basic precepts of modern finance theory primarily from the right but also from the left wing. I suggest that like much of the casual partial-equilibrium economics that finance theory is based upon, it suffers simultaneously by not being sufficiently mathematical or institutional. As such, on questions such as mergers, buy-outs, or tender offers, current finance theory has little to say of any value because its models are not rich enough to capture the essence of the process in the struggle for corporate control. But for those of us who are willing to make our theorizing neat, the mere fact that an economic model does not appear realistic to a lawyer or a nonexpert may be merely a proof that these individuals are unable to reason sufficiently abstractly.

The poor judge who might be cowed by the learned Professor Enterprise averring under oath that the just, right, and fair price for a stock whose controlling stockholder is squeezing out the minority stockholders is that which the market will pay (see, for example, Transocean Oil and Vickers, or Federated Development) may feel that the professor is somewhat cavalier about detail, fiduciary problems, and control considerations. But even so, if the abstract essay of modern finance had useful content as perceptive advice about fundamental economic principles, it would still be of great value to the judge. Unfortunately, the major underpinnings of the theory appear only as a reasonably useful first approximation for a portfolio manager who wants to place a few hundred million and have a fair chance of keeping his job and sleeping well, or it serves as an appropriate parable to let Mrs. Smith know more or less what her 100 shares of AT&T or IBM are worth in the market available to her. The theory is of little value for the topics discussed here because the bag and baggage of efficient market theory, rational expectations, and capital asset pricing are loaded with implicit or explicit counterfactual assumptions. These assumptions, as any good microeconomic theorist can see, are set up to rule out, by assumption, the possibility that the market for a few shares of the stock of a corporation and the market for control of a corporation may be fundamentally different markets.

The past few years have seen a change in the type of warfare for control with special gimmicks such as golden parachutes and greenmail to reward warriors on both sides with consolation prizes. But regardless of the variation in process, both economic theory and political science indicate that extremely stringent conditions are needed in order to make a competitive-pricing system and a stockholder-voting process logically consistent. In general, these conditions are rarely if ever satisfied in actuality.

The lawyers may talk about a premium for control. But to a true believer of efficient markets, there cannot be a premium for control. If, in contradistinction to the adherents of the single, efficient market, we suggest that there are several more or less imperfect markets involving the market for a few shares, the market for control, the market for going-business assets, and the market for assets in liquidation, then we have a structure for interpreting what is going on in terms of arbitrage among these different markets. But although this might appear to be a commonsense approach to some, good theory is neither mere fact nor just common sense. It has to have a structure which goes beyond the previous theory.

Parsimony is often a desirable feature of a theory; Occam's razor applies. If you do not need an assumption, do not use it. Theorists in general and economic theorists in particular are cognizant of Occam's razor. But there is an extra reason for the use of simplifying assumptions. There is often a trade-off between the complexity of a model and the ability to carry out a formal analysis. Simplification which allows for great in-depth analysis of the relevant variables is clearly a double blessing. It cuts out the peripheral factors and it analyzes in depth those which are relevant. Unfortunately, relevance is often in the eyes of the beholder. What constitutes a nice point to the boys in the quarterlies may be peripheral to legal fact. There is little direct connection between economic theory and legal fact. At any point in time the law is what it is, or at least it is what the current crop of lawyers and judges interpret it to be in the light of current social pressures and precedent. It is emphatically not necessarily what the logic of some economic theory says it should be. Between the law and the theory are the complex mechanisms of social process.

Many of the cases which call for economic advice involve adversarial proceedings where the money stakes are high. Can the economist being paid several thousand dollars a day be expected to maintain a scientific, scholarly, nonadversarial posture? Paradoxically, the answer is yes, because of the great distance between economic abstraction and institutional fact. The potential for qualification and the selection of different *ad hoc* models is sufficiently large and the difference in the perception of what is relevant and critical may be so great that it is not difficult to find economists of stature willing to testify on either side.

DISCOURSE

Student to professor of finance: Sir, there is a 20-dollar bill on the ground.
Professor to student: Don't be foolish; if it were really there, someone would have already picked it up.

One of the crowning achievements of economic theory has been the gradual development of general equilibrium theory and the understanding of the conditions under which a decentralized competitive-bidding system might lead to the emergence of an efficient price system.

In the popular free-enterprise mythology the freedom of markets and the impersonal discipline and justice of the price system take on a virtue associated with freedom and justice for the individual in general, as though the major purpose of government laws were to thwart the free play of the market. Yet rather than being an artifact of nature, the free-exchange market is clearly a product of society and its laws. The success of the functioning of possibly the most efficient market known, the New York Stock Exchange, has been in part due to a careful formalization of the rules of the game by its board of governors and by the Securities and Exchange Commission (SEC).

The central paradox which has led to the overemphasis by both the mythology and many professionals in finance is the concept of competition embedded in the key implicit assumption made. The paradox is that what is meant by competition is *no competition at all*. The perfect competition of the efficient market occurs when each individual can behave as though he were faced with a one-person maximization problem in the face of an impersonal, anonymous market mechanism. The individual is not in a position to influence any outcome but his own. Technically, this result requires that each individual be "small" with respect to the market. A natural way to model this condition is to consider a continuum of traders, with any individual trader having a measure of zero (Dubey and Shapley, 1977; Dubey and Shubik, 1978b). This model may serve to approximate the economic reality on impact of a small trader selling a few hundred shares of a heavily traded issue. But it does not fit groups filing 13Ds.

The theory of competitive markets has proved to be of great worth in providing insight and guidance concerning the overall functioning of mass markets, but it offers no intellectual basis for our understanding of the different markets for the paper, the real assets, and the control of a corporation, which may exist.

In the past several decades the understanding of the theory of competitive markets and its implications for finance have been marked by several important developments in economics and finance. Several of the more salient developments are noted and examined here. They include (1) the theory of general equilibrium proposed by Walras (1954) and mathematically formalized by Arrow and Debreu (1954), Debreu (1959); and McKenzie (1959); (2) the treatment of trade in shares when there are complete markets proposed by Arrow and Debreu (1954); (3) the spanning of incomplete markets proposed by Arrow (1964);

(4) the irrelevance of the debt-equity structure of the corporation under the assumptions noted by Modigliani and Miller (1958); (5) the portfolio theory of Markowitz (1959); the capital asset–pricing model originally proposed by Sharpe (1964) and Lintner (1965); (6) the strong, semistrong, and weak forms of the efficient-market hypothesis; and (7) the recent concern with the economics and game theory of nonsymmetric information and agency problems.

The work referred to here represents a significant step forward in our understanding of the properties of a competitive price system in equilibrium. They tell us little about disequilibrium or dynamics; and in markets where the host of highly specialized assumptions needed for these insights to be valid do not hold, it is an open question as to how useful these insights are. Futhermore, if they are unsatisfactory, what can we use as an alternative?

General Equilibrium and the Underlying Assumptions

The central result of general equilibrium theory is that under certain "reasonable assumptions" at least one set of prices will exist which will clear all markets efficiently. The economist's concept of efficiency is a weak one; it merely implies that no individual's welfare can be improved without decreasing the welfare of another. It is important to note that although virtues such as "fair, just, equitable" are associated with the competitive price system, much of the "justice" has already been assumed implicitly in the acceptance of individual property rights. Furthermore, since there can easily be several different price systems which are all efficient and can have highly different distributions of resources, the fairness of the distribution has considerable leeway in interpretation.

We now turn to the assumptions required to guarantee the existence of a competitive equilibrium.[3] We will try to avoid technical detail but nevertheless convey the economic substance of the conditions. The set of all consumers is such that any individual consumer has a set of preferences which can be represented by a utility function.[4] It is hard to see or measure a utility function or, for that matter, to describe the preference ordering of an individual, but these are part and parcel of the credo of the model of the rational economic agent. Most reasonable economists, lawyers, judges, and bank robbers will take the utilitarian-agent model as a good first approximation when dealing with economic affairs.

Each consumer is supposed to be of an economic size which is insignificant with respect to influencing the market. At this point the theory of efficient price splits into its centralized socialist version and its decentralized competitive version. The socialist version nicely illustrated in Debreu's (1959) proof will work for any number of individuals as long as we make the assumption that they must act as price takers. If the central agency announces that all prices and all agents are required to take them as given, then if the agency picks prices which clear all markets, they will be efficient. The key element here is that even though some agents might be large, they are not permitted to use their power to influence price.

The competitive, efficient price system can be established mathematically by two somewhat different devices. We may assume that there is a continuum of economic agents and that each individual is of measure zero—in other words, so insignificantly small that his strategic influence is zero (Dubey and Shapley, 1977). Alternatively, we may model the economy as a strategic market game[5] with a finite number of agents and study how the power of each is attenuated as the number of competitors is increased.[6] Given a model of this kind, we have proved that certain noncooperative equilibria[7] approach the competitive equilibrium (Shubik, 1973; Shapley and Shubik, 1977; Dubey and Shubik, 1978a), but they are, in general, inefficient for finite numbers reflecting the oligopolistic powers of the agents. Furthermore, the behavior of the prices depends explicitly on the price formation mechanism employed. The best candidate for efficiency with few numbers is a version of the double-auction market (Dubey and Shubik, 1980; Shubik, 1981; Dubey, 1982).

Attempts to formulate the competitive economy as a full process or strategic-game market demonstrate that, for finite number of players, institutions matter and efficiency is, at best, a function of careful institutional design. Furthermore, for many plausible mechanisms efficiency will only be approximately achieved with a finite number of players (Shubik, 1979).

Another assumption made is that firms are run by selfless, profit-maximizing managers for the benefit of nonvoting stockholders in an economy with complete markets (the full impact of the complete-market assumption is discussed later when we consider exogenous uncertainty).

The economist's definitions of profit is a far cry from that of the accountant's or the tax collector's. In a world with complex tax laws, tax-loss carryforwards, quickie refunds, interest deductibility, and differences between merger tax consequences and acquisition consequences, to paraphrase Mr. Dooley, "What appears to be a stone wall to the layman is frequently a triumphal arch to the Mergers and Acquisition Department."

The main proofs of general equilibrium theory in general assume no transactions costs. The introduction of even fairly elementary transactions costs sends up the mathematical complexity considerably (see Foley, 1970; Hahn, 1971; Rogawski and Shubik, 1986). If one is using general equilibrium theory to calculate the broad sweep of approximate prices in some parts of international trade (Scarf, 1973; Scarf and Shoven, 1984) or to give a general discourse on aggregate price movements, it is not unreasonable to argue ad hoc that for the purpose at hand transactions costs can be ignored. But when a proxy fight or tender offer can, as in the Revlon takeover contest, cost $100 million, then in this less-than-the-best-of-all-possible worlds only a select few are going to be in a position to indulge. The small stockholders can coat-tail or exit; and the bank trust, pension, and mutual fund officers will behave according to the complex of fiduciary and legal restrictions on them. This is not a model of perfect competition.

The general equilibrium model is formulated in such a way that not only are resources of worth never unemployed or misemployed, errors never occur and bankruptcy and insolvency are not logically required. These conditions do not hold when the same economic structure is modeled as a strategic process.

Summing up, in the left-hand column of Table 2.1 the conditions required for the existence of a general equilibrium, efficient price system are noted. How good an approximation these assumptions are to trading on the stock exchange and to trading in control blocks and mergers and acquisitions is noted in the next two columns.

Trade in Goods with Complete Markets and Uncertainty

Arrow and Debreu postulated an ingenious way to extend the results on the efficient price system to situations involving both time and uncertainty. Suppose trade is in M commodities and for T time periods. Furthermore, suppose that during any period the economy can randomly be in any one of K states. We may invest a host of time-dated contingent goods such as

"wheat in 1991, if the sun shines." We may regard the economy as having MKT goods. If we permit trading between all pairs of time-dated contingent goods we require

$$\frac{MKT(MKT - 1)}{2} \simeq \frac{(MKT)^2}{2} \text{ markets}$$

The use of money cuts down the number of markets to $(MKT-1)$, but even this number is enormous in comparison to what exists. Any attempt to model trade with uncertainty through time as a playable game immediately reveals the difficulties encountered in trust, accounting, clearing, and documenting ownership claims in futures markets. But without complete markets, unless one takes considerable care in the specifications of weaker, alternative assumptions, the efficient-market property may be lost (e.g., as soon as we consider trade using money, then the meaning of enough money or credit to provide sufficient liquidity for trade must be made clear).

In essence, the Arrow-Debreu technique for handling time and uncertainty was an ingenious way to extend the mathematical domain of some results which provided further insight into efficient-market-price, static equilibrium. No insights, however, were provided for either competition or the dynamics of price formation. Techni-

Table 2.1.

Assumptions for Existence of Competitive Equilibrium	Plausibility of the Assumptions	
	Stock Exchange	Mergers and Acquisitions
Many traders	Often for thickly traded shares	Generally the reverse
No transactions costs	Rough approximation	Generally the reverse
Complete markets	Possibly yes	Generally the reverse
Regular preferences	Credo	Credo
No unemployment	Often ok to ignore	Often the reverse
Profit-maximizing managers	Often ok to ignore	Usually the reverse
No voting	Often ok to ignore	Usually the reverse
No taxes	Often ok to ignore	Often important and complex
No bankruptcy	Often ok to ignore	Often important and complex
Accounting and legal	Often ok to ignore	Often important and complex

cally, uncertainty was eliminated by complete forward contracts, and time was eliminated by transforming a problem essentially posed in extensive form into a problem in strategic[8] or normal form (see von Neumann and Morgenstern, 1944; Shubik, 1982).

A further gain in this mathematical extension is that one does not need to assume that individual preferences can be represented by a utility function.[9]

Trade in Securities with Money

Arrow (1964) extended our understanding of efficient markets by introducing a securities market where when state s (out of K states in total) occurs, there will be associated with each security a money payout. In essence, a security is a lottery ticket. Arrow showed that for M commodities and K states using securities and money, efficient trade could be achieved with $M + K$ rather than MK markets provided all individuals were risk-averse or risk-neutral.

Note that the model of exchange with securities modeled as lottery tickets abstracts from all considerations of voting, control, and managerial discretion. The original Arrow article, which is a monument to elegance and simplicity, avoided details concerning production and fiduciary decision making.

As soon as we add production, fiduciary decision making, control, differential information, or insufficient numbers of securities to cover the generation of all lotteries, the promise of great generality evaporates. Yet in return, it is precisely here that a major opportunity for a reconciliation of law and economic theory appears. The law is process-oriented and institutional; much of microeconomic theory is equilibrium-oriented and noninstitutional. In contrast, much of game theory—in its requirements for the full specification of the rules of the game—when applied to economic problems, forces the development of a *mathematical, institutional* economics. The rules of the game which must be specified if the game is to be playable are, in essence, the *carriers of process*. But the economic insti-

tutions of society are the carriers of process; and law, politics, custom, and technology all combine to delimit the rules of the game.

The economic generalist could easily react to a statement such as the one just given with the observation that the development of a science must proceed at a high level of abstraction and we cannot afford the luxury of prematurely swamping ourselves in institutional detail. The argument here, however, is not merely a plea for institutional detail but is a statement that for the questions being asked, general equilibrium theory (see Shubik, 1975) and much of the theory of finance is not abstract enough and works with inadequate models. Institutions are not ephemeral complications invoked by lawyers and students of industrial organizations who are unable to cope with mathematical economics and finance. They are logical necessities in the description of the rules of the game which must account for defining outcomes which are not necessarily in equilibrium as well as those which are.

A fundamentally superior approach to general equilibrium analysis and the predominant use of partial equilibrium analysis in finance is to model in terms of *playable games* and analyze in terms of strategic market games. Both approaches are suggested for the following reasons: A playable game requires complete and consistent rules to delimit the development of process. The valid (and hopefully simplest) complete description of a playable game contains within its rules the elementary mechanisms, institutions, and laws which are logically needed to guide economic activity.[10] An intermix of logic, technology, costs, and playability forces the invention of minimal rules, laws, mechanisms, or institutions. Thus, in essence, in society as a whole there are possibly no more than around ten basically different ways that goods change hands (Shubik, 1970); and if we limit ourselves to economic allocation mechanisms, there are only a few fundamentally different market mechanisms (Shubik, 1979).

A playable game is defined without regard for equilibrium—or for that matter without a formal specification of any solution concept. It is economic theory, finance, or game theory that introduces the concept of what constitutes a solution. The two most popular solutions are the competitive equilibrium and the noncooperative equilibrium.[11] The competitive equilibrium may be regarded as a special limiting case of the noncooperative equilibrium. The latter reflects oligopolistic forces and is extremely sensitive in general to information conditions. There are two basic reasons for using the competitive equilibrium model. The first is that it is mathematically far easier to work with than the noncooperative equilibrium; the second is that the competitive market is claimed to be a reasonably good approximation of economic reality. Unfortunately, for takeovers, mergers, and acquisitions oligopolistic structure is far more plausible than competitive equilibrium.

Trade in Securities with Insufficient Markets

The Arrow model of the securities market produces an efficient market for risk if there are K uncertain states of the economy and K securities (with short sales permitted) which span all possible mixtures of risk. But what does this abstract statement of uncertain outcomes in the economy mean? In good investment banking and in virtually any profession, one of the key skills of the professional is the ability to assess risk—both to qualify and to quantify risk. How many different states of uncertainty need to be recognized to give us a good approximation of the functioning of the politico-economic system. On the order of 10,000 companies must register with the SEC. These account for the preponderant part of stock market transactions. Is the U.S. economy represented adequately by 50, 500, or 50,000 states of uncertainty?

If the number of securities is fewer than the number of independent states, the Arrow result does not hold. Furthermore, if firms producing final goods are introduced, then the proposition that the firm

should maximize its value—which in turn would be equivalent to maximizing expected profits—need not be true. Stiglitz (1972) provides a counterexample. He presents a specific example "in which firms act like competitive price takers, but which, when firms maximize their stock market value, does not lead to an optimal allocation." Since the original article of Diamond (1967)—which, in the context of partial equilibrium, one product, and one type of firm, provided a formal model of the stockholder-held firm with production—there has been an explosion of the literature. Leland (1974) developed a "unanimity" theorem showing circumstances under which all stockholders, despite differences in risk attitudes, would agree on the production decisions of the firm. The outputs will not in general maximize the value of the firm. Fama (1972) and Jensen and Long (1972) also showed a unanimity result for stockholders whose valuation of returns is based only on the mean and variance of their portfolios. Ekern and Wilson (1974) consider sufficient conditions for unanimity, presenting an arbitrage argument which also links the results of Merton and Subrahmanyan (1974), permitting the entry of new firms, to the previous unanimity results.

Grossman and Hart (1979) consider an economy which lasts for T periods where the consumers have uncertain future endowments. At the first date all firms choose production plans for the complete future; at each date consumers can trade goods and shares and obtain dividends in proportion to previous holdings. They assume that the managers present the initial stockholders with a production plan that is unanimously approved. They state: "We are making the implicit assumption that, if a firm does not act in this way, the shareholders will take it over and effect a new production plan." They use as a solution concept a variant of a noncooperative equilibrium which in general will not be efficient.

There have been many other writings since, but the purpose here is not to present a critical survey of the stockholder unanimity literature. The basic purpose here is to provide enough insight into the prevailing models, their assumptions, and results, to be able to appreciate the gap between economic theory directed toward finance and the actual problems of corporate control. In all of the literature noted previously transactions costs are assumed away; voting is not voting in the usual sense; and even with an imposing array of simplifications, market efficiency in the sense of Pareto optimality is only always achieved with the full spanning of risk insurance. In the literature noted the question "Is the assumption of completely spanned markets a reasonable or an unreasonable approximation to reality, at least for some purposes?" does not seem to be asked.

This literature represents a valuable first step in extending pure microeconomic theory. But the ignoring of transactions costs, control, corporate voting, oligopolistic effects, bankruptcy, and several other items such as taxation makes the value of the specific results of little direct relevance to problems of corporate governance. Questions concerning the long-term need for capital and the rights and responsibilities of potentially short-term owners and long-term managers are seldom formulated in this literature.

Even if we were to assume the existence of enough markets, Dubey and Shubik (1981) have noted that to be able to deduce profit-maximizing behavior by the managements of the firms requires not only competitive firms and stockholders but also explicit rules against self-dealing by management, such as selling at undermarket price to Firm B by the management of Firm A who are small stockholders of A but large stockholders of B.

Finally, returning to the simplest and possibly most hopeful of models—that of Debreu (1959) with firms owned by shareholders who are paid at the end proportionate shares of a well-defined profit—even this model, when described as a game of strategy, requires fussy institutional details and laws which are overlooked in the competitive-equilibrium formulation. In particular, if the shares are voting shares,

then for an efficient price system even to exist, minority-stockholder protection rights must be made explicit (Shubik, 1984).[12]

Another landmark in the application of economic theory to finance is the insight of Modigliani and Miller (1958) concerning the valuation of a firm. They observed and established in a competitive, partial equilibrium context that in a world without taxes, transactions costs, or bankruptcy, with competitive firms the value of the firm will not depend on the leverage of the mix between debt and equity financing. In particular, if all parties are rational and well informed and all bets are available via corporate and individual borrowing, the individual can use a homemade leveraging to change the mixture of risk implicit in the firm's leveraging. This view requires also that the individual does not run the risk of bankruptcy.

As an antidote to old wives' tales and to sloppy thinking about institutional arrangements in general, the pristine simplicity of the Modigliani-Miller result represents another step forward in showing the usefulness of the central idea from general equilibrium theory taken over to finance. That is, at equilibrium there is no opportunity for arbitrage in an economy with complete competitive markets or their equivalent.

The writings of Lintner (1962), Smith (1970, 1972), Stiglitz (1972), and Hellwig (1981), among others, indicate the difficulties of trying to extend the Modigliani-Miller results to situations with default. In particular, the main result of Hellwig is that the Modigliani-Miller result is valid only if all portfolios used as collateral by the individual borrowing have the same structure as the firm. This result, as Hellwig notes, not only requires an unreasonable restriction on borrowing but basically indicates that optimality can only be obtained by ruling out a perfect capital market.

Dubey and Shubik (1979) note that even in a world with no exogenous uncertainty, if borrowing and lending are to be accommodated, then a bankruptcy law is required to police borrowers who would otherwise elect for a strategic bankruptcy. In such a situation, without exogenous uncertainty, it is possible to define and design an optimal bankruptcy law. It is a law that is just harsh enough that at any equilibrium the marginal value to any trader of opting for bankruptcy is at least offset by the penalty. Unfortunately, when we consider a world with exogenous uncertainty and less-than-complete markets, the previously simple way to define an optimal bankruptcy law is no longer meaningful because each individual's final holdings now become state-dependent.

If an extremely high bankruptcy penalty is introduced into a society where there is at least one state in which some borrower may default, all borrowing will be stopped. The bankruptcy laws under uncertainty appear as a public good which defines in some sense (such as by majority vote or by consensus) society's willngness to accept a level of bankruptcy as part of the cost of encouraging risk taking. Thus even though overall efficiency may not be achievable in a society with exogenous uncertainty, less-than-complete markets, and a bankruptcy law which is not fully state-dependent, there is still the possibility that some laws will be better than others (in the sense that a noncooperative equilibrium with one law could be dominated by the equilibrium with another law).

The dominant attitude in the development of microeconomic theory and finance is that often the introduction of an institutionally realistic factor such as bankruptcy or transactions costs so increases the complexity of the mathematics that the models become unmanageable. Sound scientific methodology calls for parsimony and efforts to facilitate analysis. But the cost of such parsimony is a competitive-market theory that has very limited applicability to virtually all problems involving the struggle for control of large corporations and as well as to many other aspects of competition in an economy where oligopoly, taxes, limited liability, insolvency, bankruptcy, indivisibility, fiduciary decision making, incomplete markets, and voting stock are facts of life.

A reasonable reply to a criticism such as this one is to say: "Even supposing that everything you say is true, the current theories of microeconomics and finance are all that we have. What is your better alternative?"

The answer to this quite reasonable challenge must be somewhat unsatisfactory, yet it at least can be honest. For many practical purposes the gap between economic theory and the law is large. The theory itself is not merely an abstraction but is often a gross simplification which in general is static and not designed to portray process. Currently, the theory of finance for many purposes is too simple, insufficiently institutional, and too incomplete to serve as more than a guide and method of reasoning for a skilled professional who must make out an *ad hoc* argument for the case at hand.

Basic economic reasoning can serve to attach weights to factors left out of the simpler models. Thus, for example, in the Delaware evaluation, weighting was attached to stock market value, assets, and earnings. Simplistic theory would argue that they all should be the same in perfect equilibrium.

A professor of finance should bring skilled reasoning and economic insight to the law. He almost always cannot bring directly applicable theory, because it is too simple and based on too many counterfactuals which count.

A different argument for trying to fit the simplistic models of economics and finance to even complex merger and acquisition problems involves the proposition that it does not really matter that the models proposed appear to be overly simple or leave out elements that are held to be important by some as long as empirical evidence shows that they fit the facts. The difficulty with this approach lies in the selection, interpretation, and relevance of the facts which are verified. Two examples of the dangers in the interpretation of facts and their relevance to theory are given.

You cannot beat the market. This can be proved empirically by examining the performance of all individuals invested in the market and observing that on the average they do no better than the average. This somewhat extreme example is made clearer by considering a poker game. The stock market at one instance of time is a zero-sum game (leaving out the broker's cut). Over even a few days it is no longer zero-sum, since overall wealth could have been created or destroyed by the economy. A poker game, in contrast, is completely zero-sum. The average expected winnings have to be zero. But as anyone who has played poker knows (see Yardley, 1957), not all poker players have been created equal. There are the patsies or steady contributors to the game, and there are the experts. Because much of economic theory and finance is resolutely nonpsychological, an implicit assumption in these theories (and for that matter in much of political science and game theory) is that all agents are psychologically equally endowed with perceptions, intelligence, etc.

The empirical proof that superior poker players or chess players exist is relatively easy to come by since the games and measures of success are tightly defined. The proof that Buffett, Graham, Dodd, Steinberg, the Belzbergs, Basses, Pritzkers, Crowns, Icahn, Pickens, Boesky, and many other recognized players are superior in the stock market is harder, because they are in a game where they may be arbitraging among three or four different markets and competition among the few, not the anonymous market, is almost always relevant.

A second example of the problems in linking empirical results with theory is the study by De Angelo et al. (1984) which demonstrates that when a firm goes private, minority stockholders who were bought out benefited.[13] The question we must ask is, What does this correlation tell us about the virtues of the market, the virtues of takeovers, and the efficiency of process? I suggest one hypothesis which appears to fit these facts. The markets for control and for the trading of small holdings of shares are different. Owing to taxes, indivisibilities, and special organizational and control structures, large differences between the value of a share in the mass secondhand market for shares (known as the stock market) and the per-share value of a control block can come into existence. A

large gap available for arbitrage can exist until a deal maker of sufficient size and ability can simultaneously line up the financing (which may be in the billions); work out the legal, accounting, and organizational problems of taking control; and have a takeover plan (including possible buyers already lined up for the "crown jewels") ready to go. This market, by its entrance requirements, has to be oligopolistic. If a stock trading at 10 has assets liquidatable at 25 and is taken over at 15 by a raider who liquidates it, the small stockholder gets a bonus of 50% over previous markets, the raider has taken a 40% liberation fee, and an arbitrage gap has been closed by a control play. Did the stockholders do well? Was this action economically and socially desirable? It depends upon the case. In some instances the raider could be viewed as forcing an incompetent or lazy management to improve the employment of assets; in other instances the divergence could have been the result of a responsible management having long-term plans for committed capital which were out of step with a short-term stock market evaluation.

Portfolio Theory and the Capital Asset–Pricing Model

The seminal work of Markowitz (1959) is possibly one of the most important contributions of operations research and microeconomics to applied finance and to some aspects of macroeconomic theory. It has immediate application to the small, passive investor. It says, "If you are small and do not have a special edge, then there is an optimal way to diversify and hedge yourself against the unknown." Sharpe (1964), Lintner (1965), Treynor, and others developed the capital asset–pricing model for application, and it was accepted to the point that any financial analyst knows his "alphas and betas" as well as he knows his *abc*s.

The key observation of Markowitz was that a single security's contribution to the risk of a portfolio was not the same as the risk of holding the single security alone. In order to develop a theory of how an individual with a given amount of money should select an optimal portfolio, we must make the following assumptions. The individual's preferences can be represented by a utility function; market prices are given; and the future performance expected from the stock can be summed up as though the stock were a lottery ticket. In a fundamental way portfolio theory has no contribution to make to security analysis. It tells us how to mix risks only if the risks have been assessed and the correlations between the expected performance of the stocks have been taken into account. Given that our assessment is correct, the concept of an efficient portfolio as one which provides a given expected return with minimum risk provides economic insight and practical assistance.

The steps from Markowitz's theory to actual application are large. The capital asset–pricing models (CAPM) attempted to apply them. It is at this point that a subtle intermix of assumptions and facts concerning divergence of assessments and the functioning and information revelation aspects of competitive markets appear.

The CAPM assumptions are that all investors have the same information and expectations concerning the future; transactions costs and taxes are ignored. In essence, in the original CAPM the efficient portfolio will be the market portfolio or a holding of all securities in proportion to their market value.[14] Empirically, the best immediately available approximation for this portfolio is the Wilshire 5000 index, but probably Standard and Poor's Industrial Average is the most used.

The distance between theory and practice is often great. If we wished to use the Wilshire 5000 list in detail for our market calculations, we would need millions of correlation coefficients. The use of historical data to characterize stock performance is suspect. The empirical problems with the estimation of utility functions are many. Many modifications and emendations to CAPM exist and are already even well summarized in some of the textbooks (e.g., see Sharpe, 1985). The arbitrage price theory (APT) (see Ross, 1976; Roll and Ross, 1980) considers the identification of

major economic factors influencing stock valuation and postulates an equilibrium relationship.

These theories represent an important step forward in linking the economic theory of the efficient, mass, competitive-exchange market to our observations and understanding of the mass market for highly traded issues. They offer practical wisdom to the small trader who wishes to benefit from the virtually total alienation of ownership of paper from management and control of real economic assets and institutions. The game the CAPM model portrays is the ultimate abstraction of trading paper for paper with little need to be concerned with economic causality. The stocks are lottery tickets. The APT is somewhat more concerned with the linking of trade to economic factors; but even so, these approaches focus on arbitrage of paper on paper in a single set of markets, the stock markets. When companies are merged, bought, sold, liquidated, reorganized, taken public, or taken private, there are other markets which must be taken into account; and the arbitrage is between markets, with the mass stock market providing only one part of the trading arena.

Efficient Markets and the Spread of Information

Is expertise worth anything? Do markets reveal economic information? How fast does individual knowledge become common knowledge? What does economic theory have to say about the value of inside information?

These questions are some of the fundamental questions being asked in the economics of information and in finance. We begin with efficient markets. As was ably exposited by Fama (1970), there are three forms of the efficient-market hypothesis: (1) the weak, (2) the semistrong, and (3) the strong forms of market efficiency. In a weak, efficient market all information contained in previous prices is reflected. In a semistrong market all publicly known information is reflected in price. In the strong version all currently known information is reflected.

An immediate problem occurs when one tries to make sense out of any one of these hypotheses. The general equilibrium model of economic theory, the CAPM model, and the description of an efficient market are all formally specified as static, equilibrium, *nonprocess* models, but they are talked about as though they entail process. One cannot meaningfully discuss information and its flow without specifying process. This is made adequately clear when one attempts to model even the simplest of price formation mechanisms as a strategic market game. Dubey et al. (1982) have done so, and the following results have been obtained: The information efficiency of a market in the sense of it conveying signals to others, in general, can only be true in a truly mass market. If the market is thin on either side, it is easy to construct examples in which an individual purposely conceals his information. Even if we assume many traders,[15] we would not be able to build a logically consistent process model to even define the strong form coherently. The weak form can be proved but immediately has an interesting interpretation. Suppose that in every period a random event takes place which is revealed to a few experts but not to the others; the experts can act in the market and profit from it. But their market action will be reflected in the last price they have helped to form. This process can be repeated indefinitely, with the experts constantly revealing their informational edge but profiting by it on each occasion.

If markets were more than weakly efficient, there would be no use for experts, specialists, news services, analysis groups, or the whole industry devoted to selling information. The presence of experts and specialists in particular should cause us to ponder over what we mean by information and how these individuals fit into our theories of efficiency. The key factors overlooked are perception and interpretation. The mere presence of "contrarian investors" (e.g., see Dreman, 1952) calls attention to the distinction between raw information and its interpretation. Yet information theory and economic information concentrate only on a well-defined special definition of information (see von Neumann and Morgenstern, 1944; Shannon, 1948) where context and perception are irrelevant.

It is my opinion that one of the reasons why most superior financial analysts or specialists can write popular books explaining more or less what they do without necessarily endangering their competitive edge is that most individuals are not capable of seeing the distinctions they see. Of the very few who would get the message, only a few of them would have the drive and perception to do the work to become an expert; and for the few who do, because there may be more deals than expert dealers, they can be welcomed to the partnership.

An example of information retrieval and interpretation is the Getty merger, where a sensitive analyst could and did obtain the Getty family's California court proceedings and estimated from them that a Getty merger was doable.

The key element to information is interpretation, and both organizations and individuals may be slow in or incapable of understanding that the blips on the radar screen really could be an attack on Pearl Harbor, or that Hitler's *Mein Kampf* was to be interpreted seriously, or that the first audit at Penn Square could be the tip of the iceberg.

Leaving aside the questions of interpretation, there are some straight physical and sociological questions as to how fast new information is revealed in a market. For a thickly traded stock on the NYSE, it is here that weak efficiency appears reasonable.

Nonsymmetric Information and Agency Theory

The last items noted are the formal treatments of nonsymmetric information and the recent concern with problems of agency. One of the basic attractions of mass markets with only small agents is that the agent is strategically powerless to use information concerning the moves of others. This is not true if one set of agents knows something about uncertain events. The Arrow-Debreu ingenious device of inventing markets to cover all contingencies has some difficulties when some individuals do not even know that certain contingencies exist. It is possible to analyze competition with nonsymmetric information in economies with less-than-complete markets (see Radner, 1968, 1970; Dubey and Shubik, 1977); but although it is possible to find equilibrium price systems which are weakly efficient, the outcomes are usually not efficient (in the economist's sense of Pareto optimality).

Although its application to financial theory and practice has been minimal to date, along with a concern for a theory of corporate organization (Williamson, 1975; Marris, 1979), the problems of agency have recently been recognized as important to the understanding of a modern economic system. In a complex economy experts must be used, motivated, and trusted by those who do not know what they know.

Agents, trustees, brokers, fiduciaries, representatives, and managers of other people's money are the earmark of any modern economy, yet the central core of microeconomic theory and finance ignores this fact of life. This statement is *not* meant as a criticism of the development of these theories but as a *caveat* against taking theories developed to provide insights to a set of appropriate problems and applying them to problems such as corporate control, LBOs, mergers, and acquisitions where their relevance is far less. The economist's advice on these problems must be tempered with an *ad hoc* understanding of the problem and a realization that the economist or professor of finance can bring value added to the resolution of a problem by contributing the economist's mode of reasoning, not economic theory that does not fit. "A stock is worth what the market will pay for it" is a catchy slogan and holds true when Mrs. Green sells her 100 shares of AT&T; but its relevance becomes less evident when Vickers is forcing out the remaining stockholders in Transocean Oil or where in general there are elements of coercion and control such as the ability to delist.

Agency theory has concentrated on problems with two individuals, a principal and an agent. The agent's action is not directly observable by the principal, or the outcome observed by the principal is not fully determined by the actions of the agent. Arrow (1985) has recently provided a review of the literature and observes, "An example of very special economic importance is the relationship between stockholders and management."

Even relatively simple economic problems involving the construction of incentive-fee structures become highly complicated quickly. Yet the student of history and society confronted with many of the models of microeconomic theory can become uneasy, with some justification. Is loyalty to one's country, friends, or partners best explained by short-term utility maximization? In the search for economic explanation, is there an efficient market for charity or the very punctilio of honor? Are tradition, custom, and codes of ethical behavior little more than institutionally imperfect realizations of the principle of short-run maximization in an efficient market? Or could it be that much fiduciary behavior is based on longer-term concepts of codes of honesty not easily (or uniquely) explained by nonsocialized, noninstitutional, consciously short-term-optimizing economic individuals?[16]

Reprise

The survey in this section entitled "Discourse" has attempted to sketch and discuss some of the highly valuable contributions to economic and financial understanding which have been made in the development of competitive equilibrium, efficient-market, and portfolio theory. These developments have been central in the understanding of the overall mechanics of a decentralized price system and have had considerable applied value in the day-to-day business of paper asset conversion in mass markets not involving control.

Unfortunately, as work in oligopoly theory, game theory, information theory, and agency theory demonstrates, the essentially static, nonstrategic mass market results do not generalize to situations with few fiduciaries and with nonsymmetric information concerned with control. The competitive-market theories, where they apply, should have great appeal to the judge looking for an elegant, plausible, and apparently scientific means to cut the Gordian knot of institutional, societal, and legal complication. Unfortunately, the complicated problems may often require complicated analysis and have complicated solutions. At best, the attractively simple world of the mass, efficient market for the exchange of financial paper serves only as a benchmark in the analysis of the arbitrages among paper, tangible assets, and control of ongoing or liquidated corporations.

TAKEOVERS, LAW, AND OLIGOPOLISTIC COMPETITION

In this last section, in the spirit of economic analysis and political economy, some observations are made concerning hostile takeovers, tender offers, and leveraged buy-outs. Much of my thought has been influenced by the perceptive observations of Lowenstein (1983). But the full context must be viewed in terms of economic institutions and the purposes and processes of the law.

In the terms of the economist the laws concerning competition, contract, fiduciary responsibility, trading conventions, commercial codes, bankruptcy and insolvency, etc., are public goods. They are constructed by the government of a society to serve all of its members. The game theorist sees them as *rules of the game*. But as society and politics change, so does the rule. There are games within the game (see Shubik, 1984). Finance and short-term economic maximization are on a shorter time horizon than long-term investment or the development of legal codes, which reflect, as best they can, society's current views of fairness, equity, and reasonable behavior.

The great abstraction of the microeconomist—the mass, anonymous liquid market for the exchange of financial paper—is close to a reality for the small trader. But paradoxically, this reality is an artifact of law and society. The SEC and the evolution of U.S. accounting standards have done so much to enable the ideal of the efficient market to be realized. Laissez-faire and the unimpeded functioning of the price system can only be achieved by a body of delicately crafted law to prevent kicking and gouging.

The task that faces the lawyer and economist is the design of appropriate rules of the game. These mold the institutions which are the carriers of economic process. Because much of microeconomic theory and finance is static, it appears as if it were noninstitutional and hence in some sense general. Any attempt to produce a process model designs an institution to carry the process and shows that the noninstitutional view is false.

In most societies for most items ownership entails responsibilities as well as rights. Thus the ownership of a house or automobile may involve inspection and maintenance. The common stock with limited liability in the United States is not too far from the dollar bill in the amount of responsibility it calls for from its owner.

The political economy and technology of the modern corporation created the need for large masses of long-term capital guided by a single management. But as was observed by Berle and Means (1932) and many others since, the price paid for liquidity was the separation of ownership and control. As noted and stressed by both Berle and Means and by Lowenstein, the right to dispose over physical property *jus disponendi* ceases to be held by the small trader in the highly liquid market for paper. At this point a problem in agency and fiduciary relationships appears. Who controls the corporation if not the owners? The answer appears to be the managers. But "Who controls the managers?" has, in theory, the answer "The directors," but in fact most directors serve at the pleasure of the management (see Baker, 1945; Mace, 1971; Brown, 1976; Bacon, 1977; Herman 1981).

If Mr. Doe does not like the actions of the management of AT&T, he can sell his stock. The efficient market gives him the liquidity to do so. His options are "exit or voice." But is voice really an option for the small stockholder other than a devoted corporate stockholder gadfly? In theory, Mrs. Jones could challenge management with a proxy contest; but in practice, it is only a major player who can afford a proxy contest no matter how wide the divergence between market value and asset values appears to be. The tender offer at first glance might seem to be an alternative instrument to the proxy fight. But as noted by Lowenstein (1983, p. 265), the tender offer as it has developed is a fight not merely for power to benefit from the long-term control of an ongoing institution but also for the right to redeploy assets (See Whitman and Shubik, 1979).

The questions to society are, How accountable are large corporate managements to their stockholders, and how accountable should they be? How can arbitrage opportunities exist among the markets for shares, ongoing corporations, and their assets? If these gaps exist, who should close them? Is the hostile raider, with his tender offer well above the stock market but well below realization value to the control group, a popular hero, a highwayman, or a socially valuable scavenger? Is the president of the corporation, who is participating in a leveraged buy-out at above market but below potential asset conversion, a responsible fiduciary?

If all markets everywhere were competitive, then the arbitrage between any two would be removed. The mere fact that some may claim that for large corporations the stock market is efficient (however, even here, see Shiller, 1981) is only partially relevant to the problem at hand. The market is for secondhand, noncontrol paper which should more or less reflect the noncontrol, no-asset-conversion view of the world. The small investor, the bank trustee, the pension fund trustee, and the mutual fund operator are not concerned with creating "doable deals." They, like anyone else, are more than happy to coattail a deal in progress. The premium over market in a tender offer may well be interpreted as hush money to make sure that all are made happy. Lowenstein (1983, p. 273) is too kind; the problem is not efficiency merely in the stock market but across the markets.

It is well known that the dominant form of industrial competition is oligopolistic (see Scherer, 1980) and one could make a case that this form works reasonably well to provide the incentives needed to innovate in a highly dynamic, changing, and uncertain environment. However, when one combines tax laws, transactions costs, organizational indivisibilities, oligopolistic markets, and oligopolistic financing (not everyone can get a standby credit line for a billion or two) with bureaucratic control of real assets and complex institutions run by fiduciaries, the chances are high that there is a difference between the average opinion of the stock market and the opinion of worth by a control buyer working on a hand-tailored deal.

The small stockholder may well stand to gain by selling out in a hostile tender offer or leveraged buy-out. The instigators of the action, if successful, will gain considerably more. These are two questions we must ask: What responsibility does management have to close the gap between the stock market and a control redeployment of assets? Given that a hostile tender offer can give the small stockholder a premium and redeploys assets, is this arbitrage a social good, or is a different correction mechanism called for?

Whitman and Shubik (1979) suggest that asset conversion is at the core of good finance. Yet it is important to recognize the difference between good finance and good industrial policy. To a great extent, it is major financiers and not only major industrialists who are involved in the redeployment of assets. There is a considerable leeway available in how the asset use is to be restructured, such as the restructuring of debt in an LBO or the selling of the "crown jewels" after a takeover. It may be that the major measure of success of the financier is short-term profit or "point score" (see Reich, 1983), and it is by no means obvious that this is a socially optimal way to redeploy productive assets.

If the gap between a control market and the stock market exists and persists, the takeover activity of the past few years indicates that the gap will be closed by the tender offer or other means. At the formal level economic theorists, including those specializing in finance, have little if any dynamic theory which tells us how the markets close. The magic word *arbitrage* is used as though a name were equivalent to an explanation. An informal sketch of what might be going on is as follows: The potential arbitrage market between the stock market and the control market involves, at most, on the order of 10,000 firms and possibly a few hundred financial groups with the knowledge, ability, and resource base to be able to take action. These numbers are small enough that a considerable amount of hand tailoring will be done so that each firm is, to its possible buyer, an indivisible, differentiated item which may be partially or wholly dismembered later but will be bought whole. The preliminary search for control values which can be realized is not a matter of private information but, to a great extent, is private interpretation of public information on the target juxtaposed with private information about the acquisition group and its special needs, goals, and ability to control timing.

The relevance of the stock market to the dealer in corporations is to provide an index of the difference between institutional and economic reality on the one hand and the price of lottery tickets on the other. As this index swings, there is a time to go public and a time to go private; a time to acquire and a time to be acquired.[17]

If we are distrustful of the tender offer groups as the socially best, oligopolistic arbitrage mechanism, what are the alternatives? There are several candidates: management itself, the boards of directors, the institutional investors, investors as a whole, or the government.

Management would appear to have the highest responsibility in trying to bring market value and institutional control value together. But even here the fiduciary problem (which is entirely left out or assumed away in the theory of competitive markets) appears. When we consider customers, employees, local communities dealt with, and stockholders, by far the most transient and liquid group is the stockholders.

Anonymous liquidity for the stockholder is not designed to promote the deepest sense of fiduciary responsibility and trust by management. The leveraged buy-out is a monument to this proposition. The manager—especially if he is a founder of the firm—may feel that the stockholders having no sense of identity with the firm are more than adequately rewarded by the premium over previous market paid by the LBO group he has put together.

There is no clean, clear economic answer to whether the LBO by a management constitutes overreaching or a breach of fiduciary responsibility. What is clear is that if management is to be expected to forgo the LBO, then there should be a greater level of long-term community of interests between managements and stockholders. The cost of community interest is less liquidity. For example, a time-graduated capital gains tax starting at ordinary income levels for a year or two and decreasing to zero for holdings over six or seven years might generate more interest in and community with management.

An alternative scheme not involving taxation (but more radical and academic) might be to change voting rules so that stock held for, say, less than a year has no vote, and from then on the vote is proportional to the number of years held. Thus, 100 shares held ten years would have 900 votes.

In even a perfectly competitive world, it may take a few years to train new expertise. The expertise of deal makers and steelmakers is not the same. Thus, LBO may have in its favor, in contrast with the tender offer, that management involved knows the business well and intends to run it profitably.

Could directors or institutional investors serve to guide management to help to bring long-term economic and stock prices more into line? As the economic system stands, the function, purpose, and power of most directorates is best considered by viewing them as advisors to, rather than supervisors of, management. Possibly a minor improvement in the quality of directorial thought could be obtained by paying the board only in stock or stock options which cannot be sold or exercised for a period of five or six years. The role of the director in a modern mass economy needs deep reconsideration and cannot be adequately covered here.

The institutional investors with an ownership of around a third of all the shares on the NYSE (see the *1984 Fact Book*), if they chose, could serve as a form of Zaibatsu to management; but instead, they apparently prefer to concentrate on liquidity rather than identify with control. If they opted for control, then a new set of problems concerning societal interests and oligopoly behavior would be encountered.

We are left with the direct stockholders themselves. Economic reality and eventually good economic theory must take into account the critical roles both of time and timing in the understanding of economic process. Much of the mystery concerning efficient-market theory evaporates as soon as one tries to build any playable game—any mechanism, no matter how simple, that actually forms price. In doing so, time—the actual sequencing of moves—and timing play important roles. Furthermore, the relationship between stock performance and corporate performance requires the specifying and contrasting of both the stock market and the industrial process.[18] Once we raise questions involving a horizon of a year or more, society must face the trade-off between liquidity and concern and responsibility. In Lipton's (1979) view hostile tender offers are motivated by short-term speculators whose goal is a quick profit. But one could argue that in a system whose god is liquidity and anonymity, virtually all stockholders are looking for short-term gains. Keynes (1936, Chap. 12) likened the attitude of the stock market to the game of snap or musical chairs, noting that what is liquid for the individual is fixed for the community as a whole.

It is my belief that both the theory and practice of stockholder liquidity and responsibility and the fiduciary roles of management and the board of directors need drastic review. These, however, are bigger and more systemic problems than trying to make the results of hostile tenders and LBOs more socially constructive now. Lowenstein (1983) proposed an amendment to the Williams Act which in effect would change timing and enable a better

auction to develop, giving the target company more opportunity to explore alternatives. He has since (Lowenstein, 1984) concluded that it would not be adequate to cope with the emergence of greenmail with large-bank financing. Although there are many legal and institutional details to be worked out, the principle to the student of oligopoly theory and game theory is reasonably well defined. Process matters; timing matters; so does trying to design the rules so that a competent management has the opportunity not so much to defend itself as to take steps to ensure that, if there are large gains to be had in a legitimate arbitrage between the markets, most of that gain will be captured by the stockholders as a whole. Lowenstein's proposal might even go some distance toward alleviating the tug between the short-term goals of stockholders and the long-term needs of capital by leaving less on the table.

REPRISE

In economic newspeak, words such as *efficient markets, rational expectations, perfect competition,* and *perfect equilibrium* have taken on quasi-religious meaning. Judges or lawyers seeking scientific simplicity and learned authority can rest their cases on the pristine virtues of a true believer in laissez-faire. Unfortunately, the world of dynamic economies with players of different skills has scarcely been formalized by the best of theorists.

What may appear to be high abstraction to the lawyer or layman—such as the strong and semistrong assertions about efficient markets—to the takeover group accumulating its first 5% appears to be irrelevant noninstitutional unreality.

But doubts are not raised by the practitioners alone, who may not recognize or appreciate abstraction. The problem with the theory is that it does not appear to be a logically consistent and complete representation of the problems it purports to answer. General equilibrium theory provides an elegant, logically complete explanation of the static existence of a price system. It has virtually nothing to say about dynamics unless special structure or detail is added. Much of the theorizing about price in finance is watered-down partial equilibrium theory still with a lack of formal structure of process. Yet many of the key questions in law and practical finance concern process.

The leap which permits one to claim that a theory which deliberately rules out process is capable of answering questions involving process is one of faith, not knowledge. But theories are seldom overthrown by mere facts. They are overthrown by facts that do not fit and by better theories. The beginnings of better theories are available; the models in agency theory, auctions, strategic market games, oligopoly theory, and game theory[19] are for the most part process models. The mere attempt to formalize economic process models of financial competition requires a mathematical, institutional economics where bankruptcy, seniority, insolvency-secured loans, and virtually all financial instruments and institutions appear as necessary rules or important simplifications of the game. The solutions for the most part are still static—mainly the noncooperative equilibrium—because the fully dynamic models and solutions are in general too hard to formalize and solve. Yet the models and type of thought involved are more in line with the view of financial competition among the few as a game of skill and strategy.

The special limiting assumptions noted in the "Discourse" section of this chapter have produced a theory which shows that a player in a mass secondhand market for lottery tickets has no way to beat the market in the next few days. It says nothing about the next few years and little about the connections between paper and real assets and institutions. It contains valuable advice to the mutual fund manager and little advice for those who are concerned with the meeting of the markets of paper, control, and real assets.

APPENDIX

This brief explanation of terms is for the convenience of noneconomists unfamiliar with some of the economic or game-theoretic terminology. I have tried to provide intuitive insight rather than formal rigor.

Preference, Indifference Curves, and Utility Functions

Preference

Consider a set of n objects $A_1, A_2, \ldots, A_n$. The assumption that an individual has a complete (weak) preference order over all of the objects means that when he is confronted with a simple choice between any two, say A_i and A_j, he can always state which one he prefers or that he is indifferent between them. Furthermore, the condition of transitivity holds. If A_i is preferred to A_j and A_j to A_k, then A_i is preferred to A_j.

Indifference Curves

Suppose that two (or more) commodities were easily divisible and any quantity of the same commodity were completely tangible with the same quantity (e.g., a gallon of the same gasoline). We can represent the preferences of an individual for any combination of holdings of the two commodities by an indifference curve map, where the individual indifference curve shows combinations of holdings of the two commodities among which the individual is indifferent (see Figure 2.1).

The two points (7, 7) and (10, 4) which lie on the same indifference curve tell us that the individual, given the choice of 7

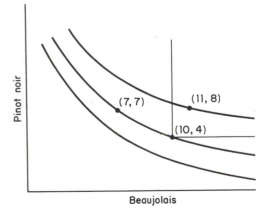

Figure 2.1

liters of both Pinot noir and Beaujolais or 10 liters of Beaujolais and 4 of Pinot noir, does not care which he chooses. He is indifferent. The point (11, 8) lies on a higher indifference curve; it is preferred to either of the others. It reflects the assumption that more of everything is better. The fact that the indifference curves are drawn as continuous and concave requires special assumptions (such as divisibility, portability, fungibility, etc.) are often important in commercial transactions but are not generally discussed in the elementary development of the basic theory. The very existence of an efficient price system depends upon the reality of these assumptions.

Utility Function

If we can order preferences for bundles of goods—i.e., if we can say that (11, 8) is preferred to (10, 4)—can we make a stronger statement and say by how much? There is a large body of literature in economic theory and in psychology which indicates that this should be possible under certain circumstances (for an expository discussion, see Shubik, 1982, Chap. 4). If we represent an arbitrary bundle of goods by (x, y), then the existence of a utility function means that there will be a number z such that $z = f(x, y)$, where f is a continuous function of x and y. A host of assumptions about individual preference, choice, and perceptions are contained in this abstraction.

Rational Expectations

A formal definition requires an almost Talmudic piling up of special assumptions. In essence, however, the idea is that intelligent individuals will take into account all second guessing so that their expectations include guesses about the guesses of others, and vice versa. If all parties are equally intelligent and industrious and have the same basic information, then their guesses should all be consistent. A better and less mysterious name for rational expectations should be consistent expectations.

Competitive Equilibrium

Assume that all individuals have preferences representable by utility functions,

and that they are all "small" with respect to every market they are trading in so that no individual alone can influence price. Then (with the appropriate list of qualifications) there exists (see Debreu, 1959) at least one set of prices such that, if all individuals were informed of these prices, trade would take place so that each individual would maximize his or her own welfare (or utility) given the total value of each person's resources and all markets would precisely balance or clear. This result implicitly assumes complete liquidity of all resources and says nothing whatsoever about how the prices are formed. Money, credit, and bankruptcy play no explicit roles in this theory.

Strategic Market Game

This and the remaining two definitions involve game-theoretic concepts.

A strategic market game is a model of an economic system involving trade or trade and production where the mechanism carrying process is modeled explicitly; i.e., details such as how price is formed are supplied (see Shubik, 1973, 1975, 1979; Dubey and Shapley, 1977; Dubey and Shubik, 1977, 1978a, 1978b, 1979, 1980).

Even at the level of high simplification and abstraction, the details required to produce a mathematically tractable model call for a description of trade via "the rules of the game," which amount to the mathematical description of the minimal elementary laws and institutions required to carry out exchange and production. In other words, concepts such as the role of money, credit, liquidity, thickness of markets (see Shubik, 1984, Chap. 15), bankruptcy, and price formation must be made explicit.

Under the appropriate conditions the results obtained from the model of competitive equilibrium can be obtained as results from the analysis of strategic market games with many small players.

Noncooperative Equilibrium

The noncooperative equilibrium is the solution concept most frequently employed in the analysis of strategic market games (or for that matter any game in strategic form; see Shubik, 1984, Chap. 3). Rather than present a discussion of the strategic form, we should be able to follow the exposition reasonably well by using an example.

A strategy is a plan of action which covers all contingencies. We can contemplate an extremely simple game where there are two players, each of whom has to choose between two strategies. There will be four outcomes to each. A game can be easily illustrated. Two examples are shown by the two matrices in Tables 2.2a and 2.2b.

We interpret Table 2.2a as follows. Strategy 1 for each is to keep price high; strategy 2 is to cut price. In each cell of the matrix there are two numbers; the first is the payoff to Player A and the second is the payoff to Player B. If both keep price high, they each earn 5. If Player B cuts price (strategy 2) and Player A keeps her price high, then Player A obtains -1 and Player B obtains 9. If both cut price, they each earn 2.

The matrix portrays a game in strategic form. The idea behind a noncooperative equilibrium solution to a game in strategic form is one of mutually consistent expectations. If Player A thinks that B is going to use his strategy j, then she will maximize given this belief. Suppose she would choose her strategy i. Then (i, j) would be an equilibrium if B would choose j. Table 2.2a can be used for illustration. If A thinks B will cut prices, so will she, and vice versa. The only equilibrium in the game illustrated by Table 2.2a is the pair of strategies (2, 2).

In the game in Table 2.2b there are two equilibria, one at (1, 1) and one at (2, 2). If A thinks B will play 1, she knows she has

the upper hand and she will play 1. If B thinks A will play 1, he will play 1. But the same sort of argument could be made for the strategy pair (2, 2) which favors B.

A more discursive and technical summary of the noncooperative solution, complete with many examples, is given in Shubik (1982, Chap. 10).

PERFECT EQUILIBRIUM (PERFECT NONCOOPERATIVE EQUILIBRIUM)

A concept that is currently popular in the analysis of oligopolistic competition and in the study of questions concerning the enforcement of contract is the perfect-equilibrium point. Consider the game illustrated in Table 2.2a played twice. At the last play the only equilibrium is that both cut price. But by backward induction, if both know they will cut price on the last play, they might as well cut price on the first play. The only strategies which are in equilibrium at all stages are that both cut price from the start.

Table 2.3 shows the game presented in Table 2.2a, modified by the addition of a "threat" strategy for each player. If either player uses his threat strategy, he can inflict considerable damage on his competitor, but at high cost to himself. The same equilibrium is still perfect. If each plays his second strategy, this is in equilibrium at each stage. Each player will get a payoff of 2 each period.

There is, however, another strategy which involves using option 3 as a threat. For example, Player A could announce to keep my prices high (1) in the first period; if B does likewise, I cut prices in the second

Table 2.2

		Player B's Strategies 1	2
Player A's	1	5, 5	-1, 9
Strategies	2	9, -1	2, 2

a

		Player B's Strategies 1	2
Player A's	1	2, 1	0, 0
Strategies	2	0, 0	1, 2

b

Table 2.3.

	1	2	3
1	5, 5	−1, 9	−20, −10
2	9, −1	2, 2	−20, −10
3	−10, −20	−10, −20	−25, −25

period (2); if B does anything else in the first period, then I engage in out-and-out war to punish him by playing (3).

If both adopt this strategy, they will earn 5 each in period 1 and 2 in period 2. But it can be argued that this equilibrium is not perfect because it should never pay a player to carry out his threat because it cannot pay him to do so after it has failed to deter. The plausibility of this argument is not a matter of logic but involves a critical view of human decision processes. The perfect-equilibrium argument is nonhistorical. It is without the context of history of society. It encapsulates the short-term view which ignores yesterday and considers enforcement only in terms of "Will it pay immediately?" The most levelheaded of humans tend to be not rational but at best *context-rational.* Their actions are based not merely on here and now but on the context of their society and history. To some, it may be the height of irrationality to spend $100 to track down a $10 theft; to others (including myself), it may be a mark of societal rationality.

The debate concerning perfect-equilibrium points may appear, at first glance to the outsider, as an argument over esoterica by the economic theorists and game theorists; yet it is at the center of arguments concerning the evolution of threats and contracts. At an even deeper level it involves a split in views in economic theory; on the one hand, that a noninstitutional, nonprocess, nonhistorical picture of the competitive markets must dominate an economy, and on the other hand, that process counts and cannot even be defined without inventing institutions and recog-

nizing the role of history and society in delimiting the scope of economic action.

NOTES

1. This comment is not meant to be pejorative; it may be that complexity is a necessary device in a democracy to provide a way to pay lip service to populist simple solutions while working out sophisticated compromises.

2. In spite of the collaboration of economists and lawyers, some of the "terms of art" used by each are not necessarily fully understood by the others. Rather than add definitions to the text, the few which may be useful are given in an appendix.

3. See Appendix.

4. See Appendix.

5. See Appendix.

6. Replication is the simplest way to do this formally. Replace each individual by k identical individuals, and let k increase.

7. See Appendix.

8. See Appendix.

9. Defined up to a linear transformation by using axioms of behavior under uncertainty (von Neumann and Morgenstern, 1944).

10. For example, if money is used instead of bilateral trade in all goods, one has to define "enough money" for efficient trade. If there is not enough money, we may wish to invent credit, but most credit mechanisms call for clearinghouses, insolvency laws, bankruptcy laws, and seniority rules if the game is to be defined out of equilibrium as well as in.

11. See Appendix.

12. This result can be deduced from cooperative game theory. If a majority in control could avoid paying the minority its proportionate share of the profits, the resultant cooperative game would have no core, from which it follows that no efficient price system exists.

13. See also the symposium on the market

for corporate control in a special issue of the *Journal of Financial Economics* (1983).

14. One can formulate the optimization as a simple type of general equilibrium exchange model where the traders own endowments of money and lotteries for money and their utility functions are von Neumann–Morgenstern utility functions for money.

15. Technically, a continuum of all agents with no atomic agents.

16. See Appendix on perfect equilibrium.

17. The work of Shiller (1981) already noted provides some indication of stock market swings around economic valuation. The stress on asset values as contrasted with concern for short-term profits would appear to indicate that those who deal in corporations as a whole are willing to arbitrage in both directions against the stock market's over- and underevaluation of assets. I conjecture that Shiller's results illustrate an arbitrage between concerned, active, specialized professionals and a mass market subject to the fashion show and "animal spirits" in both directions (Keynes, 1936).

18. In 1968, a business game was constructed and played at Stanford Research Institute (see Shubik, 1970), with the corporate results being announced by a stock exchange floor where four stocks could be traded. There were no trading costs or other imperfections. The players were, for the most part, corporate executives. The relationship between the eventual, expected money payoff at liquidation at the end of the game and market price was highly variable.

19. In extensive or strategic but not coalitional form.

REFERENCES

Arrow, K. J. (1964). "The Role of Securities in the Optimal Allocation of Risk Bearing." *Review of Economic Studies* **31**, 91–96.

————— (1985). "The Economics of Ageing." In *Ageing: The Structure of Business*, ed. J. W. Pratt and R. Zeckhauser. Cambridge, Mass.: Harvard Business School Press.

—————, and G. Debreu (1954). "Existence of an Equilibrium for a Competitive Economy," *Econometrica* **22**, 215–290.

Bacon, J. (1977). *The Board of Directors: Perspectives and Practices in Mine Countries*. New York: The Conference Board.

Baker, J. C. (1945). *Directors and Their Functions*. Boston: Harvard Graduate School of Business.

Berle, A., and G. Means (1932). *The Modern Corporation and Private Property*. New York: Macmillan.

Brown, C. C. (1976). *Putting the Corporate Board to Work*. New York: Macmillan.

De Angelo, H., L. De Angelo, and E. M. Rice (1984). "Going Private Minority Freezeouts and Stockholder Wealth." *Journal of Law and Economics* **27**, 367–401.

Debreu, G. (1959). *The Theory of Value*. New York: Wiley.

Diamond, P. A. (1967). "The Role of the Stock Market in a General Equilibrium Model with Technological Uncertainty." *American Economic Review* **57** (4), 759–776.

Dreman, D. (1952). *The New Contrarian Investment Strategy*. New York: Random House.

Dubey, P. (1982). "Price-Quantity Strategic Market Games." *Econometrica* **50**, 111–126.

—————, and L. S. Shapley (1977). *Noncooperative Exchange with a Continuum of Traders*. Discussion Paper 447, Cowles Foundation, Yale University.

—————, and M. Shubik (1977). "Trade and Prices in a Closed Economy with Exogenous Uncertainty and Different Levels of Information." *Econometrica* **45** (7), 1657–1680.

—————, and M. Shubik (1978a). "The Noncooperative Equilibria of a Closed Trading Economy with Market Supply and Bidding Strategies." *Journal of Economic Theory* **17**, 1–20.

—————, and M. Shubik (1978b). "A Closed Economic System with Production and Exchange Modelled as a Game of Strategy." *Journal of Mathematical Economics* **4** (1), 258–287.

—————, and M. Shubik (1979). "Bankruptcy and Optimality in a Closed Trading Economy Modelled as a Noncooperative Game." *Journal of Mathematical Economics* **6**, 115–134.

—————, and M. Shubik (1980). "A Strategic Market Game with Price and Quantity Strategies." *Zeitschrift fur Nationalokonomie* **40** (1–2), 25–34.

—————, and M. Shubik (1981). "The Profit Maximizing Firm: Managers and Stockholders." In *Economies et Societes* Vol. 14, 1369–1388. Cahiers de l'Institut de Sciences Mathematiques et Economiques Appliquees, Series EM, No. 6, Laboratoire Associe au C.N.R.S.

—————, J. Geanakoplos, and M. Shubik (1982). *Revelation of Information in Strategic Market Games: A Critique of Rational Expectations*. Discussion Paper 643, Cowles Foundation, Yale University.

Ekern, S., and R. Wilson (1974). "On the Theory of the Firm in an Economy with Incomplete Markets." *Bell Journal of Economics and Management Science* **5**, 171–180.

Fama, E. (1970). "Efficient Capital Markets: A

Review of Theory and Empirical Work." *Journal of Finance* **25**, 383–417.

———— (1972). "Perfect Competition and Optimal Production Decisions Under Uncertainty." *Bell Journal of Economics and Management Science* **3**, 509–530.

Foley, A. K. (1970). "Economic Equilibrium with Costly Marketing." *Journal of Economic Theory* **2**, 276–281.

Grossman, S. J., and O. D. Hart (1979). "A Theory of Competitive Equilibrium in Stock Market Economics." *Econometrica* **47**, 293–330.

Hahn, F. H. (1971). "Equilibrium with Transactions Costs." *Econometrica* **30**, 417–439.

Hellwig, M. (1981). "Bankruptcy, Limited Liability and the Modigliani-Miller Theorem." *American Economic Review* **71**, 150–170.

Herman, E. S. (1981). *Corporate Control, Corporate Power.* Cambridge, England: Cambridge University Press.

Jensen, M., and J. Long (1972). "Corporate Investment Under Uncertainty and Pareto Optimality of Stock Markets." *Bell Journal of Economics and Management Science* **3**, 151–174.

Keyes, J. M. (1936). *The General Theory of Employment Interest and Money.* London: Macmillan.

Leland, H. (1974). "Production Theory and the Stock Market." *Bell Journal of Economics and Management Science* **5**, 125–144.

Lintner, J. (1962). "Dividend Earnings, Leverage, Stock Prices and the Supply of Capital to Corporations." *Review of Economics and Statistics* **44**, 243–169.

———— (1965). "The Valuation of Risk, Assets and the Solution of Risky Investments in Stock Portfolios and Capital Budgets." *Review of Economics and Statistics* **47**, 13–37.

Lipton, M. (1979). "Takeover Bids in the Target's Boardroom." *Business Law* **35**, 101.

Lowenstein, L. (1983). "Pruning Deadwood in Hostile Takeovers: A Proposal for Legislation." *Columbia Law Review* **83**, 249–333.

———— (1984). Statement of hearings on takeover and public policy on May 24, 1984, before House Subcommittee on Telecommunication, Consumer Protection and Finance, at Rayburn House Office Building, Washington, D.C.

———— (1985). "Management Buyouts." *Columbia Law Review* **85**, 730–784.

Mace, M. (1971). *Directors: Myths and Realities.* Boston: Harvard School of Business.

McKenzie, L. (1959). "On the Existence of General Equilibrium for a Competitive Market." *Econometrica* **27**, 54–71.

Markowitz, H. (1959). *Portfolio Selection: Efficient Diversification of Investments.* New York: Wiley.

Marris, R. (1979). *Theory and Future of the Corporate Economy and Society.* Amsterdam: North-Holland.

Merton, R., and M. Subrahmanyan (1974). "The Optimality of a Competitive Stock Market." *Bell Journal of Economics and Management Science* **5**, 147–170.

Modigliani, F., and M. H. Miller (1958). "The Cost of Capital, Corporation Finance and the Theory of Investment." *American Economic Review* **48**, 261–297.

New York Stock Exchange Fact Book (1984).

Radner, R. (1968). "Competitive Equilibrium Under Uncertainty." *Econometrica* **36**, 31–58.

———— (1970). "Problems in the Theory of Markets Under Uncertainty." *American Economic Review* **60**, 454–460.

Reich, C. (1983). *Financier: A Biography of Andre Meyer.* New York: Morrow.

Rogawski, J., and M. Shubik (1986). "A Strategic Market Game with Transactions Costs." *Mathematical Social Sciences* (forthcoming).

Roll, R. S., and S. A. Ross (1980). "An Empirical Investigation of the Arbitrage Pricing Theory." *Journal of Finance* **35**, 1073–1103.

Ross, S. A. (1976). "The Arbitrage Theory of Capital Asset Pricing." *Journal of Economic Theory* **13**, 341–360.

Scarf, H. S. (1973). *Computation of Economic Equilibria.* New Haven: Yale University Press (with the collaboration of T. Hansen).

————, and J. P. Shoven, eds. (1984). *Applied General Equilibrium Analysis.* Cambridge, England: Cambridge University Press.

Scherer, F. M. (1980). *Industrial Market Structure and Economic Performance.* 2nd ed. Chicago: Rand McNally.

Shannon, C. E. (1948). "A Mathematical Theory of Communication." *Bell System Technical Journal* **27**, 379–423, 623–656.

Shapley, L., and M. Shubik (1977). "Trade Using One Commodity as a Means of Payment." *Journal of Political Economy* **85** (5) 937–968.

Sharpe, W. F. (1964). "Capital Asset Prices: A Theory of Market Equilibrium Under Conditions of Risk." *Journal of Finance* **19**, 425–442.

———— (1985). *Investments.* 3rd ed. Englewood Cliffs, N.J.: Prentice-Hall.

Shiller, R. J. (1981). "Do Stock Prices Move Too Much to Be Justified by Subsequent Changes in Dividends?" *American Economic Review* **71**, 421–436.

Shubik, M. (1970). "A Note on a Simulated Stock Market." *Decision Sciences* **1**, 129–141.

———— (1973). "Commodity Money, Oligopoly, Credit and Bankruptcy in a General Equilibrium Model." *Western Economic Journal* **11** (1), 24–38.

———— (1975). "The General Equilibrium Model Is Incomplete and Not Adequate for the Reconciliation of Micro- and Macroeconomic Theory." *Kyklos* **28** (3), 74–93.

———— (1979). "On the Number of Types of Markets with Trade in Money: Theory and Possible Experimentation." In *Research in Experimental Economics,* Vol. 1, ed. V. L. Smith. Greenwich, Conn.: JAI Press.

———— (1981). "A Price-Quantity Buy-Sell Market With and Without Contingent Bids." In *Studies in Economic Theory and Practice,* ed. J. Los et al. Amsterdam: North-Hollard.

———— (1982). *Game Theory in the Social Sciences.* Vol. I. Cambridge, Mass.: MIT Press.

———— (1984). *Political Economy: A Game Theoretic Approach.* Cambridge: MIT Press.

Smith, V. L. (1970). "Corporate Financial Theory Under Uncertainty." *Quarterly Journal of Economics* **84**, 451–471.

———— (1972). "Default Risk, Scale and the Homemade Leverage Theorem." *American Economic Review* **62**, 66–76.

Stiglitz, J. E. (1972). "On the Optimality of the Stock Market Allocation of Investment." *Quarterly Journal of Economics* **86**, 25–60.

von Neumann, J., and O. Morgensterm (1944). *Theory of Games and Economic Behavior.* Princeton, N. J.: Princeton University Press.

Walras, L. (1954). *Elements of Pure Economics* (translated from French, original 1874). London: Allen and Unwin.

Whitman, M. J., and M. Shubik (1979). *The Aggressive Conservative Investor.* New York: Random House.

Williamson, O. (1975). *Markets and Hierarchies: Analysis and Antitrust Implications.* New York: Free Press.

Yardley, H. O. (1975). *The Education of a Poker Player.* New York: Simon & Schuster.

3

Fashions, Fads, and Bubbles in Financial Markets

ROBERT J. SHILLER

For hundreds of years it has been commonly accepted that prices in speculative markets are influenced by capricious changes in investor sentiments, changing fashions, fads, or bubbles. In the past few decades this commonly accepted view has been strongly challenged by academic researchers in finance. They have posed, as an alternative to this view, the hypothesis of market efficiency and have claimed extensive statistical support for the hypothesis.

The usual definition of market efficiency given in introductory finance textbooks, while it is not as precise as we'd like, may capture the most commonly understood meaning. Sharpe (1985) wrote: "A (perfectly) efficient market is one in which every security's price equals its investment value at all times."[1] Brealey and Myers (1984) wrote: "We recommend that financial managers assume that capital markets are efficient unless they have a strong, specific reason to believe otherwise. That means trusting market prices, and trusting investors to recognize true economic value."[2]

I wish to argue here that this fundamental notion of market efficiency is not quite right and that, in fact, there is evidence that fashions, fads, or bubbles *do* importantly influence prices of speculative assets. The view of speculative markets that I wish to urge, however, is not just a return

to the common views of thirty or more years ago; rather my position is, in fact, heavily influenced by the efficient-markets literature.

Investors, of course, vary in their investment savvy. Ordinary investors are influenced by extraneous information or fads in their investment decisions and overemphasize some investments and overlook others. Other investors, whom we may call "smart money," systematically search over investments for abnormal returns. The latter group, limited in wealth, prevents the demands of ordinary investors from feeding directly into prices but does not prevent them from influencing prices. The "smart money" probably does not correspond closely to investment professionals: Among them are both ordinary investors and smart money. In one study (Pound and Shiller, 1987) survey evidence was found that suggests that among institutional investors one can find both "diffusion investors," whose interest in individual stocks is spurred by interpersonal communications, and other "systematic investors."

One possible formal model of the influence of fashions, fads, or bubbles on financial markets was discussed in an earlier paper (Shiller, 1984). In this model prices are the present value of expected (by smart money) future dividends *plus* a term proportional to the present value of the expected (by smart money) future demands by ordinary investors.

With a model like this one, we would expect that in takeovers the price increase of target firms might well be understood, in

Yale University and National Bureau of Economic Research. Michael W. Ewing supplied research assistance for this paper. This research was supported by the National Science Foundation.

some cases at least, in terms of the management inefficiency, synergy, or information effects theories discussed in the literature. However, the model would also suggest that firms may be takeover targets because they are overlooked by ordinary investors, or that their price increase at the time of takeover may not be understood without reference to the behavior of ordinary investors.

TRADITIONAL EVIDENCE ON FADS IN FINANCIAL MARKETS

The old view of fads in financial markets was supported by anecdotal evidence. Some of the anecdotes are so well known as to be part of our popular culture: the stories of the tulipomania in the seventeenth century, the South Sea Islands bubble and John Law's Mississippi scheme bubble of the eighteenth century, the U.S. stock market boom of the late 1920s, the Florida land price bubble of the 1920s, the great bull market of the 1950s and early 1960s, the Canadian stock boom of the early 1950s, the growth stock craze of 1959–1961, and the high-tech boom of the early 1980s.

What is common to all of these anecdotes is the claim that people are sometimes excessively enthusiastic for certain speculative assets and that their judgment is then not sound. For example, speaking of the tulipomania of the seventeenth century, Mackay (1841) wrote:

In 1634 the rage among the Dutch to possess them [tulips] was so great that the ordinary industry of the country was neglected and the population, even to its lowest dregs, embarked in the tulip trade. As the mania increased, prices augmented until, in 1635, many persons were known to invest a fortune of 100,000 Florins in the purchase of 40 roots. . . . Houses and land were offered for sale at ruinously low prices, or assigned in payment of bargains made at the tulip mart.[3]

Speaking of the stock market boom of the late 1920s, Galbraith (1972) wrote:

By the summer of 1929 the market not only dominated the news. It also dominated the cul-

ture. That recherché minority which at other times has acknowledged its interest in Saint Thomas Aquinas, Proust, psychoanalysis and psychosomatic medicine then spoke of United Corporation, United Founders and steel. . . . Main street had always had one citizen who could speak knowingly about buying or selling stocks. Now he became an oracle.[4]

Speaking of the "growth stocks craze" of 1959–1961, Malkiel (1981) wrote:

Growth took on an almost mystical significance, and questioning the propriety of such valuations became, as in the generation past, almost heretical. These prices could not be justified on firm foundation principles.[5]

These anecdotes necessarily concern extreme and unusual events, selected as they are for dramatic effect. The tellers of these stories wished to convince us that human judgment is sometimes faulty, and they had to pick extreme examples if the faulty judgment is to be readily apparent. It is natural, however, to suspect that if such extreme examples are indeed correctly reported, then it must also be the case that in the usual course of trading, less dramatic fads or fashions are an important cause of price variability; various speculative assets are at times overvalued because they are fashionable and have attracted undue attention, while other speculative assets are subject to adverse prejudice or are just ignored and hence underpriced.

Advocates of market efficiency correctly point out that such anecdotal evidence does not constitute solid proof that human judgment was ever faulty. The problem with the anecdotes is that they hinge on the judgment of the teller of the story (or of others the teller cites) that people did *not* have good reasons to behave as they did. Even if we believe the teller's assertion that people were unusually excited or optimistic, that doesn't prove that they weren't also right to feel so. The fact that the expected future price increases didn't materialize doesn't prove that their methods of forecasting prices weren't sound. A good method of forecasting will sometimes fail, and selecting these failures for special attention may not be a good way of evaluating the method.

THE EVIDENCE FOR MARKET EFFICIENCY

Despite the weaknesses of the anecdotal evidence, it does *suggest* that there is an important influence of faddish behavior in financial markets. Why is it, then, that so many in academic finance strongly assert the opposite position, that fads have no influence on financial prices?

There is nothing in *theoretical* finance that implies that market prices ought not to be influenced heavily by changing fashions or fads among a portion of investors. Some people seem to think that there is such a theoretical argument. If such fashions or fads influenced price, then there would be "profit opportunities" for smart money. The smart money would then, through profitable trading, take over the market and thereby eliminate the profit opportunities. There is something to this possibility, and it does give a reason to doubt that there are spectacular profit opportunities. But the argument is not strong enough to rule out the possibility that actual price changes aren't heavily influenced by changing fashions or fads. Such fashions or fads may not create spectacular profit opportunities if the future paths of the fashions or fads are not very predictable. If there exist only modest (and uncertain) profit opportunities for smart money, then the tendency for smart money to accumulate wealth through profitable trading may be a slow one and may not keep up with other tendencies that would tend to spread wealth through the population. Consider those people who, in the late 1950s and early 1960s in the United States, thought that the bull market had gone on too long and that stocks were overpriced. Even if they *knew* that the market would eventually fall, there was no way for them to get rich quickly from this knowledge. They had to wait years to be vindicated; they could not predict when the bull market would end. In fact, those people who thought the market would fall hardly took over the market.

If there is any evidence for the efficient-markets model, then it must be empirical. There is in fact a really vast statistical literature that bears on the issue of market efficiency. There are, however, fundamental problems with this literature that make it of questionable relevance to the issue at hand. The first problem is that there is no agreed-upon way to define the terms *investment value* or *true economic value* in the definitions of market efficiency, nor to define the *abnormal returns* due to departure of prices from these values. The null hypothesis of market efficiency is ill defined. The second problem is that there has been virtually no explicit consideration in this literature of how fashions or fads might be expected to influence markets. The alternative hypothesis also remains ill defined. No amount of statistical evidence can resolve such ill-defined hypotheses.

The null hypothesis of market efficiency cannot be defined just as the absence of an "abnormal profit opportunity" without defining carefully what such a profit opportunity is. It cannot be considered proof of a profit opportunity just to show that some investment strategies yield more on average than do others. The strategy of investing in stocks yields more on average than the strategy of investing in bonds. The higher return may be considered just a compensation for the higher risk of investing in stocks versus bonds. To show that markets are not efficient, one must find an investment strategy that achieves higher average return without achieving higher risk. To show this, one must rely on a model of the risk-return relationship.

The capital asset–pricing model that is the basis of many studies has been criticized on a number of theoretical grounds (Roll, 1977), and so rejection of it does not constitute evidence that markets are not efficient. Finance theorists have gone on to test rather different and new models, like the consumption-based, asset-pricing model of Breeden (1979) that measures risk by correlation of returns with consumption; but no consensus has emerged on these models. It is plain that the finance profession does not agree on how to measure risk or even on whether it can be measured with existing data.

In addition to the problems of risk, there is the problem of taxes. Investors are concerned with after-tax returns (which are influenced differentially across stocks by the dividend-price ratio), but investors differ in their tax brackets and holding periods for capital gains. Thus, the "after-tax return," which ought to be the basis of efficient-market studies, is unmeasurable.

In the absence of such a well-defined null hypothesis, critics of the basic notion of market efficiency are in a difficult position. In effect, they must try to show spectacular evidence of market inefficiency that is so dramatic that it would appear to contradict any of the different versions of the hypothesis. But perhaps it is just such spectacular evidence that we would not expect to find, if spectacular evidence means spectacular profit opportunities.

The second problem with the existing literature testing market efficiency is its lack of consideration of a well-defined alternative representing fashions or fads in financial markets. The efficient-markets literature is often described as finding only "small" departures from market efficiency. But how large are the "anomalies" that we would expect to find if fashions or fads did in fact dominate financial markets? I have argued elsewhere (Shiller, 1984), as has Summers (1986), that big valuation errors may generate only "small" abnormal profit opportunities. It is not hard to see that this is a possibility. If, let us say, a stock with a dividend yield of 4.5% is bid up by enthusiastic investors so that its price is doubled, and if the enthusiasm is unpredictable and there is no reason to think it will subside in the near future, then the anticipated yield falls only to 2.25%. This yield does not produce any dramatic, riskless profit opportunity through short sales or option markets. Similarly, if the stock is overlooked and its price falls by a third, then the anticipated yield rises by 2.25 percentage points to 6.75%. Buying this stock would not make one rich quickly. It is hardly obvious, given the uncertainties, that "smart money" will do anything effective in response to the 2.25% yield differential to prevent the mispricing of the stock.

However, the efficient-markets literature has indeed found a number of "small" anomalies of the sort that one might expect to find if fashions or fads dominated financial markets. I will cite here only those anomalies that are related to price relative to some simple measure of firm value. Returns have been found to show a small correlation with the earnings-price ratio, even after beta has been taken into account. Basu (1983) found that firms in the highest quintile in terms of the earnings-price ratio had an abnormal return (i.e., risk-corrected excess return) over the market of 4.4% per year.[6] High–earnings-price-ratio stocks tend to do slightly better, as if stocks whose price has fallen due to investor disinterest become underpriced and hence a good investment. Low–earnings-price-ratio stocks tend to do slightly worse, as if their low ratio is often the result of a fad pushing the price up, so that the stock is overpriced and a poor investment. Other studies (e.g., Black and Sholes, 1974; Blume, 1980; Litzenberger and Ramaswamy, 1982; Morgan, 1982) have shown that the dividend-price ratio predicts abnormal returns, just as does the price-earnings ratio, though this evidence is ambiguous since the dividend-price ratio also has tax conseqences whose value depends on the tax bracket of the investor. More recently, Rosenberg (1985) has shown that stocks with high (by his criterion) book-value–price ratios tend to do slightly better, with an abnormal return of 4.4% per year. DeBondt and Thaler (1985) showed that stocks whose price has dropped dramatically (by their criterion) in the last three years show an abnormal return of 6.1% per year over the succeeding three years.

Another group of studies has investigated whether professional analysts have any ability to beat the market. If markets are inefficient, then it would seem to follow that some professional investors ought to be systematically able to profit from this information. It is tricky, however, to evaluate by any casual reading of this literature whether fashions or fads exist. Most of the studies in the literature report, on average, weekly or monthly returns of some special group of investors over a relatively short calendar interval. In many of these studies investors who are doing the right thing for the long run may well do poorly owing to chance. Moreover, even if there are fashions or fads in financial markets, it does not follow, of course, that *all* professional investors will profit from them. One might think, though, that they as a group would be less vulnerable to fads and would therefore do better.

Dimson and Marsh (1984) surveyed 27 studies of the performance of brokers' advisory service recommendations. These studies reported returns over various horizons after each recommendation was made. The weighted-average return over prerecommendation price in all these studies was 0.6% on the publication day, 1.5% after one day, and 1.1% after one week.[7] To someone trained in finance, the natural next question to ask is whether transactions costs might substantially diminish the profit opportunity, or whether one could take advantage of these profit opportunities with substantial amounts of money without destroying them. But for the purpose of confirming that fashions or fads influence financial markets, these considerations are irrelevant.

While most of the efficient-markets literature turning up "anomalies" does not give us a clear idea as to the source of valuation errors, another avenue of research actually shows that the data are consistent with the notion that movements in the aggregate stock market over the past century may be attributed almost entirely to fashions and fads. This work (Shiller, 1981a, 1981c; similar to work by Shiller, 1979; LeRoy and Porter, 1981; West, 1984; Mankiw et al., 1985; and others) shows that aggregate, real–stock price indexes have moved much more than the present value of the corresponding real-dividend series, the present value behaving much like a trend through time. Some of the interpretations of this result made by these authors have been criticized (Flavin, 1983; Kleidon, 1983; Marsh and Merton, 1984; and others). These criticisms do not deny, however, that movements in aggregate, real stock prices over the past century were without any validating movements in fundamentals. If the data had shown, instead, that real, aggregate stock prices moved as if they were *successfully* forecasting funda-

mentals, we would indeed have evidence for the efficient-markets hypothesis. Since they have not, it is hard to see how any further statistical tests could be construed as proving the efficient-markets hypothesis for the aggregate stock market.

That speculative, asset price movements appear to be influenced by things other than fundamentals is further suggested by some work of Roll (1984) and French and Roll (1986). Roll showed that news about the weather seems to dominate news cited with reference to orange juice futures, and yet most price movements in orange juice futures appear to be unrelated to the weather. Moreover, the variance of orange juice changes is not as high over the weekend, when there is just as much news about the weather, as it should be. French and Roll found that the variance of stock price changes from Tuesdays to the immediately following Thursdays was lower in periods when the stock market was closed on Wednesdays, even though it would seem that as much information was forthcoming then.

DIFFUSION MODELS AND FASHIONS, FADS, AND BUBBLES

The availability to investors of instances or associations regarding speculative assets is a random process influenced by a number of factors. News stories or commonly noted events that remind people of the stock may make it more likely that individuals will talk about the stock. Thus, for example, news of severe weather in one part of the country may suggest conversation about companies headquartered there. The rate of spread of interest in one stock is likely to be inhibited by the spread of interest in another stock, since people can talk seriously about a limited number of stocks at a given time. Thus, for example, a big earnings announcement in a different firm may cause conversations that displace conversations about the stock. The lumpiness of media attention is also a factor inducing randomness in the behavior of diffusion traders. Opportunities to talk seriously about a given stock with others may be influenced by patterns of social interaction that may vary irregularly over time. Receptiveness to new interest may vary depending on economic or other circumstances.

A fad is a bubble if the contagion of the fad occurs through price; people are attracted by observed price increases. Observing past price increases means observing other people becoming wealthy who invested heavily in the asset, and this observation might interest or excite other potential investors. In the simplest bubble model, price increases themselves thus cause greater subsequent price increases until price reaches some barrier; then the bubble bursts and price drops precipitously, since there are then no further price increases to sustain the high demand. This model contrasts with the simple models of the transmission of attitudes offered by mathematical sociologists, as in Bartholomew (1982), in which increases in the intensity of the fad are related to the number of (not the increase in) involved people and the number of potentially involved people. These fad models tend to produce hump-shaped patterns, with the intensity of the fad gradually increasing, then gradually decreasing.

It is quite plausible that the effect of past price increases on demand for stocks is variable: Sometimes, people are encouraged by past price increases; at other times, discouraged. Past price increases may discourage investors by suggesting that the asset is becoming overpriced, and whether it does suggest this may depend on popular theories which may change from time to time. *Fashions* or *fads* are more general terms than *bubble*, and it will be easier to establish the existence of the former.

EVIDENCE FROM PSYCHOLOGY

The notions of speculative excesses associated with the anecdotes discussed previously are inherently psychological. More specifically, they are social-psychological, relating as they do to the behavior of crowds rather than to isolated individuals. It is logical, therefore, to look in the psychological literature for evidence on the rationality of judgments of groups of people. Presumably, the fads or fashions in financial markets would be just one manifestation of a human tendency that can be documented in a wide variety of circumstances.

There is, in fact, a truly vast psychological literature on the process of human judgment and on the behavior of individuals in groups. There are several reasons why the literature has not had much impact on finance. One reason is that psychologists are often unconcerned with the possibility that their subjects are making rational decisions, and do not construct experiments in which it is possible to prove that they are not fully rational. Experimental psychologists often give problems to their subjects that strike economists as ill posed, so that it is impossible to tell whether they are responding rationally. Instead of trying to rule out the possibility that subjects are acting rationally, psychologists often try to tabulate behavior patterns that are not directly of interest to economists. The literature on contagion of attitudes (e.g., see Wheeler, 1966) has emphasized such things as whether the authority or sex of the transmitter of attitudes has an impact on the rate of transmission, or whether such things as hunger, lack of social commitment, or recent chastisement affected the susceptibility of individuals to attitude change. Psychologists interested in group behavior have also concentrated on phenomena in which group ties are strong and consume much of the attention or emotional energy of the participants. They are often interested in the behavior of angry mobs, of fringe religious groups that try to cut members off from the rest of society, or of charismatic political movements. The informal communications among most investors usually do not take place in a large mob on a street corner nor even in the intense group sessions of many experiments.

There is still, apparently, a lot to be learned from the psychological literature if the reader is willing to generalize from human behavior in rather different situations.

GAMBLING BEHAVIOR

When the expected utility revolution in theoretical economics was born, there was some discussion of the importance of gambling behavior for economics. Now that the assumption of expected utility maximization is firmly entrenched in conventional economic theory, discussion of gambling behavior seems to have subsided in economics journals and has not kept pace with research in psychology. Studies of the behavior of gamblers reveal some aspects of human behavior that are likely to be especially important for understanding financial markets.

Gambling behavior reveals a universal aspect of human behavior and not an aspect of an individual culture:

In various forms it occurs universally in all cultures, all ages, and is participated in widely by those of all societies, and social strata. Anthropological studies indicate its frequent occurrence in the most primitive of societies, and our modern games of chance are frequently more sophisticated versions of games once played by our forbears.[8]

Kallick et al. (1975), under the auspices of the Survey Research Center at the University of Michigan, undertook a study of gambling in 1975 in which more than two thousand randomly selected people in the United States were each interviewed for more than an hour about their attitudes and behavior regarding gambling. They found that 61% of the adult population placed some kind of bet in 1974; 48% placed bets on one or more of the popular commercial forms of gambling, with (among those betting) an average total wager on these in 1974 of $387 (or about $850 in 1985 prices).

The importance of the gambling urge can be underscored by the observation that in many people the urge becomes a compulsion. Compulsive gambling is a sufficiently important phenomenon that such

groups as Gamblers Anonymous have arisen to deal with it.

Compulsive gambling was characterized by Custer (1975) as

preoccupation and urge to gamble with frequent gambling activity.... The gambling preoccupation, urge, and activity characteristically are progressive and with significant increases during periods of stress. Problems which arise as a result of gambling lead to an intensification of gambling behavior.[9]

Kallick et al. (1975) concluded that according to this characterization of compulsive gambling, 1.1% of American men and 0.5% of American women are "probably compulsive gamblers" and an additional 2.7% of the men and 1% of the women are "potential compulsive gamblers."[10]

Psychologist Igor Kusyszyn (1977) described gambling as a form of adult play yielding a sort of "high":

The gambler, very quickly, usually as soon as he or she begins to contemplate making the first wager, transports his or her self into a play world, a fantasy world in which he or she stays suspended until jarred back into reality by the finish of the last race or the disappearance of his or her money.... The uncertainty of the event and the risk that is an integral part of it provide for the cognitive-emotional-muscular arousal of the individual.[11]

Investing in speculative assets clearly shares with gambling the element of play. Lease et al. (1974), in a survey of 2500 individual investors who had accounts at a large, national retail brokerage house, asked them to rate a number of attitude statements about investing on a scale of 1 to 5 (1 meaning strongly disagree, 5 meaning strongly agree). They gave a score of 4.09 to the statement "I enjoy investing and look forward to more such activity in the future." None of the other ten attitudes [including "I am substantially better informed than the average investor" (3.31) and a variety of other statements] was given as high a score.

The satisfaction afforded by gambling is related to the individual's ego involvement in the activity; and thus individual investors must themselves play to achieve satisfaction, and most do not rely on others for decisions. Lease et al. (1974) found that the average rating given to the statement "Relying exclusively upon mutual fund investments reduces the personal satisfaction I obtain from making my own investments" was 3.94. Of their respondents, only 20% said that they "rely primarily on brokerage firm or account executive for recommendations," and only 7% said they "rely primarily on paid investment newsletters or investment counselors' advice." Similar results about reliance on others for decisions came from surveys by Barlow et al. (1966) and Katona (1975).

While there is apparently no survey of institutional investors comparable to those of individual investors, it is even more likely that the aspect of play motivates them. The institutional investors are those who have chosen investing as an occupation, and it is reasonable to assume that they enjoy it at least as much and are as ego-involved as is the average investor.

If investing is, in part, play and is done for such motivations, then we will expect some judgment errors from investors like the judgment errors of gamblers. People who take chances may not require that there be really sound reasons to expect to win. Of course, the compulsive gambler at the racetrack is not deterred by losses and must know rationally and from past experience that he or she can generally expect to lose.[12] It is thus also plausible that investors whose interest is piqued by some speculative asset may go ahead and invest in that asset even after their further analysis indicates that their initial reasons to invest in it are not really good. Not playing would result in a sort of psychological letdown.

Speculative bubbles may provide a clear example of such behavior. If the price of an asset has gone up and made some of one's friends considerably richer, one's attention is drawn to that asset. The gamble posed then by investing in the asset will certainly seem interesting. On reflection, one may well realize that one has no way of knowing whether the price of the asset will continue to go up or even reverse itself and drop. The "chain letter" nature of the speculative bubble may even be readily appar-

ent to market participants. But by the time that one has realized this, the game may have so captured one's imagination and involved one's ego that one is sorely tempted to play.

Roll's "hubris" theory of takeovers described in Chapter 14 in this volume would also appear to be related to such an effect. In his theory, managers who are fully capable of understanding the "winner's curse" persist in their beliefs because of "overweaning pride," i.e., because of their ego involvement.

If one yields to the temptation to play, then one is likely to feel the need to justify the decision on grounds other than a gambling urge. One is likely to tell one's friends that the investment has good prospects. A front will be erected to conceal the gambling aspect of the decision.

As a form of play, the satisfaction afforded by gambling is affected by how well the game captures one's imagination. The observation of one's friends involved, the stories and gossip that surround a particular investment, all might contribute to the pleasure and thus to the judgmental "errors" that result. The Survey Research Center study on gambling concluded that "we have found repeatedly that the incidence of gambling on different types of games is associated with exposure to others who gamble."[13] Thus, although gambling itself is not always a social activity, the biases on judgment that it creates may tend to be social.

SALIENCE AND JUDGMENT

The diffusion models of fashions or fads discussed earlier relied on the notion that people do not behave systematically and allow their judgment to be influenced by what happens to catch their attention.

Tversky and Kahneman (1974) asserted in what they called the "availability heuristic" that judgments are influenced by "the ease with which instances or associations come to mind." Many experiments have sought to confirm that more vividly presented arguments (involving pictures, anecdotes, etc., that would seem to make the arguments more easily remembered) have more of an effect on human judgment. The "vividness" literature, however, has not demonstrated many sharp failures of human judgment. In a survey of this literature, Taylor and Thompson (1982) concluded that "the vividness effect, at least as it has been studied to this point, is weak if existent at all.[14]

The "vividness" literature, however, has worked within some narrow bounds that may have excluded the relevant behavior. Taylor and Thompson (1982) noted that in the experiments that they cited, experimental design ensured that subjects were equally exposed to arguments whether or not they were vividly presented. Experiments confirming the effects of "salience" on judgments differ from the vividness experiments in that the former allow vivid and nonvivid presentations to compete for the subjects' attention. Taylor and Thompson find that the evidence that salience affects judgments is much stronger. Thus, a well-documented human judgment error is that people fail to collect evidence systematically and allow themselves to be distracted by attention-grabbing events.

GROUP POLARIZATION OF ATTITUDES

A number of choice dilemma experiments and observations of people gambling indicate that people in groups tend to take greater risks than do individuals separated from a group. This phenomenon, as surveyed by Clark (1971), has been called the "risky shift." Further experimental research, however, did not always confirm the risky shift, and indeed in some experiments groups behaved more cautiously than individuals.[15] It was found, though, that groups whose individual members were cautious relative to the population average tended to become even more cautious in groups, and that individuals who were less cautious relative to the population average tended to become on average even less cautious in groups. Thus, the risky-shift hypothesis was abandoned and replaced with the "group polarization" hypothesis: "The average postgroup response

will tend to be more extreme and in the same direction as the average of the pre-group response."[16] A large number of studies have confirmed such a group-induced polarization of attitudes in a wide variety of decision problems, not just those involving decisions regarding risk. One survey concluded of the group polarization effect that "seldom in the history of social psychology has a nonobvious phenomenon been so firmly grounded in data from across a variety of cultures and dependent measures."[17]

The phenomenon of group-induced polarization of attitudes would suggest that social movements might be begun by any events that cause a subgroup of the population to form to talk about the matter in question. For example, an advertising campaign that reminds people of a product may, if it engenders conversation by an already favorable subgroup, heighten the favorable attitude. (It might equally well cause a less favorably disposed subgroup to develop a very negative attitude.) Social movements may end when the events cease to enforce the group interaction.

Much of the literature on the polarization effect will seem unsatisfactory to economists, who are inclined to ask whether any observed human behavior might be reconciled with an optimizing paradigm. In fact, the "group polarization of attitudes" observed in many experiments may well be consistent with rational decision making if groups pool the information of individual members. If the experiments can be described as asking groups to estimate a parameter on which each member has some information, and if the group members are optimal Bayesian decision makers, then the group estimate may behave like an amplified transformation of the average estimate that members of the group would give without pooling information. Such an information-pooling argument was used by Burnstein et al. (1971) and by Bordley (1983) to dismiss the whole literature on group polarization as only discovering rational behavior.

This criticism of the group polarization literature is not effective against all of the studies demonstrating group polarization because in many of these studies there was no conceivable information to be pooled. Many experiments asked people not to respond to questions of fact but to make decisions about hypothetical situations, about which other group members could not have any information.

There are other reasons canvassed in this literature to think that the group polarization phenomenon may not be consistent with Bayesian decision making. For example, there is some analysis of the process by which the observed group polarization occurs. It has been found that there is a tendency for groups to concentrate in their discussions on facts and arguments supporting the dominant attitude of the group (see Lamm and Myers, 1978). Janis (1972), after a series of case studies of real-world groups that made disastrously bad judgments, found that there was a tendency for self-appointed censors to appear who would try to discourage discussion of arguments contrary to the emerging group judgment.

CONCLUSION AND SUMMARY

The notion of market efficiency has proven a useful one in many ways in the finance literature over the past couple of decades. In many ways it is a big improvement over notions that preceded it. But the academic finance profession has carried it too far, so that alternative notions based in part on the sort of psychological research discussed in this chapter are almost totally ignored in finance journals. Since psychological alternatives are virtually never discussed in academic finance journals, the profession at large is generally uninformed about these alternatives. The profession does not generally connect the various pieces of "anomalous evidence" regarding market efficiency with such alternatives and is in the habit of describing the anomalies as "small," even though they may be the consequence of sizable valuation errors.

Modern psychology does not reduce human behavior to a simple model like the expected utility model that underlies theoretical finance. The literature on gambling behavior shows the plausibility of the claims made in the usual anecdotes that there is sometimes excessive enthusiasm for certain financial assets and thus that other financial assets are sometimes ignored. The literature on salience and human judgment makes plausible the claims in the anecdotes that popular attention to certain speculative assets was capricious. The literature on group polarization of attitudes adds some further plausibility to the claim in the anecdotes that groups of individuals may tend to act together, reaching the same decisions around the same times.

How much of the variance in price changes may be attributed to changing fashions and how much to fundamentals as measured by information about future dividends? The answer will differ from one speculative asset to another, depending on how much variation there has been in dividends. For the aggregate stock market over the past century, the aggregate dividend stream has been sufficiently trendlike that we might attribute most of the price variation to fashions or fads. For some individual stocks, on the other hand, there have been very dramatic movements in dividends or other measures of fundamental value, movements sometimes spanning orders of magnitude. Clearly, price movements for these stocks primarily reflect fundamentals.

How much credence should we attach to theories in the literature on takeovers that "undervaluation" of target firms and subsequent price changes around the date of a takeover are to be understood in terms of information about fundamentals? Again, the answer will differ across firms. When, for example, there is clear evidence that the target firm is mismanaged and that the takeover will clearly imply that a new management will be installed, then it is entirely plausible to interpret the premium paid for the target firm at the time of takeover in terms described in the literature on mismanagement theories. But we should not feel compelled to interpret prices in terms of such fundamentals, and we can be just as confident that instances occur where entirely different interpretations are appropriate: where, for example, the undervaluation may be due to investors' overlooking the stock, or the takeover premium may reflect an overvaluation by those who acquire the firm.

NOTES

1. Sharpe (1985), p. 67.
2. Brealey and Meyers (1984), p. 784.
3. Mackay, (1841), pp. 141 and 147. Mackay notes that 100 florins would then buy ten fat sheep, a suit of clothes, or a complete bed (p. 143).
4. Galbraith (1972), p. 79–80.
5. Malkiel (1981), p. 53.
6. Reinganum (1981) instead concluded that the "size effect" (small firms tend to show abnormal returns) largely subsumes the E/P effect. Basu, however, found that while slightly weaker for larger firms, the abnormal return predicted by the earnings-price ratio is present in all quintiles of firm size, and he criticized Reinganum for his failure to correct for risk. Peavey and Goodman (1983) found that the P/E effect is even more dramatic among a group of firms whose market value in 1980 exceeded 100 million and after controlling for an "industry effect."
7. Dimson and Marsh (1984) p. 1260.
8. Bolen and Boyd (1968) p. 617.
9. Custer (1975) cited in Kallick et al. (1975).
10. Kallick et al. (1975) p. 75.
11. Kusyszyn (1977) pp. 25–26.
12. Note that both pari-mutuel racetrack betting (horse racing is the most popular commercial sport in the United States) and the picking of stocks involve direct competition in a marketplace against other players and the subsequent thrill of watching the horse (price) move.
13. Kallick et al. (1975).
14. Taylor and Thompson (1982) p. 172.
15. Kusyszyn (1977) argued that these group experiments do not accurately represent real-world gambling in that they fail to generate the ego involvement and enthusiasm of actual gamblers.
16. Myers and Lamm (1976) p. 603.
17. Lamm and Myers (1978) p. 146.

REFERENCES

Barlow, R., H. E. Brazer, and J. N. Morgan (1966). *Economic Behavior of the Affluent.* Washington, D.C.: Brookings Institution.

Bartholomew, D. J. (1982), *Stochastic Models for Social Processes.* 3rd ed. New York: Wiley.

Basu, S. (1983). "The Relationship Between Earnings, Yield, Market Value and Return: Further Evidence." *Journal of Financial Economics* **12**, 129–156.

Bishop, G. D., and D. G. Myers (1974). "Informational Influence in Group Discussion." *Organizational Behavior and Human Performance* **12**, 92–104.

Bjerring, J. H., J. Lakonishok, and T. Vermaelen (1983). "Stock Prices and Financial Analysts' Recommendations." *Journal of Finance* **38** (1) 187–204.

Black, F. and M. Sholes (1974). "The Effects of Dividend Yield and Dividend Policy on Common Stock Prices and Returns." *Journal of Financial Economics* **1**, 1–22.

Blume, E. (1980). "Stock Returns and Dividend Yields: Some More Evidence." *Review of Economics and Statistics* **62**, 567–577.

————, J. Crockett, and I. Friend (1974). "Stockownership in the United States: Characteristics and Trends." *Survey of Current Business* **54**, 16–74.

Bolen, D. W., and W. H. Boyd (1968). "Gambling and the Gambler: A Review and Preliminary Findings." *Archives of General Psychiatry* **18** (5), 617–629.

Bordley, R. F. (1983). "A Bayesian Model of Group Polarization." *Organizational Behavior and Human Performance* **32**, 262–274.

Brealey, R., and S. Myers (1984). *Principles of Corporation Finance.* New York: McGraw-Hill.

Breeden, D. (1979). "An Intertemporal Asset Pricing Model with Stochastic Consumption and Investment Opportunities." *Journal of Financial Economics* **7**, 265–296.

Burnstein, E., H. Miller, A. Vinokur, S. Katz, and J. Crowley (1971). "Risky Shift Is Eminently Rational." *Journal of Personality and Social Psychology* **20**, 462–471.

Clark, R. D., III (1971). "Group-Induced Shift Toward Risk: A Critical Appraisal." *Psychological Bulletin* **76**, 251–270.

Custer, R. L. (1975). Description of Compulsive Gambling. Manuscript prepared for the American Psychiatric Association Task Force on Nomenclature.

DeBondt, W., and R. Thaler (1985). "Does the Stock Market Overreact?" *Journal of Finance* **40**, 793–805.

Dimson, E., and P. Marsh (1984). "An Analysis of Brokers' and Analysts' Unpublished Forecasts of UK Stock Returns." *Journal of Finance* **39** (5), 1257–1292.

Figlewski, S. (1981). "The Informational Effects

of Restrictions on Short Sales: Some Empirical Evidence." *Journal of Financial and Quantitative Analysis* **16** (4), 463–476.

Flavin, M. (1983). "Excess Volatility in the Financial Markets: A Reassessment of the Empirical Evidence." *Journal of Political Economy* **91**, 929–956.

French, K. R., and R. Roll (1986). "Stock Return Variances: The Arrival of Information and the Reaction of Traders." *Journal of Financial Economics* **17**, 5–26.

Friend, I., and M. Blume (1978). *The Changing Role of the Institutional Investor.* New York: Wiley.

Galbraith, J. K. (1972). *The Great Crash, 1929.* 3rd ed. Boston: Houghton Mifflin.

Hall, R. E. (1985). Intertemporal Substitution in Consumption. Reproduced, Stanford University.

Janis. I. L. (1972), *Victims of Groupthink.* Boston: Houston.

Jarrow, R. (1980). "Heterogeneous Expectations, Restriction on Short Sales, and Equilibrium Asset Prices." *Journal of Finance* **35**, 1105–1113.

Kallick, M., D. Suits, T. Dielman, and J. Hybels (1975). *A Survey of American Gambling Attitudes and Behavior.* Ann Arbor: Survey Research Center, Institute for Social Research, University of Michigan.

Katona, G. (1975). *Psychological Economics.* New York: Elsevier.

Kleidon, A. W. (1983). Variance Bounds Tests and Stock Valuation Models. Unpublished paper, Stanford University Graduate School of Business.

Kusyszyn, I. (1977) "How Gambling Saved Me from a Misspent Sabbatical." *Journal of Humanistic Psychology* **17** (3), 19–34.

Kydland, F. E., and E. F. Prescott (1982). "Time to Build and Aggregate Fluctuations." *Econometrica* **50**, 1345–1370.

Lamm, H., and D. G. Myers (1978). "Group-Induced Polarization of Attitudes and Behavior." In *Advances in Experimental Social Psychology,* Vol. 11, ed. L. Berkowitz, 145–195. New York: Academic Press.

Lease, R. C., W. G. Lewellen, and G. G. Schlarbaum (1974). "The Individual Investor: Attributes and Attitudes." *Journal of Finance* **29**, 413–433.

Leroy, S., and R. Porter (1981). "The Present Value Relation: Tests Based on Variance Bounds." *Econometrica* **49**, 555–574.

Litzenberger, R. L., and K. Ramaswamy (1982). "The Effects of Dividends on Common Stock Prices: Tax Effects or Information Effects." *Journal of Finance* **37**, 429–443.

Lucas, R. E. (1978). "Asset Prices in an Exchange Economy." *Econometrica* **46**, 1429–1445.

McGuire, W. J. (1969). "The Nature of Attitudes and Attitude Change." In *The Handbook of Social Psychology,* 2nd ed., Vol. III, ed. G. Linzey and E. Aronson. Reading, Mass.: Addison-Wesley.

Mackay, C. (1841). *Memoirs of Extraordinary Popular Delusions,* London: Bentley.

Malkiel, B. G. (1981). *A Random Walk Down Wall Street.* 2nd ed. New York: Norton.

Mankiw, N. G., D. Romer, and M. Shapiro (1985). "An Unbiased Reexamination of Stock Price Volatility." *Journal of Finance* **40**, 677–687.

Marsh, T. A., and R. C. Merton (1984). *Earnings Variability and Variance Bounds Tests of the Rationality of Stock Market Prices.* Working Paper 1559–84, Alfred P. Sloan School of Management, Massachusetts Institute of Technology, Cambridge, Mass.

Morgan, I. G. (1982). "Dividends and Capital Asset Prices." *Journal of Finance* **37**, 1071–1086.

Myers, D. G., and H. Lamm (1976). "The Group Polarization Phenomenon." *Psychological Bulletin* **83**, 602–627.

New York Stock Exchange (1960). *Investors of Tomorrow.*

——— (1979). *Public Attitudes Toward Investing: Marketing Implications.*

——— (1955). *The Public Speaks to the Exchange Community.*

Paget, E. H. (1929). "Sudden Changes in Group Opinion." *Social Forces* **7**, 440–444.

Peavey, J. W., III, and D. A. Goodman (1983). "The Significance of P/E's for Portfolio Returns." *Journal of Portfolio Management* **9**, 43–47.

Pound, J., and R. Shiller (1987). "Are Institutional Investors Speculators?" *Journal of Portfolio Management,* **Spring,** 46–52.

Reinganum, M. R. (1981). "Misspecification of Capital Asset Pricing: Empirical Anomalies Based on Earnings Yields and Market Values." *Journal of Financial Economics* **9**, 19–46.

Roll, R. (1977). "A Critique of the Asset Pricing Theory's Tests. I. On Past and Potential Testability of the Theory." *Journal of Financial Economics* **4**, 129–176.

——— (1984). "Orange Juice and Weather." *American Economic Review* **74**, 861–880.

Rosenberg, B. (1985). "Persuasive Evidence on Market Inefficiency." *Journal of Portfolio Management* **11**, 9–16.

Sharpe, W. F. (1985). *Investments.* 3rd ed. Englewood Cliffs, N.J.: Prentice-Hall.

Shiller, R. J. (1979). "The Volatility of Long-Term Interest Rates and Expectations Models of the Term Structure." *Journal of Political Economy* **87,** 1190–1219.

———(1981a). "Alternative Tests of Rational Expectations Models: The Case of the Term Structure." *Journal of Econometrics* **16,** 71–87.

——— (1981b). "Do Stock Prices Move Too Much to Be Justified by Subsequent Changes in Dividends?" *American Economic Review* **71,** 421–436.

——— (1984). "Stock Prices and Social Dynamics." In *Brookings Papers on Economic Activity.* 457–497. Washington, D.C.: Brookings Institution.

——— (1981c). "The Use of Volatility Measures in Assessing Market Efficiency." *Journal of Finance* **36,** 291–304.

———, and P. Perron (1985). "Testing the Random Walk Hypothesis: Power Versus Frequency of Observation." *Economics Letters* **18,** 381–386.

Summers, L. H. (1986). "Do Market Prices Accurately Reflect Fundamental Values?" *Journal of Finance* **41,** 591–602.

Taylor, S. E., and S. C. Thompson (1982). "Stalking the Elusive 'Vividness' Effect." *Psychological Review* **89,** 155–181.

Teger, A. I., and D. G. Pruitt (1967). "Components of Group Risk Taking." *Journal of Experimental and Social Psychology* **3,** 189–205.

Tversky, A., and D. Kahneman (1974). "Judgment Under Uncertainty: Heuristics and Biases." *Science* **185,** 1124–1131.

West, K. D. (1984). "Speculative Bubbles and Stock Price Volatility." Memo No. 54, Financial Research Center, Princeton University, Princeton, N. J.

Wheeler, L. (1966). "Toward a Theory of Behavioral Contagion." *Psychological Review* **73,** 179–192.

4

Comment

FRANKLIN R. EDWARDS

The papers by Professors Shubik and Shiller provide an ideal opening gambit for a conference on takeovers and contests for corporate control. They seek to establish, right at the outset, that it is too naive an approach to simply look at stock prices and companies' equity values to determine whether a takeover is or is not in the public interest—or whether it enhances social welfare. Even if, taken as a whole, the shareholders of the target and acquiring firm both benefit, the authors are still unwilling to conclude that a takeover is necessarily in the public interest.

Both Professors Shubik and Shiller have written lengthy and insightful papers, the former attacking the entire discipline of finance theory, the latter the idea that stock prices represent sensible reflections of value. Both papers, however, seem to have only a tangential connection to the subject of takeovers (although they are of obvious interest to students of economic theory).

The experience we have already had makes it reasonably clear that stockholders of target firms do benefit from a takeover, often substantially. Less clear is whether the stockholders of acquiring firms benefit, or whether bondholders of either firm benefit.

Why is the value of a "target" firm higher to a "raider" than to current stockholders? Acquiring firms, seemingly, can reallocate or redeploy the assets of the acquired firm in a way that often substantially increases the value of the firm. One explanation is that there are substantial costs associated with discovering the alternative asset uses and with reorganizing and restructuring the firm. Furthermore, these costs may not be lowest for the managers of the target firms. A firm restructuring requires the integration of many skills and personalities and the assimilation of information that is often beyond the immediate purview of operating managers.

Another explanation is that managers of firms do not have the incentive to undertake a restructuring. A restructuring introduces uncertainty about the future position of managers. They may have comfortable positions that took years to attain. They also are unlikely to be compensated financially for taking the extra personal and managerial risks associated with restructuring. Even if stock values were to rise appreciably, managers may not benefit commensurately. Outside "raiders" are not exposed to these personal disabilities and stand to gain substantially from a rise in the firm's stock.

Takeovers would seem to increase social welfare by causing the redeployment of firms' assets to more efficient end uses. Professor Shiller, however, would have us believe that such takeovers are only part of recurring, speculative financial bubbles or fads. The high stock prices paid by raiders and received by the target firm's stockholders are temporary illusions, soon to disappear.

Professor Shubik, on the other hand, seems to argue that capital markets are not efficient in that target firms are often substantially undervalued. Thus, the increase in the target firm's stock value because of a takeover does not represent an increase in social welfare.

I do not find either Shubik's or Shiller's arguments convincing. While capital market inefficiencies exist, the large body of evidence in support of general capital market efficiency is surely on the side of general market efficiency. As anyone who has been deeply involved with financial markets and institutions knows, there are hundreds and even thousands of people working day and night to discover and exploit capital market inefficiencies. Significant inefficiencies seldom last long.

Professor Shubik also worries about whether the takeover prices paid are "fair," or whether they might be too low. There may be too few bidders, so that the price is not the "competitive" price. In this event the acquiring firm's shareholders would obtain too large a share of the net gain.

I am not overly concerned about this distributional issue. To the extent that (monopolistic) raiders earn monopoly rents, such rents may be a return to information. If only competitive returns were available, the investment in information on which takeovers are based might be less than that which is socially optimal. In any case, the value of the stock of the acquiring firm will be more efficiently priced after the acquisition, regardless of who captures the rents.

Empirical evidence also does not support Shubik's argument. Takeover benefits appear to be captured mainly by the stockholders of target firms. In addition, there is no evidence that the returns to all raiders, taken as a group, are abnormally high. Some make spectacular profits; most make nothing.

Neither Shubik nor Shiller provide theoretical or empirical arguments that are convincing enough to have us ignore the shareholder benefits that occurs as a result of takeovers. Rather than disregarding such benefits as either illusory or inaccurate, one should try to explain why they occur and to assess whether these benefits are outweighed by losses to other segments of financial markets or to society as a whole. The impact on bondholders, creditors, long-run managerial incentives, financial market stability, and even local communities (because of plant closings) may all enter the social welfare equation. A basic understanding of these potential effects is necessary before any conclusions are reached about possible regulatory interventions to curb takeovers.

The recent proposal by the Federal Reserve Board to apply more restrictive margin requirements to so-called junk bonds is an example of the kind of inadvisable regulation that can spring from an imperfect understanding of the takeover phenomenon. Almost all studies of the effects of similar margin requirements on other financial securities indicate that such margins do not accomplish the goals for which they are intended. They are not, for example, able to reallocate credit or curb speculative activity. Worse, they may have unintended income distribution effects. Margin requirements on junk bonds are not a constructive governmental response to the "takeovers" debate.

5

Comment

MICHAEL A. SALINGER

My assigned task is to discuss two very provocative papers by Martin Shubik and Robert Shiller. Before I do so, however, let me comment that I find it interesting that this conference is beginning with a session on market efficiency and that the conference organizers chose two critics of the efficient-markets hypothesis to present the papers. The efficient-markets hypothesis has two important implications for discussions about takeovers. First, if capital markets are efficient, the undervaluation of targets does not explain why takeovers occur. Second, and more important, the increase in market value associated with takeovers means that takeovers are beneficial to shareholders. The role of these two papers is to preempt some finance professor from commenting: "Shareholders benefit from takeovers and isn't that all that matters?" Accordingly, I will focus my discussion of these two papers on their implications for what we should make of the increase in stock prices associated with takeovers.

COMMENTS ON SHUBIK

Shubik makes several points that relate to what we should make of the stock market reaction to takeovers. The first is that the three forms of the efficient-markets hypothesis listed in most modern finance textbooks are not what should be meant by market efficiency.[1] Rather, capital markets should be considered efficient if they pro-

These comments represent the views of the author and do not necessarily represent the views of the Federal Trade Commission.

vide incentives to allocate society's resources efficiently. I agree in principle with Shubik's definition. Unfortunately, questions about the relationship between financial and real markets are very difficult to address. We do not currently have results about the ways in which capital markets are inefficient or about the relationship between the "rules of the game" and the economic outcome to guide economic policy.[2]

Shubik does, however, hazard some guesses about why capital markets as they are currently set up do not generate an efficient outcome. One problem he sees is that the constraints on managers to act in the interest of shareholders are not as strong as they might be. To correct this problem, he suggests schemes to enhance directors' incentives to protect shareholders' interests. It is hard to quarrel with that suggestion.

His other policy recommendation is more controversial. He claims that shareholders who hope to make short-run profits do not hold their shares for very long and, hence, do not have the long-run interests of the firm at heart. He recommends changes in the law that provide incentives for shareholders to hold onto their shares for a relatively long time.

The liquidity of stocks is what makes investors with a short time horizon willing to invest in firms that undertake long-run projects. Under Shubik's proposal, therefore, investors with relatively short time horizons would either leave the stock market altogether or pressure managers to have a shorter time horizon than they currently have. Shareholders who plan to sell in the near future want managers to maximize the current stock price. Short-run value maximization does not, however, necessarily require a short time horizon. Insofar as stock market values reflect expected future distributions to shareholders, the interests of "sellers" and "holders" are identical.

Shubik argues on theoretical grounds, however, that stock prices cannot reflect all inside information. This point raises two concerns. First, managers might maximize the value of the firm based on public information. In practice, managers are not likely to be removed instantaneously for behavior which appears not to be value maximizing based on public information. Thus, they should have no qualms about acting on inside information that will become public in a moderate amount of time, particularly if the directors approve. Managers might very well be hesitant to act on information that must remain private for many years. For example, they might not initiate long and expensive new-product developments. Restrictions on takeovers would allow managers to have a longer time horizon and, as a result, would make it more likely that such projects would be undertaken. The restrictions would, however, simultaneously allow managers to act contrary to shareholder interests. Whether the benefit from increasing managers' time horizons would outweigh the cost of additional managerial slack is not clear.

The second concern is the one that perhaps is expressed more frequently. Take-overs might occur because insiders who recognize the true value of a firm manage to acquire it for something less than that value. I am skeptical, however, of this general explanation for takeovers because, takeover premiums can be very large. Thus, to explain takeovers with stock market inefficiency, we have to believe that stock market valuations are off by a huge amount. Shubik's theoretical finding that the stock market cannot reflect all inside information says nothing about how much a stock price can deviate from its true value. I find it somewhat implausible that the market is systematically valuing firms

at half their true value. Furthermore, suppose it were true that Carl Icahn's and T. Boone Pickens's only skill is identifying undervalued companies. A takeover attempt by one of them would signal to the market that it had undervalued the target. If shareholders knew that the acquirer was paying less than the company was worth, they would refuse to sell. Of course, this argument is true only if the higher market value is appropriate regardless of whether the firm is acquired. If the increased value is due to a change in control, then the acquirers do not expropriate from shareholders anything that they would have received if the acquisition did not occur.

A related point that Shubik makes is that while the market for individual shares may be perfectly competitive, the market for corporate control is oligopolistic. His concern is, presumably, that even if a takeover benefits shareholders, another takeover might benefit them more. I question this assertion on two grounds. First, a large number of firms have active takeover programs. Thus, the number of potential bidders for a truly undervalued firm might be quite large. Second, if the market for control were not competitive, then we would expect acquirers to earn excess returns. The empirical evidence suggests, however, that essentially all the excess returns from takeovers accrue to the target's shareholders.[3]

COMMENTS ON SHILLER'S PAPER

The implication of Shiller's work and of work on anomalies in stock returns is that stock market values do not even accurately reflect all publically available information. If they do not, then an increase in the stock price does not necessarily imply an increase in shareholders' wealth. I consider it a mistake, however, to reason that if stock prices are irrational in any sense, then stock prices and stock price changes are meaningless. Just because a signal is noisy does not mean that it is not a signal. Indeed, I have an offer for any one who thinks that stock prices are meaningless. I will accept the stream of dividends from

100 shares of IBM in return for the stream of dividends from 100 shares of any publically traded penny stock.

Shiller tells us that the stock market is subject to fads and bubbles. The implications of that point for takeovers would seem to be that the willingness of acquirers to pay huge takeover premiums is a fad, that the acquirers are paying too much for the targets, and that the increase in stock market values does not represent an increase in wealth. Shubik argues that the market for corporate control is oligopolistic. The implication of that point would seem to be that acquirers can purchase firms for less than their true value. Shubik claims that he is not arguing that small shareholders need protection, and Shiller's chapter barely mentions takeovers at all. Nonetheless, some people will use their chapters to argue simultaneously that excessive takeover premiums do not represent true gains and that shareholders have to be protected from acquirers who purchase companies for less than their true value. Both claims cannot be correct; and in my view, neither is.

CONCLUSIONS

What should we say to the finance professor who says: "Shareholders benefit from takeovers and isn't that all that matters?" With regard to the need to protect shareholders, the increase in share value is all that matters. No justification for restricting takeovers to protect shareholders exists. With regard to whether takeovers are beneficial, the increase in share value indicates that shareholders benefit. Whether or not society as a whole benefits depends on whether the increase in shareholder value comes at the expense of some other group (the U.S. Treasury, bondholders, employees, consumers) or is due to efficiencies. Rather than dismissing the gains to shareholders as illusory, we should accept them

as real and try to ascertain their source. That remains the fundamental mystery about the takeover phenomenon.

NOTES

1. The three forms are labeled strong, semi-strong, and weak. Strong-form market efficiency means that no knowable information can be used to predict excess returns. Semistrong-form market efficiency means that no publically available information can be used to predict excess returns. Weak-form market efficiency means that past and current stock prices cannot be used to predict excess returns. An excess return is the difference between the *ex ante* required return on a stock and the *ex post* actual return.

2. One of Shubik's primary points is that academics should address these questions. He claims that the partial-equilibrium nature of portfolio theory severely limits the implications that can be drawn from it, and argues that game-theoretic models are more appropriate than competitive models. However, given that game theory has not yet generated a satisfactory model of oligopoly in a single market, a game-theoretic, general equilibrium model with both a financial and a real sector is unlikely to appear before Halley's comet returns at least twice.

3. Magenheim and Mueller argue that acquiring firms earn significantly negative returns after a merger occurs (see Chapter 11 of this volume). Of the chapters in this book, their presentation is potentially the most damaging to the notion of stock market efficiency and the current wisdom that mergers enhance shareholder wealth. I disagree, however, with their interpretation of their results. Acquiring companies have, on average, significant, positive excess returns in the two years before they merge. Magenheim and Mueller argue that their superior premerger performance should be the expected return by which postmerger performance should be judged. A fundamental property of efficient capital markets is, however, that excess returns in one period cannot be used to predict excess returns in subsequent periods. Thus, far from being a rejection of capital market efficiency, the Magenheim and Mueller results are precisely what the theory of efficient captial markets predicts.

MANAGERIAL BEHAVIOR
AND TAKEOVERS

6

Shareholders Versus Managers: The Strain in the Corporate Web

JOHN C. COFFEE, JR.

We have entered the era of the two-tier, front-end loaded, bootstrap, bust-up, junk-bond takeover.

Martin Lipton, *Wall Street Journal*, April 5, 1985, p. 16.

Until recently, takeovers typically involved larger firms digesting smaller firms, a process that most theorists have assumed was driven by the pursuit of synergistic gains.[1] Lately, however, this dynamic has dramatically reversed itself. To a considerable extent, the large conglomerate is now the target, and such prototypical conglomerate firms as General Foods, Richardson-Vicks, Beatrice, Revlon, SCM, CBS, and Anderson, Clayton and Co. have been forced to either liquidate or restructure themselves since 1984.[2] The new bidder in turn tends often to be one or more individuals, or a collection of individuals, smaller entities, and investment banking firms, who intend not to assimilate the target but to dismantle it. In this new era of the "bust-up" takeover, the driving force is the perceived disparity between the target's liquidation and stock market values. A new breed of financial entrepreneur, originally typified by Carl Icahn and Boone Pickens but more recently expanded to in-

Because the author is serving as a Reporter for the American Law Institute's *Principles of Corporate Governance,* it is necessary to add that the views expressed herein are strictly those of the author and do not purport to represent those of the American Law Institute or the other Reporters. The author wishes to acknowledge helpful comments and criticism from Victor Brudney, Melvin Eisenberg, Ronald Gilson, Louis Lowenstein, and Susan Rose-Ackerman, but he alone is responsible for any errors or omissions that remain.

clude major investment banking firms acting for their own account, has appeared on the scene who is essentially arbitraging this difference between stock and asset value by first acquiring control and then partially liquidating the target in order to pay off all (or most) of the acquisition indebtedness.[3] Tactically, it is easy enough to explain how this new era has arrived: New financing techniques—most notably, the appearance of the "junk bond" in late 1983—have vastly extended the capability of the smaller bidder by allowing it to borrow more and to use the liquidation value of the target as its collateral.[4] What is more puzzling is the underlying explanation for this trend. If the pursuit of synergy fuels the takeover movement (as probably the majority of recent commentators believe), one might expect the target's assets to be assimilated by the bidder, not dismantled and resold in the asset market. Nor does the more controversial "disciplinary thesis," which holds that superior managers are displacing inferior ones, provide a convincing explanation for a pattern in which the bidder increasingly intends at the outset not to rehabilitate the target's operational performance but to reduce its scope of operations by selling off or closing down marginal divisions. I will offer an alternative explanation for takeovers that places this disparity between stock and asset values at center stage. This discount theory is not intended as a definitive account of all takeover activity but as a partial explanation of those trends that raise the most serious social issues, because they suggest a fundamental realignment is under way within the American public corporation.

The implications of this transition in the nature of takeover activity are even less clear. The critical fact is that the market for corporate control is now largely complete. Few, if any, American corporations are today beyond the reach of this market because of their size or scale. The appearance of the bust-up takeover and the new financing arrangements undoubtedly facilitated this closing-off of the market, but other factors also contributed. Although it is not fruitful to debate at length whether the bust-up takeover represents a basic discontinuity in the short history of takeovers or whether it is better viewed as part of a longer-term continuum, the influence of the bust-up takeover has clearly been abrupt and decisive in several respects. First, its appearance has at least coincided with a sudden shift toward higher corporate leverage that has alarmed the Federal Reserve Board and produced the first mild intervention by that agency into the field of takeovers.[5] Concomitant with this shift has come a unprecedented spate of restructuring by large corporations; indeed, between January 1984 and mid July 1985, 398 of North America's 850 largest corporations engaged in such restructurings, largely, it will be argued, as a means of discouraging or preempting a hostile takeover.[6]

Second, as a result of both this activity and the increased number of hostile bids, the status of the manager within the large public firm has been significantly adversely affected. Put simply, employment security was once an element of the "implicit contract" that this manager had with the firm, but today that relationship has been significantly altered. Because substantial managerial layoffs are now likely after either a hostile takeover or a friendly "white knight" merger,[7] the prior pattern of career employment within a single firm may no longer be a realistic expectation. Over the long run, this development could change the internal culture of the American corporation, force significant revisions in the structure of managerial compensation, and affect the economy as a whole. In this light, the appearance of the bust-up takeover heightens the prospect of externalities and suggests that interests besides those of the immediate participants are at stake.

These developments are altering the character of the American corporation, both in terms of its goals, span of operations, and the behavior of its managers and in terms of its ability to compete against foreign rivals. These are not modest claims, and they also may not seem to be legal ones. Yet my focus is ultimately on legal issues in the broader sense of that term: how should the internal relationships between managers and shareholders within the firm be restructured? More generally, how should the law even characterize these relationships—as those of principal and agent or as those of joint venturers who each share in the residual risk of the enterprise? Should the law take cognizance of an implicit contract between the shareholders and managers of the public corporation, which may have been disrupted by these developments?[8] Should the law accord the manager a greater "voice" in, or facilitate a smoother "exit" from, the corporation? In overview, I will advocate a policy that this chapter will term "premium sharing" between shareholders and managers. My specific prescriptions are, however, less important than that these questions be directly faced and traditional answers not automatically assumed.

Both efficiency and equity-based arguments support a policy of premium sharing as a means of facilitating and cushioning managerial exit. These arguments are premised on a model of the firm that views the interests of shareholders and managers as fundamentally in conflict over the issue of risk. Such a perspective differs from most recent commentary on the hostile takeover, particularly in the following respects:

First, most critiques of the takeover have been relatively narrow and *ad hoc.* Thus, we are recurrently told that hostile takeovers divert managerial attention, enforce a myopic concentration on the short run, or discourage investment in research and development.[9] Little attempt has been made by these critics to relate their views to any broader theory of the firm. In contrast, this chapter will suggest that the implications of the hostile takeover can only be understood in terms of a basic tension between managers and shareholders that preexisted recent developments but which has been substantially intensified by them.

Second, both proponents and critics have framed their arguments as if takeovers were a game that involved only shareholders. Given this "no-externalities" assumption, they have in common focused on how a particular policy toward takeovers would affect shareholders' wealth. Thus, those who have defended managerial defensive tactics have simply argued that such tactics are in the shareholders' long-run interest, either because they promote a value-maximizing auction or because they otherwise protect shareholders from an exploitative takeover at a price below the firm's "intrinsic" value.[10] Conversely, proponents of competitive bidding in takeovers have viewed the process as simply a "competition among management teams" for control of the corporation's assets.[11] The problem with this "fairgame" perspective is that those playing this game may trample on the interests of those who are inevitable bystanders. The standard assumption of economics that voluntary exchanges produce social gains fits the takeover context rather easily, but precisely because of this close conceptual fit, proponents of this mode of analysis tend not to look for impacts on others. Yet predictably, there are affected bystanders—most notably, managers and employees, but also creditors and ultimately the state as well—who will change their behavior as the significance of the takeover's impact grows on them. Over time, the process is a dynamic one in which the changed behavior of these other constituencies will likely affect shareholders in turn.

That little attention has been given to the claims of these other constituencies is in large part attributable to the popularity of a model of the firm that sees shareholders as the principals and managers as their agents.[12] Although recent theorists have tended to view the firm as a complex web of contracts, they have stopped short of realizing the full implications of this point and continue to see the shareholder as the only residual risk bearer and the only party needing contractual or governance protections. Traditional economic theory sees the other participants in the corporate contract as receiving a largely fixed return that is essentially determined by external market rates.[13] As a result, it is assumed that the shareholder, as the critical actor who has alone accepted the entrepreneurial role, is entitled to appropriate the full takeover premium. This chapter will argue that this analysis is flawed because managers and others also share in the residual risk and are not protected fully by the external market.

Others have, of course, also asserted that hostile takeovers can produce diseconomies. The problem with their *ad hoc* critiques is that, if accepted, they prove too much and could be used to justify the total prohibition of hostile takeovers. Moreover, this species of "horseback empiricism" is largely unverifiable in the absence of any commonly accepted benchmark and also begs critical normative questions. For example, when one asserts that market forces pressure managers to concentrate on the short run, the obvious retort is: Why shouldn't they do so if this is what shareholders want? Why should not the market also penalize investment on exploration or research if it considers such expenditures either unprofitable in themselves or a signal that unprofitable operations will be continued? If shareholders today demand a higher discount rate or simply have a shorter time horizon in an inflationary world, a critic must explain why this change is not as much within the shareholders' prerogative as it is to shift their political preference from Democrat to Republican. Similarly, the claim that takeovers wastefully divert managerial attention and energy is at least incomplete, unless one makes the balancing observation that managers, to the extent that they are agents for others, should be concerned about whether their principals are satisfied. Only the monopolist enjoys the advantages of the quiet life, and to the extent that a manager's piece of mind is undisturbed, an organizational failure has occurred almost by definition.

This assessment does not dismiss the standard claims that takeovers may produce various diseconomies, but it does imply that these criticisms lack coherence unless they can be understood in terms of a broader theory of why managerial and shareholder preferences should conflict. If a systematic tension between shareholder and managerial preferences can be identified, however, then it is possible to view the hostile takeover's impact as more ambiguous than neoclassical theorists have seen it. In this latter view, the takeover may sometimes discipline management, but it also disrupts a preexisting web of contracts by which shareholders and managers had reached an equilibrium position between their conflicting interests. If the old equilibrium has been disturbed, the initial question is: In what direction are we moving? Who wins and who loses as a result of these changes? To say that the capital market is disciplining management only identifies the process but leaves unresolved the question of the direction in which we are moving. This chapter will answer this question by arguing that the new wave of takeover competition is moving us toward acceptance of a higher level of risk at the firm level. This movement may be in the shareholders' interest, but it is far from clear that it is in the interests of society as a whole.

How, then, should we analyze the hostile takeover in terms of a broader theory of the firm? Any answer to this question must recognize that there exists not a single theory of the firm but a number of well-known and intellectually serious models, each of which has its adherents and current theoreticians. For ease of exposition, this chapter will analyze these models under three headings: (1) the neoclassical model, (2) the managerialist model, and (3) the transaction cost model. None of these theories, however, has given adequate attention to a critical area where shareholders and managers have an inherent conflict, one that the existing structure of the firm does not resolve or mitigate. Notwithstanding the signficant changes in internal structure over the past half century that have been described by business historians such as Alfred Chandler,[14] there remains a deep internal strain between shareholders, on the one hand, and managers and employees, on the other. The central conflict, which this chapter will claim provides a basis for an understanding of the recent takeover movement, involves the asymmetry in attitudes toward risk held by the typical manager and the typical shareholder. Put simply, the rational manager has good reason to be risk-averse, while the fully diversified shareholder has every reason to be risk-neutral. If we see the modern public corporation as, in the phrase currently fashionable among theorists, a "web of contracts," this is the strain in the corporate web that arises because managers and shareholders have conflicting risk preferences. This strain also helps to explain the significant disparity between stock and asset values that invites bust-up takeovers.

Having suggested that recent critics of the takeover have been excessively *ad hoc* in their analyses, this chapter will attempt to explain, in its first section, why this problem of risk is fundamental. It will suggest that the hostile takeover should be conceived in its current operation, less as a device by which "good" managements drive out "bad" and more as a means by which shareholders can impose their own risk preferences on more risk-averse managements. To be sure, this is not the exclusive role of the takeover. Takeovers also compel retrenchment and redeployment of assets by overgrown target firms, sometimes (but relatively infrequently) replace inferior operating managements, and occasionally realize other synergistic gains.[15] Yet for the past three years, the bust-up takeover has predominated (at least in terms of its impact on both the media and management), and its principal contemporary impact has been to serve as a coercive measure by which managers are induced to accept risks that they would resist on their own. Indeed, takeover competitions among various bidders and the incumbent management begin to look increasingly like contests that are determined by the relative willingness of the contestants to accept risk, as each side proposes to turn a radically more leveraged capital structure. To develop this argument, it is useful to examine the ways in which the principal models of the firm have implicitly, but inadequately, recognized that shareholders and managers have conflicting attitudes toward risk. Then, this first section will survey the two recent developments that show the new impact of the takeover: (1) the movement toward "deconglomeration" and (2) the increase in corporate leverage.

This assessment that the takeover is changing the risk level of the modern corporation is a problematic one. Recognition of the conflict between shareholders and managers over risk does not imply the social desirability of the shareholders' ability to force a higher lever of risk upon the corporation. Although no level of risk aversion or preference is necessarily optimal, this chapter will focus its second section on the possible diseconomies associated with a higher tolerance for risk, in particular as the problem is compounded by the impact of increasing corporate leverage. Decomposing the corporation into its separate constituent interests,[16] it will assess the changed position in this brave new world of creditors, employees, and the state as the ultimate insurer of residual corporate liabilities. The practical question will be whether there are flaws in the bargaining process that justify regulatory intervention.

The third section will then focus on the economic position of the manager in the large public corporation, in particular by employing the concept of "firm-specific" human capital and by advocating the relative efficiency of basing management compensation on an ex post "settling up" that the takeover disrupts. Ultimately, this chapter will propose a more equitable sharing of takeover gains, in part to mitigate the strong incentive that today exists for managers to resist takeovers. But other alternatives also exist, including permitting managements to acquire a disproportionate share of their corporation's voting power and encouraging greater employee ownership in the corporation.[17] Recently, there have been movements in each of these directions, and the trade-offs among them need evaluation. In particular, these alternatives need to be examined because the one option on which much legal commentary has focused—namely, enforcing a rule of managerial passivity in the face of a hostile takeover—seems an increasingly futile hope.[18]

WHAT HATH THE TAKEOVER WROUGHT: A SURVEY OF THEORIES AND EVIDENCE

A little over fifty years ago, Berle and Means reported that the separation of ownership and control in the modern corporation had left shareholders effectively powerless, since managers could neither be ousted from office by shareholders who were widely dispersed and therefore incapable of coordinated action nor disciplined effectively by the capital market, at least as long as managers could rely on internal cash flow to finance corporate expansion.[19] Almost everyone who has since written on the theory of the firm has used the Berle and Means thesis as a point of departure.[20] Much recent work has shared two characteristics: First, it has seen the manager as having less autonomy than Berle and Means thought, because the manager's own self-interest would lead him to install various monitoring and bonding devices in order to maximize the value of his own share in the firm. Second, it has rejected the view of the firm as "owned" by shareholders in favor of a view that conceives of the firm as an equilibrium position achieved as the result of bargaining between the various participants, including managers, shareholders, and creditors.

Viewed in this light, the fundamental irony surrounding the modern bust-up takeover is that it may be taking us full circle back to the apocryphal era that Berle and Means assumed once existed when managers were in fact dutiful agents of shareholders. If bidders perceive that a firm's assets can be liquidated at a value in excess of the firm's stock value plus the takeover premium, they will launch a hostile tender offer, thereby reducing *ex ante* the permissible range for managerial opportunism. That much is clear. But what explains this margin between asset and stock value sufficient to justify current takeover premiums as high as 100% or more, when modern institutional economics has convincingly explained that managers also desire to maximize the firm's stock price? Answering this puzzle will provide the starting point for this chapter's analysis.

The Central Problem of Risk

Shareholders and managers can potentially have many conflicts: salary, dividends, self-dealing transactions—all these and other topics have long produced disputes that sometimes reach the courts. Recent theorists of the firm have argued, however, that it is in the interests of both sides—managers and shareholders—to resolve these conflicts in advance through a variety of contractual devices and institutional mechanisms. Different as the theories of Oliver Williamson and Michael Jensen will be seen shortly to be, they agree that those conflicts between the interests of shareholders and managers that most worried Adolf Berle and Gardiner Means a half century ago have been largely mediated and resolved today.[21]

Whether or not one accepts this contention that the traditional problems of corporate law have been solved, economic theory suggests that there is one area of conflict that was never addressed, even recognized, by the traditional law of fiduciary duties and that remains very much unresolved today. Modern financial theory assumes that rational shareholders will hold diversified portfolios. Although there is evidence that individual investors do not in fact hold well-diversified portfolios,[22] this generalization certainly fits institutional investors, who today dominate the marketplace. In any event, it seems clear that investors, whether individual or institu-

tional, are better diversified than managers. Managers are inherently overinvested in the firm they serve, for at least three distinct reasons.

First, the manager's most important asset is his or her job. Although the manager generally does not have a recognized property right in his or her employment relationship with the corporation, this relationship still has a present value to the manager equal to the discounted earnings stream he or she expects to receive from that job (or career path) until retirement. Both because lateral mobility among senior corporate executives is limited and because the manager may develop firm-specific human capital,[23] the manager cannot assume the existence of an external market rate of return applicable to his or her labors, as the lower-echelon employee may be able to assume. Rather, the still-prevailing pattern is one in which there are "ports of entry" within the corporate hierarchy but little opportunity exists for lateral movement at an equivalent level.[24] Managerial compensation is thus set within an internal market, and loss of a job thus means more to a manager than to those employees whose wages are determined by an external market. To sum up, the basic contrast is that shareholders own many stocks, but managers have only one job.

Second, the manager is overinvested in his own firm because the firm in its own interest awards him a generally nontransferable interest in itself through stock options and other fringe benefits. Empirically, there is no doubt that senior managers do in fact have a substantial portion of their personal wealth invested in their own firm.[25] The firm's purpose is to align the manager's interests with those of the shareholders. This concept of aligning managerial and shareholder interests is at the very heart of the Jensen and Meckling model, which demonstrates that most shareholders/manager conflicts can be minimized in part through such incentive compensation.[26] However, for present purposes, the relevant point is that the use of stock as compensation gives the manager an undiversified portfolio. Ironically, as this device cures other conflicts, it tends to exacerbate the asymmetry in risk attitudes between shareholders and managers.

Third, although shareholders have limited liability, managers and directors may well have personal liability in the event of corporate insolvency or financial distress. Recent experiences at Continental Illinois, Trans-Union, Chase Manhattan, and Bank of America indicate that corporate managers can be sued from all directions: in derivative actions, in governmental proceedings, in class actions under the federal securities laws, and by bankruptcy trustees.[27] In some circumstances, they may even face criminal liability for securities fraud or other offenses if, after insolvency, there surface allegations that they hid the corporation's financial distress.

As a result, the bottom line is that the manager may not view corporate insolvency with the same equanimity that the diversified shareholder can. Because the manager cannot spread his risks or escape them safely in the event of insolvency, he is thus economically wedded to his firm. The implications of this point are at once obvious and far reaching: Managers will be more risk-averse than their shareholders. Indeed, it is axiomatic that fully diversified shareholders should not be risk-averse at all. Portfolio theory divides the risk associated with any security into two components: a firm-specific component and a "systematic" or nondiversifiable component associated with general market conditions.[28] Once shareholders have diversified their portfolio, they are in theory largely immune from firm-specific risk, both because no individual stock will have that material an impact on their portfolios' performance and because their portfolios will include countercyclical stocks whose price movements will offset each other. Hence, the investor should in theory be risk-neutral. Under some circumstances, such an investor may even behave as a risk preferrer, because the investor may seek stocks having a high-risk level to offset the debt or low-risk components of the portfolio. The manager, however, has no real protection against firm-specific risk and hence will be risk-averse. This is both inev-

itable and in some respects desirable, because if the manager could diversify away all firm-specific risk, serious moral hazard problems would arise and the senior manager would have little incentive to monitor others.

Once this conflict is recognized, it can be seen to constitute an underlying tension that runs through the corporate landscape much like the San Andreas fault—that is, seldom overtly visible in its operation but still powerful in its impact. At the level of ordinary business decisions, the impact of this "risk aversion differential" will seldom be evident. In choosing among competing investment opportunities or business projects that do not threaten the firm's solvency, managers have little reason to act as if they were risk-averse because they are "repeat players" who understand that the firm itself is a diversified portfolio. However, when we move from the tactical to the strategic level, the conflict becomes pronounced. For example, some economists, such as Robin Marris and William Baumol,[29] have argued that corporate managers maximize sales or growth, not profits. In part, such an empire-building policy is pursued, they claim, to increase the security of the corporation's managers, because the acquisition of additional divisions and product lines both reduces the risk of insolvency and provides opportunities for personal advancement. Translated into the vocabulary of this chapter, this claim can be understood as an assertion that managers seek to build a diversified portfolio within their firm. Exactly this specific claim has been made by financial economists, most notably by Amihud and Lev, who marshall evidence that "managers, as opposed to investors, ... engage in conglomerate mergers to decrease their largely undiversifiable 'employment risk.'"[30] Where all these different writers share a common ground is in their mutual recognition that empire building may be rational for managers but inefficient for shareholders.

This perception can be generalized to cover all investment decisions.[31] In the area of corporate financial policy, there is again a close fit between this theory and empirical observations. In a well-known field study, Professor Gordon Donaldson of the Harvard Business School found that the corporations he studied as a participant observer preferred to finance through retained earnings rather than through the issuance of debt.[32] Many firms that he interviewed plainly revealed a strong bias against any financing that involved resort to the capital markets and required a considerably higher expected return from an investment before they would resort to external financing sources. In a more recent and extended study of a dozen mature industrial firms over the period of 1969 to 1978, Donaldson found that of the capital funds invested by these companies over that period, some 74% was internally generated, 26% came from long-term debt, and none came from new equity issues.[33] What explained this aversion for the public capital markets? Donaldson concluded that the policy of these firms with respect to the use of debt could be "summed up in one word: conservation."[34] In his view, managers treated their firm's debt capacity as if it were a hidden bank account to be saved for a rainy day. Leverage then is something that managers avoid, his study implies, because it consumes the firm's debt capacity, which they view as the buffer that protects them from the risk of future adverse events.

Heretical as this thesis may sound, other studies also point to this same conclusion that managers underutilize debt and avoid nonessential entanglements with the capital markets. These studies have found that the rate of return experienced by public corporations on internally generated funds was well below that on debt or equity.[35] Indeed, for firms that did not resort at all to the equity market, the return on "ploughbacked" funds has been found to be near zero.[36] This startling finding suggests both that managers are overly biased toward earnings retention (possibly because they wish to maximize growth) and that they are reluctant to use the capital markets unless the projected investment offers a much higher rate of return than is ordinarily available to the firm. Even more to the point, other studies have found that man-

agement-controlled firms have a lower return on investment than firms where ownership and control is not separated[37] and that management-controlled firms retain a higher percentage of earnings.[38]

All this data comes into clearer focus once we begin from the premise that senior management, having a fixed investment in the firm, will act in a more risk-averse manner than the shareholders. In this view, managers tend to be reluctant to accept any form of capital market discipline, not just the discipline of the market for corporate control. Accordingly, a naive "growth maximization" model misspecifies managerial incentives. Although the corporations that Donaldson studied doggedly pursued growth and enhanced market share (rather than the highest stock price or return on equity), they did so always within the constraint of seeking only that level of growth that could be "self-sustained"—i.e., financed through internally generated funds and without utilizing the corporation's much protected debt capacity. Such a portrait describes a management that can be described both as risk-averse and as extremely protective of its own autonomy.

Excessive earnings retention is, of course, another facet of this same phenomenon, but one that directly relates to the motive for bust-up takeovers. Although managerialists have seen this behavior either as motivated by a desire for growth or as proof that managers have an "expense preference" that conflicts with the shareholders' interest,[39] the more fundamental cause-and-effect relationship may be the disparity in the level of risk aversion between managers and shareholders. Thus, the less risk-averse shareholder wants a high payout, but the manager wants to hoard cash and assets to protect against future contingencies. Of course, tax motives may also play a role here, because dividends are highly taxed; but if managers were simply conforming their behavior to the incentives that the tax laws held out, they would long ago have also increased the firm's degree of leverage. Because they clearly have not, tax effects seem then to have only a partial explanatory power.[40] In particular, tax incentives cannot explain the critical empirical finding that management-controlled firms are characterized by lower levels of systematic and unsystematic risk than owner-controlled firms[41]—a finding that dovetails with the managerial risk aversion hypothesis here expressed.

Finally, risk is also the critical element that may shape managerial compensation systems. A leading model of the labor market—known as the "implicit-contract" model—assumes that employers are risk-neutral and employees are risk-averse.[42] Thus, the two sides negotiate employment contracts in which employees trade off some portion of the wages they could demand for employment stability. Because this model has the ability to explain both wage rigidity and underemployment equilibria, it has attracted considerable attention. To date, it has been chiefly used with respect to lower-level employees, but it applies at least as well to the manager, because the manager is even more dependent on the firm for his expected future wealth and may suffer a greater loss if forced to resort to the marketplace.[43] There is a profound irony here, because one tradition of neoclassical economics has long argued that managers are undercompensated and so lack true entrepreneurial spirit.[44] The short answer to this thesis is that managers have probably chosen fixed-wage contracts over more "entrepreneurial" variable-wage contracts precisely because they are risk-averse.

The point of immediate relevance is, however, that this implicit contract is disrupted if the takeover can deprive the manager of the employment stability for which he has already paid a price in terms of forgone earnings. In short, all these pieces of evidence fit a larger pattern in which managers and shareholders have a hidden conflict over the level of risk the firm should accept. This conflict affects not only the variance of the firm's expected returns but also their mean value to the shareholders, because it implies that the firm's managers will delay the payout of earnings, restrict the issuance of debt, and hoard cash and other assets that might be put to higher-valued uses by the market.

Against this backdrop, the hostile takeover may be viewed as a mechanism that compels a management to accept that level of business risk that shareholders deem appropriate. Such an assessment sounds optimal, but it considers, however, only the interests of shareholders. Other interests may merit equivalent concern. To understand why, we will next examine how the principal models of the firm treat the relationship of shareholders and managers.

Theories of the Firm

This section will analyze, in order, three groups of theories: (1) the neoclassical model (where writers such as Michael Jensen, Eugene Fama, Armen Alchian, and Harold Demsetz constitute the principal theorists),[45] (2) the managerialist model (whose leading advocates include William Baumol, Robin Marris, Harvey Leibenstein, and Dennis Mueller),[46] and (3) the transaction cost model (whose leading proponent is Oliver Williamson).[47] Although these theories ultimately may be complementary or at least can be read to reinforce each other, it is useful to take each initially on its own terms.

The Neoclassical Model

The leading neoclassical model of the firm—that offered by Professors Jensen and Meckling—begins essentially where Berle and Means left off a half century ago.[48] Initially, they recognize the potential conflicts that arise between managers and shareholders once shareownership becomes dispersed; the utility-maximizing agent, they acknowledge, does not necessarily have an incentive to act in the best interests of his principal. Accordingly, the principal will have to incur costs to monitor the agent's performance and will pay less for shares in the corporation in proportion to the magnitude of the "agency costs" that must be so incurred. At this point, Jensen and Meckling make their distinctive contribution: it is in the agent's interest, they argue, to convince investors that the firm will have an institutional structure which will minimize agency costs (a term that includes both the expenditures incurred to reduce managerial misappropriation and shirking and the irreducible mimimum of such losses). That is, because agency costs reduce the market value of the firm, the agent as the firm's promoter will wish to minimize them. These agency costs can be reduced in a variety of ways: (1) through monitoring expenditures (such as the use of outside directors, audit committees, and independent directors), (2) through bonding devices (which will be discussed shortly), and (3) through incentive compensation that gives the agent a substantial equity investment in the firm and so a desire to maximize its share value. Following Jensen and Meckling, neoclassical economists have tended to assume that market forces will alone result in the installation of the optimal level of monitoring devices and incentive systems that bring agency costs down to an irreducible minimum. At this minimal level, no additional dollar spent on internal controls or incentive compensation will yield an equivalent reduction in managerial opportunism or shirking.

One could debate at length whether market forces are alone adequate to minimize agency costs or whether the law also has a positive role to play, but the focus of this chapter is narrower: Do these forces work to align the manager's risk aversion level with those of the shareholders? It seems extremely doubtful that the contractual devices described by Jensen and Meckling do anything like this. Take, for example, the use of outside directors. If anything, they have reason to be even more risk-averse than managers. This is because their economic stake in the corporation is relatively small while their potential personal liability may be significant once the corporation becomes financially distressed. Their own individual cost-benefit calculus should therefore make them resist a high-risk course of action, even if they in general were risk-neutral, because for them the potential losses are likely to exceed the potential gains. In addition, directors are subject to severe cognitive limitations: the information they receive comes to them through management, and they have little

independent means of verifying the set of opportunities the corporation has to choose among.[49] Interestingly, business school academics have independently concluded that outside directors are inherently more likely to be a brake on, rather than a motor force for, organizational innovation or other change that would produce a higher-risk level.[50]

The other principal mechanism identified by Jensen and Meckling—i.e., incentive compensation through stock options—seems even more limited in its impact. Although the use of options does give the manager greater incentives to accept risk, it also aggravates the degree to which the manager holds an undiversified portfolio that is overinvested in a single firm; thus, their use may expose both the manager's savings and human capital to the unique risks of a single firm.

Once we introduce the institution of the hostile takeover and postulate that at least some bidders view their targets as having operated in a bureaucratic, overly risk-averse, and insufficiently entrepreneurial fashion (a description of bidders that at least fits the public prose of Carl Icahn and, to a lesser extent, Boone Pickens), then the takeover becomes comprehensible as a device that disciplines "excessive" risk aversion. Given its existence, managers may find it in their interest to turn to what can be described as a "bonding" device: They can increase corporate leverage as an *ex ante* takeover defense. As will be discussed shortly, this description seems to fit the financial restructuring that over the past three years has become the principal, long-term, takeover defense strategy of those firms that believe themselves to be potential targets.

Viewed in terms of the neoclassical model, the emphatic increase in corporate leverage that occurred in 1984 as the result of debt issuances, stock repurchases, and high dividends can be seen as a bonding device by which managements signal to the market that they will not maintain a conservative capital structure or hoard assets when diversified stockholders would prefer a high payout. Frank Easterbrook has suggested that a high dividend payout is a means of reducing agency costs by assuring investors that the firm will have to subject itself (and its policies) regularly to the discipline of the market in order to finance new projects.[51] Actually, this ingenious argument simply stands on its ear the earlier thesis of Berle and Means that the market had little disciplinary power on managers because managers relied on internal cash flow to finance expansion. Empirically, the difficulty that the Easterbrook thesis faces is that few firms do seem to pay out such a high ratio of earnings as dividends as to compel them to resort to the capital markets; in effect, the Berle and Means premise here remains substantially accurate.

Yet a further variation is possible on the Easterbrook thesis. When debt is exchanged for stock (a now-frequent phenomenon in takeover defense tactics), it is possible to recast his thesis and say that this debt issuance represents a firmer promise than does a past dividend payout record that the corporation will not pursue growth over profitability. In other words, because interest payments are mandatory but dividends are only discretionary, Professor Jensen views leverage as a tactic by which management makes a more credible promise to accept the market's judgment because more frequent returns to the market will be necessary for a firm with a high debt-equity ratio.[52]

A puzzling aspect of the Easterbrook-Jensen thesis is that although it sounds plausible in theory, it did not have much empirical confirmation prior to the appearance of the bust-up takeover. That is, managers do not seem to have voluntarily adopted their suggested technique for "bonding" themselves to follow their principals' preferences. Only with the advent of the bust-up takeover is there any evidence that suggests a process that even vaguely resembles the kind of bonding that Jensen and Meckling predict managers will engage in. Yet this takeover-induced bonding can hardly be called voluntary. This in turn suggests either that managers' aversion to risk is very strongly held or that the Jensen and Meckling model generally overesti-mates the willingness of managers to bond themselves in order to increase the firm's stock value.

The Managerialist Model

While the neoclassical model uses the market as its starting point, another variety of model begins with the manager. Rather than assume that the firm is externally controlled by the market, theorists have developed "internal" theories of the firm in which the manager is the central actor.[53] In focusing on the manager, these theorists emphasize both the severe cognitive limitations that surround business decision making and the opportunities for discretionary behavior by managers. Denied perfect information, the manager in the large organization exists in a world of "bounded rationality" in which he must search for satisfactory answers to immediate problems by adopting more or less trial-and-error strategies. As a result, the manager functions not by seeking optimal solutions but only satisfactory ones. As developed by Nobel Laureate Herbert Simon and his colleagues, this "behavioral" theory of the firm postulates that managers do not profit-maximize but, rather, "profit-satis-fice"—i.e., they seek that level of profits that will suffice to prevent external interventions by dissatisfied creditors or stockholders.[54] So viewed, managers are in effect semiautonomous, subject only to the weak external constraint that the providers of the firm's capital receive a minimal return.

How do managers exercise the vast discretion that this model sees them as possessing? In the best-known of these models, Robin Marris saw managers as using those residual funds left over after external constraints were satisfied to expand the size of the firm.[55] Why is growth maximization the goal of managers? According to Marris, growth provides managers with greater compensation, greater psychic income, and greater security. A similar theme (but absent this emphasis on the personal security of the manager as a force for growth) appears in another well-known model of the manager's utility function developed by Oliver Williamson.[56] Professor

Williamson postulates that managers have an "expense preference" and gain a personal utility from expenditures on increased staff or growth. Neither Marris nor Williamson places the problem of risk at center stage in their models, but in each case this idea is at least consistent with their analysis that managers use their discretion to reduce the insecurity to which they are subject. Ultimately, their assertions translate into a claim that managers are seeking to reduce risks that do not appear to trouble the firm's shareholders. Much this same theme that managers use their discretion to reduce their insecurity within the firm can also be found in the writings of the principal organization theorists.[57] However phrased, the claim that managers want to pursue growth or other security-enhancing objectives within the boundaries established by external profit constraints on the firm is at least in part a statement that managers will seek to reduce risk up to that point where the shareholders may oust them if they pursue this objective further.

How valid do these managerialist theories seem today? Although they are intuitively attractive in their description of managerial objectives, they also have a dated quality in their implicit assumption that firms are large, unchanging bureaucracies and that the market constitutes only a weak external constraint. Historically, these models were developed in the early 1970s based on the experience of the late 1960s, when it was still possible to write confidently of corporations as unchanging bureaucratic organizations that were only weakly constrained by the market. In short, these models predate the emergence of the takeover as a major constraining force, the rise of active institutional investors, and the traumatic series of shocks that the American economy began to experience in the 1970s.

Yet if these theories understate the external constraints on the corporate manager, there is, if anything, additional reason today to believe that they correctly describe the manager's own preferences as biased in favor of growth over profitability. The best evidence of this bias lies in the re-

cent prevalence of bust-up takeovers in which the asset value of the firm on liquidation clearly exceeds the price that a bidder pays to acquire the firm's stock. The puzzling question about such takeovers has been why the firm's asset value is so much in excess of its stock market value. From the foregoing analysis, the most plausible answer is not that these firms were inefficient in the usual sense of substandard operating performance but, rather, that they either had grown to an inefficient size or were failing to exploit opportunities to create value for their shareholders through increased leverage or a higher payout ratio. This answer also helps to explain the "deconglomeration" movement, which will be discussed shortly and which has involved a record level of spinoffs and sales of assets by large corporations under the threat of a takeover.

Ironically, this resolution implies that both sides in the debate between the neoclassical and managerial positions may be partially correct. That is, the takeover may in these instances be enhancing efficiency (at least to the extent that the market's judgment can serve as a proxy for efficiency), but it is doing so largely because the manager had a preference for inefficient growth and earnings retention, as the managerialists hypothesized.

The Transaction Cost Model

The theory of the firm developed by Oliver Williamson is unique in that it builds upon a historical base. It relies on the work of the business historian Alfred Chandler, who found that American corporations underwent a major transition during the middle of this century, as a result of which a new form of corporate structure arose that was characterized by decentralized, semiautonomous divisions coordinated by a central executive office.[58] Williamson has offered a plausible theory to explain this development by returning to a central question posed by Ronald Coase: Why are some business decisions coordinated by markets and others resolved by internal administrative decisions within the firm?[59] Williamson's answer (also suggested by Coase in a more rudimentary form) is that the internal processes within the firm involve lower transaction costs than does the use of the market system.[60] In effect, the firm exists to effect those processes that it can coordinate more efficiently than the market.

In Williamson's view, the modern multidivisional conglomerate (or M-Form firm) functions as a miniature capital market in which the central executive office reallocates funds from stagnant or low-growth divisions to high-growth winners in a manner that outperforms the capital market. Because of its superior monitoring ability, the M-Form firm gradually superseded its predecessor, the U-Form firm, which had a functionally specialized management but did not have the same multiunit, diversified scope of operations or the decentralized system of administration that developed within the M-Form firm.

Yet it is precisely with respect to this claim of superior efficiency for the M-Form firm that recent developments in corporate structure present a problem. Indeed, these developments suggest that the Williamsonian theory may be historically bounded as well as historically derived. Put simply, if the conglomerate form is more efficient than the earlier U-Form firm, why has there been a sudden trend toward deconglomeration? The specifics of this trend will be noted in the next section, but the more important issue involves identifying the motor force driving it. To say that the deconglomeration movement is takeover-induced (as it clearly is) begs the question. Why is it takeover-induced? What inefficiency does the market see in the conglomerate form, and why has this trend toward deconglomeration suddenly peaked two decades after the full-scale appearance of the modern conglomerate in the 1960s?

One possibility is, of course, that the managerialists could be more right than Professor Williamson. That is, the growth of the conglomerate could owe more to the growth-maximizing preferences of managers, who are seeking to build a diversified portfolio within a single firm, than to its greater efficiency, as Professor Williamson postulates. A satisfactory basis for empirical evaluation of these competing claims still eludes us, but some evidence has shown that diversification at the shareholder level has outperformed conglomerate firms.[61] This is hardly the result one would expect if the modern conglomerate had superior monitoring ability. In addition, the work of Dennis Mueller and others casts doubt on whether the conglomerate (or M-Form) firm has achieved greater efficiencies.[62]

Even if Williamson were more correct than the managerialists, another possibility is that the tendency toward inefficient expansion could be sufficiently prevalent to create a cloud over the use of the conglomerate form. Investors may find it difficult to distinguish these pseudo-M-Form firms that have grown to inefficient size or that intend to "hoard" earnings when shareholders would prefer a higher dividend payout from those in which use of the M-Form has achieved an efficient reallocation of funds at lower transaction costs. Such judgments involve predictions of the future, during periods when the corporation may be under a different management team, and thus are highly speculative. In short, if investors cannot distinguish "good" from "bad" conglomerates (in terms of their likely future behavior), a "market-for-lemons" effect could arise along the lines suggested by Professor Akerlof.[63] In this light, even if only a minority of all conglomerates exhibited the behavior predicted by the managerialists, the market might still penalize the stock prices of all conglomerates if monitoring by investors could not easily distinguish between these firms. As a result, arbitrage profits would still be available to bidders seeking to realize the difference between the stock market price and the asset value on all conglomerates.

Finally, the Williamsonian model gives no attention to the rise over the past 20 years of two external monitoring forces: (1) the institutional investor and (2) the takeover bidder. Inherently, any improvement in external monitoring controls reduces the significance of the disparity between the internal monitoring capacity of the M-Form firm and its predecessor, the U-Form firm.

As a result, the comparative advantage of the M-Form is reduced. In addition, because the institutional investor is already fully diversified (or nearly so), the diversification advantages of the conglomerate seem dubious from its perspective, for two quite different reasons. First, because the institutional investor is already the holder of a diversified portfolio, it has little need to invest in another diversified portfolio, which is what the large conglomerate essentially resembles. Rather, the institutional investor's need is to pick and choose stocks to fill specific holes in its own portfolio.[64] Almost by definition, a diversified conglomerate does not have such a specific profile that can match this need. Thus, the institutional investor has reason to disdain it or to purchase its stock only at a discount. To the extent that such an attitude prevails in the market, there may again be a market penalty imposed on the use of the conglomerate form. Second, the institutional money manager has a self-interest that disinclines him toward investing in diversified conglomerates. Investing in a portfolio of conglomerates is little different from investing in a market index fund. From the standpoint of the money manager, it becomes difficult to justify high management fees for transactions that are so easily and costlessly effected.[65] Hence, self-interest—whether conscious or unconscious—dictates that these managers maintain that they can outperform this simple strategy of diversification by selecting less diversified companies.[66]

Summary

The responses of these three models differ significantly in their recognition and treatment of the asymmetry in risk attitudes between managers and shareholders. The neoclassical model does not deny that managers may be more risk-averse but argues that increasing corporate leverage represents a form of bonding by which managers are compelled to accept their shareholders' preferences. Yet if this is bonding, it is curious why it is happening only today. The abrupt character of this transition suggests that managers had declined to adopt their shareholders' preferences with respect to the issues of risk, growth, and the optimal payout of earnings until the takeover forced them to do so. If so, the theory of bonding seems weak, and it is only the takeover that has compelled change. The managerialist model can easily accommodate the idea of a disparity in risk aversion between managers and shareholders, but it seems historically dated in its failure to recognize the impact of the takeover on the balance of power between shareholders and managers. It assumes that takeovers, like mergers generally, only produce more growth and more empire building. Yet the irony is that the takeover may be the one mechanism that can purge organizational slack from these corporate empires, albeit at a potentially disturbing social cost. Finally, the transaction cost model seems simply to ignore the problem of risk.

Indeed, in response to this author's arguments, Professor Williamson has explicitly argued that we should treat the manager and the shareholder as if they were both risk-neutral.[67] Although this assumption of risk neutrality disdains a well-developed literature on implicit contracting,[68] it also enables Williamson to sidestep the related claim that the modern conglomerate arose not because it was a more efficient monitor but largely because conglomerate acquisitions allowed risk-averse managers to diversify to avoid the firm-specific risk to which they were otherwise subject.[69] Recognizing that a conflict does exist between the interests of shareholders and managers, Williamson has offered a "hazard exposure" hypothesis that explains seemingly risk-averse managerial behavior as attempts to secure protection for management's substantial investment of firm-specific human capital. Once one assumes a substantial investment of firm-specific human capital by managers, it follows that if managers are compelled to resort to the market for executive services, they are exposed to a loss of this capital and so will seek contractual protections against such a loss. By this same token, however, the exposed position of the manager who has invested in firm-specific human capital can also produce an incentive for inefficient expansion that protects them from economic reversals within a single division, but injures shareholders.

Thus, using Williamson's vocabulary, one can still reach about the same end result as I do, but without recognizing a risk aversion differential between shareholders and mangers. The issue is thus joined: Do we need the risk aversion differential to model recent developments within the firm? My answer is that more than semantics is involved here and that the hazard exposure hypothesis can capture and explain only a modest proportion of the managerial behavior that the risk aversion differential more fully explains. Three distinct reasons support this conclusion.

First, it is questionable, as a general proposition, whether managers have the level of firm-specific human capital invested in their firms necessary to make Williamson's theory a generalized explanation. To begin with, an active market for senior-executive services exists, and many CEOs came to their present firm without prior service there.[70] To be sure, internal promotion is the more common route, but the existence of a substantial rate of inter-firm transfers is inconsistent with the claim that an executive must make substantial investments in firm-specific human capital to advance within the corporate hierarchy. Other barriers to lateral mobility—such as the lesser uncertainty associated with internal promotion and the forfeiture provisions in stock options and most pensions—better explain why lateral transfers are not more common. The tremendous success of executive-recruiting firms (or "headhunters") also shows that managerial talent is not logically firm-specific. Indeed, the modern business school is curricularly premised on the proposition that a broad range of executive skills can be taught that have career-long utility and wide applicability. Not only is executive mobility *among firms* increasing, but the typical career path of young executives *within the firm* will today require that they transfer among the often unrelated divisions of a diversified conglomerate. Thus, the road to executive success requires then that the executive learn "general-purpose" executive skills, not simply "special-purpose" (but dead-end) technological expertise.[71] In short, Williamson's emphasis on firm-specific human capital, although it certainly captures a piece of the problem, applies more to the lower-level technocrat—the engineer or manufacturing specialist—than to the financial executives who have increasingly come to dominate the upper ranks of management in corporate America.[72] An illustration of this point comes when we look at the profiles of the CEOs of recent target companies. While some undoubtedly have had substantial firm-specific capital invested in their firm, this characterization simply cannot be sensibly applied to executives such as Agee of Bendix, Bergerac of Revlon, Dingman of Signal, Wyman of CBS, or other highly mobile chief executives, such as those at Esmark and Beatrice.

Given the broad employment experience and fungible talents of these executives, why would they be risk-averse? Here, we come to the second basic reason, which involves not firm-specific human capital but the much simpler fact of financial overinvestment in the firm. It is in the firm's interest to compensate managers through forfeitable stock options and unvested pension rights in such a manner as to restrict their lateral mobility (hence, the term *golden handcuffs* for managerial compensation packages). But as the firm succeeds in making executives less mobile, it also makes them more risk-averse.

Finally, there is a more general methodological objection to Williamson's reliance on firm-specific human capital: namely, its existence in substantial amounts requires a leap of faith. If the market places a lower value on an executive's services than does his current firm, one cannot automatically explain this disparity as attributable to the executive's unique value to his current firm. Sometimes, this may be true, but a simpler explanation may also be that the executive is overpaid because of high agency costs. Alternatively, a subtler explanation may be that executives have entered into an implicit contract with the firm under which high, deferred returns will be paid on the basis of seniority.[73] In general, theories are soundest when they are built from an observable empirical base. In this regard, managerial overinvestment in their firms is observable, but firm-specific capital is not. Postulating that it exists in large amounts may assume what is to be proved.

In the last analysis, both the risk aversion differential and the hazard exposure hypothesis can coexist as complementary theories, which each explain a piece of the puzzle. While this chapter agrees that firm-specific human capital is exposed to loss by the takeover, this account is incomplete, and the factor of risk aversion cannot be omitted. Almost certainly, only risk aversion can explain the behavior of directors, who face real liabilities but have no human capital invested in their positions as directors.[74] More generally, the risk aversion differential has the greater explanatory power, because it can account for other forms of behavior, such as the failure of managers to make greater use of debt or to avoid the capital markets, which the "hazard exposure" hypothesis simply leaves unexplained.

The Empirical Evidence

Most attempts at empirical evaluation of the takeover phenomenon have sought to study either targets or bidders, typically through stock price studies or follow-up studies of their postacquisition performance.[75] This may be the wrong focus, or at least an overly narrow one, because the more important impact of the takeover may well be on those firms and managers who are not taken over but who change their behavior as a result of the general deterrent threat of a takeover. In principle, this deterrent impact dwarfs the takeover's specific deterrent impact on those firms that are actually taken over, if only because this former category is vastly larger than the much smaller number of firms actually taken over. As will next be shown, the landscape of corporate America has changed radically since even 1980, and these changes—whether for good or ill—seem largely takeover-related.

The Trend Toward Leverage

Federal Reserve Board data show that in 1962, the ratio of debt to equity of American corporations, as measured by the book value of assets less the face value of liabilities, was 58.2%.[76] As Table 6.1 shows, this debt level as a percentage of book value grew gradually over the next 22 years until it reached 73% in 1983, never increasing more than 3% in any one year. Then in 1984, it rose from 73% to 81.4%, a jump that exceeded the entire prior increase from 1968 to 1983. This trend has clearly continued into the first half of 1985. Particularly alarming is the fact that short-term debt stood at a record 52% of total debt at the end of 1985s first quarter, thus leaving companies more vulnerable than in the past to any increase in interest rates.[77]

What caused this sudden leap? Part of the answer lies in the fact that 1984 was a year of high merger and takeover activity. According to Federal Reserve data, 1984 witnessed a record $85 billion shrinkage in equity, which was the amount of net stock redemptions in 1984.[78] According to a New York Stock Exchange study, this shrinkage was a direct result of merger activity, since between $84 billion and $100 billion worth of equity was retired in merger exchanges of debt and cash for equity in 1984.[79] When the $12 billion in new equity issued in 1984 is subtracted from these figures, the result is a merger-related decline of at least $72 billion. Although only a relatively small portion of this equity shrinkage can be directly attributed to the appearance of the junk bond,[80] much of the balance may be indirectly attributable to takeovers, since share repurchases, which are a principal cause of this equity shrinkage, have become a favorite takeover defense. Unquestionably, target corporations have found it an effective postbid defensive tactic to increase their leverage, in large part because doing so disrupts the junk bond financing that the bidder has typically assembled. Martin Marietta, Phillips Petroleum, Union Carbide, Unocal, CBS, and Revlon are all recent examples of a common takeover defense: leveraging up and

Table 6.1. Debt-to-Equity Ratios: Nonfinancial Corporations (percent)

Year	Book Value[a]	Current Value[b]	Market Value[c]
1962	58.2	37.6	42.4
1964	59.9	41.8	37.7
1966	62.7	45.7	43.4
1968	67.2	49.4	35.6
1970	70.5	50.8	48.0
1971	70.4	51.2	46.7
1972	70.2	50.0	45.4
1973	70.9	49.7	61.9
1974	70.2	44.6	91.1
1975	66.7	42.3	72.0
1976	65.6	42.1	72.9
1977	67.7	41.4	84.0
1978	69.1	41.1	87.5
1979	69.9	39.9	79.0
1980	68.3	38.2	60.4
1981	71.0	38.9	70.2
1982	74.3	40.6	71.5
1983	73.0	40.9	63.4
1984	81.4	46.5	75.0
1985[d]	n/a	49.4	72.9

Source: Federal Reserve Board.

[a]Debt is valued at par; equity is valued at book.

[b]Debt is valued at par, and equity is balance-sheet net worth with tangible assets valued at replacement cost.

[c]The market value of debt is an estimate based on par value and ratios of market to par values of NYSE bonds; equity value is based on market prices of outstanding shares.

[d]Estimated values.

then distributing the proceeds to shareholders.[81] Although a new SEC rule has eliminated the special advantages of a discriminatory self-tender,[82] Revlon, which made a nondiscriminatory self-tender after the proposal of this rule, shows that self-tenders will remain a popular postbid defensive technique, even though the self-tender would have to be open to all shareholders. Indeed, Revlon's unsuccessful defense illustrates this tactic in its classic form: by repurchasing 10 million of its shares for $575 million in debt securities, it effectively recapitalized itself into a highly leveraged firm whose debt capacity was largely exhausted.[83]

More common than the postbid self-tender as a last-ditch defensive tactic is the use of share repurchases as an anticipatory defense that is undertaken by a corporation that realizes it is becoming a potential target. Increasing leverage and distributing the proceeds to its shareholders achieves a strategic advantage for such a target: The bidder who covets the target because of its unused borrowing capacity will realize that this objective has been frustrated and will instead seek a different target. Also, leveraging immunizes the target from a boot-strap acquisition in which a typically smaller bidder borrows against the combined assets of both companies. In effect, the target beats the bidder to the punch by borrowing up to its debt capacity and distributing the proceeds to its shareholders. From a tactical perspective, leveraging is then the new defense that stalemates the modern junk bond–financed, bust-up takeover (at least as long as the bidder cannot finance its offer solely from its own creditworthiness). To the extent that "excess" resources are distributed to shareholders through pro rata repurchases, the disparity between the corporation's stock price and its asset liquidation value should narrow or disappear, because the market would no longer have reason to penalize the stock for management's retention of "excess" assets.

As noted earlier, the optimistic view of this sharp increase in corporate debt-equity ratios sees it as a correction to the suboptimal degree of leverage that was the product of management's risk aversion. The pessimistic view is, of course, that many firms will be unable to sustain their debt service once the business cycle turns downward.[84] Those who are sanguine about leverage point out that net interest payments have not exceeded the growth in cash flow. Interest coverage ratios have, in fact, recently improved as a result of liberalized depreciation rules. At the end of the first quarter of 1985, net interest payments as a percentage of corporate cash flow stood at 23.7%, a level well below the 1982 peak of 33.0% and about equal to the level that prevailed in 1970.[85] Moreover, although corporate debt has increased as a percentage of book value, the optimists point out that book value provides a frequently misleading measure, because it is based on historical cost and we live in an inflationary world. As Table 6.1 shows, if we look instead at the replacement cost of corporate assets (rather than their book value), the debt-to-equity ratio stood at 46.1% rather than the 81.4% level that results from use of a book-value denominator. This level is below the peak level of 1968 to 1972, when debt exceeded 50% as measured on a current-value basis. Alternatively, one can also measure the debt level against the market's valuation of the corporation's net worth. As Table 6.1 shows, this denominator produces a more

volatile figure, which increased significantly in 1984 and has increased steadily since 1980 but which is still well below previous peak periods.

If we narrow our focus to Fortune 500 industrial companies, which is probably the relevant peer group for any discussion of the impact of the takeover, total liabilities as a percentage of the book value of assets rose from 35% in 1960 to 55% at the end of 1984—a sizable increase but one considerably less scary than that suggested by the Federal Reserve Board's 80% figure.[86] Still, any focus on the average level of debt can be misleading, because it may disguise a substantial growth in debt that is limited to a particular sector of the economy. Ultimately, only a sector analysis, and not aggregate data, can satisfactorily answer the question of whether serious risks of corporate insolvencies loom.

Examining the debtor's financial condition also looks at only half the equation. If there is a problem with leverage, why is it that creditors would not protect themselves adequately? Here, there are potentially disturbing answers. To the extent that the junk bond market is a new institution, it is possible that the necessary monitoring mechanisms may not yet have developed adequately.[87] One aspect of this problem involves the distinct possibility that the creditors purchasing these bonds have little incentive to monitor their debtors. Many junk bond purchasers are either savings and loan associations or pension funds, and these classes of institutions receive their capital from individuals who are largely protected by government insurance [either the Federal Savings and Loan Insurance Corporation (FSLIC) or the Pension Benefit Guaranty Corporation (PBGC)]. As a result, these investors have little reason to monitor the level of risk accepted by these financial institutions, and a classic moral hazard problem therefore arises, because the high returns paid on junk bonds are not counterbalanced by high risks to these depositors as long as they can look to government insurance.[88] This is a traditional problem in banking, and the traditional answer has been the use of regulatory monitoring by a variety of agencies. However, in the new era of deregulation, some of these constraints have been relaxed, and financial institutions, such as Continental Illinois, may themselves be under shareholder pressure to accept greater risk. Whatever the reason, the apparent result has been a wave of bank failures unprecedented since the Great Depression.[89]

Another, even more significant reason for skepticism about whether the credit risks associated with junk bonds have been properly evaluated by their purchasers has been suggested by Peter Drucker. As he points out,[90] pension funds, who are major purchasers of junk bonds, are typically "defined-benefit" plans under which the corporate employer's contribution is reduced to the extent that the pension fund's assets earn above-market returns. Because the corporation's financial managers typically also supervise the pension fund, there is a built-in conflict of interest, with the corporation having an incentive to seek above-average returns for the fund (and accept above-average risks in so doing) in order to minimize its own required contribution.

Similar observations may be made about mutual funds, and other more general problems may also compromise the efficiency of the debt market, which will be reviewed later.[91] Nonetheless, it is premature to conclude that junk bonds imperil the stability of any class of financial institutions, because they represent only a relatively trivial percentage of the total portfolio of any segment of the banking and investment industry.[92] Yet given their recent appearance, past data may not predict the future. Although junk bonds financed no more than 1% of all tender offers between 1981 and 1984, an SEC study shows that this figure rose dramatically to 25% in of 1985.[93] Moreover, at least in some regions, small government-insured financial institutions have invested very substantial percentages of their assets in this new class of debt security.[94]

So where are we left? Clearly, corporate debt, however measured, increased significantly last year, and such a rise is disquieting during a "boom" period when debt levels have classically fallen. When based on book value, debt is at a record level; but conversely, it is within prior ranges when current asset value or stock market value are used as a measure. Should we be concerned? The critical question is, of course, "Who is 'we'?" If one is a fully diversified shareholder, the prospect of a significantly increased rate of bankruptcy is not necessarily alarming. But other constituencies are affected much more adversely. Obviously, employees and managers have the most reason to fear bankruptcy, because significant managerial layoffs have followed in the wake of recent instances of leveraging up as a takeover defense.[95]

Even creditors—the group most able, in theory, to protect itself through contractual devices—have been adversely affected. In 1985, Standard & Poor's downgraded a record 272 corporate debt ratings, half again as many as in 1984.[96] According to another survey, 27% of Moody's downgrading during 1984 "resulted from takeover activity."[97] Over the long run, creditors—particularly those who purchase debt securities in the secondary market—may simply learn to pay greater attention to indenture covenants or demand higher interest when managerial discretion to increase debt levels is retained. But if the problem is deeply rooted and they are unavoidably exposed to residual risks, they may need to acquire voting rights. Such a trend is already evident in the recent popularity of "strip financing" in leveraged buy-outs where the lenders also acquire a voting equity stake. The occurrence of debt downgrading on this significant a level does suggest imperfections in the internal contracting process that neoclassical theory assumes is occurring within the firm.[98] Various interpretations are possible for this failure, but the most plausible may be that creditors had simply found it easier to free ride on management's known risk aversion than to engage in more costly and still imperfect contracting. If contracting fails, participation in voting seems the next step.

Ultimately, any balanced evaluation must today be an equivocal one. From the shareholders' perspective, the recent trend can be described as a shift toward a more optimal level of leverage, because shareholders are at last able to discipline excessive managerial risk aversion. Indeed, most market observers believe that the recent wave of equity repurchases by firms has boosted stock market values significantly.[99] Yet, from a social perspective, externalities may result, because private and social wealth can diverge. Obviously, this was the conclusion reached by the Federal Reserve Board when it subjected debt securities issued by shell corporation bidders to the margin rules. The consensus of informed opinion is that the Board's action has to date done very little to restrict the credit available to a bidder, and a host of obvious evasions appear possible.[100] In perspective, the Federal Reserve's action appears to be more an assertion of jurisdiction and an expression of concern than a serious attempt at credit restriction.

Should junk bonds then be subjected to greater regulation, either by tightening the margin rules or by denying the interest deduction with respect to them?[101] The tradeoff is a difficult one. If the bidder's access to credit is curtailed, the takeover as an external check on management will have considerably diminished force with respect to the largest U.S. corporations.[102] Moreover, discouraging junk bonds means that greater size would imply relative immunity, thereby creating a strong incentive for inefficient empire building by defensively oriented managements. Conversely, there are reasons to believe that normal market processes are not operating well in this market, that moral hazard problems are serious, and that something approaching the well-known "market for lemons" may have arisen. Indeed, instances have already arisen in which junk bond issues appear to have been seriously misunderstood and mispriced by the market.[103]

Much ultimately depends on how the public policy goal is defined: Is it the protection of bond purchasers or the curbing of corporate leverage because of anticipated future insolvencies? Bond purchasers are not as exposed to losses as employees, because they are better able to diversify. Also, changes in control do not present an occasion on which the equity holders in the firm can opportunistically renege on a prior implicit understanding (as they may be able to do with respect to the managers' expectation of deferred compensation).[104] Bondholders then may need greater disclosure, but (apart from those institutions subject to a moral hazard problem), it is difficult to justify greater interferences with market processes on their account. If, however, our concern is a chain-related series of bankruptcies, paternalism can be justified because of the third-party effects of business failures. What this means is that ultimately the central figure is the employee/manager.

The Rush to Restructure: Has the Twilight of the Conglomerate Arrived?

Leverage is not the only technique by which the disparity between asset and stock values can be reduced. Undoubtedly, the hottest buzzwords in the executive suite over recent years have been *financial restructuring* and *deconglomeration*. The overall rate of restructuring during 1984 and 1985 appears to have been unprecedented.[105] A better insight is gained when we examine specific examples during 1985 and 1986:

1. In January, ITT announced plans to sell off $1.7 billion in assets by mid 1986.[106]
2. Shortly thereafter, Textron began to restructure itself by selling off units that represented one-third of its sales in the preceding year.[107]
3. In early summer, Gulf and Western sold its consumer and industrial products group to Wickes Companies for approximately $1 billion. This division had represented 40% of G&W's operating income in the prior fiscal year; and its sale was the culmination of a program under which G&W has shed divisions following the death of its founder, Charles Bluhdorn, in 1983, until it has today shrunk itself by half.[108]
4. In late summer, Mobil spun off Montgomery Ward, thus finally ending, with a $500 million write-off, an ex-

perience that ranks as one of the most disastrous acquisitions in financial history.[109]

5. Also over the summer, Crown Zellerbach announced plans to split itself into three separate operating groups that would be separately held by shareholders.[110] Although this plan was ultimately withdrawn when the hostile bidder (Sir James Goldsmith) succeeded in gaining control, this example still shows that deconglomeration can even be a postbid defense.

6. In late August, Westinghouse indicated that it would sell its successful and much-coveted cable television business as part of a financial restructuring, because, it acknowledged, the stock market simply would not reflect the value inherent in the cable business as long as it remained buried within Westinghouse's broader portfolio of companies.[111]

7. In October, The Beatrice Companies announced plans to sell off four divisions, including Avis, Inc., whose total sales were over $1 billion; by year's end, Beatrice would nonetheless go private in the largest buy-out on record.[112]

8. Within the oil industry, restructuring has reached epidemic proportions. ARCO announced in May that it would sell or close 2000 gas stations and close its major East Coast refinery.[113] Freeport-McMoran has spun off its oil and gas operations by creating trust units that trade separately on the New York Stock Exchange.[114] Amoco has spun off its mineral divisions, the Cypress Minerals Co., and Unocal is spinning off its reserves in the Gulf of Mexico into a limited partnership;[115] Chevron is disposing of its East Coast retailing and refining operations;[116] and Mesa Petroleum, as usual leading the way, announced that it would in effect begin to liquidate itself by converting itself into a master limited partnership.[117]

9. Finally, the ink was not dry on the Allied-Signal merger agreement before that company spun off 30 subsidiary operations into an independent concern having $3 billion in annual revenues.[118]

These developments are pieces of a larger pattern. One recent study reports that 23% of the nation's leading 850 corporations have undergone an "operational restructuring" since the beginning of last year, usually selling or spinning off divisions.[119] Closely associated with this trend is the number of divestitures (900) that occurred in 1984. Although there have been prior sell-off waves in U.S. business history, the dollar volume of these transactions was a record.[120] Unlike the earlier sell-off wave that followed the conglomerate merger boom of the 1960s, the selling firms in this wave were not generally seeking to reinvest the proceeds in other acquisitions (much as in a gin rummy game) but were, instead, paying out these proceeds to shareholders in an effort to downsize the firm.

By all accounts, restructurings have been very profitable for shareholders and have helped fuel the stock market's recent advances.[121] But what else does this pattern imply? As always, different factors are at work. Within the oil industry, the basic movement was clearly to drop marginal retail and refining operations. Today, even those firms that fought Boone Pickens bitterly have conceded his point that corporate expansion should not be pursued in that industry in the face of declining profitability.[122] Thus, whether oil industry firms spun off assets and ceased to be vertically integrated or whether they repurchased their own shares (as Exxon has done[123]), they are essentially heeding the capital market's preference for the return of capital that would yield poor returns if it were retained in the firm. In this light, the oil industry experience is the best case study of the efficiency-enhancing attributes of the hostile takeover. Within this industry, the takeover threat appears to have curbed the tendency toward empire building that the managerialist theorists correctly identified as a central drive of management. The irony here is that although the managerialists have tended to view acquisitions skeptically (particularly conglomerate acquisitions) as simply another route to inefficient empire building, the net effect of takeovers may be to downsize the American corporation. Those who focus only on the bidder's motives and its tendency to overpay have missed the key fact that the general deterrent effect of the takeover on target managements has probably done more to prune corporate empires than to build them.[124]

Outside the oil industry, where most of the targets could not be described as conglomerates, the changes that are occurring are more problematic. ITT, Gulf and Western, and Textron represent the very prototypes of the modern conglomerate organization. Their collective decisions this year to spin off a material portion of their assets cannot therefore be dismissed as isolated occurrences of merely anecdotal significance. Tactically, these decisions were understood by all observers as a form of *ex ante* takeover defense: Assets were spun off or sold by these firms because the asset value of the firm on a breakup clearly exceeded the firm's market value in the stock market by a margin sufficient to attract the bust-up takeover bidder, who essentially arbitrages the differences between these two valuation standards. That these firms undertook this step represents a significant concession on their part. That is, having finally recognized that the standard operational moves available to senior management (i.e., cost cutting, increased dividends, stock repurchases) would not affect the disparity between stock and asset value sufficiently to forestall a bust-up takeover, these managements have in effect accepted the capital market's judgment and partially busted up the firm themselves in order to escape the threat of ouster. In sum, this new sell-off wave followed, and is a product of, the financial developments that have enabled the takeover to threaten the very largest U.S. corporations. What is most distinctive about this new sell-off wave is the identity of the sellers—companies within the Fortune top 20 industrial corporations who, as late as 1980, were not seriously threatened by takeovers.

Viewed strictly in terms of financial the-

ory, this trend can thus be seen as another instance of the market forcing managers to maximize value for their shareholders. Under closer examination, however, there are some anomalies that require at least a qualification of this conclusion. Curiously, it is often the highest-growth division—the "crown jewel"—that is spun off. Westinghouse's decision to divest its cable television assets represents a good illustration.[125] Under the Williamsonian model of the firm, one expects the managers of the M-Form firm to hold the winners (i.e., the high-growth division) and dispose of the losers. Instead, the reverse may be frequently happening. The "invisible hand" of the market may be here leading the "visible hand" of management to dispose of "winners," or at least those winners whose "hidden" value appears not to be recognized in the stock price.[126]

How does one explain this tendency? One answer is that there is an informational asymmetry between managers and the market with the result that the former often know more than the latter. Another possibility, which is complementary, requires that we return to the managerialist's premise that managers have a desire to maximize corporate size and growth. If valid, this premise logically applies to negative-growth decisions (i.e., divestitures) as well as to acquisition decisions, and it suggests that managers would attempt to minimize the total diminution in corporate size. Thus, they might prefer, albeit reluctantly, to spin off a small crown-jewel division that could attract a bust-up bidder than to retain the crown jewel and dispose of all other assets (which strategy would equally end the disparity between asset and stock value). As a result, although the market may be forcing a diminution in size, it is not clear that the specific portfolio that shareholders are left holding in the remaining firm was chosen on the basis of efficiency-related criteria. To be sure, the macroeconomic distortions that such a bias would cause may be minimal, because the high-growth winner can be sold for cash, which could be reinvested. Yet it is again curious that managers have frequently chosen to spin off assets to shareholders rather than sell them at the frequently higher market price that these assets could command in the asset market. Again, the determinative consideration may be that of managerial self-preservation: a cash sale would raise the corporation's liquidity level and thus might make the corporation a likely takeover target. In contrast, a spin-off (or a leveraged buy-out in which the division's management purchases the division for largely noncash consideration) does not increase the corporation's liquidity, which could make it an inviting target. Self-preservation may then dictate keeping a low profile, but there is little reason to believe that this strategy maximizes value for shareholders or economic efficiency.

To the theorist, the major issue posed by the deconglomeration movement is how to reconcile it with the Williamsonian model that sees the M-Form firm as able to outperform the market. Why should such a broad trend toward a smaller portfolio size have arisen and involved such prototypical M-Form firms as ITT, Gulf and Western, and Textron? In this author's judgment, a modification of the Williamsonian model is necessary, but not its abandonment. The deficiency in the current statement of this model is twofold: First, it omits to recognize the significance of the emergence of the institutional investor who holds a diversified portfolio of securities; second, it gives too little attention to the disciplinary impact of the takeover on the older U-Form firm.

To understand these contentions, let us begin with the principal advantages of the M-Form firm. The major claim is that the M-Form firm has superior monitoring ability because the senior management of the M-Form firm is essentially able to make capital-budgeting decisions that allocate the firm's resources among competing semiautonomous divisions better and more swiftly than can the market. In effect, the M-Form firm is itself a miniature capital market. This claim is highly credible and seems to have been accepted by most recent theorists.[127]

Now, let us place this thesis in an updated perspective as it has been affected by the appearance of the hostile takeover. Although hostile tender offers appeared in the 1960s, they were not able to threaten seriously the upper tiers of the Fortune 500 until the late 1970s. Only with the appearance of the two-tier takeover could firms as large as Conoco or Marathon Oil be attacked and forced to enter shotgun marriages with white knights (DuPont and U.S. Steel, respectively). Next, increasingly in the 1980s, the development of new financing techniques—and ultimately the appearance of the junk bond—made it possible for relatively small bidders, including collections of individuals, to tender for very large concerns (i.e., Gulf, Phillips Petroleum, Unocal, CBS, Revlon, etc.).[128] With this development in the 1980s, classic financial entrepreneurs, such as Carl Icahn and Boone Pickens, could essentially seek to arbitrage any significant disparity between stock market value and liquidation value.

The impact of these developments was arguably twofold: First, the threat of the takeover may have initially threatened U-Form firms more severely than M-Form firms, because if the former were less well monitored, then they would logically become the initial targets of takeovers as an external monitoring force. This hypothesis partially explains the tendency for the initial targets of the new takeover wave over the last five to eight years to have been U-Form firms. Essentially, oil giants such as Gulf, Cities Service, Getty Oil, and Phillips Petroleum were U-Form firms. However, as a result of these takeovers and the general deterrent threat they generated, it is reasonable to expect that "agency costs" in the U-Form firm were reduced. By the same token, the existence of this external monitoring force reduced the differential in agency costs between the M-Form firm and the U-Form firm. Hence, even though the M-Form firm could engage in much superior internal monitoring, the existence of an external monitoring system that was less costly to target shareholders reduced the comparative advantage of the M-Form firm. The predictable next step would then be that less successful M-Form firms would become takeover targets to the extent that their breakup value significantly exceeded their stock value. This, of course, is what has concerned ITT, Gulf and Western, Textron, and CBS.

Now, add to this history the impact of the institutional investor's rise. This development also occurred largely in the 1960s, but the percentage of market trading attributable to these investors has continued to rise, particularly as their performance has been more closely monitored by their clientele because of public-reporting requirements imposed in the 1970s.[129] Because the institutional investor already holds a diversified portfolio, it has less interest in investing in diversified conglomerates and certainly should not pay a premium for such stocks. The institutional investor is also engaged in a continual process of portfolio revision. Whenever an exogenous event (such as a merger or liquidation) causes a given firm in its portfolio to disappear or fundamentally change its character, the institutional investor must search for a replacement stock to fill this niche. Given this continuing search for stocks to fill specific niches in a portfolio, institutional investors would rationally tend to disinvest in broadly diversified conglomerates.[130]

In addition, institutional investors are not all alike. They differ particularly in their taste for risk. A given mutual fund may specialize in searching out high-growth, high-risk stocks (i.e., stocks with a high beta value). Here again, the diversified conglomerate will not satisfy this taste because the more it approaches full diversification, the more it resembles a market index fund. Prior to the recently acquired capacity of bidders to tender for very large firms, the large M-Form firm had less reason to be greatly concerned about the tastes and needs of institutional investors.[131] Yet, with the appearance of the bust-up takeover, this indifference to the market's taste is no longer prudent because it invites a takeover.

Viewed more broadly from an industrial organization standpoint, one is lead to the conclusion that only an inefficient industrial structure could superimpose a diversified portfolio managed by institutional investors on top of a firm structure that also manages a somewhat less diversified portfolio of operating divisions. To say that there is seeming redundancy here is not to say which level is superfluous, but it is to suggest that such an industrial structure is unstable.

So what should happen? The massive restructuring among conglomerate firms appears to be producing not a return to the traditional U-Form firm but, rather, firms whose operations span a narrower range of goods and services. In the future, the M-Form firm will still likely manage a portfolio of divisions, but these divisions may become more concentrated in a narrower sector or sectors of the economy. In the vocabulary of Wall Street, these firms will seek a sharper image; or, in our vocabulary, they will remain multidivisional firms because of the superior monitoring capacity of the M-Form firm, but they will operate over a narrower range to please investors who resist fully diversified conglomerates. This appears to be exactly what has happened at Gulf and Western, which has repositioned itself as an entertainment and financial concern, having sold its industrial and consumer divisions this year.[132] In short, the sheer size of the M-Form firm need not necessarily shrink (other than temporarily), but its span of operations should. This will occur not because the M-Form was necessarily a less efficient monitor than was theorized (although this hypothesis is also possible) but because the M-Form firm's ability to reallocate capital across divisions is not prized by institutional investors, who can do this themselves. Over the long run, the one certainty is that firm structure cannot remain unaffected by capital market structure and the tastes of the institutional investor.

THE PROBLEM OF RISK

In overview, the social implications of the foregoing trends for persons other than shareholders may seem to be partially offsetting. On the one hand, increased corporate leverage has alarmed those whose primary concern is with the possibility of a wave of corporate bankruptcies. On the other hand, the takeover's recent tendency to trim large conglomerates by forcing them to sell or spin off assets may reassure those who have been concerned about either the large conglomerate's asserted ability to engage in low-visibility anticompetitive practices or its political power.

For those who are participants in the corporation, however, there are more specific and less obvious implications in these trends, ones that ultimately lead up to the normative issue of the entitlements of the nonshareholder constituencies in the public corporation. This section will consider the impact of the takeover on the incentive of corporate managements to accept high-risk gambles, then turn to the interrelation of risk and leverage, and finally attempt a preliminary social accounting of who wins and who loses under the new takeover regime.

The Moral Hazard Problem

Let us begin with a simple example of the moral hazard problem as applied to corporate decision making. Consider the position of a CEO whose corporation is rapidly approaching insolvency and who has a choice between two investment decisions: Investment A will yield an attractive return well in excess if his company's historic cost of capital and carry relatively little risk. Investment B is much riskier but alone offers the possibility, albeit remote, of a bonanza payoff that will prevent insolvency. Ordinarily, the CEO (and his shareholders) would prefer the higher net present value associated with Investment A; but when bankruptcy looms (with the result that management will be superseded in control by the firm's creditors), it is entirely rational for them to prefer Investment B. This incentive to accept risky investments arises ultimately because the manager and the shareholders enjoy limited liability. Put simply, they have nothing to lose from Investment B and nothing to gain from Investment A (because the returns it generates will only go to the firm's creditors).

The standard literature on corporate finance recognizes that limited liability can give rise to moral hazard problems, such as that just described, and that this danger grows in direct proportion to the degree of leverage in the corporation's financial structure.[133] What has not received adequate attention, however, is that the threat of a hostile takeover can place the manager in an equivalent position.

To see this, consider now the CEO of a firm that is reputed to be a takeover target. His investment bankers tell him that unless firm's stock rises sharply, the firm will be "in play." In that event, he can anticipate that he will be ousted in the wake of an eventual takeover by someone. Once again, an incentive arises to accept risky investments (or make risky strategic decisions) that otherwise would be disdained, because the manager knows that from his perspective he will not be worse off if the investment or project fails. The only difference here is that in this variation his preference for the high-risk, high-payoff strategy conflicts with that of the shareholders, who have no desire to avoid a takeover bid or to accept high-risk gambles [whereas in the first hypothetical the shareholders as well as the CEO would wish to accept the one alternative (Alternative B) that could possibly avert bankruptcy]. This conclusion that managements may sometimes behave in a risk-preferring fashion may seem to contradict this chapter's basic premise that managers tend to be more risk averse than shareholders with regard to their corporation. Yet there is no contradiction. The manager's utility function remains constant, but whether the manager will disdain a desirable risk or accept an excessive one depends in each case on what will preserve control.

Although much commentary has recently asserted that management is forced to take a "short-term" perspective because of the threat of a hostile takeover that will displace them,[134] the underlying phenomenon, to the extent it exists, might be better described in the foregoing terms as a moral hazard problem. That is, rather than viewing managers as pressured into focusing on the short run to the exclusion of long-run considerations, we should recognize that managers are induced to accept high-risk gambles that are not in their shareholders' interests once their position is seriously threatened. This hypothesis has the comparative advantage over the "short-run" hypothesis of not requiring any explanation of (1) why the target firm's shareholders should not have the right to force its management to focus on the short run if they so desire, or (2) why the firm's stock value would not fall further if shareholders had a different time preference than the manager's short-term one. This way of understanding the problem can also help explain the trend toward higher corporate leverage, because leveraging up is inherently the acceptance of a higher-risk gamble.

The problem with this moral hazard explanation is that it is endemic to any system of accountability, corporate or political. A president whose popularity plummets in public opinion polls may have an incentive to manufacture a crisis or take some other gamble, when a more prudent course of action would be in the best interest of the citizenry.[135] But even if this is true, one would hardly suggest the abolition of elections as a remedy. Similarly, if one views the takeover as a mechanism of accountability, it—or a proxy contest or, for that matter, any other conceivable system for disciplining managers—will produce an incentive for managers to accept higher risk when they otherwise are in a position where they face being disciplined.

What then is distinctive about the takeover as a form of accountability? One answer is that its threat of discipline is constant and unrelenting, whereas other mechanisms of accountability tend to focus their threat on specific, periodic moments (e.g., a quadrennial presidential election, an annual meeting of shareholders, etc.). As a result, the moral hazard problem is generalized under the discipline of the takeover, while it would tend to exist only during periodic moments under other systems of accountability. Put differently, the regime of the takeover is analogous to a political system in which the president could be forced to stand for election at any time and recurrently at the decision of any opposition party.

If one accepts this analogy, the frequently heard argument that takeovers preoccupy management gains at least some plausibility. In turn, this suggests that more accountability is not always better. Rather, once a trade-off between diversion of managerial time and shareholder accountability is posed, it follows that there may be an optimal middle ground—i.e., a level of accountability that, if surpassed, produces greater loss in terms of forgone managerial efficiency than it yields in terms of shareholder gain because of reduced agency costs.

Risk and Aspiration Levels: The Social Psychologist's Viewpoint

Although the economist's concept of moral hazard simply assumes that individuals will gamble when they have little or nothing to lose, social psychologists have developed a subtler theory that seeks to explain in a different manner how individuals will behave with respect to risky decisions. From observations and experimental studies, Professors Kahneman and Tversky have concluded that individuals do not simply compare the expected values of different alternatives, as standard economic theory assumes.[136] Rather, they find that individuals begin with a reference point (or aspiration level) that they seek to achieve. This premise seems reasonably close to that of organization theorists, such as Herbert Simon, who long ago postulated that organizational decision making occurred against a backdrop of specific target levels of profit or growth that were desired.[137] The specific contribution of "prospect theory," as expounded by Kahneman and Tversky, is its claim that individuals will prefer lower-risk (i.e., lower-variance) options as long as they are performing above their aspiration level but will opt for higher-risk (i.e., high-variance) options when they are below their aspiration. In effect, there is a "preference reversal" as individuals move from being risk preferrers to risk averters, or vice versa, depending on whether they are performing above or below their aspiration level.[138]

Translated into the corporate context, this theory has useful applications because it helps reconcile the perspective of the "profit-satisficing" theorists with the contemporary realities. Essentially, the well-known view of such writers as Galbraith, Marris, and Baumol that corporate managers tend to behave in a highly bureaucratic manner and do not pursue profit-maximizing policies vigorously can be translated into a statement that these managers, having met their aspiration level, thereafter act in a risk-averse manner and pursue growth over higher profitability.

What has changed since Herbert Simon and his colleagues first put forward their theory of profit satisficing? Basically, the relevant reference point—i.e., the manager's aspiration level—has moved upward, chiefly because of the appearance of the hostile takeover. At the time that Galbraith, Marris, or Baumol wrote their principal pieces, the hostile takeover was not a visible threat and did not significantly constrain the behavior of the manager in the large public corporation; nor would a bust-up takeover have made sense in this era, because stock values generally exceeded asset values by a substantial margin through the "go-go" market of the 1960s. Whatever the reason, the hostile takeover was then an infrequent phenomenon (at least for large firms), and prospect theory holds that individuals tend to ignore (or discount heavily) dangers that have low–base expectancy rates. As a result, the typical manager's aspiration level then could be said to have been only to achieve that "satisfactory" level of profit that protected him from shareholder revolt or creditor dissatisfaction. Of course, the manager would still pursue greater profits, but in doing so, he would tend to opt for the safer, lower-risk alternative.

However, once hostile bidders proved able to capture large public corporations, the aspiration level of corporate managers shifted upward by a quantum leap. Although definitionally their aspiration level at all times can be said to have been the achievement of that level of profits that protected them from ouster, this level has increased substantially now that financially stable, highly solvent firms are targets because their stock prices lag behind those of other firms in the same industry or they have an asset value in excess of their stock market capitalization. The upshot then is that many, and perhaps most, senior corporate managers may today subjectively feel that they are performing below the necessary level of profitability that will protect them from ouster. In consequences, a massive "preference reversal"—i.e., a shift in attitude from risk aversion to risk preference—may have occurred within senior corporate echelons. To say this is again not to claim that human nature has changed or that the manager's utility function has been modified but only that the best empirical research gathered by social psychologists suggests that all of us are capable of behaving very differently with respect to risky decisions, depending on whether our most important goals are at stake.

Risk and Leverage

Standard finance theory recognizes that the shareholder in a highly leveraged firm will prefer a higher-risk (i.e., higher-variance) course of action than would the same shareholder in a less leveraged firm.[139] This is because the greater the degree of leverage, the more the downside risk falls not on shareholders but on the firm's creditors. As the residual claimant, the shareholders receive all the upside return; but because they have limited liability, they can avoid downside loss, except to the extent their capital is invested in the firm. Thus, the higher the degree of leverage, the less capital they have at risk and the more they would be attracted by high-variance investments or policies in which they receive the full upside return.

In this light, the claim made by Professor Jensen and others that higher leverage is simply a bonding device by which management assures the capital market that it will subject itself to the discipline of the market's judgment misses a critical point: As leverage is increased, shareholders' attitudes do not remain static. Rather, shareholders would come to favor higher-risk policies and would pressure management in that direction. Consider, for example, how the board of directors of a corporation would behave if it were elected exclusively by, and were faithful only to, the desires of an electorate consisting only of warrantholders. Logically, warrantholders would prefer that course of action that increases the volatility of a stock and thus increases their chance of making a profit on their investment. Extreme as this example sounds, the shift toward higher leverage over the past several years has been dramatic, and with it should logically come increased shareholder pressure for management to accept higher risks.

Of course, one answer to this hypothesis that increased leverage will produce a still higher level of risk preference in shareholders is that creditors will not sit by passively and permit higher risk to be imposed on them. Arguably, either creditors will contract with the corporation through such devices as bond indentures and loan agreements to restrict the risks that may be imposed on them, or they will charge higher interest, which at some point should chill the shareholders' desire for higher leverage. Although these contractual devices can restrict higher leverage, it is doubtful that they can restrict managements from accepting higher risk. Debt-equity ratios are easily monitored, but particularly in a large conglomerate, management's choice between competing investments or business strategies is not (at least not by creditors from their relatively remote vantage point).[140] Recent experiences in corporations such as Continental Illinois, Baldwin-United, EPIC, and Home State or in the recent series of insolvent thrift and savings institutions remind us that these institutions, all of which were highly leveraged, did in fact shift additional and unbargained for risks onto creditors.[141]

Assessing the Impact of Higher Risk: Who Wins and Who Loses?

Shareholders

From the preceding discussion it may seem that the clear winner in the trend toward higher leverage is the shareholder, for whom the takeover arguably maximizes value by forcing management to accept a higher level of risk in keeping with his own preferences. Yet this conclusion is subject to one potentially important qualification: It is not all shareholders who want the corporation to accept a higher risk level than managers prefer, but only diversified ones. Some empirical evidence casts considerable doubt on whether most shareholders approach full diversification,[142] and institutional investors appear to represent only around 35% of all shareholders.[143] Thus, there may be a significant and unrecognized conflict between institutional shareholders, who do approximate full diversification, and other shareholders who do not. The latter group may logically occupy a position on the continuum somewhere between managers and diversified shareholders, depending on the size of its investment in the corporation and its degree of diversification.

Should we therefore be concerned about and seek to protect the undiversified shareholder? This conclusion does not necessarily follow. It remains a puzzle why they have failed to diversify. Arguably, some of these undiversified shareholders may actually be risk preferrers and hence do not seek the benefits of diversification. If so, these shareholders would hardly want restraints placed on leverage. Or they may in fact be fully diversified, once their ownership of other risky assets other than securities is considered. Finally, they may simply be commercially incompetent and thus do not realize the ease with which full diversification could be achieved by investing in mutual funds. Only in the last case would paternalism seem justified, but it would be highly speculative to premise any reform proposals on the assumption that these investors are in the majority.

Creditors

Creditors represent an intermediate class of participants in the corporation who appear to have lost more than they have gained, although their long-term reaction may not yet be fully visible. Anecdotal evidence is now abundant that bondholders have been adversely affected by highly leveraged takeovers.[144] This evidence conflicts with earlier findings that bondholders typically either gained or suffered no loss in mergers.[145] The reason for this reversal seems intuitively obvious: Although traditional synergistic mergers typically increase the firm's assets and hence the bondholders' security, the new generation of highly leveraged takeovers has had the opposite effect. The recent series of credit downgradings by Moody's and Standard & Poor's, which have been the by-product of takeovers in a significant percentage of the cases, also provides evidence that creditors may have less ability to monitor risk taking by managements than neoclassical theory has assumed.[146] Although economists have traditionally assumed that creditors can protect themselves adequately by imposing financial tests and covenants in bond and loan indentures,[147] the empirical evidence suggests their confidence is unjustified, because contrary to the conventional wisdom, the trend is very much in the direction of eliminating most such covenants from bonds indentures.[148] No consensus exists as to why bond creditors are today abandoning contractual restrictions, but it appears that the contracting process has proven both costly and ineffective.[149] In part, this may be because there are too many ways in which the firm's level of risk can be increased that are simply not amenable to feasible contractual restrictions. Management can, for example, change its corporate strategy so as to accept more risk in a variety of invisible ways. That it has not typically done so in the past may reflect the basic managerial bias toward risk aversion that this chapter has previously stressed. Yet under shareholder pressure, this bias is being overcome; and at least over the short run, creditors suffer as a result.

Over time, creditors may devise new financial instruments, demand voting rights, or invest only in shorter-term notes (as junk bonds typically are). Yet over the interim, they are unprotected at a time when managerial behavior is shifting rapidly toward the acceptance of greater risk. As a result, one of the least noted aspects of the takeover phenomenon is that massive wealth transfers appear to be occurring from bondholders to stockholders.

Whether the end result will be that bondholders demand in the future to share in the upside return through an equity kicker or to share in control through voting rights is uncertain, but the present pattern cannot remain stable.

Employees

Employees and managers constitute the best example of a class that has had to accept the imposition of higher risk.[150] Many recent instances can be identified where corporations first leveraged up as a takeover defense and then followed this action with subsequent massive dismissals or compelled retirements of employees.[151] Another prevalent recent phenomenon has been the termination of pension plans or the transfer of "excess" funds from continuing such plans back to the corporation, particularly as leveraged firms struggle to maintain liquidity.[152]

In overview, very different evaluations of this trend are possible. Obviously, it can be said that these dismissals and plan terminations represent only the efficient pruning of surplus staff and redundant resources. There is probably some truth to this generalization, particularly given the earlier-noted tendency toward inefficient growth within large firms. On a macroeconomic level, the U.S. economy has long employed a substantially higher level of administrative and managerial personnel than other similar economies, and this tendency may be a symptom of organizational slack.[153]

In some industries, particularly the oil industry, the recent takeover wave has probably only anticipatd and hastened a shrinkage that developments in the product market and the gradual depletion of oil reserves would have eventually caused. In other industries, particularly the food and broadcasting industries where some of the largest mergers of 1985 occurred, it is more difficult to find any revolution occurring in the product market. Yet the efficiency of these staff reductions does not fully answer the critical normative issue. Should the expectations of these employees that they would have continuing employment in the absence of a financial crisis be seen as rising to the level of an "implicit contract"? This question will be the focus of this chapter's final section.

The State

Neoclassical theory sees the corporation as an exclusively private body. The state's corporations code is viewed as simply a model-form contract that the state provides to simplify the contracting process and from which the parties are free to opt out by inserting specially tailored provisions in the corporation's certificate of incorporation.[154] Historically, it is clear, however, that the corporation originated in the United States as a quasi-public body in which the state was often a very unsilent partner.[155] Yet probably not since Adolf Berle's later writings has there been much of an attempt in the academic literature to view corporate law as other than an essentially private body of law.[156]

What view then can be taken of the state's role that still treats the corporation as a private body essentially focused on wealth maximization? One answer is to view the state's role as that of an insurer for the losses that limited liability spares shareholders. It is a fundamental error to believe that costs disappear just because shareholders escape them. The costs that shareholders avoid through limited liability fall most heavily on creditors, but a significant portion are ultimately borne by the state as the ultimate residual risk bearer. At a minimum, the state's welfare rolls increase when corporations fail, and often it winds up partially compensating tort creditors. This inevitable role of the state has been neglected because significantly concentrated losses usually occurred only during recessionary periods. Also, the state's role has low visibility because the state does not in any formal sense guarantee the obligations of the firm; rather, it absorbs indirectly many of the losses initially experienced by the other constituencies that surround the firm. Axiomatically, if plants are closed and workers and managers are laid off in the aftermath of either a takeover or a defensive tactic that increases corporate leverage, much of the resulting costs will fall on the state, which typically

will be required to pay increased welfare benefits and make other transfer payments. In the case of local communities, there may also be extensive firm-specific investments that the community has funded to create the infrastructure of social services that surround a major plant or corporate headquarters.[157] To be sure, the relationship is a symbiotic one, and the state or local community also benefits; but there is no reason to believe that the community should rationally be indifferent to the level of risk accepted by such a firm.

Once again, as with bond creditors, contractual restrictions could in theory protect the community's interest. But no such contracting process appears visible. Whether this is because of intercommunity competition for corporate relocations or because smaller governmental units tend not to be sophisticated "repeat players" (and so are overreached) can be debated. For present purposes, the only contention is that the state and local communities frequently stand in the position of a creditor or partial surety for the corporation. With the creditor, they may come to demand greater "voice."

THE STATUS OF THE MANAGER: VILLAIN, VICTIM, OR SIMPLY IN FLUX?

Implicit in much recent commentary about hostile takeovers has been a view of managers as the villain of the story. Their ability to shirk or consume excessive perquisites or otherwise overreach shareholders is seen as providing the rationale for the hostile takeover. True as it is to say that managers sometimes do all of these things, they also can be presented as the victims of the story. Threatened with loss of job security in a volatile stock market in which few companies are not at some point rumored to be takeover targets, managers have been forced, as a takeover defense, to leverage up and accept a higher level of risk. They are thus left in the unenviable position of having all their eggs in one basket, with the solvency of the basket suddenly placed in doubt. Standing alone, either of these accounts, however, is unbalanced. This section will assess the manager's position by first examining the managerial labor market, then considering the implications that the concept of firm-specific human capital holds for corporate governance, and finally surveying the predictable strategies by which managers are likely to seek to reestablish a stabler equilibrium that protects their investment in firm-specific capital.

The Managerial Labor Market

The simple neoclassical model of the firm sees the shareholder as the sole residual risk bearer. As this theory was given its standard synthesis by Frank Knight,[158] the shareholder is seen as the critical actor, the risk-bearing entrepreneur who contracts for the services or capital of the other participants, agreeing to pay them a return governed by external markets while he himself retains whatever surplus, if any, remains once these fixed claims are paid. Thus, because the shareholder faces the greatest variance in possible future returns, the shareholder most needs to monitor the performance of the other participants, because any shirking or opportunistic behavior by the others will reduce the residual return that it receivees. From this perspective, it is understandable that typically only shareholders vote and that directors' fiduciary obligations run exclusively to their benefit.

Still, one can argue that this model overstates the case for shareholder sovereignty. In particular, the assumption that managerial wages are subject to external market standards is subject to at least two serious objections: First, from the implicit-contract perspective, managers may have traded off salary for employment stability.[159] Thus, if the firm fails, they may lose what from this perspective they have already paid for. Second, managers face special problems in terms of safeguarding their investment in firm-specific human capital. Others have argued that this may give managers a legitimate interest in the nature of the firm's governance structure.[160]

Although lateral mobility is today increasing, the still-prevalent pattern is one under which new managers enter the firm at relatively low level "ports of entry" and gradually move upward along steep seniority ladders.[161] Compensation is deliberately structured to defer a significant component. This pattern of internal promotion and seniority-weighted compensation may reflect an implicit contract, or it may be in the firm's interest, both in order to encourage managers to invest in firm-specific human capital and because the manager's real contribution to the firm often cannot be evaluated until a long-term project or strategic plan has been fully implemented. Which of these reasons is more important can be debated. Clearly, managers are often asked to develop expertise that only has value within a specific firm and not to the broader labor market and accept a seniority-weighted compensation structure. Properly understood, such firm-specific human capital consists not only of specialized training or knowledge but also of the ability to work within an existing corporate culture and organizational structure.[162] For present purposes, the critical point, however, is that under either explanation—firm-specific capital or inability to estimate the manager's marginal contribution during the current period—the senior manager is left in an exposed position. As several recent writers, most notably Professors Aoki and Williamson, have pointed out,[163] the manager's investment of human capital is at risk, because he will only receive the expected return that leads him to make this investment over the course of a career. Yet if the firm is taken over, his investment may be lost for one of several reasons: (1) because a different firm-specific expertise may now be necessary to operate within the acquiring firm, (2) because the manager's position duplicates that of a similar manager within the acquiring firm, or (3) because the new owners may simply refuse to recognize the implicit agreement to pay deferred compensation based on earlier performance. Like the bondholder, the manager has arguably lost bargained-for security through a transaction to which he did not consent.

Where should this argument lead us? A partial answer is that the corporation can compensate the manager for this new level of risk on either an *ex ante* or an *ex post* basis. That is, either the corporation can pay a risk premium to all managers to reflect this loss of future employment security, or it can utilize *ex post* devices, such as the "golden parachute," which compensates only those who are in fact terminated. An *ex ante* approach is inefficient if the manager's performance is best evaluated *ex post* because of the need to incorporate the ultimate success or failure of longer term projects into the compensation decision. Moreover, the important advantage of the *ex post* approach is that it better responds to the problem of risk aversion, since paying managers a risk premium at the outset will not ensure that they will not still seek to block a takeover. Because they might rationally both accept the premium and seek to oppose a takeover, the *ex ante* bargain is not easily enforced, and the *ex post* solution seems sounder.

More generally, however, other mechanisms need to be considered. In overview, the range of options were best defined by Albert Hirschman in *Exit, Voice and Loyalty*.[164] If we feel the position of the manager is unduly exposed as the result of the hostile takeover, we can respond to this perception by following one or more of essentially three options: (1) We can give the manager a greater ability to exit; (2) we can give him or her a greater voice in internal decision making; or (3) we can try to establish greater loyalty to the firm on the part of its shareholders. In this context, a greater ability to exit means essentially a greater ability to share in the takeover premium, possibly through such much-criticized devices as the golden parachute. Correspondingly, a greater voice could be achieved through such controversial devices as weighted voting stock, which could be used to give disproportionate voting power to the stock held by management and its allies.[165] Another means to greater voice is through collective employee ownership of a significant portion of the firm's stock, probably through devices such as the employee stock ownership plan (ESOP).[166] Greater loyalty could result from legal rules or charter provisions that restrict the individual shareholder's freedom of action to dispose of his or her shares or that condition his or her rights on a requisite holding period (as a newly popular takeover defense does). Obviously, there are powerful objections to each of these options, because depending on how they were implemented, they might prove an impregnable defense by which a self-interested management could block a takeover or divert the premium to itself. In balance, however, the exit option appears to be the least objectionable, because it alone both recognizes that managers do bear a portion of the residual risk and does not seek to eliminate the takeover as an external check on management.

This sanguine assessment of the golden parachute will seem naive and uncritical to some. They will point to the undeniable examples of egregious overreaching by management or to the possibility that golden parachutes can be used as a takeover defense, rather than as a means of cushioning the manager's exit.[167] Although the law of fiduciary duties has until recently placed few meaningful limits on the board's discretion in this area,[168] it does not follow from this evaluation that the current potential for abuse is serious. To the contrary, recent revisions in the tax law have accomplished what the common law never seemed able to achieve: namely, the creation of a "bright line" standard that few boards will be willing to cross. Under the Tax Reform Act of 1984, a corporate tax deduction is presumptively denied for "excess parachute payments"; these are defined as those that both (1) exceed three times the executive's average annual compensation over the preceding five years and (2) are contingent on a "change of control" (as defined).[169] In addition, a 20% excise tax must be paid by the recipient executive on "excess parachute payments." Whether this trebled salary standard is too low can reasonably be debated, but it clearly sets a ceiling that most boards will not lightly exceed, in part for fear of their own liability for waste of corporate assets.

In this light, although instances of overreaching will no doubt arise from time to time, the more pressing problem with managerial compensation may be the overly limited use of such contracts. Although such change-of-control contracts are now very common at senior managerial levels,[170] they appear to be relatively uncommon at middle management and staff levels. Yet work force reductions after a takeover tend to fall most heavily on those occupying staff positions, both at senior and middle-management levels, because these persons are essentially redundant if the bidder has similar personnel and their discharge does not threaten immediate operating performance.

If so, where does a recognition of this tendency lead us? Few would argue that the state has any right to restrict the corporation from shedding resources, including employees, that it deems redundant. Nor can middle-level managers be analogized to poverty-stricken waifs for whom a court should feel a paternalistic responsibility. However, without restricting the corporation's right to terminate its employees, other options are available. Essentially, a standard is needed that both protects shareholders from egregious wealth transfers in favor of managers and ensures that any tax subsidy inherent in these payments is not enjoyed exclusively by the most senior corporate officials.

Here, a useful analogy is suggested by the federal law applicable to pension plans. As a precondition for favorable tax treatment, qualified pension plans may not "discriminate" in favor of "officers, shareholders, or more highly compensated" employees.[171] Nondiscrimination does not, however, require that all be treated identically; rather, in a defined-contribution plan, an equivalent-percentage contribution may be made on behalf of all salaried income above a specified level. Effectively, this means that the CEO may not receive a higher percentage of covered compensation than a lower-echelon plant manager receives. Consider now the consequences of generalizing this equality constraint by also making it a condition of the corporate tax deduction for "change-of-control" payments. Although there may be technical problems associated with such a proposal, its logic is to supply a floor that matches the ceiling of the trebled-salary standard specified in current law. Such a rule would not require that change-of-control payments be made, but it would prevent senior management from protecting its interests to the exclusion of those at lower echelons. In effect, all managers would be placed on a similar footing. To be sure, it can be argued that junior managers do not have firm-specific capital invested in the corporation, but other formulas—such as a seniority-based one—can respond to this consideration and are equally acceptable on the conceptual level, which in theory demands only that any principle for the award of employment termination compensation be "nondiscriminatory."

Although costly to shareholders, change-of-control severance compensation is probably less expensive than the risk premium that managers would demand once the "old" equilibrium in the executive labor market shifts because the implicit contract has been breached.[172] In addition, a nondiscrimination rule can be monitored at low cost (and by the Internal Revenue Service), thus sparing courts the need to determine substantive fairness in complex, fact-specific cases. Any such rule would be largely self-enforcing because it would simply require that senior management "do unto others as they did unto themselves." This rule would not be a mandatory requirement (if senior management did not avail itself of golden parachutes), nor would it exclude other procedural safeguards (such as a requirement of shareholder approval). Indeed, such a ratification requirement naturally follows once it becomes the entire managerial staff receiving this largess from the shareholders.

In rebuttal, various objections are predictable. To begin with, it can be argued that the analogy just proposed between severance and pension benefits does not stand up under closer scrutiny, either because there is no tax subsidy involved in the case of the golden parachute or because the nature of the two kinds of payments is somehow qualitatively different. These arguments seem dubious. First, for employees having unvested pension or profit-sharing benefits, severance compensation may represent a payment that is largely in lieu of the tax-subsidized benefits so forfeited on termination. Second, the underlying economic nature of the golden parachute is less certain than it first appears, with the result that there is arguably a tax subsidy being provided when the corporation deducts these payments. In overview, such payments, which are frequently triggered by the bidder's decision to liquidate the target, often seem more to resemble an outright purchase of management's acquiescence than ordinary compensation. If, in fact, the bidder is purchasing the target management's consent, such a cost should logically be capitalized as part of the purchase price and amortized much like goodwill. Hence, no tax deduction need result. Alternatively, they can be seen as selective dividends to management—again with the result that no corporate tax deduction would be available. Of course, it would be cynical to characterize all such payments as discriminatory dividends or de facto bribes to management not to oppose the takeover. But given these uncertainties as to the appropriate characterization, a legislative compromise seems the soundest answer. Thus, conditioning the corporate deductibility of change-in-control compensation upon the observance of a nondiscrimination constraint seems an appropriate price to charge when there is at least a prospect of a tax subsidy being awarded. Essentially, such a trade-off is analogous to the treatment accorded qualified pension plans by Section 401 of the Internal Revenue Code. In both cases, the tax law would be striking a balance with respect to payments whose current deductibility would otherwise be debatable and difficult to assess in each individual case.

A second predictable objection to the proposed rule is that no reason is apparent to cover the managerial staff but not workers. Why draw such a line? Here, the answer is simpler. First, lower-echelon employees seldom possess firm-specific capital and can generally resort to external markets. Second, the implicit-contract theory can also be used to draw a line between the mere employee and the officer, because the former typically has an explicit contract—namely, the collective-bargaining agreement. Finally, the line is not mandatory; all that it requires is equality within a defined class, but additional largess can also be extended.

The Rival Perspectives: Fiduciary Duty Versus Implicit Contracting

Economic theory views the modern corporation as a complex set of contracts between different constituent interests.[173] From this "nexus-of-contracts" perspective, it is possible then to view recent developments as having compelled an involuntary renegotiation of the terms of the relationship between management and its shareholders. This perspective is controversial, because more traditional legal analysis sees management simply as the agents of the shareholders.[174] Yet it is useful to examine recent developments from both perspectives and then from possible intermediate positions.

From a contractual perspective, one can argue that the appearance of the bust-up takeover has disrupted a prior system of implicit contracting. By definition, an implicit contract is an incomplete contract, one in which the understandings of the parties have never fully met. Thus, each side acts over an extended period on the basis of expectations that have never been formally accepted by the other, and the legal issue becomes how a court should respond when asked to fill in a missing term that the parties never negotiated.[175] From management's perspective, this implicit contract had two key elements. First, managerial terminations were to be limited either to instances of demonstrated personal incompetence or occasions when impending insolvency threatened the viability of the firm as a whole.[176] Second, there was an expectation of an *ex post* settling up so that managers who contributed disproportionately to the firm's welfare would be specially rewarded. Although these claims may seem novel, a substantial theory underlies both. The first claim about an implicit contract for continuing employment helps explain the finding separately acknowledged by Leibenstein, Williamson, and Donaldson that firms seem to cut their managerial work force only in times of financial exigency.[177] The second claim that an *ex post* settling up was anticipated has also been stressed by neoclassical theorists, such as Professor Fama, who have viewed the managerial labor market as a more important mechanism than the takeover in preserving corporate efficiency.[178]

As a result of the disruption of this system of implicit contracting, *ex post* settling up can no longer be safely anticipated by the manager, and observers are reporting that possibly in response the sense of loyalty that the lower- and middle-level manager once felt for the firm and its senior management is rapidly eroding.[179] Of what significance is this erosion in loyalty? From this chapter's perspective, much of the gains realized by target shareholders in takeovers may represent wealth transfers from managers. In addition, if managers are discouraged from investing in firm-specific human capital or if a high rate of lateral mobility develops that interferes with the maintenance of harmonious managerial teams, corporate efficiency may suffer.

These efficiency arguments may initially seem unrelated to the claim that there is an unnegotiated missing term in the implicit contract between managers and shareholders. Yet under one well-known theory, when a contractual term is missing, the court should insert that term which it believes rational parties would have agreed upon had they focused on it.[180] Here, the term that was allegedly not focused upon is managerial compensation in the event of a takeover, and arguably a generous managerial right to exit as in their mutual interest. Why? The simplest answer is that it is difficult to believe that shareholders would not want to offer managers a relatively cheap inducement not to oppose a lucrative offer to shareholders that management can often effectively block. That is, at a time when takeover premiums average around 80% in some surveys and when the total cost of even the most generous golden-parachute compensation arrangements has been below 1% of the total acquisition cost of the takeover,[181] it is almost inconceivable that shareholders would not give up 1% of the total price in order to obtain an 80% premium. The *ex ante* impact of a strict fiduciary rule that is hostile to such compensation may be to make shareholders worse off by encouraging managerial resistance. Viewed *ex post,* however, such an argument may seem to legitimize extortion, because it implicitly permits managers to profit from their ability to block the transaction.

An alternative approach can avoid this dilemma and yet reach the same end result. It focuses not on what the parties would have done but on what they have done—i.e., create a fiduciary relationship. Such a relationship inherently requires *ex post* judicial assessment. The best analogy here might be to the use of the term *reasonable* in a contract. Inherently, the use of such a term requires an *ex post* evaluation of conduct that the parties themselves could not define to their satisfaction in advance. Such an *ex post* determination by a court often may be more efficient than attempts to draft a more elaborate, but still inevitably incomplete, contract. Similarly, the board of directors can be viewed as a body that both sides intended to mediate this conflict. Modern case law has recognized the directors' authority to make reasonable provision for nonshareholder constituencies.[182] This "rule of reason" approach is appropriate precisely because the parties could not anticipate all future contingencies. Once reasonableness is at issue, it opens the door to a judicial weighing of all relevant evidence, and here this permits both the board and the court to consider the changed position of the manager from the perspective of an *ex post* umpire who was originally delegated by the parties with the task of balancing the expectations of both sides. One attraction of this rationale is that it is far simpler for a court to recognize the board as an *ex post* referee than to mediate the dispute itself or to attempt to determine the efficient outcome. The bottom line is, however, that this broader view of both the directors' and court's role legitimizes an *ex post* settling up on a simpler doctrinal basis.

Scenarios for the Future: How Will Relationships Evolve Within the Public Corporation?

Regardless of the stance courts take with regard to change-of-control compensation, some institutional and political repercussions appear likely in the face of the disruption that takeovers are causing to the prior relationship between managers and the corporation. Inherently, the nexus-of-contracts perspective suggests that other participants may wish to join the negotiations. Perhaps the clearest indication that there are such participants who may seek to enter the negotiations emerged in the recent contest between Carl Icahn and Texas Air Corporation for control of TWA. Here, the unions in effect choose the victor (Carl Icahn), notwithstanding the initial prefernce of TWA's board for Texas Air.[183] They did so by negotiating a wage concessions package with Icahn that they presumably believed would be less drastic than the wage cuts and layoffs they anticipated Texas Air would impose on them if it obtained control. As a consequence, although the takeover still left the employees worse off than they had been prior to the change in control, the employees still minimized losses that were likely to have been worse had they not become active.

The position of the pilots at TWA is in some senses similar to that of middle management in the large corporation, both because of the existence of elongated seniority ladders in the airline industry and the sheer value of the physical assets entrusted to pilots as operational managers.[184] The analogy is imperfect for several reasons: First, pilots have little firm-specific human capital. Moreover, the pilots special negotiating leverage at TWA was the product of two factors that makes this example somewhat idiosyncratic: (1) the pilots were operating personnel, not staff, and thus their actions could have an immediate impact on the firm's short-run profit and loss, and (2) they had a preexisting institutional rep-

resentative—namely, the unions—and thus they did not have to encounter the difficult start-up problems of organizing and coordinating their efforts.

Still, the general pattern that the TWA example illustrates involves a movement toward employees seeking greater "voice" as well as a protected "exit." While the TWA control contest is an example of an *ex post* attempt to obtain "voice," there are also means by which interested constituencies can obtain greater voice on an *ex ante* basis. The most obvious means to this end is by obtaining voting power. Increasingly, Employee Stock Ownership Plans ("ESOPs") have been created as a takeover defense, essentially to create a new constituency with voting power that would be a firm ally of management.[185] Although there are obvious conflicts of interest and potentials for abuse throughout this area, this development represents a step toward exactly the form of profit-sharing contract between management and labor that some economists believe would significantly increase the overall productivity of the U.S. economy.[186] In effect, it signals a movement by employees as an interest group toward becoming greater residual risk bearers. Yet as shareholders trade off salary income for a greater share of the residual risk, this development will also compel even greater underdiversification, thereby heightening the shareholder-manager tension over risk levels. In short, precisely as employees obtain greater voice, they will desire to exercise in a manner that conflicts with shareholders' wishes.

Broader employee ownership is also arriving through individual and voluntary action as well as through collective entities, such as ESOPs or unions. Thus, for example, a majority of the stock of Grumman Corporation, a firm that has successfully resisted a takeover, is now reported to be in "friendly hands,"[187] including apparently a large portion that is held by employees, pensioners, and suppliers. By whatever route, this minitrend, if it continues, could significantly change the nature of the American corporation, moving us at least some distance in the direction of the Japanese model of the corporation, which has long been characterized by broad resid-ual risk sharing and relatively passive shareholders.[188]

Other possibilities have not yet materi-alized but can be envisioned. For example, potential target corporations could recip-rocally increase their cross ownership in each other and then protect themselves against dispositions of these defensively placed shares by entering into standstill agreements. It is curious that at a time when public institutional investors (such as state pension funds) have been organiz-ing into the Council of Institutional Inves-tors, a loose confederation under the aus-pices of Jesse Unruh of California,[189] no similar movement has yet occurred among creditors or managements. Yet such a loose confederation among potential tar-gets who each reciprocally own shares in each other is precisely the Japanese pat-tern, where it has produced stable share-holders and almost no takeover activity.[190] There are signs, however, that patterns of protective cross-ownership may also de-velop in the United States, as firms offer their securities on attractive terms to their suppliers, customers, and employees.[191]

Perhaps the most likely scenario is an in-crease in the pace of the current leveraged buy-out boom. Essentially, managerial buy-outs also represent an instance in which managers are being forced by share-holders to accept more risk than they de-sired. For managers, the leveraged buy-out is the ultimate takeover defense—the only one that ensures that their companies will not remain "in play." Indeed, as managers recognize that higher leverage will be com-pelled upon them in some fashion, the le-veraged buy-out becomes particularly at-tractive, in part because it uniquely offers the prospect of a higher return to manage-ment to compensate for the higher risk as-sumed.[192] In contrast, a simple policy of le-veraging up the firm may achieve little, except a temporary respite. For example, the management at CBS may have gained only a temporary respite when they lever-aged up their firm to defeat Ted Turner; in short order, they found that another poten-tial bidder (Loews Corporation) bought a near-controlling block in the depressed af-

termarket.[193] If the buy-out boom contin-ues at its current pace, the long-term im-pact of the hostile takeover may well be not only to purge the public corporation of excess managerial staff but also to place the public shareholder in a minority position. Once the implicit contract is opened up for renegotiation, it is simplistic to expect that all the resulting changes will produce re-duced managerial discretion and enhanced power for public shareholders.

CONCLUSION: TOWARD PREMIUM SHARING

More descriptive than prescriptive, this chapter's principal claim is that the mod-ern public corporation must be understood as an imperfect and unstable risk-sharing arrangement between managers, employ-ees, and shareholders that is today in flux rather than at equilibrium. Viewed opti-mistically, the new wave of takeovers represents a mechanism by which share-holders are at last able to counteract man-agement's inherent bias toward risk aver-sion and excess earnings retention. From this perspective, the takeover movement has begun to purge the modern corpora-tion of the organizational slack on which an earlier generation of managerialist crit-ics had focused. Viewed more pessimisti-cally, however, there may be social costs associated with this newfound shareholder power, because society as a whole may share the manager's aversion toward risk. Both views may be correct.

Important issues have a tendency to present themselves as questions of both eq-uity and efficiency. The takeover move-ment is no exception to this generalization. The paradigm issue of equity arises in the case where an acquiring firm (say Chev-ron) buys the target (say Gulf) and then dismisses a substantial portion of the tar-get's managerial staff in the aftermath of the acquisition.[194] The losses incurred by the target employees are obviously signifi-cant, but the gains received by the target shareholders are probably substantially greater.[195] If part of the gain can thus be considered a wealth transfer from employees to shareholders, a normative issue surfaces: Is it equitable for the law to encourage such wealth transfers to shareholders from nonshareholder classes? The answer of neoclassical economic theory would be that given by the Kaldor-Hicks definition of efficiency: Because the gains exceed the losses, the transaction is "efficient" (i.e., Pareto superior) and should be encouraged, on the rationale that the losers can be compensated by some other means (such as by the state).[196] The obvious problem with this theory is that the losers will generally not be so compensated, and the state may not be able to undertake complex programs of wealth redistribution. Yet there is an acceptable compromise to this problem suggested by economic theory that both mitigates the equity issue and satisfies the efficiency criterion: Society should encourage the "winners" to "bribe" the "losers." This is, of course, the standard Coasean prediction of what would occur in the absence of high transaction costs;[197] here, it implies that the obvious "winners" from takeovers (i.e., the target shareholders) can secure the acquiescence of the clearest losers (the target employees) by paying them substantial termination payments (i.e., golden parachutes).

In this light, it is curious that Professors Easterbrook and Fischel, the leading proponents of a neoclassical approach to law and economics, have seemingly deviated from the obvious Coasean prescription and have instead urged a rule of strict managerial passivity.[198] Passivity seems a strange stance for the law to require of the employee if the latter is more the victim than the villain of the story.[199] Regardless of who is entitled to claim the role of victim, it is patently obvious that both sides will believe themselves aggrieved in most future takeover battles. A policy of premium sharing represents then a constructive approach to resolving or mitigating these disputes before they arise.

Nonetheless, the propriety of encouraging side payments from shareholders to managers in the form of termination bonuses will trouble many on ethical grounds. Yet as this chapter has stressed, there is a substantial case for such pay-

ments to the extent that they compensate managers for their investment of firm-specific capital and also fulfill an implicit contract that the new wave of takeovers has disrupted. To say this is not to accept all such payments, however excessive or egregious, nor is it to reject the need for judicial monitoring of other defensive tactics. But the efficacy of such judicial monitoring remains in doubt.[200] Indeed, because the policy favored by most recent commentators—under which management may seek to promote an auction but not to preserve itself in control[201]—is a particularly difficult one to police, there would seem to be every reason to try to use positive incentives, as well as negative ones, to obtain management's acquiescence.

More generally, from a social cost perspective, there is an unnecessary "deadweight" loss incurred by society when amounts as high as $200 million are incurred as transaction expenses incident to a single takeover.[202] One need not be a cynic to observe that amounts considerably below this level might encourage the vast majority of American managements to accept a takeover gracefully, even enthusiastically, with the results that (1) substantial cost savings would be realized by society, (2) shareholders might save more on the legal and advisory fees that are incident to hostile battles than they lost on severance payments, (3) courts would be less burdened by takeover litigation, and (4) no reduction in current takeover premium levels would necessarily result, because there would on average be a net savings in transaction costs.[203]

The real difficulty with the proposal made here is a noneconomic one: The payment of vast sums to senior managers to encourage them to leave gracefully may appear indecent and even corrupting. In response, the practical standard recommended by this chapter is the adoption of an equality side constraint. By requiring that change-of-control compensation observe nondiscrimination rules that were analogous to those applicable to pension plans, one mitigates this problem and achieves a rough justice by linking the interests of senior and middle management.

Given the de facto ceiling on such compensation set by the Internal Revenue Code,[204] a nondiscrimination rule essentially supplies a floor to match the ceiling set by the code. If a requirement of shareholder ratification were substituted for the current trebled-salary ceiling, there would seem to be little reason to retain any ceiling on such compensation, other than the common law's traditional waste standard.[205] To be sure, any constraint that limits the maximum change-of-control compensation that senior managers could receive by a formula that links their interests with those of middle management works against the previously stated Coasean rationale, because it reduces the side payment that can be paid to those able to block the transaction. But it is the middle manager who today seems most exposed to a loss of human capital and who is most likely to be left out in the settling up that today frequently occurs at the twelfth hour of a takeover contest. There is thus an efficiency and an equity basis for such a regulatory constraint.

Ultimately, there is a curious irony about the implications of this chapter's analysis. For decades, reformers from the time of Adolf Berle to that of Ralph Nader have sought to increase the power of shareholders to control corporate managers by a variety of means: increased disclosures, independent directors, reform of the proxy process, etc. The advent of the hostile takeover may have succeeded in reducing agency costs beyond their wildest dreams. Yet the end result is problematic, because for at least some of these reformers the motivation underlying their pursuit of increased shareholder power was the assumption that shareholders had interests and values that coincided with those of the unrepresented constituencies they chiefly wished to protect (e.g., local communities, the poor, the environment). Even if this assumed identity of interests proved tactically useful in some instances, it has become intellectually untenable in the current era of the bust-up takeover. The point is not simply that shareholders cannot be sensibly equated with widows, orphans, and the socially dispossessed. At least where the issue of risk is at center

stage, a closer identity of interests may exist between managers, employees, and the community of unrepresented interests that surround the corporation and depend upon its solvency. Reform of corporate governance should proceed then not on the assumption that potentially "reckless" managers need to be restrained by controls that protect shareholders who want a prudent, conservative management. Rather, the biases of the participants are closer to the reverse.

Although only an apologist for management would seriously present managers as invariably paternal and benevolent in their dealings with these other constituencies, both economic theory and the "managerialist" evidence support a description that views managers and these other interests as sharing common interests arising out of their common circumstance of having a nondiversifiable investment in the firm. Both thus have reason to be risk-averse. As a result, the alliance of shareholders and reformers is a curious one. In the British Foreign Office of the nineteenth century, there was a maxim to the effect that "there are no permanent alliances, only permanent interests." On the topic of takeovers, perhaps the more natural alliance is between managers and those who fear the social dislocations and other potential externalities that the takeover movement can bring about. This chapter does not suggest that this alliance should be permitted to block takeovers, but a policy of premium sharing and a common focus on the social costs of excessive risk taking would constitute a sensible agenda.

NOTES

1. See, e.g., Bradley, Desai, and Kim, "The Rationale Behind Interfirm Tender Offers: Information or Synergy?" 11 *J. Fin. Econ.* 183 (1983) (rejecting the undervaluation rationale for tender offers based on evidence that the stock prices of targets that successfully resisted a takeover eventually declined to pretakeover levels). For a review of the various theories advanced to explain takeover activity, see Coffee, "Regulating the Market for Corporate Control: A Critical Assessment of the Tender Offer's

Role in Corporate Governance," 84 *Colum.* 1145 (1984).

2. Until recently, even in the largest transactions, the scale of the bidder generally exceeded that of the target. Thus, such megamergers as DuPont's 1981 acquisition of Conoco for $10.7 billion, U.S. Steel's 1981 purchase of Marathon Oil for $7.3 million, and the two giant acquisitions of 1984—Chevron's purchase of Gulf for $13.3 billion and Texaco's acquisition of Getty Oil for $10.1 billion—fit this pattern in that all were "friendly" deals by large bidders having related operations into which they intended to assimilate the target. Only in the Chevron deal was the acquirer (the fifth-largest oil firm) slightly smaller than the target (Gulf being then the fourth-largest firm). See K. Davidson, *Mega-mergers: Corporate America's Billion-Dollar Takeovers* (1985), 263–264. 1984 appears, however, to have been a turning point, as the Chevron-Gulf marriage was in fact a shotgun wedding precipitated by Boone Pickens's siege of Gulf. Subsequently, such individuals as Carl Icahn, Saul Steinberg, Asher Edelman, Irving Jacobs, Robert Holmes a Court, Charles Hurwitz, and the Belzberg brothers have led small groups of individuals or relatively small firms in takeover bids for much larger targets. During 1985, Carl Icahn took control of TWA; Asher Edelman, Datapoint; Sir James Goldsmith, Crown Zellerbach; Irving Jacobs, AMF; and Ronald Perelman (the CEO of Pantry Pride), Revlon. See Worthy, "What's Next for the Raiders," *Fortune,* November 11, 1985, 21. In most of these cases, the "junk bond" financing arranged by these bidders necessitates that they liquidate a substantial portion of the target's assets to amortize these short-term bonds. See note 4.

A particular target of this new takeover wave has been the conglomerate firm (whereas earlier waves focused on oil and natural resource companies). During 1985, General Foods Corporation was acquired by Philip Morris Inc. without a fight; Richardson-Vicks, Inc. accepted a "white knight" bid from Procter & Gamble in preference to a hostile bid from Unilever, N.V. See Prokesch, "Food Industry's Big Mergers," *N.Y. Times,* October 14, 1985, D-1. Revlon Inc. eventually was acquired by Pantry Pride Inc. for $2.7 billion after various attempts by Forstman, Little & Company to arrange a leveraged buyout either fell through or were enjoined by the Delaware courts. See Cole, "High Stakes Drama at Revlon," *N.Y. Times,* November 11, 1985, D-1. CBS escaped a proposed $5.4 billion hostile takeover bid made by Ted Turner, after CBS spent nearly $1 billion to buy back 21% of its stock. See "CBS's debt bomb," *Fortune,* August 5, 1985, 8. Subsequently, Loews Corporation bought a 25% interest in CBS, making its victory seem potentially Pyrrhic. See "Loews Doubling CBS Stake," *N.Y. Times,* October 17, 1985, D-1. Finally, Hanson Trust, an English conglomerate, battled Merrill Lynch for control of SCM Corp., another conglomerate, throughout the fall of 1985. See Brown, "Hanson Trust's U.S. Thrust," *Fortune,* October 14, 1985, 47.

3. For a good description of the organizational structure of these new bidders, which consist of loose networks of individuals and entities that have been assembled by entrepreneurs such as Carl Icahn, see Penn, "Raiding Parties: Friends and Relatives Hitch Their Wagon to Carl Icahn's Star," *Wall St. J.,* October 2, 1985, 1. The economic motives of these new takeover technicians are entirely orthodox. They are simply pursuing a profit opportunity that is not available to ordinary shareholders, who cannot feasibly coordinate so as to force management to liquidate a corporation whose liquidation value exceeds its going-concern value. They are, however, more constrained in their options for the target than traditional corporate bidders because the financing arrangements available to these entrepreneurs usually require a speedy amortization of the acquisition indebtedness (in part because the debt component of the acquisition price is much larger in cases where small groups of individuals make the bid than when a much larger corporation does). Thus, plans to dismantle the target and sell its assets in piecemeal fashion to third parties are often in place even before the takeover has succeeded. See Crudele, "Rorer Buys Drug Unit of Revlon," *N.Y. Times,* November 30, 1985, 29, 31 (noting that Pantry Pride had negotiated sale of Revlon's drug unit to Rorer even before the tender offer had succeeded in order arrange its financing). Similarly, Ted Turner attempted to make a "presale" of various CBS properties. See "Turner Is Said to Try Pre-Sale of CBS Assets," *Wall St. J.,* April 22, 1983, 3. GAF announced similar plans for Union Carbide had its offer been successful. As a result, although the bust-up takeover has its precursors and all takeovers threaten the job security of the incumbent target management, the distinctive financing arrangements underlying these transactions make asset divestitures and substantial layoffs marginally more likely.

The newest development in the bidder's structure has been the appearance of major investment banking houses (Merrill Lynch, Morgan Stanley & Co., Bear Stearns, First Boston

Corp.) as joint venturers in the bid who will actually acquire a substantial equity investment in the target. See Sterngold, "Wall Street Buys into the Action", *N.Y. Times,* June 19, 1986, D-1.

Courts have also recognized the special nature of the bust-up takeover and hinted that they may justify defensive tactics not otherwise appropriate. See *Moran v. Household International, Inc.,* 500 A.2d 1346, 1349 n. 4 (Del. 1985); *Revlon v. MacAndrews & Forbes Holdings,* 605 A.2d 173, 180, 181 n. 12 (Del. 1986).

4. The most complete description of this new form of takeover financing is contained in a report prepared by the Congressional Research Service for the House Subcommittee on Telecommunications, Consumer Protection, and Finance. See "The Role of High Yield Bonds [Junk Bonds] In Capital Markets and Corporate Takeovers: Public Policy Implications" (December 1985) (hereinafter called Congressional Research Service Report). For a revealing description of the unique nature of this "junk bond" market, see Sloan and Rudnitsky, "Taking in each other's laundry," *Forbes,* November 19, 1984, 207. Essentially, "junk bonds" are bonds rated at below "investment grade" by the two principal bond-rating agencies (Moody's or Standard & Poor's); such bonds pay a correspondingly high interest rate, with current rates equaling 16% or more. Prior to 1976, no well-known investment banking house would underwrite the original issue of such low-rated bonds, but in that year Drexel Burnham Lambert, which had previously made a secondary market in these bonds, began also to underwrite them. The use of junk bonds to finance takeovers apparently dates from the "latter part of 1983." See Congressional Research Service Report, p. 23. The significance of the junk bond's appearance is twofold: First, bidders, such as Boone Pickens, Victor Posner, Saul Steinberg, or Pantry Pride (all of whom have financed tender offers through Drexel Burnham), had previously had difficulty in obtaining credit from banks, some of whom have refused to finance "raiders" as a matter of policy. Second, commercial banks have traditionally followed conservative lending policies and have seldom been willing to finance more than 50% of the acquisition cost of a target, thus compelling bidders in the past to raise the balance from retained earnings. Yet commercial banks have no objection to bidders incurring additional debt that is subordinated to their own loans (because from the standpoint of these banks such subordinated debt is the equivalent of equity). Thus, a bidder who can issue subordinated junk bonds (at a high interest rate) after first borrowing from commercial

lenders (at a lower rate) can today finance as much as 90% of the acquisition cost. This fact explains much about the newfound ability of small bidders to tender for much larger targets.

5. In late 1985, by a 3–2 vote, the Federal Reserve Board announced a proposed restriction on the use of junk bonds issued by "shell corporations" to finance takeovers. Effectively, the Federal Reserve's action means that debt securities issued by such shell corporations might not be issued to finance more than 50% of the purchase price in a takeover. Procedurally, the Federal Reserve Board established a presumption that debt securities issued by a shell corporation were "indirectly secured" by the target's stock when no other credit or assets were pledged. However, the Board defined "shell corporation" narrowly as one having "virtually no business operations, no significant business function other than to acquire and hold the shares of the target, and virtually no assets or cash flow to support the credit other than the margin stock it has acquired or intends to acquire." See "Interpretation of Margin Requirements," Volume 72 *Federal Reserve Bulletin,* Number 3, p. 192 (March 1986). Given this definition, the professional reaction to the Federal Reserve Board's ruling was that creative planning by bidders could overcome this presumption, particularly if other security for the loan (such as a guarantee by those who stood behind the shell corporation) were also pledged. See Hershey, "Federal Reserve Votes for Limits On Debt Financing of Takeovers," *N.Y. Times,* December 7, 1985, 1, 36. Modest as the proposal was, it still elicited a sharply critical response from the Reagan administration, which saw it as unnecessary intervention in the marketplace and as protecting large corporations from hostile raids. See Nash, "Federal Reserve's Curb on Bonds Is Assailed by the Administration," *N.Y. Times,* December 24, 1985, 1. Nonetheless, in a slightly modified and weakened form, the Federal Reserve Board adopted its proposal on January 10, 1986: 12 C.F.R. § 207.112 ("Purchase of Debt Securities to Finance Corporate Takeovers"). See also notes 80 to 94.

6. See "Surge in Restructuring Is Profoundly Altering Much of U.S. Industry," *Wall St. J.,* August 12, 1985, 1. According to this survey, some 58 of these restructurings were classified as forced by a takeover; the rest were viewed as "voluntary." This assumption that restructurings that occur prior to a definite takeover bid are not takeover-induced seems simplistic because it ignores the *ex ante* impact of the takeover threat. See notes 106 to 131.

7. Substantial managerial layoffs have been

common in the wake of larger mergers, particularly in the recent "oil patch" mergers where the acquiring firm essentially wants only the oil reserves of the target and already possesses excess refining capacity of its own. Thus, in the wake of the Chevron-Gulf acquisition in 1984, the combined entity laid off 10,000 employees (or 12% of its work force), and it has further reduced its work force by 2000 more in 1985. Following Texaco's acquisition of Getty Oil, Texaco announced a 26% reduction in its work force. See Schmitt, "Depleted Field: Despite Raiders' Lust, Oil Industry Is Facing Retrenchment Period," *Wall St. J.,* June 7, 1985, 1, 9. Nor is this pattern unique to the oil industry. Following Baxter Travenol Laboratories acquisition of American Hospital Supply Corporation, plans were announced to lay off 10% of the combined work force, or 6000 workers. See "Baxter Plans Layoffs; Merger Is Completed," *N.Y. Times,* November 26, 1985, D-2. Even when the bidder is defeated, the target may be compelled to trim its work force substantially as the result of the added leveraged it took on in connection with its defense. For descriptions of layoffs at CBS, Martin Marietta and Phillips Petroleum following "successful" takeover defenses, see Nielsen, "Management Layoffs Won't Quit," *Fortune,* October 28, 1985, 46. See also sources cited at note 81.

Of course, changes in the product market and foreign competition are also responsible for these developments by making some industries unable to sustain the prior number of firms in them. While this explanation has considerable validity for the oil industry, it does not explain the takeover wave in broadcasting (where licenses have de facto monopolies) or the food industry.

8. The use of contract analogies to analyze the corporate governance issue has been strongly criticized by some commentators. See Brudney, "Corporate Governance Agency Costs, and The Rhetoric of Contracts," 85 *Colum. L. Rev.* 1403 (1985). Although this author partially disagrees with both Professor Brudney and the neoclassical proponents of contract law analysis, the reference in the text to "implicit contracts" is intended here only to frame the issue, not to assume the appropriate form of analysis. See text and notes 156 to 165.

9. For representative examples of these critiques, see Loescher, "Bureaucratic Measurement, Shuttling Stock Shares, and Shortened Time Horizons: Implications for Economic Growth," 24 *Quarterly Review of Economics and Business* 8 (1984); Hayes and Abernathy, "Managing Our Way to Economic Decline," 58

Harv. Bus. Rev. 67 (1980); R. Reich, *The Next American Frontier* (1983), 140–172; Drucker, "Taming the Corporate Takeover," *Wall St. J.,* October 30, 1984; Fogg, "Takeovers: Last Chance for Self-restraint," 63 *Harv. Bus. Rev.* 30 (November–December 1985); Williams, "It's Time for a Takeover Moratorium," *Fortune,* July 22, 1985, 135–136.

10. See, e.g., Lipton, "Takeover Bids in the Target's Boardroom," 35 *Bus. Law* 101 (1979); Lipton, "Takeover Bids in the Target's Boardroom: An Update After One Year," 36 *Bus. Law.* 1017 (1980). Compare Bebchuk, "The Case for Facilitating Competing Tender Offers," 95 *Harv. L. Rev.* 1028 (1982); Lowenstein, "Pruning Deadwood in Hostile Takeovers: A Proposal for Legislation," 83 *Colum. L. Rev.* 249 (1983) (arguing for an extended takeover offer period).

11. See Bradley and Rosenzweig, "Defensive Stock Repurchases," 99 *Harv. L. Rev.* 1377 (1986).

12. See, e.g., Jensen and Meckling, "Theory of the Firm: Managerial Behavior, Agency Costs and Ownership Structure," 3 *J. Fin. Econ.* 305 (1976); Cheung, "The Contractual Nature of the Firm," 26 *J.L. & Econ.* 1 (1983); Fama, "Agency Problems and the Theory of the Firm," 88 *J. Pol. Econ.* 288 (1980); Alchian and Demsetz, "Production, Information Costs, and Economic Organization," 62 *Amer. Econ. Rev.* 777 (1972); Fama and Jensen, "Separation of Ownership and Control," 26 *J.L. & Econ.* 301 (1983). For a critical review of this mode of analysis, see Brudney, note 8.

13. This is true at least in the neoclassical model of the corporation, as formalized by such thinkers as Frank Knight. See F. Knight, *Risk, Uncertainty and Profit* (1921). More recent theorists have emphasized that employees develop "firm-specific" capital on the job, which factor converts the corporation into an internal job market. See M. Aoki, *The Co-operative Game Theory of the Firm* (1984), 25–26; O. Williamson, "Corporate Governance," 93 *Yale L.J.* 1197, 1207–1209 (1984).

14. A. Chandler, Jr., *The Visible Hand: The Managerial Revolution in American Business* (1977). Chandler's description of the rise of managerial specialization and the development of internal control mechanisms is discussed in notes 58 to 60.

15. For a fuller critique of this disciplinary hypothesis, see Coffee, note 1, pp. 1163–1166. Essentially, the disciplinary thesis cannot account for the cyclical-wave character of takeover movements (because incompetence does not occur in waves) and cannot easily explain

why the worst-managed firms, such as International Harvester or Chrysler (before its change in management), have not been taken over.

16. For an excellent example of this approach that identifies the various categories of participants and the relationships among them, see W. Klein, "The Modern Business Organization: Bargaining Under Constraints," 91 *Yale L.J.* 1521 (1982).

17. Unequal or "super" voting stock has also become a major issue within the past year after over a half century of unquestioned public acceptance of the New York Stock Exchange's "one-share, one-vote" rule. Its appearance is also testimony to the repercussions of the new takeover wave. See notes 165 to 166. New devices to encourage employee ownership, such as the ESOP, have also recently become popular. See the discussion in notes 166 and 182 to 191.

18. Managerial passivity in the face of a takeover was the legal rule favored by Professors Easterbrook and Fischel in their well-known article. See Easterbrook and Fischel, "The Proper Role of a Target's Management in Responding to a Tender Offer," 94 *Harv. L. Rev.* 1161 (1981). Others have argued for a modified passivity rule that would permit only auction-enhancing tactics. See Gilson, "A Structural Approach to Corporations: The Case Against Defensive Tactics in Tender Offers," 33 *Stan. L. Rev.* 819 (1981). Although this author is sympathetic to the latter approach, it has made little headway with the courts, which continue largely to favor the business judgment's applicability to this context. For recent decisions in the federal courts, see, e.g., *Gearhart Indus. Inc. v. Smith Int'l Inc.,* 741 F.2d 707, 721 (5th Cir. 1984); *Radol v. Thomas,* 772 F.2d 244, 255–258 (6th Cir. 1985). For the recent Delaware decisions, see note 200.

19. A. Berle and G. Means, *The Modern Corporation and Private Property* (1973).

20. Proof of this contention can be found in a symposium on Berle and Means published by the *Journal of Law and Economics* on the fiftieth anniversary of their book's publication. See Symposium, "Corporations and Private Property," 26 *J.L. & Econ.* 235 (1983). John Kenneth Galbraith has termed the book, with Keynes's *General Theory of Employment, Interest and Money,* one of the two most important books of the 1930s. See Galbraith, Review, 13 *Antitrust Bull.* 1527 (1968).

21. From the perspective of Jensen and Meckling (note 12), this conclusion follows because the stock market will discount the shares of those corporations whose managements are perceived as behaving opportunistically (at least more so than average), thus reducing the value of the managers' own wealth to the extent they hold shares in the firm. For Williamson, the rise of the M-Form firm implies that a new monitoring apparatus came into being that could better check managerial opportunism. Thus, he suggests that "the corporate control dilemma posed by Berle and Means has since been alleviated more by internal than it has by regulatory or external organizational reforms." See Williamson, "The Modern Corporation: Origins, Evolution, Attributes," 19 *J. Econ. Lit.* 1537, 1560 (1981).

22. For evidence that investors in fact frequently hold undiversified portfolios, see Blume and Friend, "The Asset Structure of Individual Portfolios and Some Implications for Utility Functions," 30 *J. Fin.* 585 (1975); M. Blume and I. Friend, *The Changing Role of the Individual Investor* (1978). Of course, it is possible that these investors hold other risky assets (such as real estate) that compensate for this apparent failure of rationality. Institutional investors now own 35% of all shares on the New York Stock Exchange and even higher levels of corporations in the Standard & Poor's 500 stock index. See Lowenstein, "Pruning Deadwood in Hostile Takeovers: A Proposal for Legislation," 83 *Colum. L. Rev.* 249, 297–298 (1983).

23. Firm-specific capital is essentially a subset of the problem of asset specificity. See Williamson, note 21, p. 1548, and Williamson, note 13, pp. 1207–1208, 1215–1217. Such capital could arise either because of specific job training or technological skills that the manager acquires, which is not equally valuable to other firms generally, or because of the significance of "corporate cultures," which necessitate that special interpersonal skills be acquired to function in individual corporate environments. See T. Deal and A. Kennedy, *Corporate Cultures: The Rites and Rituals of Corporate Life,* (1982), 16–18, 83–84, W. Ouchi, *Theory Z* (1981). The assimilation difficulties that acquiring firms often experience in absorbing target firms may corroborate the significance of this culture barrier, which in turn necessitates that managers invest in learning the indigenous "culture."

24. For an economic overview of the labor market within the firm, see P. Doeringer and M. Piore, *Internal Labor Markets and Manpower Analysis* (1971); Mortenson, "Specific Capital and Labor Turnover," 9 *Bell J. Econ.* 572 (1978). These writers have suggested that promotion ladders and invested pension benefits were mechanisms by which the firm could hold onto the services of an executive who possessed firm-specific capital. See also O. Williamson,

Markets and Hierarchies: Analysis and Antitrust Implications (1975), 57–80. Historically, the rate of turnover among managers, particularly top managers, was low. See W. McEachern, *Managerial Control and Performance* (1975), 30–31. There are signs, however, that it has recently increased in direct consequence of the prevalence of hostile takeovers. See Coffee, note 1, pp. 1235–1237.

25. See Demsetz, "The Structure of Ownership and the Theory of the Firm," 26 *J.L. & Econ.* 375, 387–390 (1983); DeAlessi, "Private Property and Dispersion of Ownership in Large Corporations," 28 *J. Fin.* 839, 840–841 (1973); W. Lewellen, *The Ownership Income of Management* (1971), 150–151 ("The annual income of an executive depends very heavily, very directly, and very persistently, on the dividends received and capital gains experienced by such men in their roles as stockholders of their employer companies, and as beneficiaries of stock-related compensation arrangement").

26. See note 12.

27. The officers and directors of Continental Illinois have been sued both by shareholders and by the FDIC, which suit was pending as of 1986. The board of Continental decided not to oppose certain of these suits against former officers. See Williams, "Continental Cites Lax Lending," *N.Y. Times,* July 23, 1984 at D-1. The directors of Trans-Union were found to have recklessly breached their duty of care in accepting a merger proposal without considering other candidates. See *Smith v. Van Gorkum,* 488 A.2d 858 (Del. 1985). Senior bank officers at both Chase Manhattan and Bank of America have been directly sued by their own corporations.

See Glaberson, "Is Chase Opening the Gates to Negligence Suits by the Boss?" *Business Week,* November 5, 1984, 39. Possibly in consequence, directors' and officers' liability insurance has become increasingly hard to obtain, and recent newspaper reports suggest that directors have become extremely anxious about their exposed position. See Schatz, "Directors Feel the Legal Heat," *N.Y. Times,* December 15, 1985, F-12; Rovner, "D & O Indemnity," *Legal Times,* November 25, 1985, at 1.

28. See R. Brearley and S. Myers, *Principles of Corporate Finance,* 2nd ed. (1984), 123–127.

29. See, e.g., W. Baumol, *Business Behavior, Value and Growth* (1959); R. Marris, *The Economic Theory of Managerial Capitalism* (1964). See also notes 32 to 43.

30. Amihud and Lev, "Risk Reduction as a Managerial Motive for Conglomerate Mergers," 12 *Bell J. Econ.* 605, 605 (1981). The authors present empirical findings that conglomerate acquisitions are more likely to be made by management-controlled firms than by owner-controlled firms. See also Note, "The Conflict Between Managers and Shareholders in Diversifying Acquisitions: A Portfolio Theory Approach," *Yale L.J.* 1238, 1241–1244 (1979).

31. See Marcus, "Risk Sharing and the Theory of the Firm," 13 *Bell J. Econ.* 368, 373–375 (1982) (managers will generally prefer to pursue policies that are less risky than those that diversified shareholders would prefer, and hence the scale of investment with respect to any attractive investment will be suboptimal for shareholders if managers act in their own self-interest). See also Kihlstrom and Laffont, "A General Equilibrium Entrepreneurial Theory of Firm Formation Based on Risk Aversion," 87 *J. Pol. Econ.* 719 (1979) (different attitudes toward risk cause individuals to separate into workers and residual risk bearers). Unlike the above authors, I will argue that an equilibrium has not been achieved and substantial renegotiation of the "contract" is occurring within the large firm.

32. G. Donaldson, *Corporate Debt Capacity* (1961), 51–56. As a result, Donaldson found that some firms held to that rate of growth that they could finance internally without resort to the capital markets; other firms applied more stringent criteria to projects that would require outside finance, generally requiring a higher expected rate of return on such projects. Donaldson interpreted these findings to mean that managers sought autonomy from capital markets—a conclusion certainly consistent with the Baumol-Marris "managerial discretion" literature.

33. G. Donaldson, *Managing Corporate Wealth: The Operation of a Comprehensive Financial Goals Systems* (1984), 45–46.

34. Ibid., 45. Donaldson writes: "In essence, the managers of these mature industrial companies sought to conduct their own affairs so that they could always borrow if necessary, even in bad times. They did so by keeping their borrowing within tight limits and by providing wide margins of safety over and above the lender's minimum lending rules. They made it a practice to live within the standards of an A credit rating at the least and within moderate debt/equity ratios. As a result, they were in a position to regard debt as an automatic extension of internally generated funds and to treat it, for planning purposes at least, as though it were an assured, off-balance sheet, liquid asset reserve" (ibid., 45).

35. The best known of these studies is Bau-

mol, Heim, Malkiel, and Quandt, "Earnings Retention, New Capital and the Growth of the Firm," 52 *Rev. Econ. & Statistics* 345 (1970). These authors examined the growth in earnings from 1946 to 1960 of the 900 firms on the Standard & Poor's Compustat tape, using regression equations to differentiate earnings financed by "ploughback" (i.e., earnings plus depreciation minus dividends) from earnings financed by debt and equity. See also Grabowski and Mueller, "Life Cycle Effects on Corporate Returns on Retentions," 60 *Rev. Econ. & Statistics* 400 (1978). For an excellent review and further analysis of these studies, see M. Fox, *Finance and Industrial Performance in a Dynamic Economy: Theory, Practice and Policy* (1987), Chap. 2.

36. After methodological criticisms were made of their original study, Baumol et al. did a further study that segregated the return on "ploughback" from firms that avoided the capital markets from those that did issue debt or equity in these markets. This time, they found that firms that issued only negligible amounts of new equity had an average rate of return of near zero on their "ploughback." See Baumol, Heim, Malkiel, and Quandt, "Efficiency of Corporate Investment: Reply," 55 *Rev. Econ. & Statistics* 128 (1973).

37. For a review of nine such studies, see W. McEachern, *Managerial Control and Performance* (1975), 39–51. McEachern's own findings were that management-controlled firms have a rate of return only half that of owner-managed firms and somewhat less than that of externally controlled firms.

38. Williamson, "Managerial Discretion and Business Behavior," 53 *Am. Econ. Rev.* 1032, 1047–1051 (1963).

39. See Williamson, note 38. Williamson found both high earnings retention ratios and a pattern under which declines in profitability brought sharp staff cutbacks without a decrease in production. This tendency for staff cuts to follow earnings declines, but not to precede them, was consistent with the "expense preference" that Williamson postulated—namely, that managers derive a positive utility from increasing staff and tend to minimize these expenditures only when the firm enters a period of earnings decline. In contrast, a profit-maximizing firm would always be seeking to minimize its costs.

40. If tax motives were the only or primary explanation, the picture should be a static one with no change in earnings retention ratios. Yet during the late 1970s and early 1980s, Gordon Donaldson reports that a tension developed between corporate managements and investors, as the former sought to maintain low dividend payouts while investors began to express a stronger preference "for companies with high and sustained divided yield" (Donaldson, note 28, p. 89). This is again an instance of the same "strain" that I submit is motivating the bust-up takeover.

41. See Amihud, Kamin, and Ronen, "'Managerialism,' 'Ownerism' & Risk," 7 *J. Banking & Fin.* 189 (1983). This study also found that management-controlled firms more frequently tried to "smooth" their income (i.e., avoided sharp fluctuations). "Systematic risk" is the risk that remains after a portfolio is diversified; "unsystematic risk" is, in theory, that risk that can be diversified away.

42. See Azariadis, "Implicit Contracts and Underemployment Equilibria," 83 *J. Pol. Econ.* 1183 (1975); Azariadis and Stiglitz, "Implicit Contracts and Fixed Price Equilibria," 98 *Q.J. Econ.* 1 (1983); Hall and Lilien, "Efficient Wage Bargains Under Uncertain Supply and Demand," 69 *Amer. Econ. Rev.* 868 (1979); Rosen, "Implicit Contracts: A Survey," 13 *J. Econ. Lit.* 1144 (1985). In Chapter 9 of this volume, Professor Melvin Eisenberg takes issue with the use of the concept of implicit contracts. He seems to resist the use of the term *contract* to apply to behavior where there is not actual, identifiable bargaining. I consider this to be a largely semantic point that does not meet the real contention made here: that managers may have accepted lower, relatively fixed wages in preference to a variable-wage system as the price of obtaining some employment security. If so, these expectations have been disrupted, and they have been forced to accept unbargained-for risk. The equity arguments here strike me as similar to those relating to creditors, although the efficiency losses may be greater.

43. This would be the case if the manager has invested in firm-specific human capital (discussed in notes 70–71, 160–163) or if the implicit contract deferred payments according to a seniority ladder.

44. Henry Manne in particular has claimed that existing systems of managerial compensation are inadequate to motivate managers and make them true entrepreneurs. See H. Manne, *Insider Trading and the Stock Market* (1966), 110–158. Professor Manne uses this argument to justify insider trading.

45. See sources cited at note 12.

46. See Baumol, note 29; Marris, note 29; Leibenstein, "Allocative Efficiency vs. 'X-Efficiency,'" 56 *Amer. Econ. Rev.* 392 (1966); FitzRoy and Mueller, "Cooperation and Conflict in Contractual Organizations," 24 *Q. Rev.*

of Econ. & Bus. 24 (1984); Marris and Mueller, "The Corporation, Competition and the Invisible Hand," 18 J. Econ. Lit. 32 (1980).

47. See Williamson, notes 13, 21, and 24.

48. Jensen and Meckling acknowledge, however, that their model chiefly applies to the smaller, entrepreneurially managed firm (Jensen and Meckling, note 12, p. 354). However, they speculate that the same principles apply to the larger public corporation analyzed by Berle and Means.

49. For a discussion of these limits on the board as a monitoring body, see Coffee, "Beyond the Shut-Eyed Sentry: Toward a Theoretical View of Corporate Misconduct and an Effective Legal Response," 63 Va. L. Rev. 1099 (1977).

50. J. Worthy and R. Neuschel, Emerging Issues in Corporate Governance (1983), 77–79.

51. Easterbrook, "Two Agency-Cost Explanations of Dividends," 74 Amer. Econ. Rev. 650 (1984).

52. For a concise statement of this view, see Chapter 20 of this volume.

53. See sources cited at note 46.

54. See H. Simon, Models of Man: Social and Rational (1957); H. Simon and J. March, Organizations (1958), 47–50; R. Cyert and J. March, A Behavioral Theory of the Firm (1963), 9–10; R. Gordon, Business Leadership in the Large Corporation (1961).

55. Marris, note 29. See also Donaldson, note 33, pp. 11, 36–42 [discussing the "compulsion to grow" in firms studied and postulating the manager's objective as "the maximization of corporate wealth (as distinct from shareholder wealth)"].

56. See Williamson, note 38.

57. V. A. Thompson and Herbert Simon have, in particular, emphasized this theme, which views large organizations as generating great anxiety and insecurity for their members. For a recent restatement of this theme that views the middle-level manager as a virtual paranoiac as a result of the political power struggles within large firms, see E. Shorris, The Oppressed Middle: Politics of Middle Management (1981).

58. A. Chandler, Jr., The Visible Hand: The Managerial Revolution in American Business (1977).

59. R. Coase, "The Nature of the Firm," 4 Economica (n.s.) 386 (1937); reprinted in R. Posner and K. Scott, Economics of Corporation Law and Securities Regulations (1980).

60. Originally, Williamson's work primarily stressed the historical side of his story, relying on Chandler and arguing that the M-Form firm had superior monitoring properties. More re-

cently, he has stressed the theme of asset specificity as his starting point. See Williamson, note 21, pp. 1548–1549. To the extent that asset specificity is present, he maintains that firms can outperform markets at reducing the transaction costs associated with recurring transactions.

61. See Mason and Goudzwaard, "Performance of Conglomerate Firms: A Portfolio Approach," 31 J. Fin. 39 (1976) (finding that a randomly selected, diversified portfolio of securities outperformed conglomerate firms). See also Weston and Mansinghka, "Tests of the Efficiency Performance of Conglomerate Firms," 26 J. Fin. 919 (1971); Melicher and Rush, "The Performance of Conglomerate Firms: Recent Risk and Return Experience," 28 J. Fin. 381 (1973). Thus, although the M-Form firm may outperform its predecessors at the firm level, it is not clear that the shareholder could not do as well at lower cost by himself.

62. For an overview of the evidence that conglomerate acquisitions have not increased efficiency, see Mueller, "The Case Against Conglomerate Mergers," in The Conglomerate Corporation, ed. R. D. Blair and R. F. Lanzillotti (1981); see also, D. Mueller, ed., The Determinants and Effects of Mergers: An International Comparison (1980).

63. There is a well-known economic argument that when consumers (or investors) cannot distinguish the quality of a particular product, they will discount all similar products by the same average factor that reflects their skepticism over quality. See Ackerlof, "The Market for 'Lemons': Quality Uncertainty and the Market Mechanisms," 84 Q.J. of Econ. 488 (1970). The force of this argument in this context arises from the fact that investors cannot ordinarily assure themselves that managements will not in the future pursue growth-maximizing or excessively risk-averse policies, because the future is inherently uncertain. Hence, investors may apply an average agency cost discount to all conglomerate stocks.

64. Portfolio revision is a constant process. Exogenous changes—mergers, bankruptcies, changes in the business strategy or environment of firms—are always occurring. Hence, even a money manager who is content with his portfolio will find from time to time that an exogenous change has caused it to become less well diversified and thus requires him to engage in stock trading.

65. This argument is closely related to the much-discussed topic of whether too much is paid for securities research. See Langbein and Posner, "Market Funds and Trust Investment Law," 1976 Am. Bar Foundation Research J. 1

(1976); Pozen, "Money Managers and Securities Research," 51 *N.Y.U. L. Rev.* 923 (1976).

66. They may, of course, be right in this belief. See sources cited at note 61.

67. See Chapter 10 in this volume.

68. The "implicit-contract" model of labor contracts, whose insights I believe apply to the takeover context, essentially sees employers as risk-neutral and employees as risk-averse. Because employees want a full-employment, fixed-wage contract, they are prepared to accept lower wages in return for employment stability. See Azariadis, "Implicit Contracts and Underemployment Equilibria," 83 *J. Pol. Econ.* 1183 (1975). In my analysis, the takeover can disrupt this bargain by denying the stability which has been purchased at the price of lower earnings.

69. See Amihud and Lev, note 30; see also Note, note 30.

70. A 1981 study by *Forbes* magazine found that 121 out of 888 chief executives had become chief executives at their present firm without prior service at the firm. This seems a high rate, given the inherent advantages that other executives already at those firms would have in the competition to succeed the former CEO. See Vagts, "Challenges to Executive Compensation: For the Markets or the Courts," 8 *J. Corp. L.* 232, 237, note 27. Another survey found that lateral transfers account for 13% of changes in senior management. See Roche, "Compensation and the Senior Executive," *Harv. Bus. Rev.,* November–December 1975, 33. Robert Reich has collected data showing that each year 15% to 25% of all American executives leave their jobs and that at any given time 30% of American managers are seeking new employment. See R. Reich, *The Next American Frontier,* (1983), 161. To be sure, most executives are promoted from within, and the executive labor market is still largely an internal one. See note 24. However, this rate of external mobility suggests that executives need not invest in firm-specific capital to rise to the CEO level. The preference for internal promotion and seniority ladders may again reflect an aspect of the implicit contract that risk-averse managers choose.

71. A similar point has been made by Martin Weitzman, who also argues that labor as a factor of production is unique because it is more redeployable than capital. See M. Weitzman, *The Share Economy: Conquering Stagflation* (1984), 28–29. Williamson has disputed this characterization. See Williamson, "A Microanalytic Assessment of The Share Economy," 95 *Yale L.J.* 627, 631–632 (1986). As discussed, Williamson's arguments about "asset specificity" seem overstated when applied to human capital,

given the increasing rate of executive mobility.

72. Indeed, Professors Hayes and Abernathy of the Harvard Business School decry the fact that the senior-executive layers of Corporate America are now largely populated by executives with either a financial or a legal background but little manufacturing experiences. See Hayes and Abernathy, "Managing Our Way to Economic Decline," *Harv. Bus. Rev.,* July–August 1980, 67. Still, whether for good or ill, this trend is visible to most.

73. This would be consistent with the premise of managerial risk aversion, since it would reduce uncertainty.

74. That directors behave in a risk-averse manner seems plainly obvious at a time when many outside directors are fleeing the board as a result of the decreased availability (or higher cost) of D&O liability insurance. See "Business Struggles to Adapt As Insurance Crisis Spreads," *Wall St. J.,* January 21, 1986, 31; Lewin, "Director Insurance Drying Up," *N.Y. Times,* March 7, 1986, D-1.

75. The literature on stock prices studies is endless. For an overview, see Jensen and Ruback, "The Market for Corporate Control," 11 *J. Fin. Econ.* 5 (1983). But see Malatesta, "The Wealth Effect of Merger Activity and the Objective Functions of Merging Firms," 11 *J. Fin. Econ.* 155 (1984). Longer-term studies of the stock price and earnings performance of acquiring firms have only recently been conducted, and they give a far less optimistic picture of the wealth effects of merger and takeover activity. See Chapters 11 and 13 of this volume.

76. Table 6.1 is a composite of data published by the Federal Reserve Board is taken from an April 21, 1986 letter to the author by then Congressman Timothy Wirth, Chairman of the Subcommittee on Telecommunications, Consumer Protection, and Finance of the House Committee on Energy and Commerce. For similar data published by Merrill Lynch based on Federal Reserve data, see Straszheim, "Are Corporations Overextended?" *Merrill Lynch Business Outlook Weekly Economic and Financial Commentary,* August 5, 1985, 2. The remaining two columns came from a table supplied by Federal Reserve Chairman Paul Volcker to Senator William Proxmire. See the letter dated November 8, 1985, from Chairman Paul Volcker to Senator William Proxmire.

77. See Labich, "Is Business Taking on Too Much Debt?" *Fortune,* July 22, 1984, 82. In 1983 and 1984, short-term borrowing by nonfinancial corporations accounted for 62% of their total external financing. This contrasts with about a 35% share during the 1970s. See H.

Kaufman, Dangers in the Rapid Growth of Debt—the Need for a National Policy Response (speech given before the National Press Club, January 1985; printed by Salomon Brothers, Inc., p. 3). Mr. Kaufman is chief economist at Salomon Brothers, Inc.

78. See Straszheim, note 76, p. 1. Others place the figure even higher. See Saul, "Hostile Takeovers: What Should Be Done?" 63 *Harv. Bus. Rev.* 18, 22 (1985) (placing the figure at $90 billion in 1985, or 4.5% of the total equity outstanding).

79. See Silk, "Economic Scene: Preventing Debt Disaster," *N.Y. Times,* September 6, 1985, D-2.

80. According to the Congressional Research Service Report (note 4, p. 23) only $11 billion of the $32 billion in below-investment-grade bonds issued in 1984 were used in mergers or leveraged buy-outs. On this basis, junk bond financing amounted to only 1.4% of all merger activity (ibid., 26). See also Nash, "'Junk Bond' Role Called Small in 1984 Mergers," *N.Y. Times,* January 4, 1986, 33. Yet the small relative size of junk bonds should not lead to a conclusion that their importance can be dismissed. The use of these bonds as a source of takeover financing began in 1983, grew significantly in 1984, and skyrocketed in 1985. See "Junk Bond Financing Up," *N.Y. Times,* June 20, 1986, D-5 (reporting that junk bonds accounted for 13.5% of takeover financing in the first half of 1985). The potential for the future use of this financing source has influenced the behavior of potential target firms, who have begun to leverage up as an anticipatory defense. As Warren Buffet has remarked to an audience at Columbia University, the attempt to dismiss the junk bond on the basis of the still low volume associated with its current use is similar to dismissing the AIDS epidemic on the basis of the number of deaths it caused in 1980.

81. See Hertzberg, "Borrowing Time: Takeover Targets Find Loading Up on Debt Can Fend Off Raiders," *Wall St. J.,* September 10, 1985, 1. According to a Salomon Brothers' estimate, $24.9 billion was spent on stock repurchases in 1984, up from $7.6 billion in 1983. For example, when Ted Turner made a hostile bid for CBS, his highly leveraged bid would have raised CBS's debt to 83% of its total capitalization. In response, CBS purchased 21% of its stock for $955 million, thereby increasing its debt to 66% of capitalization. To finance this acquisition and also to signal that it could make still more repurchases, CBS increased its outstanding debt from $508 million to $1.35 billion. This left few unencumbered assets for

Turner to leverage, and the loan agreement limited further borrowing by CBS to 75% of its capitalization. See "CBS's debt bomb," *Fortune,* August 5, 1985, 8.

82. SEC Rule 13e–4 now sets forth an equal-treatment rule that precludes the tactic used by Unocal to foil Boone Pickens under which Unocal repurchased its shares at a substantial premium from all shareholders except Boone Pickens and his allies. Under the rule, an issuer may not discriminate among shareholders of the same class but is required to extend the offer to all such shareholders. See Sec. Exch. Act Rel. 34–23421 (July 11, 1986).

83. See Cole, "High Stakes Drama at Revlon," *N.Y. Times,* November 11, 1985, D-1, D-8. Revlon also employed a highly toxic poison pill and secured negative covenants from its lenders that would have precluded further borrowing. However, Revlon later rescinded its poison pill once the bidding went over $57.25. The net effect of Revlon's repurchases were to double its long-term debt and slash shareholder's equity by 56%. See Hertzberg, note 81, p. 1. That this tactic failed may only tell other target managements that they must go to even more extreme levels of leverage.

84. Probably the most careful and disturbing statement of this view is to be found in a recent speech by the president of the Federal Reserve Bank of New York on September 18, 1985. See Corrigan, "Public and Private Debt Accumulation: A Perspective, "*FRBNY Quarterly Review,* Autumn 1985, 1. Corrigan estimates that after "abstracting from internally generated equity, the 1984–85 period will, if current trends continue, see the net retirement of $150 billion of equity in the nonfinancial corporate sector—an amount which in nominal dollars exceeds the net issuance of equity by nonfinancial business over at least the entire post–Korean War period" (ibid., 3). Moreover, this increase in private debt has largely "occurred on the upside of the business cycle and the downside of the nominal interest rate cycle" (ibid.). Nor can it be explained as an attempt to beat inflation (by paying back debts with cheaper dollars on their maturity), because the rate of inflation is lessening. Corrigan attributes the growth in private debt in substantial part to "a very rapid retirement of equity which, in turn, importantly—but not exclusively—related to leveraged buy-outs and the threat of hostile takeovers" (ibid.).

85. See Straszheim, note 76, p. 2.

86. See Labich, note 77, p. 82.

87. Some accounts suggest that junk bond purchasers are essentially relying on Drexel Burnham to make a secondary market into

which they can quickly dump their securities if credit conditions worsen. In effect, this suggests that whatever monitoring occurs is being done by the one underwriter that today holds a near monopoly on this market. See Sloan and Rudnitsky, note 4. Yet given the existence of limited liability, Drexel Burnham may have inadequate incentive to monitor as long as the fees its partners receive from this business (up to $15 million per annum in the case of the principal partner handling these transactions) exceed their equity that would be lost if the firm became insolvent.

88. For such an analysis, see Barth, Bisenius, Brumbaugh, and Sauerhaft, Regulation and the Thrift Industry (unpublished paper by economists at the Federal Home Loan Bank Board, October 2, 1985).

89. Eighty percent of the 650 thrift institution failures since the establishment of FSLIC in 1941 have occurred since 1979, and 50% of the 362 commercial bank failures since 1942 have occurred during this same period. See Barth et al, note 88.

90. Drucker, "Corporate Takeovers—What Is to Be Done?" The Public Interest, Winter 1986 (No. 82), 3, 11–12.

91. Mutual funds currently hold $17 billion in junk bonds. See "Junk Bonds: Why the Yields Are Still Fat," Fortune, July 7, 1986, 107, 109. Some commentators believe that the competition among mutual funds has inhibited their ability to function as prudent investors. See note 129. For a more general discussion of imperfections in the debt market, see notes 140 to 149.

92. According to data gathered by the Federal Home Loan Bank Board, FSLIC-insured institutions held $4.0 billion of below-investment-grade bonds on March 31, 1985. This amounted to only 0.4% of industry assets on that date. See Congressional Research Service Report, note 4, p. 38.

93. See Office of the Chief Economist, "Non-investment Grade Debt as a Source of Tender Offer Financing," (June 20, 1986), Fed. Sec. L. Rep. (CCH), para. 84,011 at p. 88,168. This percentage rose to 33% in the case of the 30 largest tender offers in 1985.

94. Although junk bonds are a trivial percentage of the total industry's portfolio, they loom larger on a regional basis. Fifty-two percent of the junk bonds held by the 200 largest institutions were held by institutions in the San Francisco FHLB district, 24% by institutions in the Dallas district, and 18% by institutions in the Atlanta district. See Congressional Research Service Report, note 4, p. 38. This localized growth is consistent with their recent appearance and suggests high future growth, because financial institutions compete increasingly on a nationwide basis. One large savings and loan institution in Beverly Hills, California, already holds over $2 billion of junk bonds, or 28% of its total portfolio. See Hilder, "Heard on the Street: Thrifts with Junk Bonds Recover Some Losses, But Uncertainties Linger," Wall St. J., December 19, 1986, 55.

95. For recent descriptions of takeover-produced layoffs, see note 7. See also Buzzota, "A Quiet Crisis in the Work Place," N.Y. Times, September 4, 1985, A-27; "Middle Managers Are Still Sitting Ducks," Business Week, September 16, 1985, 34; Prokesch, "'People Trauma' in Mergers," N.Y. Times, November 19, 1985, D-1; Nielsen, "Management Layoffs Won't Quit," Fortune, October 28, 1985, 46. Of course, any balanced account must acknowledge that product market competition is probably the principal reason for managerial layoffs—and in some cases (such as that of American Telephone and Telegraph, which is currently laying off 24,000 workers) is the exclusive cause. But for other companies, such as CBS, which laid off 2000 workers one month after leveraging up its financial structure to defeat Ted Turner's hostile bid, or Phillips Petroleum, which fought off Boone Pickens, the takeover phenomenon appears to be the principal explanation. See Smith, "Sweeping Staff Cuts at CBS News," N.Y. Times, September 20, 1985, C-30; "The Shrinkage at Phillip Pete," Business Week, May 27, 1985, 46 (noting a 10% work force cut).

96. See Editorial Commentary, "Bondholders, Unite: Issuers Are Getting Away with Highway Robbery," Barron's November 24, 1986, 9; see also Labich, note 77, p. 84 (discussing recent instances at Chesebrough-Ponds, Phillips Petroleum, Unocal, and Martin Marietta where takeover battles were the cause of the credit downgrading). In his letter to Senator Proxmire, Federal Reserve Board Chairman Paul Volcker also connected the recent number of credit downgradings to the takeover-induced degree of leverage. See note 65.

97. See "Takeovers and Buyouts Clobber Blue-Chip Bondholders," Business Week, November 11, 1985, 113.

98. Jensen and Meckling, however, recognized that it was uniquely difficult for creditors to restrict risk taking by the conglomerate firm, which could change its business strategy to accept more risk. Thus, they theorized that such firms would be more equity-financed than other corporations. See Jensen and Meckling, note 12,

pp. 338–340. Recent developments appear to have proven them half right: Creditors seem not to have restricted risk taking, but equity levels are declining.

99. See "Changing the Rules: Attacking Junk Bonds, Fed Becomes a Player in the Takeover Game," *Wall St. J.,* December 9, 1985, 1, 16 (noting that market traders and investment bankers predicted that a substantial reduction in takeover credit would have a "profound impact on the stock market" because the supply of stock has recently declined in light of stock retirements and takeover activity).

100. Ibid. The Federal Reserve Board's action applied only to bidders that fell within the "shell corporation category." If, for example, a Mesa Petroleum were to guarantee the debt of its shell subsidiary that bid for Unocal, or if it were to place substantial assets in the subsidiary, then the presumption that the loan was indirectly secured by the target's stock would probably be overcome. See 12 C.F.R. § 207.112. See also note 5.

101. The idea of limiting interest deductions has been most notably advanced by Peter Canellos, a tax partner at Wachtell, Lipton, Rosen & Katz, who has recommended legislation that would deny interest deductions in connection with mergers if the resulting debt-equity ratio of the surviving corporation exceeded three times the standard for the industry in which the corporation principally operated. See Canellos, *The Over-Leveraged Acquisition,* Tax Forum Paper No. 419, April 1985. For an evaluation of this proposal, see Congressional Research Service Report, note 4, pp. 40–41.

102. One spokesman for the Reagan administration has attacked the Federal Reserve's action on the grounds that "[t]he board's proposal would destroy the market for corporate control." See Nash, "Federal Reserve's Curb on Bonds Is Assailed by the Administration," *N.Y. Times,* December 24, 1985, 1 (quoting Douglas H. Ginsberg, Assistant Attorney General for Antitrust). This characterization seems a serious overstatement, given the modest likely impact of the Federal Reserve's action, but it does point correctly to the values in play.

103. See Nulty, "Irwin Jacobs Stirs a Junk Bond Brawl," *Fortune,* June 9, 1986, 104 (purchasers of junk bond issue were surprised to find that high–interest rate debentures were redeemable by the issuer under a special covenant despite their belief that indenture conferred call protection until 1990). In this author's view, the most likely consequence will be a shorter maturity on junk bonds if investors distrust them. Some evidence suggests this is already occur-

ring. See "Junk Bonds: Why the Yields Are Still Fat," *Fortune,* July 7, 1986, 107–109.

104. For a fuller statement of this view, see Knoeber, "Golden Parachutes, Shark Repellents and Hostile Tender Offers," 76 *Amer. Econ. Rev.* 155, 159–161 (1986). Essentially, the argument runs that the corporation could not itself renege on the implicit contract because it would suffer reputational injury, but after a change in control the new owners can.

105. See note 6.

106. See "G&W's Crash Diet," *Fortune,* July 8, 1985, 8, 9. See also Magnet, "Is ITT Fighting Shadows—or Raiders?" *Fortune,* November 11, 1985, 25 (in which one former ITT executive describes the decision making of his colleagues as "panic-stricken").

107. Ibid.

108. Ibid. See also Landro, "Reversing Course: Davis Reshapes G&W Into an Entertainment and Financial Concern," *Wall St. J.,* June 10, 1985, 1.

109. See Lieb, "Mobil Plans to Divest Ward Unit," *N.Y. Times,* May 7, 1984, D-1.

110. Stevenson, "Settlement for Crown, Goldsmith," *N.Y. Times,* May 27, 1985, 33.

111. Cole, "Electrical Maker Sets Buyback," *N.Y. Times,* August 29, 1985, D-1.

112. "Beatrice Will Sell Avis and Three Other Units," *N.Y. Times,* October 2, 1985, D-5.

113. Hayes, "Atlantic Richfield to Dispose of 2000 Gas Stations in East," *N.Y. Times,* April 30, 1985, 1.

114. Curran, "Corporate Moves to Lift Stocks," *Fortune,* July 22, 1985, 121, 124.

115. Hayes, "The Oil Industry Shake-Up," *N.Y. Times,* May 7, 1985, D-1.

116. "Chevron Properties on Block," *N.Y. Times,* September 4, 1985, D-1.

117. Cohen, "Mesa Holders Could Get Annual Return Up to 13.4% Under Partnership Plan," *Wall St. J.,* September 4, 1985, 6.

118. Crudele, "30 Allied-Signal Units to Form New Company," *N.Y. Times,* November 21, 1985, D-1. Those companies spun off were those not "highly regarded in the financial community," according to the *New York Times,* which again suggests that the focus was on the disparity between asset and stock values.

119. Buzzotta, note 95. Another study by Eugene Jennings of Michigan State University found that since 1980, 89 of the 100 largest U.S. companies have reorganized to reduce management levels. See "Middle Managers Are Still Sitting Ducks," *Business Week,* September 16, 1985, 344.

120. Prokesch, "U.S. Companies Weed Out

Many Operations," *N.Y. Times,* September 30, 1985, 1, D-5 (quoting data from W. T. Grimm & Company, which also placed a record market value of $29.4 billion on the assets divested in 1984). The figure of 900 divestiture transactions in 1984 is not a record, although it is above the average level of 767 that prevailed between 1978 to 1981. See Chapter 12 of this volume. Unlike the earlier sell-off waves described in Chapter 12, the divesting firms are today reducing their total asset size by as much as 30% to 50%. See notes 106 to 109.

121. A study in late 1985 by Goldman, Sachs & Company, the investment banking firm, estimated that "70% of the Standard & Poor's 500 stock index's 13% price appreciation since the start of 1984 came from actual and anticipated restructurings." See "Takeovers and Buyouts Clobber Blue-Chip Bondholders," *Business Week,* November 11, 1985, 113.

122. For recent statements by industry leaders that the oil industry has largely accepted the need for restructuring along the lines organically advocated by Boone Pickens—which strategy emphasized reduced exploration expenditures, buying reserves rather than searching for them, and a self-liquidating approach that views an oil corporation as a "wasting asset"—see Daniels, "Restructuring the Oil Industry," *N.Y. Times,* September 2, 1985, 27; Schmitt, "Depleted Field: Despite Raiders' Lust, Oil Industry Is Facing Retrenchment Period," *Wall St. J.,* June 7, 1985, 1; Williams, "Big Oil Starts Thinking Smaller," *N.Y. Times,* March 17, 1985, F-1.

123. Although probably the least threatened of all oil companies, given both its size and its ability to find cheap reserves, Exxon has been repurchasing its shares at the rate of one million shares per week since the last half of 1983. See Vartan, "Market Place: Some Caution on Oil Stocks," *N.Y. Times,* November 1, 1985, D-8.

124. Those who have been most critical of the efficiency claims made for conglomerate acquisitions—such as Dennis Mueller, Robert Reich, and F. M. Scherer—have tended also to doubt the disciplinary thesis that the hostile takeover replaces less efficient managements with more efficient ones. See sources cited at notes 62 and 75. Although this author has also examined and expressed reservations about the disciplinary thesis (see Coffee, note 1), the efficiency claims that can be made for the recent operation of the hostile takeover are much broader than this narrow disciplinary thesis. Rather, the more sustainable claim is that the takeover is squeezing the organizational slack out of Corporate America. The problem with

this claim is that it is doing so in a way that also may produce serious diseconomies.

125. See Cole, "Electrical Maker Sets Buyback," *N.Y. Times,* August 29, 1985, D-1. A corporate spokesman for Westinghouse said that the cable properties were being sold "because our stock price doesn't reflect the value of the cable" (ibid.).

126. For a fuller discussion of this problem, which I have elsewhere described as reducing the manager's margin for error, see Coffee, note 1, pp. 1229–1234. Put simply, if managers know more than the market, it may be unwise to make them constantly hew closely to the market's less informed judgment. To be sure, managers are also biased in favor of thinking that their past judgments were correct, and thus market discipline is necessary; but accountability is not necessarily a virtue when the agent knows more than the principal. This informational asymmetry may often make the disciplinary power of the takeover counter-productive.

127. See also Donaldson, note 33, pp. 144–151 (offering an alternative model of how a corporation strategically handles its portfolio of companies over their life cycle). Donaldson compares his approach to that of the Boston Consulting Group's matrix (p. 151, note 4). Both Donaldson and the Boston Consulting Group see a life cycle to the typical division or product group, whereas Williamson makes no such assumption.

128. See notes 2 and 3.

129. See Lowenstein, note 10, pp. 297–304 (noting the possible impact of Schedule 13–F, which was adopted in 1978 and requires quarterly reports from portfolio managers holding more than $160 million in funds). Professor Lowenstein's provocative thesis is that quarterly disclosure has compelled more active and even frenetic trading among fund managers.

130. Another possible reason is that institutional fund managers justify their high fees by searching for "undervalued" stocks, even if this search is futile, and not by investing in index funds or diversified conglomerates. See text and notes at notes 65 and 66.

131. Gordon Donaldson views management's attention to have essentially focused on the product market and the goal of self-sustaining growth, not return on capital. However, he notes a shift over the period of his study. See Donaldson, note 33, pp. 5–6, 84–86.

132. See Landro, note 108.

133. See Jensen and Meckling, note 12, pp. 338–340. Jensen and Meckling describe the incentive effects on the owner-manager of the

highly leveraged firm as follows:

Potential creditors will not loan $100,000,000 to a firm in which the entrepreneur has an investment of $10,000. With that financial structure, the owner-manager will have a strong incentive to engage in activities (investments) which promise very high payoffs if successful even if they have a very low probability of success. If they turn out well he captures most of the gains; if they turn out badly, the creditors bear most of the costs.

In effect, this is a moral hazard problem, and an unlimited supply of junk bonds would raise both this problem and its corollary, the "adverse-selection" problem, which suggests that those wanting to take such extreme risks would be the first to leverage up.

134. See note 7.

135. Professor Susan Rose-Ackerman has developed a formal theory that captures this intuitive point. See S. Rose-Ackerman, "Risk-Taking and Reelection: Does Federalism Promote Innovation?" 9 *J. Legal Studies* 593 (1980).

136. Kahneman and Tversky, "Prospect Theory: An Analysis of Decision Under Risk," 47 *Econometrica* 263 (1979). See also Fishburn, "Mean Risk Analysis with Risk Associated with Below-Target Returns," 67 *Amer. Econ. Rev.* 116 (1977); Payne, Laughhunn, and Crum, "Translation of Gambles and Aspirational Level Effects in Risky Choice Behavior," 26 *Mngt. Sci.* 1039 (1980).

137. H. Simon, *Models of Man* (1957).

138. Some research shows that decisions are reached by first classifying the outcomes of each choice as gains or losses in terms of whether the outcome is above or below the aspiration level. When expected values are above the target point, decision makers are risk-averse—i.e., they will tend to prefer the choice with least downside risk (or variance extending below the aspiration level). Conversely, managers become risk preferrers when each choice has an expected value below the aspiration level. See Payne, Laughhunn, and Crum, "Further Tests of Aspiration Level Effect in Risky Choice Behavior," 27 *Mngt. Sci.* 953 (1981); Laughhunn, Payne, and Crum, "Managerial Risk Preferences for Below-Target Returns," 26 *Mngt. Sci.* 1238 (1980).

In terms of this chapter's terminology, managements might logically prefer a risk-averse, profit-satisficing policy that maximized growth, not profit, as writers such as Baumol, Marris, and Donaldson have argued, as long as they were operating above their aspiration level, which I would loosely define as that level of profits that avoids their ouster; but once legal and institutional changes have increased the threat of a takeover, the aspiration level shifts upward to that profit level necessary to maintain them in office, and they may, as a result, tend toward a more risk-preferring style at the same level of profitability.

139. See note 133. This statement does not necessarily conflict with those writers who maintain that capital structure is irrelevant to the firm's value. Cf. Modigliani and Miller, "The Cost of Capital, Corporation Finance and the Theory of Investment," 48 *Amer. Econ. Rev.* 261 (1958). The focus here is on the conflict between debtors and creditors, not the aggregate value of their claims.

140. This point is acknowledged by Jensen and Meckling (note 12), who argue that therefore conglomerates should rely more heavily on equity financing, given the higher risks and monitoring costs that creditors would face (ibid., 338–340).

141. Until recently, regulatory supervision within the financial industry might have curbed this incentive to take excessive risk (from a social standpoint), but with deregulation, there is little incentive for creditors to monitor adequately (given depository and other forms of governmental insurance). See text and notes at notes 88 and 89. Hence, a moral hazard problem arises, and these recent insolvencies tend to confirm this theory.

142. See note 22.

143. See note 23.

144. See Prokesch, "Merger Wave: How Stocks and Bonds Fare," *N.Y. Times,* January 7, 1986, 1 (citing recent examples and quoting securities industry experts that "[b]ondholders on both sides are often left holding the bag"); "Takeovers and Buyouts Clobber Blue-Chip Bondholders," *Business Week,* November 11, 1985, 113 (viewing takeovers and buy-outs as wealth transfers from bondholders to stockholders).

145. Earlier empirical studies had suggested that wealth transfers from bondholders to stockholders seldom occurred in mergers, but these studies predate the appearance of the bust-up takeover. See Asquith and Kim, "The Impact of Merger Bids on the Participating Firms' Securityholders," 37 *J. Fin.* 1209 (1982).

146. See text and notes at notes 96 to 99.

147. For a statement of the conventional view, see Smith and Warner, "On Financial Contracting: An Analysis of Bond Covenants," 7 *J. Fin. Econ.* 117 (1979) (arguing that there is an optimal set of financial covenants and restrictions for each company which is reached through bargaining and market pricing).

148. See McDaniel, "Bondholders and Cor-

porate Governance," 41 *Bus. Law.* 413, 425–426 (1986) (reporting results of a survey of Fortune 500 corporations which finds that few corporations today included traditional or even related covenants in their indentures).

149. Ibid., 428 ("In the real world, even a rough approximation of an optimal bond contract is out of the question.")

150. It is, of course, possible that managers have already received a higher return on an *ex ante* basis to compensate them for this higher risk, but at least with respect to middle management, little evidence suggests this. Indeed, product market competition has grown more severe across the landscape of Corporate America, particularly as the result of foreign entrants, and this has produced substantial efforts, that are independent of the takeover phenomenon, to trim costs and pare down staff size.

151. See sources cited in notes 7 and 95. The oil industry provides a particularly good illustration, because it is here that the takeover pressure has been the most dramatic. Annual reports for the 12 largest oil companies show that they had 124,000 fewer employees at the end of 1983 than at the end of 1981. The Chevron/Gulf combination resulted in a reduction of the combined entity's work force by 12%, or about 10,000 jobs (and 2000 more were eliminated in the first half of 1985); Texaco trimmed its work force by 26% during 1985. See Schmitt, note 7, p. 9.

152. Over the past five years, employers have terminated over 700 pension plans and collected $6.7 billion in "surplus" assets; $3 billion was recaptured in 1984, equal to the prior three years and thus showing a rising tide. Probably the largest and best-known recent case involved United Airlines, which announced in 1985 that it intended to recapture over $1 billion for general corporate purposes. See Farnsworth, "Washington Watch: Pension Plans' Surplus Assets," *N.Y. Times,* August 12, 1985, D-2. As of August 28, 1985, $3.1 billion had been recaptured during 1985, thus exceeding 1984's level. See Williams, "Raking in Billions from the Company Pension Plan," *N.Y. Times,* November 3, 1985, F-1.

In United's case, the recapture was announced as a defensive move designed to thwart a raider, because the surplus assets were placed in a trust that could only be used to finance corporate expansion. See Byrne, "UAL Will Use Some of Unit's Pension Funds," *Wall St. J.,* June 11, 1985, 2. In other cases, the raiding of the pension fund's assets appears to have been designed to help finance future acquisitions. See "Pension Plan Shift Is Planned by FMC," *N.Y. Times,* November 8, 1985, D-4.

153. Administrative and managerial personnel constituted 10.8% of total nonagrarian employment in the United States in 1980, as opposed to 3% in West Germany, 2.4% in Sweden, and 4.4% in Japan. See Green and Berry, "Taming the Corpocracy: The Forces Behind White-Collar Layoffs," *N.Y. Times,* October 13, 1985, F-3. This evidence is difficult to evaluate, but it is revealing to learn that the percentage of nonproduction workers as a percentage of total employment rose by more than 50% between 1947 and 1980. This rise coincides with the appearance and growth of the conglomerate and provides some ammunition for those who doubt that it has curbed the problem of organizational slack.

154. For a statement of this view, see R. Posner, *Economic Analysis of Law,* 2nd ed. (1977), 292–296.

155. See L. Friedman, *A History of American Law* (1973), 166–178. Almost all colonial-era corporations in the United States were quasi-public in charter: churches, charities, or cities and boroughs. Throughout the entire eighteenth century, corporate charters were only issued to 335 businesses, and only 7 of these during the colonial period (ibid., 166).

156. See A. Berle, *The Twentieth Century Capitalist Revolution* (1955); for a review of this literature, see Werner, "The Berle-Dodd Dialogue on the Concept of the Corporation," 64 *Colum. L. Rev.,* 1458 (1964); Romano, "Metapolitics and Corporate Law Reform," 36 *Stan. L. Rev.* 923 (1984).

157. This trend is increasing as small towns now bid for major industrial plants by offering to install special improvements and to develop a surrounding infrastructure of schools and other social services. Such investment represents a form of firm-specific capital, even if it does not show on the firm's balance sheet. The recent negotiations surrounding the GM Saturn plant show this. See Ansberry and Sasaki, "Ohio Town Gives Look at Future for Site of GM's New Saturn Plant," *Wall St. J.,* August 30, 1987, 17 (discussing GM's proposed plant at Spring Hill, Tennessee; Honda's plant at Marysville, Ohio; and Nissan's plant at Smyrna, Tennessee). Of course, local communities can negotiate, and even contract formally, with a large employer to protect their firm-specific capital, but in these negotiations they tend to be novices matched against a "repeat player" who sees that it is in a "buyer's market" full of communities eager to attract such employers.

158. See F. Knight, *Risk, Uncertainty and Profit* (1921), 279–280, 359. Knight viewed the shareholders as exercising the critical authority in selecting the manager of the firm; he does not

appear to have focused on agency cost problems. Following Knight, neoclassical economics has seen the shareholders as the residual risk bearers; others—manager, employees, creditors—are viewed as being guaranteed a contractual rate of return. Knight's theory has been extended by Alchian and Demsetz to explain why only the residual risk bearers should be the monitors of the firm. See Alchian and Demsetz, "Production, Information Costs and Economic Organization," 62 *Amer. Econ. Rev.* 777 (1972). Only a monitor elected by those holding the residual claimants' interest in the firm, they argue, has an adequate incentive to prevent shirking. In this chapter's view, this form of analysis gives insufficient attention to the fact that managers bear residual risk along with shareholders, given their limited mobility in the managerial labor market, the prevalence of seniority-weighted salary structures, and the existence of firm-specific capital.

159. See sources cited in note 42.

160. See Williamson, "A Microanalytic Assessment of 'The Share Economy,'" 95 *Yale L.J.* 627, 632–633 (1986).

161. See note 24.

162. See Deal and Kennedy, note 23.

163. See Aoki, note 13, pp. 25–26; Williamson, note 13, pp. 1207–1209.

164. A. Hirschman, *Exit, Voice and Loyalty* (1970).

165. A variety of techniques have been used to place weighted or super voting stock in management's hands. In 1984, Coastal Corporation obtained shareholder authorization for a new class of shares having 100 votes per share which it then distributed in a fashion that shifted voting power to its management. See Hector, "The Flap over Super-Shares," *Fortune,* September 16, 1985, 114. Another device has been to issue super voting stock to all shareholders but to provide that these voting rights lapse on a transfer until the new holder has held them for defined period (say, three years). This again denies the bidder the ability to obtain a voting majority in that period. Since 1926, the New York Stock Exchange has insisted, as a condition of listing eligibility, upon rule of "one share, one vote," but in 1985, it indicated that it is reconsidering this rule. See Whitehead, "Don't Bend the Big Board's Rules," *Fortune,* March 18, 1985, 185.

166. The use of ESOPs has risen dramatically, but substantial issues of fairness also surround their use because employees may be overreached by them. See Note, "The False Promise of Worker Capitalism: Congress and the Leveraged Employee Stock Ownership Plan," 95 *Yale L.J.* 148 (1985). See also text and

notes at notes 188 to 189. The use of the "leveraged" ESOP as a takeover defense has also become common. See Simmons, Ward, and Watson, "An ESOP Can Be an Effective Anti-Takeover Device," *Nat'l L.J.,* June 30, 1986, 25 (discussing the use of ESOPs in several recent takeover battles). In terms of this author's analysis, the fundamental problem with the ESOP is that it forces employees to invest in an undiversified portfolio.

167. Some recent examples of golden parachutes do indeed seem extreme, but largely because of factors distinct from the dollar amounts in question. In connection with its leveraged buy-out, the Beatrice Companies granted golden parachutes totaling $23.5 million to six officers. One of these officers had been with the corporation for only 13 months and yet received a $2.7 million package; another, the chief executive officer, received a $7 million package, even though he had emerged from retirement only 7 months before. See Johnson and Morris, "Beatrice Cos. Grants Golden Parachutes Totaling $23.5 Million to Six Officials," *Wall St. J.,* November 25, 1985. In neither such case would there appear to be much firm-specific capital at risk. Indeed, it has been estimated that Beatrice's chief executive would receive, under his contract, $5000 for each hour that he had worked at Beatrice since emerging from retirement. See Greenhouse, "Golden Chutes Under Attack," *N.Y. Times,* December 10, 1985, D-2. In another well-known case, Michel Bergerac, the former chairman of Revlon, received a $35 million package consisting of severance pay and stock options. See Stevenson, "Decisions for Owner of Revlon," *N.Y. Times,* November 4, 1985, D-1. Yet in both cases these amounts were trivial in comparison to the total acquisition price ($6.2 billion in the Beatrice buy-out and $1.74 billion in the Revlon acquisition). Similarly, when the 50 top officers of Allied and Signal received slightly over $50 million in golden parachutes in connection with their merger, this amounted to only about 1% of the total merger price of $5 billion. See "Allied-Signal Tie Proves Lucrative to Executives," *N.Y. Times,* August 13, 1985, D-2.

Most commentators have doubted that golden parachutes are an effective takeover defense, because the cost of golden parachutes has been estimated at less than 1% of the total cost of a takeover. See Morrison, "Those Executive Bailout Deals," *Fortune,* December 13, 1982, 86.

Frequently, the manager's right to receive the special termination compensation specified in the golden-parachute clause of his employment contract is triggered by a "change in control" of the corporation employing him; this means that the manager need not be terminated by the successful bidder but may voluntarily resign and collect the specified payment. For a fuller description of these clauses, see R. Winter, M. Stumpf, and G. Hawkins, *Shark Repellents and Golden Parachutes* (1983), 425–428. One recent survey by Ward Howell International, Inc., of Fortune 1000 corporations found that 21.8% of these contracts providing for a lump-sum termination payment were triggered by their terms even if the employee resigned voluntarily. See Note, "Golden Parachutes and the Business Judgment Rule: Toward a Proper Standard of Review," 94 *Yale L.J.* 909 (1985), 909 n. 3.

168. Several recent cases have invalidated or granted preliminary injunctions against the exercise of golden parachutes, especially when the officers could trigger the payment at their own election. In one of the most publicized of these cases, a Wisconsin appellate court ruled that any golden parachute without a mitigation or offset clause was unenforceable as against public policy. See *Koenings v. Joseph Schlitz Brewing Co.,* 368 N.W. 2d 690 (Wisc. Cir. Ct. 1985). However, this decision was reversed by the Wisconsin Supreme Court, which found the principal issue to be the reasonableness of the stipulated damages clause and recognized the impact of a hostile takeover on employee morale to be a factor that could be considered in this determination. See *Koenings v. Joseph Schlitz Brewing Co.,* 377 N.W. 2d 349 (Wisc. 1985). For other recent decisions, see *Weinberger v. Shumway,* No. 547586 (Super. Ct. San Diego County, Calif.) (preliminary injunction granted with respect to Allied-Signal merger payments to executives); *Minstar Acquiring Corp. v. AMF, Inc.,* No. 85 Civ. 3800 (S.D.N.Y. 1985). See Moore, "Golden Parachutes Appearing Vulnerable," *Legal Times,* September 30, 1985, 1. Recent settlements also show that managers cannot rely on their change-of-control contracts as written. In *Weinberger v. Shumway,* the former executives of The Signal Companies agreed to a $25 million reduction in benefits after a preliminary injunction was granted. See Greenhouse, "Golden Chutes Under Attack," *N.Y. Times,* December 10, 1985, D-2. Prior to these recent cases, there does not appear to have been a decision invalidating a golden-parachute contract on the merits. See Note, note 167, p. 909, note 6. Many commentators have argued that the business judgment rule would protect such agreements (ibid., p. 912, note 17).

169. See Internal Revenue Code, Sections 280G and 4999. For a history and closer analysis of these new provisions, see Lear and Bagley, "Excess Golden Parachute Payments Specially Taxed," *The National Law Journal,* November 4, 1985, 15.

170. According to Ward Howell's survey of Fortune 1000 companies, 48% of such companies protected senior management with employment contracts, almost half of which contained change-of-control provisions. As of October 1984, 180 of 485 corporations surveyed from Standard and Poor's 500 list of companies had change-of-control provisions with some of their senior executives. See Lear and Bagley, note 169, p. 16.

171. See Internal Revenue Code, 401(a)(4) and (5). In substance, these sections require a qualified pension or profit-sharing plan not to discriminate, but they permit the contributions made on behalf of employees to "bear a uniform relationship to the total compensation or the basic or regular rate of compensation of such employees" and to exclude that portion of an employee's compensation on which FICA payments are made. In effect, this permits an employer to make contributions on a percentage-of-salary basis, excluding that portion of an employee's salary on which Social Security contributions must be paid.

172. To date, employee termination payments do not appear to have exceeded 1% of the total cost of a takeover. See Morrison, note 167. Even in a case such as that of the Chevron-Gulf acquisition where 10,000 employees were laid off, the cost of a three-year employment guarantee, subject to an offset for income received from other employment if the employee resigned voluntarily, would not exceed $1 billion. High as this number sounds, it would still represent less than 8% of the $13.3 billion acquisition cost of that megatransaction.

173. See sources cited in note 12.

174. For the counterview, see Brudney, note 8. See also Clark, "Agency Costs Versus Fiduciary Duties," in *Principals and Agents: The Structure of Business,* ed. J. Pratt and R. Zeckhauser (1985).

175. Professors Easterbrook and Fischel have argued that the most sensible approach to this problem is to implement the fiduciary principle by asking what the parties would have rationally bargained for with respect to the unforeseen contingency. See Easterbrook and Fischel, "Corporate Control Transactions," 91 *Yale L.J.* 698, 700–703 (1982). They then argue that the parties would bargain so as to maximize the aggregate gains without regard to their distribution. For a critique, see Brudney, note 8, pp. 1408 and 1415, note 31. Presumably, Professor

Brudney would say that managers are to be held strictly to the preexisting corporate contract (i.e., the corporate charter and bylaws), unless they possessed explicit contractual rights in an employment agreement. For the general rules as to how a court should proceed when there is a missing term in a contract, see Farnsworth, "Disputes over Omissions in Contracts," 68 *Colum. L. Rev.* 860 (1968).

176. Such an implicit contract of continuing employment has been described by students of the labor market as a widely prevalent phenomenon. See Azariadis, "Implicit Contracts and Underemployment Equilibria," 83 *J. Pol. Econ.* 1183 (1975); see also Aoki, note 13, pp. 5, 7, and 70, for a discussion of implicit bargaining. On the managerial level, Gordon Donaldson reports that the senior managements he studied identified with their managerial staffs and saw themselves as a collective managerial team whose interests lay in minimizing the power of other constituencies, such as labor or the shareholders. See Donaldson, note 33, pp. 155–156. For a strong statement to this effect by the chief executive officer who is chairman of the Business Roundtable's Corporate Governance Committee, see Lueck, "Building a New Empire Out of Paper," *N.Y. Times,* August 12, 1984, F-6, F-7 (quoting Andrew Sigler of Champion International).

177. See sources cited in notes 34, 39, and 44.

178. See Fama, note 12 (emphasizing the desirability of a system that compensates managers through "*ex post* settling up").

179. For such a conclusion, see Kiechel, "Resurrecting Corporate Loyalty," *Fortune,* December 9, 1985, 207.

180. The Easterbrook and Fischel thesis is that the parties to the corporate contract would bargain to maximize the total gain, regardless of its distribution among them; thus, they claim when a court is confronted with an apparent missing term in the corporate relationship of shareholders and managers, it should attempt to reconstruct this hypothetical bargaining process and determine what term would lead to the greatest enhancement of aggregate value. Professor Brudney has replied that this form of bargaining is indeterminate and that the burden under traditional principles should be on the party seeking protection from this "implied" term. See sources cited in note 158. Finally, as takeovers have now become frequent and indeed pervasive, it seems to torture words to believe that any term is "missing," because the contingency is now clearly foreseen by all. The real issue becomes the degree of deference the court should give to the board's judgment to

award seemingly very generous change-of-control compensation. Here, courts are at present differing. See note 168.

181. See Morrison, note 167.

182. For example, § 2.01 of the American Law Institute's *Principles of Corporate Governance: Analysis and Recommendations* (Tentative Draft No. 2, 1984) provides that "whether or not corporate profit and shareholder gain are thereby enhanced, the corporation in the conduct of its business

(b) may take into account ethical considerations that are reasonably regarded as appropriate to the responsible conduct of business, and

(c) may devote a reasonable amount of resources to public welfare, humanitarian, educational, and philanthropic purposes.

In principle, both clauses (b) and (c) could be cited to justify change-of-control consideration or the creation of an ESOP after a takeover bid had commenced. See Illustration 14 to § 2.01 (permitting the purchase of an annuity for an employee without retirement income on a firm's liquidation). The key issue is "reasonableness" under subparagraph (c) or whether an "ethical" principle is discernible under subparagraph (b). Although one can dispute whether change-of-control payments can be analogized to other efforts by a corporation to protect its employees, some courts have already drawn this analogy. See *GAF Corp. v. Union Carbide Corp.,* Fed. Sec. L. Rep. (CCH) para. 92,408 at p. 92,507 (S.D.N.Y. 1985) ("The protection of loyal employees, including managers, of the organization is not anathema in the Courthouse. To be compared are the situations in which similar protection to the well being and security of employees, pensioners, and loyal members of management is regularly accorded when a business is moved or substantially liquidated; they are similarly directly affected by unfriendly raids on control.") In *GAF Corp. v. Union Carbide Corp.,* the court went on to suggest that the fiduciary position of the board required it to consider the interests of its employees in a bust-up takeover (ibid., 92,508). This may overstate the prior precedents, but it does suggest that the concept of the fiduciary relationship is more open-ended and multifaceted than either the positions of Professor Brudney or Professors Easterbrook and Fischel describe it to be.

183. Salpukas, "The Long Fight for TWA: Unions Decided the Winner," *N.Y. Times,* August 31, 1985, 1.

184. It would be an exaggeration to claim that pilots have firm-specific capital, because their skills are essentially fungible. Rather, the

TWA pilots were protecting their seniority rights. However, as Professor Aoki has argued, the use of seniority ladders may be efficient as a means of curtailing rivalry, and some empirical evidence supports this view. See Aoki, note 13, p. 103. See also Freeman and Medoff, "The Two Faces of Unionism," 57 *Public Interest* 69 (1979).

185. See Blumstein, "The New Role for ESOP's," *N.Y. Times,* January 2, 1985, D-1. From 843 plans in 1976 covering 520,000 workers, the number of ESOPs at the beginning of 1985 had risen to 5700 covering 9.6 million workers. Although ESOPs in effect exploit a tax subsidy, a shift of this magnitude does show a broadly based reaction among employees to threat of a takeover.

186. In his recent book, *The Share Economy: Conquering Stagflation* (1984), Professor Martin Weitzman of MIT has argued that the central problem of Western economies is wage rigidity, which produces both high unemployment and inflation. His solution would be a profit-sharing system under which a portion of a worker's pay would be tied to the firm's profitability per employee. Although he does not focus on the problems of implementation, he favors a Japanese-style economy which he sees as having devised a superior form of profit-sharing capitalism. New techniques for resisting a takeover, such as the ESOP and the management buy-out, are in effect moving in this direction by leading workers to invest in their firm. An equity investment in the corporation, particularly when it is closely held, gives the employee a reasonably close equivalent of Weitzman's profit-sharing scheme. Thus, while the employees are overinvesting in the firm from the standpoint of portfolio diversification, they are also entering into a serendipitously created profit-sharing agreement from this other perspective. Residual risk sharing may then be arriving by the back door. Realism requires the observation that the recent history of the ESOP has also been characterized by serious abuses. See Note, note 166.

187. See Crudele, "A Fresh Look at Grumman," *N.Y. Times,* June 12, 1985, D-10.

188. See J. Abegglen and G. Stalk, *Kaisha: The Japanese Corporation* (1985); W. Ouchi, *Theory Z* (1981); Aoki, note 13, pp. 189–194.

189. See Bleakley, "A Trustee Takes on the Greenmailers," *N.Y. Times,* February 10, 1985, F-6.

190. The typical large Japanese corporation "has ten or twenty important institutional shareholders, in which it in turn holds shares" (Aoki, note 13, p. 183). In effect, the Japanese system creates a reciprocal alliance of "stable shareholders" who protect each other from attack. See also Note, "Corporate Governance in Japan: The Position of Shareholders in Publicly Held Corporations," 5 *U. Hawaii L. Rev.* 136, 146–152 (1983).

191. In 1985, the Wachtet, Lipton firm introduced a new variation on the "poison pill" security that they also originally designed. This new security, called a "PIP" [for participating incentive preferred (stock)], would carry a special dividend and voting rights (including an 80% class vote on mergers) and would have limited transferability; it would be held by suppliers and customers of the target and thus it might begin to approximate the Japanese system of stable shareholders.

192. Some estimates have placed the historical annual return to investors in a leveraged buy-out at levels as high as 40%. See Wane, "Buyouts Altering Face of Corporate America," *N.Y. Times,* November 23, 1985, 1, 37. Such a return can be achieved in part because of high leverage and tax subsidies but also because management is itself here arbitraging the difference between the stock value of the firm and its higher asset value. When such gains are preempted by senior management, it may be middle management that suffers most.

193. See "Loews Doubling CBS Stock," *N.Y. Times,* October 17, 1985, D-1.

194. See notes 7 and 95.

195. Sometimes, however, the capitalized value of the layoffs occurring in the wake of a takeover may equal the total premium paid to the shareholders. Salter and Weinhold argue that in the acquisition of The Continental Group by Peter Kiewit & Sons, the capitalized value of the salary expense saved as a result chiefly of dismissing the senior managerial team of Continental equaled the premium paid to the target shareholders. See M. Salter and W. Weinhold, Corporate Takeovers: A View from the "Buy Side" (paper prepared for Columbia Law School Conference on Takeovers and Contests for Corporate Control, 1985), 17. In such a case, it is arguable that simply a wealth transfer is occurring, with no enhancement of economic efficiency. However, it seems more likely that even in these cases the loss to employees is still less than the gain to the target shareholders, because most employees will eventually secure employment elsewhere, even if at a reduced salary.

196. Economic theory usually avoids the question of equity by assuming only that "more is better than less." This is the basic notion of Pareto efficiency, which assumes that if a change

or transaction makes some better off and none worse off, it is efficient. What happens, however, if there are both winners and losers? The Kaldor-Hicks approach postulates that if the gains exceed the losses, the transaction or legal change giving rise to this net gain is efficient because the winners can compensate the losers for their losses and still come out ahead. See Hicks, "The Foundations of Welfare Economics," *Econ. Journal* LXIX, 696 (1939); see also A. M. Polinsky, *An Introduction to Law and Economics* (1983), 7–11, 115–117.

197. The Coase Theorem, which is at the core of neoclassical economics, postulates that in the absence of high transaction costs, the parties will bargain to the efficient solution, because in effect the "winners" will bribe the losers. See R. Coase, "The Problem of Social Cost," 4 *J.L. & Econ.* 1 (1960). Proponents of this view often argue that where transaction costs are high, the law should "mimic" what the market would otherwise have accomplished.

198. See Easterbrook and Fischel, "The Proper Role of a Target's Management in Responding to a Tender Offer," 94 *Harv. L. Rev.* 1161 (1981) (arguing for a rule of passivity). The Easterbrook and Fischel position seems anti-Coasean because they rely on judicial action rather than bargaining among the participants. This chapter does not dispute the need for judicial oversight but would recommend relaxing some of the barriers to a Coasean solution through the payment of change-of-control compensation to managers.

199. See Knoeber, note 104 (arguing that managers are exploited by opportunistic shareholders in takeovers because they lose bargained for rights to *ex post* compensation).

200. Recent decisions by the Delaware Supreme Court upholding a discriminatory self-tender by Unocal to fend off Mesa Petroleum and a "poison pill" plan adopted by Household International suggest there is little current willingness on the part of state courts to monitor defensive tactics in corporate-control contests.

Compare *Moran v. Household International, Inc.,* 500 A.2d 1346 (Del. 1985), and *Unocal Corporation v. Mesa Petroleum Co.,* 493 A.2d 946 (Del. 1985). Although the Delaware Supreme Court has restricted the use of lockups [see *Revlon, Inc. v. MacAndrews & Forbes Holdings,* 506 A.2d 173 (Del. 1986)], this decision restricts managerial tactics only once a decision has been made to liquidate or sell the firm.

201. See sources cited in note 199.

202. Pantry Pride paid approximately $1.7 billion to the stockholders of Revlon but incurred total costs of $2.7 billion, including "some $200 million in expenses for lawyers, investment bankers and severance payments." See Cole, "Takeover Accepted by Revlon," *N.Y. Times,* November 2, 1985, 35, 37. While this $200 million figure presumably includes the $35 million paid to Michael Bergerac, the former CEO of Revlon, it apparently includes even greater amounts paid to Pantry Pride's lawyers and investment bankers. Thus, the interesting question is whether, on average, increasing severance payments would produce more than offsetting savings in terms of the expenses incident to a hostile fight (in comparison with a friendly acquisition). Arguably, a rule that liberalized change-of-control compensation would cause a wealth transfer from lawyers and investment bankers, who today profit enormously from takeovers, to managers, who today lose.

203. See Morrison, note 167, p. 86; see also examples described at note 167.

204. See text and notes at notes 169 to 171. Admittedly, there have been cases in which this trebled salary has been exceeded. See note 167 (discussing recent golden parachutes awarded by Beatrice Cos.). Case law, however, has begun to restrict such payments. See cases cited at note 168.

205. The "waste" standard is a permissive one. See *Lieberman v. Becker,* A.2d 467 (Del. Ch. 1982); *Bergstein v. Texas International Co.,* 453 A.2d 467 (Del. Ch. 1982).

7

Corporate Takeovers: Financial Boom or Organizational Bust?

MALCOLM S. SALTER
WOLF A. WEINHOLD

The year 1984 was a banner year for mergers and acquistions in the United States. According to W. T. Grimm & Company, more transactions were announced in 1984 than in any year since 1974.[1] A record $122.2 billion was paid to sellers. The number of transactions larger than $100 million reached a record 200, a level 50% higher than the previous record set in 1983. Seventeen transactions greater than $1 billion in value were consummated, almost double the record set in 1983. In addition, the value of international merger transactions were near historically high levels. (See Figures 7.1, 7.2, and 7.3 which summarize key trends in merger activity.)

Tender offer attempts for publicly traded companies in 1984 more than doubled 1983's total, rising from 37 to 79—the highest count since 1979, when 106 attempted tenders were recorded. Hostile tenders accounted for 23% of all tenders. Although below the average for the preceding decade, many of these hostile bids came from speculators more interested in making capital gains than in acquiring ownership and managing a business. For senior managers of target companies, the most salient fact of life was that nearly 60% of all hostile tender offers for publicly traded target companies were successful.

The year 1985 was another noteworthy year. While the oil patch frenzy that culminated in the takeovers of Getty, Gulf, and Superior died down, large-scale merger activity shifted into previously untouched areas. The $3 billion acquistion of American Broadcasting Companies by Capital Citites Communications signaled that communications companies were hot prospects. By the end of the third quarter nearly $10 billion in broadcasting, publishing, and cable properties were sold, with properties worth several billion dollars more still on the auction block. Similarly, Beatrice's acquisition of Esmark pointed out the attractiveness of food companies as takeover targets. In short order, Nestle's acquisition of Carnation, R. J. Reynold's acquisition of Nabisco, and Philip Morris's acquistion of General Foods established new records as the largest nonoil takeovers. Even such old-line consumer products companies as Unilever and Procter & Gamble—which had never pursued large-scale acquisition—found themselves in a bidding war over Richardson-Vicks.

The search for a balanced analysis of the beneficial and harmful effects of current merger and takeover activity continues to pit economists against economists, bankers against bankers, lawyers against lawyers, and managers against managers. In light of the many conflicting views held by those participating in or observing corporate takeovers, our goals in this chapter are to review the managerial economics underlying corporate strategies involving mergers and takeovers and, in this context, to probe two basic questions posed by the current spate of takeovers: First, how can real economic value be created or de-

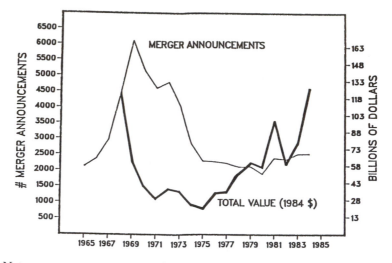

Figure 7.1. Net merger announcements and total value paid, 1965–1984. (*Source:* W. T. Grimm & Company.)

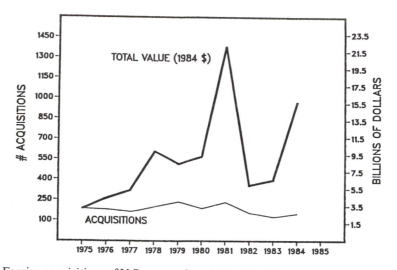

Figure 7.2. Foreign acquisitions of U.S. companies, 1975–1984. (*Source:* W. T. Grimm & Company.)

stroyed for the constituencies comprising bidding firms? And in light of the concept of value creation, where do the benefits from corporate takeovers flow from and where do they flow to? Second, how does the nature of the takeover event—negotiated or hostile—affect the capacity of acquisitive firms to capture whatever potential economic value exists?

It should be clear from the phrasing of

these questions that our concerns center on surviving firms' ability to create real economic value for their relevant constituencies. Thus, rather than broadening our discussion to include issues facing the constituencies comprising the target firms— such as the growing tension between the rights of shareholders and the discretion of managers—we will focus here on how takeovers can enhance or detract from the

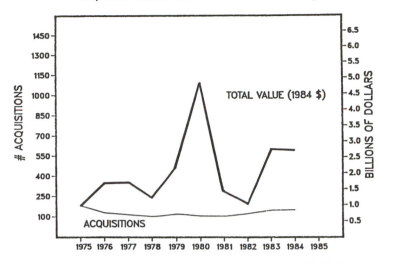

Figure 7.3. U.S. acquisitions of foreign companies, 1975–1984. (*Source:* W. T. Grimm & Company.)

long-term performance of acquisition-minded firms.

We will develop three pivotal points in this chapter:

- Despite empirical evidence suggesting that many takeovers destroy buyers' economic wealth, many opportunities exist for the managers of bidding firms to create real economic value over the short- and long-term. Doing so, however, requires that the managers of acquisition-minded companies identify more carefully than many of their predecessors the sources, timing, and ultimate beneficiaries of whatever potential for value creation exists.
- Contrary to the beliefs of takeover critics, many opportunities to create real economic value for the surviving firm are open to managers pursuing hostile as well as friendly transactions. However, these opportunities tend to be one-shot improvements in the financing and organization of the surviving firm—improvements that lead to higher, but not increasing, returns.
- The most important source of long-term value creation, involving the recombination of separate businesses into a more competitive entity, is *rarely* available to companies pursuing hostile tenders or to financial entrepreneurs

with limited operating experience. While financial entrepreneurs often serve as catalysts to get a value creation process going, their typical strategies are unlikely to enhance the long-term value of the surviving corporation.

THE CONCEPT OF VALUE CREATION

Since we use value creation as a principal criterion for evaluating both corporate performance and the benefits of corporate takeovers, the concept merits an explanation at the outset. The concept can best be understood by a return to basics—i.e., by reviewing both the role that firms play in our market economy and what this role implies in terms of the work of top-level managers.[2]

Economic organizations, such as business firms, arise in our economy to exploit the profit opportunities and inefficiencies of poorly performing or dynamically changing markets. They serve to process information and bear risks that individual players cannot easily handle, and they assume explicit responsibility for the coordination functions otherwise filled by the market. In this role, firms must assemble resources from the marketplace and distribute output into the marketplace. Their managers must define boundaries between the enterprise and the marketplace by deciding which activities should be performed within the firm and which outside the firm by others. In setting these boundaries, an organization's leadership must also define the purposeful intent of the enterprise and, on that basis, induce numerous constituencies to participate in the enterprise rather than in the marketplace as independent players or in other organizations. Inducements include economic payments to capital and labor, a variety of social and psychological rewards for the firm's participants and, as noted previously, the assumption by the organization of economic uncertainty otherwise borne by participants.

Management's task of securing each constituency's participation and institutional commitment at the least possible cost is extremely complex. For example, in addition to bringing intangible psychic and social rewards, participation in a business enterprise must also make capital and labor better off economically. Since an economic organization cannot keep operating for very long unless all participants are rewarded at least at market rates, survival depends on its ability to process and act upon information and to coordinate activities at least as efficiently as the marketplace. This ability, in turn, depends upon how well the organization can structure relationships or terms of exchange among its membership, and upon what decision-making processes it adopts to monitor and alter these relationships.

Managing the evolution of corporate purpose and policy is also a complicated task: It requires that senior management continually revise many of the implicit and explicit contracts linking the firm's constituencies together—contracts between the firm and its employees; contracts between the firm and its suppliers of technology, raw materials, and capital; and contracts between managers and the owners of the firm. Where required changes cannot be effected through negotiation and other means, intervention from outside the organization may occur. New top management, unfettered by previous commitments, agreements, and policies, may be brought in to perfom the entrepreneurial act of restructuring the organization and the relationships among the constituencies. Such intervention can be triggered by management's failure to satisfy the firm's constituencies, typically represented by the board of directors, or by the interests of capital mobilized by outside investors.

For incumbent managers, their success in negotiating changes in corporate purposes, policies, and practices in any one time period is greatly facilitated by the generation of an economic surplus in previous time periods. Economic surplus refers to profit after all participants have been compensated for their involvement in the enterprise, and all direct and indirect costs of that enterprise's productive efforts have been paid. (As such, it is difficult to measure by generally accepted accounting conventions.) Economic surplus facilitates organizational adaptation because it gives senior managers the flexibility to make new resource commitments to participants in the firm apprehensive about opportunity costs resulting from these changes.

Economic surplus also determines whether economic activities coordinated through organizations can sustain themselves. If firms fail to compensate their participants at or above competitive rates, they will eventually find them reducing their participation in the enterprise in favor of more rewarding economic (and noneconomic) relationships elsewhere. Furthermore, firms that cannot generate surplus will be unable to attract new resources—human, technological, or financial—to maintain their competitive position. Indeed, unless a firm can outperform its competitors in generating economic surplus, critical resources will tend to flow away, diminishing the firm's capacity to innovate and expand. The inevitable result is reduced competitive strength and the eventual disintegration of the enterprise as a viable entity.

Similarly, since resources tend to flow through market mechanisms to those firms promising the highest rates of present and future expected risk-adjusted returns, the more productive economic entities will attract greater amounts of capital resources with which to compete, expand, and innovate. In this way, economic surplus enables a firm to attract both financial and nonfinancial resources in the present for use in the future. This "call option" on future resources is a basic source of competitive advantage. Throughout this chapter, we will refer to the process of generating economic surplus as *value creation.* We will use this phrase to indicate the accumulated and expected worth of participation by capital, labor, and management in an enterprise over and above the level of well-being or return that they might anticipate from alternate economic exchanges. We will also employ this notion of value creation as a principal standard of managerial and corporate performance.

There are three principal sources of value creation for firms. Tapping these sources is an immense managerial task. It includes (1) gaining and retaining an information advantage over other players in the marketplace, (2) assembling and marshalling resources with unique competences around a production or transformation process, and (3) coordinating the production process more efficiently than the marketplace. The first two sources of value creation are easy to grasp: The greater the information advantage achieved or the more unique the set of technological, human, and financial resources assembled, the greater is the organization's ability to exploit environmental opportunities more efficiently and effectively than other competitors. The third source of value creation, coordination, is a bit more complicated and deserves a special comment since it is critical to our observations about corporate takeovers.

Coordination in firms can occur at two levels: within discrete business or production units or among business units. Efficient coordination at the business unit level requires decision-making systems that are highly responsive to environmental stimuli. To provide competitive advantage, these systems must be efficient in processing relevant information. They must limit the organizational equivalent of friction, which is inaccurate or incomplete

information about transactions. Shared value systems and the formal structures of bureaucracies represent attempts to meet this information-processing challenge. The common premises that any coherent organization seeks to promote as a basis for decisions are equivalent to automatic rules. These premises help filter important data from the organization's environment. In addition, when decision making is localized and a pattern of responses to recurring problems is reinforced, these common decision premises reduce internal dissonance and conflict. Furthermore, formally articulated organization structures and relationship attempt to guarantee that critical information travels to the right decision-making centers with a minimum of biases and unnecessary processing. By specializing information-processing needs, a firm can limit biases and mistakes to small segments of the operation. Cumulative errors are controlled and more accurate information sources are retained. Cost-conscious managers will also try to establish organization structures that gather and process only information that is critically important.

Efficient coordination among business units, especially in widely diversified public firms, is largely a matter of disciplined resource allocation. Large corporations must continually assess whether or not the expected returns in its various businesses compensate capital for the risks and opportunity costs of operating in the businesses. Senior managers in these firms typically develop elaborate financial control and information systems as aids in monitoring their ongoing capital commitments. In this sense, most corporate offices of widely diversified firms serve a function similar to the external capital market in allocating resources. Indeed, as the current takeover interest in such diversified firms as AMF, City Investing, Continental Group, and SCM Corp. dramatically indicates, the external capital market serves as a sort of competing decision-making system that reviews the efficiency and productivity of a diversified firm's internal capital market.

With this notion of value creation and

the related tasks of senior management in place, we can now turn to the potential benefits and costs of corporate takeovers. In our discussion, we will have the opportunity to stress how takeovers affect the sources of value creation just discussed.

VALUE CREATION AND CORPORATE TAKEOVERS

The current surge in mergers and takeovers is the result of many forces—increased economic uncertainty, lower economic growth, permissive public policy in the United States, large pools of risk capital available for investment on short notice, the increasing willingness of institutional investors to put companies into play in order to help them achieve their performance goals, and industrial restructuring forced upon U.S. industry by international competition and deregulation. For many operating managers and corporate entrepreneurs, however, the issue is less complicated. With the productivity of capital declining in their establishing businesses and with attractive capital investment programs diminishing, why not, they ask, simply invest surplus cash and available debt capital in financial assets that are priced well below their replacement value? This, of course, is what has been going on since 1974. (See Figure 7.4 showing the long-term decline in both the real rate of return earned by nonfinancial corporations and the market value/replacement value ratio.)

In this current economic context, the wealth position of shareholders of bidding and target firms can be enhanced through both short-term gains in stock prices associated with a takeover transaction and longer-term gains arising from improved capital productivity. Evidence, reported by Michael C. Jensen and Richard S. Ruback in a detailed review of many studies of the shareholder effects of successful takeovers, shows that the short-term gains to the target companies' shareholders are approximately 30% from tender offers and 20% from mergers.[3] In marked contrast to the substantial gains for selling shareholders, Jensen and Ruback also found that the short-term gains for the shareholders of acquiring companies appear to be negligible. An important new study by Lois Shelton at the Harvard Business School offers an enlightening qualification to this last finding.

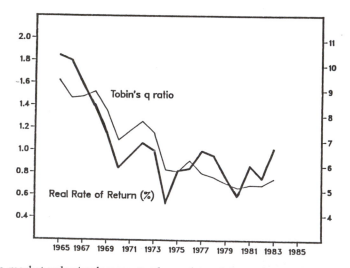

Figure 7.4. The market value/replacement value ratio and the real rate of return earned by nonfinancial corporations, 1965–1984. (*Source:* Daniel M. Holland, ed., *Measuring Profitability and Capital Costs: An International Study.* Lexington, Mass.: Lexington Books, 1984; *Economic Report of the President,* Washington, D.C.: U.S. Government Printing Office, 1983; authors' analysis.)

If one differentiates mergers and takeovers according to the corporate strategy, it appears that whenever short-term gains do accrue to bidding firms, they tend to be associated with related acquisitions.[4]

Evidence concerning the long-term effects of takeovers on the shareholders of bidding or acquiring firms is less detailed and more ambiguous than that for short-term effects. There is a gathering stream of evidence, however, to suggest that many takeovers lead to worse financial performance for acquiring firms rather than better. For example, Michael Lubatkin and Hugh O'Neill recently examined years of performance before and after large mergers by 314 firms that were not involved in any other mergers during that five-year period.[5] They found that all types of mergers led to a decrease in market return and an increase in business-specific risk. Evidence of positive gains over a five-year period only turned up in their analysis when considering, on a transaction-by-transaction basis, a unit of return for a unit of risk and controlling for market trends. Frederic M. Scherer, in a detailed clinical study of 15 takeovers that ended up in divestiture, found that in 7 of the 15 cases corporate control contributed to a deterioration of the acquired firm's performance.[6] As part of a larger survey of over five thousand mergers, Scherer and David J. Ravenscraft estimated that perhaps 30% of previously acquired businesses were subsequently divested in poorer financial condition than when they were acquired.[7] Finally, a recent study by McKinsey Economics of 400 acquisitions found that only half of them worked.[8] The other half destroyed shareholder's wealth in the acquiring company, even though the shareholders in companies taken over made big gains. Nevertheless, it is also clear from this developing research stream that not all mergers destroy economic value for the shareholders of bidding firms. In those combined firms that end up more competitive after a takeover, gains to shareholders may accrue in the form of higher security prices and to employees without ownership interest in the form of enhanced job security and compensation. To the extent that a take-over involves firms that are inefficient in processing information or in coordinating their economic activities, there may be losses to managers and employees—in the form of layoffs or reduction in compensation—as new owners search for ways to increase competitiveness.

Buried in these generalizations are a set of conditions related to the sources of the value created (or destroyed) and the time horizon which managers must adopt in working to create new economic value. In summary form, there are *transaction-related sources* and *operation-related sources* of value creation in corporate takeovers. Benefits stemming from the former are typically irreversible, arising from one-shot moves made during or shortly after the time of the takeover or merger transaction. Benefits from the latter typically require the sustained attention of operating managers over many months and years. In exploiting transaction- and operation-related sources of value creation, managers can pursue strategies of *resource restructuring* and *coordination restructuring*. In many takeovers today, both types of restructuring are being pursued. Figure 7.5 summarizes four principal sources of value creation in mergers and takeovers: Refinancing assets, renegotiating "contracts," reconfiguring assets and the portfolio of businesses, and recombining businesses into more competitive entities.

In the following discussion, we will elaborate the four principal sources of value creation associated with takeovers. As explained previously, we will focus primarily on the interests of bidding firms since recent research indicates that these seem to have been the most difficult to serve successfully.

Refinancing Assets

The takeover event provides an opportunity for successful bidders to restructure the financial assets and liabilities of the target company to the benefit of the newly combined or successor company. This process is commonly referred to as "financial entrepreneurship." The classic case of financial entrepreneurship is replacing eq-

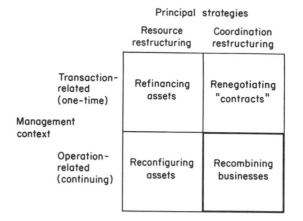

Figure 7.5. Value creation in mergers and takeovers.

uity with debt by financing the takeover with borrowed money, thereby lowering the successor company's cost of capital employed. For example, in its "friendly" takeover of The Continental Group—a conglomerate comprised of packaging, timber, energy, and insurance business units, which, at the time, was trying to escape a "hostile" bid from Sir James Goldsmith—Peter Kiewit and Sons ran up a debt-to-equity ratio of nearly 8 to 1 (three times higher than Continental's). Similarly, in its junk bond takeover attempt at CBS, Turner Broadcasting intended to use no equity at all. The resulting company would have had a debt-to-equity ratio in excess of 18 to 1 (in contrast to CBS's pre-takeover ratio of 0.4 to 1). In addition to the benefits of leverage, takeovers also provide the opportunity of writing up the assets of the newly acquired company, thereby creating new depreciation tax shields for the successor company. CBS in its purchase of Ziff Davis's magazine business wrote up the assets—principally subscription lists—nearly tenfold. The depreciation flowing from a write-up of these assets from under $30 million to nearly $300 million provided CBS with nearly $75 million in additional cash flow. In a maneuver that eventually led to revisions in the tax law concerning partial liquidations, U.S. Steel recouped over $1 billion in tax benefits from its write-up and sub-

sequent depreciation of Marathon Oil's Yates oil field. Even tightened regulations, however, have not prevented General Motors from writing up the book value of EDS's existing contracts and software, thereby realizing new amortization tax benefits in excess of $1 billion.

From an administrative point of view, not only are the benefits of refinancing assets easiest to achieve, but they may well be largest, too. For the right company, increased leverage and depreciation tax benefits might lead to a 60 to 70% increase in the value of the transaction to the successful bidders. We should hasten to add, however, that these benefits are not necessarily automatic or significant. Certain economic assets—namely, those with little accumlated depreciation, such as Ziff Davis's magazine subscription list and Marathon's Yates oil field—are far more valuable than others, such as Continental's packaging plants.

Tax benefits such as these are readily available to all takeover players, since they flow from the U.S. government through its tax codes. In the case of Continental, the more than $1 billion in value created for Continental's shareholders in the form of a tender premium is approximately the same as the financial benefits accruing to Peter Kiewit and Sons from the tax shield provided by increased interest and depreciation charges. While these benefits can accrue to the company over many years, their present value is readily capitalized. Thus, the benefits associated with these financial moves are typically throught of as being one-time or one-period returns. (Whether or not these benefits represent net tax losses to the government is debatable. At the very least, however, they do result in the transfer of tax bills from one set of taxpayers to another.[9])

Renegotiating Contracts

The takeover event can also provide an opportunity for acquiring firms to create economic value through coordination restructuring—e.g., by negotiating more favorable "contracts" or agreements with managers, employees, suppliers, and shareholders of a target firm. Such revisions of agency contracts comprise an important form of co-ordination restructuring; in contrast to asset restructuring, this strategy can lower the cost of running the enterprise relative to the market or competing organizations.

In today's environment, there are multiple ways that such coordination restructurings are employed. Some are formalized into policy processes of firms such as periodically negotiated labor contracts and supply arrangements. Others, like bankruptcy proceedings, are administered by the judicial system to ensure widespread confidence in the process. Some, like the Chrysler bailout or failing-firm ESOPs, are dealt with on a more or less *ad hoc* basis when one constituency feels enough pressure to change. While bankruptcy is perhaps the best-understood form of coordination restructuring, takeovers also provide opportunities to review and revise existing relationships. Thus, in its takeover of McLough Steel, Tang Industries renegotiated long-term supplier contracts on much more favorable terms. Similarly, Frank Lorenzo, shortly after his takeover of chronically unprofitable Continental Airlines, filed for bankruptcy in order to revamp totally an uncompetitive cost structure. High-cost labor agreements were broken as Lorenzo turned Continental into a low-cost, discount carrier. So distasteful were these wage deductions to organized labor that the unions representing TWA's pilots and mechanics joined Mr. Carl Icahn—a noted corporate "raider" and "greenmailer"—in making a counter-tender offer against a board-approved tender offer for TWA by Lorenzo's Texas Air. In this case, competition between bidding firms for TWA provided the incentive for TWA's unions to make concessions to their preferred bidder. As a result, the airline's future cost of retaining and coordinating critical human resources may decline by several hundred million dollars in the near term—a clear benefit to Mr. Icahn and his backers who have taken on a large debt burden to purchase a chronically unprofitable airline, and to TWA's employees who are understandably interested in job security in a stagnant industry. Such open conflicts are a rare, but nonetheless instructive, example of a one-time, downward revision of agency or contracting costs associated with the takeover event itself.

A particularly dramatic example of value creation stemming from transaction-related coordination restructuring is the takeover of The Continental Group, referred to earlier. Despite being cast as the "white knight" in a friendly (friendlier) deal, Kiewit's senior managers recognized that not only would substantial assets have to be sold to pay off the takeover debt but the company's coordinating mechanism, the corporate office, was not working efficiently. Kiewit thus moved to restructure the coordinating mechanism of this multi-business corporation by closing the corporate office and, in effect, canceling the contracts between the corporation and headquarters managers and staff through involuntary layoffs. It is reported that 300 to 500 managers and supporting staff at the Darien corporate office were laid off. Not surprisingly, Continental's management turned very bitter about Peter Kiewit's friendly merger. As it turned out, the value created for Kiewit's shareholders (and its managers) who bought into the new company flowed in large part from Continental's prior management cadre. Indeed, the nearly $800 million in estimated value accruing to Kiewit from its takeover of The

Continental Group is very close to the capitalized value of the $50 million savings in annual corporate-office coordination costs that were eliminated.

Reconfiguring Assets

Over the months and years following a corporate takeover or merger, there are often potential opportunities to create real economic value through restructuring the business' assembly of resources around a production or transformation process. Usually, this entails basic strategic decisions about the boundaries between the business and the marketplace and what assets or unique competences the business really needs to compete successfully in those businesses. Asset restructuring can include reconfiguring or reshaping the business of the acquired company into a more profitable format, as in the case of Black and Decker's acquisition of the McCulloch chain saw business and GE's small–household appliance group or Emerson Electric's acquisition of Poulan chain saw, Insinkerator, and Hobart's small appliances. Numerous companies have built their strategies around these asset-restructuring opportunities—companies like James River in paper, White Consolidated and Magic Chef in appliances, Hasbro in toys, and Petri Stores in women's apparel retailing. Figuring out the right competitive strategy, getting the acquired organization to accept it, and implementing it effectively are not, however, skills for which many acquisitive companies have become well known or admired. Even such high-powered organizations as Philip Morris, Coca-Cola, and General Mills have had their share of problems in making acquisitions fit (as PM's experience with Miller Beer and Seven-Up, Coke's trials with wholesale beverages, and General Mills' divestiture of Parker Brothers toys and Lacoste apparel testify).

Reconfiguring or reshaping the portfolios of businesses of diversified companies is another potential source of value creation. To a large extent, this entails unraveling past strategic mistakes or divesting businesses that have no synergy with each other or are worth more to other investors than to the company. Although corporate takeovers are not a prerequisite to creating value through the reshaping of business portfolios—as the large number of divestitures by Gulf & Western Industries during 1984 and 1985 has shown—a change in ownership can be an effective catalyst. Sometimes this is a clear part of the takeover strategy, as it was in Hanson Trust's takeover battle for SCM Corp., Pantry Pride's takeover of Revlon, or GAF's bid for Union Carbide. More often, it is the result of refinancing pressures following a takeover where the successful acquirer can no longer afford unproductive, yet valuable, assets. Following its takeover of Continental, Kiewit sold Continental's capital-intensive, low-free-cash-flow energy and insurance businesses while retaining its highly profitable packaging and timber businesses. Similarly, Allied Corporation totally reconfigured the Bendix portfolio of businesses following that bizarre takeover battle. Within a year of this "white knight" takeover, Allied generated sufficient cash to cover the $925 million cash component of its $1.8 billion payment for Bendix. Although referred to by the press as "asset stripping," Allied successfully sold the businesses, real estate, and securities that did not fit the needs or skill base of the newly combined operations. This reconfiguration of assets left Allied in a position to pay for the entire Bendix acquisition in just three years and to profit over the long term from integrating the remaining Bendix assets into Allied's diversified operations.

Recombining Businesses

In contrast to the unraveling of past strategic mistakes through asset divestitures and financial restructuring, mergers and takeovers can also help companies create real economic value by recombining the assets and revising coordination mechanisms of their portfolio businesses. A successful recombination of businesses is most likely to follow related business mergers where (1) increased productivity of corporate resources through operating efficiencies, (2) improved competitive position accuring from increased size of the business, and (3) reduction in long-run average costs can lead to an improved risk-return profile for the business through a reduction in the variability of a company's income stream and/or a larger income stream than that available from simple portfolio investments by investors.

In the world of takeovers, these business recombinations are normally closely related to each other. A related-supplementary target provides the acquirer with greater access to new customers and markets rather than totally new assets or products. Related-complementary target businesses provide the acquirer with new products, assets, or skills for currently served product markets rather than access to new markets. Shelton's new study of 114 mergers between 1962 and 1983, referred to earlier, shows that bidding firms gain the most from related mergers, in general, and related-supplementary mergers, more specifically. While Shelton's methodology only captures estimates of value created for the successful bidding firm over a limited period surrounding the merger transaction, the study strongly suggests that the potential for long-run value creation is greatest in related-supplementary mergers where the top executives of both bidding and target firms (1) share similar functional skills and common managerial premises and (2) are therefore in a good position to develop collectively and implement programs that use the assets of the target firms in new or more efficient ways.

Three recent combinations—Champion's acquisition of St. Regis, IBM's of Rolm, and General Motors' of Electronic Data Systems—highlight the intensely *managerial* process of recombining business in ways that create real economic value. For example, Champion International found that its "friendly" rescue of St. Regis led it to a strategy quite different from the one it had envisioned. By combining the superior controls systems and production quality of St. Regis with Champion's low-cost supplies and established distribution system, the recombined "Champion" was the largest, lowest-cost

competitor in coated white papers—the most attractive segment in the forest products industry. With the ability to concentrate resources on a high-payoff marketplace, Champion is now following an asset divestiture program at St. Regis comparable to that undertaken by James Goldsmith in his less friendly takeovers of Diamond International and Crown Zellerback. Nevertheless, the principal item on the agenda of the new senior-management group is how to integrate their two paper manufacturing organizations successfully.

In the IBM-Rolm case, the problem was how to overcome a corporate culture which did not share information with outsiders. To "Big Blue" it did not matter that it owned 30% of Rolm, that Rolm was a stunning success and IBM a dismal failure in PBXs, and that PBXs were crucial to IBM if it was to successfully enter the telecommunications market. With Rolm in the role of a stepchild, IBM could not push itself to share information, particularly information about its future product plans. Only after Rolm's senior management recognized the futility of battling this corporate culture did it give up its cherished Silicon Valley independence and convince IBM senior management that the substantial benefits of working together were available only through a full merger.

Finally, GM's Roger Smith recognized that the one important way he could alter the course of his company's automotive business that was becoming increasingly incapable of competing in the global marketplace was through restructuring and streamlining its information system. By merging with Ross Perot's EDS, a company characterized by both high technical competence and aggressive on-site management, Smith has achieved more changes in its information and control system in 2 years than in the previous 30. Such change has not come easily to GM, however. Policy disputes between Smith and Perot over the management of GM's automotive operations and controversies over intracompany billing led to Perot's controversial and costly buy-out by GM. Yet by giving EDS management a far larger role in GM management, Smith was able to accelerate the process of organizational change that GM needed to ensure future competitiveness.

Here is where coordination restructuring and asset restructuring become inevitably intertwined. In order to exploit the potential benefits of "reconfiguring" a portfolio of businesses, through asset divestitures or product line acquisitions, senior managers often need to "recombine" the operating businesses into a new set of organization relationships comprised of reporting structures and coordinating mechanisms. This resource and coordination restructuring is precisely the managerial agenda of the new GM/EDS merger, the partial mergers leading to the recent IBM/Rolm/MCI linkup, and the Champion/St. Regis and the Chevron/Gulf acquisitions. A successful recombining of businesses will lead to increased asset utilization and bureaucratic efficiency.

Each of the situations discussed here (and depicted in Figure 7.5) has the potential for creating value for the various constituencies comprising the bidding firm. Anecdotal evidence and a deepening stream of empirical research suggest that at least some companies have been able to turn this potential value into reality. Whether or not future mergers and takeovers will be more likely to serve the long-term interests of bidding firms is not clear. Our casework and analysis suggest, however, a cautious answer. Value creation depends, to a large extent, on the management context as well as the business strategy being pursued by the bidding firm. The benefits of refinancing assets, revising contracts comprising a business enterprise, and reconfiguring businesses will accrue primarily to outside investors who can mobilize the interests of capital. The auction process that currently characterizes takeovers means that many of these benefits will also be passed on to selling shareholders through higher acquisition prices. The benefits of recombining businesses into organizations that can compete more effectively and efficiently than disassociated firms operating in relevant product markets also appear to offer significant potential for value creation. But this increased

effectiveness and efficiency is based upon shared goals and a willingness to cooperate among the managers of merged enterprises. Where this condition does not exist, prospects seem less bright.

IMPACT OF HOSTILE TENDERS ON VALUE CREATION

In conventional Wall Street parlance, a hostile takeover is usually described as any offer not currently favored by the management of the target firm. Yet as every experienced merger participant knows, few mergers are ever completely friendly. Continental Group's management found this out when their white knight rescuer, Peter Kiewit & Sons, subsequently eliminated the corporate office and liquidated much of the corporation. In a vastly different kind of merger, many of General Motors' managers began wondering who had acquired whom as EDS's managers began dismembering and rebuilding GM's computer-based information systems.

To complicate matters further, takeovers that are deemed "hostile" by the target company's management are often warmly embraced by the company's investors or other constituencies. None of Boone Pickens's recent forays against major oil companies can be labeled "friendly," yet merely the rumor of a takeover attempt by Mesa Petroleum brings dozens of investors and billions of dollars to Pickens's doorstep. Similarly, TWA's management vehemently resisted Carl Icahn's initial overtures and embraced Texas Air's Frank Lorenzo, only to find the company's unions, united in their dislike of Lorenzo's labor policies, negotiating their own deals with Icahn. Finally, a "hostile offer" at one point in time may be warmly embraced at another. Richardson-Vicks initially scorned Procter & Gamble's advances, only to leap into its arms three months later in order to avoid Unilever's tender offer. Similarly, General Foods recently found it hard to say no to Philip Morris's sweetened terms.

In short, it is very difficult to come up with a clear definition of a hostile takeover.

The degree of hostility in a transaction depends upon who is describing the event and at what time. If looked at as a purely contextual issue, however, the role that hostility plays in analyzing corporate takeovers becomes more understandable. One way to structure the analysis is to begin with the presumption that hostility—in contrast to integrity, for example—can be readily bought and sold in the market for corporate control. A second useful presumption is that the issue of hostility for each constituency comprising the firm inevitably comes down to whether or not it expects to be better or worse off from the takeover. From the perspective of each participant, a takeover is hostile or friendly to the extent that it reduces or increases the incentives and rewards for those participating in the enterprise.

As an example of such a contextual analysis, consider the differing interests that often arise between investors and managers. Investors want returns in excess of risk-adjusted rates, returns which give rise to market values for assets in excess of replacement costs. They rely upon the economic competition of the marketplace to drive both corporate and managerial performances in this direction over time. With diversified portfolios, investors tend to focus most on overall portfolio performance and less on individual company performance. Managers, on the other hand, have a very different agenda. They are totally focused on their company's performance from which their compensation, perquisites, social prestige, and psychological rewards flow. Since managers' portfolios are not diversified, they must be concerned with the task of protecting their business-specific and personal performance.

The takeover event often introduces a wedge between the interests of investors and managers. As passive suppliers of capital to the modern corporation, investors have had virtually no choice but to accept or reject the corporate performance and allocation decisions of incumbent management. The takeover, however, offers investors an alternative—i.e., a performance contract with a new set of managers. By offering the suppliers of capital a much better deal for their investment, the bidding firm seeks to become the new architect of the organization's strategy. No wonder that it is incumbent management that labels takeovers as either "friendly" or "hostile." When threatened with the loss (or reduction) of their jobs, and therefore, their "personal" value creation, incumbent managers obviously label the takeover "hostile." If, on the other hand, incumbent managers become part of the governing management structure, thereby preserving the opportunity for personal-value creation, the takeover is termed "friendly." Similarly, a takeover which is hostile to their managerial well-being can become friendly if the financial rewards on their stock options are high enough or their severance payments substantial enough.

Understanding that perceptions of hostility reflect the different interests of participants in the soon-to-be-combined enterprise, we can now turn to the impact of hostile tenders on value creation. The most salient observation that we can make, after a decade of study, is that there is little empirical evidence suggesting that hostile takeovers eliminate the chance to create value for bidding firms pursuing strategies of resource restructuring—i.e., what we have called "refinancing assets" and "reconfiguring businesses." Neither is there reason to expect that the success of strategies focused on "renegotiating contracts" with suppliers of financial or human capital depend upon friendly mergers. Indeed, revising such contracts and related expectations is normally a highly stressful, conflict-laden activity where existing constituencies in the enterprise openly question each other's motives and actions. For firms pursuing such restructuring strategies, hostile takeovers may actually lead to the creation of more economic value than so-called friendly acquisitions.

As previously pointed out, however, the benefits accruing from strategies shown in the northeast, northwest, and southwest quadrants of Figure 7.5 are not sustainable over time. Furthermore, takeover strategies focused on transaction-related resource restructuring do not affect the capacity of the core business to respond and adapt to a dynamic, competitive environment. In contrast, the takeover strategies represented by the southeast quadrant do. Here the production process and coordination systems of two formerly distinct organizations are combined into a new enterprise which, hopefully, can compete more successfully in the changing marketplace. This increased competitive ability only comes about, however, through the dedication of the firm's top managers to identifying, implementing, and exploiting those opportunities for value creation. Difficult under the best of conditions, this strategy of "recombining business" places great demands upon managers of a bidding firm involved in a hostile takeover. Without shared goals and a willingness to cooperate no top manager can successfully perform those tasks basic to value creation discussed above. Thus, in light of our framework of analysis, the major source of value creation, represented by the integration of operations and coordination systems in the southeast quadrant of Figure 7.5, is severely threatened by most hostile takeovers.

Recombining businesses, we hasten to add, is not the natural realm of financiers or takeover artists. Rather, it is the realm of operating managers who have mastered the tasks of value creation in large organizations. To these managers, the successful meshing of either two production systems which emphasize very different performance criteria or two organizations whose cultures value different beliefs requires an infinite attention to detail at every level in the organization. Production process must be rationalized, coordination systems integrated, information flows redirected, reporting relationships restructured, and disparate beliefs harmonized. Managerial dissention can derail the most brilliant strategy. When a business recombination requires the support of a disenfranchised management group—such as that arising in any unfriendly takeover—many of these activities stop dead in their tracks. Critical information is lost as the losing managers leave, compliance costs jump as unwilling managers refuse to cooperate, and control costs skyrocket as functional activities no longer smoothly coordinate themselves.

To sustain the process of value creation, therefore, it is not enough for a takeover artist to renegotiate contracts, engage in refinancing assets, or to reconfigure asset portfolios. Each can be a significant source of value creation, but each contributes little to the ongoing competitiveness of the surviving enterprise. If the takeover is to result in a business with an enhanced competitive position and the ability to generate returns at least as great as those of the marketplace, then the takeover must eventually entail some sort of recombination where the productive assets and coordination systems are restructured into a unique package. It is by no means clear that for many of today's takeover entrepreneurs, overseeing the trials and tribulations of living in and coping with the idiosyncrasies of organizations and product markets is to their liking or aptitude.

CLAIMS ON VALUE CREATED IN TAKEOVERS

In the most up-to-date research report on the goals of U.S. enterprise, Donaldson and Lorsch show that senior managers seek—above all else—growth and financial self-sufficiency.[10] When these goals are achieved, senior managers have the opportunity to act independently and to allocate resources and rewards according to their own judgments and vision. Corporate takeovers challenge this self-sufficiency.

In contests for corporate control, managers of bidding firms end up competing with the managers of target firms, each promising their investors better returns. Since many managers of bidding firms are willing to accept less financial self-sufficiency than incumbent managers, bidding firms can drive their cost of capital down by assuming a heavy debt burden and, therefore, afford to offer higher prices to investors for their shares. Managers of the target firm are, in turn, forced to demonstrate how they can match these increased returns. Thus, in a takeover situation, power over the future of the enterprise tends to flow from incumbent management to investors.

As investors exercise their power to select who receives the right to manage a specific enterprise, they directly influence the distribution of potential gains flowing from a takeover or merger. But so, too, do the strategies being pursued by the bidding firm. Our sense of the matter is that when takeovers do not involve the recombination of businesses into new entities with new coordination requirements and ongoing operating management needs, firms pursuing hostile takeovers can create value for both selling and bidding shareholders—with selling shareholders receiving the lion's share in an auction environment. However, when takeover strategies are aimed at gaining unique competitive advantages from the recombination of businesses into a new entity, negotiated transactions generally increase the changes that whatever value is created will accrue to the bidding firm. For this reason we have argued that the managers and directors of bidding firms need to think through the details of their takeover strategies if they are to serve the long-term interests of their shareholders. Creating value through recombining businesses depends to a large extent upon a cooperative internal environment where new coordinating arrangements with incumbent management can be negotiated. In the absence of such negotiations, a promising takeover can quickly turn into a financial and organizational bust.

NOTES

1. W. T. Grimm, *Mergerstat Review,* 1984.

2. For a full discussion of value creation, see M. S. Salter and W. A. Weinhold, *Value Creation and General Management* (Harvard Business School Working Paper 9–384–080, 1984). See also C. I. Barnard, *The Functions of the Executive* (Cambridge, Mass.: Harvard University Press, 1938); J. L. Bower, *Managing the Resource Allocation Process* (Boston: Harvard Business School, 1970); R. M. Cyert and J. G. March, *A Behavioral Theory of the Firm* (Englewood Cliffs, N.J.: Prentice-Hall, 1963); G. Donaldson, *Managing Corporate Wealth* (New York: Praeger, 1984); P. F. Drucker, *The Practice of Management* (New York: Harper & Row, 1954); E. F. Fama, "Agency Problems and the Theory of the Firm," *Journal of Political Economy* **88** (2), 288–307 (1980); M. C. Jensen and W. H. Meckling, "Theory of the Firm: Managerial Behavior, Agency Costs, and Ownership Structure," *Journal of Financial Economics* 3(4), 305–360 (1976), M. S. Salter and W. A. Weinhold, *Diversification Through Acquisition* (New York: Free Press, 1979); H. A. Simon. *Administrative Behavior,* 2nd ed. (New York: Free Press, 1965); O. S. Williamson, *Markets and Hierarchies* (New York: Free Press, 1975); O. S. Williamson, "The Economics of Organization: The Transaction Cost Approach," *American Journal of Sociology* 83(3), 548–577 (1981).

3. M. C. Jensen and R. S. Ruback, "The Market for Corporate Control: The Scientific Evidence," *Journal of Financial Economics* **11,** 5–50 (April 1983). See also M. C. Jensen, "Takeovers: Folklore and Science," *Harvard Business Review* **62** 109–121 (November–December 1984).

4. L. M. Shelton, The Role of Strategic Business Fits in Creating Gains to Acquisition (Ph.D. dissertation, Harvard University, 1985).

5. M. Lubatkin and H. M. O'Neill, Risk, Return and Acquisition Strategy (paper presented to Strategic Management Society Meetings, Barcelona, 1985).

6. F. M. Scherer, Mergers, Sell-DPFS, and Managerial Behavior (mimeo, November 1984).

7. D. J. Ravenscraft and F. M. Scherer, Chapter 12 of this volume.

8. McKinsey Economics, Creating Value with Acquisitions and Divestitures (mimeo, May 1985).

9. For a discussion of tax effects associated with mergers, see Chapter 19 of this volume, also see L. Lowenstein, "No More Cozy Management Buyouts," *Harvard Business Review* **64,** 147–156 (January–February 1986).

10. G. Donaldson and J. W. Lorsch, *Decision-Making at the Top* (New York: Basic Books, 1983).

8

Comment

VICTOR BRUDNEY

Professor Coffee has offered a novel and imaginative thesis to explain the import of recent variations in the takeover phenomenon. I do not know if he intends it to have broader implications for the theory of the firm in general—not merely in the takeover context. But examining its broader implications may shed light on its acceptability as an analysis of the takeover.

Coffee's thesis appears to be that in evaluating the takeover phenomenon, it is improper to view the shareholder "as the critical actor who has alone accepted the entrepreneurial role [and] is [therefore] entitled to appropriate the full takeover premium." He suggests that "other constituencies—most importantly managers and employees, but also ultimately the state . . . have a legitimate claim either to share in the takeover premium or participate in the [takeover] negotiations."

Why should this concern for the entitlements of constituencies other than shareholders arise at the occasion of takeovers but not at other times? If there are legitimate claims for them to share in the residual returns on the occasion of takeover, why not at all times in the operation of the firm? In particular, for example, why is not management entitled to all it can get from stockholders in management buy-outs? And why aren't workers and the community entitled to protection, by way of compensation or otherwise, against plant closings caused by sales of divisions that are not takeover-induced?

Coffee answers that only in recent years has the operation of the takeover phenom-

enon produced an effect that justifies special concern with allocating the residual returns only to stockholders, a concern not present during normal operation. The relentless cupidity of stockholders has fueled a pattern of takeover which has resulted in a significant increase in risk to the enterprise and a shifting of a fair portion of that risk to other participants without any compensating increase in returns to those other participants—particularly top management and middle management.[1] In effect, altered circumstances, brought on by stockholder cupidity, have altered the import of the implicit contract between stockholders on the one side and managers, employees, and presumably the community on the other side—to the advantage of stockholders; the terms of that contract, therefore, should be adjusted.

The unusual increase and shift in risk in recent years Coffee explains by two phenomena which he identifies as the increased leverage produced by junk bonds and the bust-up acquisition designed to realize the difference between the breakup asset value of a firm and its lower stock market value.

It is not clear that (1) the cost of bust-ups to others than management or (2) the added risk caused by the junk bonds is either as new to the takeover process or as significant as he suggests. The bust-ups are not sales of enterprises or parts of enterprises piece by piece under the hammer. They are transfers of going concerns, presumably for better use by the purchaser. If the purchaser is local, few jobs are lost—

except possibly for management and middle management—and the community is not likely to be seriously affected.

If the purchaser moves the enterprise, the old community is indeed adversely affected, but presumably another community gets the jobs and related goodies.

There may well be obligations to the community and the enterprise's displaced lower-income employees for mitigation of the effects of any such move. But the case is less clear for entitlements of middle management, and certainly less clear for top management. There is reason to believe that loss of jobs to middle management is not a function of takeovers. It is going on all over the country, as operations are tightened to meet competition: Presumably the paring down of middle management is economically efficient in a private, for-profit economy whether or not it is the takeover that induces leaner operations and the associated human costs.

If top management's loss is not anticipated by it in the *ex ante* arrangements, there seems to be no dearth of "compensatory" management buyouts. The latter raise more problems about treatment of stockholders than about disadvantaging managements.

Junk bonds apparently create two evils—first, a risk that the business will fail because it is too heavily indebted and cannot meet its fixed charges and payback schedules, and second, a risk that the lenders (and society) will suffer when the borrower defaults. Whether the junk bonds are an evil either to lenders or to borrowers requires considerably more information than we presently have.

At least so far as concerns all employees and probably most constituents other than management, it is important to distinguish between *financial* failure of the enterprise because of the debt load and the nonfailure of the *productive* enterprise. The enterprise is likely to continue to exist through the insolvency reorganization process, as is appropriate if it is operationally viable. In that case, the effect of the junk bonds may not be seriously to injure the community or the workers or related enterprises. To be sure, management and middle management may be hurt. But whether they should be protected against the consequences of such hurt raises questions about who should bear the consequences of managerially tolerated slack and excess debt. Certainly, there is a problem with suggesting that, *ex ante,* the stockholders of the target should share their takeover premiums with the architects of the junk bonds and the target's inefficiencies.

Whether the lender will—or should—suffer from the risk of junk bonds depends, in fair part, upon how knowledgeably they acquired them.

Possibly Coffee's fear of junk bonds is justified, at least as a threat to the lenders. But even if so justified, it is hard to see it as a reason for requiring shareholders to transfer part of the premiums they receive to nonshareholder constituents of the enterprise, who either have little or no relationship to any ultimate worthlessness of such bonds to their holder or may indeed be responsible for their issuance.

Passing those issues, Coffee's suggestion seems to be that the stockholders receive unique returns from the takeover process. If the takeover premium is, as all or most of it seems to be, economically justified by the criteria of a free-market, profit-seeking economy, it is hard to see why the stockholder is less entitled to those "unique" premiums than to any other aspect of the firm's residual return. Possibly the free-market, profit-seeking economy does not provide adequately for many of the participants in the firm. But that is a reason for examining generally how to redistribute costs and benefits from the operation of the firm among its participants and others—including the workers and the community which creates the firm-specific infrastructure that Coffee talks about. Possibly the cost of capital should reflect the need to care for unrepresented constituents. But any such examination requires development of criteria by which to tell which constituents of the firm are giving or getting too much and which too little, and who should redistribute what to whom.

The suggestion that top management (or even middle management) should be regarded as the proxy for, or agent of, such other constituents as are entitled to share in stockholder premiums raises all the problems embraced in the concept of agency costs and management discretion in functioning as agents of stockholders—and lacks even a theory for, let alone a basis for systematic constraints on, managerial discretion as agent for the other constitutents.

In any event, even if stockholders should be deemed to receive some unusual gain in takeovers, questions remain as to (1) why they should have to distribute a portion of it to other constituencies and (2) how to identify those constituencies and divide the redistribution among them.

To the first question, Coffee answers that takeover is becoming the "mechanism by which shareholders may impose their risk preferences on managers and employees" and "their entitlement to do so . . . remains open to debate."

It is unclear which shareholders Coffee has in mind, unless he homogenizes them all, on the theory that they can all diversify and gain as target shareholders what they lose as bidder shareholders and therefore may be treated as a homogeneous group. But as Coffee recognizes, not all stockholders are diversified; and there is evidence to suggest that institutional investors do not act uniformly or unequivocally to favor the takeover phenomenon.

Coffee's analysis raises the question of whether it is shareholders or managements that stimulate bidders to seek bust-up takeovers and corporations to issue junk bonds and to incur the possibly wasteful transactions costs imposed by bankers, lawyers, accountants, etc., in the takeover process.

What proportion of bids is fueled by greenmailers or investment bankers financing bust-ups is hard to tell. But it is difficult to believe, in the absence of evidence, that most bids are not made by substantial operating corporations and have been decided upon by stockholders rather than by well-established managements.

By the same token, junk bonds are issued by corporations at the direction of managements.

If a shift in risk is occurring by reason of the takeover phenomenon, it occurs largely by act of bidders' managers (and defensively by the target's managers). And by the same token, if wasteful costs are incurred for bankers, lawyers, etc., they are generated by managers, not stockholders. The nice question is whether the managers are pursuing their own interests at the expense of their stockholders' interests.

If managements thus contribute significantly to increased risk to non-stockholder constituencies, should they (as well as stockholders) be asked to compensate others? Coffee seeks to have them compensated for the very risk they create for, and shift to, others.

With respect to *how much* of the premium the stockholders should distribute, questions arise as to whether other beneficiaries of the process should contribute—e.g., the investment banking community that stimulates the transactions and distributes the junk bonds? The commercial banks that underpin much of the inflated credit involved? The lawyers, accountants, and other beneficiaries of the transactions costs that Coffee deplores? The new workers and communities to which the "sold" business moves? How much should stockholders be allowed to keep so as to permit the cost of capital to be most efficiently and equitably determined?

With respect to *who* should be the distributees, there may be good reason to consider whether the community and the lower-level employees are entitled to some portion of the premium—for retraining or otherwise. But why should any of the windfall be redistributed to management?

Among the array of possible claimants to share in such windfalls, many could not have played much of a role either in causing or in averting the disaster on which their claim to compensation or offset rests. And many have no resources to offset the consequences of their displacement. Management is, if not the only constituency that can protect itself against the disaster, at least the one best able to do so. It is pure fiction to suggest that stockholders and management have a bargained-for contract or that the arrangements on entry and during management's tenure are other than unilaterally determined by management, constrained only by management's perception of how much it can take and how little it need give. It is hard, therefore, to see the case for equity requiring a protective adjustment in management's status at takeover time.

Efficiency raises still a different question. To the extent that another cost of the bust-up takeover phenomenon is said to be the loss of management's loyalty, and Coffee seeks remedies to preserve that loyalty, he indeed is opening a Pandora's box. Possibly the risk of such displacement will result in loosening management's loyalty and thereby causing it either to charge more for its services or to put less into its work—to the ultimate detriment of society. There are some who suggest that management's loyalty runs (and inevitably must run) more to itself than to any other constituency. Whether or not that is true, each of Coffee's propositions about the role of management vis-à-vis either stockholders or employees raises complex problems of social psychology and organization theory that transcend the takeover phenomenon and indeed go beyond privately owned enterprise—how to stimulate and how to constrain management in order to induce optimal performance. His references to the state or society as the ultimate bearer of the losses resulting from management disaffection suggest the need for a much broader inquiry than simply into management's role and stockholders' entitlements.

Finally, there are questions about the nature and efficacy of Coffee's remedy for the evil he sees. He appears to believe that enough societal good is produced by the takeover process to require that it not be prohibited or even impeded. His primary prescription seems to be to entitle management to enjoy some part of the premiums that bidders pay to acquire the target. Whether characterized as golden parachutes or by any other name, the remedy

would give managers discretion to decide how to add to their benefits in the event of a takeover. Coffee does not spell out how giving management greater access to the trough at takeover time than it has at other times either will be a deterrent to the takeovers that cause the problem or can be justified by the legitimate needs of management.

The case for management's need for more protection at takeover time is hard to see in light of the immense discretion that it has during the operation of the company to reward itself generously for its sacrifice in limiting its talents to firm-specific dimensions. Moreover, it is well able, as the history of the past few years demonstrates, to spend great quantities of company funds resisting takeovers which it says it thinks are not in the interests of stockholders, and to itself become the new owner of the enterprise by way of management buy-outs. To give management additional rewards when its resistance fails requires some justification that I don't think Coffee offers.

If there is little justification for giving management a larger share of the takeover premium, there is even less efficacy in doing so if the goal is to induce it to dampen efforts at bust-up takeovers or resort to junk bonds. The takeover is not fueled by the target's management. It originates with bidders' managements and is stimulated by financial intermediaries. Neither of those will be deterred one whit by increasing the rewards to targets' managements in the event of takeover. Possibly, as Coffee suggests, to the extent that targets' managements are thus rewarded, they may resist takeovers less determinedly and thus save on the transactions costs involved in resistance. But what criteria should determine how to allocate the benefits of that saving (as well as the takeover premium) among the assorted constituencies? How will Coffee's proposed relief for management operate to curtail the growth of the evils he fears? Why will it not have the opposite effect—of encouraging such takeovers—unless a comprehensive scheme is adopted for regulating the process and allocating its costs and benefits among all the "legitimate" claimants on the enterprise? I do not understand Coffee to advocate any such scheme.

NOTE

1. Coffee's suggestion that stockholders thus compel managers to take added risks is offered as in some sense a correction of the counterproductive risk averseness of management that is said (by Berle and Means and others) to reflect the divergence of interest between management and stockholders. The suggestion assimilates increased *business* risk (which, in a rational world, should increase the firm's return) with increased *financial* risk, which is likely to have a more remote and much smaller impact on the firm's aggregate return.

9

Comment: Golden Parachutes and the Myth of the Web

MELVIN A. EISENBERG

A major question posed by the modern takeover phenomenon is what role law should have in this area. More specifically, the question is, what limits, if any, should be placed on offerors, target managers, and target shareholders, and what affirmative steps, if any, should be taken to change the legal rules of play? In answering this question, as in answering all questions of what the law should be, three broad types of criteria are relevant: policies, moral norms (that is, considerations of fairness), and administrative considerations. I will focus in this chapter on certain issues of policy and fairness.

As regards strictly economic issues, the underlying policy aim of the law is the faciliation and encouragement of an economic system that promises to deliver goods and services in the most efficient manner, thereby maximizing national wealth. The maximization of shareholder wealth is often a means toward that end, because legal standards that maximize shareholder wealth serve to hold managers to an efficiency objective and to promote continuing infusions of capital into the equity market. Furthermore, if shareholders invest in the justified expectation that managers will act to maximize shareholder wealth, the law should take that expectation into account as a matter of fairness. And all other things being equal, the creation of shareholder wealth is obviously a good thing in itself.

There is evidence that takeovers create wealth for shareholders of particular target corporations. It also seems safe to assume that shareholders invest in the justified ex-

pectation that managers will act to maximize shareholder wealth. The issue then is, are there considerations suggesting that a legal regime that facilitates takeover bids would subserve the policy of maximizing national wealth, would create unfairness, or, for that matter, would not maximize wealth for shareholders as a class?

Many economists have argued that the interests of managers may not be wholly aligned with that of shareholders because (among other things) managers may have a preference for corporate growth, and for expense on such matters as perquisites and staff, beyond what is profit maximizing. John Coffee's paper adds significantly to this line of analysis by bringing out the extent to which managers' interests may also fail to be aligned with those of shareholders because of a difference in attitude toward risk. While shareholders may hold a diversified portfolio, managers are typically overinvested in their own corporations and often tied closely to their corporations by bonds that are often not easy to sever. Therefore, managers may be more risk averse in making corporate decisions than shareholders would want them to be. So, for example, managers may have a preference for greater retained earnings and equity and less debt than would be efficient, because as corporate debt increases, so typically does risk.

Building on this base, Coffee goes on to convincingly argue that the takeover phenomenon has increased the general level of managerial risk. The very potential for a takeover increases managerial risk, because it makes managerial tenure less se-cure. Furthermore, a frequent response to the threat of a takeover is leveraging up (i.e., increasing the corporation's debt level), and that response increases corpo-rate risk because the greater the leverage, the greater are the fixed-interest payments that must be covered. Coffee suggests that the law should respond to this increase in risk by taking a tolerant view of golden parachutes (contracts for extremely large severance payments that are triggered by a change of control), subject to the con-straint that such payments would not be tax-deductible unless made pursuant to a plan that did not discriminate among higher- and lower-echelon managers. This suggestion is based on an argument of pol-icy and an argument of fairness. The ar-gument of policy is that the long-run inter-est of shareholders, and presumably of the economic system, is best served when managers are at least moderately secure. The argument of fairness is that the in-creased level of risk resulting from the takeover phenomenon violates an implicit contract with managers.

The argument of fairness is founded in large part on intellectual constructs that originated with certain economists and have now entered some of the legal litera-ture. One such construct is that a corpora-tion is a "web" or "nexus" of contracts. This construct seriously misuses the term "contract." Most types of persons who might be thought of as associated in some significant way with the corporation do not in fact have contracts either with the cor-poration or with each other. Managers be-neath the very top level usually have no contracts, although that may be slowly changing. White-collar workers and unor-ganized blue-collar workers usually have no contracts. Organized blue-collar work-ers have only a very unusual kind of con-tract. Vendors and consumers are likely to have no ongoing contracts, except in a triv-ial sense (such as protection under warran-ties). The local community normally has no contracts. Finally, while the share-holder relationship to the corporation is sometimes characterized as a contract, that

characterization is at best highly oversim-plified. A contract consists of terms that each of the parties has normally seen and signed. The typical shareholder sees noth-ing and signs nothing. To the extent that common stock can be characterized as, or analogized to, a contract, the correct met-aphor is not that the classical bargained-for contract, in which each party is bound by the contract's explicit terms, but the mod-ern form contract of adhesion, in which fair expectations can override explicit terms.

To make up for this lack of real con-tracts, the web-of-contract theorists bor-rowed from labor economics the term "implicit contract." As used in labor economics, that term refers to a noncon-tractual (or at least, not necessarily con-tractual) relationship between a firm and its employees that is treated, for purposes of analyzing the market for labor, *as if* it were a contract.[1] An example is a relation-ship in which employees take lower wages than they could get elsewhere in exchange for a job that has a prospect of less vari-ance in wages, or less prospect of layoff, than would prevail elsewhere. When a law-yer characterizes a state of affairs as a con-tract, he means, normally, that two or more parties have made reciprocal prom-ises in the form of a bargain, or if he is being very precise, that the parties have made a bargain that is legally enforceable. In contrast, the term implicit contract, as used in labor economics, does not require either real promises (express or implied) or a real bargain, still less a legally enforceable bargain. The employee does not (or may not) tell the employer, "I agree to lesser wages if you promise less wage variance, or if you promise not to lay me off," and the employer does not (or may not) make such promises even implicitly.

In many of the relationships that labor economists would call an implicit contract, each party has at best a hope that for rea-sons of self-interest, or perhaps altruism, the other party will act in a certain manner. But a hope that is not rested on a promise is not even a bargain, still less a contract. What the term implicit contract describes is a sociological relationship involving a certain degree of tacit reciprocity. Almost any social relationships, including marriage and friendship, could be analyzed in this manner, as the literature of exchange theory in sociology demonstrates. That a relationship entails hopes and tacit reciprocity does not make it a bargain unless the reciprocity is based on a promise, and does not make it a contract unless the reciprocity is based on a legally enforceable promise. The terms bargain and contract can be used to describe such relationships only metaphorically. "Implicit contracts" are not contracts. "Implicit bargains" are not bargains. Those terms bear no more relationship to real contracts and real bargains than marginal cost bears to average cost.

This metaphorical use of contract and bargain terminology probably didn't matter too much as long as labor economists used the terminology. Perhaps it wouldn't even have mattered too much that it was picked up by economists who called the corporation a web or a nexus of contracts or bargains, despite the fact that it isn't either one of these things, if the metaphors had been confined to strictly economic discourse. Indeed, some of the analysis that has used these metaphors, such as that of Oliver Williamson, has arrived at important results. By and large, however, as in Williamson's work, those results did not turn on the accuracy of the contract and bargain terminology.

Unfortunately, the terminology was also picked up by scholars who began to talk as if "implicit contracts" were real contracts, as if "implicit bargains" were real bargains, and as if the corporation really was a web or nexus of contracts or bargains. To put this differently, the terminology was picked up by scholars who wrongly thought that the terminology was not metaphor but reality, and who derived results from the terminology. For example, some of the scholars who use the web-of-contracts terminology then go on to argue that any provision in a certificate of incorporation should be enforceable, like any other contract term—even, say, a provision in the certificate of a publicly held corporation that varies the duty of loyalty. Others go on

to argue that "managers are not simply hired hands," who serve as agents of the shareholder-owners, but "members of the organization," just as much as shareholders.[2]

Similarly, the web-of-contracts construct leads Coffee to argue that the increased level of risk resulting from the takeover phenomenon violates the manager's implicit contract that he will be discharged only for demonstrated incompetence or impending insolvency. Contracts can be violated. So can bargains. Implicit contracts cannot, because they are neither contracts nor bargains. Managers, of all people, are well able to bargain for themselves. All managers today know the risks of takeovers, and it may safely be assumed that the risks entailed by takeovers have been impounded into managerial salaries.

It might be argued, though, that managers whose employment began before the modern takeover phenomenon are unable to change the terms of their employment so as to impound the resulting increased risk in their salaries, because the lateral mobility of managers is limited. Such an argument would be much too strong. The argument would not apply to managerial employees hired laterally since the takeover phenomenon began. It would also not apply to managers who have lateral mobility but don't exercise it, because the corporation will impound takeover-based insecurity into their salaries to retain them. Nor would the argument apply to entry-level managers, for whom the corporation must bid against other corporations (and for whom, taken as a class, the corporate sector must bid against other sectors). Finally, the argument would apply only weakly to remaining managers—that is, managers who were hired before the modern takeover phenomenon and who have little lateral mobility. Most corporations want to maintain a salary structure that is equitable both horizontally and vertically, at least on a divisionwide basis. Therefore, if increased risk is impounded in the salaries of incoming managers and of managers with lateral mobility, comparable adjustments will normally be made in the salaries of the remaining managers as well.

In short, while golden parachutes may be justified by market considerations, by policy, or even by certain elements of fairness in a particular case, they cannot be justified by the concept that the increased risk level resulting from the takeover phenomenon violates managers' implicit contracts. Whether a particular golden parachute is fair depends on a variety of factors, but the concept of implicit contracts should not figure in that determination.

This brings us to the issue of policy. Even if managers are not entitled as a matter of fairness to protection against the increased risk entailed by a permissive takeover regime, it may be that they should be afforded such protection as a matter of policy, because the increased risk of losing one's job through a corporate takeover may cause a manager to focus unduly on the short term, or even to take unduly high risk gambles. This is certainly plausible, but it should be stressed that these issues are highly indeterminate. Managers act for noneconomic reasons as well as for economic reasons. It may be that because of noneconomic reasons, such as pride in making proper decisions, the change in managerial behavior resulting from increased risk are only marginal.

In any event, to the extent golden parachutes are justified by a desire to make managers secure against the prospect of being discharged, the justification imposes certain limits that not all such arrangements reflect. For example, that justification will not support parachutes that are extended to executives who are very near retirement age, or parachutes that permit the executive to pull the rip cord, or parachutes that don't reflect a mitigation-of-damages principle. That many golden parachutes have these features suggests that the goal of preventing managerial insecurity is not always the sole reason such arrangements are made, and that this justification cannot be used to validate golden parachutes on an across-the-board basis.

NOTES

1. See, e.g., S. Rosen, "Implicit Contracts: A Survey," *Journal of Economic Literature* **23,** 1144 (1985).

2. See W. Klein, "The Modern Business Organization: Bargaining Under Constraints," *Yale Law Journal* **91,** 1521, 1532 (1982).

10

Comment: Shareholders *and* Managers— A Risk-Neutral Perspective

OLIVER E. WILLIAMSON

John Coffee's discussion on shareholders versus managers (Chapter 6) deals with a large number of important and controversial issues. Although I frequently find myself in disagreement with him, all students of corporate governance stand to benefit from his provocative treatment of the issues.

I begin with a brief examination of alternative theories of the corporation. Whereas Coffee treats managerialist, organization form, and contractual theories of the corporation as rival theories, I regard these as successive evolutionary developments with complementary properties. I then contrast the risk aversion with the hazard exposure approach to the study of contract. I maintain that risk aversion is a much overused argument and that the study of contract is better served by focusing on hazards (and adaptive responses thereto). A series of particular issues on which Coffee and I differ are then discussed.

THEORIES OF THE CORPORATION

The theory of the firm occupies a prominent place in microeconomics. The orthodox theory of the firm characterizes the firm as a production function to which a profit maximization objective is ascribed. Inasmuch as the modern corporation is plainly a firm, albeit of a complex kind, and since economists are presumed to have analytical apparatus that is germane to the study of such entities, it is natural that the orthodox theory of the firm as production function is invoked when issues of corporate organization are posed.

Indeed, for many purposes, this is the appropriate place to start. A large number of investment issues can be usefully addressed with the neoclassical apparatus. Effects of taxes and changing factor prices can be investigated. Transfer-pricing criteria can be derived.

But there are a large number of other issues with which this "black box" conception of the firm makes little or no useful contact. Modern theories of the firm owe their origins to that condition. In order of appearance, these theories have successively addressed issues of (1) managerial discretion, (2) organization form, and (3) contractual conceptions of the enterprise.

Managerial Discretion

Although concern over managerial discretion has early origins (Adam Smith was sensitive to this condition), efforts to formalize such arguments did not appear until the late 1950s and early 1960s. The main models were William Baumol's sales maximization hypothesis,[1] Robin Marris's growth maximization formulation,[2] and my expense preference treatment of the managerial utility function.[3]

These models did not yield a large number of refutable implications, and some of the apparent differences between the profit maximization hypothesis and managerial discretion models have been disputed.[4] I submit, however, that an appreciation for managerial discretion is an absolutely crucial concept, without which follow-on models of the corporation are quite without purpose. Thus although managerial discretion models have not spawned a large theoretical or empirical literature, they constitute a useful transition stage between the neoclassical profit maximization hypothesis and the models described here.

Indeed, almost everyone now agrees that managers are not reliably given to unremitting profit maximization. Most of the interesting puzzles of economic organization vanish if agents (managers) are assumed to behave in such a stewardship manner. Faithful stewardship of assets being the exception rather than the rule, veridicality is better served by assuming that managers, like other economic agents, pursue their own interests when and as the opportunities permit. Whatever one's view of the Baumol-Marris-Williamson models,[5] therefore, it is instructive to record that *all students of the modern corporation take managerialism seriously.* (In much the same sense that all macroeconomists "are Keynesians now,"[6] we students of the modern corporation are all managerialists now.)

Organization Form

The main checks against managerial discretion were originally thought to be competition in the product market and competition in the capital market. Managerial discretion does not, however, vanish since product market competition is not everywhere intensive and the proxy contest is a severely limited capital market control.

Product and capital market competition do not, however, exhaust the possibilities. Might the internal organization of the firm be reshaped in a manner that brought managerial discretion under more effective control?

My reading of Alfred Chandler, Jr.'s historical study[7] of the appearance and evolution of the multidivisional structure, under which the large functionally organized (U-Form) business firm was reshaped as a divisionalized (M-Form) enterprise in which operating and strategic purposes were separated, led to the following multidivisional hypothesis: *"The organization and operation of the large enterprise along the lines of the M-Form favors goal pursuit and least-cost behavior more nearly associated with the neoclassical profit maximization hypothesis than does the U-Form organizational alternative."*[8] Although the first M-Form firms were relatively specialized enterprises (in automobiles, chemicals, and petroleum), the divisionalization concept was subsequently extended to diversified lines of commerce. The more well managed conglomerate enterprises were those that respected M-Form organizing principles.[9]

Indeed, an unanticipated systems consequence materialized. Since the M-Form organizational innovation permitted a firm to acquire and manage new assets more effectively than the older U-Form structure allowed, takeover by tender offer took on operational significance. The market for corporate control was thereby provided with a more credible instrument by which to upset incumbent managements which refused merger proposals. Latitude for managerial discretion was thus reduced both directly (in firms which adopted the M-Form structure) and indirectly (through the capital market) as a consequence.

Contractual Models

Three kinds of contractual models of the enterprise can be distinguished: team models, agency models, and transaction cost.

Team

The original team model was advanced by Armen Alchian and Harold Demsetz.[10] It had two parts. First, they argued that hierarchical organization was explained by the need for a monitor to oversee the performance of workers who were engaged in nonseparable production activities. A condition of technological nonseparability was thus central to their formulation.[11] Second, Alchian and Demsetz argued that "long term contracts between employer and employee are not the essence of the organization we call a firm."[12] Since it was possible to motivate the crucial monitor/residual claimant relation by invoking nonseparability, parsimony evidently argued against any appeal to long-term contracting.

Formalisms aside, however, the adequacy of nonseparability, taken by itself, depends on how many tasks are appropriately described in this way. If, as I have argued elsewhere, the symphony orchestra is the largest organization to which nonseparability applies,[13] then presumably other factors must be invoked to explain the large corporation with it tens of thousands of employees. Alchian concurs and now accords a prominent place to transaction cost reasoning.[14]

Agency

Michael Jensen distinguishes between formal and informal branches of agency theory and associates his work (and that of William Meckling and Eugene Fama) mainly with the latter.[15] The more formal literature deals with a series of principal-agent issues in which crafting *ex ante* incentives for an employment relation is key.[16] All of the relevant contracting action is packed into the *ex ante* bargain, the only limitation on comprehensive contracting being that some of the information relevant to an efficient exchange is private. But for private information (information impactedness), however, the contract is complete in all other respects. The formal-agency literature thus maintains the assumption that the agents have unrestricted cognitive powers to reach contracts of bewildering degrees of complexity.

The informal literature is less concerned with the analytics of incentive contracting than it is with the nature of the contracting process. The informal literature features the "nexus-of-contract" conception of the firm and examines the uses of bonding, monitoring, residual claimant status, etc., as these serve to perfect contracting relationships.[17] Albeit subject to bounded rationality, economic agents are nevertheless assumed to be perceptive. Changes in the incentives of managers that attend the sale of ownership are thus reflected in the terms under which equity is purchased. New owners are not therefore "surprised" when managers, as their participation in the marginal net receipts of the firm is reduced, choose to take more or their compensation as slack.[18] Numerous refutable implications obtain.

Transaction Cost

Transaction cost economics expressly assumes that human agents are subject to bounded rationality—which is to say that they are "intendedly rational but only limitedly so."[19] It furthermore assumes that human agents are given to opportunism—which is akin to moral hazard but has a somewhat more expansive quality.[20]

Transaction cost economics holds that the transaction is the basic unit of analysis and employs a comparative institutional approach to the study of contracting. Unlike agency theory, of either formal or informal kinds, transaction cost economics focuses on the *attributes of transactions.* The object is to align transactions (which differ in their attributes) with governance structures (which differ in their costs and competencies) in a discriminating (mainly transaction cost economizing) way.

Of the several relevant dimensions for describing transactions, the condition of asset specificity turns out to be the most important. Asset specificity has reference to the extent to which investments are durable and are specialized to the needs of a particular buyer or supplier. Classical market contracting works well where asset specificity is slight; transactions are apt to be taken out of the market and organized internally as asset specificity is progressively deepened (this is the vertical integration response); and complex intermediate forms of contracting (bonding, arbitration, reciprocity) arise to support intermediate degrees of specificity. The condition of asset specificity has numerous ramifications for corporate financing (when to use debt rather than equity), managerial compensation (including golden parachutes), and constituency representation on the board of directors. These matters are elaborated elsewhere;[21] selective aspects are discussed next.

Overview

Coffee discusses managerial discretion, organization form, and contractual models of the corporation as rival theories. I see them mainly as complements. The principal linkages are these:

1. But for opportunism, managerial discretion would vanish, and the internal organization of the firm need only be concerned with bounded rationality.[22]
2. Organization form, however, can and does have a bearing on opportunism. The M-Form innovation both economizes on bounded rationality and attenuates opportunism.
3. The diffusion of the M-Form structure served to activate competition in the capital market by making takeover a more credible corporate-control technique. Control over corporate assets could thereby be transferred more easily from managments with a greater propensity for slack to those who would use these same assets to realize greater productive value.
4. Self-corrective actions by incumbent managements who were previously disposed to run slack operations were elicited as a result.
5. As discussed later, the appearance of takover upset the previous equilibrium set of contracts and induced further adaptations by managers and others whose expectations were affected.

RISK AVERSION VERSUS HAZARD
EXPOSURE

Differential risk aversion has been widely invoked to support implicit-contracting models of the labor market[23] and to explain multiperiod supply contracts between firms.[24] Excessive reliance on this assumption has been noted by others.[25]

As I have observed elsewhere, differential risk aversion appears to be the modern counterpart for monopoly as the main basis by which to explain nonstandard forms of contracting. Thus whereas it was once the case that "when an economist finds something—a business practice of one sort or another—that he does not understand, he looks for a monopoly explanation,"[26] the new orthodoxy is to substitute differential risk aversion for monopoly and to ignore other possibilities. The earlier preoccupation with monopoly deflected attention from the possibility than nonstandard forms of contracting arise, often if not always, in the service transaction cost economizing. The recent preoccupation with differential risk aversion has had precisely the same effect.

I submit that reference to differential risk aversion is not only problematic—as Clive Bull puts it, "unambiguous comparisons of risk aversion between multidimensional utility functions can only be made for very special cases"[27]—but is often unneeded. Indeed, a deeper understanding of the contractual phenomena in question will often be realized by assuming risk neutrality and focusing on the contractual *hazards* which are presented under different contracting scenarios.

A Simple Contractual Schema[28]

The rudimentary contracting apparatus described here makes contact with and helps to illuminate a wide variety of nonstandard contracting practices. It is specifically relevant to an assessment of the disequilibrium contracting issues of concern to Coffee.

Assume that a good or service can be supplied by either of two alternative technologies. One is a general-purpose technology, the other a special-purpose technology. The special-purpose technology requires greater investment in transaction-specific durable assets and is more efficient for servicing steady-state demands.

Using k as a measure of transaction-specific assets, transactions that use the general-purpose technology are ones for which $k = 0$. When transactions use the special-purpose technology, by contrast $k > 0$. Assets are then specialized to the particular needs of the parties. Productive values would therefore be sacrificed if transactions of this kind were to be prematurely terminated.

Whereas classical market contracting—"sharp in by clear agreement; sharp out by clear performance"[29]—suffices for transactions of the $k = 0$ kind, unassisted market governance poses hazards whenever nontrivial transaction-specific assets are placed at risk. Parties have an incentive to devise safeguards to protect investments in transactions of the latter kind. Let s denote the magnitude of any such safeguards. As $s = 0$ condition is one in which no safeguards are provided; a decision to provide safeguards is reflected by an $s > 0$ result.

Figure 10.1 displays the three contracting outcomes corresponding to such a description. Associated with each node is a price. So as to facilitate comparisons between nodes, assume that suppliers (1) are risk-neutral, (2) are prepared to supply under either technology, and (3) will accept any safeguard condition whatsoever as long as an expected break-even result can be projected. Thus node A is the general-purpose-technology ($k = 0$) supply relation for which a break-even price of p_1 is projected. The node B contract is supported by transaction-specific assets ($k > 0$) for which no safeguard is offered ($s = 0$). The expected break-even price here is $\bar{p}$. The node C contract also employs the special-purpose technology. But since the buyer at this node provides the supplier with a safeguard ($s > 0$), the break-even price $\hat{p}$ at node C is less than $\bar{p}$.

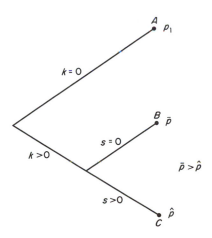

Figure 10.1. A simple contracting schema.

The protective safeguards to which I refer normally take on one or more of three forms. The first is to realign incentives, which commonly involves some type of severance payment or penalty for premature termination. A second is to create and employ a specialized governance structure to which to refer and resolve disputes. The use of arbitration, rather than litigation in the courts, is thus characteristic of node C governance. A third is to introduce trading regularities that support and signal continuity intentions. Expanding a trading relation from unilateral to bilateral exchange—through the concerted use, for example, of reciprocity—thereby to effect an equilibration of trading hazards, is an example of that last.

This simple contracting schema applies to a wide variety of contracting issues. It facilitates comparative institutional analysis by emphasizing that technology (k), contractual governance/safeguards (s), and price (p) are fully interactive and are determined simultaneously. It is gratifying that so many applications turn out to be variations on a theme. As Friedrich Hayek observed, "whenever the capacity of recognizing an abstract rule which the arrangement of these attributes follows has been acquired in one field, the same master mould will apply when the signs for those abstract attributes are evoked by altogether different elements."[30]

By way of summary, the nodes A, B, and C in the contractual schema set out in Figure 10.1 have the following properties:

1. Transactions that are efficiently supported by general-purpose assets ($k = 0$) are located at node A and do not need protective governance structures. Discrete market contracting suffices. The world of competition obtains.
2. Transactions that involve significant investments of a transaction-specific kind ($k > 0$) are ones for which the parties are effectively engaged in bilateral trade.
3. Transactions located at node B enjoy no safeguards ($s = 0$), on which account the projected break-even supply price is great $\bar{p} > \hat{p}$). Such transactions are apt to be unstable contractually. They may

revert to node A [in which event the special-purpose technology would be replaced by the general-purpose ($k = 0$) technology] or be relocated to node C (by introducing contractual safeguards that would encourage the continued use of the $k > 0$ technology).

4. Transactions located at node C incorporate safeguards ($s > 0$) and thus are protected against expropriation hazards.

5. Inasmuch as price and governance are linked, parties to a contract should not expect to have their cake (low price) and eat it too (no safeguard). More generally, it is important to study *contracting in its entirety*. Both the *ex ante* terms and the manner in which contracts are thereafter executed vary with the investment characteristics and the associated governance structures within which transactions are embedded.

Applications to Takeovers

Assume that a firm has struck an equilibrium set of contracts with each of its constituencies—labor, suppliers, management, finance, etc. Consider, in particular, the contracts with labor, management, and equity finance. Assume, arguendo, that labor is of a fully general-purpose ($k = 0$) kind; while management develops significant firm-specific knowledge and skill during the course of its employment ($k > 0$). Stockholders are residual claimants and are awarded *de jure* control over the board of directors to safeguard their investment in the firm.

Assume, however, that stockholders are actually able to exercise control over the board of directors only if management fails "obviously and even ignominiously,"[31] which condition was believed to prevail in the pretakeover era when challenges to incumbent managements took the form of proxy contests. Stockholders thus expected that managers would exercise considerable discretion. And managements did not disappoint these expectations.

Managers were thus reasonably secure in their jobs in the pretakeover era and took their compensation in both pecuniary and discretionary forms. The specific assets of managers were nevertheless protected against arbitrary dismissals by providing for severance pay if a manager were fired without cause. And the management further operated under the norms of protection afforded by "informal organization."[32]

Labor in this firm would be located at node A. Assume that it received a payment of w_1. Management would be located at node C. Assume that it was paid pecuniary compensation of $\hat{p}$. And assume that equity is priced so as to earn a fair rate of return under the prevailing (expected) degree of managerial discretion.

Suppose, however, for the reasons discussed previously, that takeover now bursts onto the scene. What are the contractual ramifications?

A new instrument now exists which makes it easier to displace incumbent managers. Since managerial discretion can be brought under more effective control, greater profits can be realized. But the earlier contractual equilibrium will have been disturbed and will need to be reequilibrated. How will labor, equity, and management be affected?

Induced marginal productivity effects aside, general-purpose labor will continue to be paid the wage w_1. The price of equity will be bid up to restore a fair rate of return to stockholders. And management ($k > 0$) will ask that its contract be renegotiated.

Of course, the specific asset investments of incumbent managements have already been sunk. But successor managements cannot be expected to strike the same deal. For one thing, they will demand greater pecuniary compensation since managerial discretion has been wrung out of the deal. For another, since incumbency is less secure, incumbent managers are confronted with added employment hazards. This added hazard will induce reequilibration in one or more of three ways: (1) the specific nature of the assignment can be reduced; (2) a front-end premium can be paid to induce managers to accept the hazard (this corresponds, approximately, to a node B solution); or (3) added protection against displacement can be offered. As I have discussed elsewhere, the so-called golden parachute can be thought of as a response of this last kind.[33]

While this description is merely a sketch, it nevertheless identifies some of the core issues that need to be faced and demonstrates wherein transaction cost economics helps to inform the study of these matters. Refinements and qualifications, moreover, can be introduced as needed. The critical thing is to get the basic contractual framework in place. Absent this, discussion of these matters easily has a diffuse and piecemeal quality. The study of "contracting in its entirety" demands that assets (k), price (p), and safeguards (s) be considered simultaneously. Corporate governance needs to be assessed from this combined perspective.

SOME PARTICULARS

Conglomerates

Coffee makes a series of statements about my treatment of conglomerates that seem to me to be unwarranted. Among those with which I take stronger exception are the following:

Recent developments in corporate structure present a problem ... [for] Williamsonian theory. . . . Put simply, if the conglomerate form is more efficient than the earlier U-Form firm, why has there been a sudden trend toward "deconglomeration."

As a closer reading of my work discloses, however, I made favorable reference to deconglomeration in 1972 and have repeated this since. Thus I observed that while voluntary divestiture is sometimes undertaken because of pressing cash needs, it is also "undertaken out of recognition that large size and proliferating variety eventually result in diseconomies. . . . This process of 'mitosis' represents a variety of organizational self-renewal that warrants a sympathetic public policy response."[34] And I followed this up by observing that "freeing the market for corporate control ought ... to be considered as a means by which to encourage very large firms to trim their operations when excessive size and

variety are reached; anxious to forestall takeover, otherwise passive firms may be induced voluntarily [to divest]."[35] Coffee plainly needs another candidate on which to hang the "troublesome" recent developments to which he refers.

The Williamsonian model omits virtually any reference to ... the institutional investor. Because it is already fully diversified (or nearly so), the diversification advantages of the conglomerate seem dubious.

Coffee does not indicate where I characterize diversification as a conglomerate advantage but merely imputes such views to me. A reading of the literature would disclose, however, that although others, in particular Morris Adelman, attribute portfolio diversification advantages to conglomerates, I specifically take exception with this interpretation of the conglomerate. Since "individual stockholders, through mutual funds and otherwise, are able to diversify their own portfolios, ... the portfolio diversification thesis is a very incomplete explanation for the postwar wave of conglomerate mergers."[36]

According to Coffee: Under the Williamsonian model of the firm, one expects the managers of the M-Form firm to hold the winners (i.e., the high-growth division) and dispose the losers. Instead, the reverse may be happening.

Note that whereas previously Coffee had claimed that voluntary divestiture was inconsistent with my view, now he argues that I favor divesting losers. This too is gratuitous. Thus although I do not recall making statements as to which divisions should be or would be divested, I will now. As to "should," my view is that, monopoly and other social cost exceptions aside, resources ought to be placed in the hands of highest-valuing users. Sometimes a firm should divest "losers." Sometimes it should divest "crown jewels." As to what will actually happen, I predict that the M-Form hypothesis will be borne out in practice. Note that my prediction does not imply that the previously stated good policy will be implemented faultlessly and without internal politiking.[37] The Williamsonian paradox to which Coffee refers is of his own making.

> The Williamsonian model . . . gives too little attention to the disciplinary impact of the takeover on the older U-Form firm.

Whether my emphasis is "too little" is hard to say, but I have been *very explicit* on this point:

> Unitary form enterprises that anticipate takeover efforts may attempt to shrink the potential displacement gain by making appropriate internal changes: subgoal pursuit may be reduced or, possibly, self-reorganization along M-form lines may be initiated. . . . Once the number of multidivision firms becomes sufficiently large . . . , the effect on unitary form enterprises that are otherwise shielded from product market pressures is equivalent to an increase in competition in so far as subgoal pursuit is concerned.[38]

One Job

Coffee observes that "shareholders own many stocks, but managers have only one job" and regards this as the "basic contrast."

I agree but believe that the contrast is easily exaggerated. As I have observed elsewhere, "One labor power and one job regarded nakedly and one labor power and one job embedded in a protective governance structure have very different connotations."[39] Although much more work on the governance structure features of management jobs needs to be done, the fact is that it is in the mutual interest of both owners (equity) and managers to craft protective governance structures.

Disequilibrium Contracting

Timing

Although economists are very adept in supplying *ex post* rationales for observed events, they are much less successful in anticipating these developments. Our knowledge of economic organization being very primitive, perhaps that is as much as can be expected.

Inasmuch, however, as an endless number of *ex post* explanations can be invented, choice among these alternatives

needs to be made. My sense is that competition in the capital market often has origins in organizational innovations—the effects of which work themselves out through capital market processes. More systematic study of this hypothesis, however, is needed. Coffee's concerns about *ad hocery* are warranted.

Unbargained-for Hazards

Coffee makes reference to unbargained-for hazards in his discussion of the managerial labor market and seems to feel that rules to protect the stake of middle managers are needed.

I agree that unbargained-for hazards are troublesome and further agree that protective rules may sometimes be warranted.[40] I am not at all sure, however, that the rules favored by Coffee are apt to be either timely or useful.

To be sure, incumbent middle managers may be caught in an awkward transition. Once a takeover threat has materialized, they may be unable to renegotiate their contracts to reflect the new hazard. But successor generations of managers will presumably be alerted and will contract accordingly. Since Coffee does not propose retroactive compensation for those caught in the transition, his regulatory rules may be of little purpose. (They are akin to locking the barn door after the horse has been stolen.) Indeed, if they have an effect, it is that they appear to be too sweeping. In general, contractual remedies should be developed in a discriminating way to reflect the particulars of the situation. If managerial asset specificity varies widely, an across-the-board application of the golden rule of golden parachutes, which is what Coffee proposes, is not apt to be optimal.

NOTES

1. W. Baumol, *Business Behavior, Value and Growth* (1959).
2. R. Marris, *The Economic Theory of Managerial Capitalism* (1964).
3. O. Williamson, *The Economics of Discretionary Behavior* (1964).

4. R. Solow, "Some Implications of Alternative Criteria for the Firm," in *The Corporate Economy,* eds. R. Marris and A. Wood, 318 (1971).

5. See Alchian, "The Basis of Some Recent Advances in the Theory of Management of the Firm," 14 *J. Indus. Econ.* 30 (1965), for an assessment of the several strands.

6. M. Friedman, "The Role of Monetary Policy," 58 *Am. Econ. Rev.* 1 (1968).

7. A. Chandler, Jr., *Strategy and Structure* (1962).

8. O. Williamson, *Corporate Control and Business Behavior* (1970), 134.

9. Ibid, also see O. Williamson, *Markets and Hierarchies* (1975); "The Modern Corporation: Origins, Evolution, Attributes," 19 *Jour. Econ. Lit.* 1537 (1981).

10. Alchian and Demsetz, "Production, Information Costs, and Economic Organization," 62 *Am. Econ. Rev.* 777 (1972).

11. Surprisingly, this emphasis on technological nonseparability, which is central to the Alchian and Demsetz formulation, has been ignored in recent political science surveys of the literature. See Miller and Moe, "The Positive Theory of Hierarchies," in *Political Science: The Science of Politics,* ed. H. Weisberg (1986).

12. See Alchian and Demsetz, note 10, p. 777.

13. See Williamson, "Modern Corporation," note 9, p. 1565 (note 44).

14. Alchian, "Specificity, Specialization and Coalitions," 140 *Journal of Institutional and Theoretical Economics* 34 (1984).

15. Jensen, "Organization Theory and Methodology," 50 *Accounting Rev.* 319 (1983).

16. For a survey and references, see MacDonald, "New Directions in the Economic Theory of Agency," 17 *Can. Jour. Econ.* 415 (1984).

17. See Jensen, note 15.

18. Jensen and Meckling, "Theory of the Firm: Managerial Behavior, Agency Costs and Ownership Structure," 3 *Jour. of Fin. Econ.* 305 (1976).

19. H. Simon, *Administrative Behavior* (1961), xxiv.

20. O. Williamson, *The Economic Institutions of Capitalism* (1985), 51 (note 8).

21. Ibid., Chap. 12.

22. The theory of teams as set out in J. Marschak and R. Radner, *The Theory of Teams* (1972), would then suffice.

23. For a survey, see Azariadis and Stiglitz, "Implicit Contracts and Fixed Price Equilibria," 99 *Quar. Jour. of Econ.* 1 (1983).

24. Townsend, "Optimal Multiperiod Contracts and Gain from Enduring Relationships Under Private Information," 90 *Jour. Pol. Econ.* 1166 (1982).

25. Akerlof and Miyazaki, "The Implicit Contract Theory of Employment Meets the Wage Bill Argument," 47 *Quar. Jour. of Econ.* 34 (1980); Bull, "Implicit Contracts in the Absence of Enforcement and Risk Aversion," 73 *Am. Econ. Rev.* 658 (1983).

26. Coase, "Industrial Organization: A Proposal for Research," in *Policy Issues and Research Opportunities in Industrial Organization,* ed. V. Fuchs (1972), 67.

27. See Bull, note 25, p. 660.

28. This subsection is based on Williamson, "Assessing Contract," 1 *Jour. of Law, Econ. and Organization* 177 (1985).

29. MacNeil, "The Many Futures of Contract," 47 *Univ. of So. Cal. Law Rev.* 714 (1974).

30. F. Hayek, *Studies in Philosophy, Politics, and Economics* (1967), 50.

31. O. Knauth, *Managerial Enterprise* (1948), 45.

32. The importance of informal organization was emphasized by C. Barnard, *The Functions of the Executive* (1938). Further study of this governance structure is greatly needed.

33. See Williamson, note 20, Chap. 12.

34. O. Williamson, "Antitrust Enforcement and the Modern Corporation," in *Policy Issues and Research Opportunities in Industrial Organization* ed. V. Fuchs (1972), 29. Also see O. Williamson, note 8 p. 144 and [*Markets and Hierarchies*], note 9, pp. 170–171.

35. Williamson, ["*Antitrust*"], note 34, p. 31.

36. See Williamson [*Modern Corporation*], note 9, p. 1558; see also Williamson, note 8, p. 142; Williamson [*Markets and Hierarchies*], note 9, Chap. 9, and Williamson, note 20, p. 287.

37. As set out earlier, the M-Form hypothesis is a comparative statement. The refutable implications of organization form analysis for divestiture are likewise comparative. The principle implications are these: (1) An M-Form firm will be more prepared to divest itself of acquired assets in response to changed circumstances than will a comparable U-Form enterprise; and (2) if assets are divested by both U- and M-Form firms, those divested by the M-Form will be more consonant with efficient investment principles.

38. Williamson [*Markets and Hierarchies*], note 9, p. 160.

39. Williamson, note 20, p. 259.

40. Williamson, ["Assessing Contract"], note 28, pp. 199–200.

EVIDENCE ON THE GAINS
FROM MERGERS AND TAKEOVERS

11

Are Acquiring-Firm Shareholders Better Off after an Acquisition?

ELLEN B. MAGENHEIM
DENNIS C. MUELLER

Out of the massive amount of research on acquisitions that has been conducted over the past 20 years, some consensus on major issues has emerged. But perhaps surprisingly, several key issues remain in dispute. On the positive side, early theoretical contributions showed that diversification through mergers was an inefficient method for spreading risks (Levy and Sarnat, 1970; Smith, 1970; Azzi, 1978), and empirical findings have corroborated this result (Smith and Schreiner, 1969; Mason and Goudzwaard, 1976). All observers have found that shareholders of acquired companies enjoy substantial immediate gains from the acquisitions, and no disagreement exists on this point. But the pattern of results with respect to the returns to acquiring-firm shareholders has been varied. One study claims to find positive gains; another records negative returns. Nor do reviewers of this literature reach a consensus (e.g., compare Mueller, 1977, 1980; Scherer, 1980, pp. 138–141; Halpern, 1983; Jensen and Ruback, 1983).

This lack of consensus carries over into the explanations for why acquisitions occur. One group of observers sees acquisitions as a means for improving the allocation of assets by transferring assets to more capable management or achieving other synergistic gains from the transfer of control (Manne, 1965; Mandelker, 1974; Dodd and Ruback, 1977). Adherents to this view claim that the existing evidence indicates that acquiring-firm shareholders are slightly better off or, at minimum, no worse off as a result of acquisitions (Halpern, 1983; Jensen and Ruback, 1983).

Although this interpretation of the evidence, if valid, would appear to vindicate a liberal antimerger policy (acquired-firm shareholders are better off; acquiring-firm shareholders are not worse off), it still raises fundamental questions about the theory of the firm and the market for corporate control, which feed back onto the broader policy issues. Acquired-firm managers may sometimes be unwilling partners to an acquisition, as in a hostile takeover, but acquiring-firm managers need never be. Why do the latter enter so readily into the market for corporate control, given its well-known large risks and apparently modest returns?

Several observers have answered this question by hypothesizing that managers undertake acquisitions which increase their utility but do not necessarily increase shareholder wealth (Mueller, 1969; Firth, 1980; Amihud and Lev, 1981; Greer, 1984). To the extent that these hypotheses are valid, the possibility must be entertained that acquisitions neither enhance acquiring-firm shareholder wealth nor confer broader social benefits. Thus, the issue of what the gains to acquiring-firm shareholders are is central to both the theory of the firm and public policy regarding acquisitions.

For this reason, the seemingly contradictory results regarding the effects of acquisitions on acquiring-firm shareholders and the lack of consensus among observers of what the results signify are disconcerting. It is the thesis of this paper that disagreement regarding the impact of acquisitions on acquiring-firm shareholders stems in part from the different methodologies individual studies have used. Measures of the impact of an acquisition on acquiring-firm shareholders are quite sensitive to the choice of methodology. In effect, authors have been asking different questions about the performance of acquiring-firm shares and, not surprisingly, have come up with different answers. We shall show that when one attempts to ask the same question in each study, the results turn out to be far more consistent than was heretofore apparent.

To do so, we reexamine the basic methodology used to measure the effects of acquisitions, placing particular emphasis on the pattern of returns to acquiring-firm shareholders before and after the acquisition (the first section). In the second section, we demonstrate the sensitivity of the results to the choice of methodology, i.e., to the particular question asked, using data for 78 mergers and takeovers in the years 1976 to 1981. In the light of the methodological issues raised in the first two sections, we reexamine the results of several published studies in the third section. Conclusions follow.

METHODOLOGICAL ISSUES IN MEASURING THE EFFECTS OF ACQUISITIONS

The basic assumption underlying the use of stock market data to estimate the effects of acquisitions is, of course, that share prices reflect future profit and dividend streams, and that any changes in future profit and dividend streams an acquisition is expected to bring about are reflected in changes in the prices and returns of the company's shares. Granting this assumption, one can test for the *expected* effect of an acquistion on future profit and dividend streams by measuring the change in returns to acquiring-company shareholders

accompanying an acquisition. To measure such a change, two questions must be answered: When is the effect of the acquisition on stockholder returns to be measured? How is the effect of the acquisition separated from other coterminous events that affect stockholder returns?

The first question could be easily resolved if all of the relevant information regarding an acquisition were to become public on the day the acquisition is announced and the market could be assumed to adjust fully in that day to the new information. But news of an acquisition is known to leak into the market prior to the first public announcement, and it is unrealistic to assume that the market is capable of predicting the full future consequences of an acquisition immediately upon learning of it. The latter point is a key part of our critique of the existing literature and requires some elaboration.

Robert Shiller (1981) has shown that swings in stock market prices exceed by factors of five and more those which should have occurred given the actual movements in dividend streams that occur. In a bull market, prices rise by far more than subsequent increases in dividends will warrant; in a bear market, they fall too far. The market has historically continually shifted from being too optimistic in bull markets to being too pessimistic in bear markets. Shiller (1984, 1986) hypothesizes that the behavior of individuals in the stock market is best explained through the psychology of fads and bandwagon movements.

Shiller's findings and his explanation of them are particularly relevant to the literature on mergers and takeovers, since it is well known that acquisition activity has been highly correlated with stock market activity.[1] Mergers and takeovers have occured most frequently at times when stock market prices are rising and the market in general is known to be overly optimistic about the future performance of companies. Since acquisition and stock market activity seem to respond to the same underlying economic environment and psychological factors (Geroski, 1984), it is reasonable to suppose, or at least prudent to allow for the possibility, that the stock market might be overly optimistic in its evaluation of acquisitions at the time they are first announced. Shiller's results, combined with the positive correlation of acquisition and stock market activity, suggest the importance of tracing the effects of an acquisition's announcement on a stock's price over a long enough period to ensure that any changes in stock prices are an unbiased reflection of the future effect of the acquisition on profits and dividends.

The second conceptual issue to be resolved is the separation of the effects of the acquisition from other coterminous events, i.e., the prediction of what the return on the firm's shares would have been in the absence of the acquistion, over whatever period is chosen to record this event. The counterfactual can never, of course, be truly predicted. Three approximations have been employed in the literature: (1) to assume the firm's returns post-event would have been the same as its returns preevent in the absence of the acquisition, (2) to select a control group and assume the firm's returns postevent would have been the same as those of the control group firm(s), or (3) a combination of (1) and (2), i.e., to assume that the change in returns of the acquiring firm following the acquisition's announcement would have been the same as the change in returns for the control group firm(s) for the same time period. The difference between this predicted change and the change actually observed is attributed to the acquisition. The third method is obviously the best. If one simply compares a firm's postevent performance to its preevent performance, one ignores all of the other events that may be occurring coterminously with the acquisition and affecting its returns. But if one predicts a firm's returns in the postevent period entirely from the control group (method 2) one ignores any systematic difference between the merging firm(s) and the control group that may exist. This latter point proves to be very important because, as we shall see, there are sizable differences between the performance of acquiring firms and the usually employed control groups over the preevent period.

If all events other than the acquisition that affect a firm's returns have the same effect on the firm's control group, then one should be able to isolate the effect of an acquisition by predicting the *change* in returns for the acquiring firm from the observed change in returns for the control group firms, and calculating the difference between observed and predicted returns as the effect of the acquisition. The most frequently employed control group in acquisition-stockholder returns studies is the market portfolio, the returns on all securities each weighted by its aggregate market value.

More formally, the returns for a given firm i are predicted from the characteristic line

$$E(R_i) = R_f + \beta_i [E(R_m) - R_f] \quad (11.1)$$

where $E(R_i)$ and $E(R_m)$ are the expected returns for firm i and the market portfolio, respectively, R_f is the return on a riskless $(0 = \beta)$ asset, and β_i is the covariance of i's returns with the market portfolio divided by the variance of the market portfolio. Equation (11.1) is one of the central results of the capital asset pricing model (CAPM). It states that the return on any firm i's shares, R_i, varies directly with the return on the portfolio of all shares, R_m, and thus that changes in R_i can be predicted from changes in R_m if β_i is unchanged.[2] The β_i term can be estimated from a time-series regression of R_{it} on R_{mt} or, as is frequently done, from a regression of $(R_{it} - R_{ft})$ on $(R_{mt} - R_{ft})$. By Equation (11.1), the intercept of this equation should equal zero. But if the intercept is not constrained to equal zero, regressions of the following sort typically yield nonzero estimates of $\hat{\alpha}_i$:

$$(R_{it} - R_{ft}) = \hat{\alpha}_i + \hat{\beta}_i (R_{mt} - R_{ft}) + e_{it} \quad (11.2)$$

Now $\hat{\alpha}_i$ is basically the average residual from the characteristic equation (11.1) for firm i implied by the CAPM. As such, it is a measure of the performance of the company over the sample period used to estimate $\hat{\beta}_i$ (Jensen, 1969), and has been so used in some acquisition studies (e.g., Weston, Smith, and Shrieves, 1972). A company with $\hat{\alpha}_i > 0$ has on average earned higher returns than are predicted by the CAPM. If $\hat{\beta}_i$ were not affected by the acquisition, one way to estimate the effects of the acquisition would be to estimate $\hat{\alpha}_i$ from data from before the acquisition and again from data following its announcement. The *change* in $\hat{\alpha}_i$ between the two periods would then be an estimate of the effect of the acquisition on firm i's returns assuming all other effects are captured through the movement of $(R_{mt} - R_{ft})$ over the two periods. Alternatively, one can estimate (11.2) by using preevent data, and then use the $\hat{\alpha}_i$ and $\hat{\beta}_i$ estimated from the preevent data to predict R_{it} from the postevent R_{mt} and R_{ft}. The difference between the actual and predicted R_{it} based on the preevent $\hat{\alpha}_i$ and $\hat{\beta}_i$ is a second measure of the effect of the acquisition on shareholder returns.

Both $\hat{\alpha}_i$ and $\hat{\beta}_i$ are likely to vary with the choice of time period used to estimate them. If this variation is random, measures of the effects of acquisitions are not biased by the choice of time period for estimating $\hat{\alpha}_i$ and $\hat{\beta}_i$, although the power of the tests is weakened. But there is considerable evidence, reviewed later, that acquiring firms earn substantial, positive abnormal returns over a period running anywhere from 18 to 66 months prior to the acquisition announcements. Given this evidence, the estimates one obtains of the effects of acquisitions are sensitive to how the preevent data are treated when estimating $\hat{\alpha}_i$ and $\hat{\beta}_i$. Studies differ widely as to how they treat the preevent period when estimating the $\hat{\alpha}_i$ and $\hat{\beta}_i$ used in predicting postevent performance, and this difference will be shown to have a significant influence on one's evaluation of the impact of the acquisition on stockholder returns.

Although substantial excess returns for acquiring firms have been estimated over prolonged preevent periods in several studies, little attention has been paid to these returns. Perhaps the neglect of the returns to acquiring firms prior to acquisitions can be explained by the prevailing view among many of those working in this area that it is deficiencies in the *acquired*

firm's performance that precipitate acquisitions. But if managers undertake acquisitions which worsen the performance of their companies' shares, it is logical to assume that they would choose to announce the acquisitions at times when the performance of their shares is above average. Also, the above-normal return performance of acquiring-firm shares prior to acquisitions may signal above-normal profit flows which can be used to finance the acquisitions. Thus, the above-normal performance of acquiring firms' shares over sustained intervals prior to their making an acquisition may explain why these particular firms' managements have chosen to make an acquisition at these particular points in time. Whether or not this conjecture regarding casuality is correct, it seems obvious that one should take into account this preevent performance of the acquiring firms when measuring the change in performance the acquisitions bring about.

We face now three conceptual problems: (1) How does one pinpoint the first arrival of information concerning the acquisition to the market? (2) Over what period should the preevent performance of the firm be measured to determine the change in performance caused by the acquisition? (3) How long a period after this event should one allow to measure the full effect of the acquisition on the acquiring firm's returns?

Somewhat surprisingly, the first question is the easiest to answer. While acquisition announcements do not seem to have had a large, systematic impact on acquiring-firm share prices, they have a predictable and large positive impact on acquired-firm share prices owing to the substantial premiums offered. An individual with nonpublic information of an acquisition will make a more certain and substantial gain by purchasing the shares of the to-be-acquired firm. Thus, the date of the first impact of the acquisition on firm share prices can be determined by examining the share price performance of the acquired firm. The month (day) in which its returns begin the sustained rise that culminates in the acquisition can be taken to be the point in time at which knowledge of the acquisition reaches the market. Most studies seem to indicate that information of an acquisition reaches the market in the month of the announcement or the month before. No study which we have seen presents evidence suggesting that information of the acquisition reaches the market more than four months prior to its announcement. Thus, we should expect to see the effects of acquisitions on acquiring-firm share prices commencing over a short time interval prior to the announcement month.

The question of what preevent period should be used against which to measure postevent performance is obviously somewhat arbitrary. It seems to us more reasonable to judge the effect of an acquisition against the period immediately preceding the market's learning of the acquisition than against a period some distance removed, since the acquiring firm's performance over the three preceding years is more relevant than over the interval four to six years before the acquisition, if one wishes to measure the *change* in performance caused by the acquisition.

If Equation (11.2) estimated on preevent data is used to predict post-acquisition performance, then an improvement in performance upon the market's obtaining information of an acquisition should appear as an upward movement in the residuals one obtains when preevent estimates of $\hat{\alpha}_i$ and $\hat{\beta}_i$ are used to predict postevent performance. Should one observe a systematic rise (fall) in the cumulative residuals from (11.1) commencing around the time of the acquisition, one might reasonably attribute this movement to the acquisition. As long as the cumulative residuals continue the rise (fall), which commenced with the acquisition, one can assume that the market is continuing to reevaluate the expected effects of the acquisition on the acquiring firm's performance. When the rise (fall) stops, the adjustment process is complete.

On the other hand, the market may reevaluate a firm's prospects as a consequence of an acquisition at almost any point in time following its announcement at which new information is received (e.g., a manager leaves; a contract is lost). If all subsequent movements in share prices not caused by the acquisition are assumed to be random, then a prudent strategy for ensuring that all possible effects on share prices caused by the acquisition are captured is to measure the acquiring firm's postevent performance over as long a period as possible. Here again, as we shall show, one's interpretation of the effects of an acquisition is in some cases sensitive to just how long an interval one allows the market to complete its evaluation after the acquisition.

ESTIMATES OF THE EFFECTS OF ACQUISITIONS ON THE PERFORMANCE OF A SAMPLE OF ACQUIRING FIRMS

In this section, we examine the implications of the methodological issues just discussed for a specific sample of acquiring firms. A description of the sample is presented, and the techniques for measuring returns are discussed. Particular emphasis is placed on the sensitivity of the conclusions to the choice of a time period for measuring the market model, and the length of time over which postevent returns are measured.

Description of the Sample

The sample of 78 acquiring firms is composed of companies completing takeovers valued at $15 million or more. Of the 78 acquiring firms, 51 entered into mergers and 26 into tender offers.[3] All of the firms are listed on the New York or American Stock Exchanges. To ensure data availability, only firms listed on Price-Dividend-Earnings (PDE) tapes are included. The sample period begins in 1976. To ensure three full years of postevent data, we specify 1981 as the end of the sample period. Announcement and completion dates and the mode of acquisition in each case were checked in the *Wall Street Journal*.

These acquisitions span a more recent time period than do samples previously analyzed. We describe here some characteristics of this sample. The distribution of initial bid announcements is reported in Table 11.1. These bids were made within an active market for acquisitions.[4] The

Table 11.1 Distribution of Initial
Announcement of Acquisition Bid by Year

Year	Number of Acquisition Bids
1976	9
1977	9
1978	21
1979	18
1980	7
1981	14

level of acquisition activity intensified in
the mid 1970s following a fairly placid period; the end of the sample period coincides with a leveling off in the number of
transactions recorded (W. T. Grimm,
1984). This wave of activity coincides with
a periodically depressed stock market
which makes it an anomaly among acquisition waves.

On average, 16 weeks elapsed between
the bid announcement and completion of
the transition; the median level is 13
weeks. The length of the interval ranges
from 1 week or less in three cases to more
than 80 weeks in two cases. The average
ratio of the preevent equity value of acquiring to acquired firm is 3.77. The average percentage premium over stock value
paid by sample firms is 81%, and the
average value of the premium paid to acquired-firm shareholders is $191.58
million.

Methodology for Measuring Abnormal
Returns

To measure the effect of acquisitions on
stock price returns, we follow the Fama,
Fisher, Jensen, and Roll (1969) event study
technique. This technique relies on the use
of the market portfolio as a control group
to capture the effect of marketwide fluctuations in stock prices. Any remaining unexplained abnormal performance can be
attributed to the effect of a specific
event—in this case, an acquisition bid
announcement.

We estimated the following market
model using ordinary least-squares
regression.[5]

$$R_{it} = \alpha_i + \beta_i R_{mt} + e_{it} \qquad (11.3)$$

where

R_{it} = return on stock i at time t

R_{mt} = return on the market portfolio at
time t

e_{it} = homoscedastic, normally
distributed, serially uncorrelated,
zero-mean-error term with
variance $\hat{\sigma}(\hat{e}_{it})$

The coefficient on R_{mt}, β_i, measures the
sensitivity of the ith firm's return to fluctuations in the market index. The intercept
measures the risk-free return plus the average abnormal performance of the firm
over the sample period used to estimate
(11.3). The error e_{it} measures that part of
R_{it} which is due to neither movements in
the return on the market portfolio nor to
the firm's average abnormal return.

Each R_{it} is calculated from monthly data
taken from the PDE tapes, with stock
prices adjusted for splits and dividends.
The New York Stock Exchange equally
weighted index is used as a proxy for the
market portfolio. Monthly residuals for
each firm i are calculated as $\hat{e}_{it} = R_{it} - \hat{R}_{it}$.
From these monthly residuals for each
firm, average abnormal returns are calculated for each time t:

$$AR_t = \sum_{i=1}^{I} \frac{\hat{e}_{it}}{I}$$

where I is the total number of firms and t
= 0 is the event date, i.e., the month of the
initial announcement. This yields, for each
time period, a measure of the average divergence between actual and forecast returns, adjusted for each firm's normal level
of performance and for marketwide fluctuations. Cumulated average abnormal returns are then calculated as

$$CAR_{xy} = \sum_{t=x}^{y} AR_t$$

where x and y are the start and end dates
of the cumulation period. To test the statistical significance of the average and cumulative average abnormal returns, we

construct a test statistic following the commonly used procedure (Linn and McConnell, 1983; Malatesta, 1983).

Results

In this section, the sensitivity of conclusions regarding the effect of acquisitions on firm returns to the time period used to estimate the market model coefficients and the length of the postevent measurement period is shown. We first review what we define as our basic case; then we show how results change with the choice of different estimation periods. To understand these changes more fully, we examine how $\hat{\alpha}$, the measure of the firm's abnormal performance over the estimation period, varies with the choice of time period.

To allow for information reaching the market prior to an acquisition's announcement, all preevent periods are ended four months prior to the announcement month, an interval which seems prudent on the basis of existing studies (see the third section). Consistent with previous research, we find significant positive gains being earned in the two years preceding the event. During the period [−24, −4] acquirers earn returns that are 18.4% in excess of the expected returns based on their performance over the [−60, −25] period (Table 11.2). These abnormal returns are significant at the .05 level. The pattern of returns for each firm was examined over this preevent period. Of the 78 firms, 71 experienced a preevent upward trend in abnormal returns which, on average, began at $t = -33$. For the 48 merging firms, this upward trend began, on average, at $t = -29$; for 21 firms making tender offers the upward movement begins, on average, at $t = -36$.

The returns for the [−3, −1] period, measured by using coefficients estimated from [−60, −4], introduce a trend of negative but insignificant returns that continues for the two years following the event. In the third postevent year, however, significant losses of −9% occur. A pattern emerges in which acquirers earn substantial positive gains until shortly before the

Table 11.2 Cumulative Average Abnormal Returns: All Sample Firms

Forecast Period	Estimation Period	
	[−60, −25]	[−60, −4]
[−24, −4]	.1839 (3.4161)[a]	
[−3, −1]	—	−.0148 (−.5683)
[0]	—	.0019 (−.3386)
[1, 6]	—	−.0336 (−1.273)
[7, 12]	—	−.0121 (−.6261)
[13, 24]	—	−.0096 (−.3403)
[25, 36]	—	−.0883 (−.2115)
[−3, 36]	—	−.1565 (−1.2364)

[a]The numbers in parentheses are the test statistics which are distributed standard normal.

event, following which returns begin to drop.

Breaking the full sample down by type of transaction, we see similar patterns (Table 11.3). Firms engaging in tender offers and mergers earn large positive gains prior to the event; the level ranges from 28% for the former group to 12.7% for the latter. Around the event month and over the next three years, a mixed pattern is observed. Bidders in tender offers experience a sharp drop in returns in the second year after the event, a sharp rise in the third year. In the third year, [24, 36], acquiring firms in mergers exhibit a significant decline in returns. Despite these differences, we confine most of our attention to the combined sample of 78 acquisitions, since we do not have enough observations on tender offers to undertake a meaningful separate analysis for this group. For both groups of acquiring firms the pattern emerges that the preevent period is one of positive abnormal performance; returns in the postevent period reflect a lower level of performance.

The high performance in the three years

Table 11.3 Cumulative Average Abnormal Returns by Mode of Acquisition

| | Estimation Period | | | |
| | [−60, −25] | | [−60, −4] | |
Forecast Period	Mergers	Tender Offers	Mergers	Tender Offers
[−24, −4]	.1271 (1.9472)[a]	.2804 (2.6400)	—	—
[−3, −1]	—	—	−.0300 (−.9918)	.0122 (.3078)
[0]	—	—	−.0037 (−.6769)	.0138 (.4500)
[1, 6]	—	—	−.0495 (−1.3182)	.0022 (−.1339)
[7, 12]	—	—	−.0252 (−.6257)	.0209 (.0968)
[13, 24]	—	—	.0281 (1.0110)	−.0908 (−1.0091)
[25, 36]	—	—	−.1971 (−3.709)	.1309 (1.7843)
[−3, 36]	—	—	−.2774 (−2.6039)	.0892 (.5633)

[a]The numbers in parentheses are the test statistics which are distributed standard normal.

prior to the event suggests that the treatment of this period in estimation of the market model coefficients may significantly affect the measurement of abnormal returns. Since the intercept measures firm performance over the estimation period, an intercept calculated from this period of above-normal performance is larger than if calculated from a lower-performance period. With a higher benchmark the residuals calculated relative to this "normal" performance level are lower.

Table 11.4 provides evidence of how the performance benchmark embodied in $\hat{\alpha}_i$ varies with differences in the estimation period. The first estimate of mean $\hat{\alpha}$ is

Table 11.4 Average Intercepts by Estimation Period, All 78 Firms

Estimation Period	Mean $\hat{\alpha}$	$\hat{\sigma}_{\hat{\alpha}}$
[−60, −25]	.0091	.0150
[−60, −4]	.0134	.0127
[−36, −4]	.0181	.0189
[−3, 36]	.0107	.0147
[4, 36]	.0080	.0300

.0091, based on [−60, −25]. It is small relative to the estimate of .0134 calculated from the period [−60, −4], reflecting the upward trend in returns that begins approximately three years prior to the event. While the first estimation period stops short of much of the rise in returns, the second period captures most of it. The estimates from [−36, −4] are from a period of almost exclusively higher returns and are much larger. The mean $\hat{\alpha}$ from [−36, −4] is double that estimated over [−60, −25]. The measures in the last two rows are based largely on the postevent periods over which lower average returns are observed. The mean $\hat{\alpha}$ from [−36, −4] is more than double that of the postevent period [4, 36].

These differences in $\hat{\alpha}$ lead one to expect sizable differences in the residuals from the market model depending on the choice of estimation period, and one observes them (Table 11.5). The cumulative residuals are uniformly lower when measured against the last 33 months of the preevent period [−36, −4] than when measured against the last 57 months [−60, −4]. Acquiring-

Table 11.5 Cumulative Average Abnormal Returns Based on Selected Estimation Periods: All Sample Firms

Forecast Period	Estimation Period		
	[−60, −4]	[−36, −4]	[13, 36]
[−3, −1]	−.0148 (−.5683)[a]	−.0298 (−.7743)	—
[0]	.0019 (−.3386)	−.0028 (−.4784)	—
[1, 6]	−.0336 (−1.2730)	−.0620 (−1.7100)	−.0175 (−.8249)
[7, 12]	−.0121 (−.6261)	−.0508 (−1.5890)	−.0146 (−.7386)
[1, 12]	−.0457 (−1.3429)	−.1128 (−2.3328)	−.0321 (−1.1057)
[13, 24]	−.0096 (−.3403)	−.0940 (−1.5520)	—
[25, 36]	−.0883 (−2.1150)	−.1826 (−4.5930)	—
[−3, 36]	−.1567 (−1.2464)	−.4221 (−4.9307)	—

[a]The numbers in parentheses are the test statistics which are distributed standard normal.

firm shareholders experienced an insignificant decline in returns of 15.67% over the period [−3, 36] as measured against the acquiring-firms' performance over [−60, −4]. They experienced a significant decline in returns almost three times greater than that when returns are measured against performance over [−36, −4].

Table 11.5 reveals that the choice of preevent period against which postevent performance is measured can have a significant effect on one's conclusions as to the change in performance following an acquisition. Several studies measure acquiring-firm postevent performance not against a preevent period, however, but against a subsequent postevent period.[7] But the average performance of acquiring firms in the postevent periods is systematically lower, as measured by $\hat{\alpha}$, as is evident in Table 11.4. Thus, use of postevent-period estimates of the market model yield systematically higher residuals than do preevent estimates. The third column of Table 11.5 reports the cumulative residuals for the first 12 postannouncement months measured against the acquiring

companies' predicted performance from [13, 36]. They are an insignificant −3%. In contrast, if the acquiring companies' performance over these 12 months is measured against how they did over the last 33 months of the preevent period, one observes a significant 11% lower return in the first year after the announcements. The differences in estimates of postevent normal returns, depending on choice of base period against which performance is judged, are depicted in Figure 11.1.

Acquiring firms performed substantially better over the period [−24, −4] than they did over [−60, −25]. If we define the latter as normal, then acquiring firms exhibit above-normal performance starting between two and three years before the acquisition announcements, an interpretation which is consistent with that of other studies reviewed later. Assuming this preevent performance is above normal, then acquiring firms must eventually exhibit some worsening of performance postevent. At some point in time, the market must adjust fully to whatever it is that causes the above-normal performance. A key methodological issue in judging the ef-

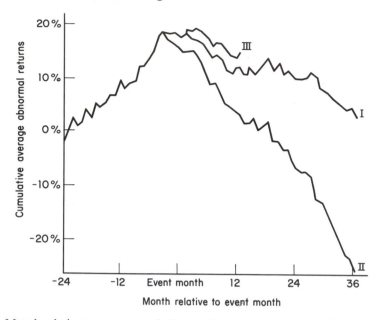

Figure 11.1. Month relative to event month. For all three cases, errors in [−24, −4] are calculated relative to performance in [−60, −25]. For case I, errors in [−3, 36] are based on [−60, −4]; for II, they are based on [−36, −4]. Case III is identical to case I for [−24, 0]; errors for [1, 12] are calculated relative to performance in [13, 36].

fects of acquisitions is the relationship between this point in time and the announcement month.

To begin to answer this question, one must explain why acquiring firms earn above-normal returns long *before* an acquisition. One possible explanation is that managers choose to acquire other companies when their own firms and their shares are doing relatively well. If this assumption is valid, the next question is whether the acquisitions are announced toward the beginning, middle, or end of these periods of above-normal performance. This is the kind of counterfactual question that never can be answered in a merger study. Our acquiring firms exhibit an upward trend in returns for roughly three years prior to the announcements. If the announcements come in the middle of the period of above-normal performance, then comparison of the first three postevent years with the last three preevent years would be appropriate.

Bradley and Jarrell's calculation of postevent performance in their comment (Chapter 15) effectively assumes that the announcements occur at the end of the period of above-normal performance. That the acquiring companies' period of above-normal performance just happens to end around the time the acquisitions are announced strikes us as an unlikely coincidence. Their estimate of the cumulative return to acquiring-firm shareholders over the three postevent years, which is almost identical to our estimate of −15.65% using the [−60, −4] interval as benchmark, we thus regard as an upper-bound measure of acquiring-firm performance. The −42.2% estimate using the interval [−36, −4] as benchmark, which implicitly assumes that the announcements occur in the middle of the above-normal performance period, is perhaps a reasonable lower bound.[8]

Our main results are summarized in Table 11.6, in which we again break out the merger and tender offer subsamples. If one assumes that the market's adjustment to news of an acquisition takes place entirely within the announcement month,

Table 11.6 Cumulative Average Abnormal Returns for Different Time Periods

Cumulation Period	Estimation Period $[-60, -4]$		
	All Firms	Mergers	Tender Offers
[0]	.0019	−.0037	.0138
	(−.3386)	(−.6769)	(.4500)
[−3, 6]	−.0465	−.0832	.0282
	(−1.4039)	(−1.7776)	(.2070)
[−3, 12]	−.0586	−.1084	.0491
	(−1.4932)	(−1.7885)	(.2229)
[−3, 24]	−.0682	−.0803	−.0417
	(−1.3513)	(−.6900)	(−.4920)
[−3, 36]	−.1565	−.2774	.0892
	(−1.2464)	(−2.6039)	(.5633)
	Estimation Period $[-36, -4]$		
[0]	−.0028	−.0070	.0065
	(−.4784)	(−.8527)	(.4637)
[−3, 6]	−.0946	−.1144	−.0514
	(−1.8993)	(−1.4770)	(−1.004)
[−3, 12]	−.1454	−.1692	−.0859
	(−2.4746)	(−1.8976)	(−1.2304)
[−3, 24]	−.2394	−.2125	−.2857
	(−2.8866)	(−1.4076)	(−2.7711)
[−3, 36]	−.4220	−.4909	−.2734
	(−4.9307)	(−4.2564)	(−2.1715)

The numbers in parentheses are the test statistics which are distributed standard normal.

then acquisitions have no significant impact on acquiring-firm shareholders. If, however, one allows the market three years following the announcement to evaluate an acquisition's effects, then acquiring-firm shareholders are significantly worse off following an acquisition than they would have been had the acquiring firms continued to perform as they had over the three years (i.e., the $[-36, -4]$ interval) prior to the acquisition. The hypothesis that acquiring-firm shareholders are better off as a result of acquisitions fares better if one uses the longer preevent period $[-60, -4]$ and, in general, if one uses shorter postevent periods.

Studies on this subject vary considerably in their choices of pre- and postevent-period lengths when estimating the effects of acquisitions. We favor a longer postevent period, because we doubt that all relevant information regarding an acquisition's likely effects reaches the market in the an-

nouncement month, and that the movements of stock prices in the few months surrounding an acquisition are, necessarily, unbiased estimates of the future consequences of the acquisitions.

Both the merger and tender offer subsamples reveal substantial declines in stockholder returns over the three years following the announcement month, as judged against the $[-36, -4]$ time-period performance. For the merging firms, the biggest decline occurs in the third year following the announcement; for the tender offer bidders, in the second. We do not place much weight on this difference. Indeed, we anticipate significant changes in stock market values for individual companies at different points of time following the initial announcement as additional information reaches the market. This anticipation is what leads us to favor a relatively long postevent interval for measuring the effects of acquisitions.

Jensen and Ruback (1983) stress the importance of differentiating between mergers and tender offers in event studies, and some support for the position is present in our results. Acquiring-firm shareholders are noticeably better off in tender offers than they are in mergers. But the similarities between the two subsamples are also noteworthy. Both groups experience an upward trend in abnormal returns over roughly three years prior to the acquisition's announcement. Commencing roughly with the announcement, the paths of abnormal returns for the two groups are refracted. After another three years, both groups of shareholders are significantly worse off than they would have been had their companies continued to perform in the postevent period $[-3, 36]$ as they had prior to the event $[-36, -4]$.

If our study were the only one to expose such a pattern of returns, one might be inclined to dismiss the substantial differences between the post and preannouncement acquiring-firm share performances as curiosa of our sample. But as we shall now illustrate, the same pattern has been observed in several studies from different time periods and countries.

A REEXAMINATION OF THE LITERATURE

The results of the previous section indicate that, at least for our sample, acquiring firms do earn substantial, positive abnormal returns prior to the market's learning of acquisitions and that acquiring-firm shareholders are not better off, relative to this preevent performance, after information of the acquisition reaches the market. Moreover, whether the acquiring-firm shareholders are judged no better off or significantly worse off depends on both the pre- and postevent periods used in the comparison.

In this section, we further illustrate the importance of these methodological issues by examining results reported in several other studies. While all take inspiration from the CAPM, they actually differ in a surprisingly large number of respects, and

it is not possible to comment on each in detail. We focus upon the general patterns.

Our thesis emphasizes the possible importance of the return pattern both before and after an acquisition, and thus we exclude from consideration studies that leave out entirely or severely truncate these pre- and postevent periods (e.g., Halpern, 1973; Bradley, 1980; Dodd, 1980; Asquith et al., 1983). To facilitate comparisons, we focus upon only those studies that measure returns by months or days surrounding a single-event announcement, i.e., we do not consider studies which measure returns on an annual basis (Hogarty, 1970; Lev and Mandelker, 1972; and those in Mueller, 1980).

The first group of studies we wish to consider measures a firm's return performance in any day or month relative to that of a control group. Bradley (1980), Asquith (1983), and Asquith et al. (1983) use Center for Research in Security Prices excess returns and thus use as a control group companies with $\hat{\beta}$'s similar to those of the acquiring firms. The prediction in these studies is that an acquiring firm would earn a return each day equal to that of firms with similar $\hat{\beta}$'s. Of the three, only Asquith (1983) presents sufficient returns data before and after the announcement date to allow comparison with the other studies in this section.

Table 11.7 summarizes his main results. Asquith reports 22 months of returns data prior to the announcement day. The acquiring firms earn positive cumulative excess returns over this entire preannouncement period. Acquiring-firm shareholders enjoy cumulative abnormal returns above those earned by shareholders in the control group of 14% between the first month in Asquith's data series (-22) and the last month before the market learns of the merger (-2). The cumulative excess returns for acquiring-firm shareholders reach a peak of 14.5% above the control group on press day and level off through the period between announcement and consummation; 30 trading days after the merger a decline begins that continues for as long as Asquith reports figures (roughly 17 months after announcement). An individual who purchased an acquiring firm's shares just prior to the first signs of market knowledge of the merger (-1) and held them throughout the period over which Asquith reports data would have experienced a cumulative return 7.2% *below* that of shareholders of nonacquiring firms with similar β's over the same period.

An analogous procedure to that just described uses Fama-MacBeth residuals. These are calculated from the following equation:

$$ e_{it} = R_{it} - \hat{\gamma}_{1t} - \hat{\gamma}_{2t}\hat{\beta}_i \quad (11.4) $$

where R_{it} and β_i are defined as before. The $\hat{\gamma}_{1t}$ and $\hat{\gamma}_{2t}$ parameters are the cross-section estimates of the intercept and slope from monthly regressions of average portfolio returns on average $\hat{\beta}$. Thus, $\hat{\gamma}_{1t}$ and $\hat{\gamma}_{2t}$ differ from month to month, but for any single month they are the same for all firms. The acquiring firm's predicted return for each period t reflects market factors common to all firms. Thus the use of Fama-MacBeth residuals effectively treats the market portfolio as the control group. Table 11.7 summarizes the main results for three studies which employ Fama-Mac-Beth residuals (Mandelker, 1974; Ellert, 1976; Kummer and Hoffmeister, 1978). All three studies again exhibit positive premerger returns for acquiring-firm shareholders commencing in Ellert's study with the first month of data, some 100 months prior to the merger. Mandelker's study exhibits a leveling off and slight decline in returns commencing around the time of merger announcement, as Asquith's study did. Ellert's sample is more difficult to interpret, since it consists of firms whose mergers were challenged by the FTC or Justice Department. The firms, which eventually succeeded in consummating the mergers, experienced a very slight decline in returns relative to the market portfolio over the 48 months after the challenge to the merger was settled.

The Kummer and Hoffmeister (1978) results indicate substantial positive abnormal returns for acquiring-firm shareholders in the month the tender offer is

announced, followed by no clear pattern. It is the only study in Table 11.7 for which the acquiring-firm shareholders do better than their control group over the combined announcement-event–postevent period.

The four studies examined so far are similar in that they all measure a firm's excess return in any month relative to a control group's performance. Any inference regarding the *change* in acquiring-firm performance must be drawn by comparing the preevent performance of the acquiring firms relative to their control groups and their postevent performance relative to these control groups.

All four studies report positive, abnormal return performance for acquiring-firm shareholders over periods ranging from 17 to 100 months prior to announcement. All report a poorer relative performance for the acquiring companies' shares over the announcement-event–postevent period than observed for the preevent period. Indeed, only one study reports significant positive gains relative to the control group for this period (Kummer and Hoffmeister), but the abnormal gains they report for the 21 months commencing with an acquisition's announcement are only a third of the abnormal returns the same firms earned over the preceding 28 months. In the Mandelker and Ellert studies, the acquiring firms perform roughly the same as the control group firms following the merger announcements. In Asquith's study, the acquiring firms perform significantly worse than their control group after the mergers, where they had performed significantly better before.

Before turning to the next set of studies, let us briefly reconsider Mandelker's results. Although the general pattern of return performance in Mandelker's study resembles the others, the premerger rise in returns is much smaller. Mandelker's sampling of mergers stops in 1963. Unlike the other three studies, it does not include mergers from the peak years of merger and stock market activity, 1967–1969. Consistent with our earlier arguments that merging firms' returns may be particularly af-

Table 11.7. Before- and After-Acquisition Performance of Acquiring Companies in Nine Studies

Study	Time Period (Country)	Control Group Against Which Preacquisition Abnormal Performance Measured	Month Information of Acquisition Reaches Market (t_i)	Month in Which Cumulative Residuals Begin Upward Trend (t_u)	Cumulative Abnormal Returns at Month t_{i-1}	Control Group Against Which Postmerger Abnormal Performance Measured	Month Following Acquisition in Which Fall in Cumulative Residuals Stops (t_f)	Difference Between Cumulative Residuals in t_f and t_{i-1}	Last Month for Which Return Performance Reported (t_e)	Difference Between Cumulative Residuals in t_e and t_{i-1}	Notes
Asquith (1983)	1962–1976 (USA)	Companies with similar βs	−1	−22[a]	14.0	Companies with similar βs	17	−7.2	17	−7.2	Returns reported in days. We have converted to months by dividing by 22 trading days per month. Interval between announcement day and merger completion assumed to equal 6 months.
Mandelker (1974)	1941–1963 (USA)	Fama-MacBeth residuals	−1	−17	3.5	Fama-MacBeth residuals	46	+0.2	46	+0.2	Mandelker's data centered around merger completion. We have assumed announcement is 6 months before completion.
Ellert (1976)	1950–1972 (USA)	Fama-MacBeth residuals	−3	−100[a]	23.6	Fama-MacBeth residuals	82	−3.4	82	−3.4	Ellert's data centered around month a merger complaint is made by antitrust authorities. We assume announcement month is same as complaint month. Premerger returns are for all acquirors; postmerger returns are for only those which completed the acquisition.
Kummer and Hoffmeister (1978)	1956–1974 (USA)	Fama-MacBeth residuals	0	−28	17.0	Fama-MacBeth residuals	No systematic movement following merger		20	+5.8	

Study	Time Period (Country)	Control Group Against Which Premerger Abnormal Performance Measured	Month Information of Merger Reaches Market (t_i)	Month in Which Cumulative Residuals Begin Upward Trend (t_u)	Cumulative Abnormal Returns at Month t_i-1	Control Group Against Which Postmerger Abnormal Performance Measured	Month Following Merger in Which Fall in Cumulative Residuals Stops (t_f)	Difference Between Cumulative Residuals in t_f and t_i-1	Last Month for Which Return Performance Reported (t_e)	Difference Between Cumulative Residuals in t_e and t_i-1	Notes
Dodd and Ruback (1977)	1958–1976 (USA)	Acquiring firm's performance relative to market portfolio −73 through −14	−1	−43	10.47	Acquiring firm's performance relative to market portfolio +14 through +73	60	−1.85	60	−1.85	
Franks et al. (1977)	1955–1972 (UK)	Acquiring firm's performance relative to its industry, −29 through +8	−3	No systematic movement prior to merger	−0.3	Acquiring firm's performance relative to its industry, −29 to +8	15	−2.4	40	−0.1	Sample is for acquisitions in brewing and distillery. Returns are measured net of industry index.
Langetieg (1978)	1929–1969 (USA)	Acquiring firm's performance relative to market portfolio and its two-digit SIC industry, −72 to −12	0	−60	13.58	Acquiring firm's performance relative to market portfolio and its two-digit SIC industry, +12 to +72	78	−29.0	78	−29.0	Langetieg's data centered around merger completion month. We have assumed announcement is 6 months before completion based on acquired-firm return performance.
Firth (1980)	1969–1975 (UK)	Acquiring firm's performance relative to market portfolio in 48 preceding months	−1	−48[a]	1.5	Acquiring firm's performance relative to market portfolio in 48 preceding months (omitting −12 to +12)	1	−7.4	36	−4.8	
Malatesta (1983)	1969–1974 (USA)	Acquiring firm's performance relative to market portfolio in 36-month period from −62 to −1	−4 (?)	−60[a] (?)	3.6	Acquiring firm's performance relative to market portfolio in 36-month period in +13 to +60	12	−7.7	12	−7.7	

Notes: Month 0 is the announcement month.

[a]First month for which data are reported.

fected by stock market swings, both the more modest premerger increases and postmerger declines recorded by Mandelker may stem from his having employed a merger sample drawn from a more tranquil period of stock market–merger activity.

The last technique for estimating the effect of acquisitions we consider uses the residuals from some variant on Equation (11.5):

$$e_{it} = (R_{it} - R_{ft}) - \hat{\alpha}_i$$
$$- \hat{\beta}_i(R_{mt} - R_{ft}) \quad (11.5)$$

Recall that the value of $\hat{\alpha}$ for the average firm is zero and that $\hat{\alpha}_i$ thus captures a firm's abnormal performance over the time period from which (11.5) is estimated. Thus, if (11.5) is estimated over a period prior to the event's announcement, the residuals from (11.5) at and after announcement do measure the *change* in performance for the firm relative to the preevent period over which (11.5) was estimated. More generally, the inferences one draws from residuals from (11.5) are sensitive to the time period over which it is estimated.

This point is illustrated by the bottom five entries of Table 11.7. We first consider the study of Dodd and Ruback (1977) in some detail, since it clearly illustrates the issues. They estimate Equation (11.5) separately on data from $[-73, -14]$ and $[14, 73]$. If the pre– and post–tender offer performance of acquiring firms in their sample resembles that of the studies just discussed, then acquiring firms exhibit above-normal performance over some part, if not all, of $[-73, -14]$ and normal or below-normal performance over part or all of $[14, 73]$. The $\hat{\alpha}$'s from (11.5) over $[-73, -14]$ will be higher than those for $[14, 73]$.[9] The residuals they report for $[-60, -1]$ are for $\hat{\alpha}$ and $\hat{\beta}$ estimated over $[-73, -14]$ and those for $[0, 60]$ from $[14, 73]$. Thus, the reported residuals for the preevent period are calculated against a benchmark of above-normal performance and are thus smaller than if they had been measured relative to a period of poorer performance. Residuals for the an-

nouncement month and postevent period are calculated against a benchmark of poorer performance than the preevent period and thus are certainly larger than they would be if they were measured against the acquiring firms' preevent performance.

That these inferences are likely to be valid can be seen by an examination of the cumulative residuals for the bidding firms in the Dodd and Ruback study (Figure 11.2).[10] As with the studies using CRSP and Fama-MacBeth residuals, a period of sustained above-normal performance is observed commencing at A some 43 months prior to the initial tender offer month (B), where *normal* is now defined as how these firms did over the period $[-73, -14]$. Since acquiring-firm performance over $[-73, -14]$ is, if anything, above that predicted from the market portfolio and Equation (11.1), these residuals probably understate the extent of abnormal, positive performance of acquiring firms prior to the acquisitions. A period of gradual but sustained decline in share returns commences at C, month 6, about the time the takeovers are probably consummated.[11] It continues through month 60 and conceivably through 73. It is against this period of deteriorating performance $[14, 73]$ that the abnormal returns $[0, 60]$ are calculated. Thus, the level of returns in the interval $[0, 12]$ is judged relative to how the firms did from one to six years after the tender offers, not to how they did before. A comparison of Figures 11.2 and 11.1 reveals that Dodd and Ruback's acquiring-firm residuals pattern resembles the pattern for our sample when a postevent estimation period is used as benchmark (our case III). Had preevent period α's and β's been used by Dodd and Ruback, their postevent residuals probably would have exhibited a steeper decline, as with our cases I and II.[12]

Similar reasoning calls into question Dodd and Ruback's conclusion that acquiring-company shareholders are better off from the acquisitions on the basis of the statistically significant average residual of 2.83% in the announcement month. The rise in "abnormal" returns in month 0 stems in part from the switch at this month from the higher performance period

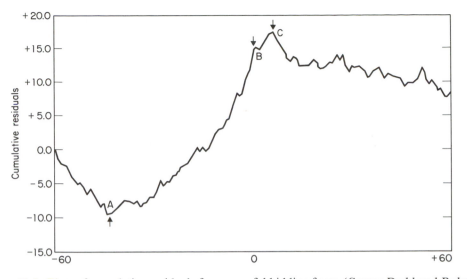

Figure 11.2. Plots of cumulative residuals for successful bidding firms. (*Source:* Dodd and Ruback, 1977.)

[−73, −14] $\hat{\alpha}$'s and $\hat{\beta}$'s to the lower-period [14, 73] estimates. That is, acquiring-firm shares appear to have gained in abnormal performance in month 0 partly because the benchmark of normality has shifted downward.

The importance of the treatment of $\hat{\alpha}$ and thus the choice of time period over which $\hat{\alpha}$ is estimated is further illustrated by Malatesta's (1983) study. Residuals over the period [−60, −13] are calculated by using the first available 36 observations from the preceding 50 months. The cumulative average $\hat{\alpha}$ over [−24, −4] is 10.7, and the forecast error is −1.6. Thus, acquiring firms in Malatesta's sample also were earning significantly higher returns than the market portfolio prior to the market's learning of the mergers. The modest cumulative residuals Malatesta reports for the premerger period relative to the acquiring firms' performance over this period merely indicate that the above-normal performance for the acquiring firms was fairly uniform throughout the entire premerger period [−62, −1] and thus is adequately represented by his $\hat{\alpha}$ estimates.

The residuals for months 1 through 60 are calculated from $\hat{\alpha}$ and $\hat{\beta}$ estimated from the first available 36 months in the interval

[13, 60]. The cumulative residuals over [1, 12] are negative and significant even relative to the acquiring firms' subsequent performance in the postmerger period. While Malatesta does not report the $\hat{\alpha}$'s for the postmerger residuals, one presumes from Asquith's results that they would be substantially less than the 10.7% cumulative $\hat{\alpha}$ obtained prior to the mergers. Thus, the acquiring firms probably did even worse during the first 12 months after the announcements, compared with how they were doing before, than is implied by the residuals Malatesta calculates relative to the postmerger period's $\hat{\alpha}$'s and $\hat{\beta}$'s.

The importance of how one treats the $\hat{\alpha}$ estimates from Equation (11.5) is further illustrated by the results of Langetieg's (1978) study. Langetieg estimates a variant on Equation (11.5), which also controls for movements in acquiring-firm returns common to all firms in the acquiring firm's two-digit SIC industry. His measure of abnormal returns for firm i is the sum of $\hat{\alpha}_i$ and $\hat{e}_{it}$. Thus, although Langetieg estimates separate $\hat{\alpha}$'s and $\hat{\beta}$'s for the pre- and postmerger periods, his measures of abnormal returns do not suffer from the same problems as the Dodd and Ruback and Malatesta measures do, because Langetieg includes the respective $\hat{\alpha}$'s as part of the abnormal returns, thus building into his results the systematic change in the intercept.

The cumulative excess returns for the acquiring firms turn positive 60 months prior to the point in time when information of the merger reaches the market. Over these 60 months, shareholders of acquiring firms enjoy excess returns of 13.58% over what one predicts from movements in both the market portfolio and the acquiring firm's two-digit industry.[13]

In what is now a familiar pattern, we witness in Langetieg's data a leveling off of excess returns between the market's first knowledge of the mergers and their consummation, and then a sustained decline. The acquiring-firm returns decline continuously over the 72 months following a merger. A shareholder who bought into an acquiring firm just prior to the market's learning of the merger and held its shares for the next 78 months would experience a cumulative loss relative to the market portfolio and shareholders of other firms in the same industry of 29%.

Firth (1980) calculates the residual at month t from $\hat{\alpha}$ and $\hat{\beta}$ estimates for the 48 months immediately preceding t, when t varies from -48 to -13. Thus, if acquiring firms earned above-normal returns uniformly over a substantial interval prior to the mergers, this fact would not be apparent in the residuals for the premerger period.

The residuals over the entire interval $[-12, 12]$ are calculated by using $\hat{\alpha}$'s and $\hat{\beta}$'s estimated from $[-60, -13]$. Thus, unlike the results in both Dodd and Ruback and Malatesta, the immediate pre- and postannouncement residuals are all calculated relative to the acquiring companies' premerger return performance. As it turns out, in Firth's study this difference does not prove to be important. The market adjusts fully in the announcement month, at which time the acquiring-firm shareholders suffer a significant 6.3% loss relative to premerger performance. The residuals for the postmerger months reveal no distinctive pattern.

The Franks et al. (1977) study of 94 ac-

quisitions by United Kingdom breweries and distilleries is difficult to analyze. They first present, for the combined merging companies, cumulative average residuals which "display a strong upward bias throughout, thus exhibiting effects which cannot be attributed to mergers" (1977, p. 1521). Since the residuals for the acquiring and acquired firms are combined, one cannot determine whether it is the performance of the former or the latter which accounts for this positive abnormal premerger performance. But if it were the acquiring firms that were exhibiting above-normal premerger performance, the Franks et al. results would correspond closely to those of the other studies we have discussed. When they control for industry performance, the acquiring firms exhibit no above-normal returns prior to the merger. But since the acquiring firms are part of the industry index, this choice of control group introduces a bias toward zero in the residual estimates.

Franks et al. estimate Equation (11.5) over the time period $[-29, 8]$, omitting an interval around the announcement, which "is adjusted on the basis of the resulting estimates of abnormal residuals" (p. 1515). Given that the excluded interval varies from firm to firm, it is difficult to determine against what yardstick abnormal performance is being gauged. Nevertheless, returns initially rise (from -4 through 0) and then decline, leaving acquiring shareholders no better off as a result of the mergers. "Indeed since some gain would have been anticipated as a result of premerger interests [of the acquiring firms in the targets], one could argue that there may have been losses exclusive of these interests" (p. 1523).

SUMMARY AND CONCLUSIONS

To acquire another firm, a buyer must pay a substantial premium over the current market value of the target. In our sample, this premium averaged 81% of the target firms' market value. Thus, over the period between the initial decision to acquire and the completion of an acquisition, shareholders of acquired firms enjoy substantial increases in their wealth. The key question for the theory of the firm and for antimerger policy is whether these wealth increases measure net increases in wealth for society as a result of some synergistic efficiency gain, or mere wealth transfers from acquiring-firm to acquired-firm shareholders.

To answer this question, one must measure the effects of the acquisitions on acquiring-firm shareholder wealth. While it is reasonable to assume that the changes in acquiring-firm shareholder wealth related to the acquisition begin about the same time as the changes in acquired-firm shareholder wealth begin, somewhere between the announcement and four months before, it is arguable whether all changes in acquiring-firm wealth caused by the acquisition are complete by the date of its announcement or its completion. Conceivably, new information about its future consequences might reach the market at intermittent intervals for some time after the market's first knowledge of the acquisition. This consideration suggests that a longer-run perspective of the consequences of acquisitions for acquiring-firm shareholders might be appropriate than is warranted for acquired-firm shareholders.

Several studies have measured the performance of acquiring firms relative to the average firm in the stock market or in the acquiring firm's industry, both before and after acquisition announcements.[14] A consistent pattern emerges. Acquiring firms begin to experience significant positive abnormal returns as early as 100 months prior to the acquisition announcements. The cumulative preacquisition gains of acquiring-firm shareholders are inevitably positive and are typically large.[15]

Starting around the time the market begins to learn of an acquisition, or at its consummation, the performance of the acquiring firm's shares begins to deteriorate relative to their preevent performance. In some cases, they exhibit a roughly normal postevent performance (e.g., Mandelker, 1974); in others, a significant relative decline (Langetieg, 1978; Asquith, 1983).[16]

A second set of studies measures an ac-

quiring firm's performance as a result of an acquisition, relative to this performance over another period, controlling for general shifts in the economy by using the basic CAPM equation (11.5). Given that the acquiring firm's performance relative to the market (or its industry) differs significantly over the pre- and postevent time intervals, estimates of "abnormal" returns to acquiring-firm shareholders are sensitive to the choice of time period over which the "normal" $\hat{\alpha}$ and $\hat{\beta}$ of Equation (11.5) are measured. Our own results indicate significant above-normal returns are earned by acquiring-firm shareholders over the immediate two to three years prior to the market's learning of an acquisition, relative to the performance of these firms in the three preceding years. Following the market's receipt of information of the acquisition, the acquiring firms' shareholders experience lower returns than they enjoyed over the preevent period. Moreover, the deterioration in performance is more dramatic if comparison is made with the immediate three years' performance than if comparison is with the five preevent years.

Our findings are consistent with those of other studies using Equation (11.5) and the CAPM, although comparisons are made difficult by the differing choices of time periods for estimating (11.5). A significant decline in acquiring-firm returns is observed by Firth (1980) in the announcement month and perhaps by Franks et al. (1977) in the first few months following the merger announcements. Malatesta (1983) observes a significant decline in acquiring-firm performance in the first 12 months after the announcement, relative to the acquiring companies' performance over a postmerger period; Dodd and Ruback (1977) record a steady decline in performance over 54 months following the acquisition's completion, again measured relative to the acquiring companies' own normal postevent performance. Since acquiring firms perform worse after acquisitions than before, when measured against the market, the decline in returns measured by Malatesta and Dodd and Ruback following the acquisitions is in all likelihood considerably smaller than it would have been had these authors measured the decline against the predicted performance of acquiring firms on the basis of their preevent histories.

Thus, the answer to the question posed in the title of this chapter, "Are acquiring-firm shareholders better off after an acquisition than they were before?" seems to be no, if by *before* we mean the three years or so prior to the time information reaches the market, and if by *after* we mean the three years or so after this point in time.

The evaluation of the effects of acquisitions on acquiring-firm shareholders' wealth presented here is considerably more negative than that found in some other parts of the literature. Others have reached more positive conclusions than we in part because they have posed different questions from ours. To the extent that one focuses on the acquiring companies' performance only at the time of the announcement (e.g., Dodd and Ruback, 1977; Bradley, 1980) and makes one's comparison not to the acquiring firms' own preevent performance but to that of the market portfolio (e.g., Mandelker, 1974; Kummer and Hoffmeister, 1978; Bradley, 1980), one obtains a more optimistic assessment of the performance of acquiring-company shares. Halpern (1983) ignores the evidence on postevent acquiring-company returns entirely in his survey; Jensen and Ruback (1983) clearly give more weight to the figures regarding the gains at the time of acquisition in their Table 3 than they do to the figures which include postacquisition performance in Table 4. Neither survey has much to say about the substantial positive abnormal returns acquiring-firm shareholders earn before the market learns of the acquisitions.

The stock market is subject to substantial swings in returns that cannot be justified by an application of the rational-expectations assumption to subsequent dividend streams. Acquisition activity is correlated with stock market activity and is arguably subject to the same underlying psychological factors and motivations. The stock market may be over- or under optimistic about the future consequences of acquisitions at different points in time. Moreover, an acquisition is a sufficiently complex event that it might take the market more than a single month or year to form an accurate estimate of its future effect. These considerations suggest to us the need for a longer-run view of the consequences of acquisitions. But whether or not one agrees with us on this point, we do hope we have achieved our goal of demonstrating that one's answer to the question "Are shareholders of acquiring firms better off after an acquisition than they were before?" is sensitive to both the choice of time intervals over which before and after performance is defined and the choice of benchmark against which performance is measured.

NOTES

1. Nelson (1959, 1966); Melicher et al. (1983); Geroski (1984). Casual observation suggests that this correlation may have weakened in the most recent years. But the cited studies carry the analysis up through the midseventies. Since all of the empirical work discussed in this chapter, save our own, is from the period in which the positive correlation has been found to exist, our point with respect to the existing literature and its interpretation is valid even if it should prove that acquisition activity is no longer strongly correlated with stock market price movements.

2. Recent critiques by Roll (1977) and Levy (1983), among others, call into question some of the assumptions of the CAPM. While these papers pose serious challenges to many of the conclusions drawn from the CAPM, they carry less weight with regard to the literature on the effects of acquisitions. The market portfolio may be a reasonable choice as a control group for predicting changes in an acquiring firm's returns, even if it is not a reasonable portfolio for an individual to hold.

3. The total number of firms exceeds the number of firms involved in mergers and tender offers because one of the firms could not be classified.

4. The pattern of overall acquisition activity during the sample period can be seen in this record of completed acquisitions:

Year	Number of Acquisitions	Percent Change
1976	1145	16.7
1977	1209	5.6
1978	1452	20.1
1979	1564	7.7
1980	1583	1.2
1981	2314	46.2

Transactions counted here are valued at $1 million or more; the list includes partial acquisitions (*Mergers and Acquisitions,* Winter 1984).

5. See Fama (1976) for a full description of the market model.

6. Each firm error $\hat{e}_{it}$ is divided by its standard deviation $\hat{\sigma}(\hat{e}_{it})$, where

$$\hat{\sigma}(\hat{e}_{it}) = \left\{ S_i^2 \left[1 + \frac{1}{T} + \frac{(R_{mt} - \overline{R}_m)^2}{\sum_{\tau = 1}^{T} (R_{m\tau} - \overline{R}_m)^2} \right] \right\}^{1/2}$$

and

S_i^2 = error variance calculated from the market model regression for firm i

$\overline{R}_m$ = average return on the market portfolio over the estimation period

T = number of months in the estimation period

The standardized errors $\hat{e}_{it}/\hat{\sigma}(\hat{e}_{it})$ are summed and divided by I, the total number of firms, to obtain AS_t, the average standardized error for each time period. We define z, the test statistic, as $z_t = \sqrt{I_t}\,(AS_t)$, where z is distributed as approximately a normal variable for large samples. To obtain the test statistic for the null hypothesis that the CAR_{xy} are insignificantly different from zero, we calculate

$$\overline{z} = \sum_{t=x}^{Y} \frac{z_t}{(y - x + 1)^{1/2}}$$

where z is also distributed approximately normally for large samples.

7. The typical justification for choosing a postevent period against which to measure postevent residuals is that the $\hat{\beta}$'s may change as a result of the acquisition. But those studies which test for shifts in the $\hat{\beta}_i$ report no *systematic* shifts in them (see the third section). Nor do we find any. For example, only two of the $\hat{\beta}$'s estimated over [−3, 36] are significantly different from those estimated over [−60, −4], one being larger, the other smaller. The other 76 insignificant changes divide almost evenly between increases and decreases.

8. Michael Jensen also argues that the postevent benchmark should be the normal performance of the acquiring firms, not their above-normal preevent performance. We thank Michael for his comment at the conference, which helped clarify our thinking on this point.

9. Although Dodd and Ruback (1977) report the differences between the $\hat{\beta}$'s for the two periods, they unfortunately do not report the differences in $\hat{\alpha}$'s (p. 358).

10. Dodd and Ruback (1977) do not report the cumulative residual series, so we have added the averages they do report to obtain Figure 11.2. Our Figure 11.2 corresponds to and resembles very closely their Figure 2.

11. Both Mandelker (1974) and Langetieg (1978) center their data around the consummation of the acquisition, not its announcement. Judging from the acquired firms' returns in these studies, information regarding the mergers would appear to reach the market about six months before the mergers are completed. In our sample, four months elapse on average between first announcement and consummation, which corresponds to these other studies if one allows two months for preannouncement information leakage. We assume the gap between announcement and consummation to be six months in the Mandelker, Langetieg, and Asquith studies.

12. The reason Dodd and Ruback (1977) give for using separate $\hat{\alpha}$ and $\hat{\beta}$ estimates from before and after the announcement is that for 34 of the 184 firms in their sample (18%), there is a significant change in $\hat{\beta}$ (pp. 358–359). But changes in $\hat{\beta}$ are equally divided between increases (10 for successful bidders) and declines (9). Thus, no *systematic* shift in residuals should result if preannouncement $\hat{\beta}$'s are used. But if postannouncement $\hat{\alpha}$'s are significantly lower than preannouncement $\hat{\alpha}$'s, postannouncement residuals are systematically raised by their choice of period against which to measure postannouncement performance.

13. Langetieg (1978) reports four sets of similar results (Table 1, p. 373). We quote from only the first set, using an equally weighted industry index.

Langetieg also reports residuals net of the market portfolio, industry index, *and* the performance of a "well-matched non-merging firm" (p. 371). The latter is selected from the acquiring firm's two-digit industry by the criterion that its residuals from the market portfolio regression (11.5) have the highest correlation with the residuals for the acquiring firm. This criterion for selecting a control group firm biases Langetieg's findings for this comparison toward zero. With an infinitely large population from which to select control group firms, one would find for any acquiring firm a nonacquiring firm whose residuals correlate perfectly, leaving nothing to be explained. A two-digit industry is not an infinite population, but it is large enough to introduce serious bias toward zero. Nevertheless, the same preevent-positive-excess-returns, postevent-negative-excess-returns pattern appears even after netting out the movements in the control group returns (see Table 2, p. 377).

14. Since Langetieg (1978) adds $\hat{\alpha}_i$ back into his estimate of abnormal returns, his is really an estimate relative to both the market portfolio and the two-digit SIC industry and should be included with this group.

15. Other studies reporting substantial positive premerger returns for acquiring firms are Lev and Mandelker (1972) and Cosh et al. (1980).

16. Other studies reporting postmerger period declines include Hogarty (1970); Cosh et al. (1980); Dodd (1980); Jenny and Weber (1980); and Mueller (1980).

REFERENCES

Amihud, Y., and L. Baruch (1981). "Risk reduction as a Managerial Motive for Conglomerate Mergers." *Bell Journal of Economics* 12, 605–617.

Asquith, P. (1983) "Merger Bids, Uncertainty, and Stockholder Returns." *Journal of Financial Economics* 11, 51–83.

————, R. F. Bruner, and D. W. Mullins, Jr. (1983). "The Gains to Bidding Firms from Merger." *Journal of Financial Economics* 11, 121–139.

Azzi, C. (1978). "Conglomerate Mergers, Default Risk, and Homemade Mutual Funds." *American Economic Review* 68, 161–172.

Bradley, M. (1980). "Interfirm Tender Offers and the Market for Corporate Control." *Journal of Business* 53, 345–376.

Cosh, A., A. Hughes, and A. Singh (1980). "The Causes and Effects of Takeovers in the United Kingdom: An Empirical Investigation for the Late 1960s at the Microeconomic Level." In *The Determinants and Effects of Mergers: An International Comparison,* ed. D. C. Mueller, 227–270. Cambridge, Eng.: Oelgeschlager, Gunn, and Hain.

Dodd, P. (1980). "Merger Proposals, Management Discretion and Stockholder Wealth." *Journal of Financial Economics* 8, 105–137.

————, and R. Ruback (1977). "Tender Offers and Stockholder Returns: An Empirical Analysis." *Journal of Financial Economics* 5, 351–374.

Ellert, J. C. (1976). "Mergers, Antitrust Law Enforcement and Stockholder Returns." *Journal of Finance* 31, 715–732.

Fama, E. F. (1976). *The Foundation of Finance.* New York: Basic Books.

————, L. Fisher, M. C. Jensen, and R. Roll (1969) "The Adjustment of Stock Prices to New Information." *International Economic Review* 10, 1–21.

Firth, M. (1980). "Takeovers, Shareholder Returns, and the Theory of the Firm." *Quarterly Journal of Economics* 94, 315–347.

Franks, J. R., J. E. Broyles, and M. J. Hecht (1977). "An Industry Study of the Profitability of Mergers in the United Kingdom." *Journal of Finance* 32, 1513–1525.

Geroski, P. A. (1984). "On the Relationship Between Aggregate Merger Activity and the Stock Market." *European Economic Review* 25, 223–233.

Greer, D. F. (1984). "Acquiring in Order to Avoid Acquisition." Mimeo, San Jose State University.

Halpern, P. J. (1973). "Empirical Estimates of the Amount and Distribution of Gains to Companies in Mergers." *Journal of Business* 46, 554–575.

———— (1983). "Corporate Acquisitions: A Theory of Special Cases? A Review of Event Studies Applied to Acquisitions." *Journal of Finance* 38, 297–317.

Hogarty, T. F. (1970). "The Profitability of Corporate Mergers." *Journal of Business* 43, 317–327.

Jenny, F., and A. P. Weber (1980). "France, 1962–72." In *The Determinants and Effects of Mergers: An International Comparison,* ed. D. C. Mueller, 133–162. Cambridge, Eng.: Oelgeschlager, Gunn, and Hain.

Jensen, M. (1969). "Risk, the Pricing of Capital Assets, and the Evaluation of Investment Portfolios." *Journal of Business* 42, 167–247.

————, and R. S. Ruback (1983). "The Market for Corporate Control." *Journal of Financial Economics* 11, 5–50.

Johnston, J. (1972). *Econometric Methods.* 2nd ed. New York: McGraw-Hill.

Kummer, D. R., and J. R. Hoffmeister (1978). "Valuation Consequences of Cash Tender Offers." *Journal of Finance* 33, 505–516.

Langetieg, T. C. (1978). "An Application of a Three-Factor Performance Index to Measure Stockholder Gains from Merger." *Journal of Financial Economics* 6, 365–384.

Lev, B., and G. Mandelker (1972). "The Microeconomic Consequences of Corporate Mergers." *Journal of Business* **45**, 85–104.

Levy, H., and M. Sarnat (1970). "Diversification, Portfolio Analysis and the Uneasy Case for Conglomerate Mergers." *Journal of Finance* **25**, 795–802.

Levy, H. (1983). "The Capital Asset Pricing Model: Theory and Empiricism," *Economic Journal* **93**, 145–165.

Linn, S. C., and J. J. McConnell (1983). "An Empirical Investigation of the Impact of 'Antitakeover' Amendments on Common Stock Prices." *Journal of Financial Economics* **11**, 361–399.

Malatesta, P. H. (1983). "The Wealth Effect of Merger Activity and the Objective Functions of Merging Firms." *Journal of Financial Economics* **11**, 155–181.

Mandelker, G. (1974). "Risk and Return: The Case of Merging Firms." *Journal of Financial Economics* **1**, 303–335.

Manne, H. G. (1965). "Mergers and the Market for Corporate Control." *Journal of Political Economy* **73**, 110–120.

Mason, R. H., and M. B. Goudzwaard (1976). "Performance of Conglomerate Firms: A Portfolio Approach." *Journal of Finance* **31**, 39–48.

Melicher, R. W., J. Ledolter, and L. J. D'Antonio (1983). "A Time Series Analysis of Aggregate Merger Activity." *Review of Economics and Statistics* **65**, 423–430.

Mergers and Acquisitions, 1984 Almanac and Index, p. 21.

Mueller, D. C. (1969). "A Theory of Conglomerate Mergers." *Quarterly Journal of Economics* **83**, 643–659.

———— (1977). "The Effects of Conglomerate Mergers: A Survey of the Empirical Evidence." *Journal of Banking and Finance* **1**, 315–347.

———— (1979). "Do We Want a New, Tough Antimerger Law?" *Antitrust Bulletin* **24**, 807–836.

————, ed. (1980). *The Determinants and Effects of Mergers: An International Comparison.* Cambridge; England: Oelgeschlager, Gunn, and Hain.

Nelson, R. L. (1959). *Merger Movements in American Industry, 1895–1956.* Princeton: Princeton University Press.

———— (1966). "Business Cycle Factors in the Choice Between Internal and External Growth." In *The Corporate Merger,* eds. W. Alberts and J. Segall. Chicago: University of Chicago Press.

Roll, R. (1977). "A Critique of the Asset Pricing Theory Tests." *Journal of Financial Economics* **4**, 129–176.

Scherer, F. M. (1971). *Industrial Market Structure and Economic Performance.* 2nd ed. Chicago: Rand McNally.

Shiller, R. J. (1981). "Do Stock Prices Move Too Much to Be Justified by Subsequent Changes in Dividends?" *American Economic Review* **71**, 421–436.

———— (1984). "Stock Prices and Social Dynamics." *Brookings Papers on Economic Activity,* December, 457–498.

———— (1986). "Fashions, Fads, and Bubbles in Financial Markets." Chapter 3 of this volume.

Smith, K. V., and J. C. Schreiner (1969). "A Portfolio Analysis of Conglomerate Diversification." *Journal of Finance* **24**, 413–427.

Smith, V. L. (1970). "Corporate Financial Theory Under Uncertainty." *Quarterly Journal of Economics* **84**, 451–471.

Weston, J. F., K. V. Smith, and R. E. Shrieves (1972). "Conglomerate Performance Using the Capital Asset Pricing Model." *Review of Economics and Statistics* **54**, 357–363.

12

Mergers and Managerial Performance

DAVID J. RAVENSCRAFT
AND F. M. SCHERER

This chapter provides a nontechnical summary of our research since 1982 on the economics of mergers and sell-offs.[1] It deals only peripherally with contested takeovers, the conference's central focus. During the time period spanned by our principal data, contested takeovers were more of a rarity than in the 1980s, and so relatively few cases are covered. Rather, we are concerned with mergers of all kinds, friendly and hostile, large and small: why they are made, how they are managed, and what their financial consequences have been.

Our work was inspired by a paradox and an opportunity. Many scholarly studies have inferred from the behavior of stock prices immediately surrounding merger "events" that merger activity was unambiguously efficiency increasing. The underlying hypotheses, implicit or explicit, are (1) that premerger financial performance of the acquired firm was deficient and improvable, and (2) that profitability increases would on average follow after mergers were consummated. Yet since the early 1970s, the business press has been reporting vast numbers of "sell-offs"—mergers that were made and then, because of ill fit, disappointing performance, or other problems, were being undone. The high incidence of postmerger divorces—up to

Scherer's work was supported under National Science Foundation Grant SES-8209766 and two Swarthmore College faculty research grants. Use is made of line-of-business data collected by the Federal Trade Commission. A review by FTC staff has determined that individual company data are not disclosed. The conclusions are the authors' and not necessarily those of the FTC.

40% of acquisition transactions during the 1970s, according to W. T. Grimm data—seemed hard to reconcile with efficiency hypotheses. The opportunity that coincided with recognition of this paradox was the availability of richly segmented performance data under the Federal Trade Commission's line-of-business program. For the first time ever, it became possible to analyze microscopically, using a large statistical sample, the postmerger financial performance of corporate units.

At the heart of our research strategy was a desire to understand the actual internal events that preceded and followed mergers and thus to go beyond stock market manifestations. To this end, three main research thrusts were pursued simultaneously. First, historical case studies were compiled on 15 mergers (or merger clusters) that led to sell-off. These were based on 70 interviews, mostly at the division-head level or higher, as well as considerable research in documentary materials. Second, 27 years of merger history were linked to financial performance records for over 3600 individual manufacturing lines of business (LBs) operated by some 450 corporations. Altogether, more than five thousand mergers and acquisitions, with accompanying size, timing, and accounting treatment information, were coded to the company LBs, permitting a well-controlled analysis of the relationship between merger activity and postmerger profitability. Third, an attempt was made to identify all sell-offs occurring between 1974, the first year for which segmented financial performance data were available, and 1981. In this way, the financial performance patterns that preceded sell-off could be isolated. The insights flowing from these three efforts and several related subprojects are what we summarize here.

PREMERGER PERFORMANCE OF ACQUIRED ENTITIES

Among merger phenomenon commentators whose reading is confined to works with a "Chicago" imprimatur, there persists a hypothesis that acquisition candidates are characteristically sluggards— poorly performing companies which, with the proper postmerger change in management, could achieve substantial profitability gains. One key source of this view was the seminal article by Henry G. Manne. Distinguishing voluntary "mergers" from tender offers and proxy fights, he wrote:

Mergers seem in many instances to be the most efficient of the three devices for corporate takeovers. Consequently, they are of considerable importance for the protection of individual non-controlling shareholders and are desirable from a general welfare-economics point of view.... Among the advantages of [the market for corporate control] ... are a lessening of wasteful bankruptcy proceedings, more efficient management of corporations, the protection afforded non-controlling corporate investors, increased mobility of capital, and generally a more efficient allocation of resources.... One real problem [of antitrust policy] will be in devising statistical methods for distinguishing mergers motivated by a quest for monopoly profit from those merely trying to establish more efficient management in poorly run companies.[2]

Statistical studies of merger activity since the time of Manne's article have provided, at best, modest support for the deficient-performance hypothesis. Steiner's overview of the literature through 1973 concluded that "acquired firms were not all that different from the average in their industry: perhaps slightly below average in their premerger profitability but certainly not on the brink of financial disaster."[3] More recent studies by Scherer[4] and Harris

et al.[5] found acquired firms of the mid-1970s to be somewhat *more* profitable than population norms or nonacquired-company control samples.

The early premerger profitability studies were severely constrained by their focus on "public" acquired companies—a small subset of all acquired firms. A largely untapped data source escaping this constraint is the collection of "listing applications" filed when corporations with securities traded on the New York Stock Exchange make acquisitions entailing the issue of new shares. Such listing applications normally include recent income statements and balance sheets for the acquired entity, whether public or private. These were consulted for a sample of 634 domestic manufacturing company acquisitions made in three years: 1968, at the peak of the 1960s conglomerate merger wave; 1971, for which recession-year 1970 profitability data were disclosed; and 1974, by which time acquisition-prone firms had fallen out of favor on the stock market. The sample covers all manufacturing acquisitions with relevant data, not only acquisitions made by the line-of-business companies analyzed later, although there is considerable overlap. The median premerger asset size of the acquired companies in our sample was $2.4 million. In contrast, the "public" corporations on the Federal Trade Commission's list of large manufacturing corporations acquired in 1968 had median assets of $29 million.[6] Thus, our new study covers a population quite different from, and largely ignored in, previous premerger profitability analyses.

To maximize comparability with available line-of-business data, our measure of profitability is the ratio of annualized operating income (before capital charges, income taxes, and extraordinary items) to end-of-period assets. Table 12.1 presents simple averages of the premerger profitability ratios defined in this way for the acquired-company sample and for all manufacturing corporations. The acquired-company profit averages are significantly higher than the all-manufacturing figures (derived from *Quarterly Financial Report* universe totals), but the acquired-company

Table 12.1. Profitability in Last Year Before Merger for Premerger Company Sample, Compared with All Manufacturers

	Sample of 634 Acquired Companies	All Manufacturing Corporations	Differential
1968 acquisitions	20.8%	11.3%	+9.5%
1971 acquisitions	19.6%	8.6%	+11.0%
1974 acquisitions	18.9%	11.6%	+7.3%
All three years	20.2%	10.9%	+9.3%

differentials do not differ significantly from one another across individual years.

How can our results diverge so much from those that have formed the basis of conventional wisdom, in Chicago or elsewhere? There are three plausible explanations. First, as noted already, our sample is much more heavily weighted toward small companies—the infantry of the 1960s and 1970s conglomerate merger campaigns. In a more complex analysis than is reported here,[7] we found a negative association between premerger profitability and size. For every tenfold increase in assets, acquired firms' average profit premium declined by 2.3 percentage points. Yet this is not enough to reconcile the various samples' results. To have the whole-sample profit differential of 9.3 percentage points vanish, an acquired company's assets would have to increase from the sample median of $2.4 million to approximately $25 billion—a size attained by few takeover targets even today.

Second, our sample is nonrepresentative in the sense that new securities were issued to consummate the merger transaction. Mergers made without new securities (and listing applications) may have been different. Still, it is noteworthy that there is no marked difference in the results between 1968, when the use of convertible preferred stock and other funny-money securities to make acquisitions was common, and 1974, when that device had become costly owing to deflated conglomerate price-earnings ratios. Third and related, we found sharp differences in premerger profitability between companies acquired in transactions accounted for as poolings of interests and those handled as purchases (i.e., with post-

merger assets stepped up above premerger book values to reflect premiums paid). Pooling-of-interests acquisitions, comprising 79% of our NYSE listing-application sample, had average premerger operating income/assets ratios of 22.0%, whereas purchase acquisitions were only slightly (and statistically insignificantly) more profitable than their manufacturing peers. Thus, in emphasizing a set of acquisitions that lent themselves to the use of pooling accounting and the swap of securities (which are correlated), we have slighted the different (purchase accounting) set, which is less profitable and which comprised 47% of all the mergers covered by the more comprehensive sample to which we shall turn. If our premerger sample results are reweighted to reflect the relative pooling vs. purchase frequencies observed more generally, the simple average surplus of acquired-company over manufacturing universe profitability would be on the order of 6.7 percentage points.

This statistical evidence is consistent with the results of our 15 case studies, which were selected to illuminate sell-off conditions but had no deliberate premerger characteristics bias.[8] With at most one or two exceptions, the buying companies perceived their acquisitions as highly promising, not as businesses in trouble. One manifestation was that none of the acquiring companies intended to purge the acquired firm's managerial ranks. In six cases, acquirers established control by installing their own chief executives, but even then, they showed in a number of ways their satisfaction with the inherited managers and their desire to keep them, if they were willing to remain.

Thus, from both statistical analysis and case studies, it appears that acquisition activity in the United States, at least during the late 1960s and 1970s, was characteristically a search for gold nuggets, not for dross that could, by some managerial alchemy, be transformed into gold.

WHY MERGER LED TO SELL-OFF:
QUALITATIVE INSIGHTS

If merger makers began with acquisitions of generally superior performance, why did they subsequently sell many of them off? Our case study research provided numerous preliminary insights.

One of the most important is that acquisition making is appropriately viewed as a process of sampling under considerable statistical uncertainty. On average, as we have seen, the companies acquired during the late 1960s and early 1970s were of above-average profitability and with generally good perceived future prospects. But there was much uncertainty about those prospects, posing an "inspection problem" for the acquirer. Some acquisitions would turn out much better than anticipated. Others would develop problems. Our sell-off case studies emphasized the more problem-ridden acquisitions, and so our evidence on how problems emerge is especially comprehensive. Some emerging problems came from a new roll of the business environmental dice and could not, under any reasonable circumstances, have been predicted. Examples include the OPEC shock that undercut the demand for Bendix's newly acquired recreational-vehicle business and for automobiles of a size requiring Great Lakes Screw's traditional fasteners, the whims of fashion that moved dresses toward using more buttons and fewer of Talon's zippers, and the quadrupling of prices for cobalt used in J. B. Lansing's loudspeakers. The 1970s were perhaps unusually turbulent in this respect, and so more postmerger problems intruded than might have been expected in "normal" times.

Other problems were latent at the time of acquisition, more or less clearly perceived by the to-be-acquired-firm's management. They included such things as the accelerating erosion of Talon's highly profitable home-sewing zipper market, the approaching obsolescence of some companies' equipment compared with that of competitors, and weaknesses in accepted product development strategies. Such latent problems are difficult for an outside acquirer to identify under the most cooperative circumstances. When the acquisition is conglomerate and the acquirer lacks in-depth knowledge of the business, detection is even more difficult. From our two case studies of hostile takeovers, latent problems are most difficult to pinpoint when the target refuses to talk in detail with the would-be acquirer about its internal operations and plans. Still other problems stemmed from the "chemistry" postmerger organizational changes engendered. Since the phenomena here are subtle, we defer examples and further discussion until the path has been prepared.

Our case study research revealed three and perhaps four principal (and partly overlapping) patterns underlying the sell-off of acquired units. Most frequent was the emergence or persistence of some problem that reduced profits and left top management dissatisfied with acquired-unit performance. Also common were cases in which Division A was performing well, but divisions B and C, with similar market characteristics, had developed problems. Sensing that Division A might become equally troublesome in the future, corporate management, stressing considerations of "fit" and "strategic compatibility," decided to divest A along with B and C. Third, companies sometimes found themselves in cash flow binds and sold off "crown jewels" along with the problem-ridden units to stem the crisis. Fourth, but often interacting with the first three scenarios in difficult-to-disentangle ways, companies sold off units because a would-be buyer made them an offer too good to refuse.

This summary prompts more questions than it answers. American managers take some pride in their can-do skills. Why should they sell off problem-ridden acquisitions rather than pitching in and working to improve their performance? And why should there be buyers willing to pay a price for problem-ridden units higher than the value to the incumbent parent of retaining the units and implementing remedial measures?

Wisdom begins by asking, "What do you do when you are a conglomerate corporation's group executive and one of your wards gets into trouble?" The options are surprisingly limited. One can sit back and do nothing but offer encouragement, hoping that matters improve. The troubled unit's key managers can be replaced. One can move in and offer corrective advice or "take over" to varied degrees. Or the unit can be sold off.

At least for our case study companies, which spanned a diverse array of circumstances, the more interventionist alternatives tended to work poorly. Conglomerates seldom have a ready stock of managers who understand the details of subsidiary operations. The typical manager with general experience, transplanted to an unfamiliar business, takes a year or so to grab hold. When a business is already in trouble, deterioration can snowball during the transitional period. Increased top-management intervention in the operations of troubled units has other problems. If the operating-level managers are able— and as we have seen, they were good enough on average to earn substantial pre-merger profit premiums—they know they are in trouble and what the menu of potential correctives is. Intervention by top management is commonly seen by them as nit-picking, the setting of unattainable objectives, and/or downright derogation of their authority. Morale and motivation fall. If the operating-level managers have alternatives, they leave; if not, they soldier on sullenly while the problems worsen.

Conglomerates such as Beatrice Foods Co. wise enough to recognize that they had very limited interventionist problem-solving capabilities followed a rule of selling off units quickly when they experienced problems that persisted over several quarters. Others intervened but saw the situation deteriorate and then resorted to sell-off. In either event, our case study research showed that there was an interaction between the emergence of problems, latent or totally unpredictable, and the impaired problem-solving ability of conglomerate organizations that sooner or later made sell-off likely. The buyer's side of the sell-off market existed because there were alternative organizational forms that could solve the problems better. Most of the units covered by our sell-off case studies became self-standing unitary orgaizations (e.g., through leveraged buy-outs) or were acquired in horizontal mergers. In these new organizations, authority was more closely linked with problem-solving knowledge, and especially in the leveraged buy-outs, motivation was strengthened greatly. The behavioral changes were dramatic. Previously igored cost-cutting opportunities were seized, new sales strategies were adopted, labor relations became less bureaucratic and more constructive, and much else. In our studies, we observed only occasional efficiency increases and many efficiency decreases with a shift from unitary to conglomerate organizational forms. But with the shift through sell-off from conglomerate toward unitary or tightly integrated organizations, efficiency increases abounded.

There are further implications of the conglomerates' intervention dilemma. The job of a conglomerate group vice president or equivalent group executive is peculiarly difficult. He or she is in charge but, if the operating-level managers are good, ought to show it only in a minimal and supportive way. Yet to do so is contrary to a good deal of human nature. There is a strong temptation to intervene and "manage," but its consequence is frequently the souring of operating-level morale and motivation and the magnification of problems that otherwise would have been innocuous.[9] Our case studies provided several clear examples. Sell-off was the eventual corrective for this negative interaction between conglomerate organization and operating efficiency.

Finally, the financial policies of parent corporations precipitated difficulties that eventually led to dissatisfaction with unit performance and sell-off. Several case study parents imposed upon their acquired units stringent cash flow return requirements or consciously treated the units as "cash cows" from whom funds were to be drawn for supporting other, supposedly more promising divisions. For the units treated in this way, results included the scrimping on capital equipment and R&D outlays, with an eventual loss of operating efficiency and competitive advantage, and the setting of high prices that attracted competitive inroads. Market shares declined as a consequence. A further consequence was more subtle. In principle, pursuing a "matrix strategy," of which cash cow treatment is one component, improves the efficiency of resource allocation, channeling funds from cash-rich but slow-growth lines to promising rapid-growth lines.[10] However, partly because of the extraordinarily turbulent economic conditions of the 1970s and early 1980s, companies were not very good at identifying high-growth lines. And more importantly, cash cow status is a fragile thing that cannot be taken as given. People matter, and motivation matters. When lines run by highly motivated managers are deprived of investable funds for which they see profitable uses, the milk soon sours. Motivation flags, and what could be a continuing source of good profits crosses the matrix and becomes a "dog." The end result, at least in several of our case studies, was sell-off.

Thus, having acquired thousands of characteristically small but profitable and promising firms, the conglomerates found that they could not manage them consistently. Many acquisitions, especially those lucky enough not to experience significant business setbacks, did do well under conglomerate control. The parent corporations sometimes made positive contributions to their growth by providing funds at lower cost, and in more elastic supply, than would have been possible had the acquired units remained independent. In a subset of cases, the conglomerates maintained sufficiently enlightened managerial policies to work with their subsidiaries toward the satisfactory solution of emerging prob-

lems. But in a quantitatively substantial set of cases, the conglomerate acquirers proved to be inept problem solvers and even created new problems by undermining operating management morale and depriving subsidiaries of funds for modernization. Profits turned to losses, pulling down overall parent corporation returns. Sooner or later the trouble-ridden subsidiaries were sold off to organizations that could manage them better, and further strategic pruning eliminated still-successful units for which the risk of future control loss was appreciable.

STATISTICAL EVIDENCE

Our case study research was necessarily limited in scope and, by design, biased toward acquisitions that ended in sell-off—by our findings, a manifestation of failure. Do the case study results hold up for a broader sample of sell-offs? And were the disappointing profits observed in many (but not all) sell-off case study acquisitions offset, or more than offset, by above-average profits in the more successful acquisitions? More generally, how profitable *has* merger activity been? Has acquisition *on average* raised or lowered the basic profitability of the acquired units? These are questions that can only be answered through the analysis of a large, well-controlled statistical sample. For that, we turn to Federal Trade Commission line-of-business data.

The Profitability of Sold-Off Units

Under the FTC's line-of-business program, a panel of from 437 to 471 corporations provided for the four reporting years 1974–1977 income statement and balance sheet data disaggregated into a maximum of 261 manufacturing and 14 (broader) nonmanufacturing industry categories. We focus here on the manufacturing industry line-of-business (LB) reports. The average reporting company in 1977 broke its operations down into eight manufacturing LBs (excluding a residual catch-all category), with a range of from 1 to 53.

For each manufacturing line of each sample company, an attempt was made to identify and date all sell-offs occurring during the years 1974 through 1981 (with a few observations trailing into 1982). Because published information on sell-offs is much sparser than the data on mergers, the survey is undoubtedly incomplete, especially after 1977, when line-of-business reporting ended. Over the eight-year period covered, 450 individual lines of business were totally sold off. Of these, 83% had prior merger activity, and 70% are believed to have entered the parent company's operations through acquisition. In addition, 479 lines experienced partial sell-offs, i.e., leading to a less-than-total cessation of operations by 1981 in the relevant industry category.

The basic question addressed here is, What financial performance pattern preceded sell-off? Was divestiture the sequitur to disappointing profitability, as suggested by our case studies, or was the typical divested unit not significantly different from retained operations? The measure of profitability used is the ratio of operating income (before capital charges, extraordinary items, and income taxes) to end-of-period assets. The results are summarized in Table 12.2. All four years' data for manufacturing LBs are combined. For lines experiencing either total or partial sell-offs, each row measures the average operating income/assets percentages for LBs commencing a sell-off program the stated number of years following the period for which profits were recorded. Thus, the row entries for three years before sell-off include 1974 profits of LBs with initial 1977 sell-offs, 1975 profits of LBs with 1978 sell-offs, 1976 profits for LBs with 1979 sell-offs, and 1977 profits for LBs with 1980 sell-offs. In each row for either total (left-hand numerical column) or partial (right-hand) sell-offs, the first entry is the operating income average, the second entry (in parentheses) the number of observations, and the third entry (also in parentheses) the sampling error of the mean profit figure.

For the 10,912 cases without total or partial sell-offs, the average profit return was 13.93%, with a standard error of .17%. Throughout the seven years of pre-sell-off

Table 12.2. Average Operating Income as a Percentage of Assets for Lines of Business with Sell-offs, by Interval Between the Years of Profit Reports and Sell-Off Initiation

Years from Profit Report to First Sell-off	LBs with Total Sell-off	LBs with Partial Sell-off
7	8.77% (58) (2.94)	10.66% (57) (1.80)
6	9.32% (110) (1.99)	11.00% (104) (1.44)
5	8.29% (155) (1.38)	12.35% (155) (1.40)
4	7.07% (191) (1.24)	12.38% (189) (1.23)
3	3.46% (204) (1.14)	10.04% (218) (0.93)
2	2.93% (201) (1.15)	9.26% (226) (1.08)
1	−1.09% (210) (1.60)	9.72% (219) (0.97)
0	−0.29% (121) (2.27)	11.43% (198) (1.06)
<0 (profits reported after first sell-off)	7.49 (39) (3.74)	13.02 (238) (0.91)
Unknown sell-off date	−4.35 (19) (5.13)	12.97 (147) (1.55)

Note: The values in parentheses report the number of observations and the standard error of the mean.

history, lines of business subjected to total sell-off had returns averaging 4.76%—significantly less than those of nondivested lines.[11] In the third year before total sell-off began, profitability deteriorated sharply, turning negative in the year before sell-off.[12]

It might be conjectured that the deficient financial performance of divested units was inherited from the time when the units were acquired. This hypothesis receives no statistical support. For 215 line-of-business company acquisitions that were subsequently sold off, it was possible to obtain profitability data for the reporting year prior to acquisition. The average premerger ratio of operating income to assets for those divested firms was insignificantly different from that for the previously discussed premerger sample of 634 firms, most of which were not divested, controlling also for acquired-company size and the merger accounting method adopted. Thus, sell-offs during the 1970s do not in general appear to have been a facet of some "asset redeployment" plan contemplated at the time of acquisition. Rather, they are manifestations of failure. Something went wrong after acquisition.

The 7.49% profitability average for totally sold off units in <0 years, i.e., years after the first recorded sell-off occurred, warrants special consideration. This subset covers LBs for which divestiture proceeded in stages. It provides verification for our case study insight that the most seriously distressed components of a multiunit line are sold off first, leaving the more profitable components for later "tidying-up" divestitures.

The data for LBs with only partial sell-offs by 1981 (right-hand numerical column) exhibit a somewhat different but plausible behavioral pattern. Their seven-year predivestiture profitability average was 10.64%, which is significantly lower than the nondivested line average of 13.93% but diverges much less than the average for totally divested LBs. Two to three years before the first partial sell-off, profitability erodes. In the postdivestiture period (year < 0), the tumor had been excised and profitability returned to levels only slightly different from those of lines without recorded sell-offs. The relatively large cohort of LBs with unknown sell-off dates (last line) mainly involved divestitures in the 1978–1981 period, after line-of-business reporting ceased. For them, the average lag between profit reports and partial divestiture was probably three to four years—too long to encompass the period of noticeable profit deterioration. Also, the difficulty of pinpointing divestiture dates may imply that the units sold off were relatively small, so that their impact on the profitabiilty of the LBs to which they belonged may have been modest.

In sum, the evidence on sell-offs is un-

ambiguous. Sell-off was characteristically a response to disappointing performance. With the excision of low-profit units and the retention of the stronger operations, the parent companies' average profitability rose.

The Profitability of Acquired Units

Approximately 6% of the manufacturing LBs with a merger history were fully divested during the 1974–1977 period for which line-of-business profitability data were available. Many unsuccessful acquisitions had been sold off before then. According to W. T. Grimm & Company data for a population broader than the line-of-business company sample, "divisional" sell-off activity peaked in absolute terms in 1971 at 1920 transactions, averaged 1193 transactions per year in the 1974–1977 interval, and declined to 767 transactions per year over 1978–1981.[13] We now analyze the sample for years on which line-of-business data were available, asking how profitable acquisitions were *on average*, taking into account both the successful units and the unsuccessful ones that had not yet been divested.

Our assessment of acquired units' basic profitability began by compiling exhaustive lists of acquisitions made between 1950 and 1977 by companies included in the FTC's line-of-business surveys. Each acquisition not known to have been sold off by 1977 was coded to the line(s) of business it entered (or originated). The information coded included acquisition dates, type of acquisition, accounting treatment, and the (often estimated) value of the assets acquired. When an acquired company's activities extended to two or more LBs, its assets were divided among them. In some cases, it was difficult to determine who acquired whom. This problem was handled by creating a special "merger-of-equals" coding for pooling-of-interests mergers in which the merging parties' premerger assets differed by no more than a factor of 2.

Altogether, the 2955 manufacturing LBs operated by line-of-business survey companies in 1977 and surviving diverse data quality control deletions received codings for 5552 nonequals acquisitions and 270 mergers of equals. Of the 2955 sample LBs, 717 had no recorded (nonequals) acquisitions, 723 were already occupied by the parent companies in 1950 and had subsequent acquisitions, and 1515 were new to the parent since 1950 and had acquisitions (the first of which usually marked the parent's entry into that line).

As before, our measure of profitability is the ratio of operating income to end-of-period assets. However, in analyzing the impact of mergers on this variable, it is crucial to recognize the role merger accounting plays. Under pooling-of-interests accounting, the assets of the acquired entity are taken onto the acquirer's books at their premerger book value. Any premium (deficit) of the acquisition price over book value is debited (credited) to the acquirer's stockholders' equity account. Under purchase accounting, the acquired assets are stepped up or written down to reflect the difference between their premerger book value and the purchase price. On purchase acquisitions, which tended to be less profitable on average premerger than pooling acquisitions, average premiums paid over book value were smaller than on poolings, but they tended to be positive. To the extent that positive premiums were paid, the use of purchase accounting implies higher average postmerger asset values and depreciation charges than with pooling-of-interests, all else equal. Thus, an identical acquisition will show lower postmerger operating income/assets ratios under purchase accounting than under pooling. Purchase acquisitions may also exhibit lower returns because their lower premerger profitability persisted into the postmerger period. To disentangle these effects, pooling and purchase acquisitions must be distinguished.

Our key merger history variables are therefore three. POOL is the ratio of the value of acquired-nonequals' assets treated as poolings to the total value of assets at the end of the year whose profits are analyzed. PURCH measures the ratio of nonequals' assets acquired under purchase accounting to total end-of-year assets. Because one cannot have more than 100%

merger origination of a line, and because one must guard against possible extreme-value biases, the ratio of assets acquired in an LB, under purchase plus pooling, to total assets for the year whose profits are being analyzed was truncated at 1. (Sensitivity tests showed this truncation assumption to have no significant impact on the results.) Our third basic merger variable, EQUALS, has a value of unity if an LB experienced a merger of equals and zero otherwise.

The method of determining how merger activity affected profitability is multiple-regression analysis. Using techniques that need not detain us in this nontechnical exposition, each individual line's profits were related to the mean profit level in the four-digit industry category to which it belonged. Thus, industry-specific effects were controlled. Also controlled was the market share of the individual LBs. The "control group," then, is lines of equivalent market share in the same industry that had no acquisitions or minimal acquisition activity. Nearly a fourth of all LBs in the 1977 analysis had zero acquisition activity, and for half, 15% or less of 1977 assets originated from acquisition. To simplify the presentation of results, we suppress the coefficients for the control variables and present only the coefficients for the merger effect variables. Coefficients significantly different from zero at the 90% statistical confidence level are marked with one asterisk; those significant at the 95% level or better, with two asterisks.

With operating income as a percentage of assets as the dependent variable, the estimated merger effect coefficients are as follows for three years:

	1975	1976	1977
POOL	+1.25	−1.60	+3.36**
PURCH	−3.31**	-3.48**	−3.74**
EQUALS	+2.00*	+1.55	+2.29**
Mean full-sample profitability	11.7%	13.4%	13.9%

Taking 1977 as an example, the coefficients are interpreted in the following way: Moving from having had no pooling-merger activity (POOL = 0) to having 1977 assets 100% pooling-merger-originated (POOL = 1) raises baseline profitability on average by 3.36 percentage points, or 24% above the full-sample mean of 13.9%. Purchase accounting mergers, on the other hand, were much less profitable. Moving from no–purchase merger assets (PURCH = 0) to all–purchase merger assets (PURCH = 1) reduces profits by 3.74 percentage points relative to nonmerger LBs and by 7.10 percentage points (the algebraic difference between the POOL and PURCH coefficients) relative to pooling-of-interests mergers. Having had a merger of equals was associated in 1977 with profitability 2.29 percentage points higher on average than the no-merger control group.

The POOL coefficients are in some respects the most interesting, since, barring for the moment an important qualification, they are on the same asset accounting basis as no–merger control group lines and can be interpreted as an index of relative efficiency (holding industry effects and market share constant). POOL is small in 1975, a year of sharp but brief recession, negative in 1976, and significantly positive in the strong recovery year 1977. This evidence has several possible interpretations. The most agnostic view would be that the profitability effects of acquisition (again excluding mergers of equals) jump around a fair amount and, averaged over three years of the business cycle, are mildly positive. An interpretation that reads more into the apparent pattern would say that management of acquired companies had more trouble coping with the recession of 1975 than their industry peers in no-merger lines but, through sell-offs and other changes, got their acts in order again by 1977 and then exhibited significantly superior baseline profitability. A third possibility is that the acquired companies were, again relative to their industry peers, unusually susceptible to business downturns, and indeed, this vulnerability may have been part of their owners' reason for entering a merger. However, this "selection bias" explanation is at odds with the premerger profitability evidence presented in the second section. The companies acquired in 1971, whose premerger profit results were for the recession year 1970, actually fared a bit *better* relative to their peers than did acquired companies whose premerger profits were recorded for the boom years 1967 and 1973.

Selection bias is important, however, in another way. Suppose we embrace an even more optimistic interpretation: that 1975 and 1976 were anomalies and that "normal" 1977 (with unemployment of 6.9%) best reflects the baseline profitability of acquired entities. Does it follow that the average merger yielded efficiencies (e.g., synergies)? Not necessarily, since baseline profits might also be high because the units acquired were of above-average earning power. This, of course, is what we found in our study of premerger profitability. In fact, compared with the average 9.8% pre-pooling-merger profit premiums identified through our listing-statement survey, the 3.36 percentage point POOL premium for 1977 implies a *fall* in postmerger profitability. On this point we shall expand in a moment.

The merger-of-equals coefficient EQUALS has an interpretation similar to that of POOL, but its statistically significant positive values are more consistent over the business cycle. They are also more plausibly interpretable as evidence of merger-related synergies. Premerger operating income data were available for 45 of the 69 mergers of equals. After adjustment for business cycle influences, average operating income/assets ratios in the last reporting period before merger were 12.1% for the larger of the partners, 14.5% for the smaller, and 12.6% for the weighted average of the two. The weighted average is slightly but statistically insignificantly below the 1975–1977 all-sample average return of 13.3%. Thus, a modest increase in returns following mergers of equals is indicated. Conceivably, mergers of equals were more successful in raising baseline profitability because fewer managerial hierarchy tiers were superimposed upon their premerger organizations and because more managerial effort could be concentrated on making them work.

The PURCH coefficient shows how postmerger profits were reduced as a consequence of takeover premium-related asset write-ups and increased depreciation. It also reflects the selection bias associated with the demonstrated inferior premerger earning power of purchase accounting acquisitions. For all three years, the PURCH coefficients are strongly negative, revealing postmerger returns lower on average than the acquiring companies realized in pre-1950 lines with no mergers or in lines developed through internal growth without the help of acquisitions. Given evidence that purchase acquisitions were no less profitable premerger than the all-manufacturing average, the PURCH effect must be interpreted as indicating that baseline profitability deteriorated and/or that, on average, acquirers paid takeover premiums above acquired-firm book value sufficiently high to drive postacquisition returns below the returns in their established merger-free businesses.

The premium effect is measured explicitly only for acquisitions subjected to purchase accounting. For pooling-of-interests acquisitions, takeover premiums are concealed in stockholders' equity account debits rather than asset account step-ups. For a subsample of 1409 manufacturing acquisitions on which comparable data were available, the consideration paid averaged 1.75 times the book value of assets for acquisitions treated as poolings, but only 1.05 times assets for purchase acquisitions. Assuming this to be representative, consider an LB whose 1977 assets of $100 million were 100% pooling-merger-originated. Let the line's operating income be $17.25 million, i.e., the 1977 all-sample average of 13.89% plus the 3.36% differential associated with 100% pooling-merger origin. If a 75% takeover premium above book value had been paid, the acquirer's actual investment in the line would have been $175 million, not the $100 million debited to asset accounts. Then the line's return under purchase accounting (ignoring added depreciation charges) would have been $100(17.25/175) = 9.86\%$, or 7.4 percentage points below the return revealed

under pooling accounting and well below all-sample averages.

Time-Lag Effects

The results discussed thus far come from an analytic model assuming that mergers have equal profitability effects, no matter how long ago the acquisition was consummated. This assumption must be tested. The tests focused on 1977, the most "normal" year macroeconomically and the only one for which significant positive baseline (pooling) profitability effects were observed. Alternative linear and nonlinear lag structures were imposed upon the POOL and PURCH variables, and tests were conducted to see which lag structure best explained profitability. The best-fitting lag structure (significantly better than the constant-effects structure assumed thus far) was a simple linear structure in which the merger effects, and especially the POOL effects, decline, the greater was the time interval between 1977, on the one hand, and an LB's asset-weighted average year of acquisition, on the other. Using this structure, we found that pooling-of-interests acquisitions consummated in 1976 yielded profits 9.1 percentage points above control group norms on average. For older acquisitions, e.g., those made in 1968, the differential had declined to 4.8 points. By 1959, the differential goes to zero and was negative for earlier years' acquisitions.

These results are extremely important. The largest POOL premiums (for 1976) are of roughly the same magnitude as those our premerger profit analysis shows acquirers to have inherited at the time of a pooling acquisition. After that, it is all down hill. The question is, Why?

A benign interpretation would be that the declining-profit effects reflect the quite natural tendency, abundantly documented by Dennis Mueller,[14] for abnormally high (or low) profits to regress over time under most circumstances toward "normal" levels. This tendency would be reinforced if acquisition candidates chose a time of peak (and nonsustainable) profitability to fetch the highest possible acquisition price—a phenomenon observed in some of our case studies.

Alternatively, baseline profits could have declined with longer postmerger experience because of the managerial control problems and cash cow behavior identified by our case studies. Three strands of statistical evidence support this interpretation. First, for a subsample of 67 lines originating from pooling-of-interests mergers and with perfectly matched pre- and postacquisition profit data, 43% experienced an *absolute* decline in current-dollar profits, even though assets more than doubled on average. Second, in our sample, the average market share of acquisition-making LBs that had not been part of the parent's operations in 1950 was only slightly higher (at 2.1%) than the average market share (2.0%) of post-1950 LBs without any acquisitions. The latter were presumably started internally from a zero–market share base some time after 1950. The former, though new to the parent since 1950, typically had much longer histories before their acquisition. It is at least striking that, despite their history, they had 1977 market shares only slightly higher on average than those of new internal start-ups. Third, Dennis Mueller has analyzed before and after data quite independent of ours and found that lines with sizable mergers, especially conglomerate acquisitions, experienced much more serious market share declines between 1950 and 1972 than a minimal-merger control group.[15] The combination of market share decline evidence with profitability decline evidence points strongly toward managerial control loss and/or cash cow interpretations.

The Effects of Merger Type

This view is reinforced by a further analysis of how baseline (i.e., pooling-of-interests) merger profitability effects vary with the type of acquisition—i.e., horizontal, vertical, conglomerate, and "related business." An acquisition was counted as horizontal if the acquirer had at least five years' prior experience in the same four-digit FTC industry category. For "related-business" acquisitions, the acquirer had to have five years' prior experience in the encompassing two-digit manufacturing industry group. In this way, an attempt was made to emphasize the accumulation of experience that could make the difference between well- and ill-informed management.

When the regression equation, whose basic results (i.e., assuming constant effects over time) are presented on pages 202–203, was reestimated taking into account merger type, there was no significant difference among types in the PURCH coefficients. However, the pooling-of-interests profitability effects varied considerably, as the following values show:

Horizontal acquisitions	+4.18*
Related-business acquisitions	+5.61**
Vertical acquisitions	+1.77
Conglomerate acquisitions	+1.18

The horizontal and related-business acquisitions exhibit pooling profitability effects appreciably higher than those for the conglomerate and vertical acquisitions, and only the coefficients for the first two pass conventional statistical significance tests. Moreover, the related-business effect is higher than the horizontal effect, suggesting that it is managerial experience, rather than monopoly power (plausible at best only for the horizontals), that distinguishes the two from more poorly performing conglomerate acquisitions. The relatively low profitability of vertical acquisitions is more surprising. It may be attributable to the low incidence of such acquisitions (only 11% of total acquired assets) or internal-transfer-pricing choices that shifted profits to other lines.[16]

Tender Offer Acquisitions

Our sample consists preponderantly of larger corporations, and the years 1975–1977, on which our profitability analysis focuses, predated the period when large, well-established companies were a common instigator or target of tender offer takeovers. Nevertheless, 150 of the 1977 sample LBs were taken over through tender offers, in 39 of which the successful tenderer's efforts had been opposed overtly by incumbent management. We exploit this limited subset to determine whether appreciable profitability impacts follow tender offer mergers.[17]

The lines acquired through tender offers were divided into three categories: 39 "hostile" acquisitions to which there had been active management opposition, 34 acquisitions made by an incumbent-management-favored "white knight" following an offer opposed by management, and 77 "others" in which management maintained at least overtly a neutral position with respect to solitary tenders (62 cases) or multiple tenderers (15 cases). Controlling also for accounting method, 1977 asset fractions resulting from merger, market share, and other variables, as in the analysis summarized on pages 202–203, the estimated tender offer effect coefficients for 1977 operating income as a percentage of assets are as follows:

	Three Effects Separated	Hostile and Other Offers Combined
Hostile	−2.97	
Other	−5.99*	−4.77**
White knight	+1.38	+1.36

Results covering the years 1975 and 1976 (reported in a separate paper) were similar for the hostile and (with one minor exception) other takeovers, but the white knight coefficients moved from positive to negative. Over the three years together, having been subjected to a takeover of any sort was associated with a significant negative impact on profitability. It is conceivable that tender offers were biased toward companies of inferior profitability that persisted after takeover. In fact, however, the targets' average premerger profitability, adjusted to be macroeconomically comparable to the 1975–1977 data, was 11.88% in the year preceding (or overlapping) the first tender offer announcement and 12.21% two years earlier. Both years' averages differ from the all-manufacturing average

of 12.50% by statistically insignificant amounts. Thus, the average observed tendency was for operating income/assets ratios to *decline* following takeover through tender offer. Yet in view of the small sample size, there is a need for further research tapping the richer sample generated by the more recent proliferation of tender offers. Unfortunately, the end of line-of-business reporting will render analyses such as ours difficult or impossible.

CONGLOMERATE MERGERS AND THE STOCK MARKET

Recapitulating, large numbers of highly profitable enterprises were acquired by line-of-business sample corporations during the 1960s and early 1970s. Substantial takeover premiums were paid—the more so, the greater the acquired entities' premerger profitability was. Baseline (i.e., pooling-of-interests) profitability of the acquired units subsequently declined at an average rate of about 0.36 percentage points per year, with the sharpest profitability drops occurring for pure conglomerate acquisitions. Many lines suffered more severe profit erosion and were sold off in whole or in part, leaving the more profitable operations and raising companywide profitability averages.

These events were reflected in an interesting way by movements in conglomerate corporation stock values. To explore this linkage, we track the common stock performance of the thirteen leading (and relatively more successful) conglomerate acquirers, defined according to the following criteria:

1. The company had at least 99 mergers recorded on the Federal Trade Commission's historical file for 1950–1978.
2. The company's acquisitions were mainly conglomerate (rather than horizontal or vertical, as with some acquisition-prone natural resource companies).
3. The company was one of the 20 most active acquirers of manufacturing and mineral industry companies.

For each corporation, we assumed that a $1000 common stock investment was made in 1965 (before the conglomerate merger boom accelerated) or in 1968 (at the boom's peak).[18] Stock splits and dividends were accounted for, and each year's cash dividends were assumed reinvested at midyear. Accumulated market values were tallied as of June 30, or for holidays, on the first trading day before, of each year. A similar procedure was followed to track the market value of a comparable investment (with dividends reinvested) in the Standard & Poor's 425 industrials portfolio. The results are summarized in Table 12.3.

As always, how investors fared depends upon how good their timing was. If they bought into the thirteen budding conglomerates in 1965 (top half of the table), they did 3.6 times better than the S&P by 1968, when conglomerate mergers were viewed enthusiastically by the market, but only 86% as well in 1974. By 1983 they had recouped nicely, with a portfolio value 2.7 times that of the S&P (but only 1.6 times the S&P's value if they had excluded from their purchases the spectacularly successful

Teledyne, omitted from the right-hand side of the table).

The picture (bottom half of the table) is quite different for investors who bought at the peak of the conglomerate merger wave in 1968. By 1974, their holdings had lost 56% of their value, but S&P investors gained by 10%. Although the conglomerate investors' position improved greatly by 1983, they had still not recouped, with or without the Teledyne bonanza, to a position of parity with those who had invested more conservatively in the S&P portfolio.

These movements parallel in a crude way the chronology illuminated by our case studies and statistical analyses. In 1968, conglomerates were acquiring highly profitable entities, albeit at high premium prices. By 1974, their managerial indigestion problems had become painfully evident, they had begun selling off the least successful acquisitions, and their growth had slowed appreciably. By 1983, the sell-off programs had pruned out the least profitable units while retaining those that were on average most successful.

However, the violence of the market's

Table 12.3. Cumulated Stock Market Value of $1000 Initial Investments in Thirteen Leading Conglomerates

	All Thirteen Conglomerates				Teledyne Excluded			
	1965	1968	1974	1983	1965	1968	1974	1983
$1000 invested in each conglomerate in June 1965	$13,000	63,009	16,543	144,482	12,000	55,340	14,490	79,019
Equivalent amount invested in S&P 425 industrials	$13,000	17,382	19,177	53,377	12,000	16,046	17,701	49,271
Conglomerates as percentage of S&P portfolio value	100.0	362.5	86.3	270.7	100.0	344.9	81.9	160.4
$1000 invested in each conglomerate in June 1968	—	$13,000	5,686	31,115	—	12,000	5,418	22,578
Equivalent amount invested in S&P 425 industrials	—	$13,000	14,342	39,919	—	12,000	13,238	36,848
Conglomerates as percentage of S&P portfolio value	—	100.0	39.6	77.9	—	100.0	40.9	61.3

reaction to these changes raises doubts about the quality of stock investors' foresight. Why were investors willing to pay $63,009 in 1968 for conglomerate stocks that would sell for only $16,543 six years later? Were they carried away by Keynes's "animal spirits"?[19] Or did they fail to foresee the cessation of profit growth and the managerial difficulties that would befall the conglomerates—a failure that speaks poorly for the use of contemporary merger-related stock price valuations as an indicator of future profitability?[20] And what about the depressed valuations prevailing in 1974 (and indeed all of the early 1970s)? Had the animal spirits now lurched toward excessive pessimism? Or did investors fail to foresee the management purges and widespread sell-offs that would restore profit growth for some conglomerates? Or did they foresee the coming share-value growth but discounted it—e.g., at the 24% discount rate necessary to make the present value of $144,482 in 1983 equal $16,543 in 1974? At such a high discount rate, very few farsighted investment projects could pass muster. Quite generally, it is hard to conceive a nontautological rationalization of the conglomerates' long-term stock price experience with the assumption that stock markets correctly forecasted the actual consequences of merger. If the market can err so badly in evaluating the leading conglomerate acquirers of the 1960s and 1970s, will it not err again?

The leading conglomerates' stock price experience between 1965 and 1983 is also troublesome in a more technical sense. As Table 12.4 shows, the distribution of individual companies' stock value growth was extremely skewed. Six conglomerates performed worse than the S&P 425, three did slightly better, three considerably better, and one (Teledyne) 16 times as well. The distribution of gains is similar to what one would expect from investing in *individual* high-technology company stocks—a far cry from the risk-reducing performance that was supposed to come from pooling the business fortunes of numerous unrelated entities under one corporate mantle.[21] Plainly, the conglomerates were something

Table 12.4. 1983 Value of a $1000 1965 Investment in Each of Thirteen Leading Conglomerates or the S&P Industrials

Rank	Company	1983 Value
1	Teledyne	$65,463
2	Whittaker	24,025
3	Gulf & Western	16,287
4	U.S. Industries	7,152
5	Textron	4,947
6	Walter Kidde	4,813
7	Chromalloy-American	4,672
	S&P 425 industrials	4,106
8	Beatrice	3,992
9	Consolidated Foods	3,820
10	ITT	3,625
11	Litton Industries	2,691
12	W. R. Grace	2,587
13	Genesco	408

radically different from simple mutual funds. Rather, they appear to have been "asset plays" with unusually high risks in terms of both their economic prospects, assuming managerial control of constant quality, and the quality of the managerial control that would actually be achieved.

CONCLUSION

In the long run, the stock price evidence shows, those who invested early in the leading conglomerates of the 1960s prospered. Perhaps all's well that ends well—at least for the early birds. But this is too simple. Good companies were acquired, and on average, their profits and market shares declined following acquisition. A smaller but substantial subset of those good companies experienced traumatic difficulties, triggering sell-off to nonconglomerate organizations that could manage them more effectively. There was considerable distress and wreckage on the road to conglomerate riches. Left to be resolved are what economic historians call "counterfactual" questions. Would acquired company profits have deteriorated even without merger? Would the average acquired and then divested company have plunged into unprofitability had it retained its independence? Would the companies that did well under conglomerate ownership have fared as well independently, among other things receiving the injections of capital required to sustain their growth? Like all counterfactual questions, these cannot be answered confidently. On the negative side, it is clear from our case studies and many accounts in the press that eventually divested units experienced sometimes severe managerial problem-solving breakdowns aggravated by the conglomerate form of organization and ameliorated, at least partially, by a transition to simpler organizational forms. And Mueller's evidence of sharp market share declines following conglomerate merger is hard to reconcile with any "business-as-usual" hypothesis. On the positive side, the unanswered counterfactual is how much the units favored in capital allocation—units that on average were highly profitable and had good perceived growth prospects—would have been held back had they been forced to obtain financing on the open market. If there would have been significant retardation, a policy counterfactual is also posed. One might be well advised to correct the problem by working directly to perfect capital markets rather than embracing the conglomerate merger solution, with its clear negative-side control loss consequences.

That even after the pruning of many worst cases through sell-off baseline (pooling-of-interests) profitability had declined on average is hard to square with the hypothesis that conglomerate mergers were on balance efficiency increasing. At the very least, the defense of that hypothesis would appear to demand a substantial injection of detailed evidence on how efficiency was raised more in the successful cases than it declined in the unsuccessful cases.

NOTES

1. A complete analysis will appear in David J. Ravenscraft and F. M. Scherer, Mergers, Sell-offs, and Economic Efficiency (Washington, D.C.: Brookings, 1987), as well as in several shorter articles.

2. H. G. Manne, "Mergers and the Market for Corporate Control," *Journal of Political Economy* **73**, 110, 119–120 (April 1965). See also D. Dewey, "Mergers and Cartels: Some Reservations About Policy," *American Economic Review Papers and Proceedings* **51**, 255 (May 1961).

3. P. O. Steiner, *Mergers: Motives, Effects, Policies* (Ann Arbor: University of Michigan Press, 1975), 188.

4. Testimony before the House Committee on the Judiciary, Subcommittee on Monopolies and Commercial Law, *Mergers and Acquisitions,* 97th Congress, 1st session, 1981, 255.

5. R. S. Harris, J. F. Stewart, and W. T. Carleton, "Financial Characteristics of Acquired Firms," in *Mergers and Acquisitions,* ed. M. Keenan and L. J. White (Lexington, Mass.: Heath, 1982), 235–239.

6. The line-of-business-company sample members made three-fourths of the acquisitions, calculated in terms of acquired asset value, on the FTC "large" merger list for the years 1950–1976.

7. See Ravenscraft and Scherer, note 1, Chap. 5.

8. The case study findings are summarized more fully in F. M. Scherer, "Mergers, Sell-offs, and Managerial Behavior," in *The Economics of Strategic Planning,* ed. L. G. Thomas (Lexington, Mass.: Heath, 1986). The case studies were, with acquirer given first and the acquired unit(s) after the comma, as follows: Philip Morris, American Safety Razor; Consolidated Foods, Robert Bruce; Bendix, Boise Cascade Home Systems Division; Bendix, Caradco; Chromalloy-American, Sintercast; Chromalloy-American, various glass companies; Inco, ESB; U.S. Industries, Great Lakes Screw; AMF, Harley-Davidson; Beatrice Foods, Harman International; W. R. Grace, Letisse; Gulf & Western, Marquette Cement; Textron, Talon; Pennwalt, S. S. White; and Lykes, Youngstown Sheet & Tube.

9. The problem is not limited to conglomerates, on which our case study research focused. See the thoughtful discussion of the automobile group vice president's role in J. P. Wright (for J. Delorean), *On a Clear Day You Can See General Motors* (Grosse Pointe, Mich.: Wright, 1979), especially 16–31, 112, 194–195, and 209–210.

10. On the theory, see, e.g., G. A. Steiner, *Strategic Planning* (New York: Free Press, 1979), Chap. 9; W. E. Cox, Jr., "Product Portfolio Strategy, Market Structure, and Perfor-

mance," in *Strategy + Structure = Performance,* ed. H. B. Thorelli (Bloomington: Indiana University Press, 1977), 83–102.

11. The *t* ratio in a test of equality of means is $(13.93 - 4.76)/.58 = 15.80$.

12. Note that for parent corporations, sell-off is an exit decision—one of the most fundamental decisions in the economic theory of firm. The strong pattern of deteriorating and then negative profitability before this decision is implemented goes far to refute the allegation that line-of-business profitability data are economically meaningless. See G. J. Benston, "The Validity of Profits-Structure Studies with Particular Reference to the FTC's Line of Business Data," *American Economic Review* **75,** 37 (March 1985); F. M. Scherer et al., "The Validity of Studies with Line of Business Data: Comment," *American Economic Review* **77,** 205–217 (March 1987).

The observations for a zero lag stem from reporting-year mismatches, e.g., when a company's fiscal year ended in June and sell-off occurred in November of the same calendar year, and also from remnants persisting after the first of multiple-sell-off stages occurred.

13. From W. T. Grimm & Co., *Merger Summary* (Chicago: January 1974–January 1981) and *Mergerstat Review* (Chicago: 1981, 1982, and 1983).

14. D. Mueller, *Profits in the Long Run* (Cambridge, Eng.: Cambridge University Press, 1986).

15. D. C. Mueller, "Mergers and Market Share," *Review of Economics and Statistics* **67,** 259 (May 1985).

16. See D. J. Ravenscraft, Transfer Pricing and Profitability (manuscript, 1985).

17. This hypothesis was suggested to us by Michael Jensen, who urged an extension of an earlier analysis focusing only on overtly contested takeovers.

18. On levels and timing of manufacturing and mineral company acquisition activity, see F. M. Scherer, *Industrial Market Structure and Economic Performance,* rev. ed. (Boston: Houghton Mifflin, 1980), 120.

19. J. M. Keynes, *The General Theory of Employment Interest and Money* (New York: Harcourt, Brace & World, 1936), 161–162. See also R. J. Shiller, "Do Stock Prices Move Too Much to Be Justified by Subsequent Changes in Dividends?" *American Economic Review* **71,** 421–436 (June 1981); and Chapter 3 in this volume.

It should be recognized that the notions of stock market "efficiency," strong or weak, used to justify merger "event" studies do not imply that stock prices forecast the future accurately but only that they impound all currently available information. The use of merger event–related, short-run stock price movements to draw inferences about future merged-firm performance goes beyond the standard market efficiency assumptions.

20. By June 30, 1968, the Williams Act, sometimes blamed for the conglomerates' stock price declines, had already cleared the Senate and was near passage. The Justice Department's new Merger Guidelines had been out for a month.

21. Indeed, the frequency distribution of conglomerates' 1983 stock values is well characterized as Paretian with an alpha coefficient of approximately .6. This means that in its limit, the distribution has neither finite mean nor variance, making it difficult to apply conventional statistical tests in evaluations of long-run performance. The observed variability is only slightly less than for the profitability of individual patented inventions. See F. M. Scherer, *Innovation and Growth: Schumpeterian Perspectives* (Cambridge, Mass.: MIT Press, 1984), 176.

13

The Efficiency Effects of Hostile Takeovers

EDWARD S. HERMAN
LOUIS LOWENSTEIN

In this chapter we provide a dissenting view on the purposes and social consequences of the recent takeover movement and on the evidence needed to test that process. The currently dominant analyses have rested heavily on weak assumptions regarding market structure and behavior, corporate control, and managerial objectives. This has contributed to their preoccupation with the movement of stock values as the measure of the costs and benefits of takeovers. In our view, stock price data offer an extremely tricky basis for evaluating takeovers, and correspondingly, the scientific evidence resting on that empirical foundation is not very scientific. We have assembled data in this chapter that we believe measures more directly and accurately the impact of hostile tenders on efficiency and other relevant performance variables. The evidence we develop suggests many doubts about the net social benefits in the takeover boom.

First, we provide a critique of the logical and theoretical underpinning of recent claims that the takeover process is enhancing efficiency by displacing less efficient managers by those who will manage better. Then we examine briefly the empirical evidence developed in support of the efficiency enhancement models. In the bulk of the chapter, we offer our own empirical analysis of the efficiency effects of takeovers, based on a study of the profitability of acquiring and acquired firms both before and after the acquisitions. Finally, we draw some conclusions from the data.

THE STRESS ON EFFICIENCY

The traditional view of economists toward mergers and takeovers was that they constituted a mixed bag, with some fraction economically justifiable, others without redeeming features. But as the latter set was thought to be of nonnegligible size and capable of threatening enlargement in the absence of social controls, there has always been an undercurrent of suspicion and belief that mergers should be viewed with caution. The social costs of mergers were believed to include both the sociopolitical effects of increased centralization of economic power and the enhancement of monopoly power in individual markets. Greater monopoly power would confer private benefits on stockholders and merger entrepreneurs, but at the expense of the country at large. Private and public benefits would result if the merger had an efficiency-enhancing effect, and economists have long recognized this as applicable in a significant number of cases. But they have tended to regard efficiency enhancement as the special case, not the general rule, no doubt biased by historic special cases like the 1901 steel merger, which brought together a disparate and badly fitting collection of iron and steel facilities and ended the threat posed by the most efficient steel producer by buy-out and retirement.[1]

Recent defenses of takeovers have entirely ignored the sociopolitical dimension, despite the necessary interconnection between economic structure and the social and political environment. One version of conservatism (Jeffersonian) would give such developments serious attention and weight; another conservative tradition (Hamiltonian) accepts without question structural changes and consequences that flow out of dominant centers of power. Where a Hamiltonian conservatism is combined with a reductionist social science and ideology that finds its own discipline all-encompassing,[2] sociopolitical effects drop out of sight.

In this reduced world there is also a strong tendency to find that whatever is—barring unnatural intrusions (government intervention)—is good. As regards takeovers, they are definitely found to be good; but the new proponents do nevertheless ultimately rest their case on the claim that public benefits flow from takeovers. They concede, implicitly or explicitly, that if the gains to stockholders and other participants in the merger transaction were based on increased monopoly power, the takeover would not be justified. Fortunately, it turns out that monopoly power effects of mergers are as scarce as hen's teeth. Other factors motivating mergers that convey no social efficiency advantages, such as tax gains, are sometimes mentioned and presumably would weaken the case for takeovers if quantitatively important as a factor in mergers,[3] but they are usually mentioned only in passing.[4] The general thrust of the new defenses is that prospective and actual efficiency enhancement is the key factor in takeovers. This is sometimes obscured by euphemisms, such as that the takeover market is one in which managers "compete for the right to manage resources," but the basic implication is that higher bidders can manage the assets better.[5]

The development of the idea of the "market for corporate control" and takeovers as a mechanism for improving efficiency filled an important gap in modern classical thought. The Berle and Means revolution entrenched the notion that corporate democracy did not work, that stockholders had very limited power, and that corporate managers had significant discre-

tion with which to pursue ends which were not invariably compatible with those of the stockholders. This still left product market competition as a means of keeping managers in line. The institutionalization of oligopoly as the primary industrial market structure suggested limits to this traditional constraint on managerial discretion, although it is still surprising that the new defenses of takeovers have given so little weight to competition in product markets as a control over managerial abuse. In the Jeffersonian tradition of conservatism, an increase in product market competition would have the double advantage of constraining managers and preserving a more decentralized structure of economic and sociopolitical power. Working in the Hamiltonian tradition, the new conservatives not only ignore the possibility of enhanced product market competition but also opt for a mode of disciplining managements that increases concentration and should thus weaken the traditional constraint on managers.[6]

The conception of takeovers as an efficiency-enhancing and equilibrating machinery has grown *pari passu* with the growth and refinement of capital market modeling and stress on information arbitrage equilibrium. As far back as 1962, Alchian and Kessel noted that "the absence of competition in product markets does not imply a different quality of management in monopolistic as compared with competitive enterprises ... [as] competition in the capital markets will allocate monopoly rights to those who can use them most effectively."[7] Even earlier, Dewey had mentioned takeovers as a "civilized alternative" to failures, "that transfers assets from falling to rising firms."[8] Manne developed this idea further in stressing an ongoing market for corporate control, which gives shareholders "both power and protection commensurate with their interest in corporate affairs."[9] Manne also focused attention on the stock market as providing the only "objective standard of managerial efficiency."[10] For Manne, a low stock price is a reflection of managerial inefficiency, and the difference between the actual price and the price under efficient management is the relevant capital gain—the reward that "provides the primary motivation for most take-over attempts"[11]—which we will call the "Manne opportunity value." Manne gave no evidence that this opportunity value *was* the primary motive in actual mergers, but the idea represented a possibility, and an attractive one to conservatives pleased to find a resolution to an unsettling claim of arbitrary managerial power.

In subsequent writings of the Manne school there is an equal stress on efficiency enhancement by pruning managerial deadwood as the prime motive for and justification of takeovers. Easterbrook and Fischel assert that

when the difference between the market price of a firm's shares and the price those shares might have under different circumstances becomes too great, an outsider can profit by buying the firm and improving its management. . . . The source of the premium is the reduction in agency costs, which make the firm's assets worth more in the hands of the acquirer than they were worth in the hands of the firm's managers.[12]

Jensen and Ruback are equally confident of the primacy of efficiency enhancement by managerial displacement as the motive and function of takeovers:

Competition among managerial teams for the rights to manage resources limits divergence from shareholder wealth maximization by managers and provides the mechanism through which economies of scale or other synergies available from combining or reorganizing control and management of corporate resources are realized.[13]

Note that whereas Manne and Easterbrook-Fischel focus almost exclusively on bad management, Jensen and Ruback speak of economies of scale and synergies as well as plain management deficiencies. Management failings are still given great prominence, however, and efficiency improvement in all its dimensions remains the core motivation and effect of takeovers. The Council of Economic Advisers' *1985 Report* also goes beyond merely bad management as the rationale for mergers, although it still gives substantial weight to the possibility that "managers are poor

agents for their stockholders because they do not act in the stockholders' best interests."[14] But while admitting exceptions, it generalizes that mergers "improve efficiency, transfer scarce resources to higher valued uses, and stimulate effective corporate management."[15]

SOME FUNDAMENTAL POSTULATES OF EFFICIENCY ENHANCEMENT MODELS

Analyses that feature takeovers as efficiency enhancing start with the premise that the acquiring firms' managements are striving to maximize shareholder wealth. In their search for ways of improving shareholder wealth, these managements observe that other firms are badly run or fail to put their resources to best use. These managers are thereby induced to acquire such badly managed firms to take advantage of the Manne opportunity value. They frequently and regrettably encounter target managements who go to great pains to prevent takeovers that would provide large stockholder windfalls. It would appear, then, that the *defending* managements are not striving to maximize shareholder benefits. This dichotomous treatment of the motivation of the managers of bidding and acquired firms is partially bridged by the concession that there exists one dimension—the evaluation and hiring of management services—in which managerial and stockholder interests may deviate seriously.[16] There may be "agency costs" as the agents fail to police themselves adequately—hence the service of takeovers in keeping such agency costs under control.

The flaw in this argument is that it opens a Pandora's box and gives no reason for closing it with only "defenses against takeovers" and "agency costs" removed. If managements can so egregiously waste opportunities where stockholder wealth could be quickly and obviously increased by more than 50%, it will not suffice to make this an exception to management loyalty by mere assertion or reference to stock option plans.[17] If managers can openly ignore stockholder interests in the one case—an obvious and public one—the reasonable presumption to be rebutted is that they may pursue nonstockholder interests in other cases, most relevantly here, in *acquiring* other companies. Efficiency enhancement may be only a partial and special-case explanation of takeovers.

If managements defending against takeovers can pursue their private ends in serious violation of shareholder interests, this also raises questions about the meaning of the "agency" relationship and the parallel asymmetry of *its* applications. If the "agent" (management) is not subject to the control of his principals in the one case, why should we assume control in other cases? If the agent himself controls or substantially influences the board of directors,[18] the control that the board then imposes on his activities may be largely nominal. The gearing of managerial and shareholder interests via executive compensation arrangements, for example, may be illusory if the fixing of the salaries and bonuses is under the control of the agent (who may adjust them *ex post facto* to accomplish his goals).[19] The agreement of the board to a new acquisition program may be as compelling an illustration of the control by the agent as board approval of management's compensation arrangements.

The recent literature in defense of takeovers treats too lightly the role of the board and the dynamics of power within the corporation. Sometimes, on occasions when the virtues of the market for corporate control are being extolled, the thoroughgoing domination of the organization by the management is stressed.[20] At other times, when it is desired to show that the managerial interest may still be kept in line with that of the shareholders by devices such as stock option plans, reference is made to the independent directors who, according to Fama, act "as professional referees [and have the] task . . . to stimulate and oversee the competition among the firm's top managers. . . . [The] outside directors are in their turn disciplined by the market for their services which *prices* them according to their performance as referees."[21] If the board is dominated by the management and the management dominates the proxy

machinery, however, the "price" will be a function of service to the controlling management. And there would seem to be no independent source of power to contract that would effectively limit the actions of the "agent." The ability of the agent to resist value-enhancing takeover bids points up the fact that the agency contract is an elusive construct, which permits an evasion of the realities of corporate control and power.[22]

The new defenses of takeovers as efficiency enhancing also rest their case heavily on stock prices as providing reliable measures of asset and managerial worth. Efficient markets digest all available information and yield prices that show the only true valuation of the assets of each company and their potential in the hands of existing managements. Takeover bid prices thus reflect the anticipated enhancement of values based on the perceived superiority of the new management and its plans for redeployment, etc. The efficient-markets hypothesis denies that the stock market could undervalue corporate assets in any meaningful way. There is, it is true, substantial evidence of information arbitrage market efficiency, meaning that prices respond quickly to new information and "their correlations with past histories are too weak to be exploited profitably."[23] But this technical efficiency is very different from the claimed ability of the market to value stocks in accordance with the expected stream of future earnings or dividends. On the contrary, there is substantial evidence that fundamental value equilibria are special cases. Traders and institutional investors, having extremely short time horizons, are influenced by their perceptions of what other market traders and the public will be thinking of stock prospects. This is not irrational. The stock market is almost entirely a secondary market, and the pricing of shares depends on extremely difficult projections of earnings and dividends, on the one hand, and an essentially subjective valuation process—fixing the price-earnings ratios—on the other. In the face of such uncertainty, it is not surprising that investors react by looking as much or more to each other—playing the "performance" game, as it is currently called—than to the underlying fundamentals. What financial economists frequently characterize as quantifiable risks are in reality uncertainties of such large and incalculable proportions as to intimidate investors and send them scurrying to the seemingly safer ground of follow-the-leader. Such markets can be influenced by fads.[24] The result is that stock prices do not move in any systematic relationship to changes in expected returns.[25]

There is good evidence, also, that investors who look at the value of corporate assets as a whole and as a producing entity value them differently than traders and passive investors.[26] No coherent explanation consistent with the efficient-markets hypothesis has ever been given as to why acquiring firms will regularly pay large premiums for companies whose managements they intend to retain and whose assets they have no plans to redeploy or recombine.[27]

It may be argued, of course, that the acquisition which reduces undervaluation in trading markets is performing a valuable function, pushing market values closer to whole company values and at the same time paying shareholders of the target firms sums reflecting those more valid market values. This may be true, but there are numerous costs involved in this rectification of prices, including both the transaction costs and, more importantly, a huge diversion of managerial effort into devising ways to reduce a vulnerability that did not grow out of managerial inefficiency. Some of the policies that may be employed to counter this threat, such as loading up on debt and "defensive acquisitions,"[28] may be seriously detrimental to the long-term interests of the shareholders. In short, it requires a giant leap to conclude that in order to correct market disequilibria we should encourage an active, day-to-day trading not merely of *shares* of firms but of the firms themselves. The main point, however, is that takeovers rooted in a market undervaluation of corporate assets are not designed to prune managerial dead-

wood or improve asset utilization—on the contrary, they reflect a flaw in the market machinery and valuation process. Furthermore, an acquisitions route based on undervaluation can be pursued by bad as well as good managers. In fact, it may be the preferred path for those managers who can not perform well in their own productive domains.[29]

The efficiency enhancement perspective also rests on a vision of a market for corporate control that gives only a very partial version of reality. There can be no doubt that Manne was pointing up a very significant development in formulating the idea of a market for corporate control. It is certainly important that by means of takeover bids outsiders can bypass managements and appeal directly to stockholders, a process that has made it possible to displace managements by operations and strategies in the financial markets. The former stability of corporate control and irrelevance of shareholder ownership and voting rights to corporate power has been badly shaken and weakened. Furthermore, the "market" has become quantitatively significant.

But several caveats are in order. The number of buyers who bid in particular takeover transactions is not large and does not meet a competitive standard.[30] The assumption that these buyers are well informed is also implausible as a general rule, given the frequent lack of familiarity of the acquirer with the target's business, the lack of access to sometimes crucial inside knowledge, the great speed with which major decisions are frequently made, and the considerable evidence of unpleasant *ex post* surprises. We have also argued earlier that the Manne vision of the players in the market as competing managers seeking to control resources in order to manage them more efficiently is at best unproven. A substantial number of acquisitions are explained by the bidders themselves in terms of plans to enter fields with greater growth prospects, or to round out a product line, or to achieve some kind of advantage through vertical integration.[31] Acquisitions made in connection with these strategic plans and efforts appear to be based only marginally on efficiency considerations.[32]

The expansion of the takeover market has also brought with it numerous players who do not fit well the behavioral requirements of the efficiency enhancement vision. There are now a substantial number of professional sharks in the business of putting companies "into play," not to acquire and manage these companies themselves but to force bids and counterbids by unknown third parties. There are also "wolf packs" of substantial investors now prepared to fund takeovers by plausible bidders on high-yield terms. The ability to mobilize in advance vast sums for bidding in takeover contests is a significant development. It has increased the size of potential targets and reduced the size and financial requirements of potential bidders. The risk to the lending syndicate is small, since the actual lending will occur simultaneously with the bidder's obtaining control and the subsequent availability of the target's assets and income for payoff. The risk is greatly reduced by bidding with cash for only a bare majority of the target's shares, so that the lending syndicate is, in effect, assured of roughly $2 in purported value for each $1 invested in the takeover. (The target company's shareholders will then receive for their remaining interest new securities that are subordinated to the interests of the original lenders.) Whether the bidder's effort will "enhance efficiency" or allow him to dismantle and/or loot the acquired target would appear irrelevant to the calculations of the lenders, secured by the assets and short-term income flow of the captured prize.

The new institutional arrangements that are now in place are being steadily enlarged by the force of competitive pressure and short-run profitability calculations of investment bankers and investors, some of whom, such as thrifts urgently seeking short-term earnings, are under heavy pressure to take a "piece" of each new offering in order to stay in good standing with the underwriter. These developments have already pushed us into a promotional environment in which the largest companies are now potentially "in play" and within the grasp of promotional interests.

EMPIRICAL STUDIES OF THE EFFICIENCY EFFECTS OF TAKEOVERS

Empirical evidence bearing on the question of the efficiency effects of takeovers has grown substantially in recent years. One form of this proliferating body of evidence is qualitative, based on selected episodes and providing admittedly limited bases of comparison or generalization. Such information, easily dismissed as merely anecdotal, is nonetheless worthy of closer attention, at least as a check on global generalizations and as a lead to fresh hypotheses. For example, if it can be firmly established from U.S. Steel officials that they had no substantial knowledge of the oil industry, had no plans for any kind of restructuring, and planned on retaining the prior management of the acquired Marathon Oil Company, which they bought at an 87% premium, something must be substituted for the hypothesis that a large premium is based on prospective managerial improvements. Scherer's case study of 15 divestments, with its finding that in a majority of cases the acquired firms had been deemed efficiently managed by the acquirers who intended no managerial renovation, is similarly suggestive.[33] Questions are posed by this kind of evidence that for a valid science would provoke an intensive search for similar oddities to see whether prior hypotheses were seriously flawed.[34] Scientific research involves utilizing all resources to attain the truth, including in the case of corporate takeovers the intensive examination of the individual unit and the direct questioning of its decision makers.

Aggregative studies of the effects of takeovers have fallen into two categories: those measuring effects on corporate profit rates and those testing their impact on shareholder returns on equity. Most of the traditional studies were of the former character and focused mainly on pre- and postmerger returns of the constituent units. These studies almost uniformly concluded that mergers typically had a neutral or negative effect on company profitability.[35] More recently, instead of the earlier dominant stress on pre- and postmerger profit performance, attention has been extended to include performance comparisons between the acquiring and acquired firms and between the acquiring firms and a universe sample of firms. The study of conglomerate firms by Weston and Mansinghka in 1971[36] set off a small flurry along these lines. Their own study was most notable in showing that the acquiring conglomerate firms were less profitable than the acquired firms, that the acquisitions did raise the profitability of the acquirers between 1958 and 1968, but that this enhancement was bought at the expense of greatly increased leverage.[37] The superior returns shown by Weston and Mansinghka were quickly dissipated during the subsequent bear market that followed just after the termination date of their study.

The Weston-Mansinghka study, the early one by Boyle,[38] and those that followed by Melicher and Rush[39] and Conn[40] were all inconsistent with the hypothesis that the acquiring firms were generally superior performers (as measured by profitability) and thus likely to be purchasing other firms in order to enhance efficiency. Mueller's analysis of a large set of mergers for the years 1962 to 1972 showed the acquired firms to have higher profit rates than their industry means and to suffer from no significant profitability disadvantage relative to acquiring firms.[41] Ravenscraft and Scherer's extensive analysis based on line-of-business data confirms the findings of traditional profitability studies. They conclude that acquired firms were highly profitable on average prior to merger; that merger-prone companies did less well in acquired lines than in old lines, new internal-growth lines, and low-merger lines; and that there was a tendency toward deterioration of returns the longer the period of postmerger control.[42]

Over the past decade there has been a marked shift away from profitability stud-

ies and toward empirical studies that focus on returns on shareholder stock. Within this set there has been a further division between those studies that look at returns over a long time span that includes a substantial postmerger period and those that focus on stock price performance only in the period up to the consummation of the merger. The latter set has tended to increase in importance and is featured heavily in the summary of the "scientific evidence" in Jensen and Ruback's "The Market for Corporate Control: The Scientific Evidence."[43]

We question whether the shift to stock price–based analyses has been a boon to scientific understanding. Although marginally useful, they have inherent disadvantages that, in our view, make them less valuable than profitability studies and more readily subject to abuse. First, stock price movements of the acquiring and acquired firms will be affected in advance of the merger transaction by knowledge of the forthcoming merger, but the exact timing and effects of market acquisition of that knowledge is difficult or impossible to ascertain. Thus, even assuming that the stock market accurately reflects the expected gains from the merger, as Magenheim and Mueller make clear the choice of benchmarks affects the results to an astonishing degree.

A second problem is potential uncertainty concerning the line of causality. The rise in the bidder's price at an early date in the preannouncement period may reflect a positive market view of the anticipated effects of the merger, but it might also reflect internal improvements and prospects of the bidder wholly unconnected with the merger. These favorable developments may even help *explain* the merger, with the acquiring company's prosperity and enhanced cash flow leading it into implementing an acquisition plan.[44] Without convincing evidence of the correctness of the assumed direction of causality, citing the rise in market price of the bidder as demonstrating market anticipation of the benefits of the anticipated merger is scientifically dubious.

A third problem relates to the proper valuation of the firm. As Professor Roll notes in Chapter 14, stock price data do not accurately value the firm because they fail to capture the redistributions to and from bondholders.[45] These transfers of wealth have tended to be from bondholders to shareholders, and they have often been of significant magnitude.[46]

A further problem with stock price behavior as a measure of the expected social benefits and/or efficiency effects of a takeover is that it is an indirect measure at best. The market values show what stock market investors, traders, and arbitragers think about the company's stock and its prospective yield. They may have moved heavily into the stock, pushing up its price, because it became better known by virtue of the takeover bid itself or even before the bid, as in the recent cases of General Foods and Beatrice, if the "arbs" start to focus on a particular firm. They may have expected the merger to enhance returns because of greater monopoly power, which they believed to be correlated with size even if Chicago School studies assure them otherwise. They may be capitalizing expected tax gains[47] or claimed synergies that may or may not exist.

Given the loose and problematic connection between stock price movements of bidder and target up to merger day, the *least* scientific use of such information in measuring the efficiency effects of mergers would be to confine the analysis to premerger stock price behavior. In brief, we believe that one should also take into account price movements after the merger transaction because premerger price behavior is subject to numerous distorting and speculative effects and problems of timing (as discussed earlier); at best stock prices do not measure efficiency but only market participants' estimates of efficiency effects (among other things); postmerger price behavior will allow time for an adjustment of some of the prior distortions; and postmerger price behavior will give prices time to reflect the actual, material efficiency consequences of the merger.

Earlier stock price studies found a relatively low rate of return performance for acquired firms but statistically insignificant effects of mergers on the returns to shareholders of acquiring firms as well.[48] Jensen and Ruback find that the "scientific evidence" on the effects of takeovers shows positive gains to bidder company shareholders. But they concentrate their attention on the studies of stock price changes that occur around the time of the merger announcement or for the period from announcement to the merger transaction.[49] As an afterthought, they present evidence showing that there are "systematic reductions in the stock price of bidding firms following the event."[50] These findings are not incorporated into their net conclusions on the effects of takeovers on the welfare of bidder company shareholders; even though "systematic," they are treated as anomalies: "These post-outcome negative abnormal returns are unsettling because they are inconsistent with market efficiency and suggest that changes in stock price during takeovers overestimate the future efficiency gains from mergers."[51] We would submit that this is not scientific procedure. The body of evidence that has least credibility as a meaningful proxy for efficiency or real bidder gains is elevated to preeminence, and that which begins to take into account actual performance is set aside because it does not conform to the hypothesis to be proved.

A FINANCIAL ANALYSIS OF HOSTILE TAKEOVERS

We turn now to our own analysis of the efficiency effects of hostile takeovers. We focus on hostile takeovers and use company accounting data to develop pre- and postmerger rates of return and risk for bidding and acquired firms as our base for assessing relative efficiency. Hostile bids are an especially useful device for testing the disciplinary role and efficiency effects of the merger and acquisition process generally. Bidders must pay very large premiums over preannouncement market prices, much larger on average than in negotiated, friendly transactions. Winning bidders in the takeovers we studied paid an average premium of about 80%,[52] reflecting the obviously strong convictions of the original bidders, the usually vigorous defensive responses of the target managements, and the competitive bidding for the targets that often ensued. These were not casual marriages of convenience.

We have studied hostile takeovers by collecting a broad array of information from the published financial statements of successful bidders and targets as contained in the COMPUSTAT data base prepared by Standard & Poor's. We were particularly interested in what the data would tell us about the profitability of the successful bidders and targets in the years before the bid, the profitability of the bidders in the years after the bid, and the prices paid by the bidders as a function of the reported earnings of the targets they had purchased. In substance, we worked from the premise that stock prices, on which most other studies rely, are but a mirror of the underlying realities and that these realities would be better revealed by a study of the financial data.

As noted in the previous section, the new analyses of the costs and benefits of takeovers claim superiority for stock market price measures of performance and denigrate those based on financial data.[53] We examined earlier the serious limitations of market price data. Whatever the shortcomings of accounting data, and they are not minor, the correlation with economic rates of return has been well demonstrated, as Long and Ravenscraft noted. Accounting data are relied on heavily by those who are in the marketplace:

The broad use of accounting profit data in the private sector suggests that ... general conclusions about the uselessness of the data must be wrong. ... Given the amount spent in the private sector on analyses of accounting profit data, a substantial market failure is required to explain such an occurrence if the data are valueless.[54]

Corporate executives plan operations and capital budgets in terms of return on sales and invested capital, debt-equity ratios, and other data drawn directly from the income statement and balance sheet. They do not think of themselves as stock jobbers, and they surely do not allow their subordinate managers to report to them on that basis. It is true that issues are analyzed in part by their impact on reported earnings and earnings per share, which in turn affect share prices. But while share prices may mean cash to investors, they are not cash to the company. They are not the primary analytic tool.

Published financial data are particularly important in analyzing hostile takeovers, because unlike friendly merger partners, hostile bidders normally only have access to publicly available data about the target. The identity and extent of the turnaround opportunities at the target may not be apparent solely from the Forms 10–K, 10–Q, and 8–K on file at the SEC, but they will give a bidder a good deal more detailed information about such matters than stock price charts. To think otherwise, to denigrate financial data in favor of stock price analyses,[55] is to believe that a bidder can get bank financing in the hundreds of millions of dollars on the basis of something other than the customary accounting data. To be sure, projections are often a part of the analysis, but it would be the rare banker who did not insist that an analysis of the future begin with an accounting of the past.

The same is true when we take the measure of bidders. Their prowess ought not to be a secret that is revealed best—and only—to stock market chartists. On average the bidders ought to be more than ordinarily profitable before the bid. And the income statements of the bidders *after* the takeover should confirm those skills. If, on the other hand, the acquisition of other businesses proves to be more difficult than ambitious managers would like to believe, if the acquirers are sometimes too willing to pay $40 for a share that has been selling at $25 in the vain belief that they can by kissing toads turn them into princes,[56] then that, too, should be revealed in the financial statements.

At the least, and even assuming that stock price changes at or about the time of the takeover—the usual empirical tool of financial economists—are useful, we should be able to test them by observing whether the results they project have in fact been realized. The results should be reflected somewhere as cash in or cash out. Years after the takeover, when one is seeking merely to verify what has already happened, not to make predictions about future returns, the published data ought to be more than a little relevant.

We have gathered financial data for 56 hostile tender offers that were initiated in the years 1975–1983. The target firms and the successful bidders are listed in the Appendix (Table 13.14). These 56 transactions include, we believe, substantially all significant unfriendly takeovers in that nine-year period that satisfied the following criteria:

1. The proposed takeover was hostile in the sense that it began as an unsolicited offer. In the event, it was often a friendly "white knight" which captured the target company, but that did not change our characterization of the bid as hostile. The debate turns on the desirability of unfriendly bids rather than on the identity of the high bidder. The primary sources for the list of tender offers, and for determining whether the offers were solicited, were W. T. Grimm, Kidder, Peabody, and Morgan Stanley.[57]

2. The target company was ultimately acquired by some other company be it colored black, grey, or white. A primary purpose of our study was to see how well the target company compared with the successful bidder, whether or not the latter was the original, hostile bidder. The successful bidder was not only the firm for which the target had the highest value but also the one whose subsequent verifiable history records the impact of the takeover. It is, of course, possible that by leaving out the 20% or more of targets that retained their independence, we have skewed the data somewhat. On the other hand, it is appropriate to judge the process as a whole by the transactions that are in fact consummated.

3. Neither the successful bidder nor the target was a bank, insurance company or other financial institution, or a real estate firm. Income statement and balance sheet data for such firms tend not to be comparable to that for industrial and commercial enterprises. For real estate companies, reported earnings understate the cash flows by which such companies are usually valued. In recent years particularly, banks and insurance companies have often overstated earnings and understated their loss reserves, making comparisons more than ordinarily difficult.

4. The bidder and target were both domestic firms for which adequate data was available on the COMPUSTAT data base. The purpose was to have operating data for the bidder after the takeover as well as before, and in the case of both firms to have data that was prepared on a presumably comparable basis. Foreign firms were excluded because the accounting conventions are often dissimilar or simply because of a lack of data.

Additional information about the scope and character of the data base, and some of its potential limitations, is contained in the Appendix to this chapter.

We gathered the available data for each of the 112 firms for five fiscal years preceding the year of the initial announcement of the bid. Thus the year immediately preceding the year of that announcement is designated as year $B - 1$, the year before that as year $B - 2$, etc. For the successful bidders, we gathered data for the year the takeover was completed and, to the extent available, for the five subsequent years, which we designated years $T + 0$, $T + 1$, $T + 2$, etc. The data for the $T + 0$ years understandably contained so many extraordinary adjustments and "not available" data items that we eventually eliminated it from our base. For transactions completed later than 1979, we do not yet, of course, have data for five full $T+$ years.

The data itself falls into several broad categories: (1) size of targets and bidders, (2) their capital structure or leverage, (3) their profitability, and (4) miscellaneous other data, such as dividend payout ratios, effective tax rates, inventory accounting methods, stock prices, price-earnings ratios, and Q values. In this chapter we report on the first three data categories.

Company Size

The most obvious distinction between the targets and bidders in our study is their size, bidders being on average more than twice as large. Table 13.1 sets forth the mean total assets and common equity of bidders and targets for the fiscal year immediately before the announcement of the bid (B − 1). Both targets and bidders had grown in the years prior to the bid. The mean total assets for the B − 5 year were $557 million for targets and $1294 million for bidders. Growth over the four-year period ending in B − 1 was 63% and 64%, respectively, or more than twice the average annual increase in total assets of the Fortune 500-Industrials over the same period.[58]

After the takeover, the bidders continued to grow. Their mean total assets for the T + 1 year were $3640 million, an increase of 72% over B − 1 that reflects the acquisition of the target, to be sure, but also reflects the fact that hostile tender offers sometimes being protracted contests, T + 1—the first fiscal year after completion of the takeover—can be as much as three years after B − 1, the last year before the bid.

The firms involved in the takeovers in the later years, both bidders and targets, were larger than those in the earlier transactions. The targets, however, grew much more rapidly than did the bidders. For the group of bids begun in the years 1975–

1978, the mean total assets in the year B − 1 were $430 million for targets and $1450 million for bidders. Several years later, for the group of bids begun in the years 1981–1983, the mean total assets in the year B − 1 were $1548 million for targets and $2987 million for bidders. Over the intervening period of approximately five years, the average bidder grew by 106%, and the average target grew by 260%.

The particularly rapid growth in target firm size was part of a similar phenomenon affecting mergers and acquisitions generally. Although the total number of announced transactions was roughly unchanged, the total dollar volume of all mergers and acquisitions rose from $12 billion in 1975 to $83 billion in 1981.[59] The value of the average transaction rose from $14 million to $73 million. The number of billion-dollar transactions rose from 1 to 12. That trend has continued, even after the period of our study. In 1984 there were 18 billion-dollar transactions, and the total value of all transactions was $122 billion.[60] By 1985, there were 36 billion-dollar transactions, and the total dollar volume reached $180 billion.[61]

How did the bidders manage to swallow fish that grew more rapidly than they themselves? In the earlier, 1960s wave of acquisitions, the explanation would have been that bidders were paying with large blocks of their own common stock, a currency without limit. Not so, of course, in hostile tender offers. Cash is the currency of tender offers, especially unfriendly ones, because of the fear of competitive bidding and the delays involved in registering securities under the Securities Act of 1933. The increasing ability of bidders to finance these cash transactions lies in the changing credit market. Banks have aggressively sought to participate in business acquisitions, whether by conventional loans or by managing leveraged buy-outs.[62] In recent years, additional financing came from so-called junk or high-yield bonds issued to public or private investors.

Whatever its source, of course, the added debt ought to be reflected in the bidders' balance sheets after the transaction—to which we now turn.

Table 13.1. Average Size of Targets and Bidders in 56 Hostile Takeovers, 1975–1983 (Millions of Dollars)

	Total Assets	Common Equity
Targets	907	365
Bidders	2121	956

Leverage

It is desirable to look at the capital structures of bidders and targets to see to what extent the two groups differ, to see the impact of the takeover on the finances of the bidder, and finally to see to what extent the capitalization of the bidders was affected by their willingness to purchase ever larger targets. Did the bidders' debt become excessive? With respect to targets, is there any substance to the widespread perception that they are cash-rich, or at least have large, untapped borrowing power?

We measured leverage by two tests, debt-equity ratios and coverage of fixed charges.[63] Coverage of fixed charges was calculated as income before taxes and before interest and rental expense, divided by interest and rental expense. The two measures, both of which are widely used, approach the leverage issue from quite different perspectives, one being based on the balance sheet and the other on the income statement. One measures debt relative to net asset values or shareholders equity; the other measures more immediately a firm's ability to pay its obligations when due by measuring the availability of income to pay interest and rents.

Debt-equity ratios are useful; but since the equity figure is the item in a balance sheet that may tell the least about current values—sometimes reflecting hardly more than the historic cost of bricks and mortar—the ratio may reveal little about the ability to service debt. When interest is payable at the bank, one cannot tender bricks and mortar, at least not in the first instance. The value of the bricks and mortar, whether measured by historic cost or

replacement or market value, is ultimately a choice between a largely irrelevant history, on the one hand, or of earning power, on the other. It is for good reason, therefore, that lenders and security analysts look to the coverage of fixed charges as a primary measure.[64]

Targets

One might have expected targets to have less leveraged capital structures than bidders, either because the early and still common image of a target is that of a firm that does not use its borrowing power to the fullest or because bidders seem to be firms eager to maximize their earnings. The data did not fulfill these expectations.

When the data for the size of the firm was not adjusted or weighted, the mean ratio of debt to equity for the five years B − 5 to B − 1 was, as shown in Table 13.2, 74% for bidders and 76% for targets.[65] Where useful, as in Table 13.2, we have also weighted the results for the group of bidders and/or targets by the total assets of each of the firms in the group (a "weighted basis"). On this weighted basis the data may tell less about particular firms but more about overall economic impact and efficiency. With the data thus adjusted, the targets as a group had borrowed more heavily than the bidders.

Table 13.3 describes the coverage of fixed-charges data for targets, which may seem at first blush to be inconsistent with the debt-equity data in Table 13.2. On a weighted basis, the all-targets' coverage for the years B − 5 to B − 1 varies from 5.0 to 6.8, averaging a rather good 5.7. That may appear to be inconsistent with the relatively high debt-equity ratios of targets

Table 13.2. Mean Debt-Equity Ratio of Targets and Bidders, Prebid

	B − 5	B − 4	B − 3	B − 2	B − 1
			Unweighted		
Targets	74%	75%	82 %	73%	74%
Bidders	75	78	73	70	71
			Weighted		
Targets	76	79	78	77	82
Bidders	62	63	59	54	52

Table 13.3. Mean Coverage of Fixed Charges, Targets, Prebid

	B − 5	B − 4	B − 3	B − 2	B − 1
Unweighted basis					
	5.7	5.5	5.2	5.6	5.5
Weighted basis (All Bids)					
	5.4	5.0	5.0	6.6	6.8
(1975–1978 bids)					
	3.8	3.0	3.6	4.4	4.4
(1981–1983) bids					
	6.0	5.7	5.5	7.3	7.5

reported in Table 13.2. Second, and perhaps more curious, is the fact that on the same weighted basis, the targets as a group, even while *increasing* their debt-equity ratios in the two years B − 2 and B − 1 immediately before the bid, were also increasing their coverage of fixed charges. Thus the sharply improved coverage for targets in years B − 2 and B − 1—at least on a weighted basis—did not seem to have resulted from any substantial retirement of debt or additional equity investment.[66] Indeed, for B − 1 the weighted debt-equity ratio was a rather high 82%, no better and in fact slightly worse than the ratio in any of the preceding years. The explanation of the improved coverage in B − 2 and B − 1 seems to lie, as we shall shortly see, in the improved operating results enjoyed by targets in those two years rather than any shyness about going to the banks.[67]

The distinction is very important. If the targets were not a group of overcapitalized firms, one of the common justifications for unsolicited takeovers is missing.[68] There is a vigorous debate as to whether firms should generally be encouraged to borrow more aggressively, but the issue is mooted if the targets were not underleveraged by the standards of the marketplace. And they were not.

In addition to gathering data for all targets as a group, it was desirable to see whether there were changes within the group over time. Accordingly, the weighted data on target company coverage in Table 13.3 was broken down to separate the targets of the early 1975–1978 bids from those of the later 1981–1983 bids. The effect was dramatic. The later group had remarkably higher coverage—the result, as we shall shortly see, of a profit performance that not only was far better than that of the early targets but also was outstanding by any standard. By separating the companies in this fashion, we can also see that the good coverage ratio of *all* targets as a group is a function almost entirely of this excellence of the 1981–1983 targets. The earlier 1975–1978 targets reported coverage ratios that averaged only 3.9, a mediocre showing.

Bidders

For the bidders, the data on leverage reported in Table 13.4 tells a different tale. The debt-equity ratios of bidders before the target takeover varied, depending on whether we look at the weighted or the unweighted data. For the year preceding the bid, B − 1, the bidders' ratios were 52% and 71%, respectively. Obviously, the

Table 13.4. Debt-Equity Ratio, Bidders

	B − 3	B − 2	B − 1	T + 1	T + 2	T + 3	T + 4	T + 5
Weighted	59%	54%	52%	77%	80%	69%	68%	66%
Unweighted	73	70	71	84	81	92	78	81

weighted data gives substantial effect to the relatively low debt-equity ratios of some very large bidders, such as DuPont, U.S. Steel, and Phillips Petroleum. But in both cases, there was a prompt and sharp jump in the debt-equity ratio after the takeover. The jump was proportionately much larger in the weighted data, from 52% in B − 1 to 77% in T + 1, compared with the increase in the unweighted results, from 71% to 84%. That difference is no more than one would have expected. Those relatively few, relatively large bidders with conservative capital structures had more untapped borrowing power to use, and not surprisingly, they used it.

While average data for all bidders is useful, it necessarily gives an incomplete picture. As in the story about drowning in a lake that averages only 6 inches in depth, firms do not fail in the aggregate but, rather, one by one. Looking at individual transactions, we found that 12 of the 54 bidders for which data was available had total debt in T + 1 in excess of stated equity. And even these numbers are incomplete because they do not reflect the growing willingness of many companies to seek substantial off-balance-sheet financing.[69]

We measured the bidders' leverage also by the coverage of their fixed charges. We also thought it desirable to see what changes in coverage took place over time. Accordingly, Table 13.5 sets forth the coverage on both a weighted and unweighted basis for (1) all bidders, (2) those bidders that won the bids that were first announced

during the period 1975–1978, and (3) those that won the later 1981–1983 bids.

For all bidders as a group, the decline in coverage of fixed charges as a consequence of the target takeover was substantial. Furthermore, the coverage failed to improve very much with the lapse of time, even in the years T + 4 and T + 5. Coverage of fixed charges in the year T + 5, about 3.75, was low, which helps to explain the frequent credit downgrading of bidders by the rating services.[70]

The degree of risk taken on by the bidders was probably even greater than that reflected in Table 13.5, because much of that acquisition debt was short term, or at least the interest charges fluctuated with short-term rates.[71] The problem was not peculiar to the merger market. Total short-term debt of firms other than farms and financial companies had been less than 45% of their long-term debt in 1960, but it now exceeds long-term debt.[72] It has become fashionable, even for the Council of Economic Advisers, to contend that financial structures should be "more in line with prevailing market conditions."[73] Such fashionable doctrine misses the dynamics of credit expansion, whereby competition, myopia, and a confusion between individual and systemic liquidity regularly pushes out the risk frontier to levels that virtually ensure a financial crunch and widespread "surprise." We think that the wisdom of increased leverage and of borrowing short to invest long will be tested eventually, as it always has been, not by market condi-

Table 13.5. Coverage of Fixed Charges, Bidders

	B − 3	B − 2	B − 1	T + 1	T + 2	T + 3	T + 4	T + 5
			All Bids					
Weighted	5.3	5.2	4.9	3.2	3.5	4.1	3.9	3.9
Unweighted	5.6	5.2	4.9	3.2	3.8	3.8	3.4	3.6
			1975–1978 Bids					
Weighted	4.4	4.0	4.8	3.7	4.0	3.9	4.0	4.1
Unweighted	5.2	4.9	5.2	4.1	4.5	4.0	3.6	3.9
			1981–1983 Bids					
Weighted	5.7	5.6	4.9	2.9	3.0	n.a.	n.a.	n.a.
Unweighted	5.6	5.0	4.4	2.4	2.7	n.a.	n.a.	n.a.

tions at the time the debt is *floated* but by subsequent business downturns, renewed inflation, or even deflation.[74]

The data in Table 13.5 also discloses a second important feature of the deterioration in coverage. Those who won the 1981–1983 biddings suffered particularly severe declines in coverage, such that in the years T + 1 and T + 2 their income available for fixed charges averaged no better than 2.7 times fixed charges. The change from the corresponding coverage figures for the earlier 1975–1978 bids—an average of about 4.1—is particularly striking. What we are witnessing, at least in part, is the generally greater tolerance for debt in recent years, but aggravated in this case by the willingness of the later bidders to swallow proportionately larger targets.

What kinds of targets, then, did the bidders swallow? Did they offer opportunities for improvement, and did the bidders reap rewards? Or did they suffer indigestion?

Profitability

An increasing reliance on borrowed money often produces, over time, significant overpricing. In the 1920s, such "instances of overreaching" were vigorously defended as producing substantial economies—through what today would be called "restructuring"—and "this impression [was] industriously disseminated through self-interested propaganda."[75]

By one standard, that of the market, there has been severe overpricing in these hostile takeovers. For all transactions for which we have data,[76] the average premium over the market price prevailing 30 days before the first announcement of the bid was 80.2%. Expressed differently, the average price-earnings ratio of the winning bids to the trailing four-quarters earnings of these targets was 17.0, a very large premium over 8.9, the average price-earnings ratio of Standard and Poor's 500 stock index during the relevant years.[77] Ultimately, however, it would generally be agreed that whether bidders overpaid should be determined not by the mere fact of a premium price but by what they got for their money. These premiums do tell

us, however, that to justify their enthusiasm, the bidders must have *systematically* uncovered very major opportunities. Perhaps that is what happened, but in approaching the data, we are entitled to be skeptical.

If there has been overpricing, it should appear in lower returns on the capital and equity of the bidders after the acquisition. If, on the other hand, "takeovers generate [the] aggregate net benefits to the economy" that the Council of Economic Advisers claims, these, too, should be reflected in the bidders' income statements. Or if, as is sometimes said, the takeover process is based on a healthy competition among managers for the right to manage resources, this too should be reflected in the financial data.

We would thus expect, first, the successful competitors—i.e., the winning bidders—to display superior performance *ex ante*. Second, we would anticipate that the new managers, as they improve and synergize, would improve on the target's performance. Third, if takeovers are to impose discipline on a discriminating basis—otherwise, it is not discipline at all—the targets should as a group show the significantly inadequate rates of return on capital that would justify such heavy-handed and costly intervention. In short, even before the bid the targets' published results of operations should reveal the existence of these possibilities. Since hostile bidders do not have access to inside information—they are no better off than we—there is in fact no better place to begin.

The central focuses of our entire study, therefore, have been (1) the profitability of bidders and targets before the bid and (2) the impact of the acquisition on the profits of the successful bidder. For these purposes, we measured profitability by pretax returns on total capital (ROC) and after-tax returns on common equity (ROE).

Targets

Table 13.6 shows the ROE for all targets for the years B − 5 to B − 1 on a weighted and also on an unweighted basis. On a weighted basis, the one that best measures the overall economic impact of these

Table 13.6. Return on Common Equity, Targets (ROE)

	B − 5	B − 4	B − 3	B − 2	B − 1
Weighted	13.1%	11.5%	13.5%	17.2%	16.4%
Unweighted	12.2	11.8	11.9	13.0	12.5

tender offers, the targets' ROE is remarkably good. American nonfinancial firms earn on average about 13% on total equity, preferred as well as common.[78] The targets as a group earned about that much, or slightly better, on common equity in the early years before the bid announcement, and then in B − 2 and B − 1 they earned 16 to 17% on equity. Those last are "gee whiz" numbers. Returns that high are earned by very few companies—a fact known, of course, to the bidders.

We cannot be sure that these 56 targets were not engaged in activities that were especially profitable. In that case, bidders might yet have seen opportunities for substantial improvement, and the disciplinary-synergy thesis of takeovers might yet be validated by the data. We are inclined to doubt any such striking congruence of factors, however, for several reasons. First, our sample is quite large; it covers nine years of bidding; and there is no apparent indication that it is skewed in such a fashion. Second, we have data for five full fiscal years before the bids, a period usually considered sufficient by security analysts to compensate for cyclical factors. Third, on a weighted basis the earnings of the group rose dramatically in the years immediately before the bid, and that is not typical of firms that are underutilizing their resources.

Mr. Pickens and his academic supporters tell us that potential targets are much in need of restructuring—a concept that often entails the sale of cyclically depressed businesses, at of course cyclically depressed prices. What we found, however, when we looked first at the early bids, those announced in the years 1975–1978, and then the later ones, those announced in 1981–1983, was a very non-Pickensian pattern. The ROE data in Table 13.7 suggest that there existed targets appropriately ripe for picking a decade ago—well before Mr. Pickens's emergence, however, as a financial economist's folk hero—but that the takeover game greatly changed thereafter. For 21 targets of bids first announced in 1975–1978, the mean return on equity on a weighted basis was a not-very-good 8.8% for the five years ending B − 1.[79] The two latest years, it is true, showed markedly better results, but the returns for the period as a whole suggest that some of these targets may have offered meaningful opportunities. Calculated on a similar basis, the mean ROE for 25 targets of hostile bids in the years 1981–1983, however, was 15.9%, almost twice as high. And again, the two latest years showed the highest returns, averaging over 18%. These are once again remarkable numbers. To adopt Buffett's metaphor, these are not toads but ready-made, off-the-shelf princes, and kissing

Table 13.7. Return on Common Equity (ROE), Targets

	B − 5	B − 4	B − 3	B − 2	B − 1
		1975–1978 Bids			
Weighted	8.7%	6.0%	7.8%	10.0%	11.5%
Unweighted	9.5	8.8	10.1	11.5	12.8
		1981–1983 Bids			
Weighted	14.5	13.1	15.3	19.0	17.4
Unweighted	13.8	14.7	14.7	14.3	11.5

them would appear to have required little skill but may have run large risks.[80]

These Table 13.7 figures, in short, are scarcely the results one would expect from the better–resource-utilization thesis. Instead, it appears that the supply of promising targets having dried up,[81] the game continued and even accelerated but with much larger, more profitable targets brought into play. That much seems common knowledge. W. T. Grimm & Company, which studies acquisitions systematically, has noted that "many of the merger participants in the last decade [1975–1984] were large, well-managed concerns acquiring financially healthy and *well-managed* companies enjoying strong market positions. The acquired companies, in most cases, ranked first or second within their industries."[82]

The weighted data for the later 1981–1983 bids is perhaps influenced by the presence in the group of four large oil companies that had shown excellent rates of return. Applying industry controls, as we intend to do, will help to deal with such concerns. But the likely benefits of such controls should not be overstated. Assuming even a modest degree of efficiency in product and capital markets, the consistently high operating returns over a five-year period enjoyed by the 1981–1983 targets make it unlikely that the bidders could have found major sources of real gains. The targets' particularly strong showing in the years B − 2 and B − 1 makes it even more unlikely.

Bidders

In the early years (B − 5 and B − 4) before the bid was made, the bidders enjoyed returns on equity that were also good, though not quite as good as those of the target firms. Like the targets, too, the bidders' weighted ROE improved in the three years

immediately before the bid, though not as dramatically as did those of the targets (see Table 13.8). Using weighted ROE as a proxy for efficient asset utilization, it does not appear that the assets of the bidders were being more effectively employed than those of the targets.[83] In the years immediately before the bid announcement, B − 1 and B − 2, the years that would be of most concern to a prospective bidder, the targets were distinctly more profitable than the bidders. For those two years the targets' weighted ROE averaged 16.8%, compared with the bidders' 13.8%.

In Table 13.9 we show the relative ROE performance of matched bidders and targets, deal by deal. On this basis, bidders outperformed their matched targets in the five years prior to merger in 31 of 56 cases. On the other hand, in 25 of 56 mergers (45% of the total) the targets outperformed the bidders. The second column indicates that in 23 of 56 cases the bidders outperformed the targets by 3 percentage points or more, whereas in 16 cases (29%) the targets outperformed the bidders by the same difference. These data give some credence to the notion of bidder superiority in efficiency, but not much. Apart from the large fraction of cases of target ROE superiority, we found that the superiority of bidders over targets was confined to small transactions. When we separated the 56 transactions into quintiles by size of target company assets, we found that more targets had a higher mean ROE than their matched bidders for the five years ended B − 1 in those two quintiles that described the largest transactions. (See Table 13.10, which groups the targets with the largest total assets in the year B − 1 in the first quintile and those with the smallest in the fifth quintile.)

Arguably comparisons of the profitability of bidders and targets ought to be very

Table 13.8. Return on Common Equity (ROE), Bidders Prebid

	B − 5	B − 4	B − 3	B − 2	B − 1
Weighted	10.7%	10.0%	14.2%	13.5%	14.1%
Unweighted	11.7	11.9	14.2	14.6	15.3

Table 13.9. Comparison of ROE of Each Bidder and Its Matched Target, Prebid

	Superior ROE for 5 Years Ended B − 1	Superior ROE for 5 Years Ended B − 1 and by at Least 3 Percentage Points	Superior ROE for 2 Years Ended B − 1
Bidders	31	23	37
Targets	25	16	19

and systematically favorable to the bidders, rather than neutral or even modestly favorable. Because of the large transaction costs and presumed efficiency differentials resulting in the payments of premiums of 80%, the bidders' ability to utilize assets more efficiently than managers of acquired companies not only is a necessary assumption but also ought to have been reflected in substantially higher rates of return than those of the targets. (One must ask not only for whom does the bell toll but also who is swinging the clapper.) What is surprising, therefore, is that the targets came even close to matching the bidders in profitability.

Looking separately at the earlier (1975–1978) and later (1981–1983) bidders, as we have already done for targets, we find no important differences in their returns on common equity (ROE) for the years preceding the bid. Both groups, early and late, showed steadily rising returns (see Table 13.11). But for the years after the takeover, the differences between the two were striking. The steady improvement in profitability experienced by the early 1975–1978 bidders *before* the bid continued quite steadily during the years *after* the takeover. Thus for this earlier group of bidders, the ROE grew from about 14% in the year B − 1 to about 16% in T + 3 and about 17% in T + 5. (Those results are little affected by

whether or not they are weighted by size of company.) As already mentioned, T + 1 may be a fiscal year two to three years after B − 1, depending on the time required for the bidding process to unfold and for the completion of a second-step merger. Thus for the early-1970s bidders the data extends for as much as seven years after the initiation of the bid. And the improvement in ROE continued almost consistently throughout that period.

For the later 1981–1983 bidders, there is not yet, of course, significant data available except for the first two years, T + 1 and T + 2, following the takeover. Such data as is available, however, suggests a dramatic deterioration from the pattern of the earlier transactions. The later bidders experienced precipitous declines in profitability, declines that were severe on any basis but were particularly severe on a weighted basis. That is to say, the larger the bidders, the worse the results. Like the ROE of the earlier bidders, the ROE of the later 1981–1983 bidders was about 14% for the year (B − 1) just before the year of the bid. But then it fell to an average of less than 9% in the first two years after acquiring the target company.[84]

Quite often in corporate finance, it is the early bird that catches the worm. Finding an opportunity, the innovators exploit it with success, whether it be new issues, real

Table 13.10. Comparison of Mean ROE for 5 Years Ended B − 1 of Matched Bidders and Targets Sorted by Target Company Total Assets in B − 1

	1st Quintile	2nd Quintile	3rd Quintile	4th Quintile	5th Quintile
Bidders had superior ROE	5	5	7	7	7
Targets had superior ROE	7	6	4	4	4

Table 13.11. Return on Common Equity (ROE), Bidders

	B − 3	B − 2	B − 1	T + 1	T + 2	T + 3	T + 4	T + 5
			All Bids					
Weighted	14.2%	13.5%	14.1%	7.8%	11.5%	13.3%	16.7%	16.5%
Unweighted	14.2	14.6	15.3	11.9	12.4	11.0	14.6	15.7
			1975–1978 Bids					
Weighted	11.4	12.0	13.9	14.8	15.3	16.6	17.6	17.3
Unweighted	12.0	13.0	14.6	15.4	16.6	16.7	15.3	16.9
			1981–1983 Bids					
Weighted	15.6	14.1	14.1	4.3	9.3	n.a.	n.a.	n.a.
Unweighted	16.0	15.9	15.6	8.7	8.9	n.a.	n.a.	n.a.

estate investment trusts, leveraged buyouts, casino stocks, or venture capital investments in Silicon Valley.[85] Observing that success, others seek to imitate it, but either because they mistake form for substance or simply because the supply of attractive opportunities is limited, the investments deteriorate. For a while the bubble persists. The business of security analysis is so inherently difficult that the decline in quality is not immediately apparent. Indeed, for a while the market rewards the imitators because they are in the mainstream. They are selling what is in demand.

Tobin defined a bubble as a speculation on someone else's speculation. If the bubble does not last for long or if it is relatively minor in scale, then it may have little if any effect on the enterprise of the nation. But if, as Keynes noted, the impact is such that "enterprise becomes the bubble on a whirlpool of speculation, [and] the capital development of a country becomes a by-product of the activities of a casino, the job is likely to be ill-done."[86]

The evidence suggests that there may have been a casino effect at work in hostile tender offers. As time went by, bidders sought out ever-larger targets. The targets were increasingly firms with excellent profit histories, so that it was difficult to see how the enterprise of the nation would be enhanced by a takeover. Still the bidders persisted. They continued to pay price-earnings ratios almost two times the market average. Had the price-earnings ratios diminished over time, perhaps the pursuit of already successful firms could more easily be explained; but the price-earnings ratios for the later 1981–1983 bids were in fact slightly above those for the group as a whole.

The bidders in turn also changed. In the mid 1970s, they consisted largely of operating firms seeking, for whatever reason, to own and operate other enterprises. By the 1980s, the bidders were a new group, one that consisted in part of those who played the game for its own sake—those who threatened a takeover but were willing enough to be bought off or out—and profited on an *entrepreneurial* scale without either entrepreneurial risk or entrepreneurial contribution, and in part of those who, although they made acquisitions, seemed unlikely to profit.

That dour view of the changing character of the market in hostile tender offers was then ultimately confirmed, though not until a while later, by the operating histories of the "winning" bidders.[87] The bidders in the early years were able to take over targets earning lower rates of return than their own and yet achieve for the combined operations profitability rates commensurate with their own. Better yet, they maintained their upward momentum. Their combined operations were more profitable than those of either bidder or target beforehand. But as time passed, as the speculative aspects of the tender offer game came to overwhelm the original economic rationale, the results were the reverse. Bidders' returns on equity dropped to low levels that could not be explained by the history of either bidder or target before the event. Rather than kissing toads in order to reveal princes, the bidders seem to have paid a twice-princely price for firms that were currently performing like princes but may, like most, have harbored some toad-like qualities.

In Table 13.12 we show return-on-total-capital data on a weighted basis for targets and bidders for the five years preceding the bid. Table 13.13 contains similar data for bidders for the years after the acquisition, with the early and late bids shown separately. In most respects the return-on-capital (ROC) data confirms the data for return on common equity (ROE). Thus on a weighted basis the targets as a group are significantly more profitable in the two years immediately preceding the bid than in the earlier years. The later targets are more profitable than the earlier ones by such a wide margin as to suggest again a drying up of opportunities. The targets as a group have been moderately more profitable than the bidders, or at least not less profitable. The data does not support the better–resource-utilization thesis.

The major difference to be seen between the ROE and ROC sets of data is that although in both the bidders as a whole experience lower returns immediately after the takeover, and although the bidders in the later 1981–1983 bids experience particularly severe declines, the reduction is proportionately much less in return on total capital than in return on common equity.

That is to be expected, of course, since ROC is calculated before interest expense, and we know from the data on leverage in Tables 13.4 and 13.5 that the bidders borrowed heavily. Again, data for the years T + 3 to T + 5 for the bidders in the recent 1981–1983 bids would have been preferable, but the decline in return on total capital for the two years T + 1 and T + 2 is sufficient to raise serious concerns as to whether these are indeed gain-producing transactions for the bidders' shareholders, much less real gains for the economy as a whole.

By borrowing heavily, the bidders' managers have put a wolf at the door, but is it a "useful" wolf, as suggested by Professor Jensen, or just a voracious one? It is not a very useful wolf that produces for shareholders the Scylla and Charybdis of lower returns together with higher risk. Nor is it a wolf that any financial economist has written about. The lower returns on total capital might have been predicted if they had at least produced *higher* returns on common equity, that is, if the added leverage had paid off on any level; but alas, such was not the case.

SOME IMPLICATIONS OF THE DATA

The best single explanation of the data is that there is no single, systematic explanation of hostile tender offers. Bids made in the early years of the nine-year period of

Table 13.12. Return on Total Capital (ROC), Bidders and Targets, Prebid (Weighted Basis)

	B − 5	B − 4	B − 3	B − 2	B − 1
		All Bids			
Targets	19.2%	18.3%	20.0%	25.2%	27.6%
Bidders	15.2	15.9	19.8	22.0	21.3
		1975–1978 Bids			
Targets	11.2	9.2	11.6	14.7	16.7
Bidders	11.8	12.8	14.3	15.5	19.0
		1981–1983 Bids			
Targets	21.8	21.0	22.7	28.1	30.4
Bidders	16.4	17.2	22.5	25.0	22.6

Table 13.13 Return on Total Capital (ROC), Bidders, Postbid (Weighted Basis)

	T + 1	T + 2	T + 3	T + 4	T + 5
All bids	16.5%	18.9%	20.0%	20.4%	20.2%
1975–1978 bids	17.7	18.9	19.5	21.0	21.0
1981–1983 bids	15.9	19.4	n.a.	n.a.	n.a.

our study seem to have been productive in several respects. The bidders in 1975–1978 generally were able to find targets with relatively poor operating histories. The bidders themselves, on the other hand, were companies already enjoying high rates of return; and yet after paying premium prices for their targets, they did even better. Earning a weighted average of 14.7% on their total capital in the years before the tender offer, these bidders earned a weighted average of 19.6% in the years after completion of the acquisition. The only shadow on that bravura performance is that the targets of these mid-1970s bids had already begun a turnaround by the time of the tender offer, but any such prospects for continued improvement by the targets may well have been discounted in the high price-earnings ratio at which they acquired. The bidders in these mid-1970s transactions did, it is also true, assume substantial amounts of acquisition-related debt. Nonetheless, they did not allow their coverage of fixed charges, for example, to fall below the relatively conservative level of 4 to 1.

There are no such good marks, however, for the later 1980s bids, which in all respects seem to have been much more speculative. The 1980s targets were relatively much larger than the earlier ones; and compared with the bidders, they had little if any excess borrowing capacity. These 1980s targets were already quite profitable concerns. Their weighted-average return on total capital for the years prior to the bid was a stunning 25%. To buy these targets, the bidders, on the other hand, incurred quite heavy levels of debt and interest charges because of the very high price per dollar of earnings at which the deals were struck. As a consequence, even in the

1980s, a period of relative prosperity, the bidders suffered an immedate and sharp decline in profitability.

These changes over time should not now surprise us. When Henry Manne first "invented" the market for corporate control, there was a good deal to be said for it. But that market grew and developed. It did not develop in a vacuum. The targets took steps to reduce their vulnerability. Listening to Mr. Flom and other counsel,[88] they got rid of their cash and drained their "excess" borrowing power. Tender offers became respectable, and having become so, they were soon targeted at much larger and more profitable firms. The bidders changed, too, particularly as the sources and depth of financing changed. Ultimately, the impact of these changes was reflected in the operating histories of the successful bidders.

Eventually, those who bid for companies in order to operate them showed mediocre results, even while those who played the game for speculative purposes only were able to profit handsomely. The game itself often became the objective. Yet one looks in vain for any suggestion from the financial economists that the process was dynamic and not static, changing and not rooted in a model of perfect pricing that, by ignoring the changing context, eliminates this rich complexity and variety from intruding on the analysis.[89]

It is remarkable how much of the debate on tender offers has centered on theories of rational expectations that insist that markets, if not people, behave sensibly and that a willingness to pay a premium price necessarily implies a better allocation or utilization of resources. As Professor Ruback in Chapter 21 of this volume concedes, the proponents of these theories still cannot identify the source of these gains. Even so, they "know" that the gains are there. Or as one of them, Assistant Attorney General Ginsburg, asserted at the conference, even if in a given case a bidder errs and the process fails, the error will be redeemed by yet another takeover . . . and another?

But the data does not bear out any such single-dimension, exclusive view of the process. For example, the targets were simply too profitable and they were climbing up the earnings slope, not down, as the bidders approached. The bidders on average were no better, and perhaps worse, than the targets at utilizing their resources. Where were the systematic gains in such a process?

By now, managers of potential target companies have seen that a strong product market position and efficient operations offer no protection. W. T. Grimm knows that;[90] the managers know that. If business skills are not sufficient to ward off raiders, what is? Without approving them, we can at least better understand the panoply of defensive tactics: shark repellents, poison pills, greenmail, defensive and dilutive acquisitions, lockups, golden parachutes, and leveraged buy-outs.

Having rejected simple answers, we are left with messy, complex questions. The financial economists focus on target company behavior. Perhaps we should continue to explore, as Salter and Weinhold, Magenheim and Mueller, and Ravenscraft and Scherer did in their chapters of this volume the behavior of bidders. Perhaps the less-than-optimal efficiency, the excessive agency costs, are as much on the bidder's side as on the target's. We know that there are powerful pressures to grow bigger and not just better.[91] Perhaps, too, as Mr. Frazer's chapter (27) on the British rules suggests, we should be more willing to think about the fairness to shareholders of partial and two-tier bids, greenmail, and tender offers that remain open for less than half the 60-day period that is customary in Britain. If the tender offer process does not bring systematic gains in asset utilization, the fairness of the process is of increasing importance. These are not new concerns, but they need to be taken out from under the rug of conventional wisdom.

The most troublesome set of issues raised by our data concern, however, neither the bidder nor the target, as such, but rather the takeover process itself. As Professor Bebchuk explains in Chapter 25 of this volume, tender offers are not a model market in which buyers and sellers negotiate from positions of equal strength. Target shareholders generally depend, in mergers as well as elsewhere, on management to represent them. But the peculiar genius of a takeover bid is that the management is taken off the ice, put in the penalty box, so to speak, long enough for the bidder to make a "score." We need to think more, therefore, about whether such a playing field is ever level or appropriate. The decision to put a company into play, almost irrevocably we might add, is made neither by the shareholders, who are not active participants, nor by management, which the tender offer process is designed to circumvent, but by persons outside the company who may or may not intend to operate the business or to do anything more than exact tribute. Should the decision to liquidate the venture be lodged there?

If tender offers are *not* consistently value enhancing, what room is there for greenmail prizes of $50 million or more? Absent a divinely inspired invisible hand, the greenmailers are not doing God's work but are exacting from managers a ransom payable with other people's money. Perhaps the takeover process should at a minimum be reserved for those who bid to buy, in which case short-swing trading restrictions or the like might be used to discourage those who seek only to put companies into play.

Ultimately, to reject the financial economists' model as the sole explanation is to face up to serious, unanswered questions about the role and responsibility of the modern American shareholder. Shareholders come and go; they turn over their portfolios with increasing frequency. If they do not seem to act as owners of a business, to what extent should we treat them as such?

The issue is not shareholder democracy or fairness but the search for a rational structure for American industry.

We have no immediate answers, but our data suggests that these are at least the proper questions.

APPENDIX

Of the computer data bases we examined, only COMPUSTAT continues to make available data for firms no longer in existence. That left us with little choice, but it was not an unhappy one. In order to capture data for the minimum of 50 transactions that we had set as a goal, we reached back to bids begun in 1975. The data was cut off at bids no later than 1983 in order to have data in every case (with but one exception) for at least one full year after the completion of the takeover. Table 13.14 lists the paired bidders and targets in our data set.

A computerized data base is unavoidable for a study of this magnitude. We gathered in all about 40 separate data items for a period of 5 to 10 years for each of 112 firms, or 25,000–30,000 data items in all. COMPUSTAT makes such a study feasible, but we spent over a year gathering and checking data and then analyzing, sifting, and sorting it. We then added a substantial block of additional items to our data base in order to have industry yardsticks or controls for measuring profitability, leverage, and other financial ratios. For example, it would have been the rare oil company in our data base, and there were 12 in all, that was not highly profitable in 1980 and much less so in 1982. It is useful to adjust these returns for industry characteristics.

A data base made our study possible, but data gathered in this fashion is not altogether satisfactory to those accustomed to reading their financial statements neat. Accounting is as much art as science, and some inaccuracies are inevitable. With minor exceptions, we resisted the temptation to read annual reports, Moody's, and the like. It was not simply that the authors are both beyond the age when one still

dreams of immortality, but the financial statements would not have had even the degree of comparability that COMPUSTAT presumes to have achieved.[92] Even so, comparability was a problem. COMPUSTAT discloses whether a firm accounts for its inventories on, for example, a LIFO or FIFO basis, or even a combination of the two. But it is obviously beyond the ken of COMPUSTAT to adjust for unrealistic pension plan assumptions or any of the other "generally accepted" methods for manipulating earnings that might have been discovered by a reading of financial statements. Unlike stock price movement studies, therefore, our data potentially harbors problems of comparability. The assumption has been that these problems would tend to wash out in our large data base—and in any event ought not to affect the comparison of bidders before and after the takeover or of bidders and targets before the takeover. We found no reason to believe that either bidders or targets as a group are more aggressive than the other about reporting earnings or that bidders' accounting practices change with an acquisition.

The COMPUSTAT data base has two significant limitations. One is that while it digests extensive data drawn from the published financial statements, for example, the income statement and balance sheet, it does not directly report events or transactions such as business acquisitions. Thus the data base does not disclose the closing of any particular transaction, the price at which it took place, or even the method—purchase or pooling—used to account for it. We had to go outside COMPUSTAT—to Kidder, Peabody—for data such as the price-earnings ratios at which the target was acquired. We did not, however, seek to adjust our data for purchase/pooling considerations. It is an accounting distinction that can be quite significant in acquisitions, with pooling treatment often producing for the purchases much higher levels of reported earnings.[93] For hostile takeovers, however, pooling treatment is extremely unlikely, because (1) it depends on the bidder paying for the target almost

Table 13.14. List of Paired Bidders and Targets (within each pair, bidder first, target second)

Company Name	Company Name	Company Name	Company Name
Clabir Corp. HMW Industries Inc.	Manor Care Inc. Cenco Inc.	Tiger International Seaboard World Airlines	Northwest Industries Microdot Inc.
Brown-Forman Distillers	Allegheny International Inc.	Brown Group Inc. Outdoor Sports Industries	Harcourt Brace Jovanovich
Lenox Inc.	Sunbeam Corp.		Sea World Inc.
CSX Corp. Texas Gas Resources Corp.	Allied Stores Garfinckel, Brooks Brothers	National Medical Enterprises Hillhaven Inc.	Lear Siegler Inc. Royal Industries Inc.
Diamond Shamrock Corp. Natomas Co.	Sherwin-Williams Co. Gray Drug Stores	W. R. Grace & Co. Daylin Inc.	Eli Lilly & Co. Ivac Corp.
Burlington Northern Inc. El Paso Co.	Bairnco Corp. Lightolier Inc.	United Technologies Corporation Carrier Corp.	Allegheny International Inc. Chemetron Corp.
Quaker Oats Co. Stokely-Van Camp Inc.	Du Pont (E. I.) de Nemours Conoco Inc.	IC Industries Inc. Pet Inc.	Northwest Industries Coca-Cola Bottling Co. of L.A.
Phillips Petroleum Co. General American Oil Co.-TX	Fluor Corporation St. Joe Minerals Corp.	Philip Morris, Inc. Seven-Up Co.	Interpace Corp. Allied Thermal Corp.
Masco Corp. Evans-Aristocrat Inds.	American Medical International Brookwood Health Services	Norton Simon Inc. Avis Inc.	Humana Inc. American Medicorp Inc.
Allied Corporation Bendix Corp.	Ampco-Pittsburgh Corp. Buffalo Forge Co.	Kennecott Corp. Carborundum Co.	
Waste Management Inc. Chem-Nuclear Systems Inc.	Dart & Kraft Inc. Hobart Corp.	McDermott Inc. Babcock & Wilcox Co.	
Occidental Petroleum Corp. Cities Service Company	Cooper Industries Inc. Crouse-Hinds Co.	Morton Thiokol Inc. Ventron Corp.	
Anacomp Inc. DSI Corp.	Tyco Laboratories Inc. Ludlow Corp.	Southland Royalty Co. Aztec Oil & Gas Co.	
Valley Industries Burgess Industries	NCR Corp. Applied Digital Data Systems	United Technologies Corporation Otis Elevator Co.	
Lukens Inc. General Steel Industries	Wheelabrator-Frye, Inc. Pullman Inc.	Colt Industries Inc. Garlock Inc.	
U.S. Steel Corp. Marathon Oil Company	Clausing Corp. Fife Corp.	Emhart Corp. USM Corp.	
Witco Chemical Corp. Richardson Co.	Moore McCormack Resources Florida Mining & Materials	Atlantic Richfield Co. Anaconda Co.	

entirely with common stock, and (2) the Williams Act has never been amended to permit tender offers by securities, that require prior registration under the Securities Act of 1933, to compete on an even basis with cash offers. In short, pooling treatment is quite unlikely.

That still leaves a question whether even the consistent use of purchase accounting might introduce a bias in our results. The takeovers in our study were done at prices that averaged about 25%–30% over the book value of the targets, making it possible that the bidders' reported earnings suffered as a result of the amortization of goodwill. COMPUSTAT does not report such charges separately. We doubt, however, that this significantly affected our principal findings. First, it is usual for an acquiring firm to write up the assets of the acquired company as much as possible in order to maximize tax savings and to reduce goodwill. Premiums over book of 25%–30% are not large for these purposes, so that any remaining goodwill items affecting earnings were presumably modest, particularly if written off over the 40-year period that is permitted. Second, the premium over book value paid by the bidders was almost constant over the 9-year period of the study, so that it does not help to explain why the bidders' performance declined so sharply from the early 1970s bids to those in the 1980s. What appears to have changed primarily was the profitability of the targets and, secondarily, their relative size, not the impact of the accounting treatment.

A second, perhaps more serious limitation of COMPUSTAT is that it does not contain even the line-of-business data required by the SEC. It would have been useful to have been able, as Ravenscraft and Scherer are doing, to have observed the impact of the transaction on the relevant business segment, as well as on the bidder as a whole. Some of the targets were, in fact, quite small relative to their bidders—e.g., Ivac Corp. which was acquired by Eli Lilly. But as a group, the targets were not small. They had mean total assets of $921 million in the year preceding the bid, compared with $2121 billion for the bidders. The bidders were much larger, no doubt, but not so much larger as to be able to pay premium prices and not show significant overall effects.

NOTES

1. E. Jones, *The Trust Problem in the United States* (1921), 201; Bureau of Corporations, *Report on the Steel Industry* (1911), 85–86; A. Chandler, *The Visible Hand: The Managerial Revolution in American Business* (1977), 266–269, 361–62. It is, of course, ironic that the same firm, United States Steel, that provided the earlier negative paradigm of merger for inefficient monopoly should provide a new counterexample for the efficient-markets analysis of takeovers in its 1981 acquisition of Marathon Oil, where it paid an 87% premium over market while openly acknowledging little familiarity with the new line of activity and no plan for any kind of renovation (as if one were needed for a firm that had earned a pretax return of 51% on total capital and 19.7% after-tax on common equity in its latest fiscal year).

2. A recent trend led by Gary Becker of the University of Chicago has extended the satisfaction-maximizing premise of neoclassical economics to previously sacrosanct areas, on the supposition that economic calculations in human decision making are virtually universal. Thus cost-benefit calculations have been extended to choices in marriage and divorce, number of children, sexual behavior, cheating and lying, crime, and drug addiction, among others. G. Becker and D. Landes, eds., *Essay in the Economics of Crime and Punishment* (1974); G. Becker, *The Economic Approach to Human Behavior* (1976); R. McKenzie and G. Tullock, *The New World of Economics: Explorations into the Human Experience* (1975). One area still sacrosanct thus far, however, is the economics profession itself.

3. An exception is Easterbrook and Fischel, "The Proper Role of a Target's Management in Responding to a Tender Offer," 91 *Harv. L. Rev.* 1161, 1169 (April 1981), where it is argued that mergers based on tax losses have neutral or positive efficiency effects.

4. See, e.g., Council on Economic Advisers, *1985 Annual Report,* 199; Carney, "Fundamental Corporate Changes, Minority Shareholders and Business Purposes," 1980 *Am. Bar Found. Res. J.* 69, 119–128; Easterbrook and Fischel, "Corporate Control Transactions," 91 *Yale L.J.* 698, 708 (1982).

5. Another line of new defense, not explicitly addressed here, is efficiency enhancement by forced "restructuring." In this analysis, the primary efficiency effect of a takeover or takeover threat lies in the resultant selling off of unprofitable assets, the enforced increase in leverage, and a trimming of unjustified expenses. These effects are independent of the capabilities of the incumbent or successor management; they are more closely related to managerial objectives and a willingness to take drastic actions that will raise the present value of shareholders' stock. These restructurings are complex, however. In

part, they may represent forced wealth transfers from public bondholders to the stockholders, so that stockholder gains should be offset by bondholder losses (see Prokesch et al., note 46). Stock market gains from restructuring are also paper gains, not real wealth changes, so that whether they rest on faddish movements of the stock market or something more substantial remains to be proved and should be reflected in effects on realized rates of return.

6. The practical counterpart of this view is the softening of antitrust policy against corporate mergers and economic concentration under the Reagan administration. See "How Justice Encourages the Momentum for Mergers," *Business Week,* November 30, 1981, 53; "A Loosening of Merger Rules," *Business Week,* May 17, 1982, 120; "The Tide of Mergers Picks Up Speed" (interview with William Baxter), *U.S. News & World Report,* December 19, 1983, 73–74.

7. A. Alchian and R. Kessel, "Competition, Monopoly and the Pursuit of Pecuniary Gain," in *Aspects of Labor Economics* (1962), 160.

8. D. Dewey, "Mergers and Cartels: Some Reservations About Policy," 51 *Am. Econ. R.* 255, 260 (1961).

9. H. Manne, "Mergers and the Market for Corporate Control," 73 *J. Pol. Econ.* 112 (1965).

10. Ibid., 113.

11. Ibid.

12. Easterbrook and Fischel, note 3, p. 1173.

13. Jensen and Ruback, "The Market for Corporate Control: The Scientific Evidence," 11 *J. of Fin. Econ.* 5, 6 (1983).

14. Council of Economic Advisers, note 4, p. 188.

15. Ibid., 196.

16. As Manne put it, "Generally speaking, managers' incentives and interests coincide with those of their shareholders in every particular except one; they have no incentive, as managers, to buy management services for the company at the lowest possible price" (note 9, p. 117).

17. An important alternative strand of "reductionist" analysis stresses an active managerial labor market and a labor market for directors to discipline managers. Fama, for example, elevates managerial-directorial labor markets to primacy, leaving the market for corporate control as a "last resort"; see "Agency Problems and the Theory of the Firm," 88 *J. Pol. Econ.* 288, 295 (1980). Among its other weaknesses, the institutional premises of this alternative line of analysis seem to us farfetched. See notes 18 and 19 and associated text.

18. See C. Brown, *Putting the Corporate Board to Work* (1976); V. Brudney, "The Independent Director—Heavenly City or Potemkin Village?" 95 *Harv. L. Rev.* 597, 625 (1982); Conference Board, *The Board of Directors: New Challenges, New Directions* (1971); M. Eisenberg, *The Structure of the Corporation* (1976) 140–148; E. Herman, *Corporate Control, Corporate Power* (1981) 17–52; M. Mace, *Directors: Myths and Realities* (1971).

19. W. Lewellen, "Recent Evidence on Senior Executive Pay," 28:2 *Nat. Tax J.* 161–164 (1975); Herman, note 18, pp. 95–96. In a 1982 study of 140 large corporations, Carol Loomis found "some examples of consistency in which pay and performance match. But there were many more examples of irrationality and contradiction." Peter Grace, of W. R. Grace, received, for example, a bonus of $1 million in 1981 in "recognition of his accomplishments during his 36-year tenure," a period in which the shareholders earned an annual return of 7.4%. See C. Loomis, "The Madness of Executive Compensation," *Fortune,* July 12, 1982, 42–46.

20. Easterbrook and Fischel, note 3, pp. 1170–1171.

21. Fama, note 17, pp. 293–294; emphasis added.

22. Brudney, "Corporate Governance, Agency Costs and the Rhetoric of Contract," 85 *Colum. L. Rev.* 1403 (1985).

23. Tobin, On the Efficiency of the Financial System (Hirsch Memorial Lecture, May 15, 1984), 6.

24. R. Shiller, Chapter 3 of this volume.

25. See, e.g., Goodman and Peavy, "Industry Relative Price-Earnings Ratios as Indicators of Investment Returns," *Fin. Analysts J.,* July–August 1983, 60; R. Shiller, "Do Stock Prices Move Too Much to Be Justified by Subsequent Changes in Dividends?" 71 *Am. Econ. Rev.* 421 (1981); R. Shiller, *Stock Prices and Social Dynamics,* Cowles Found. Disc. Paper No. 719R October 1984; Wang, "Some Arguments That the Stock Market Is Not Efficient," 19 *U.C. Davis L. Rev.* 341 (1986).

26. See M. Whitman and M. Shubik, *The Aggressive Conservative Investor* (1979), 51; Shubik, Chapter 2 of this volume.

27. See note 2.

28. See, e.g., *Panter v. Marshall Field & Co.,* 646 F.2d 271 (7th Cir. 1981), cert. den. 454 U.S. 1092.

29. Analysts of the thrift crisis have stressed the problems of "moral hazard" and "adverse selection" that arise when financial institutions are insured and are permitted to survive with low or negative net worth. See J. Barth, R.

Brumbaugh, G. Wang, and D. Sauerhaft, "Insolvency and Risk-Taking in the Thrift Industry: Implications for the Future," in *Contemporary Policy Issues*, Vol. 3, November 1985, 1–32. Outsiders of dubious moral character may seek control to sell insured deposits to lend at high risk in a "go-for-broke" strategy, especially if minimal equity investment is required. Why should moral hazard and adverse-selection factors not also impel inefficient managers with limited personal investment in their controlled companies to opt for rapid growth and trading in other companies as a preferred strategic option?

30. See Shubik, Chapter 2 of this volume.

31. In diversifying acquisitions, the acquirer is generally relying heavily on the skill and experience of the acquired company's managers. That seemed clear enough in the 1982 tender offer for Giddings & Lewis, which AMCA International made only after searching the industry and picking a firm that it openly admired. When Eli Lilly, in 1977, purchased Ivac, a manufacturer of surgical instruments with the minuscule annual sales of $17 million, it was seeking to round out a product line and not to improve on the skills of the Ivac executive team. DuPont, intending to ensure itself of a source of raw materials for petrochemicals, also gave every indication of desiring to mollify and retain the Conoco management. See also note 82 and associated text.

32. Robert F. Anderson, chairman of M. A. Hanna Company, recently informed security analysts that his company was seeking acquisition candidates that would diversify its risks and provide outlets for its materials supplying facilities. He pointed out to the analysts that he would like to acquire a profitable company to enable M. A. Hanna to utilize its tax loss carryforward that totals more than $100 million. See "M. A. Hanna Co. Seeks Acquisitions," *N.Y. Times,* October 16, 1985.

33. F. Scherer, "Mergers, Sell-Offs, and Managerial Behavior," in *The Economics of Strategic Planning*, ed. T. Thomas (1986), 143–170.

34. In astronomical studies, e.g., the star 40 Eridani B presented what Professor H. N. Russell called "an exception to what looked like a very pretty rule of stellar characteristics [with its] extreme inconsistency between what we would have then called 'possible' values of the surface brightness and density." The astronomer W. H. Pickering observed that "it is just these exceptions which lead to an advance in our knowledge." Quoted in R. Burnham, *Burnham's Celestial Handbook,* Vol. 1 (1976), 400.

35. "A host of researchers, working at differ-

ent points of time and utilizing different analytic techniques and data, have but one major difference: whether mergers have neutral or negative impact on profitability." T. Hogarty, "Profits from Mergers: The Evidence of Fifty Years," 44 *St. John's L. Rev.* 378, 389 (1970).

36. J. Weston and S. Mansingkha, "Tests of the Efficiency Performance of Conglomerate Firms," 26 *J. Fin.* 919 (1971).

37. See D. Mueller, "The Effects of Conglomerate Mergers: A Survey of the Empirical Evidence," 1 *J. of Bank. and Fin.* 315 (1977).

38. S. Boyle, "Pre-Merger Growth and Profit Characteristics of Large Conglomerate Mergers in the United States 1948–68," 44 *St. John's L. Rev.* 152 (Spring 1970).

39. Melicher and Rush, "The Performance of Conglomerate Firms: Recent Risk and Return Experience," 28 *J. Fin.* 381 (1973).

40. R. Conn, "The Failing Firm/Industry Doctrine in Conglomerate Mergers," 24 *J. Ind. Econ.* 181 (1976).

41. "No difference existed in profitability on assets, but the profit-to-sales ratio for the acquiring firms was weakly greater than that of acquired companies. The acquiring firms grew significantly faster than the firms they acquired over the five years preceding the merger and had significantly higher leverage ratios in the year before the merger." D. Mueller, "The United States, 1962–1972," in *The Determinants and Effects of Mergers*, ed. D. Mueller (1980), 281–282.

42. D. Ravenscraft and F. Scherer, Mergers and Financial Performance (mimeo, rev. ed., July 1985). Mueller also found a relative profit deterioration for acquiring firms over a five-year postmerger period; see note 41, p. 283.

43. 11 *J. of Fin. Econ.* 5 (1983).

44. D. Mueller, "The Case Against Conglomerate Mergers," in *The Conglomerate Corporation*, ed. Blair and Lanzillotti (1981), 71, 83.

45. Roll, chapter 14 of this volume.

46. S. Prokesch, "Merger Wave: How Stocks and Bonds Fare," *N.Y. Times,* January 7, 1986.

47. So also may the bidding firms. Consider, for example, the Economic Recovery Tax Act of 1981 (ERTA), which created large, new incentives to acquire certain kinds of assets that could be revalued upward and then depreciated on an accelerated basis for tax purposes. Not all bidders are influenced primarily by such cash flow considerations rather than reported earnings, but many are and they play an important role in the merger market. Even if the bidder's shares were to leap in value after a merger announcement, how is one to know whether it was because of some contemplated real gain in asset

utilization or because of tax considerations of lesser social utility? The impact of the tax factor is only to be found by reading financial statements, including the *projected* statements that often accompany takeover proposals. If targets have latent values to acquirers for tax reasons, their price-earnings ratios might reflect these potential gains. Financial data after the event should be particularly helpful. The bidders, if they are pursuing latency with potency, should show returns on capital that reflect these skills. The effective tax rates they pay should help us separate tax from other considerations. Stock price changes taken alone, however, can tell us almost nothing about tax factors.

48. For a summary of these studies, see Mueller, note 37, pp. 330–333.

49. See note 13, p. 19.

50. See note 13, p. 20. See particularly, P. Malatesta, "The Wealth Effect of Merger Activity and the Objective Functions of Merging Firms, 11 *J. of Fin. Econ.* 155 (1981) ("the long-run wealth effect of the ... merger is significantly negative for acquiring firms").

51. See note 13, p. 20.

52. See text at note 76.

53. See, e.g., Easterbrook and Jarrell, "Do Targets Gain from Defeating Tender Offers," 59 *N.Y.U.L. Rev.* 277, 284–285 (1984).

54. Long and Ravenscraft, "The Misuse of Accounting Rates of Return: Comment," 74 *Am. Econ. Rev.* 494, 499 (1984); but compare Fisher and McGowan, "On the Misuse of Accounting Rates of Return to Infer Monopoly Profits," 73 *Am. Econ. Rev.* 82 (1983).

55. See M. C. Jensen, Chapter 20 of this volume, at note 6. While regarding stock market pricing with something akin to reverence, Professor Jensen paradoxically rejects the data base used by those whose activities fix these prices—bankers and bidders—as contaminated and irrelevant. Not always, however—even he relies on financial data when the cloth fits (see Chapter 20, p. 349). The heavy emphasis of financial economists on stock price studies may be a function of the easy availability of the data. As noted by Warren Buffett, and earlier by Mark Twain, to a man with a hammer, everything looks like a nail. See Buffett, "The Superinvestors of Graham-and-Doddsville," *Columbia University School of Business Magazine,* Fall 1984, 4, 8. The current fashion in finance theory is that one determine the risk and potential rewards of an investment not by analysis of company or even industry operating results but, rather, by the single tool of stock price fluctuations relative to the market average. Happily, it is a hammer whose application, its designers acknowledge, does not require intelligence. Com-

pare Graham, Dodd, and Cottle, *Security Analysis,* (1962), 523–524; Graham, *The Intelligent Investor,* (1973), 60–61; with Brealey and Myers, *Principles of Corporate Finance,* (1981), Chaps. 7–8.

56. Compare the Berkshire Hathaway, Inc., annual report to shareholders 1981, p. 4 ("Many managements apparently were overexposed in impressionable childhood years to the story in which the imprisoned handsome prince is released from a toad's body by a kiss from a beautiful princess").

57. Kidder, Peabody & Co., Inc. and Morgan Stanley & Co., Inc. furnished particularly extensive and useful computer-based data, and we are delighted to acknowledge our gratitude.

58. Both groups included firms of widely varying size. Target companies, for example, had total assets in the year B − 1 ranging from $12 million to $11 billion. The median total assets of all targets or bidders did not, however, vary substantially from the mean. It is difficult to adjust the data for inflation, because the four-year period B − 5 to B − 1 covers various years, depending on the year of the bid. Suffice it to say, however, that the increases in the size of firms noted in the data outstripped, and often far outstripped, the general increases in prices.

59. W. T. Grimm & Company, *Mergerstat Review* 1984, 6.

60. Ibid.

61. Vartan, "New Climate for Mergers," *N.Y. Times,* March 13, 1986.

62. W. T. Grimm, note 59, p. 7.

63. Although they are not used in this chapter we also collected data for the debt–total assets ratio.

64. Compare J. C. Coffee, Chapter 6 of this volume. Those who rely largely on debt–asset value ratios may not have paid adequate attention to the wisdom of the marketplace. See Graham, Dodd, and Cottle, *Security Analysis* (1962), 353 ("soundness of the ... bond ... depends primarily upon the ability of the obligor corporation to take care of its debts, rather than upon the value of the property"); Merrill Lynch, Pierce, Fenner & Smith Inc., *How to Read a Financial Report* (1984), 21.

65. A recent study for the Investor Responsibility Research Center, *Are Takeover Targets Undervalued? An Empirical Examination of the Financial Characteristics of Target Companies* (1985), came to the same conclusion that targets are not underleveraged. Our data reported higher debt-equity ratios for both targets and bidders, apparently because our definition of debt included the portion that is shown as a current liability on balance sheets.

66. We are interpreting a lower debt-equity

ratio and improved coverage as reductions of risk and therefore "good," although recognizing the obvious point that under many circumstances increases in debt may increase returns to shareholders enough to more than offset the added risk. The problems we are addressing here, however, are twofold: Is there evidence that targets were taking too little risk prior to their being taken over? Is there any evidence that the bidders were levering to excess in the takeover process? In helping to answer these questions, our measures are serviceable. There is, to be sure, a view that high debt-equity ratios are a consistently positive signal of a willingness and ability to achieve "more efficient resource utilization." See Pound, *Are Takeover Targets Undervalued?: An Empirical Examination of the Financial Characteristics of Target Companies* (Washington, D.C.: Investor Responsibility Research Center, 1985), 22. The fallacy, and it is a serious one, is in the assumption that because some risk is a necessary aspect of any investment and quest for profit, greater-than-moderate risk will systematically produce greater-than-moderate profit. Taking on substantial added debt was not, however, profitable for the bidders in our study, nor was it for the conglomerates of the 1960s. See M. Salter and W. Weinhold, *Diversification Through Acquisition: Strategies for Creating Economic Value* (1969), 22–34. Perhaps an analysis that rigidly equates risk taking with gain overlooks the agency cost, i.e., the temptations, of speculating with someone else's money and relies too much on notions of rational expectations. It also overlooks the macrodynamics of risk taking and the reasonable concern that because "markets and institutions lock together . . . risks [may] spill over in previously unexpected ways." See Federal Reserve Bank of N.Y., *Annual Report for 1985,* 24.

67. See Tables 13.6 and 13.7.

68. See Jensen, "How to Detect a Prime Takeover Target," *N.Y. Times,* March 9, 1986 (arguing on basis of anecdotal evidence that targets tend not to borrow as much as others).

69. See H. Kaufman, Dangers in the Rapid Growth of Debt (speech to the National Press Club, January 1985); "Playing with Fire," *Business Week,* September 16, 1985, 78; see also Wyatt, "Efficient Market Theory: Its Impact on Accounting," *Journal of Accountancy,* February 1983, 56, 58–60 (full-cost leasing and other off-balance-sheet-financing devices, while costly, create additional borrowing power).

70. "Downgrades of Firms' Debt Surged to Record in 1985," *Wall St. J.,* January 27, 1986.

71. See Kaufman, note 69.

72. *The Economist,* October 5, 1985, 83 (citing Federal Reserve Board data). In 1984, non-

financial firms liquidated $77 billion of equity, a sum that exceeded the aggregate $60 billion in net new equity issues by these firms in the previous 10 years (ibid.). In 1985 there occurred additional net liquidations of $63 billion. See H. Kaufman, Salomon Brothers, Inc. Comments on Credit, March 21, 1986.

73. Council of Economic Advisers, note 4, p. 196.

74. For the "private sector as a whole, the ratio of debt is at an unprecedented level and is still rising. . . . [S]ervicing even the existing levels of debt in a less favorable economic and interest environment could prove very difficult." Corrigan, "Public and Private Debt Accumulation: A Perspective," *Federal Reserve Bank of New York Quarterly Review,* Autumn 1985, 1, 3.

The favorable loss experience of the early junk bond issues tells us nothing about what the future is likely to bring. That market has deteriorated, growing in size while declining in quality. The early junk bonds had not been marketed as such; they were "fallen angels," once-good issues of companies that had fallen on hard times or even filed for insolvency reorganization. Such firms often had large compensating virtues, not the least being huge tax-loss carryforwards and the ability to emerge from reorganization with squeaky-clean balance sheets. Compare these with the 1984, $1.3 billion junk bond financing by Metromedia Broadcasting Corporation, where there was *admittedly* no conceivable set of circumstances under which the interest charges could be paid out of the operating cash flows of the Metromedia business. While the company's operating cash flow was barely more than half its interest charges and debt discount amortization, accounting conventions permitted the purchasers of these securities to report as "income" what was neither paid in cash nor earned by the debtor, Metromedia, nor supported by any underlying book equity in Metromedia. See Metromedia Broadcasting Corporation prospectus dated November 24, 1984; see also Scovill, Inc. prospectus dated August 12, 1985; Rohatyn, "Junk Bonds and Other Securities Swill," *Wall St. J.,* April 18, 1985.

75. W. Ripley, *Main Street and Wall Street* (1927), 287.

76. This data for our group of transactions was furnished by Kidder, Peabody and covers essentially those bids first announced during the years 1976–1983.

77. The premiums over market are very consistent with those reported in an earlier study of management buy-outs, particularly in those cases where there was, as there usually is in a hostile tender offer, contested bidding. See Lowenstein, "No More Cozy Management Buy-

outs," *Harv. Bus. Rev.,* January–February 1986, 147, 149; E. B. Magenheim and D. C. Mueller, Chapter 11 of this volume. In addition to premium prices, bidders also incur increasingly heavy transaction costs. See Lowenstein, p. 154; "Kohlberg Kravis to Get $45 Million Fee If Its Purchase of Beatrice Is Completed," *Wall St. J.,* March 19, 1986 (total fees estimated at $248 million).

78. The Fortune 500-Industries earned, during the period 1975–1983, the years of the hostile bids studied by us, an average return on equity of 13.2%. For 1983–1984 the average was 12.2%. See also Buffett, "How Inflation Swindles the Equity Investors," *Fortune,* May 1977, 250 ("over the years ... the return on book value tends to keep coming back to a level around 12 percent").

79. On an unweighted basis, the ROE was a better but still subpar 10.5%. While presenting both weighted and unweighted data, our analysis is generally expressed in terms of the former. The weighted data conveys a more useful picture of the overall economic impact of these transactions. For example, DSI Corp., Cenco, Inc., HMW Industries, Gray Drug Stores, and Burgess Industries were targets that suffered significantly declining returns on equity in the years B − 3 to B − 1, thus depressing the unweighted ROE results in Table 13.6. But the total amount of assets under their management was less than 1% of the total of all targets. Their poor results had little effect, of course, on the weighted ROE figures.

80. See note 56. For further evidence that targets do not chronically underperform, see Ravenscraft and Scherer, Chapter 12 in this volume.

81. Lowenstein, "Pruning Deadwood in Hostile Takeovers: A Proposal for Legislation," 83 *Colum. L. Rev.* 249, 305 (1983).

82. W. T. Grimm, note 59, p. 7 (emphasis added). The explanation of the change in size and profitability of target companies, according to W. T. Grimm, was twofold: the bidders were not seeking to redress undermanaged enterprises but rather only to "add new sources of earnings"; and second, with well-established firms participating, respectability was reinforced by the tremendous growth of the merger and acquisition departments of investment and commercial banks, law firms, etc. (ibid.). See also a recent Federal Reserve Board study that concluded that bank mergers do not tend to rid the system of poorly performing (presumably poorly managed) firms (Rhoades, "The Operating Performance of Acquired Firms in Banking before and after Acquisition," Bd. Gov. Fed. Res. Sys. (April 1986, 229).

83. On an unweighted basis, the data are more favorable to bidders in the years B − 2 and B − 1. As to the significance of such data, see note 79.

84. Table 13.11 includes data also for all bidders as a group. But the good results in the years T + 4 and T + 5 for all bids are less meaningful than one would like, because they take account of less than half of all bidders and are largely a product of the early transactions.

85. See R. J. Shiller, Chapter 3 of this volume; Lowenstein, note 81, pp. 286–287; see also "Troublesome Issues: Real Estate Securities, Increasingly Popular, Can Pose Big Problems," *Wall St. J.,* March 4, 1986 ("the old syndrome of too much capital chasing too little property").

86. J. M. Keynes, *The General Theory of Employment, Interest and Money* (1936), 159 (Royal Economics Society edition, 1973).

87. Some of the individual tales are pathetic. Fluor Corporation, for example, paid $2.2 billion for St. Joe Minerals Corp. in 1981, at a time when both firms looked princely. After writedowns resulting from losses in both the acquired and the acquiring firms' operations, Fluor's net shareholders' equity for the combined venture fell to $1.2 billion. See "Fluor Is Taking Big Write-Offs," *N.Y. Times,* October 19, 1985.

88. *Panter v. Marshall Field & Co.,* 646 F.2d 271 (7th Cir. 1981), cert. den. 454 U.S. 1092.

89. Compare, for example, the much more subtle, sensitive search for potential gains by Salter and Weinhold in Chapter 7 of this volume, in which they distinguish those forms of value creation in business acquisitions that represent real gains from those that do not and explain why major real gains are less likely to be found in hostile bids.

90. See text at note 82. As Salter and Weinhold explain in Chapter 7 of this volume, although hostile takeovers may be a useful disciplinary device, they are a rather blunt, clumsy tool for creating value in the intensely *managerial* process of recombining already successful businesses.

91. As Professor Roll suggests in Chapter 14, the process may also be skewed by the ability to expropriate bondholder wealth. See also McDaniel, "Bondholders and Corporate Governance," 41 *Bus. Law* 413 (1986); Prokesch, "Merger Wave: How Stock and Bonds Fare," *N.Y. Times,* January 7, 1986.

92. The data were gathered from the COMPUSTAT files at Columbia, Wharton, and Denver.

93. See Ravenscraft and Scherer, Chapter 12 of this volume.

14

Empirical Evidence on Takeover Activity and Shareholder Wealth

RICHARD ROLL

The available empirical results about take-over activity can be summarized as follows: Takeovers provide substantial economic benefits to shareholders of *target* firms. However, there is more doubt that takeovers, on average, provide gains to the shareholders of bidding firms, and there is similar doubt that gains accrue in aggregate and on average to all shareholders.

"Doubt" means simply that the evidence is insufficient to reach a definite conclusion. There have been takeovers in which the bidding firm's shareholders (and all shareholders) gained, but other cases have displayed the opposite pattern. Empirical studies have disagreed about the extent and sign of bidding firm and aggregate gains. Indeed, the measurement of gains is fraught with econometric difficulty. I believe that neither an unbiased statistician nor a policymaker could find much comfort in the empirical evidence to support any particular inference or action.

From the policy perspective, there is no empirical justification for limiting takeover activity because of potential damage to target firm shareholders. There is no empirical justification for restricting the activities of bidding firms, even for the paternalistic prevention of self-inflicted economic loss. Finally, the empirical evidence on private antitakeover activity is not conclusive. At present, it could support no particular social policy.

In the first section, I will give a brief survey of the empirical results obtained on the takeover question over the past decade and will suggest an interpretation based on what a skeptical econometrician can read into them. The next section presents a discussion of takeover theories and, to the extent possible, interprets existing empirical results as confirmations or denials of those theories. The final section gives a summary and conclusion.

MARKET PRICE RESPONSE TO TAKEOVER ACTIVITY

Target Firms

Virtually *every* empirical study has found that target firms display statistically significant positive price response to the announcement of a takeover attempt. Jensen and Ruback (1983) averaged the results of about twenty scholarly papers and found an increase (over the preannouncement market price) of 20% for mergers and 30% for tender offers in the period around the takeover event.

In a more recent paper, Dennis and McConnell (1985) found that the average target firm's shares increase by 8.7%, adjusted for market movements, on the day of bid announcement and the previous trading day. This is an annualized return of several thousand percent!

Although there is a mystery about the motives of bidding firms in takeovers, there is absolutely no doubt that a bid is good economic news for the target. No matter what might happen to target firm shareholders subsequent to the original announcement bid, the bid per se is beneficial. If the target firm's shareholders were concerned about subsequent damaging action by the bidder (say in a two-tiered offer), they could simply sell at the prevailing price just after the bid. In doing so, they would realize a total return considerably higher than what would have obtained in the absence of a bid.

The empirical support for the value of receiving a bid is bolstered further by studies of target firms after the original bid. Perhaps the most dramatic and persuasive evidence was uncovered by Bradley et al. (1983) in a study of unsuccessful tender offers. When an unsuccessful tender offer is followed by another offer within a few years, the original price increase around the first bid is maintained permanently. However, when the original (unsuccessful) offer is not followed by a successful offer within five years, the entire market price increase associated with the original bid is reversed.

Before turning to the more complex issues surrounding the bidding firm, I want to emphasize that bids are apparently surprises to target firm shareholders. Most studies have found a large price increase in the few days surrounding the original bid announcement; and this announcement effect is much larger per unit of time than observed price movements either before or after. This result points to the essentially passive role played by the target firm, which is an important contrast to the active role of the bidding firm. It is much easier to ascribe price movements to the bid when the firm is surprised. The bidding firm is not surprised, and this complicates the attribution to price movements of *its* shares to the takeover event.

Bidding Firms

The empirical results for bidding firms permit a variety of interpretations. Different papers have found different results. Methods, time periods, and samples of firms vary across studies, making it difficult to draw conclusive inference. (Incidentally, the same factors differ across papers for target firms but, nevertheless, the results agree.) Just to mention a sample of papers, Bradley (1980), Asquith (1983), and Dennis and McConnell (1985) report positive price movements of bidding firms; Dodd (1980), Firth (1980), and Eger (1983) report negative price movements. Some papers, e.g., Malatesta (1983), report both, depending on the method and sample.

Whether bidding firm price movements are positive or negative on average, they are generally small in percentage terms (much smaller than target firm returns), and are less statistically significant. Again, just to give an example, Dennis and McConnell (1985) report a market-adjusted return in the equities of bidding firms of −0.12% on the day of the announcement and the previous trading day. This tiny, negative, two-day return is to be contrasted with the large, positive 8.74% two-day return they found for target firms.

The return on the two-day announcement period is negative for bidders in the Dennis-McConnell sample, but it is not statistically significant. Interestingly, the authors conclude that the effect on bidders actually is positive, not negative, because of a positive price movement during a long period around the announcement. The announcement day itself displays a negative return of −0.34%, which is marginally significant, but when the authors calculate returns for other periods, (day −19 to −2 day −19 to 0, day −6 to +6), they find overall positive returns! Strangely, the greatest positive returns occur *after* the announcement.

The Dennis-McConnell paper is the most recent and one of the very best empirical papers on this subject, which is why I cite it extensively here. It seems to me that their results make something less than a persuasive case for the proposition that bidding firms' stockholders gain around merger events. Their paper is typical in this regard.

Dennis and McConnell also investigate the possibilities (1) that total potential gains to bidding firms may be larger than gains to stockholders (e.g., bondholders may also benefit), and (2) that returns may be a less useful gauge of benefits than dollar price movements, particularly when assessing the relative gains of target and bidder firms, which generally differ substantially in size.

Results for other classes of stakeholders in the bidding firm are as follows: Convertible preferred stockholders gain (even more than equityholders) in a wide period around the merger announcement, but the announcement day return is virtually zero. Convertible bondholders gain over a wide period but not by a statistically significant amount, and the announcement day return is negative (but insignificant). Nonconvertible preferred stockholders receive no statistically reliable returns. Nonconvertible bondholders have negative returns in all periods, but they are only marginally significant.

Dollar gains are reported only for a chosen period (for equities, the period is 20 days before until 20 days after the announcement). For all classes of stakeholders combined, target firms gain an average of $30 million and bidding firms an average of $40 million during this period. Keep in mind that the figure would be quite different for other periods around the announcement. For example, it would likely be negative for bidding firms on the announcement day itself.

The results for bidding firms reported in the Dennis-McConnell paper are typical of every empirical paper. Depending on the paper, the sample, the period, and the biases of the reader, widely differing conclusions can be reached. This state of affairs is possible, moreover, even ignoring what I believe is a more critical problem of interpretation of bidding firm market price reactions: the fact that the bid itself may convey information about the bidder unrelated to the takeover event.

To put this problem in perspective, one should remember that many types of public announcements by firms cause market prices to react. Dividend declarations, earnings results, splits, new products, personnel changes, etc., have been associated with market price movements. *Any* public announcement has this potential because it leads investors to revise their opinions about the value of the firm. The announcement of a takeover bid discloses at least two pieces of information: first, that the takeover will be attempted, and second, that the internal affairs of the bidding firm are in such a state that a takeover bid is possible. The second item is new information about the firm that is not necessarily related to whether a takeover will ever occur. It can signal good things, e.g., that cash flow over the recent past has been higher than previously estimated and high enough to elicit a takeover attempt. It can also signal something less favorable, e.g., that the managers are going to use the company's cash in pursuit of an expensive and elusive target, for which they may overpay.

The problem is that the bid is a "polluted" information item. The bidding firm is an activist, unlike the target firm, and its actions can be interpreted in the market as conveying more than just information about the takeover per se.

THEORIES OF TAKEOVER ACTIVITY AND RELATED EMPIRICAL EVIDENCE

A number of distinct hypotheses have been advanced to explain the motivations in takeover activity. They are not mutually exclusive; different motives could explain different individual takeovers and more than one could be present in any particular case. Most takeover hypotheses make the natural presumption that economic benefits will flow from the corporate combination. Potential sources of gains include the following:

Monopoly: Increased market power from a corporate combination.
Information: The current market price does not contain all relevant information about the value of the target. This information is revealed, and the revelation results in an upward market revaluation, during the process of a takeover.
Synergy: Reductions in production or distribution costs.
Elimination of inferior management of the target firm.
Financial motivation: Increased utilization of tax shields, lower expected bankruptcy costs, etc.

There are also existing hypotheses of takeover motivation which do not involve gains for shareholders:

Management self-interest: Managers increase their remuneration and their psychic gratification by taking over other firms.

Hubris: Bidders overvalue their targets and pay too much; thus, the takeover is merely a wealth transfer from bidder to target.

The Monopoly Hypothesis

The acquisition of market power is probably the most obvious "theory" of mergers. The (horizontal) merger of two large firms in the same industry brings an immediate increase in concentration; but whether this is translated into gains for shareholders remains in doubt.

In fact, on the basis of the work of Eckbo (1983), and Stillman (1983), monopoly does not appear to be a significant motive. Both Stillman and Eckbo reach their conclusion from indirect evidence, the lack of market price reaction of competitor firms when two other rivals in the same industry announce a combination.

There is little direct evidence to the contrary. Furthermore, many corporate combinations simply could not be motivated by monopoly because they do not involve firms in the same or closely related industries. For example, the recent increase in the rate of leveraged buy-outs could not be motivated by monopoly.

The Information Hypothesis

The information hypothesis is based on financial market inefficiency in the strong-form sense. The market price is too low because positive information about the target firms is not yet publicly known. Such information is obtained by the bidding firm, who therefore regards the target as a bargain.

This hypothesis was given a substantial boost in papers by Dodd and Ruback (1977), Bradley (1980), and Firth (1980). The results presented there indicate that a tender offer, even if unsuccessful, causes a permanent upward revaluation in the target firm's market price. However, Bradley et al. (1983) question the information hypothesis because of a further examination of unsuccessful tender offers. Unsuccessful tenders are often followed by further (successful) bids. When an unsuccessful tender offer is not followed by a successful offer within five years, the original market price rise is completely reversed. It is only those targets of unsuccessful offers followed by later successful bids that experience permanent increases in value.

On the basis of these results, and also on the stock price behavior of bidding firms, Bradley et al. argue against the information hypothesis and in favor of synergy. If information were revealed by a tender offer per se, they reason, the upward revaluation should be permanent even for firms which are never targets in subsequent successful tenders. To the contrary, the revaluation induced by synergy will accrue only when a corporate combination is actually effected. The price rise caused by potential synergy will be lost to shareholders of firms that never enter a combination.

This conclusion seems quite plausible, but there is another, perhaps less palatable, possibility: What if the tender offer revealed the *probable* existence of private positive information about the target, not the certainty of such information? One would expect that those firms for which such information did exist might be more likely candidates for further bids. Since each bid has some chance of success, such firms would also be more likely to enter a subsequent combination. Firms for whom there was no private information in the first place would be less likely to elicit further bids since there would be little incentive for a potential acquiring firm to make a bid. Thus, firms which never enter a combination should experience a fall in price back to the original level. Information whose *possible* existence was revealed by the initial unsuccessful tender offer turns out not to exist in these cases.

The price behavior of unsuccessful bidding firms is advanced by Bradley et al. as further evidence against the information hypothesis. When an unsuccessful bid has been made for a firm which received no further bids, the bidding firm's price is virtually unchanged from its original level. But when a bid is first announced by what turns out to be a successful rival, the first bidder's stock price drops by a statistically significant 2.84% (Bradley et al., 1983, p. 203).[1] The authors argue:

The information hypothesis makes no prediction concerning the relation between the share price behavior of unsuccessful bidding firms and the ultimate disposition of control of the target resources. (Bradley et al., 1983, p. 203)

However, the synergy hypothesis implies "that when a firm loses the competition for a target firm to a rival bidding firm, the market perceives it to have lost an opportunity to acquire a valuable resource" (p. 203). But doesn't the information hypothesis really imply the same thing? The appearance of a rival bid increases the probability that there exists positive nonpublic information about the target firm but it *decreases* both the probability that the initial bidder has exclusive possession of the information and the probability that the initial bid will succeed.

The Synergy Hypothesis

The hypothesis of synergy as an explanation for merger gains has considerable appeal. Jensen and Ruback (1983) support its possibility: "Some of the gains are also likely to result from ... synergies in combining independent organization" (p. 25).

Asquith (1983) argues that merger gains are caused by synergy, but he includes inefficient target firm management in the synergy category and he seems to be saying (p. 83) that the evidence really supports the inefficient-management hypothesis. Bradley et al. (1983) conclude that "the synergy hypothesis is a better description of the nature of tender offers than the information hypothesis" (p. 205); but they, too, include "more efficient management" (p. 184) under the synergy rubric.

The Jensen-Ruback characterization of synergy that excludes inefficient management is probably more useful for under-

standing the empirical results. Their concept of synergy is "potential reductions in production or distribution costs" (p. 23) through various devices available to the combined firm but not to the two firms operated separately. This is quite different from inefficient target firm management. Better management could bring the same gain in value if the target firm were operated independently. [The value gain in proxy contests (Dodd and Warner, 1983) might be an appropriate measure of the gain to replacing inefficient managers, abstracting from any other information effect in the proxy contest announcement.]

Let us hereafter define synergy as something which causes an increase in value *only* if there is a successful corporate combination. Exclude from synergy new information, inefficient management, or anything else which could conceivably imply the same increase in value to the target firm *without* a successful takeover.

Many authors have presented evidence that the stockholders of acquired (target) firms obtain most and perhaps all of the economic benefits. Why should this occur if synergy is the cause? Synergy requires *both* firms in order to secure gains in value. On average over many takeovers, there is no reason to expect that most or all of these gains would go to the same side of the transaction. True, in some transactions, competition among bidding firms for a given target might result in the (apparently) observed asymmetry; the synergy would be available to several competing bidders but only in combination with a single target. But the opposite situation might be equally as likely; there could be instances of synergy available to a single bidder combining with several possible targets. In this case, competition among targets would ensure that most of the gain accrued to the bidder. There might well be other cases, e.g., synergy available only to two *specific* firms and to no others, either target or bidder. The division of gains would then be determined by bargaining, not by competition.

On average over all observed takeovers, there seems to be no reason to think that synergy gains, as we have defined them, would be unevenly split. Rejection of the hypothesis on this basis is not possible, however, because there may be some reason, as yet undiscovered, why bidding firms are more frequently at a competitive disadvantage relative to target firms.

If the gains in takeovers actually are positive and if they turn out under further study to be approximately evenly divided, synergy would be a strong candidate for explaining the takeover phenomenon. The recent Dennis and McConnell (1985) paper does find a roughly even dollar division; so synergy is, in my opinion, a hypothesis that is empirically viable.

One puzzle remaining about synergy is why these firms undertook the combination at the observed time rather than at an earlier date when the synergy may also have been available. Perhaps synergy arises suddenly, or perhaps managers discover its existence according to some random process. The synergy hypothesis could be further developed to explain why synergy elicits a takeover bid at a particular time.

The Inefficient-Management Hypothesis

Inefficient management could be replaced by a variety of devices, not just by a takeover. Perhaps takeover costs are lower than the costs of alternatives such as proxy fights, replacement of operating managers by the board of directors, or simply replacement of directors by stockholder vote.

But if most target firm stockholders agreed with the bidding firm that incumbent management was inefficient, there would be no necessity to incur the expense of a takeover bid. Disagreement between bidding firm managers and a voting majority of target firm stockholders could necessitate a takeover as the method of target firm management replacement. Rather than convincing target firm shareholders by newspaper advertisements, speeches at the annual meeting, or by direct mail, the bidding firm offers the more persuasive argument of a higher price for the target firm's shares.

An interesting experiment concerning the synergy and management inefficiency hypotheses was conducted by Dodd and Ruback (1977). In conjunction with their broader study of tender offers, they collected results for a sample of 19 "clean up" tender offers, offers by bidding firms who already owned over 50% of the target. As Dodd and Ruback (1977) note: "since bidders already had control of the target firm, these abnormal returns (around the bid announcement) cannot reflect synergy, monopoly, or internal efficiency gains" (p. 371). Yet the returns observed in the announcement month (see Table 14.1) were similar in magnitude to those observed in their sample of ordinary successful tender offers (consisting of 124 bidders and 136 targets). (The smaller size explains the smaller t statistics in the "clean up" sample.) Dodd and Ruback argue that the premium paid to "clean up" target shareholders "include(s) the savings in litigation costs to the majority stockholder" (p. 371). Perhaps so; but there is remarkable similarity between the two samples, one of which cannot be subject to either synergy or efficiency gains. The elimination of litigation costs might just happen to bring about the same empirical results as, say, synergy, but this would indeed be fortuitous.

The Tax Hypothesis

The final hypothesis of gains is that tax benefits of some kind accrue to corporate combinations. The tax law offers many possible merger motives; Ginsburg (1983)

Table 14.1. Abnormal Percent Return in Announcement Month

	Bidder	Target
Cleanup offers	2.71 (1.89)	17.41 (6.68)
Ordinary offers	2.83 (2.16)	20.58 (25.8)

Source: Dodd and Ruback (1977), pp. 368, 371.

Note: The number in parentheses is the t statistic.

requires 142 pages to discuss recent changes in the relevant code. One prominent scenario involves a firm with sizable embedded losses that would bring valuable tax deductions to any firm with sufficient earnings. There are few reported empirical results about this scenario even though direct evidence on tax benefits would seem easier to uncover than evidence about, say, synergy or inefficient management.

An indirect implication of this particular tax hypothesis is that mergers should be more frequent during and just after business contractions when more firms have generated tax-deductible losses. Of course, at such times it may be difficult to find a merger partner with positive earnings against which losses can be deducted. Perhaps this explains why Chung and Weston (1982) find a positive relation between the dollar amount of merger activity and the real growth rate in GNP from 1957 to 1977. The general frequency of mergers appears to be higher since the early 1950s; the only other comparable period was 1927–1931. There were relatively few mergers in the 1930s and 1940s regardless of the market's performance.

A further indirect implication of the tax hypothesis is that the federal tax law change in 1981, which allowed firms to sell tax depreciation and investment tax credits directly and without merging, should have caused a reduction in the rate of merger activity *ceteris paribus,* since it reduced the tax incentives for merging. This change was in effect for only about sixteen months, so its impact may be hard to spot. It is certainly not evident in time series of the extent of merger activity.

Another tax scenario is the allegation that tax-depreciated but still valuable assets constitute a tempting target; see Weston and Chung (1983) and Dertouzous and Thorpe (1982). The latter authors conclude that this motive in conjunction with estate taxes explains many acquisitions in the newspaper industry. The acquirer is supposedly willing to pay a premium in order to "step up" the basis of the depreciated assets, thereby obtaining a further tax shield in the combined firm that would not have been available to the target firm operating alone. However, the actual advantage is complicated by the liability created for target shareholders by the recognized capital gain.[2]

Another possible financial motivation for a corporate combination is reduction in bankruptcy costs through diversification (Jensen and Ruback, 1983, p. 24). This has been termed the "coinsurance hypothesis" by Lewellen (1971). Presumably, diversification allows the use of more debt capital, thereby bringing larger tax deductions from interest. Reduction of direct backruptcy costs cannot alone explain large gains in takeovers, because even the perfect certainty of reducing such costs would result in only a small change in value, at least according to the empirical evidence in Warner (1977); but indirect backruptcy costs of the type discussed in Titman (1984) may be material.

An indirect test supporting diversification as a merger motive is provided by Marshall et al. (1984). They find that mergers are more likely between partners in less correlated manufacturing industries and that conglomerate firms are more likely to be composed of industry divisions that are less correlated than the average pair of industries.

The diversification motive has been directly tested by Kim and McConnell (1977), Asquith and Kim (1982), Dennis and McConnell (1983), Eger (1983), and Settle et al. (1984). The first of these five papers finds that "merged firms do make greater use of financial leverage" (p. 362), but consistent with the coinsurance hypothesis, bondholders do not lose value from increased leverage, presumably because the probability of default is reduced by the combination. The second paper, however, using different methods and data, finds no evidence to support a "diversification effect." The third paper concludes that the evidence is "partially consistent with the co-insurance hypothesis," because the abnormal returns to senior securityholders are "negatively correlated with the correlation coefficient between the returns on the merging companies' common stocks" (p. 27). This result indicates that bondholders gain when the risk of default decreases. The paper by Eger finds direct evidence of bondholder gains at the expense of stockholders in "pure" stock exchange mergers (mergers which involve an exchange of shares only, with no increase in leverage). This is consistent with the coinsurance hypothesis in that default risk is reduced by the merger, but it raises another puzzle in that shareholders allow bondholders to obtain part of the resulting gain. The Settle et al. results also indicate significant gains to bondholders but *prior* to the merger announcement month. In private correspondence, the authors showed me further results which seem to suggest that part of the bond price increase could be attributed to non-merger-related positive news about acquiring firms. The results do not eliminate the possiblity that news about the merger leaked out before the announcement and that this leak caused the bonds to react positively. However, the peak price occurred three months prior to the month of the first public announcement; this may be a rather long time in advance for a leak to occur.

There is a peculiar theoretical problem in interpreting movements around a takeover event when the firms involved have outstanding debt. Shastri (1983) proves that stock price increases do not necessarily imply increases in the economic value of the total firm nor does a lack of stock price increase imply that no economic value has been created by the corporate combination. The reason for this involves the complex interaction of the options implicit in the corporate debt and the opportunities these options offer for redistributing wealth from bondholders to stockholders, or vice versa, during a takeover event. [Dennis and McConnell (1985) do provide information about all classes of stakeholders.]

Finally, another tax-related motive for takeovers involves cash-rich bidding firms who might acquire other firms instead of paying dividends, provided that there is an effective personal tax differential between dividends and capital gains (but see Miller and Scholes, 1978). This particular tax ex-

planation implies that bidding firms would receive most of the takeover gain because the personal tax savings would accrue regardless of the target's identity. It also implies more merger activity with higher *personal* tax rates, which does seem consistent with the postwar increase in merger frequency.

Management Self-interest

The management self-interest explanation of takeovers is based on the strong positive empirical relation between firm size and management compensation. Penrose (1959), Williamson (1964), and many others have argued that the connection between executive rewards and the size of the firm provides an incentive for growth, including growth by takeover, even when there is no anticipated gain for the shareholders. The idea is sometimes referred to as the "size maximization hypothesis," (see, e.g., Malatesta, 1983, p. 157).

There are both logical and empirical difficulties here. Perhaps the most apparent conceptual problem is that a correlation (between size and management compensation) does not imply causation *for a given manager.* Larger enterprises undoubtedly require more management skill, but making an enterprise larger does not make its manager more skillful. Thus, a manager with a known level of skill could not expect to improve his financial remuneration by taking over another firm provided that his compensation was already at a level commensurate with his talent.

A rescue of the concept might be attempted either by making managers' utilities depend on nonfinancial reward (e.g., power) or by arguing that managers signal their skill levels through bids and that some skillful managers move into more appropriate positions by effecting corporate combinations. The latter possibility is merely a variant of the synergy hypothesis; a manager with unexploited skills is a wasted resource whose more efficient use would bring gains to someone. Presumably, the unrecognized manager would not obtain all of the gain in every case.

The spirit of the management self-interest hypothesis is that there really are *no* gains and that stockholders confuse correlation with causation. However, even admitting to the existence of such confusion or to the possibility that managers are motivated by psychic rewards, there are unexplained empirical phenomena around takeover events. The most anomalous is that target firms receive unambiguously large premiums. If takeovers were motivated purely by manager self-aggrandizement, there would be no neccessity for such payments. The target firm could be acquired by open-market purchases or by offering a very modest premium. Even a manager motivated exclusively by size maximization would see no necessity to squander resources currently in hand, not to mention any hesitation induced by possible *ex post* penalties (such as unemployment) which might be imposed by disgruntled shareholders.

The Hubris Hypothesis

A recent paper of mine (Roll, 1986) advances a behavioral explanation for the takeover phenomenon. My argument is that bidding firm managers intend to profit by taking over other firms, possibly because they *believe* that synergy is present, that the target has inefficient management, etc. Their intentions are not fulfilled, however, because the market price already reflects the full value of the firm, (i.e., there is actually no synergy nor inefficient management involved). Why, then, do bidding firms persist in their pursuit of the target? Because the *individual* decision makers in the bidding firm are infected by overweaning pride and arrogance (hubris) and thus persist in a belief that their own valuation of the target is correct, despite objective information that the target's true economic value is lower.

The hubris explanation is heavily dependent on improper recognition of the "winner's curse," a concept familiar to scholars of bidding theory. The idea of the winner's curse is simple: Whoever makes the winning bid for a valuable object is likely to be a bidder with a positive valuation error. In auctions with only a few bidders, the winner is likely to have made the biggest (positive) error. Optimal-bidding theory recognizes this problem and prescribes a lower bid than the valuation in general. The extent of downward bias in the bid depends on the variability in the bidder's distribution of values, perhaps subjectively determined, and the number of competitors.

I point out that all takeover bids are preceded by an independent valuation of the target. Although the valuation is often quite formal and extensive, it can be rudimentary. If the market price fully reflects value, only positive valuation errors will be observed because a valuation below the market price will not elicit a bid. This implies that takeover activity results in a straightforward wealth transfer from bidding firm shareholders to target firm shareholders, and that there is a slight aggregate net loss due to the expenses of the takeover. Target firm prices should increase when a bid is announced, but bidding firm prices should decrease.

After the initial bid, there is an interim period when the outcome of the takeover is in doubt. The hubris hypothesis predicts that the prices of ultimately successful bidding firms will decline during this period as the probability moves to 100% that the offer will succeed. Evidence from mergers (Asquith, 1983) seems to support this prediction, but evidence from tender offers, (Bradley, 1980) does not. In both mergers and tender offers, the statistical reliability of the interim-period price movement is low.

Another prediction of hubris is that the premium paid for the target (above the initial market price), should be negatively related to the price movement of the bidding firm's shares on the announcement date. Evidence by Firth (1980) and Varaiya (1985) strongly supports this prediction. Varaiya's empirical work also supports the presence of the winner's curse among bidders. The empirical test is too complicated to describe here, but it involves measures of the quantity of information about the target available in the market. Less information is accompanied by bigger valuation errors by bidders.

Hubris cannot be the sole explanation of the takeover phenomenon because it implies that every bid announcement should elicit a price decline in the bidding firm's shares. Some papers have even found an average increase. Furthermore, if all bids were inspired by hubris, stockholders could easily stop them by the simple expedient of a prohibition in the corporate charter. On the other hand, a strict prohibition would be irrelevant to a fully diversified shareholder since a hubris-driven takeover is a wealth transfer, from one of his or her issues to another (ignoring the deadweight takeover costs). We do not observe such stringent antibid charter provisions, which must imply that stockholders at least believe that an occasional bid by a firm might have positive individual and aggregate benefits.

SUMMARY AND CONCLUSION

The empirical evidence indicates that target firm shareholders are materially benefited by a takeover attempt. There is a positive price reaction in the few days surrounding the bid. It is statistically significant in all studies and amounts to 8% to 30%, depending on the study. The fact that the price reaction occurs in the few days around the bid announcement indicates that the market is surprised, at least to some extent, by the bid.

The empirical results for bidding firms are much less conclusive. Depending on the method, sample period, and data, different authors have reached differing conclusions. Some have found small, positive price reactions while others have found price declines. In all cases, the absolute magnitude and the statistical significance of the price reaction are smaller for bidding firms than for target firms. It is also more difficult to ascribe the price reaction of a bidding firm to the takeover per se. Simply by issuing a bid, the bidding firm may be disclosing other information about itself, information unrelated to the takeover.

A few studies have examined the relation between the price reaction of the target and the price reaction of the bidder. In all cases, they are strongly negatively related. This probably indicates that the market interprets high bids to be too high, thereby transferring wealth from the bidding firm's shareholders to the target shareholders.

There have been at least seven distinct theories of takeovers advanced in the financial economics literature. They are not mutually exclusive, so different theories could conceivably account for different takeovers. The available empirical results provide no support for the theory that monopoly is a takeover motive nor for the theory that information about the target firm is available to the bidding firm but not to other market participants. The other theories, ranging from tax effects, synergy, and elimination of inferior management to noneconomic motives such as management self-interest and hubris, seem to be consistent with the empirical evidence (however, the extent of formal statistical testing is still quite limited).

In conclusion, takeovers provide a significant economic benefit to target firm shareholders. It is not yet clear whether bidding firm shareholders benefit as well; the effect on them is relatively small, and its sign is still in doubt. There is a number of competing theories to explain the motives in takeovers, and much empirical analysis remains to be done before the truth or falsity of each theory is proved.

NOTES

1. It is interesting to note that the first bidder's stock price drops on average despite the fact that sizable positions are often taken in the target's stock by the first bidder. One might have thought that the first bidder's own stock price would increase upon the announcement of a rival bid, merely because those shares of the target already owned would increase in value; yet this effect is apparently more than offset by other factors.

2. For example, consider a sale for cash of depreciated assets. Let G be the difference between the cash sale price and the seller's tax basis and let x be the ordinary tax rate; for simplicity, assume $x/2$ is the capital gains rate. The buyer can deduct G in increments over time depending on

a depreciation schedule; the value to the buyer of a "stepped-up basis" is the discounted present value of these deductions. For example, with the sum-of-the-years'-digits method, a useful life of n years, and a discount rate r, the benefit to the buyer is

$$\frac{2xG}{n(n+1)} \sum_{t=1}^{n} \frac{n+1-t}{(1+r)^t}$$

and the tax cost to the seller is $xG/2$.

There is no net benefit when

$$\frac{4}{n(n+1)} \sum_{t=1}^{n} \frac{n+1-t}{(1+r)^t} < 1$$

Remembering that the tax deduction to the buyer is risky (it is available in any period only to the extent of prededuction income), the discount rate should be fairly large. For $r = 20\%$, for instance, the condition is satisfied for $n > 11$; i.e., for useful lives beyond eleven years, there is no net tax benefit in a stepped-up basis. Even for much shorter useful lives, the benefit is only a fraction of the capital gain; e.g., with a tax rate of 46%, the net benefit is only 7.8% of G when the useful life is five years. For a lower interest rate, e.g., $r = 10\%$, the benefit is only 14.1% of G, ceteris paribus.

This analysis applies to either the corporate or the personal taxpayer, but is probably understates the true tax advantage of a change in ownership because corporations can sometimes avoid immediate tax liability by structuring "stock-for-stock" deals. The overall net benefit is complex and clearly deserves further analysis.

There is also one other wrinkle to consider: Dertouzous and Thorpe (1982) argue that estate taxes often "force" a sale because the heir has no cash. However, this argument can be criticized on the ground that an heir can borrow to pay the tax, pledging the inherited firm's assets as collateral, thus obviating the necessity of sale.

REFERENCES

Asquith, P. (1983). "Merger Bids, Uncertainty, and Stockholder Returns." *Journal of Financial Economics* **11**, 51–83.

————, and E. H. Kim (1982)."The Impact of Merger Bids on the Participating Firm's Security Holders." *Journal of Finance* **37**, 1209–1228.

————, R. F. Bruner, and D. W. Mullins, Jr. (1983). "The Gains to Bidding Firms from Merger." *Journal of Financial Economics* **11**, 121–130.

Bradley, M. (1980)."Interfirm Tender Offers and the Market for Corporate Control." *Journal of Business* **53**, 345–376.

————, and L. M. Wakeman (1983). "The Wealth Effects of Targeted Share Repurchases." *Journal of Financial Economics* **11**, 301–328.

————, A. Desai, and E. H. Kim (1982). Specialized Resources and Competition in the Market for Corporate Control. Unpublished working paper, University of Michigan, September.

————, A. Desai, and E. H. Kim. (1983), "The Rationale Behind Interfirm Tender Offers: Information or Synergy?" *Journal of Financial Economics* **11**, 183–206.

Chung, K. S., and J. F. Weston, (1982). "Diversification and Mergers in a Strategic Long-Range Planning Framework." In *Mergers and Acquisitions*, ed. Michael Keenan and Lawrence I. White, Chap. 13. Lexington, Mass.: Heath.

Dennis, D. K., and J. J. McConnell (1983). Corporate Merger and Security-holder Returns: Tests of the Investment Hypothesis, the Incentive Hypothesis, and the Co-Insurance Hypothesis. Unpublished paper, Texas A & M University and Purdue University, August.

————, and J. J. McConnell (1985). "Corporate Mergers and Security Returns." *Journal of Financial Economics* **16**, 141–187.

Dertouzous, J. N., and K. E. Thorpe (1982). *Newspaper Groups: Economics of Scale, Tax Laws, and Merger Incentives.* Publication R–2878–SBS, Rand Corporation (June).

Dodd, P. (1980). "Merger Proposals, Managerial Discretion and Stockholder Wealth." *Journal of Financial Economics* **8**, 105–138.

————, and R. Ruback (1977). "Tender Offers and Stockholder Returns: An Empirical Analysis." *Journal of Financial Economics* **5**, 351–374.

————, and J. B. Warner (1983). "On Corporate Governance: A Study of Proxy Contests." *Journal of Financial Economics* **11**, 401–438.

Eckbo, B. E. (1983). "Horizontal Mergers, Collusion, and Stockholder Wealth." *Journal of Finanical Economics* **11**, 241–273.

Eger, C. E. (1983). "An Empirical Test of the Redistribution Effect in Pure Exchange Mergers." *Journal of Financial and Quantitative Analysis* **18**, 547–572.

Firth, M. (1980). "Takeovers, Shareholder Returns and the Theory of the Firm." *Quarterly Journal of Economics,* March, 235–260.

Ginsburg, M. D. (1983). "Taxing Corporate Acquisitions." *NYU Tax Law Review* **38**, 177–319.

Jensen, M. C., and R. S. Ruback (1983). "The Market for Corporate Control." *Journal of Financial Economics* **11**, 5–50.

Kim, E. H., and J. J. McConnell (1977). "Corporate Mergers and the Co-Insurance of Corporate Debt." *Journal of Finance* **32**, 349–363.

Lewellen, W. G. (1971). "A Pure Financial Rationale for the Conglomerate Merger." *Journal of Finance* **26**, 521–537.

Malatesta, P. H. (1983). "The Wealth Effect of Merger Activity and the Objective Functions of Merging Firms." *Journal of Financial Economics* **11**, 155–181.

Marshall, W. J., J. B. Yawitz, and E. Greenberg (1984). *Incentives for Diversification and the Structure of the Conglomerate Firm.* Working Paper 12–80, National Bureau of Economic Research, February.

Miller, M. H., and M. S. Scholes, (1978). "Dividends and Taxes." *Journal of Financial Economics* **6**, 333–364.

Penrose, E. T. (1959). *The Theory of the Growth of the Firm.* Oxford: Blackwell.

Roll, R. (1986). " The Hubris Hypothesis of Corporate Takeovers." *Journal of Business* **59**, 197–216.

Settle, J. W., H. Petry, and C. C. Hsia (1984). "Synergy, Diversification, and Incentive Effects of Corporate Merger on Bondholder Wealth: Some Evidence." *Journal of Financial Research* (forthcoming).

Shastri, K. (1983). The Differential Effects of Mergers on Corporate Security Values. Unpublished paper, University of Pittsburgh, Graduate School of Business, November.

Stillman, R. (1983). "Examining Antitrust Policy Toward Horizontal Mergers." *Journal of Financial Economics* **11**, 225–240.

Titman, S. (1984). "The Effect of Capital Structure on a Firm's Liquidation Decision." *Journal of Financial Economics* **13**, 137–151.

Varaiya, V. (1985). *A Test of Roll's Hubris Hypothesis of Corporate Takeovers.* Working paper, SMU.

Warner, J. B. (1977). "Bankruptcy Costs: Some Evidence." *Journal of Finance* **32**, 337–348.

Weston F., Jr., and K. S. Chung (1983). "Some Aspects of Merger Theory." *Journal of the Midwest Finance Association* **12**, 1–33.

Williamson, O. E. (1964). *The Economics of Discretionary Behavior: Managerial Objectives in a Theory of the Firm.* Englewood Cliffs, NJ.: Prentice-Hall.

15

Comment

MICHAEL BRADLEY
GREGG A. JARRELL

The primary purpose of the research presented in this part of the volume is to challenge the consensus among financial economists that corporate mergers in general, and hostile tender offers in particular, channel resources to higher-valued uses. The view under attack is nothing more than a simple extension of the neoclassical notion that there are mutual gains from voluntary trade—that through the process of voluntary exchange, resources will flow to their highest-value use. The evidence offered in support of this proposition is the empirical fact that the securityholders of combining corporations realize significant capital gains as a result of these transactions.

We should note from the outset that the neoclassical theory of takeovers simply states that corporate acquisitions channel resources to higher-valued uses. In its most general form, the theory does not specify the source of these gains. Quoting from Bradley's work:

The gains from corporate acquisitions may stem from more efficient management, economies of scale, improved production techniques, the combination of complementary resources, increased market power, the redeployment of assets to more profitable uses, or any number of value-creating mechanisms that fall under the general rubric of corporate synergy.[1]

However, several of the authors on this panel have elected to ignore this most general form of the theory and focus on a variant that is attributable to Henry Manne, who was the first to define and articulate the workings of a market for corporate control. Manne viewed the takeover process as a mechanism for disciplining corporate managers. However, we wish to stress that we, along with many financial economists, consider the removal of inefficient target managers to be only one possible rationale for corporate takeovers. To put the point more directly, showing that target firms are well-managed prior to their acquisition is not an indictment of the neoclassical theory of takeovers. Indeed, there are well-known cases in which acquisitions were effected specifically to secure the superior management skills of executives of the target firm.

Moreover, it is not clear whether the behavior of inefficient or self-dealing target managers can be detected in the preacquisition performance of target firms. It may well be the case that the most egregious cases of inefficiency occur in profitable and growing firms. Also, the fact that mergers occur in waves with targets clustered in specific industries does not easily conform to the inefficient-management theory. These facts are more consistent with the general economic theory, which predicts that sudden and significant changes in the economic environment will trigger a burst of merger and takeover activity, as the pairing of management teams to assets reaches the new (more efficient) equilibrium. Recent merger activity in the transportation and financial services industries more likely can be traced to deregulation rather than to a sudden increase in managerial inefficiency. Finally, the magnitude of the average takeover premium—over 50% since 1980—is hard to explain by the removal of inefficient managers. The size of these premiums must be cold comfort to those who argue that the primary purpose of takeovers is to discipline corporate managers.

The point is that there is no generally accepted theory as to the specific rationale behind corporate acquisitions. To quote from Jensen and Ruback's survey paper: "Knowledge of the sources of takeover gains still eludes us."[2] And the fact that we have disguised our ignorance by shrouding it in a fancy term like *corporate synergy* does not clarify the issue.

As our presenters have convincingly argued, we must add to the extensive stock market data on takeovers to more fully understand the economic effects of corporate acquisitions. What is required is an empirical documentation of what assets are redeployed, what operations are discontinued, and what new investments are made in order to generate the observed increase in security values. It is instructive to note that in three recent cases where target managers were able to defeat an unwanted takeover bid (CBS, Unocal, and Union Carbide), the target managers essentially mimicked the drastic asset redeployments and share repurchases that had been proposed by the hostile bidders. Michael Jensen has done some creative work in this regard by providing a logical (if yet untested) rationale for the recent flurry of acquisitions in the oil industry. We applaud this type of research and encourage more of it.

Before we turn to our specific comments on each of the chapters, we make a general point concerning the nature of empirical work, particularly since the title of this part of the volume is "Evidence on the Gains from Mergers and Takeovers." The most important aspect of an empirical paper is that the data be presented clearly and unambiguously so that the readers can judge for themselves the veracity of the evidence. The least important aspect of an empirical paper is the author's interpretation of his or her results. Empirical papers stand or fall largely on the basis of how well the data

are presented. A sufficient condition in this regard is to provide enough information so that an independent researcher can replicate the study. A necessary condition is that the author explain fully his or her research design. The reader must be told how the sample was gathered, what observations were deleted and why, what transformations have been performed on the data, and what statistical tests have been used. Sample statistics should be provided so that the reader can get a feel for the data under analysis.

The least important aspect of an empirical paper is the author's interpretation of his or her findings. One hopes that the research will have been motivated by a specific theory so that interpretation of the results simply involves accepting or rejecting a specified null hypothesis. However, many empirical papers are written and published with little or no explanation of the results. In fact, in 1983 the *Journal of Financial Economics* devoted an entire issue to papers dealing with anomalous empirical findings in finance. The fact that purely empirical papers are published and widely disseminated throughout the profession is a testimony to the relative unimportance of the researcher's explanation of his or her findings. In our opinion, several of the authors in this part of the volume have reversed this priority. Too much ink is wasted on overinterpreting results that are based on data that are not well described. These authors would do the profession a great service if they spent more time describing their data and less time interpreting their results.

Let us now turn to a discussion of each of the chapters presented in this part.

MAGENHEIM AND MUELLER

The Magenheim and Mueller chapter addresses what we have long recognized is a critical issue in the debate over the economic desirability of hostile takeovers: Specifically, do these transactions create value, or do they simply redistribute wealth from one stockholder group to another (Roll's hubris hypothesis)? The answer to this question is central to our null hypothesis stated earlier that, on net, hostile takeovers reallocate corporate resources to higher-valued uses.

Magenheim and Mueller correctly point out that the issue is an empirical one and centers on the measured gains to acquiring firms, since researchers on both sides of the current debate concede that the stockholders or target firms realize significant positive gains. Thus the relevant issue, therefore, is how to measure the gains to acquiring firms. What method should be used to estimate abnormal returns, and what is the relevant time frame for such an analysis?

Following standard financial economics, Magenheim and Mueller use stock market data to estimate the wealth effects of 78 hostile takeovers. Note that these authors disagree with the general conclusion, as summarized in Jensen and Ruback,[3] that there is a significant difference between the returns to acquirers in tender offers and the returns to acquirers in mergers, the former being significantly greater. Using monthly data, they show that indiscriminate use of the market model can lead to different and often conflicting conclusions regarding the profitability of corporate takeovers. However, having discredited this empirical technique, the authors ignore their own analysis and proceed to use the market model to estimate the returns to acquiring firms.

Magenheim and Mueller also show that the time frame used to estimate the gains to acquiring firms is critical in drawing appropriate inferences. Specifically, they find that the longer the period over which the returns to acquirers are measured, the greater the losses incurred by the firm's stockholders. In the one year following a hostile takeover, the average acquirer in the Magenheim-Mueller sample has lost 11% of its preoffer value; in the second year following the acquisition, acquiring firms lost an additional 9%; and in the third year acquirers in the sample lost an additional 18%. All told, acquiring firms lost 42% of their value over the three years following

their acquisitions, which, the authors assert, more than offsets the 81% gain realized by the (smaller) targets of these acquisitions. Again, we should point out that the estimates of the returns to acquiring firms are based on a market model that the authors demonstrate is misspecified and generates negatively biased residuals.

We fully agree that the postoffer behavior of the shares of acquiring firms is relevant to the current debate. And indeed, finding a three-year secular decline in the value of acquiring firms is troublesome for the neoclassical theory—troublesome in at least two respects. First, such a trend is inconsistent with the basic tenets of an efficient capital market. If the Magenheim-Mueller results can be generalized, then market participants can earn an average of 42% abnormal return over three years simply by selling short the shares of acquiring firms. It is troublesome that the market is this inefficient and we are still so poor. The second troubling aspect of a postacquisition decline in the value of acquiring firms is that such a secular decline casts doubts on empirical studies that measure the gains from mergers over substantially shorter intervals. Indeed, this is the point of the Magenheim-Mueller chapter.

However, before we start shorting the shares of acquiring firms or rejecting most of the existing empirical literature in this area, let us examine the Mageheim-Mueller analysis a bit closer. The measurement of the economic effects of corporate events has long been an issue in financial economics. It is well known that market model parameter estimates based on monthly data are inefficient and nonstationary. Indeed, that is why the profession has moved toward using daily data. Parameter estimates are much more efficient using daily rather than monthly data. Moreover, when looking over longer time periods, one should account directly for changing parameter values or use some other technique for estimating abnormal returns.

Myron Scholes has developed a method for estimating abnormal returns that does not involve estimating market model parameters. Using so-called Scholes's daily excess returns, we reestimated the gains to the acquiring firms in the Magenheim-Mueller study. We thank the authors for sharing their data with us. Consistent with the Magenheim-Mueller results, we find these acquiring firms, on average, did lose money—but far less money than reported in their chapter. Using Scholes's excess returns, we find the following:

6 months	−1.7%
Year 1	−2.4
Year 2	−5.0
Year 3	−6.0
Total	−16.0 ($t = 1.01$)

Thus, we find that the acquiring firms in the Magenheim-Mueller sample lost a statistically insignificant 15% over the three-year period. This loss is almost a third of the loss reported in the conclusion of their chapter. We therefore conclude that any policy proscription based on the Magenheim-Mueller results is compromised severely by the fact that these authors significantly overstate the losses to acquiring firms.

Finally, we should point out that the social desirability of hostile takeovers does not turn on whether or not the stockholders of acquiring firms realize a capital gain as a result of these transactions. Rather, the real issue is whether or not these transactions create total value. In other words, it may well be the case that on average the stockholders of acquiring firms suffer a capital loss but the stockholders of target firms realize an even greater capital gain. In order to answer this question, one must examine the total gains realized by both stockholder groups. Bradley et al. examine 163 "matched pairs" of targets and acquirers and find that on average (hostile) tender offers result in an 8% increase in the market value of the combining assets. Moreover, even in the subsets of their data in which acquiring firms suffer capital losses, the gains to targets outweigh these losses, and the net effect is a significant increase in the value of the combined assets.

RAVENSCRAFT AND SCHERER

By their own admission, the Ravenscraft and Scherer chapter sheds little light on the central issue of this conference. It is not clear what can be learned about the economic effects of hostile takeovers by studying 15 mergers that ultimately led to sell-offs. This line of inquiry seem analogous to trying to understand the institution of marriage by talking only to divorced people, and to only a few of them, at that.

Moreover, the less-than-satisfactory way in which the data are described renders almost impossible an independent assessment of their results concerning the profitability of acquiring firms. For example, the authors casually mention that they "normalize" their data, without giving the reader the slightest hint of what actually was done. They mention the use of a control group that they define as those lines of business in the same industry that had little or no merger activity over the preceding 27 years. There is no description of this control group, nor are sample statistics given. One can only imagine the strange lines of business that have had no merger activity over the past quarter of a century.

Data problems notwithstanding, let's review what the Ravenscraft-Scherer chapter purports to show:

1. Targets are well-run firms premerger.
2. Some acquired businesses are later sold off.
3. Acquiring firms performed relatively poorly in the 1974–1977 period.

We have already discussed this first issue: Finding that target firms are not on the brink of financial disaster prior to their acquisition is not an indictment of the neoclassical view of takeovers. The fact that some acquired businesses are later sold off is neither surprising nor very informative. Finally, the fact that conglomerates performed poorly in the mid to late 1970s has been documented by others. Schipper and Thompson,[5] for example, attribute this decline in the value of conglomerates to the rash of state and federal antitakeover regulations that were put into place during this time period.

HERMAN AND LOWENSTEIN

The Herman and Lowenstein chapter represents a growing literature that attempts to take the next step in the empirical investigation of the gains from hostile takeovers. While most financial economists would argue that stock market data are far superior to accounting data in assessing the economic effects of corporate events, most would also agree that examining the latter is not a fruitless exercise. If corporate combinations do in fact create value, then the accounting numbers of acquired firms should reflect these synergistic gains.

The Herman-Lowenstein study examines the accounting numbers of the firms involved in 56 hostile takeovers effected over the period 1975–1983. They begin by analyzing the preacquisition performance of these firms. Like Ravenscraft and Scherer, Herman and Lowenstein find that by and large target firms were well run preacquisition. They also find that targets are no more or no less levered than acquiring firms. Let me make two points regarding their analysis of the leverage issue.

First, Herman and Lowenstein argue that the fact that targets are not significantly underlevered is inconsistent with the neoclassical theory of tender offers. In response, let us just suggest that the authors review the neoclassical position on the existence of an optimal capital structure and the potential gains from financial diversification at the level of the firm.

Second, the authors report that the average debt-to-equity ratio of all the firms in their sample (targets and acquirers) is in excess of 70%. The surprising aspect of their data is not that targets and acquirers have roughly the same leverage but that the leverage for the entire sample is so high. There is a vast empirical literature on corporate leverage, and most of these studies indicate an average debt-to-equity value of around 40% for nonfinancial corporations over this period. The Herman-Lowenstein estimates are almost twice this

amount. In a recently published IRRC paper, John Pound[6] finds that the average debt-to-value ratio is about 25%, which is comparable to that of all U.S. manufacturing firms. Pound also finds that targets are indistinguishable along a whole host of accounting measures. In other words, Pound finds that target firms represent a typical cross section of the firms in the economy.

Herman and Lowenstein, finish their piece with an examination of the ROE of the 56 acquiring firms in their sample. Much to their surprise, they find that the ROE of half their acquirers increased in the years following their acquisitions. However, they elect to ignore these findings and concentrate their discussion on those acquirers that showed a deterioration in ROE. On the basis of the results for the latter group alone, they conclude that hostile takeovers are not value-increasing transactions.

Before leaving this study, let me make one last point. The authors assert that security prices around acquisitions are systematically biased upward and therefore one must resort to accounting numbers to determine the economic gains to takeovers. What the authors fail to realize is that this is a testable proposition and especially testable with their sample. Just by chance, these authors have found two groups of acquirers distinguished by their postacquisition ROEs. An obvious test of the authors' assertion that stock prices are biased is to see whether or not the market was about to distinguish between these two groups when the acquisition was first announced. We suspect that the stockholders of acquirers in the increasing-ROE group fared far better than those in the decreasing-ROE group around the time of announcement. But, as we said, this is a testable proposition and one that should be tested directly—if not by these authors, then by someone else.

RICHARD ROLL

Richard Roll's chapter is a must-read for anyone working in the area, not because his general thesis is necessarily correct but because he articulates many of the suspicions that we all have with respect to the source of the gains from corporate acquisitions. It is hard for us who advocate the neoclassical theory of takeovers to understand some of the recent acquisitions and particularly the enormous premiums often paid for target firms. It's hard to imagine just what synergies were realized in Exxon's acquisition of Reliance, in DuPont's acquisition of Connoco, and in U.S. Steel's acquisition of Marathon. And as you recall, the market was equally skeptical of the value-creating potential of these acquisitions. Surely, Roll's observation of the hubris attitude of many corporate executives and the persuasive logic of the "winner's curse" explain some of the more outrageous corporate-control transactions.

However, Roll readily admits that his is not a general theory of takeovers. Quoting from his chapter:

Hubris cannot be the sole explanation of the takeover phenomenon because it implies that every bid announcement should elicit a price decline in the bidding firm's shares. Some papers have even found an average increase. Furthermore, if all bids were inspired by hubris, stockholders could easily stop them by the simple expedient of a prohibition in the corporate charter (p. 250).

POLICY PROSCRIPTIONS

What, then, are the policy proscriptions that one can draw from these chapters? As developed earlier, any policy proscriptions flowing from the Magenheim-Mueller study are based on overestimates of the losses incurred by acquiring firms. We suspect that if this study were redone by using the appropriate empirical techniques, the authors would find net positive gains to the stockholders of the firms involved in these acquisitions. We suspect that these mergers are not anomalous: Target stockholders probably gained; acquiring stockholders probably did not lose.

The Ravenscraft-Scherer study has little if anything to say regarding the appropriate public policy toward hostile takeovers.

Herman and Lowenstein base their policy proscriptions solely on the subset of acquiring firms in their sample that experienced a deterioration in ROE. They completely ignore those acquiring firms that realized an increase in ROE subsequent to their acquisitions. This rather selective use of their results notwithstanding, the policy proscriptions advanced by Herman and Lowenstein seem to be contradictory to their findings. Having concluded that hostile takeovers do not create value, Herman and Lowenstein proceed to argue that many of the defensive tactics used by target managers—greenmail, poison pills, discriminatory share repurchases, and scorched-earth tactics in general—should be outlawed. This conclusion seems to us to be a complete nonsequitor. If hostile takeovers do not create value but, rather, represent a drain on society's resources, then why should defensive tactics be prohibited? It seems to us that if one believes hostile takeovers to be welfare-decreasing transactions, then one should encourage the development and proliferation of these and other antitakeover measures.

Perhaps the best summary of the public policy implications of the chapters presented in this part of the volume is found in Richard Roll's assessment of the current state of empirical work on the gains to corporate mergers and acquisitions. Quoting from his chapter:

From the policy perspective, there is no empirical justification for limiting takeover activity because of potential damage to target firm shareholders. Furthermore, there is no good empirical justification for restricting the activities of bidding firms (p. 241).

Both of us would be interested to know whether Professor Roll feels compelled to rewrite this passage in light of the evidence presented in this volume. We strongly suspect that he does not.

NOTES

1. M. Bradley, A. Desai, and E. H. Kim, "Synergistic Gains from Corporate Acquisitions and Their Division Between the Stockholders of

the Target and Acquiring Firms." Working Paper, Graduate School of Business, University of Michigan, Ann Arbor, Michigan (February 1987).

2. M. C. Jensen and R. Ruback, "The Market for Corporate Control: The Scientific Evidence." *Journal of Financial Economics* **11**, 5–50 (April 1983).

3. Ibid.

4. See note 1.

5. K. Schipper and R. Thompson, "Evidence on the Capitalized Value of Merger Activity for Acquiring Firms." *Journal of Financial Economics* **11**, 85–119 (April 1983).

6. J. Pound, *Are Takeover Targets Undervalued? An Empirical Examination of the Financial Characteristics of Target Companies* (Washington, D.C.: Investor Responsibility Research Center, 1985).

16

Comment

WARREN A. LAW

I shall comment primarily on the three empirical chapters. I like all of them, possibly because their conclusions fit my own preconceptions.

There is a well-known anecdote in the history of the Royal Society. Charles II proposed this question: "Why does a vessel of water not weigh more if a dead fish is put in it, but does weigh more if the fish is alive?" Solutions of great ingenuity were proposed, objected to, and defended. In the end, of course, someone thought to conduct an experiment, and the royal hypothesis was disproved.

For some time we have been enduring a similar experience. The question has been: "Why is the productivity of a collection of assets improved when those assets are acquired by another firm?" Professor Roll has discussed several possible answers of great ingenuity, even going so far as to suggest that managers may discover the existence of synergy according to some random process. He states that "the evidence is insufficient to reach a definite conclusion" as to whether gains accrue in aggregate to all shareholders. It is not clear whether he believes that if gains *do* accrue, this indicates an increase in social efficiency, as many observers have claimed.

I submit that, to my satisfaction at least, the results are in. The data in the three other chapters persuade me that there is no credible evidence that social welfare has been increased by any of the acquisition binges of the postwar period. Moreover, I doubt that there is reason to believe that the present wave of "bust-up" takeovers will have a different outcome.

The interesting question is why anyone ever believed in the dead-fish theory of takeovers in the first place. The answer, of course, is the efficient-market syndrome—the belief that because one can't beat the stock market, the market must know the intrinsic value of a firm. Professor Shubik has already outlined the flaws in applying the theory to takeovers, but I am more concerned with whether the short-run behavior of stock prices tells us anything useful about the true efficiency aspects of takeovers. Professors Herman and Lowenstein state, "We question whether the shift to stock price–based analyses has been a boon to scientific understanding" (p. 217). I wish I had their flair for understatement.

Professor Shiller has presented persuasive evidence that the stock market overreacts.[1] DeBondt and Thaler have confirmed this unsurprising position.[2] In a simple experiment they demonstrated that portfolios constructed by buying stocks which have been the biggest losers in the past substantially outperform both the market and portfolios of the biggest winners, when held for several years. The evidence is so clear that one must question why there aren't more contrarians in the market.

Keynes, who has been quoted often in this conference, provided the answer when he noted that "worldly wisdom teaches that it is better for reputation to fail conventionally than to succeed unconventionally." (I sometimes think professional investors should be required annually to read Chapter 12 of the *General Theory,* just as crews of naval vessels were once mustered regularly to hear the Articles of War read aloud.) Keynes also pointed out that "in the field of economic and political philosophy there are not many who are influenced by new theories after they are twenty-five or thirty," which may account for some of my remarks.[3]

The search for a stock price–based *answer* to the social costs-benefits of takeovers is an illusion. I much prefer Herman and Lowenstein's emphasis on *process,* the dynamic nature of takeover history, with changes in types of targets, bidders, methods of financing, etc. Similarly, theoretical discussions of a "market for corporate control" describe a world with which I am not familiar. I am a director of several firms and could not with a straight face read to my fellow directors Fama's description of a market for their services, with prices based on their performance as referees.[4]

Let me offer an oversimple history of takeovers which seems nevertheless more realistic than the equally simplistic ones presented by some financial economists, in which by some Darwinian process good managers drive out bad, with toadlike firms converted to princes by the magic kiss of Carl Icahn.

In the 1960s we saw a wave of conglomerate acquisitions. (These are the acquisitions analyzed by Ravenscraft and Scherer.) Most of these were uncontested, partly because the typical acquisition price was well above the replacement cost of the assets acquired. Using "make-or-buy" logic, one may question why a rational buyer would pay substantially more than it would cost to reproduce the assets. The answer (clearer now than it was then, at least to sellers) was that the acquirer usually paid in "funny money," i.e., his own grossly overvalued stock. By using pooling-of-interest accounting, the acquirer was able to generate increased earnings per share even with the poor after-acquisition performance described by Ravenscraft and Scherer.[5]

This was a period of voodoo finance, and it gave voodoo a bad name when rationality eventually prevailed and investors asked why they were paying 30 times earnings for a collection of firms which, standing alone, would command a P/E ratio of 10.

In the 1970s stock prices declined until by 1979 the typical industrial firm had a market value less than two-thirds its replacement cost.[6] Acquirers were then able to pay premiums of up to 50% and still acquire firms for less than reproduction cost. Here the make-or-buy decision was obvious, especially when one recognized that it is safer to buy an existing firm, with a known product line, market, and track record, than to invest in a new product or plant, especially in a perceived environment of low growth.

At least the raiders during this period tended to be CEOs of large firms, who stalked targets they wanted to fold into their operations. Today, however, we are in a era of financial opportunists who want to "put a target into play" and rarely intend to keep it if successful. At best, they may keep some assets, but primarily they hope to liquidate assets at higher values than they commanded in the market. At worst, they simply hope for greenmail, or a profit on their holdings when a white knight appears. This game has been facilitated by (1) the institutionalization of stockownership, since institutions are under pressure to perform and eager to tender to a raider, (2) the rise of the arbitragers, who now command large pools of capital, and (3) the arrival of the junk bond.[7]

The topic of this part of the volume is "evidence on the gains" from takeovers. It is undisputed that stockholders of target firms are big winners. In fact, Goldman, Sachs has estimated that 70% of the increase in Standard and Poor's Index since the start of 1984 has been due to actual or anticipated corporate restructuring. Do stockholders of acquiring firms lose? Magenheim and Mueller convince me they do, over the longer run. By that time, however, the stock has probably changed hands several times.

A more important question is whether society in general gains from takeovers. Admittedly, that is not the question to which these chapters are addressed, although Herman and Lowenstein raise the issue. Some apologists contend that stock prices alone answer the question, but it is impossible by some Benthamite calculus of pleasure and pain to reach a scientific conclusion. Among the many considerations often ignored are the following:

- *Entertainment value:* Free and substantial amusement is afforded to detached observers of such public circuses as the Bendix-Martin Marietta debacle.[8]
- *The brain drain:* James Tobin has described his unease at the fear that "we are throwing more and more of our resources, including the cream of our youth, into financial activities remote from the production of goods and services, into activities that generate high private rewards disproportionate to their social productivity."[9] Certainly, the $126,582 per hour of work received by one investment banker in the Texaco-Getty takeover is likely to attract emulators.[10] On the other hand, Samuel Johnson pointed out long ago that men are seldom so innocently occupied as when in pursuit of money, and there is no evidence about how the bright people in the takeover game would otherwise occupy themselves.
- *Impact on employees:* Previously in this conference, Professor Coffee described the "severe and hitherto unprecedented" risk of unemployment now faced by employees as a result of the present orgy of corporate "restructuring." Surely he is correct in his judgment that this changes a preexisting implicit contract, and that it is misleading to describe the shareholder as the only residual risk bearer.[11]
- *Creditor risk:* Obviously, the junk bond takeover increases corporate risk, and Herman and Lowenstein point out that lower returns and higher risk are an unattractive duo. Often overlooked is the impact of restructuring on *existing* creditors. Unocal bondholders, for example, saw the rating on their securities cut from AA+ to BBB when the firm piled on new debt to deter raiders. More

than one-fourth of Moody's 134 downgrades in the first ten months of 1985 resulted from takeover activity.[12]

One cannot quantify these and other consequences of takeovers. My purpose is only to underline the complexity of the question. I confess I don't *know* whether the net result of our present binge will be an increase in social welfare. But neither do the apologists, and the results of previous periods of acquisitions should make them skeptical. Toads may be converted into princes, but my daughter has a poster which proclaims, "To marry a prince, you first have to kiss an awful lot of toads."

NOTES

1. See R. J. Shiller, Chapter 3 of this volume; R. J. Shiller, "Do Stock Prices Move Too Much to be Justified by Subsequent Changes in Dividends?" *American Economic Review* **71**, 421–436. (June 1981).

2. W. F. M. DeBondt and R. Thaler, "Does the Stock Market Overreact?" *Journal of Finance* **40**, 793–805 (July 1985).

3. J. M. Keynes, *The General Theory of Employment Interest and Money* (London: Macmillan, 1936), 158, 384.

4. Quoted by Herman and Lowenstein, Chapter 13 of this volume, p. 214.

5. For a hypothetical example, see B. G. Malkiel, *A Random Walk Down Wall Street,* 4th ed. (New York: 1985), 55–59.

6. *Economic Report of the President,* Washington, D.C.: U.S. General Accounting Office, (1980), Table B-85.

7. Euphemistically called "high-yield bonds." The ability to raise very large sums by issuing these risky instruments more than anything else explains the recent spate of billion-dollar raids. See "How Drexel's *Wunderkind* Bankrolls the Raiders," *Business Week,* March 4, 1985, 90–91.

8. At one point each company appeared to own the other. See "Inside the Bendix Fiasco," *American Lawyer,* February 1983, 35–39.

9. J. Tobin, "On the Efficiency of the Financial System," *Lloyds Bank Review* **153**, 14 (July 1984).

10. "Shop Talk" column, *Wall Street Journal,* January 17, 1984. Texaco paid almost $10

billion, and one investment banker said, "You can consider the fees in this deal as tips." One year later it was unclear whether Pennzoil had successfully overturned the entire deal in the courts, long after all fees had been collected.

11. Chapter 6 of this volume.

12. "Takeovers and Buyouts Clobber Blue-Chip Bondholders," *Business Week,* November 11, 1985, p. 113. Unocal issue $4.2 billion of new debt and retired 29% of its equity. For a view critical of the outcome, see M. C. Jensen, "When Unocal Won over Pickens, Shareholders and Society Lost," *Financier* **9,** 50–52 (November 1985).

17

Discussion

SUSAN ROSE-ACKERMAN, Moderator

Saul Levmore: I think my question is best directed to Mike Scherer. In reading the literature and listening today, I found myself sympathizing with the critics of the empirical work because I am not really sure what you're going after or what you expect to find when you try to assemble evidence. For example, it is not surprising to me to find target shareholders making money. Eighty percent premiums may seem excessive, but I'm not sure what excessive or too little is. Bidders might have nonpublic information; there might be management hubris. There are many things that can explain why people make money on property that they hold. But what would you have expected to find happening to the bidders or acquirers? If you had found that the acquirers made a great deal of money, then we would all say, "Gee, people are irrational; there are not enough acquirers." I mean, if you are drilling for oil, you should keep drilling for more oil until the marginal, and eventually the average, rate of return approaches the market rate of return. Now, we don't have a lot of evidence that the acquirers' returns are very much subaverage. If acquirers' excess returns are a little negative, that's not so troubling either. After all, the average restaurant doesn't do too well either, so why should the average acquirer? In any event, from a policy point of view the average really doesn't matter as long as we think that

The following is an edited transcript of the discussion which followed the presentation of the papers.

there are *some* good folks out there increasing value. And, indeed, I guess that means we should be happy with the actor whose returns exceed the market average. But my point is really that *averages* in most industries will be close to one another, for otherwise there's insufficient entry and activity.

F. M. Scherer: Actually, we were surprised in several senses. We were very much surprised to see how profitable the acquired companies were premerger. No one has reached out to such a large sample before, and our results differed greatly from the conventional wisdom. Second, we had completely open hypotheses about whether the gain to acquirers would be plus or minus. We really didn't know. We wanted to know what happened. What we found out was that averaging over three years, the returns on pooling-of-interests acquisitions were mildly positive. But when you put that together with the premerger data, you find a *huge* drop from what existed premerger. You ask, "Aren't we happy that there were some good mergers?" Yes, there were some *very* good mergers. An interesting statistic is that on average, the acquisitions that survived—that is, the 70% or so that were not subsequently sold off— grew a little bit more rapidly than their industries. But some grew like gangbusters: They had a spectacular performance that I suspect can be attributed to mergers. But, again, if you're interested in finding out, on balance, what the merger wave of the sixties has done, you've got to look at the averages. You've got to look at the virtually zero relevant-to-control profitability of the survivors in the period 1975 to 1977. You've got to look at the minus 1% operating income/assets performance of the sell-offs—roughly 30% of the sample. You've got to look at the whole picture to determine on average how these mergers turned out.

Richard Roll: In response to Levmore, one would indeed anticipate that the returns to the *marginal* bidder would be zero, but the empirical work measures the *average.* If the average bidder gains nothing, and can expect to gain nothing, why bid?

Michael Jensen: The fundamental error being made in the work presented at this panel is the notion that the appropriate standard of comparison is the premerger performance of merging companies. Let's take the Magenheim and Mueller study for example, where it's most clear, and compare the postmerger performance of the firm to the premerger status. That is not the right standard of comparison unless you *know* something very specific about the decision process that leads to the announcement of an acquisition. Let me give you a simple example. When Dick Roll and I were graduate students, we wrote a paper investigating the effects of stock splits on prices. When you look at what's happened in the few years prior to a stock split, you will find that there's been an abnormally high rate of return. You'll find the same thing if you look at firms that have increased their cash dividends. If you look at what happens to them *after* that period of time, you would expect to find those firms earning normal rates of return if the market is efficient. If you *didn't* find that, the market would not be efficient.

The notion that premerger performance is the standard for judging where the merger has harmed shareholders (if the postmerger returns are not equal to or greater than they were premerger) is a fallacy that involves a sample selection bias. I believe the stock split example is an easy way to see it. I don't think you'd argue that

the mere announcement of a stock split—that anyone who had two shares before now has three—is going to hurt shareholders. Yet that's exactly what you find if you look at the data—stock returns are lower, on average, after a stock split than before. That is not surprising because managers split their stock when its price rises substantially out of its normal trading range. In effect, the abnormally high returns cause the stock split, and after those abnormally high returns we expect, of course, normal returns. There is evidence that abnormally high returns cause mergers also. And you'll find the same things if you look at the year *after* the announcement of positive earnings. The same argument as the stock split argument applies to the Ravenscraft-Scherer study—which uses accounting data—only it isn't quite as simple, and I needn't belabor the point.

Louis Lowenstein: I think one of the difficulties when we debate is that it's not the data but how you read it. I read the Fama, Fisher, Jensen, Roll study of stock splits that Mike just mentioned and I came away from it with the empty feeling I often get when I read an event study. What it showed was that prices are corrected very quickly after the announcement of stock splits. But a stock split is a very simple event—in large measure it's a nonevent. And one explanation of it is that it takes place rather late in the earnings increase cycle, after which the company's earnings tend to level off. So the stock split announcement is often little more than an act of celebration; there's nothing much for the market to react to. It's not the data but who it is that's reading it.

F. M. Scherer: Mike Jensen raised the question of what counterfactual assumption to use, and that is a devilishly difficult problem. What is the historical counterfactual assumption? What would have happened but for a merger? What Magenheim and Mueller are saying is that what you conclude is *critically* sensitive to the way you define the counterfactual conditions. That's a major contribution, one that has been insufficiently appreciated in the capital asset–pricing model work. Let me describe very briefly some work we did. We've been trying to disentangle the reasons for the decline in profitability, and we've chosen a different kind of control group. We chose a group in 1965 that *didn't* get acquired but that had size and profitability similar to the group of firms that *did* get acquired. We tested the post-merger profit behavior of those that *were* acquired versus those that weren't. We also controlled for accounting method by limiting our analysis to pooling mergers, so there were no reevaluations. It's a reasonable way of establishing a control. We got the results I summarized, namely, that the merged units had their profitability decline significantly more rapidly than the non-merged units of similar premerger size and profitability.

Richard Ruback: I thought that Mike Jensen was making a logical point rather than an empirical point and that he failed to emphasize one of the steps of the syllogism. I believe he was saying that if firms that do better tend to acquire, then we will get a selection bias. One way to see this is to notice that the firms that made it onto the best-performers-for-1984 list in terms of stock appreciation did much worse this year than they did in 1984. One explanation is the hubris hypothesis—once managers got on the best-performers list, they started to get lazy and underperform. Another hypothesis is Jensen's selection bias that managers' performance, on average, will be average. But if you look at people who retrospectively did very well last year, they will have a very high historical standard to match.

Dennis Mueller: I've been engaged in this debate on and off for several years now and it's the first time I've actually gotten people from the protakeovers side to pay any attention to what happens before the announcements. This time period by and large has been ignored in this literature. I think it *is* one that's fascinating, and the different interpretations of this period have to be resolved. Presumably, firms make a lot of announcements over the 33, 43, 63

months that precede the announcements of acquisitions, and these announcements don't seem to change the upward trend in the residuals. Why isn't it a reasonable null hypothesis to assume that *this* announcement of the acquisition really isn't much news at all and that things would continue to go upward further and further afterward?

M. Jensen: There's another way to put my basic point for those who are baseball fans. When I was much younger, I heard about something called the "sophomore slump." You get to the big leagues because you had an exceptionally good year in general, and if you look how the rookies do in their sophomore year, they, on average, don't do as well as they did the first year. It's a simple selection bias problem, but it's made complicated by the nature of the particular problem we're looking at. And I think what you have done has been an important contribution. What I'm saying, though, is that there's one major point that calls into question the conclusions you make. The benchmark is zero, not the premerger performance. And it applies to the accounting data used by the other researchers just as well.

Wolf Weinhold: I'd like to extend Michael's point about what we're looking for. It seems to me that we need to understand how the takeover process occurs and how prices are set. My experience has been that managers do not ask the question, "What can you buy it [the acquisition company] for?" Rather, they ask the question, "How much can we afford to pay?" It's exactly the same question that each of us ask when we buy a house. It's not "How much is the house worth?" but "What is the monthly payment?" What we do is figure out what monthly payment we can afford and from that we scale up to the price we can pay for the house. Contained within that decision are some interesting points. What happens if we guess wrong on how much we can afford to pay. i.e., what our monthly payments are going to be? Or what happens if we guess wrong about interest rates in the future? If we guess right, we can afford the house we have purchased, i.e., the expected outcome, after the fact, is zero. If we guess wrong about how much we can afford to pay, we have to sell, i.e., we end up with a great big loss—or what we have been calling "management hubris." Maybe we should expect some hubris—that's how people get into the big leagues. What we find in the takeover events is a very simple feedback mechanism. Those who have done well, continue to have chances at more deals; yet the nature of the takeover mechanism is to extract all the value out of the buyer so that you end up with zero excess returns. Those who *can't* deliver end up with major losses. I don't think there's anything unusual about the events that we're looking at. We have bidders bidding on the basis of what they think they can do. Some can perform and some can't. That performance or nonperformance results in a bimodal distribution of *ex post* measurements—lots of measurements around zero and some major disasters. You shouldn't expect to find anything else in a reasonably efficient market atmosphere.

William Kenneth Jones: If I try to assimilate the findings of the three studies that take a negative view of the postacquisition period, two points seem to emerge. First, in the process of bidding for the acquired company, the acquiring company may find that it paid too much. Second, the acquiring company may have been excessively optimistic in its view about how well it would be able to manage the assets of the acquired company. My problem is this: How do I distinguish that phenomenon from entrepreneurship generally? My understanding is that most people in both large and small firms rather consistently underestimate the difficulties that they confront, so the failure rate is very high. Now, my problem is this: The assumption is that the general negative appraisal of post-takeover activity suggests that this is not socially useful behavior on balance. If *that's* true, then how does one justify entrepreneurship? After all, the failure rate for new businesses is much higher than the failure rate associated with takeovers. Anybody taking a sample population of new

entrepreneurs and weighing the gains and the losses will come out with a negative conclusion.

F. M. Scherer: The first thing I want to say in response is that the companies being acquired are almost always companies that have gone through this period of infancy when the mortality rate is very high. Studies show that after a few years, the mortality rate drops off sharply.

W. K. Jones: I accept the proposition *arguendo* that the takeover movement, on balance, yields negative results. On balance, the takeover movement leaves us worse off than we would have been had there been no takeovers. But I'm not sure where that leads, because I believe that, on balance, entrepreneurship leads to a negative result in the sense that the losses of the losers are more than the gains of the winners. Business is very risky.

F. M. Scherer: Schumpeter said that spectacular gains to a few drive the efforts of the thousands who gain nothing or less than nothing.

W. K. Jones: I think we discount the entrepreneurial losses of the new business on the theory that these are private losses. If people want to engage in risky activities and lose their life savings by trying to do more than they can, those are private losses, but society as a whole gains because there are winners. And those winners provide something of social value. Why doesn't the same hold true here? Are the losses private losses? It seems to me that they are private losses unless either the transaction costs are very high and are borne by persons other than the losers, or the agency costs that are involved in this process are such as to somehow transform private losses into public losses. I don't think either of those conditions holds but I think that those are the two lines along which we should proceed, accepting your negative empirical results.

F. M. Scherer: Again, you pose a difficult counterfactual condition. What you're saying is that there is a *peculiar* form of entre-preneurship known as acquisition entre-preneurship. And if I understand your statement of our analysis, that entrepreneurship on average produces negative results. Maybe one should say, then, that some sorts of entrepreneurships ought to be discouraged, at which point I get upset because of both a policy problem and a counterfactual problem. The policy problem is, What are you going to do if a guy *wants* to sell his business and see it managed *worse* by somebody else?

W. K. Jones: Let him sell it.

F. M. Scherer: I'm reluctant to interfere in that process. However, the reason we're here is that there are some who don't want to sell their businesses, but there are some buyers who want to buy them. If, on average, it turns out those buyers really don't manage the businesses any better—and maybe manage them *worse* than the people who don't want to sell—then maybe there *are* some important policy implications. The tough problem that remains is: Here's this guy who's willing to sell his business voluntarily to somebody who's going to manage it arguably worse. What's the

counterfactual condition? Suppose the would-be seller wasn't able to sell the business but somehow had to find another way to keep the business going independently. How would that business do independently? And that's a really tough one. You try to solve it, but you never can perfectly.

L. Lowenstein: Ken, maybe the answer in part depends on whether you're looking at the negotiated acquisition market, which obviously in large part Mike was looking at, or whether you focus in particular on the hostile takeover market. I don't know that anyone is suggesting as a result of the studies presented here that we outlaw mergers and acquisitions. But the takeover game may be different. It's not a classical market. One doesn't have buyers and sellers negotiating on equal terms. It resembles in some respects a prisoner's dilemma, and we see factors such as greenmail at work, so that often the people who are putting the companies in play do not really want to buy. If all that's so, then the process, the rules by which the game is being played, is open to examination, even though one might not want ro reexamine negotiated transactions.

MERGERS AND TAKEOVERS:
TAXES, CAPITAL STRUCTURE, AND
THE INCENTIVES OF MANAGERS

18

Taxation and the Dynamics of Corporate Control: The Uncertain Case for Tax-Motivated Acquisitions

RONALD J. GILSON
MYRON S. SCHOLES
MARK A. WOLFSON

The claim that the tax system favors acquisitions has been a familiar and important element of the long-standing public policy debate concerning the social value of corporate acquisitions.[1] Indeed, the claim, if accurate, is treated as something of a showstopper—there seems to be little dispute over the proposition that tax-motivated acquisitions have no social value.[2] Despite its prominence, however, the accuracy of the claim has remained difficult to assess, in large measure because precisely what is meant by the statement that the tax system favors acquisitions has never been clear. The first step in such an assessment, then, is to specify just what *tax favoritism* means in this context.

Three quite different meanings can be ascribed to the statement, each of which reflects a different belief about the importance of the tax system in determining the level of acquisition activity. The first sense in which the tax system might favor acquisitions, and the least powerful claim with respect to taxes as a determinant of acquisition activity, is that acquisitions can result in pure "tax gains," i.e., an increase in after-tax cash flows from the combination of assets without any change in pretax cash

We appreciate the comments of Martin Ginsburg, Richard Ruback, Elliott Weiss, and the participants at the Conference on Takeovers and Contests for Corporate Control, as well as those of colleagues at the Stanford Law School and Stanford Graduate School of Business.

flows.[3] The most familiar example of this meaning of favoritism is the claim that a taxable acquisition can step up the basis of the target company's assets, thereby increasing the depreciation deductions associated with the assets and, as a result, the associated cash flow (by decreasing the taxable income and ultimately the tax). The second meaning of tax favoritism, which reflects a stronger claim concerning the importance of taxes to acquisition activity, is that the tax gain in question is best achieved by an acquisition as opposed to the next best alternative. The third meaning of tax favoritism, which makes the strong claim that taxes are the principal determinant of the level of acquisition activity, is that tax gains explain the size of premiums observed in acquisitions—that tax gains explain the pricing of the transaction.

Although each of these concepts of tax favoritism has been featured in the debate, the conditions necessary to establish their verity have not been clearly delineated. Consider, first, the tax-gain concept of favoritism. Returning to the example just discussed, a step-up in basis as a result of an acquisition is not alone sufficient to demonstrate the presence of a tax gain. Although the acquiring company can achieve a step-up in the basis of the target company's assets by an acquisition, the target company may pay for that step-up through a shareholder-level capital gains tax (and by a corporate level tax after the Tax Reform Act of 1986 [the 1986 Act]), and one or the other company may incur a recapture tax. Moreover, the value of the step-up in basis to the acquiring company will be a function of how much of that basis is allocated to depreciable, depletable, or amortizable assets, the useful life of those assets and the related amortization schedule, expected future tax rates, and the discount rate applied to the tax savings resulting from increased depreciation in the future. In short, the existence of a tax gain must be determined on an *equilibrium* basis, netting out the target's costs against the acquiring company's gains, because the explicit tax costs to the target will be reflected as an implicit tax[4] to the acquiring company through the price of the acquisition.

Even if a tax gain can be demonstrated on an equilibrium basis, an additional condition must be satisfied before that gain actually can be realized. Any tax gain that would result from an acquisition must be reduced by the transaction and information costs associated with effecting the acquisition. And here we have in mind more than just the legal and investment banking fees, however substantial, associated with making the deal. Additionally, and more significantly, there are substantial costs to becoming informed[5] that result in information asymmetries and create the potential for problems of moral hazard and adverse selection. For there to be a net tax gain as a result of an acquisition, the tax gain must exceed the transaction and information costs associated with the combination.

A similar problem of specification is present with respect to the conditions necessary to satisfy the stronger tax favoritism claim that an available tax gain can better be achieved by an acquisition than by the next best alternative. Here the problem is that too often the discussion assumes that an acquisition is a unique solution—that it is the *only* method by which the tax gain can be achieved. This unyielding focus on acquisitions may be explainable; if the tax professionals are brought into the transaction only after the principals have determined that an acquisition will take place,

then it is understandable that the professionals view the optimization problem as maximizing the tax gains available by means of an acquisition rather than considering other, perhaps nontransactional, means of achieving the tax gain. For example, a step-up in basis might be better achieved by a sale and leaseback or by a sale of less than all of the target company's assets, because fewer information and incentive problems are associated with these methods of achieving the tax gain, or simply because tax disadvantages result from the sale of a subset of seller's assets. In short, acquisitions must be compared with a broader range of alternatives to demonstrate their dominance as a means of achieving tax gains.

The conditions necessary to establish the strongest claim of tax favoritism—that tax gains explain the size of premiums paid in acquisitions—are the most difficult of all to demonstrate. For tax benefits to result in a premium, they must be unanticipated. Otherwise, they already would have been incorporated into the price of the target company's shares. And much of the data required to calculate the potential for tax gains from acquiring a company are freely available from public information sources concerning the company; thus, information costs may not be a major barrier to anticipation. To be sure, even anticipated tax gains might be discounted to reflect the likelihood and expected timing of an acquisition,[6] so that some announcement effect would result, but the problem of explaining the magnitude of observable premiums remains.

In this chapter we build an analytic framework with which to answer the questions concerning the tax motivation for acquisitions, and then we apply it to the three most commonly identified sources of tax gains from acquisitions during the period prior to the passage of the 1986 Act: the change in asset basis available through taxable acquisitions; the faster use of net operating losses available through nontaxable acquisitions; and the tax deduction for interest available for interest paid on funds borrowed to finance acquisitions. We emphasize these three sources of tax gains both because of their large potential effect and because of their prominence in the policy debate. The framework, however, extends easily to the analysis of other extant or proposed tax rules, whether or not acquisition-related.

The framework stresses two central points. The first is that there are many substitutes for acquisitions as a means of garnering tax gains; acquisitions are but one of a broad class of alternatives. Any analysis that singles out for attention only acquisitions and ignores these alternatives misses entirely the real issue. To understand the economic consequences of tax-motivated acquisitions, the analyst must focus on the reasons why an acquisition is chosen as the most efficient of the alternative ways to achieve the tax gains. And here we emphasize that while many competing tax-planning alternatives are imperfect substitutes along the tax dimension, the same is true along nontax dimensions. Hence, efficient tax planning does not coincide necessarily with tax minimization.

The framework's second point is that analysis of acquisitions and its alternatives with respect to change in tax basis of assets, utilization of net operating losses, or creation of interest deductions requires inclusion of implicit taxes as well as explicit taxes. Those investments offering investors lower explicit taxes, such as municipal bonds, common stock, or real estate, when compared with less favorably taxed investments, such as ordinary bonds, also offer investors lower risk-adjusted, before-tax returns. If not paid *explicitly,* the tax is paid *implicitly* through realization of lower before-tax returns. For purposes of selecting the most efficient way to structure a transaction, both forms of taxation must be taken into account.

To isolate the role of tax rules alone, we begin consideration of each of the three sources of tax gains by examining acquisitions and the related alternatives in a perfect-market setting in which there are no transaction costs, asset divisibility costs, or information costs associated with adverse-selection or moral hazard problems. The analysis demonstrates that under these conditions, the alternatives weakly dominate acquisitions as a way to achieve each of the three sources of tax gains. In all cases, the same tax gains available through acquisitions can be achieved in alternative ways, and in some cases, the alternatives avoid certain tax costs associated with acquisitions. The principal alternative to effect a change in basis is selective asset sales without liquidation. The principal alternative to net operating loss transfer through acquisition is for the firm to change its asset and liability structure to generate current taxable income to reduce the delay in eliminating its net operating loss. The principal alternative to increase interest deductions is for the corporation to borrow for nonacquisition purposes, such as repurchasing its own stock. The opportunity to increase leverage is not unique to acquisitions.

This analysis shows that the claim that the pre-1986 Act tax system favors acquisitions—that acquisitions dominate alternative means to achieve the same tax gains—is false in a perfect-market setting. Thus, if acquisitions were dominant in the real world (and we are not convinced that they were, empirically), it was not because of acquisition-specific tax rules but because they have an advantage in reducing transaction and information costs that exceed their disadvantage in achieving tax gains. Our discussion of each of the three sources of tax gains then proceeds by introducing transaction and information costs into the comparative analysis of acquisitions and the alternatives. We find that, in certain situations, these costs reinforce the results observed in a perfect market: The alternatives are less costly and provide greater tax gains than acquisitions. In other situations, however, acquisitions display a comparative advantage at reducing transaction and information costs, such as those relating to asset indivisibilities, to offset their lesser tax benefits. Finally, in some situations these costs exceed the tax gains from either acquisitions or any other tax-planning alternative, thereby transforming the potential tax gain into a mirage. Empirically, we observe that far less than all potential tax gains are achieved, thus providing support for our conclusion that transaction and information costs are pervasive and have first-order effects on the choice among alternative ways to achieve tax gains, including the choice of "standing pat," rationally leaving apparent gains on the table.

Our analysis of the importance of transaction and information costs in analyzing tax gains from acquisitions and alternative transactions also has an interesting policy dimension. We show that a tax subsidy to asset transfers, at least with respect to the change-in-basis rules, may be efficient rather than socially wasteful, as is commonly argued. Our analysis suggests that in a setting of imperfect information, such subsidies may operate to mitigate the problem of underinvestment in a search for enhanced operating efficiencies.

Our purpose in this chapter is to establish a framework through which the debate over the role of taxation in the dynamics of corporate control can be resolved. Although we cannot canvas here every transactional permutation that might have been considered by the tax planner or organization designer in the pre-1986 period, the framework developed provides a means to evaluate, on a consistent basis, the myriad forms in which transactions can be cast and tax gains achieved.

SOURCES OF POTENTIAL TAX GAINS: CHANGE IN ASSET BASIS FROM A TAXABLE ACQUISITION

Analysis in a Perfect-Market Setting

Assessing the claims that acquisitions can result in tax gains by changing the basis of the target company's assets, and that acquisitions are the best way to achieve those gains, is complicated by the presence of transaction and information costs. Potential tax gains may not be realizable at all if these costs are high enough. Similarly, alternative ways to realize the potential tax gains may differ not only in their tax treatment but also in the transaction and information costs associated with them. So, for example, the sale of an entire company and the sale of just that company's depreciated assets might be equivalent in the extent to which each succeeds in realizing the tax gains from a step-up in basis (although this is not generally the case, as later analysis indicates), but the sale of depreciated assets alone also might impose transaction costs, such as the loss of operating efficiencies and removal costs, not imposed by an acquisition. In order to separate the influence of tax factors from that of transaction and information costs, we first assess the two claims in a world of perfect markets where, by definition, there are no transaction and information costs and no operating efficiencies from acquisitions. We then consider the impact of moving to the real world, where transaction costs are large and information asymmetries pervasive, on the comparative value of acquisitions as a means of realizing tax gains.

In a world of perfect markets, there are no costs to negotiating transactions, no informational asymmetries that interfere with pricing transactions, and no costs of physically removing assets from their location in the hands of the seller and transporting them to where they will be used by the buyer. Additionally, there are no indivisibilities with regard to the assets employed by any company. That is, the market value of the entire company is simply the sum of the market value of its parts; the company can sell an asset or a division without affecting the operations or the value of the company's remaining assets.

This world, of course, is a fantasy. As George Stigler has put it: "If this [world] strikes you as incredible on first hearing, join the club. The world of zero transaction costs turns out to be as strange as the physical world would be with zero friction."[7] Moreover, if perfect markets existed, our current tax rules probably would not; their design and many of the problems to which they respond are the product of our imperfect world. Nonetheless, consideration of the perfect-market setting does provide a foundation on which we can build an analysis of the extent to which potential tax gains can be achieved at all and the comparative advantage of alternative means of achieving tax gains in the real world. It also allows evaluation of the role of market frictions in determining the extent to which the quest for tax gains leads to acquisition activity.

The Weakest Claim: The Potential for a Tax Gain

Prior to the 1986 Act, the potential for a tax gain from a taxable acquisition resulted primarily from two factors: an increase in the basis of the target company's assets and a decrease in the time period over which that basis is depreciated for tax purposes.[8] The acquiring company's basis in the assets it acquired in an acquisition was its cost—the portion of the acquisition price allocated to the assets in question. If that cost exceeded the target company's basis in the assets, and if the assets were depreciable, depletable or amortizable, the acquiring company's higher basis would yield larger tax deductions after the acquisition than before. This relation between the acquiring company's cost and the target company's basis is a common occurrence, especially in periods following unanticipated inflation, because allowable tax depreciation is typically faster than nominal economic depreciation. Moreover, tax depreciation allowances are sufficiently generous that the necessary conditions for a step-up in basis and increased depreciation deductions following an acquisition—that an asset's market value exceeds its tax basis—can exist even if the market value of the target company's assets have not increased relative to expectation.

The increased deductions, however, are not immediately available to the acquiring company; they are spread over the useful life of the assets. The present value of the increased deductions then depends on the discount rate and the rate at which the deductions are permitted to be amortized over the assets' useful life. This led to the second factor contributing to the potential for a tax gain from a step-up in basis in a taxable acquisition. Assets acquired after the passage of the Economic Recovery Tax Act of 1981[9] (ERTA) can be depreciated under the Accelerated Cost Recovery System (ACRS), which dramatically shortened the depreciation period for most assets. Because ACRS is available for used as well as new assets, an acquisition may serve to shorten the period over which depreciation deductions can be taken for assets that were in place prior to 1981.[10]

These two factors—increased depreciation over a shorter period—are not, however, enough to establish the potential for a tax gain from an acquisition. From the perspective of the acquiring company, the benefits of increased, faster depreciation are unremarkable. Except in the case of a nonrecognition transaction, anyone purchasing an asset obtains a cost basis for depreciation purposes and, after 1981, may make use of ACRS, whether the asset is acquired in a corporate acquisition or not. Thus, the impetus to use an acquisition to capture the tax gains from a step-up in basis must have come from the seller. If the asset could generate greater after-tax cash flow in the hands of a buyer, the current holder of the asset would sell it if the price received was greater than the present value of the asset's cash flow in the current holder's hands, i.e., if the seller shares in the after-tax cash flow increase resulting from the transfer. Thus, calculation of the potential for a tax gain from an acquisition must be on an equilibrium basis: Tax costs that the transaction imposes on the target company must also be taken into account.[11]

These costs can be significant. First, the target company (or its shareholders) would likely incur immediate capital gains taxes.[12] This tax liability alone would not eliminate the potential of an equilibrium tax gain from the acquisition; during the pre-1986 Act period, each dollar of increased depreciation deduction resulting from the acquisition was worth 46¢ (assuming a maximum corporate tax rate of 46%), but the cost was only a 20¢ capital gains tax (assuming a maximum capital gains tax of 20% at the shareholder level).[13] If, however, depreciation recapture is imposed under Internal Revenue Code (IRC) Sections 1245 or 1250, the tax cost of achieving the higher basis was to that extent increased to ordinary income rates. Indeed, in the extreme case where all gains were subject to recapture, there would be an equilibrium tax *loss* from the acquisition because the recapture tax would be due immediately, but the higher depreciation deductions would be available only over the depreciation period specified under ACRS.[14] Second, any investment tax credit (ITC) taken in connection with the assets disposed of in the acquisition might have been recaptured without offsetting ITC benefits for the buyer.[15]

An example illustrates the trade-offs just discussed. Assume that the acquisition will result in (1) a $100 increase in basis, 90% of which is allocable to depreciable assets; (2) a useful life of the target company's depreciable assets of five years and straight-line depreciation; (3) a $120 gain to the target company's shareholders,[16] 15% of which is subject to recapture at the corporate level; (4) a shareholder capital gains tax rate of 20% (versus 0% in present-value terms if this gain were deferred) and an ordinary corporate income tax rate on recapture and other income of 46%; and (5) an after-tax discount rate of 8%. The calculation of the equilibrium tax gain is shown in the table below.

The point of the illustration is not that an equilibrium tax gain is always possible from an acquisition. For example, increasing the useful life of the asset in the example from five years to ten years will reduce the annual depreciation charge to $9.00, the after-tax value to $4.14, and the present value of the tax benefit to $27.78, with the result that the outcome of the transaction changes from an equilibrium tax gain to a relatively large equilibrium tax loss. Rather, it demonstrates how weak the claim about the relation between taxes and the level of acquisition activity really is. At

most, the illustration shows that in some circumstances the sale of an asset could have resulted in a tax gain. As yet, nothing has been offered to explain why that tax gain would have been best achieved by an acquisition as opposed to other means of stepping up basis. Now we will consider the second, and stronger claim for tax-motivated acquisitions: that acquisitions were the best way of capturing the potential for tax gains from asset transfers.

The Intermediate Claim: Acquisitions as the Best Way to Capture Tax Gains

The primary alternative to sale of the company as a means of achieving a step-up in basis is sale of particular assets. We will show that, given perfect markets, an acquisition was not uniformly the best means to realize a potential tax gain. In fact, conditions exist under which asset sales were the equivalent of acquisitions, under which asset sales dominated acquisitions, and under which the dominant strategy would have been to forgo the potential tax gain and not transfer the asset at all. Our analysis will concentrate on the period from 1980 to the 1986 Act. Although tracing the tax treatment of corporate acquisitions and their alternatives since the adoption of the Sixteenth Amendment in 1913 would be interesting, that is a much larger undertaking than is possible here. Moreover, the 1980–1986 period is of special interest. During this period, we have seen a quantum leap in the dollar volume of acquisitions relative to any other period in our history. Additionally, this period has been

	Benefit of Increased Depreciation Deductions		Cost to Achieve the Step-up in Basis
Increase in depreciable basis	$90.00	Shareholder-level capital gain tax on $120 gain	$24.00
Annual depreciation charge	$18.00	Corporate-level ordinary income tax on 15% of $120 gain	$ 8.28
After-tax value	$8.28		
Present value	$33.06	Total tax	$32.38
	Equilibrium tax gain = $0.78		

affected by important changes in the relevant tax law, especially those resulting from ERTA, the Tax Equity and Fiscal Responsibility Act (TEFRA), the Tax Reform Act (TRA) of 1976, and that of 1984. Thus, the impact of taxation on the level of acquisition activity may be more readily observable during this period.

We begin our analysis with the assumption that a company has only a single depreciable asset, thereby putting aside for the moment the complication that in an acquisition a multiasset firm must sell all of its assets to a single buyer. Suppose that the company is formed at time 0, with shareholders contributing an amount A_0, which is used to acquire an asset. Thus, at time 0, the market value of the company, the market value of its single asset, the company's tax basis in the asset, and the shareholders' basis in their stock all equal A_0.

The potential for a tax gain from a step-up in basis arises one period later, at time 1, by which time the company has used its asset to earn income. At time 1, the company has cash in the amount C_1 equal to the pretax operating cash flow O_1 earned from the business, less the related corporate income tax O_1tc, plus the tax shield provided by the depreciation taken during the period, D_1tc; thus, $C_1 = O_1(1 - tc) + D_1tc$. At time 1, the shareholders' tax basis remains A_0, and the company's tax basis in its depreciable asset becomes $A_0 - D_1$. The market value of the asset, however, is A_1, which may differ from the company's basis for a variety of reasons. This market value will reflect the value of a step-up (or step-down) in basis resulting from the transfer of the company's asset.

We now consider under pre-1986 Act rules which method of achieving the potential tax gain from a step-up in basis—an acquisition or an asset sale—is most attractive to this company in three different cases, each representing a different relation among A_1, C_1, and A_0. In our first pass at the three cases, we simplify the analysis by assuming that the installment sale method of reporting gains from either form of transaction is not available. We then enrich the analysis in a second pass by treating the installment sale as an available alternative.

No Installment Sale—Single Asset

CASE I: $A_1 < A_0 < D_1$. Assume the market value of the asset at time 1 is less than the company's basis. In an asset sale, the company recognizes an immediate ordinary loss under Section 1231 of $(A_0 - D_1)$ $- A_1$ with a value of $T_1 = [(A_0 - D_1) - A_1]tc$.[17] The potential tax gain from the transaction results from the fact that the value of an immediate ordinary income deduction will exceed the cost of the reduced depreciation deductions because the depreciation deductions are available only some time in the future, and thus, their reduction must be discounted to present value.[18]

In this case, an asset sale weakly dominated an acquisition as a means of realizing this tax gain. If $C_1 + A_1 + T_1 > A_0$, that is, if the market value of the company, including the tax benefit of the corporate write-off from disposition of the depreciable asset, was greater than the shareholders' tax basis because of company earnings between times 0 and 1, the shareholders would incur a capital gains tax as a result of an acquisition that, in an asset sale, was deferred.[19]

CASE II: $A_0 - D_1 < A_1 < A_0$. Now assume that the market value of the asset is less than its cost but greater than its depreciated basis. In this case, no tax gain is possible from a step-up in basis, and hence, there is no tax incentive to sell either the asset or the company. If the asset is sold, the step-up in basis is equal to $A_1 - (A_0 - D_1)$. The cost of this step-up is the recognition of gain by the company in an identical amount, but since $A_0 > A_1$, all of that gain would have been recaptured and taxed as ordinary income under Section 1245.[20] Under these assumptions, the transaction results in a tax *loss* because ordinary income tax would have been incurred immediately, and the increased depreciation, which would shelter an equivalent amount of income, would be of value only in the future.[21] The analysis is identical with respect to an acquisition except that, as in case I, there was a possibility that the company's earnings would have resulted in a capital gains tax at the shareholder level that would have been deferred in an asset sale. Thus, an asset sale again weakly dominates an acquisition, but the more important point is that there is no incentive to transfer the asset by any technique.

The case is more complicated if the asset is not subject to recapture. Assume that the asset is nonresidential real property placed in service after 1980, where depreciation has been taken on a straight-line basis so that there is no recapture under either Section 1245 or 1250.[22] Then the existence of a tax gain would depend on (1) the portion of the step-up, $A_1 - A_0 + D_1$, that is allocated to depreciable improvements as opposed to the nondepreciable land; (2) the schedule governing how the step-up can be depreciated; (3) the interest rate; and (4) the difference between capital gains and ordinary income rates. We will have more to say about this later. The numerical example presented in the introductory section illustrated some of the relevant trade-offs.

CASE III: $A_0 < A_1$. In this case, the value of the asset has appreciated despite physical depreciation. Analysis of the trade-off between, on the one hand, corporate-level capital gains under Section 1231 plus ordinary income from recapture and, on the other hand, the present value of the increased depreciation deductions from a step-up in basis should be familiar by now. What changes in this case, however, is the potential under pre-1986 Act rules for avoiding a double tax on the asset's appreciation—a tax at the corporate level when the asset was sold and again at the shareholder level when the shares were eventually sold—if the transaction was cast as an acquisition rather than as an asset sale. The trade-off required in evaluating the desirability of avoiding a corporate-level capital gains tax is that the shareholder-level capital gains tax was accelerated. This acceleration applied not only to the gain on the depreciated asset for which there was a desired step-up in basis but also to the entire accumulated increase in the market

value of the corporation above the shareholder's basis of A_0 (e.g., as a result of accumulated earnings or an increase in the value of nondepreciable assets). This trade-off would be difficult to calculate on an aggregate basis because it would depend on how many shares were held by tax-exempt entities such as pension funds, how long shareholders would hold their shares in the absence of a corporate acquisition or liquidation, and how many shareholders would die prior to a taxable event taking place, thereby eliminating entirely the shareholder-level capital gains tax through a tax-free step-up in basis at death.[23] In any event, an asset sale did entail double taxation—once at the corporate level when the asset was sold and potentially again at the shareholder level. This possibility did not exist in cases I and II because in those cases $A_1 < A_0$.

The opportunity to avoid a corporate-level capital gains tax in an acquisition prior to the 1986 Act set the stage for its potential dominance over an asset sale as a means of realizing the potential tax gain from a step-up in basis in the not uncommon case where the company and its asset had appreciated in value.[24] Even here, however, comparative analysis of the two techniques is complex. Where the company's accumulated earnings are significant relative to the appreciation in the value of the asset, the benefits of postponing shareholder tax in an asset sale may swamp the costs of corporate-level capital gains tax on the sale of the depreciable asset.

Installment Sale Available—Single Asset

To this point, the potential for tax gains from a step-up in basis has been largely a function of the trade-off between the cost of current capital gains and recapture tax versus the benefit of increased depreciation deductions in the future. As a result, the useful life of the asset and the discount rate used to determine the present value of the increased depreciation greatly influenced the outcome of the calculation. Expanding the transactional alternatives to include the possibility of an installment sale under Section 453 adds significantly to the tax-planning possibilities. Most important, installment sale treatment serves to defer payment of the capital gains tax and, prior to the Tax Reform Act of 1984, also served to defer recapture tax. The impact of deferral, by reducing or perhaps even reversing the timing difference between the payment of the tax cost (the capital gains and recapture tax) and the receipt of the tax benefit (the increased depreciation), increases the potential for a tax gain from asset transfers.

The critical characteristic of an installment sale is that at least one of the promised payments is made in a tax year following the year of sale. In that event, Section 453 allows the taxpayer to recognize the gross profit from the transaction (the total of principal payments to be received from the transaction[25] less the taxpayer's basis in the asset sold) over the years that payments are received. Each installment is allocated first to interest and then to principal. The principal amount of each installment payment received, divided by the total sales price, is multiplied by the gross profit on the sale and reported as gain; the balance of the principal payment is treated as a nontaxable return of basis. The length of the deferral, and hence the present value of the gains tax, is then a function of the period of time over which installment payments are made: The longer the "duration" of the installment note, the longer the deferral. For example, if a taxpayer facing a capital gains rate of 20% sells an asset with a basis of $150 for $200 cash, a tax of $10 is payable immediately. If, alternatively, the taxpayer receives $20 of principal payments per year for 10 years and elects installment sale treatment, so that the tax is paid $1 per year for 10 years, the present value of the tax payments, assuming a discount rate of 10%, is only $6.14, a savings of nearly 40%. If the annual principal payment is reduced to $10 and the period extended to 20 years, the present value of the tax declines further to $4.26, a tax savings of nearly 60% relative to ordinary sale treatment.

Prior to the Tax Reform Act of 1984,[26] the deferral available by use of the installment method was even more powerful. Not only could capital gain be deferred,

but amounts representing recapture under Sections 1245 and 1250, and therefore taxable as ordinary income, could also be deferred. Although the Treasury regulations required that the gain recognized in connection with each installment would be ordinary income until all recapture was recognized (rather than dividing the gains associated with each installment proportionately between recapture and capital gain), the value of the deferral remained powerful. The Tax Reform Act of 1984 amended Section 453(i) to alter this result. For contracts entered into after March 22, 1984, all recapture income was treated as if it were received in the year of sale, even if no actual payments were made; as a result, recapture income could no longer be deferred at all.

One might object to treating an installment sale as a fungible alternative to a cash sale on the ground that the seller's deferral of receipt of the proceeds decreases the risk-adjusted price. In a perfect market, however, any increase in risk will be offset by an increase in the interest rate on the installment obligation, so that the seller will be indifferent between receiving cash now or installment payments later. A third-party guarantee of the buyer's obligation under the installment sale does not even affect the seller's tax treatment.[27] Moreover, careful planning has permitted tax deferral where the installment obligation is pledged as collateral for loans.[28]

CASE I: $A_1 < A_0 - D_1$. When the market value of the asset is less than the corporation's basis in it, so that a sale of the asset results in a loss, its immediate recognition is desirable. Deferring recognition of a loss by an installment sale therefore had no attraction. Besides, the tax deferral option applied only to gains.

CASE II: $A_0 - D_1 < A_1 < A_0$. In Case II, the availability of installment sale treatment substantially alters the analysis. In the absence of deferral opportunities, sale of the asset or sale of the company resulted in a tax *loss* because all gain was recaptured as ordinary income at the time of sale, but the increased depreciation was of value only over the depreciable life of the asset. Before the Tax Reform Act of 1984, installment sale treatment could alter this result. If the installment payments were structured so that the recapture income was recognized more slowly than the increased depreciation deductions, a tax gain would result because of the impact of discounting. The interesting outcome is that the introduction of installment sale treatment shifts the result from one where the dominant result is never to transfer the asset to one where transfer would always be desirable with a suitably structured contract.

The availability of an installment sale does not alter the dominance of the asset sale as a means of achieving the increased potential for a tax gain; indeed, the advantage of an asset sale over an acquisition is strengthened. In the pre-1984 period, the use of an installment sale in connection with an acquisition, in contrast to an asset sale, could not defer recognition of recapture income, although an installment sale would allow shareholders to defer the tax on their capital gain.[29] Thus, an asset sale was preferable. After March 22, 1984, however, an installment sale did not defer recapture in either an asset sale or an acquisition, and our previous analysis of case ii is then unaffected by the existence of an installment sale opportunity.

CASE III: $A_0 < A_1$. The availability of an installment sale alters the analysis of Case III in the same two ways as in Case II. First, the ability to defer recognition of capital gains tax in either an asset sale or an acquisition simply increases the magnitude of the potential tax gain.[30] Second, in the pre-1984 period, the comparison between an asset sale and an acquisition is shifted in favor of an asset sale because of the ability to defer recognition of recapture through use of the installment sale. As we discussed, this deferral of taxes was not possible with an acquisition.

Multiple Assets

The effect of introducing multiple assets into the analysis is to increase the comparative advantage of asset sales over acquisitions as a means to have achieved potential tax gains in the pre-1986 Act period. For this purpose, the critical distinction

between an asset sale and an acquisition is that, by definition, the acquiring company in an acquisition must take *all* of the target company's assets whether or not it desires all of them. To be sure, in a perfect-market setting the acquiring company could always costlessly resell any undesirable assets, and we have assumed away any indivisibilities that would cause those assets to be worth less in the hands of a subsequent purchaser. There may, however, be tax costs to the initial acquisition and resale that could not be avoided even in a perfect market. Recall that in our single-asset analysis, Case II firms would wish to engage in neither an asset sale *nor* an acquisition in the absence of installment sale opportunities. The ability of a buyer in an asset sale to pick and choose among the assets to be acquired increases the buyer's opportunity set and, therefore, the attraction of an asset sale. The number of situations in which an acquisition would have been preferable to an asset sale, as when a firm's assets are predominantly those with characteristics described in Case III of our single-asset analysis (if installment sale treatment is not available), is reduced in a multiple-asset setting.[31]

Relaxing the Perfect-Market Assumption

When we relax the perfect-market assumption, the analysis becomes, predictably, much more complex. In the perfect-market setting, whether to transfer assets, and if so, how—acquisition or sale of assets— was determined entirely on the basis of the trade-off between tax costs and tax benefits. In the real world, however, nontax costs (which, for our purposes consist of two categories of information costs— moral hazard or hidden-action costs and adverse-selection or hidden-information costs[32]—and transaction costs generally) intrude on the trade-off. If these nontax costs are large relative to the potential tax gain from asset transfer, then the *net* gains from transferring an asset may be negative even though *tax* gains are possible. The result will be that some potential tax gains are left on the table. Thus, the validity of the weakest claim concerning the link between taxes and acquisition activity—that taxes create a net gain from an acquisition—is directly affected by introducing information and transaction costs. Furthermore, if the magnitude of these nontax costs vary depending on the technique used to achieve the potential tax gains, then analysis of the intermediate claim of a tax motivation for acquisitions—that they were the most effective way to achieve potential tax gains—is also affected.

Moral Hazard or Hidden-Action Problems

Consider first the impact of introducing moral hazard or hidden-action problems. A potential moral hazard problem exists in connection with any contractual relationship. In the simplest setting, when an agent is hired to perform specified services for a principal, the problem arises because the principal cannot perfectly and costlessly monitor the agent's performance. The agent knows this and takes the magnitude of the principal's information cost problems into account in his decision—e.g., how hard the agent really works is in part a function of how expensive it is for the principal to discover the agent's shirking.

The effect of moral hazard on the achievement of tax gains from acquisitions can be seen if we consider the situation of the sole owner of a business for whom it would have been optimal to sell the business to achieve a tax gain from a step-up in basis. Assuming that the pretransaction owner remains the most effective manager of the business (consistent with our continuing assumption that no operating efficiencies, such as a shift in control to a more efficient manager, are possible as a result of the transaction), the transfer of the business could have created a moral hazard problem because the pretransaction owner was thereby transformed from a principal to an agent. The new owner then bore a nontrivial portion of the risk of the residual cash flows of the business (else the transaction would be a sham) and the agent/pretransaction owner had a reduced incentive to manage the business efficiently. If the moral hazard–induced decrease in expected risk-adjusted cash flow resuting from the sale of the business ex-

ceeded the potential tax gain from a step-up in basis, then the transfer would not take place.[33] Thus, the weak claim concerning the relationship between taxes and acquisition activity can be dramatically affected by moral hazard: To allow some potential tax gains to go unrealized because of moral hazard–related costs would have been rational.

The intermediate claim—that acquisitions were the best way to achieve potential tax gains—is also affected by moral hazard problems. Here the point is that different techniques for achieving the step-up in basis result in differences in moral hazard–related costs. We have just seen that the sale of a business by its owner to achieve a tax gain from a step-up in basis may result in moral hazard costs owing to the agency relationship created between the manager and the new owner. Suppose, instead, that the step-up in basis was achieved by a sale and leaseback. At their high point, the safe-harbor leasing rules would have allowed a step-up in basis in a sale-and-leaseback transaction without the lessor bearing any residual risk of a change in the value of the assets.[34] Under present law, the lessor must bear some economic risk with respect to the assets, and to this extent a moral hazard problem is introduced;[35] however, the moral hazard problem is mitigated because the bulk of the residual profit risk remains with the original owner/lessee.

The reduction in moral hazard problems from a sale and leaseback may be offset by differences in tax treatment; sale-and-leaseback transactions were not perfect tax substitutes for acquisitions or asset sales. For example, assets placed in service prior to 1981 were not eligible for ACRS treatment following a sale and leaseback.[36] Thus, the best means of achieving a step-up in basis—and, indeed, of achieving a net gain from the step-up at all—depends in our example on the trade-off between tax gains and information costs. Moreover, a sale and leaseback is not the only form of transaction that can be seen as a lower–information cost alternative to an acquisition as a means to achieve tax gains. For example, although a management buy-out of a division or entire firm typically in- cludes a much broader range of assets than are generally thought to be candidates for a sale and leaseback, the buy-out responds to the same moral hazard problem. A care- fully structured management buy-out is in- tended at the very least to ensure that man- agement retains as strong an incentive to manage efficiently after the transaction as before; indeed, one might claim that the in- crease in the management's percentage ownership as a result of the transaction[37] mitigates the moral hazard problem, al- though this must be balanced against the cost of inefficient risk sharing that may be created by a management buy-out. Simi- larly, a "rollout" transaction—as, for ex- ample, when Mesa Petroleum spun off assets into a publicly traded limited part- nership run by pretransaction manage- ment—also can be understood as a lower– information cost alternative to achieving a step-up in basis by means of an acquisition.

Adverse-Selection or Hidden-Information Problems

An adverse-selection problem arises when- ever parties who seek to effect an economic exchange have asymmetric information concerning an attribute important to the transaction, and the cost of eliminating this asymmetry is high, thereby leading the better-informed party to take strategic ad- vantage of its superior knowledge. Sup- pose, as before, that the sole owner of a business is considering a sale to achieve the potential tax gains from a step-up in basis. While both the owner and prospective buyer may agree on the value of the poten- tial tax gain from a step-up in basis as a function of the price paid for the business, they may not be equally well informed about the future nontax cash flows that can be expected from operating the firm's as- sets. An adverse-selection problem arises if businesses that have similar observable characteristics to prospective buyers none- theless have different values that are known only to sellers; the correct value might be discerned by buyers only if eco- nomically excessive amounts are spent on investigation or signaling mechanisms.

The distortion in behavior that may re- sult is illustrated in the following example. Assume that high-value businesses have a value of $V_h = H + T$, where H is the value of the business exclusive of the potential tax gains from sale (and the value to be re- alized by the owner if no sale takes place) and T is the value of the tax gains condi- tional on a sale taking place; also assume that low-value businesses have a value of $V_l = L + T$, where L is the value of the business exclusive of the potential tax gains from sale and T is the value of the tax gains conditional on a sale taking place.[38] Further assume that prospective buyers as- sess a prior probability of any business being of high value of P_H and that $0 < T < (H - L)(1 - P_H)$; prospective sellers know whether the firm is of type H or L.

The buyer knows that if a price below H is offered, only type L firms will be at- tracted. But an offer of H is unprofitable, because it will return

$$-H + P_H V_h + (1 - P_H) V_l$$
$$= -H + P_H (V_h - V_l) + V_l$$
$$= -H + P_H (H - L) + L + T$$
$$= -(1 - P_H)(H - L) + T < 0$$

Hence, buyers will offer only price $L + T$ to attract type L firms, and type H firms will remain unsold. The result is that ad- verse selection—the inability to distin- guish high-value from low-value firms— prevents the potential tax gains from a transfer of high-value firms from being realized.

This result is altered, from a (trivially) separating to a pooling equilibrium, if the tax gains from the transaction are in- creased to a value in excess of $(H - L)(1 - P_H)$. Assuming that buyers are risk-neu- tral, the price offered B increases to

$$B = P_H V_h + (1 - P_H) V_l$$
$$= P_H (V_h - V_l) + V_l$$
$$= P_H (H - L) + L + T > H$$

At this price both high- and low-value firms are sold, because sellers of both types of firms realize an amount in excess of what they would realize without a sale, al- though type H firms still sell for an amount below V_h. Thus, there remain both distributional and allocational consequences to the inability to distinguish between high- and low-value firms. The distributional effect is a wealth transfer from owners of high-value firms to owners of low-value firms; the allocational effect is reduced incentives to create high-value firms, resulting in lower aggregate firm values than would be forthcoming in the absence of adverse selection.

Just as with moral hazard problems, the presence of the adverse-selection problem directly affects the weak claim that tax gains were possible from acquisitions: Some potential tax gains go unrealized because of information costs. Matters cannot be left here, however. The potential tax gains left on the table provide owners of high-value firms with a substantial incentive to signal—to reveal their type (high-value) to buyers in a way that cannot be imitated by low-value firms. This can lead, for example, to elaborate acquisition agreements containing detailed representations, warranties, indemnification, and contingent pricing agreed to by the seller as proof of value. Or it can lead to hiring experts (e.g., investment bankers or accountants) that specialize in investigative actions designed to remove some of the information asymmetries.[39] Adverse-selection problems can also lead to preferences for alternative means of achieving tax gains, even if the alternatives result in smaller tax gains. An example is the selective sale of those assets suffering least from adverse-selection problems, despite the common knowledge that further tax gains would have been available from the sale of *all* assets.

The potential for adverse selection to influence the manner in which tax gains are achieved, as well as whether they can be achieved at all, thus also affects the intermediate claim linking taxes and acquisition activity—that during the pre-1986 Act period, acquisitions were the best way of achieving tax gains from the transfer of an asset. As with moral hazard problems, the impact would be to favor low–information cost transactions, like sale-leasebacks, in situations where the adverse-selection-related costs are high[40] and acquisitions

where the adverse-selection costs are relatively unimportant and the costs of dividing up the assets of the firm are relatively high.

Transactions Costs

In a perfect-market setting (and with installment sales opportunities), asset sales dominated acquisitions because an asset sale allows the selective sale of only those assets that give rise to tax gains, but an acquisition limited the buyer's opportunity set by requiring that all the target firm's assets be transferred. When transaction costs are introduced, some of this advantage may be offset. First, piecemeal sales of assets impose removal costs—the costs of physically separating the assets purchased from other assets of the seller and transporting them to a new location—that are not incurred in an acquisition.[41] Second, as the number of transactions increases, so too can the total transaction costs; e.g., the number of contracts and the aggregate investigation and negotiation costs increase.[42] Finally, there may be divisibility costs associated with piecemeal asset sales—the firm may be worth more than the sum of the separate values of its assets because efficiencies associated with their combination cannot costlessly be duplicated outside the firm. If the sum of the transaction costs exceeds the potential tax gain from a step-up in basis, no transfer will occur; and the weak claim that the tax system motivates acquisitions will fail.

Depending on the particular transaction, the intermediate claim of tax motivation—that acquisitions were the best way to have achieved tax gains from a step-up in basis—also may fall short. While the presence of divisibility costs reduces the benefit of selective asset sales, acquisitions do not necessarily emerge as the desired vehicle to achieve tax gains; there remain other alternatives to an acquisition that also avoid divisibility costs. The comparison then shifts to the relative advantages of acquisitions as opposed, for example, to sale-leasebacks as a means to maximize tax gains in light of positive transaction costs. To be sure, the two techniques are not perfect tax substitutes,[43] but neither are they perfect substitutes along other relevant dimensions. Information costs can be significantly lower in a sale and leaseback simply because the transaction minimizes the transfer of rights to residual earnings. Hence, the intermediate claim that acquisitions best realized potential tax gains must be qualified considerably in a world in which information and transaction costs are important.

Relaxing the No-Operating-Efficiencies Assumption

To this point we have ignored what would seem to be the most fundamental motivation for transactions: to effect a productively more efficient allocation of property rights (i.e., to achieve operating efficiencies). The purpose of this narrow focus was to isolate the extent to which the pre-1986 Act tax system could have motivated socially wasteful transactions, i.e., asset transfers that require nontrivial resources to effect but have no purpose other than to capture tax gains. When we ignore enhanced operating efficiencies, restructurings that achieved tax gains resulted in deadweight transaction costs at best. At worst, they could result in reductions in productive efficiency up to the magnitude of the gross tax gains that motivated them. Once we acknowledge the possibility that acquisitions also may result in operating efficiencies (or inefficiencies), the social desirability of providing tax incentives for acquisitions becomes more complex.

Suppose we abandon our focus on tax motives for economic exchanges for the moment but acknowledge the existence of operating efficiencies in a setting of imperfect information. Suppose further that the identification of socially desirable operating efficiencies requires investment in costly information. Finally, suppose that competition for the right to garner operating efficiencies in a production environment in which firms face (imperfectly) correlated production opportunities results in a free-rider problem with respect to investment in costly search and that the result is an underinvestment in search relative to the social optimum. The source of the free-rider problem could be either target share-holders, as considered by Grossman and Hart,[44] or competing bidders for the right to control the assets of the target.[45]

One of the familiar roles of tax policy is to affect the propensity of economic units to engage in economic activities whose private values diverge from their social value. Surprisingly, this argument has never, to our knowledge, been applied to merger and acquisition activity. Rather, where the role of taxes has been considered, the open question has been not *whether* tax benefits available through such transactions result in socially wasteful activity but, rather, the *severity* of the tax-induced hemorrhaging.

We have already argued that corporate acquisitions were not unique in facilitating opportunities to exploit tax gains in the pre-1986 Act period, and that in a great many circumstances they were not even the most cost-effective way to exploit such gains. Focusing criticism on acquisition activity simply because it is more readily publicly observable seems both misdirected and shortsighted. But we wish to go a step further here. We find it intriguing to note that certain important tax benefits in an asset sale or an acquisition (e.g., a step-up in basis) have a value that is an increasing function of the price paid for such assets. Thus the most efficient purchaser of assets should also be able to secure privately some of the tax benefits (i.e., the next most efficient purchaser of the nontax benefits from control of the assets of a particular company will find the tax benefits to be less valuable as well). This association will serve to mitigate the free-rider problem and potentially improve social efficiency.

To summarize and conclude this section, in the pre-1986 Act period all asset transfers, not just corporate acquisitions, receive the "subsidy" of a step-up in basis on transfers. Thus, the transactional domain that should be considered in the social policy debate is considerably broader than simply corporate acquisitions; it is the subsidy for asset transfers generally that is implicated. Corporate acquisitions may or may not be appropriate objects of subsidy, but for our purposes, the end of the inquiry is not demonstrating the existence of the subsidy but assessing the value of the subsidized activity: Do acquisitions lead to efficiency gains? If the answer to that question is no, then the subsidy can be eliminated.[46] If the answer to that question is yes, only then do the real tax law issues arise. From this perspective, the various tax rules we have been discussing reflect at any time the strategic interaction of society's efforts to balance the efficiency gains from reallocation of assets against the deadweight losses resulting from aggressive exploitation of the subsidy by those taking advantage of tax rules that may be over inclusive in the transactions identified for subsidy.

Tax gains from asset transfers perhaps may be understood as a public subsidy that operated to facilitate efficient transactions that might not otherwise occur. Issues of tax policy do not disappear in this case; however, they do change character substantially. The central issues of tax policy are no longer whether the tax system motivates acquisitions but how to prevent the subsidy from being exploited in situations where it is not warranted. This type of analysis, of course, is among the most familiar in tax law, and tax policy concerning acquisitions no longer would present unique issues.

In the end, the case for tax-motivated acquisitions is uncertain because of two unanswered questions. The first, a question that, as we will see in the next section, is difficult to answer empirically, is whether and to what extent acquisitions do take place because of taxes: How many unicorns are there? The second question, which we do not discuss here but which is the subject of empirical study in a broad existing literature, is whether acquisitions result in efficiency gains.[47] Only after this question is answered can the follow-up "tax" questions be addressed: Are there too many or too few unicorns, and what should we do about it?

Evaluating the Strong Claim: Tax Gains as the Determinant of the Size of Acquisition Premiums

Under what conditions should the potential for tax gains result in acquisition premiums? As discussed earlier, the fact that tax gains can be achieved by an acquisition is not sufficient for a premium to result. If the market were aware of the potential for tax gains from an acquisition, those gains, as with any other sources of increase in expected future cash flows, would have been incorporated into the target company's stock price. For a premium to exist, the increase in cash flows it represents must be *unanticipated*.

One explanation for why a premium that reflected potential tax gains from an acquisition might not have been anticipated is that the acquiring company had unique information concerning the potential for tax gains from the target's acquisition (e.g., the tax basis of the target's assets, potential recapture amounts, and remaining depreciable life of the assets). In the unusual circumstance where the acquirer has discovered a new tax technology, as perhaps with the Esmark-Transocean transaction that led to the amendment of Section 311,[48] a tax-related premium may result, at least the first time the new technology is unveiled. But unless a technological change is present, the tax analysis underlying the potential for a tax gain from a step-up in basis (or from any of the other sources of potential tax gains that have been the center of active policy debate) is widely known.[49] Moreover, a good deal of the firm-specific information concerning the potential for a step-up in basis with respect to a particular target is available through publicly disclosed financial statements. If the costs and nontax benefits of combination (including operating efficiencies) are known, the market's lack of information about the potential for tax gains from an acquisition would appear to be a weak candidate for explaining why these gains would not be anticipated.

One explanation for an unanticipated tax-based premium that does not depend on the acquiring company possessing unique information concerning the potential for tax gains is poor target management. Suppose target management resisted relinquishing control to achieve a tax gain from selling the company. In that event, the premium associated with a successful offer that sought to achieve potential tax gains could be unanticipated, although what is unanticipated is not the potential for tax gains but that target management could be displaced. Even here, however, one must recognize that associating the entire premium with the takeover is inaccurate. Some portion of the tax gain might have been achieved by a technique that did not require a change in control (e.g., a sale and leaseback). Thus, the maximum potential *acquisition* premium in this case is only the difference between the tax gain achievable through an acquisition and the tax gain achievable through the most effective technique that does not require a change in control, multiplied by the probability that entrenched management can block a change in control.

Note that if the relevant issue is the link between tax gains and change in control, we must focus not on the total tax gains that result from an acquisition but on the acquisition premium, the increase in tax gains available from an acquisition over those available from the next best alternative that does not require a change in control. Unfortunately, this fact significantly complicates efforts to conduct empirical research because analysis of the next best alternative may require a considerable amount of company-specific information.

A rather different picture emerges when the explanation for unanticipated tax-induced premiums is based on the interaction of tax gains and firm-specific operating economies (or diseconomies) that are imperfectly known by the market, rather than on the market's lack of knowledge about the potential for tax gains. Assume that the market knows all of the relevant tax characteristics of the target's depreciable assets. As discussed in the previous section, the magnitude of tax gains achievable through an acquisition in the pre-1986 Act period would have been an increasing function of the target price (which determines the size of the step-up in basis), which, in turn, is a function of both the tax gains and the operating efficiencies resulting from the combination. Further assume that the potential for operating efficiencies—and therefore, tax gains—differs among acquiring companies. In this situation, the market would anticipate a tax gain based on expectations of the operating efficiencies associated with prospective acquirers. Search is then conducted by competing acquiring companies. If the target company is "discovered" by an acquiring company that possesses higher-than-anticipated operating efficiencies, the price offered and the associated tax gain may be higher than was anticipated by the market. A real premium, reflecting both unanticipated tax gains and unanticipated operating efficiencies, would then result.[50]

Although this analysis might explain an unanticipated premium in individual cases, it does not explain an unanticipated premium for all target companies or even a positive *average* premium across all successful acquisitions. Those cases where the acquiring company offered lower-than-anticipated operating efficiencies would offset those where the company offered higher-than-anticipated operating efficiencies, which could well cancel over the entire sample.

Still, we acknowlege that we *can* create examples in which, even in the absence of operating efficiencies, the potential tax gains from a step-up in basis available under pre-1986 Act rules are of a magnitude comparable to that of observable premiums;[51] however, we cannot offer satisfactory explanations for why much of this premium would not have been anticipated.

Empirical evidence that would facilitate an evaluation of the role of taxes in the dynamics of corporate control might include the following:

1. Estimates of the magnitude of potential tax gains from acquisition versus selective asset sales versus sale-leasebacks, etc.
2. Estimates of *ex post* operating efficiencies realized by combining firms (e.g., time-series analysis of performance measures).

Another point needs mention here. With a taxable acquisition prior to the 1986 Act, target shareholders who did not elect to use the installment sale method had to pay capital gain taxes. Empirical evidence by Robinson[52] indicates that premiums resulting from taxable acquisitions were approximately 10% higher than premiums resulting from nontaxable acquisitions. Obviously, if the tax benefits of change in basis are small relative to the tax costs to shareholders, a nontaxable reorganization might dominate a taxable reorganization. Although the usual self-selection problems contaminate the experimental design (tax-free reorganizations versus taxable acquisitions are rather unlikely to be selected randomly, to say the least), we are not surprised to see a differential premium, although the exact magnitude of the premium to be expected is uncertain. A premium is particularly likely when we consider the mix of shareholder tax characteristics (taxable versus tax-exempt and corporate versus individual), the possibility for installment sale treatment in an otherwise taxable acquisition, and the fact that shareholders may anticipate whether the transaction will be taxable or nontaxable. Another potential motive for nontaxable transactions will be discussed in the next section, namely, net operating losses of target companies.

SOURCES OF POTENTIAL TAX GAINS: TRANSFER OF NET OPERATING LOSS CARRYOVERS

The idea that the ability to transfer net operating loss carryovers (NOLs) by an acquisition can give rise to tax gains and that such gains are socially wasteful has an old and distinguished history. Professor Bittker reports a 1943 *New York Times* advertisement offering: "For sale. Stock of corporation having 1943 tax loss deduction $120,000. Sole assets are $80,000 in cash and equivalent."[53] In the same year Congress enacted IRC Section 269 providing for disallowance of deductions and benefits resulting from corporate acquisitions when the principal purpose of the acquisition was tax avoidance.[54] In this section we examine NOLs as a source of potential tax gains from acquisitions in the pre-1986 Act period. To an even greater extent than with respect to tax gains from a step-up in basis, information and transaction costs shape whether acquisitions or alternative techniques were the best way to realize the

value of NOLs in this period. Indeed, we will see that in a perfect-market setting the substitutes for acquisitions are sufficiently rich that they permit a company to utilize its NOLs fully and instantaneously at no cost, and hence, there would be no motivation for acquisitions.

The Concept: Tax Gains and Tax Restrictions

To begin, we set forth, at the outset, the traditional argument that there can be a tax gain from transferring NOLs by an acquisition and describe the pre-1986 Act tax law restrictions that constrained efforts to secure the gain. For there to be a tax gain from such a transfer, the NOLs must be worth more to the acquiring company than to the target company. The current value of a company's NOLs depends on several factors, including existing and anticipated future NOLs and tax rates, the likelihood that the company will earn sufficient income in future periods to make use of its NOLs, and discount factors to reflect the timing and the probabilities of *when* the NOLs might be used. Assume, for example, that a potential target company has fallen on hard times and has accumulated NOLs of $50,000. Further assume that there is only a 50% chance that the company will return to profitability so that the NOLs could be used. Ignoring for the moment the discount factor relating to *when* the NOLs would be used, the value of the NOLs to the company would be

$$\$50,000 \times 46\% \times 0.5 = \$11,500$$

In contrast, if an acquiring company is certain of at least $50,000 in earnings, the last term in the calculation becomes 1, and the value of the NOLs increases to $23,000.

The potential for a tax gain from the acquisition increases when timing considerations are taken into account. Assume that the loss company will break even for two years and faces a 50% chance of earning $50,000 or nothing only in the third year; the acquiring company is certain of having at least $50,000 in earnings to offset the NOLs immediately. If the loss company's operating and financing decisions are taken as fixed, the value of its NOLs must be reduced because they cannot possibly be used for three years. If an after-tax discount rate of 8% is used, the calculation of the value of the NOLs to the loss company becomes

$$\$50,000 \times 46\% \times 0.05 \times 0.79383$$
$$= \$9129$$

It is important to recognize that the tax gain from transferring NOLs by acquisition depends on whether the NOLs are available to reduce the postacquisition income of the acquiring company. For example, suppose that the tax law allowed the loss company's NOLs to survive an acquisition, but that the NOLs could only be used to offset the future earnings of the loss company's preacquisition business.[55] In this situation, no tax gains result from the acquisition. The probability and timing of income that could be offset by the NOLs remain precisely the same after the acquisition as before, *unless* one assumes that the acquiring company's management is more skillful at operations or will take other steps[56] to increase the loss company's near-term earnings. This, however, is simply a bad-management argument. If the NOLs are worth more to the acquiring company than to the loss company, because the acquiring company can improve the distribution of future earnings, a tax-motivated acquisition need not be socially wasteful. This is especially so if there is underinvestment by acquiring companies in search for such ineffectively managed NOL companies, owing to the free-rider problems alluded to in the section on step-up in tax basis.

Thus, if we ignore real operating efficiencies created by taking over NOL firms, the existence of an NOL *tax* gain is essentially a function of the ability of the acquiring company to use the transferred NOLs against its income. This use of NOLs, in turn, depends on the restrictions in the tax law. In fact, in a wide range of situations, tax law allowed this result, although not without costly restrictions. Under IRC Section 381, 23 tax attributes of a target company, including, most importantly, its net operating loss carryover,[57] passed to the

acquiring company in A and C reorganizations (under IRC Section 368, involving, respectively, mergers and purchases of substantially all of the target company's assets, in both cases achieved largely through the transfer of voting stock of the acquiring company). The target company's tax attributes also survived transfer following the liquidation of a controlled subsidiary under IRC Section 332, provided that the target's basis in its assets also survives the transfer. The most familiar example of the latter situation was the second step typically taken after a B reorganization (under IRC Section 368, involving an exchange offer), when the liquidation serves to freeze out the remaining minority shareholders. If the acquisition fell within Section 381, then the value to the acquiring company of the NOL in our example is $23,000, because the NOLs can be used completely and immediately.

Although we cannot survey here the application of the complex set of pre-1986 Act restrictions on the survival of NOLs in acquisitions, two general constraints capture the character of the limits. The first constraint on an acquiring company's ability to have used a loss company's NOLs to offset its own income was the requirement that it continue to operate, in one form or another, the loss company's preacquisition business. For an acquisition to qualify as a reorganization, and therefore to have fallen within Section 381, Treasury Regulation Section 1.368–1(b) requires "a continuity of the [loss company's] business enterprise."[58] To meet this standard, an acquiring company must either "(i) continue the [loss company's] historic business or (ii) use a significant portion of [the loss company's] historic business assets in a business."[59] The upshot was that the acquiring company could use the loss company's NOLs to offset income from other businesses, but at the price of continuing to run the very business which generated the loss in the first place. This result had the potential to reduce the value of the NOLs to the acquiring company if it required the continued investment in negative net present value projects.

The obligation to continue operation of

the loss company's business was not eliminated by altering the form in which the loss company was acquired. Although the restrictions of the continuity-of-business-enterprise doctrine under Section 368 could be avoided by an acquirer first purchasing the loss company's stock and then merging its profitable business into the loss company, Section 382(a) imposed a similar restriction. If more than 50% of the ownership of a company with NOLs changes hands in a year, the NOLs were lost unless the company's business was continued.[60]

The second constraint on the acquiring company's use of the loss company's NOLs was that the acquiring company give up any tax gain from a change in the loss company's basis in its assets that might otherwise have resulted from a taxable (to stockholders) acquisition. Under IRC Sections 362 and 332, the acquiring company retains a target company's basis in the assets acquired in any transaction covered by Section 381. Thus, in our example, any step-up in basis that would have resulted from the transaction had the acquiring company not sought to preserve the loss company's NOLs was lost.

Prior to the enactment of Section 338 in 1982, the ingenuity of tax planners had substantially weakened the constraint that, in an acquisition, either all or none of the target's tax attributes, like NOLs and asset basis, survived. A number of techniques had been developed to acquire assets that presented the potential for a tax gain from a step-up in basis in a taxable transaction, while the rest of the target, and its NOLs, were acquired in a second transaction falling within the terms of Section 381. Section 338 was intended to eliminate the opportunity "to have your cake and eat it too" by requiring an acquiring company, in effect, to elect between a step-up in basis and the survival of tax attributes, and then to treat all transactions between the acquiring and target companies consistently with that election.

In a perfect-market setting, this second constraint, even as buttressed by Section 338, was less significant than would first appear. Although the acquisition could not be used to step up the basis of the loss company's assets if its NOLs were to be acquired, our earlier analysis considered several effective alternatives to acquisitions as a means of stepping up asset basis. For example, the sale of individual assets will capture the gain, and this approach was available to an acquiring company on a postacquisition basis as long as the acquiring company did not sell so many assets that continuity of the loss company's business was not maintained; but even this limit evaporates if a sale and leaseback was used.

Both constraints could be weakened even further by reversing the standard transaction pattern of a profitable company acquiring a loss company. If the loss company was the acquirer, its tax attributes survived regardless of the terms of Section 381 because nothing had happened to alter its tax status. Although Section 269 would likely have applied to prevent a simple reversal of the surviving company in a merger, a debt-financed acquisition of a profitable company by a loss company (technically preventing a large change in ownership of the loss company's stock) likely was free of all restrictions, including the requirement that the loss company continue to operate its losing business. As we will observe, however, it is in these situations that the problems of strategic behavior and the resulting information-related costs are particularly severe. In addition, because interest deductions reduce the income available to offset the NOLs, debt financing may not be the cheapest form of financing for a loss company, unless the taxable profits being purchased are sufficiently large.

Thus, pre-1986 Act current tax rules governing the treatment of a loss company's NOLs following its acquisition did not eliminate the potential of securing a tax gain from a transfer of NOLs by acquisition.[61]

Acquisitions as the Best Way to Capture Tax Gains: The Intermediate Claim

Stated generically, the effect of an acquisition on the value of a target company's

NOLs is that it increases the likelihood of income against which to offset the NOLs. In a frictionless world, however, a company with NOLs but without the future income from its current business to use them has a broad range of alternatives that accomplish the identical result as an acquisition without selling the company and without the costly restrictions imposed by the pre-1986 Act Internal Revenue Code on acquiring a company with NOLs. In a frictionless world, these alternatives would allow a loss company to utilize its NOLs fully and immediately.

In this perfect-market setting, we assume that the returns to assets are such that tax-exempt assets bear an implicit tax at the full corporate tax rate. For example, if the maximum marginal tax rate on corporate income is 46% (as was the case prior to the 1986 Act), and fully taxable assets (e.g., corporate bonds) return a risk-adjusted rate of 10%, then tax-exempt assets (e.g., land or municipal bonds) return a risk-adjusted rate of 5.4%.[62] Assume then that we observe a company whose operating decisions (which we take to be fixed) will give rise to $10 of NOLs at the end of the forthcoming period. In addition, the firm has $1000 in funds to be invested. If the company acquires $100 in taxable bonds and $900 in municipal bonds, it will earn $10 on the fully taxable bonds, thereby eliminating its NOLs, and $48.60 on the municipal bonds for a total after-tax return of $58.60. At the end of the year, the loss company's after-tax earnings on the $1000 investment would be $4.60 greater than those of a fully taxable company ($58.60 − $54.00). On the other hand, if a fully taxable company were to bid for the loss company, it would pay $4.60 (at the end of the period) for the NOLs (0.46×10) and then use the NOLs to offset its own taxable income. If the acquiring firm's offer was accepted, the shareholders of the loss company would earn $54.00 ($0.054 \times $1000) in addition to the bid of $4.60, or a total of $58.60, exactly the same as if they had adopted an internal investment strategy to use up their NOLs through the purchase of taxable bonds. In this equilibrium, it

makes no difference whether the loss company buys taxable bonds, buys a combination of taxable and municipal bonds with taxable bonds sufficient to use up its NOLs, or sells its NOLs to another fully taxable company through a merger.

With this structure of implicit taxes, a large set of nonacquisition alternatives is available for securing full value for the NOLs by rearranging the company's assets and liabilities. Unless the company generates sufficient income to use up its NOLs in the forthcoming period, it becomes a low–marginal tax rate taxpayer. Consider first the asset side of the balance sheet. Suppose that the loss company holds as assets either common stock or municipal bonds. Both of these assets are tax-favored. They bear low explicit taxes. As a result, their market prices are bid up to reflect their respective tax advantages. By holding an asset for which the marginal investor is in a high bracket, the low-bracket loss company is in the wrong tax clientele. The implicit tax is then too high relative to the explicit tax that can be paid on tax-disfavored assets—those with returns that are taxed at full rates—such as taxable bonds. For NOL companies, selling tax-favored assets and purchasing tax-disfavored assets reduces the total (implicit plus explicit) tax burden by generating taxable income that reduces the company's NOLs.

A different form of asset restructuring involves not the loss company's passive investments but its operating assets. Assume that some of the company's operating assets are depreciable. The loss company cannot use the depreciation deductions these assets generate as effectively as can fully taxable firms; moreover, if a tax gain from a step-up in basis is possible, the loss company cannot make effective use of the increased depreciation. A sale of these assets to a fully taxed firm is a substitute for selling part of the loss company's NOLs. The loss company can then invest the proceeds of the sale in taxable bonds, thereby increasing income at the same time that deductions are reduced. For a brief period between the Economic Recovery Act of 1981 and TEFRA, tax rules allowed sale-

and-leaseback transactions that amounted to a simple sale of these deductions; the lessor bore no risk concerning the residual value of the investment. Although these rules were tightened somewhat by TEFRA so that now the lessor must bear some investment risk, during the pre-1986 Act period the use of a sale and leaseback remained an alternative to an acquisition as a means of altering the target company's balance sheet to increase the value of the company's NOLs.[63]

The same type of restructuring is possible on the equity side of the balance sheet. The market interest rate on taxable debt reflects its tax-disfavored status to investors—interest receipts are fully taxable. The cost of equity, the required return on common or preferred stock, is lower than that of taxable bonds on a risk-adjusted basis because it represents tax-favored investments to the marginal investor. Put differently, an issuer must pay for the opportunity to take the interest deduction associated with debt by paying a higher interest rate. The loss company is better off refinancing its debt with lower-cost equity. The increase in taxable income that results reduces the NOLs.

A loss company also could issue equity and use the proceeds to buy taxable bonds. This strategy is functionally identical to the sale of NOLs through an acquisition of the loss company by a profitable company. In one case the loss company's shareholders' equity in the NOLs is sold to the public, and the proceeds are used to enhance the value of the NOLs by increasing taxable income in the form of taxable bonds. In the other case, equity in the NOLs is sold directly to a profitable company, and the NOLs are used to shelter the acquiring company's future income. Indeed, this approach simply generalizes the technique of having the loss company make the acquisition, rather than being acquired, as a means to avoid Internal Revenue Code restrictions. The generalization is important, however, because buying taxable bonds may be more effective at increasing the value of the NOLs than buying a profitable business. Whether cast as a purchase of

stock or assets, an acquisition of a profitable business can be a tax-favored investment because at least some of the assets acquired result in deductions like depreciation. In contrast, a purchase of taxable bonds is tax-disfavored, and for a company with NOLs, the latter is preferable.

On the other hand, to use up NOLs either to eliminate depreciation recapture on taxable acquisitions, to absorb the ordinary income resulting from termination of an overfunded pension plan, or to absorb a LIFO inventory reserve is inefficient: Care must be taken to avoid confusing the nonpayment of current taxes with the most efficient means to use NOLs. For example, prior to the Tax Reform Act of 1984, an installment sale with deferral of both depreciation recapture and capital gains tax coupled with additional investment in taxable bonds dominated a strategy of using NOLs to eliminate recapture tax. Obviously, the use of taxable bonds and deferral would produce higher after-tax profits than the use of NOLs to reduce current taxes on depreciation recapture. After 1984, installment sales cannot be used to defer the tax on depreciation recapture. If, after 1984, a fully taxable company would choose not to sell an asset to step up its basis because of recapture, in a perfect market a loss company's decision would be exactly the same. It would be more efficient to issue equity, invest in fully taxable assets to eliminate the NOLs, and retain the depreciable asset. Therefore, if, in an imperfect market, the information and transaction costs of a sale and leaseback (or an asset sale) exceed the costs of buying bonds and issuing equity, bonds and equity would dominate as a means of using up NOLs. As discussed more fully in the next section, we again must consider the relative costs of alternative strategies to determine the most efficient way to eliminate NOLs.

Similar arguments apply to excess assets in defined-benefit pension plans. Since the returns on pension fund assets are exempt from tax, eliminating NOLs by buying bonds and issuing equity dominates a taxable reversion of excess pension fund assets if the loss company cannot restore the excess in the fund once its NOLs are safely behind it.

Acquisitions Versus Substitutes: The Role of Information Costs

Let us turn next to an emphasis on problems of information asymmetry—adverse-selection or hidden-information and moral hazard or hidden-action costs—and transaction costs. The presence of these costs affects both the potential for any tax gain from increasing the value of a loss company's NOLs and the relative effectiveness of an acquisition in achieving that gain.

When an acquisition is used to increase the value of a company's NOLs, moral hazard and adverse-selection problems potentially are severe. The change in the position of the target company's owner-manager from an owner to an agent creates the potential for moral hazard or hidden-action costs; the information asymmetry in favor of the seller of the business creates adverse-selection or hidden-information costs. When these costs are high, some acquisitions will not take place, and tax gains—in the form of observable net operating losses—will be left on the table. By the same token, some methods of using up NOLs internally (i.e., without an acquisition) will also prove too costly. For example, issuing stock to purchase fully taxable bonds suffers from the same sort of adverse-selection costs as the sale of the company in an acquisition.

This result is consistent with empirical observation—we do observe the existence of companies with NOLs, and in nontrivial amounts (hundreds of millions of dollars for some companies). For example, start-up companies commonly accumulate NOLs. In the absence of information-related costs, anticipation of these losses should lead to a start-up company's early acquisition; indeed, considered *ex ante,* the difference in the expected value of the NOLs will make every start-up project more valuable to an existing profitable company than to a start-up company. Start-up companies could avoid the wasteful existence of early-stage NOLs by issu-

ing larger quantities of stock and using the proceeds to purchase ordinary income-generating assets. That this strategy is not exploited is prima facie evidence of the importance of adverse-selection and moral hazard problems. We note that research-and-development limited partnerships can be understood as an attempt to increase the value of early-stage NOLs. This technique, however, presents its own tax, adverse-selection, and moral hazard problems which account for its limited use.

The impact of the introduction of information and transaction costs is even more significant with respect to the relative effectiveness of acquisitions as a means to secure tax gains from increasing the value of NOLs—the intermediate claim that acquisitions were the best method to use up NOLs. In this setting, the returns to tax-exempt assets may be such that on a risk-adjusted basis, they bear an implicit tax at less than the full corporate rate. In our previous numerical example, tax-exempt assets returned a risk-adjusted rate of 5.4% when fully taxable assets returned a risk-adjusted rate of 10%. If the tax-exempt risk-adjusted return was 6% when the return on fully taxable assets was 10% (an implicit tax rate of 40%), it would not have been profit maximizing for the loss company to buy taxable bonds in a quantity just sufficient to offset its NOLs and to buy municipal bonds with its remaining assets. Merging with a fully taxable company would have generated higher after-tax profits, ignoring information costs. If the loss company bought $100 of taxable bonds to eliminate its NOLs, it would earn $10 in addition to $54 (0.06 × $900), or a total of $64 after tax. A fully taxable company investing in municipal bonds would earn $60 after-tax, a difference of only $4.00. Yet the fully taxable company would still be willing to pay $4.60 for the NOLs. The acquisition alternative would dominate. A 40% implicit tax on municipal bonds coexistent with a 46% tax rate on ordinary bonds, however, would not be supportable as an equilibrium absent information and transaction costs. In the face of such costs, acquisitions could still be dominated by the various alternatives that we have discussed if the costs of these alternatives are sufficiently low relative to the costs of an acquisition. The combination of implicit taxes and implicit costs (information costs) is such that the alternatives to an acquisition seem likely to dominate, even when the implicit tax on tax-exempt securities is less than the full corporate rate.

Many nonacquisition strategies share the common feature of lower information and transaction costs relative to acquisitions. The restructuring of the asset side of a loss company's balance sheet by altering its passive investments, if it has any, in favor of tax-disfavored assets involves low costs beyond such brokerage fees as early recognition of capital gains tax or the costs of negotiating installment sales. Adverse-selection-related costs specific to these transactions should be minimal. When it is a loss company's operating assets that are sold and then leased back, information and transaction costs should also be relatively small compared with those that arise in a complex acquisition.

The information and transaction cost advantages of nonacquisition alternatives also extend to more active strategies such as issuing equity to acquire tax-disfavored assets. Because NOLs of a loss company only survived an acquisition if the consideration received by its shareholders included a substantial amount of voting stock,[64] adverse-selection and other information-related costs appeared on *both* sides of the acquisition: The acquiring company must worry about the price it pays for the loss company, and the loss-company shareholders must worry about the value of the acquiring-company shares they receive. In contrast, the issuance of stock by the loss company and the purchase of taxable bonds with the proceeds of that issuance largely eliminates one layer of adverse-selection problems. The costs, however, could be so great in either situation that the NOLs remain unused.

Relaxing the No-Operating-Efficiencies Assumption

Our discussion of the differential impact of both tax restrictions and information and

transaction costs on acquisitions and non-acquisition alternatives to increasing the value of a loss company's NOLs suggests that the nonacquisition alternatives are viable contenders. Empirically, however, NOLs are frequently sold through tax-free reorganizations rather than "used up" internally. One plausible explanation for these acquisitions is efficiency gains: Companies with significant NOLs are likely candidates for improved operation. This explanation, however, is not a tax explanation for acquisitions.

Evaluating the Strong Claim: Tax Gains as the Determinant of the Size of Acquisition Premiums

Evaluating the strong claim concerning the importance of the tax system in determining the level of acquisition activity is relatively easy in the case of transfers of NOLs by acquisition. First, the existence of NOLs is easily observable by investors (and potential acquirers). Gains from the sale of NOLs are likely to be anticipated. Second, our analysis suggests that alternative means of achieving this tax gain may well be more cost-effective. As a result, when we observe that the tax gain has been achieved by acquisition, the likely motive—and the likely cause of any sizable premium—is something other than the attempt to secure a tax gain.

SOURCES OF POTENTIAL TAX GAINS: LEVERAGE

The most persistent recent claim in the policy debate over the influence of the tax system on the level of acquisition activity is that the deductibility of interest on debt encourages acquisitions.[65] The argument, of course, is not new. It was prominent in the late 1960s when the consideration in conglomerate acquisitions was frequently some form of convertible subordinated debt. Congress responded then by enacting Internal Revenue Code Section 279 as part of the Tax Reform Act of 1969, which denies a deduction for interest payments in excess of $5 million on acquisition-related subordinated debt that has an equity feature such as convertibility and is issued by a highly leveraged company (i.e., with a ratio of debt to book net worth of greater than 2 to 1). Section 279 does not, however, apply to debt that is either unsubordinated or without an explicit equity feature, such as the high–interest rate bonds prominent in the current acquisition market. As a result, the same claim—that the deductibility of interest on debt encourages acquisitions—has again become prominent. In response, a number of bills have been introduced in Congress that would deny an interest deduction to one or another form of debt issued in acquisitions. When viewed from the perspective adopted in this chapter, however, the claim does not withstand scrutiny.

In its most general form, the claim is simply that there is a tax advantage to increased debt because interest payments are deductible. So stated, the claim has nothing to do with acquisitions; rather, it calls forth the debate over whether the presence of taxes alters the optimal capital structure for the firm. While this is not the place to rehearse the complete debate, Miller suggests that a firm *cannot* increase its market value by increasing its leverage.[66] In his equilibrium model, the after-tax return on fully taxable assets will equal the return on tax-exempt assets. If the implicit tax on taxable assets is less than the corporate rate, there is a tax advantage for firms to issue debt. The after-tax cost of debt to the corporation would be less than the return on tax-exempt assets such as municipal bonds. Without transaction or information costs, the result is arbitrage, as we discussed earlier in connection with the efficient use of NOLs. Even when the implicit tax rate on tax-exempt assets is below the corporate tax rate shielding the interest deductions on the firm's debt, to issue bonds to finance the purchase of tax-exempt assets in the face of transaction costs and other information-related costs may not be tax-efficient. To sustain the claim that the deductibility of interest encourages acquisitions, one must demonstrate why deductibility is more valuable when the proceeds of the debt are used to make an acquisition

than when the proceeds are used to make any other investment.

Consider the most familiar explanation for why debt-financed acquisitions are particularly favored. The argument is that a diversified company, because its income is subject to less variance, will support a larger amount of debt or, alternatively, will pay a lower interest rate for the same amount of debt, than a company with a single line of business. As a result, there is an incentive to diversify to reduce risk, and it follows that diversification can be profitably financed with debt. The problem with the argument, however, is that it stops short. Even taken at face value, the most it can explain is why debt is the preferable way to finance diversification. Without consideration of the relative transaction and information costs, it says nothing about the manner in which the debt-financed diversification is best accomplished—by acquisition or by internal expansion. If the legislative response is to deny interest deductions only for acquisition-related indebtedness, as current proposals appear to do, then the proposed legislation's motive cannot be that the tax system uniquely favors acquisitions. Rather, the tax system would be used as a tool to discourage acquisitions, as compared with other means of corporate growth, for reasons that must be found outside the Internal Revenue Code.[67]

CONCLUSION

Our objective here has been to set the issues commonly conflated under the rubric of whether the tax system favors acquisitions in terms precise enough that they can be addressed meaningfully. Our investigation considers the most prominent claims that tax gains were possible from acquisitions in the pre-1986 Act period—change in asset basis, transfer of net operating losses, and leverage. Central to our approach has been an equilibrium view of tax planning and a realization that there exists a rich set of potential transactional substitutes that can yield similar productive outcomes and tax results. The efficiency of these transactional alternatives depends importantly on the information and transaction costs associated with each. Thus, the social desirability of particular tax subsidies cannot be determined in isolation from the desirability of the underlying activity that the tax system may encourage and the level of associated information and transaction costs. In fact, without these costs, there are few instances in which the pre-1986 Act tax law favored acquisitions over asset sales or other balance sheet restructurings as a way to change basis or as a way to eliminate NOLs. On the other hand, when information and transaction costs become important, whether acquisitions were the most efficient way to garner tax benefits depends upon the particular circumstances.

We also have explored the intriguing notion that the opportunity to step up asset basis might have acted as an efficient subsidy to encourage costly search for operating efficiencies among firms in a competitive setting in which, because of free-rider problems, the social value of such search exceeds the private value that can be captured. This view of our tax system contrasts sharply with the alternative view that tax-induced acquisitions result only in deadweight losses to the system. In all events, our analysis should advance the ongoing policy debate by making it more difficult to resolve nontax issues bearing on the social value of corporate acquisitions under the guise of tax neutrality.

NOTES

1. See, e.g., Federal Trade Commission, *Economic Report on Corporate Mergers* (1969), 142–48; Hellerstein, "Mergers, Taxes, and Realism," 71 *Harv. L. Rev.* 254 (1957); Lintner, "Expectations, Mergers and Equilibrium in Purely Competitive Securities Markets," 61 *Am. Econ. Rev.* 101, 107 (Papers and Proceedings, 1971); Bebchuck, "The Case for Facilitating Competing Tender Offers: A Reply and Extension," 35 *Stan. L. Rev.* 23, 34 (1982); Weston and Chung, "Do Mergers Make Money? A Research Summary," 18 *Mergers & Acq.* 40 (Fall

1983); F. M. Scherer, testimony before the Subcommittee on Telecommunications, Consumer Protection, and Finance, House Committee on Energy and Commerce, March 12, 1984, 15; Williams, "It's Time for a Takeover Moratorium," *Fortune*, July 22, 1985, 133; Saul, "Hostile Takeovers: What Should Be Done?" 63 *Harv. Bus. Rev.* 19 (September–October 1985).

2. See, e.g., Bebchuck, note 1; Scherer, note 1; Williams, note 1.

3. The point of the definition is to exclude the possibility of operating efficiencies from acquisitions. If these were present, pretax cash flows would also change.

4. An implicit tax represents the *pretax* differences in cash flows between investments that are taxed differently, such as municipal bonds and taxable bonds. See M. Scholes and M. Wolfson, *Employee Compensation and Taxes: Links with Incentives and with Investment and Financing Decisions*, Working Paper, Graduate School of Business, Stanford University, October 1984; M. Mazur, M. Scholes, and M. Wolfson, *Implicit Taxes and Effective Tax Burdens*, Working Paper, Graduate School of Business, Stanford University, September 1985.

5. For a discussion of the information costs associated with a corporate acquisition, see Gilson, "Value Creation by Business Lawyers: Legal Skills and Asset Pricing," 94 *Yale L.J.* 239 (1984).

6. The size of the premium would then reflect not uncertainty about the potential for tax gains but, rather, about when and whether they would be realized.

7. Stigler, "The Law and Economic Policy: A Plea to the Scholars," 1 *J. Leg. Stud.* 1, 12 (1972).

8. Another important source of potential tax gains is the recognition of a loss when the market value of assets is below their tax basis. Because step-ups are mentioned more frequently than step-downs, we use *step-up* generically to describe a change in basis. We analyze the less pervasive case of step-downs later.

9. P.L. No. 97–34, 95 Statute 172.

10. An acquisition that converts assets to an ACRS depreciation schedule may not be desirable if the preacquisition remaining tax life of the asset is less than the relevant ACRS period and the depreciation step-up in basis is not enough to make up for the lengthening of the depreciation period.

11. This does not mean, however, that the incidence of the tax is on the target company.

12. The statement in the text assumes that only a single capital gains tax is paid, either by

the target company or by its shareholders. It also assumes that even the single capital gains tax is not deferred through the use of an installment sale. The amount of the capital gain and the amount of the step-up in basis need not be the same. The amount will depend on the relation between the market value of the company's assets and the shareholders' bases in their stock, and the two will often diverge because of accumulated earnings in the company to be acquired. We consider this relationship later.

13. A single capital gains tax would have been paid by the target shareholders, either because the acquisition takes the form of a direct purchase of the target company's stock from its shareholders and a basis step-up achieved by election under IRC Section 338 [or under Section 334(b)(2) prior to enactment of Section 338 in 1982], or because the acquisition takes the form of a purchase of the target company's assets followed by a liquidation of the target pursuant to Section 337.

The elimination of the corporate-level tax on asset sales in connection with liquidation has been the subject of persistent criticism over the years. See, e.g., American Law Institute, *Federal Income Tax Project,* Subchapter C, "Proposals on Corporate Acquisitions and Dispositions," (1982), 102–150. The Tax Reform Act of 1986, which we do not consider here, requires a recognition of gain on asset sales at the corporate level regardless of whether a liquidation follows. Availability of a tax gain from a step-up in basis has been reduced by the increase in taxes paid by the target as a result of a corporate-level tax.

We will not attempt here to analyze the impact of specific proposed legislative changes on acquisition activity. The *framework* we develop, however, is as applicable to these proposed changes as it is to extant rules.

14. Counterexamples to this assertion can be offered when the marginal corporate tax rate is increasing over time.

15. IRC § 47.

16. See note 13.

17. Under Section 1231, the sale of depreciable personal and real business property held for the requisite time period gives rise to capital gain if the net effect of the sale of all such property is a gain (subject to recapture after the Tax Reform Act of 1984 to the extent of Section 1231 losses in the previous five years), and to ordinary loss if the net effect of the sale is a loss.

18. This result depends on marginal tax rates not increasing over time. If this assumption were altered, we could construct counterexamples that would favor postponing tax deductions.

19. If the inequality were reversed, such that the shareholders could generate a capital loss through the sale of stock, the asset sale route and the acquisition route would be equally effective. An asset sale then would be accompanied by complete turnover of shareholder ownership.

20. Under Section 1245, depreciation of tangible personal property generally is recaptured to the extent that the amount realized in the sale exceeds the seller's adjusted (i.e., net of depreciation) basis.

21. Again, this result depends on marginal tax rates not increasing over time.

22. Under Section 1250, depreciation of residential real property is also recaptured only to the extent that accumulated depreciation exceeds that amount which would have been taken on a straight-line basis. However, unless tax rates are increasing over time, it will still be optimal to depreciate such assets using an accelerated depreciation schedule. Depreciation of nonresidential real property placed in service after 1980 is subject to recapture under Section 1245 only if an accelerated method is used.

23. Under Section 1014, the basis of stock in the hands of a person who acquired it from a decedent is the stock's fair market value at the time of death, and none of the predeath appreciation is taxed to the decedent or to the decedent's estate.

24. A corporate-level capital gains tax could be avoided in a pre-1986 Act acquisition by structuring it as a taxable merger, as a sale of stock followed by liquidation under Section 332, or as a sale of assets followed by liquidation under Section 337. But see note 13 with respect to changes in the rules that would render asset sales weakly dominant over acquisitions in Case III *in addition to* Cases I and II.

25. Determination of the principal payments to be received must take into account imputed interest if the installment note does not provide for at least the minimum rate of interest as specified under IRC Section 483.

26. P.L. 98–369, 98 Statute 678.

27. Prior to the Installment Sales Act of 1980 there was uncertainty as to whether a third-party guarantee of the purchaser's installment obligation would cause the obligation not to be that of the purchaser and, therefore, not eligible for installment sales treatment. Section 453(f)(3) now makes clear that the existence of a third-party guarantee will not affect the tax treatment of an installment obligation.

28. See M. Ginsburg, *Tax Reform: Revisiting Installment Sales,* Working Paper, Georgetown University Law Center, February 1985.

29. If the acquisition took the form of a stock

purchase, the target shareholders could receive the benefit of installment sale deferral, but recapture would be assessed against the target company when the acquirer sought to step up the basis in the target's assets either by liquidation under Section 334(b)(2) prior to 1982 or, after 1982, by election under Section 338. Prior to the Installment Sales Act of 1980, the distribution of an installment note in liquidation, following a sale by the target company of all of its assets, would cause shareholders to recognize gain when the installment note was received rather than when payments were received under the installment note. However, several routes to shareholder-level capital gains tax deferral were available. For example, (1) the acquisition could take the form of a stock purchase rather than an asset sale; (2) even in an asset sale, shareholders could sell their stock in an installment transaction before the corporate reorganization took place; the new generation of shareholders would have no capital gain to recognize; (3) rather than an installment transaction as in example (2), shareholders could exchange their shares for preferred stock in a tax-free IRC Section 351 transaction. This alternative carries the potential for *permanent* capital gain avoidance, either through indefinite deferral (e.g., for a corporate taxpayer) or through a tax-free step-up in basis of the preferred stock upon death (for an individual taxpayer).

30. Prior to the Installment Sales Act of 1980, distribution to shareholders in a Section 337 liquidation of an installment note arising out of the sale of the company's assets would have required the shareholders to recognize income to the extent the value of the note exceeded their basis in their stock. See the three examples in note 29 for ways to secure the benefits of installment sale deferral during this period. The Installment Sales Act allows shareholders to treat receipt of payments under the note as payments for their stock in the liquidation, thereby allowing them the benefit of the installment sale deferral even when the acquisition takes the form of a sale of the target company's assets.

31. Techniques are available that will allow some asset selectivity even in an acquisition. They do not, however, provide the flexibility of a selective asset sale. See, e.g., Handler, "Variations on a Theme: The Disposition of Unwanted Assets," 35 *Tax L. Rev.* 389 (1980).

32. The use of the terms *hidden action* and *hidden information* to describe these categories of asymmetric information problems derives from K. Arrow, "The Economics of Agency," in *Principals and Agents: The Structure of Business,* ed. J. Pratt and R. Zeckhauser (1985).

33. This problem is difficult to remedy. Although performance incentives can be designed in an effort to align the interests of agent and owner, these have the unavoidable impact of imposing inefficient-risk-bearing arrangements. The problem is not confined to the acquisition of a private company. One effect of the acquisition of a public company is that market price is no longer available as a measure of the performance of management. The value of this measure may explain some of the recent equity carve-outs. See, e.g., Schipper and Smith, "A Comparison of Equity Carve-outs and Equity Offerings: Share Price Effects and Corporate Restructuring," 15 *J. Fin. Econ.* 153 (1986).

34. See, e.g., Warren and Auerbach, "Transferability of Tax Incentives and the Fiction of Sale Harbor Leasing," 95 *Harv. L. Rev.* 1752 (1982).

35. For a discussion of moral hazard problems in leasing contracts, see Wolfson, "Tax, Incentive, and Risk-Sharing Issues in the Allocation of Property Rights: The Generalized Lease-or-Buy Problem," 58 *J. Bus.* 159 (1958).

36. The differences in the tax treatment of sale and leasebacks, however, are not all unfavorable. For example, a sale and leaseback does not trigger recapture of ITC. Leasing requires sacrificing depreciation deductions in exchange for implicit tax subsidies in the form of lease payments, but if there are cross-sectional differences in tax rates, the lessee may be in the wrong clientele with the sale-leaseback.

37. Lowenstein, "Management Buyouts," 85 *Colum. L. Rev.* 730, 737 (Table 1) (1985), reports that in a sample of 28 management buyouts between 1979 and 1984, management's equity interest increased from a pretransaction average of 6.5% in the publicly held company to a posttransaction average of 24.3% in the newly formed entity.

38. In the example, we assume that the tax benefit T available if a sale takes place is identical for both types of firms. This assumption will not be true in general; it is assumed here simply to make the example more transparent. More realistically, we would expect $T_h > T_l$. This complication would change nothing of substance in the example.

39. For a discussion of the terms of a standard acquisition agreement as a means to reduce information costs and of the informational role in an acquisition played by various information intermediaries, see Gilson, note 5.

40. The same forms of transactions that reduce moral hazard costs also can reduce adverse-selection costs. In the context of an acquisition, the potential for adverse selection exists because of an information asymmetry between

the acquirer and target, and it is minimized by truthful disclosure by the seller. Where the transaction involves no real shift in ownership, like a sale and leaseback, the importance of the information asymmetry is minimized. Where the future income of the party making the disclosure also will depend on the accuracy of the disclosure, as in a management buy-out, or even where target management merely contemplates continued employment by the acquirer (see Gilson, note 5, pp. 283–285), the incentive for truthful disclosure is increased.

41. The absence of removal costs in an acquisition results in part from our continued assumption that there can be no operating efficiencies from the transaction. If operating efficiencies were possible, a complication we defer until the next section, removal costs might be incurred in an acquisition in an effort to realize them.

42. Adverse-selection costs may also go up depending on whether the value of individual assets is less costly to verify than their combined value. While a piecemeal sale of assets may require multiple valuations, firm valuation may also require multiple valuations if there is no external market price for the entire firm. Additionally, if indivisibilities exist, the glue linking the assets together may be intangible and difficult to value.

43. For example, as discussed earlier, pre-1981 assets acquired in corporate acquisitions are eligible for ACRS; those acquired in a sale and leaseback are not. In contrast, prior to 1984, sale and leasebacks allowed deferral of recapture through the use of an installment sale; taxable acquisitions did not.

44. Grossman and Hart, "Takeover Bids, the Free-Rider Problem, and the Theory of the Firm," 11 *Bell J. Econ.* 42 (1980).

45. For a discussion of whether an underinvestment problem exists in light of the information and transaction cost characteristics of the search market, see Gilson, "Seeking Competitive Bids Versus Pure Passivity in Tender Offer Defense," 35 *Stan. L. Rev.* 51 (1982); see also Bebchuck, note 1; Y. Amihud, *The Case Against a Mandatory Delay Period in Tender Offers,* New York University Graduate School of Business Administration Working Paper, August 1985; A. Schwartz, *Imperfect Information and the Tender Offer Auction,* University of Southern California Law Center Working Paper, June 1985.

46. In fact, the subsidy for acquisitions may not be so easy to eliminate if the general subsidy for asset transfers is to be retained. For a discussion of the difficulty of policing regulatory regimes which define the objects of their atten-

tion in formal terms, see R. Gilson, *The Law and Finance of Corporate Acquisitions* (Foundation Press, 1986), Chap. 13.

47. This literature is surveyed, and an extensive bibliography provided, in Jensen and Ruback, "The Market for Corporate Control: The Scientific Evidence," 11 *J. Fin. Econ.* 5 (1983). A different empirical approach to the issue is taken in Rosencraft and Scherer, *Mergers and Managerial Performance* (1985).

48. See, e.g., Axelrod, "Esmark's Tax Free Disposition of a Subsidiary: Too Good to Be True?" 9 *J. Corp. Tax* 232 (1982).

49. See the sources referred to in note 1.

50. This analysis assumes that the market cannot forecast with certainty either the efficiencies available through the most suitable acquirer or that the most efficient acquirer will make the acquisition. For a discussion of search models in the market for corporate control, see Schwartz, note 45.

51. For example, assume a company owns a depreciable asset with a zero dollar basis for tax purposes that will generate $100 of future taxable income. Assuming a discount rate of 0% and a 46% tax rate, the value of the asset to the current owner is $54. The value to a purchaser of the asset, however, is $100, since depreciation of $100 will render the $100 of taxable income completely tax-exempt. Hence, the potential tax gain upon sale of the asset is $46/54$, or 85% of the value of the asset in the hands of the present owner. Also note that if the present owner had financed the asset with equal amounts of debt and equity, the increase in equity value generated by a sale of the asset would have been $46/27$, or 170%.

Increasing the discount rate reduces these premiums unless the asset is fully and immediately tax-deductible. For example, a 10% after-tax discount rate and a three-year straight-line depreciation schedule give rise to an equity premium of 62% (123% if the assets are 50% debt-financed). A five-year straight-line schedule reduces the premium further to 54% (and 107%). Note that the premiums are independent of the timing of the cash inflows and the related tax on these cash inflows. If we let V denote the value of the asset to the current owner and P denote the value of the asset to the prospective owner, then P solves as

$$P = V + d(P, r, t, s(\ ))$$

where d is the present value of the depreciation deduction, which is a function of P, the discount rate r, the tax rate t, and the depreciation schedule $s(\ )$.

As stressed in earlier sections, however, there are several sources that reduce the value of the step-up: (1) some portion of the asset may be nondepreciable; (2) some portion of the purchase price may be recaptured as ordinary income to the seller; and (3) that portion of the gain that is not recaptured as ordinary income may be subject to corporate-level capital gains taxation.

52. T. Robinson, An Analysis of Selected Tax Variables and Corporate Combinations (mimeo, University of Kansas, 1984).

53. B. Bittker and J. Eustice, *Federal Income Taxation of Corporations and Shareholders* (1979), 16–35 (note 67).

54. Congressional efforts to restrict transfer of NOLs dates to the Revenue Act of 1924 when the predecessor of Section 482 was enacted. Ibid., p. 16–6.

55. This situation arose, for example, in a taxable stock acquisition where no Section 338 election was filed, whether or not the acquiring company sought to file returns on a consolidated basis. See Reg. Section 1.1502–21(c). Like much of the tax treatment of acquisitions, the rules governing survival of NOLs were changed drastically by the Tax Reform Act of 1986.

56. Nonacquisition techniques to increase the value of NOLs are considered in the next subsection.

57. Other tax attributes covered by Section 381 include historical earnings and profits, tax accounting methods, and investment tax credit history.

58. The requirement that the acquisition qualify as a reorganization also limits the form of consideration that can be used. In an A reorganization, a substantial amount of the consideration must be the acquiring company's voting stock. For ruling purposes, the Internal Revenue Service requires that 50% of the consideration consist of the acquirer's voting stock (Rev. Proc. 77–37, Section 3.02, 1977 −2 C.B. 568). The courts have been more lenient, however, having approved transactions where as much as 62% [*Nelson v. Helvering*, 296 U.S. 374 (1935)] and 75% [*Miller v. Commissioner*, 84 F.2d 415 (6th Cir. 1936)] of the total consideration was cash. In a B reorganization, all consideration must be voting stock, and in a C reorganization, for practical purposes all consideration must be voting stock. In a perfect market the form of required consideration would impose no restriction, because those shareholders that preferred cash could sell their stock following the transaction. The requirement that the acquiring company's stock be used does, however, limit the impact of the re-

quirement of Section 382(b) that the loss-company shareholders receive at least 20% of the stock in the acquiring company if the NOLs are to survive intact.

59. In its present form, the regulation applies to acquisitions occurring after January 1, 1981.

60. Section 382(b), in turn, imposes restrictions on the survival of the loss company's NOLs in a reorganization transaction, scaling down the NOLs that survive by 5% for each percentage point below 20% of the acquirer's stock that the loss-company shareholders receive in the transaction. Unlike Section 381(a), there is no requirement (other than that imposed by the definition of a reorganization; see text at notes 59–60) that the target's business be continued.

61. These restrictions have been altered substantially by the Tax Reform Act of 1986.

62. By inclusion of land in the set of tax-exempt assets, we are assuming a zero capital gains tax rate in present-value terms (e.g., a complete installment sales market). We are also assuming that the explicit tax on shares of common stock (i.e., the personal tax on dividend income and capital gains) is such that the risk-adjusted return on shares after both corporate and personal tax is 54% of the return on taxable bonds. This assumption is consistent with the Miller equilibrium. See Miller, "Debt and Taxes,' 32 *J. Fin.* 261 (1977).

63. The formation of limited partnerships to sell tax deductions to high–tax bracket taxpayers relating to such diverse activities as research and development, oil and gas exploration, real estate investment, and agricultural investment is also a rational alternative to selling NOLs through an acquisition.

64. See note 58.

65. See, e.g., A. Feld, *Tax Policy and Corporate Concentration* (1982); also see sources referred to in note 1.

66. See Miller, note 62.

67. Some ways of taking advantage of the interest deduction do not involve corporate growth at all. A company can increase its leverage by borrowing to repurchase its own stock, thereby shrinking at least the company's equity. Management, however, still might prefer to make use of the interest deduction through expansion if, because of agency problems, they are free to indulge a preference for size maximization. But even in this case to describe management's choice as tax-motivated would be incorrect. Rather, agency problems have determined the choice among alternative means of achieving the same tax benefit.

19

Taxes and the Merger Decision

ALAN J. AUERBACH
DAVID REISHUS

There are many economic explanations for the acquisition of one firm by another or for the combination of two firms through a merger. Some, such as synergy, better organization of production, or the improvement of the management of one of the firms, are associated with the generation of social benefits through more efficient resource allocation. Others, such as increased market power and managers seeking empires, are associated with private gains that may very well be more than offset by the losses of others in society. Hence, the motives underlying a merger must be understood for a judgment to be made about its social desirability.

One particular motive that is often cited as generating private rather than social gains is the avoidance of federal income taxes by corporations and their shareholders. At first blush, merging for tax reasons alone must seem to be socially undesirable, since it leads to a revenue loss that must be made up with distortionary taxes on others in the economy. Note, however, that by reducing their own taxes, combining firms *may* also facilitate more efficient behavior on their own part. For example, wiping out tax losses may increase the incentive to invest, particularly in the presence of a system of accelerated depreciation.[1] Hence, there can be no presumption that merging

for tax purposes reduces aggregate economic efficiency. Nevertheless, there are many cases in which the tax benefits are essentially lump-sum transfers to the merging firms; such outcomes cause concern and generate proposals for policy action.

The recent rise in merger activity, coupled with frequent publicity about tax benefits generated by some of these mergers, has provided an impetus for such proposals. One plan currently under congressional scrutiny would substantially reduce the tax benefits gained from merging.[2] Yet there is little empirical evidence on the tax consequences of merger activity or on the postmerger effects on financial and investment policies of tax-motivated behavior. Indeed, though there have been theoretical analyses over the years of the tax benefits to be derived from different types of mergers and acquisitions,[3] there have been, to our knowledge, no serious attempts to evaluate the importance of these incentives beyond the consideration of particular mergers. From a policy standpoint, we must know not only what the potential tax benefits are, and what benefits certain companies have been able to avail themselves of, but also the aggregate importance of such incentives. This knowledge requires a broader empirical investigation than the case study method permits, one which considers enough mergers so that patterns can be discerned.

In this chapter, we present some initial results based on a large sample of mergers and acquisitions that occurred over the period 1968–1983. Our aim is to assess the

We thank Brenda Chamberlain, Laurie Dicker, and Kevin Hassett for research assistance. Financial support by the National Science Foundation (Grant No. SES–8409892), the Alfred P. Sloan Foundation, and the Institute for Law and Economics at the University of Pennsylvania is gratefully acknowledged.

potential tax benefits that these merging firms could have gained in the process and to take a preliminary look at one of the distortions to firm behavior often associated with the acquisition process, increased leverage of the combined entity. The analysis is largely descriptive in that we do not estimate behavioral models to measure the relationship between tax incentives and merger activity. In the future, we hope to determine the extent to which tax factors induce mergers by comparing the tax characteristics of pairs of firms that choose to merge with those that do not. This work will require considerably more data preparation than has been done for the results reported here. However, in the development of behavioral models, an important first step is to establish the potential importance of tax factors in the merger decision and to see whether the change in financial policy hypothesized to come from tax motivations (i.e., increased leverage) is present in the data.

The first section reviews the tax treatment of mergers and discusses the various ways in which taxes can be reduced when two firms combine. The next section describes the data set which we have constructed from a variety of public sources. The third section presents the empirical methodology and the results themselves. In the final section, we interpret these findings, discuss their limitations, and consider directions for future research.

Our results suggest that potential tax benefits associated with the relaxation of constraints on the use of tax losses and tax credits are present in approximately one in five mergers and acquisitions. In about a third of this subsample, the benefits may exceed 10% of the acquired company's market value. There is less evidence of substantial gains being available through the achievement of higher asset bases and associated tax deductions, though this measure is not calculated very precisely. Finally, we find little evidence, for the pre-1984 sample period studied, that significant changes in leverage are associated with mergers and acquisitions, even when acquired companies are large relative to those making the acquisition.

TAXES AND MERGER ACTIVITY

In this section, we discuss the key tax provisions involved when firms combine through a merger or an acquisition. This discussion is not exhaustive, in that it does not touch on every section of the Internal Revenue Code that might be relevant to a particular merger. It is intended to highlight the tax factors that are likely to arise in any merger.

An ambiguity that must be addressed at the start is that in determining whether merger activity is encouraged by the tax code, one must know what the best alternative activity would be in the absence of a merger. For example, the tax law may favor a merger relative to the continued operation of the two firms in question but might be neutral with respect to the merger choice if the alternative were that the target firm liquidated in the absence of a takeover. Likewise, a cash acquisition might be favored relative to the retention of earnings but not relative to repurchases of the firm's own shares. In most situations, mergers are associated with tax benefits that may be potentially available without the occurrence of a merger. Here, one must carefully assess whether the costs of achieving such benefits are reduced substantially when a merger occurs.

Stockholder Taxation

Shareholders can receive many forms of payment when they sell their shares as part of a merger or acquisition. If they receive cash or stock as part of a taxable transaction, they must pay capital gains taxes on the difference between sale price and basis. If they receive voting stock as part of a tax-free reorganization, they carry over the basis on their old stock and defer capital gains taxes until the new stock is sold. If they receive debt as part of an installment sale, they are not taxed until the deferred payments are received.

From a tax standpoint, some types of transactions are better than others. Compared with the taxable receipt of voting stock, for example, the receipt of such stock with taxes deferred is obviously better. Likewise, an installment sale allows sellers to defer taxes on payments until they are received, even though the purchaser establishes a liability immediately for the amount that must be put aside to satisfy the debt. In effect, the seller can accumulate interest tax-free on unreceived portions of the sale price. Thus, an installment sale is preferable to a straight sale for cash.

In comparing a cash sale with a nontaxable stock sale, however, and in comparing each with the situation in which no acquisition occurs, one must make additional assumptions in order to determine whether a particular activity is favored. If the alternative to a stock sale were continued ownership of the acquired entity, then there would be no tax consequences of the sale. If, however, the investor is less likely to sell shares in the acquiring company, a tax saving is realized. To the extent that the acquiring company is larger and offers the investor greater diversification, the probability of holding onto the stock may very well be increased.

A cash sale has tax costs and tax benefits relative both to a nontaxable stock sale and the no-merger situation. The shareholders pay extra taxes, but the taxes saved by the acquiring company may more than offset these. Suppose that in performing the acquisition, the parent company borrows the amount needed for the purchase. The result is then similar to a firm borrowing to repurchase its own equity. In each case, there has been a change in the debt-equity ratio, with cash passing out to equityholders being subject to partial capital gains taxation. If the debt-for-equity swap could occur equally well in the presence or absence of an acquisition, there is no particular tax benefit to a cash-financed merger. The same logic holds for any cash purchase, no matter where the cash comes from. If the purchasing firm always has the alternative to use the cash to repurchase its own shares, there is no direct tax benefit from a cash purchase of another firm's shares.

This equivalence could break down for one of two reasons. First, purchasing one's own shares could be more difficult than purchasing those of another firm. In this case, increased leverage without an acquisition could only be achieved by an increase in fully taxable dividends (either immediately or, realistically, gradually over time). Second, the ability to borrow to purchase shares might be more difficult if the shares were in one's own company.

There is some presumption, or at least a fear, that it is easier to borrow to distribute cash through the acquisition of another firm's shares than through the acquisition of one's own shares. For example, the Tax Reform Act of 1969 restricted the use of convertible debt in takeovers. According to the general explanation of the act issued by the Joint Committee on Taxation (1970), the focus on debt involved in mergers was justified because

although it is possible to substitute debt for equity without a merger, this is much easier to bring about at the time of merger. This is because, although stockholders ordinarily would not be willing to substitute debt for their stockholdings, they may be willing to do so pursuant to a corporate acquisition where they are exchanging their holdings in one company for debt in another (the acquiring) company. (p. 123)

There is, indeed, a view expressed by many policymakers that increased merger activity is leading to increased leverage in the corporate sector because it is associated with borrowing that would not otherwise occur. While we might contemplate economic models to *explain* such an outcome,[4] we may be able here, without doing so, to test the hypothesis that it occurs. We develop a preliminary test in this chapter.

Corporate Taxation

At the corporate level (assuming each firm's shareholders are not themselves corporations), the tax treatment of a merger or acquisition depends on whether the acquiring firm elects to treat the acquired firm as having been absorbed into the parent with its tax attributes intact or first liquidated and then received in the form of its component assets. While a tax-free reorganization must follow the first path, a taxable transaction can be either type.

Once again, each form of transaction has potential tax benefits, whose magnitude depend on the alternative activities of the acquired firm in the absence of a merger. The acquisition of a firm as a collection of assets leads typically to a stepped-up basis for the assets, with depreciable or depletable assets then receiving higher allowances than would otherwise have been permitted. At the same time, the liquidating target company (and therefore, its new parent) must pay some taxes because of recapture provisions but avoids capital gains taxes that would have been due on a simple sale of assets. For some assets, like equipment, this is not a major benefit, since recapture at the ordinary income tax rate applies to all excess of sale price over basis up to the original purchase price. For structures, however, recapture is much more limited and the exemption from capital gains taxes more valuable.[5]

Such an exemption may constitute the difference between a net tax increase and a net tax decrease. For example, suppose a structure has a basis of b and a sale price of s. Assuming that depreciation allowances follow a declining-balance formula,[6] and ignoring the truncation of such allowances at the asset's actual tax lifetime, we may approximate the present value of its remaining depreciation allowances as bz, where z is the present value of depreciation deductions per dollar of new assets. The allowances received on the stepped-up basis would be sz. If the depreciation followed the straight-line method, there would be no recapture, so the increased value of depreciation allowances net of capital gains taxes and would be $(s - b)(tz - c)$, where t is the ordinary tax rate and c is the capital gains tax rate. For corporations, $c = 0.28$ and $t = 0.46$, so z would have to exceed 61%, which it generally does not. If $c = 0$, of course, the gain could be substantial.[7]

Such gains could be received without any acquisition taking place. The capital gains exemption, based on the General Utilities doctrine, applies to the distribution of property to stockholders and would apply in any liquidation, not just one associated with an acquisition of the company. However, that a large, widely held company could be reconstituted after distributing its assets to its individual shareholders as part of a real liquidation seems implausible. Hence, if the firm would have continued operating in the absence of an acquisition, the ability to obtain stepped-up asset bases without suffering capital gains taxes constitutes a tax benefit for the merger.

When an acquiring firm takes over the tax attributes of the acquired company, it does not get the opportunity to step up asset bases,[8] but it does get the benefit of any unused tax credits or tax losses that the target firm has carried forward because it was not able to use them in prior years. The use of such tax benefits is limited by Sections 269 and 382 of the Internal Revenue Code, which require the acquisition to have economic substance and impose either conditions requiring the continuation of the target's operations (in the case of a taxable transaction) or restrictions on the extent to which losses can be used based on the relative sizes of target and parent (in the case of a tax-free reorganization).[9] Even with restrictions, the parent firm may be able to use the acquired losses and credits more easily than the acquired firm would have on its own, given its projected taxable income and other vehicles available, such as leasing, to make its losses fungible.

This incentive to merge was used to justify the liberalized leasing provisions introduced in 1981 as part of the Economic Recovery Tax Act, when legislators feared that the increased depreciation allowances introduced at the same time would lead to more firms with tax losses and that these firms would come under takeover pressure. More recently, the Treasury has supported pending revisions to the Internal Revenue Code that would impose further restrictions on the ability to apply prior losses and credits of a target against income of a parent.[10] This legislative history, along with the observed presence at any given time of large numbers of firms carrying-forward large amounts of unused credits and losses, suggests that to transfer such benefits without a merger taking place may be difficult.

Finally, however the assets and tax attributes of the acquired company are treated, there is an additional tax benefit that may be obtained if the *parent* company has unused tax losses and credits, since it may set these against the otherwise taxable income of the company it acquires. Restrictions on this strategy are weaker than those of parent using the losses of the acquired company. For example, the rule regarding reorganizations would not be binding as long as the loss company represented more than 20% of the new entity's total value, which it almost certainly would it if were the parent.

Thus, given that liquidation of an ongoing enterprise and the sale of tax losses and credits already being carried forward appear to be facilitated by the act of merger, these must be considered tax incentives for the merger activity itself.

DATA

We have used several sources to construct a data set containing information over time on several hundred mergers that occurred over the past two decades. All of the mergers and acquisitions actually studied occurred during the period 1968–1983. Since tax returns themselves are confidential, our tax data are limited to what the firms have chosen to disclose in their financial statements. Fortunately, standard accounting practice is to disclose tax attributes of the type in which we are interested when they are of material importance.

The COMPUSTAT 1983 industrial file provides balance sheet and income statement information over the 20-year period leading up to 1983 on a larger number of corporations currently listed on the New York and American Stock Exchange. A companion COMPUSTAT file, the industrial research file, provides similar information for firms that were included on previous versions of the regular industrial file but were removed because they were delisted from their exchanges. The most common reasons were bankruptcy and merger. For each firm on the research file that was dropped because of a merger, we consulted

the Directory of Obsolete Securities to ascertain the year of merger and the parent into which the firm in question merged. We then determined whether the parent was included on the ordinary industrial file. If it was, then we had time-series data on both firms involved in the merger, and we included this data as one of the observations in our sample. This procedure led to 422 mergers. Many firms from the industrial file appear more than once, having engaged in more than one merger over the period that was captured by our collection method.

While a typical annual observation from COMPUSTAT provides information on federal taxes paid and tax losses carried forward, the former sometimes includes deferred taxes as well as taxes currently payable, and the latter frequently is an accounting measure that does not reflect the actual value of taxes carried forward, indicating instead what taxes would have been carried forward if the company were taxed on its accounting income rather than its taxable income. Moreover, tax losses carried forward on operations in other countries are usually combined with domestic losses. Hence, the tax-loss, carryforward data provided by COMPUSTAT are mostly entirely useless for our purposes; they do not necessarily indicate the value of losses that could be used by another firm to offset its own domestic taxable income.

Fortunately, the original annual reports of the companies usually do include the appropriate tax information. For every firm in our sample for which tax data were missing or for which the tax data indicated a potential presence of unused tax benefits,[11] we consulted the reports themselves to obtain information on federal taxes paid, tax losses carried forward, and investment and foreign tax credits carried forward. Where data were still substantially missing, or when the year of merger listed by the Directory of Obsolete Securities differed by more than one from that indicated by the disappearance of the acquired company from COMPUSTAT, we were forced to drop this firm (and its merger companion) from our sample. In a few additional cases, what was called a merger was really just the reorganization of an existing company under a new name; these were also dropped from consideration. What remained was a sample of 318 mergers for which we had usable tax information on both firms involved in the merger. Each observation consists of time-series information on both firms until the merger date and data on the new entity thereafter.

To give the precise calendar year in which each merger occurred is often difficult because of differences in fiscal years and mergers which did not happen instantaneously. However, the data usually indicate when the acquired company ceased to exist as an independent entity. We use the convention of calling the merger year the year after that for which information on the acquired company is last available. By this classification, we have mergers in each year of the period 1968–1983, with the bulk (all but 25) falling in the period 1972–1982 and over three-quarters (247) occurring between 1976 and 1982. This was a period during which the tax treatment of mergers was essentially unchanged.

As might have been expected, the acquiring companies are larger on average than those acquired. Parent companies had an average value of debt plus equity of $1.957 billion; the average target firm's value was $204 million.[12] There was relatively little difference in financial structure between the two groups, with the ratio of long-term debt to long-term debt plus equity averaging 29.7% for acquiring firms and 27.4% for those acquired.

Not surprising is the positive sample correlation between the sizes of parent and target firms. A breakdown of the relative sizes of the merger pairs is given in Table 19.1. Over a fourth of the mergers involved cases where the acquiring company had value less than $250 million and the target less than $50 million. At the other extreme, there were over 10% where the parent's value exceeded $1 billion and the target's $250 billion. There were relatively few cases in which the parent company was not substantially larger than the target.

There is also a positive correlation in the sample between the debt-equity ratios of the two firms merging, but this can only be partly explained by the positive correlation between firms' sizes and the tendency for debt-equity ratios to fall with firm size. From the ratio of long-term debt to equity plus long-term debt as a measure of financial policy, there remains a partial correlation of .27 between the target and acquiring firms' ratios after controlling for the market value of each.

A majority of companies in the sample are in manufacturing (i.e., have a primary SIC classification beginning with 2 or 3): 65% of the targets and 74% of the parents. Of the remaining companies, 23 firms in the energy and mining exploration area were acquired, 10 by companies in the same industry. (There was only one case of a company in this industry acquiring one in another industry.) Likewise, in the transportation industry, where there were 19 parents and 21 targets, 13 mergers involved 2 firms in the industry. The same general pattern was also observed in the financial industry, where of the 16 acquired companies and 16 acquiring companies, 10 were matched.

Table 19.1. Sizes of Merging Firms (Millions of Dollars in Market Value)

Parent Size	Target Size				
	0–50	50–100	100–250	250+	Total
0–250	86	18	7	0	111
250–500	18	11	9	2	40
500–1000	31	8	11	0	50
1000+	30	21	27	33	111
Total	159	58	54	35	312

MEASURING TAX INCENTIVES

As a measure of the tax incentives for two firms to merge, the conceptually correct measure would be the reduction in the present value of taxes owed by two firms because of the merger. Ideally, one would project the distribution of future tax payments for each firm in isolation and for the two firms combined and then discount the expected tax payments under each situation by an appropriate discount rate. There are a number of difficulties in doing so. The most important limitation is on the number of years for which data are available for the acquired firms. We may typically have two or three years of federal income tax payments. In cases of firms with tax losses, we may have even less. Hence, to know how such firms would have fared in the absence of a takeover is extremely difficult. Also unclear from our data is whether acquiring firms chose to step up the bases of assets or to assume the tax attributes of acquired companies. Hence, projections for the combined entity are also difficult to construct.

What we can do is identify mergers in which there were obvious potential tax benefits involved from the transfer of losses and credits or the step-up in asset bases, or in which a substantial change in the debt-equity ratio of the combined companies occurred.

Losses and Credits

If one company with taxable income takes over another with taxable income, and neither has unused tax credits, there are no evident tax benefits to be transferred through merger. There may still be future benefits to be gained by a pooling of fluctuations in taxable income that reduces the possibility of subsequent unused losses and credits, but we have little hope of measuring such effects. Likewise, we do not see the obvious tax benefits if two firms that are unable to make full use of their credits and deductions combine. The clearest case for benefits being present is when one of the firms is fully taxable and the other is not. Here, a more rapid use of the con-

strained firm's tax benefits is likely to occur because of the merger. How much more rapid we cannot tell, but we can at least get a sense of the order of magnitude of the incentive from the extent to which the taxable firm can use the other firm's losses and credits against its own taxable income.

In this spirit, we classify firms (both target and parent) into four categories according to their tax status in the year before the merger. Group I has positive federal taxes payable and no credits carried forward. This group does not face tax constraints as we have defined them. Group I contains the majority of firms on both sides of the merger. Group II firms have no current federal taxes but are able to carry back current losses and credits against prior years' taxable income. These firms have no tax benefits to transfer, but they also have little capacity to absorb such transfers from other firms. Group III firms possess unused tax credits that have been carried forward but no tax losses. Group IV firms have tax losses and credits carried forward. In estimating the gains from the transfer of tax benefits, we assume these to be zero except for mergers between firms from group I and those from groups III and IV. For cases where the benefit is assumed to be present, we measure it as the maximum amount of the constrained firm's tax benefits that could be used by its group I partner over a three-year period, assuming that the latter firm has the same taxable income in each year as in the year before the merger.

For example, suppose Firm A has taxable income and takes over Firm B, which has tax losses and credits carried forward. We multiply A's taxable income by three and compare this to B's losses. If the losses exceed A's three-year income, the latter figure, multiplied by the corporate tax rate, is the measured benefit. If not, we then offset the credits against the remaining income, taking into account the relevant limitations that applied in each year on the use of credits to offset taxes. We do not take account of the potential restrictions imposed by Sections 269 and 382 of the code, nor do we account for the potential expiration of transferred losses and credits. Finally, we do not attempt to measure the use that the group III or IV company would have made of its tax benefits had it not merged. Our choice of a three-year horizon is meant to prevent an overstatement of benefits that might come from ignoring these various factors. The notion is that benefits that the taxable firm could not use almost immediately are benefits that might have expired or been used by the other company.[13]

Table 19.2 presents a cross-tabulation of target and parent firms by their tax status, as measured by the groupings I–IV just described. We also include an additional group, V, which has ambiguous group membership because firms reported having both tax losses carried forward *and* positive federal taxes currently payable, which presumably results from the presence of more than one entity for tax purposes being combined on the financial statements. Typically, this combination occurs for financial companies which have a life insurance subsidiary. Fortunately, there are relatively few such cases.

As mentioned earlier, most of the companies are in group I: 234 of the acquired companies and 260 of the acquiring companies. There are a total of 40 mergers where a group I parent acquires a company in group III or group IV, and 21 mergers where a group I company is acquired by a group III or group IV parent. There are

Table 19.2. Mergers by Tax Status

Target Group	Parent Group					
	I	II	III	IV	V	Total
I	199	7	18	3	7	234
II	20	0	2	1	2	25
III	13	3	4	0	0	20
IV	27	3	0	5	2	37
V	1	0	0	0	1	2
Total	260	13	24	9	12	318

Notes: Group I firms have positive tax payments. Group II firms have negative tax payments but no tax losses or credits carried forward. Group III firms have tax credits but not losses carried forward. Group IV firms have tax losses carried forward. Group V firms report both positive tax payments and tax losses carried forward.

only 9 mergers in which both firms are in one of these groups. Hence, there appear to be potential tax benefits in nearly 20% of all mergers.

Interestingly, mergers between pairs of group III/IV firms occur slightly more often than would be predicted by chance.[14] Given the size of this sample, however, this is not a very conclusive finding. In addition, most of the mergers of two constrained firms involved firms in the same industry, for which cyclical profitability would tend to be highly correlated. Hence, the absence of a clear pairing of firms with tax losses and gains may simply be due to the offsetting effect of the tendency of firms in related businesses to merge.

Using the method described earlier, we calculated the potential tax benefit in each merger of a type I and type III/IV firm. For the sake of completeness, we reclassified the 14 group V firms by assuming their measured tax losses to be zero, which led to an additional two mergers falling into the tax gain set, both with group I targets and group III parents.[15] The results are summarized in Table 19.3, with the estimated tax gains being expressed as a percentage of the combined value of the acquired firm's equity plus debt.[16]

Overall, potential tax benefits are estimated to be present in nearly a fifth of the mergers, with the average gain in these cases being just over a tenth of the target firm's value. In the majority of these cases, the benefits come from losses and credits of the acquired entities. The largest such gain, over $100 million, is estimated for the takeover of Anaconda by Atlantic Richfield in 1976. There are, however, two particularly important cases of parent companies providing the tax benefits; in each case, the company is involved in more than one takeover in the sample. Allied Corporation's acquisitions of Bunker Ramo, Fisher Scientific, and Supron Energy in 1980–1981 were estimated to provide benefits of over $80 million, and Penn Central's absorption of GK Technologies and Marathon Manufacturing in 1978–1980 had measured tax benefits of over $180 million.

Though the ability to transfer unused tax

Table 19.3. Potential Gains from Tax Benefit Transfer (as a Percentage of Target Firm's Market Value)

Potential Gain	Source of Gains (Number of Mergers)						Grand Total
	Target			Parent			
	Losses	Credits	Total	Losses	Credits	Total	
None	291	290	278	315	298	295	259
<5%	15	24	22	0	10	10	32
5%–10%	1	2	6	0	4	4	10
10%–25%	7	2	8	2	6	8	16
>25%	4	0	4	1	0	1	5
No. > 0	27	28	40	3	20	23	63
Percent > 0	8.4	8.7	12.4	0.9	6.2	7.1	19.6
	Average Gain, Conditional on >0						
Unweighted	14.4	3.1	11.9	22.3	5.9	8.0	10.5
Weighted by market value of target	9.3	2.4	5.0	20.9	4.3	8.25	6.1

benefits seems to be of some relevance in a substantial number of mergers, it is likely to be economically important in only a relatively small fraction of these. Of the 63 mergers with positive estimated tax benefits, only a third (21) have benefits in excess of 10% of the acquired firm's market value. Given the mean benefit of 10.5%, this result indicates substantial skewness in the distribution of tax benefits. When weighted by the market value of the target firm, the average declines to 6.1%, indicating that the mergers for which this tax attribute is of importance tend to be for the smaller targets.

Gains from Basis Step-up

In this area special circumstances may play a major role. We do not have sufficiently detailed data to identify such cases. Broadly speaking, however, we know that the step-up in basis is most valuable for assets which are classified as structures, including those in the minerals area, for these are subject only to limited recapture. We use a mechanical procedure, described in the Appendix, to identify the step-up in basis that each target firm would receive on its structures, and then we estimate the in-

crease in the present value of after-tax income due to the higher associated depreciation allowances. The procedure assumes that the firm's earliest reported book assets that we have available are correctly reported, estimates the fraction of these assets that are structures, and calculates the market and book values of these and subsequently acquired structures at the time of the merger under the assumption that the assets grew in nominal value at the general rate of price inflation, adjusted for economic depreciation of the assets. We do this calculation for all acquired firms.

The estimated benefits from basis step-up are substantially smaller in value than those estimated to have come from the transfer of losses and credits. We must point out, however, that at our level of aggregation of assets we may be missing some important variation in the types of assets being transferred. Our algorithm may greatly understate the step-up in basis possible for assets that have risen in value substantially faster than the general price level or were on the target firm's books for many years before the date at which our data became available and, hence, incorrectly valued at that date.[17]

For 43 of the 318 target firms, there are

additional data problems that prevent a calculation of this benefit. Of the remaining 275 firms, only 7 are estimated to produce a gain from basis step-up in excess of 5% of the target firm's value. Of the 40 cases where the target firm also has estimated tax benefits from unused credits and tax losses, the benefit from basis step-up is larger in only 2. However, in the past one could get the advantages of both step-up in basis and unused tax losses and credits through a variety of mechanisms, such as partial liquidations to the parent company of the property to be stepped up without a liquidation of the acquired company itself.[18]

Changes in Leverage

The final calculation we perform concerns the change in leverage for firms in our sample, to evaluate the hypothesis that the tax benefits from leverage are made accessible by mergers. Such an investigation might well be limited to cases where a substantial portion of the consideration received by shareholders of the acquired firm was cash, but we do not have sufficient information at present to make this distinction. Hence, we have considered all mergers in our sample.

There is a very serious conceptual problem in trying to estimate how much leverage changes *because* of a merger. Presumably, one measures the fraction of the two firms' total capitalization that is debt both before and after the merger. But an increase in the debt-equity ratio when the merger occurs is not necessarily evidence in support of the hypothesis. Suppose, for example, that a firm accumulates retentions for several years, in anticipation of a merger program, and then makes its acquisition by using borrowed funds in addition to its own internal accumulations. There would be an immediate increase in its debt-equity ratio because of the "lumpiness" of the project but, viewed from a longer perspective, no real change in its underlying financial policy. If a firm makes large investments every five years, we might observe its debt-equity ratio jump

with each investment and then decline gradually until the next jump. To describe this jump as a recurring change in its financial policy would be misleading, however.

We consider this to be an important problem in assessing the impact of mergers on leverage. To deal with it, we look at debt-equity ratios two years before and two years after the merger, rather than immediately before and immediately after. We hope to obtain better estimates of the firms' "long-run" debt-equity ratios, but caution is still advised.

We measure equity by the year-end market value of common stock and debt by the book value of long-term debt. The use of book values for long-term debt may cause problems. However, given the lack of information on the maturity structure of each firm's debt, we found there to be little alternative. We also performed the same calculations including short-term debt. However, the data on short-term debt are of poorer quality, and we are less confident about results that include them.

As already mentioned, we attempt to measure changes in debt and equity over the period beginning two years before the merger and ending two years after the merger. We have only 162 pairs of merging firms for which all data necessary for this calculation are available. The sample size can be increased to 207 by allowing minor variations in the base years for the calculation (one to three years before to one to three years after). The results of the two samples are quite similar.

We find that long-term debt as a fraction of long-term debt plus equity increases in each sample from an average of 30.0% to 32.1%. Weighting by the value of long-term debt plus equity of the combined firms gives smaller changes: The weighted-average ratio increases from 25.4% to 26.7%.

Given that our data ends in 1982 and we require debt-equity ratios two years after the merger for this calculation, no mergers beyond 1980 are included in these calculations. Thus, most of the four-year changes averaged here are from 1972–1976 to 1978–1982. According to data presented in Taggart (1985)[19] of the first six of these seven four-year periods (data on the last are not given), aggregate market debt-equity ratios increased over two, decreased over two, and increased quite negligibly (by 1 percentage point) over two. These year-to-year changes in average debt-value ratios were sufficiently large to make it difficult for us to view the increases in the sample as significant.

Indeed, this conclusion is reinforced by an examination of mergers where the acquired company was large relative to the acquiring company. One might expect the use of debt to be especially important in such cases. Yet the average combined debt–market value ratio for mergers in which the target's market value was between 25% and 50% of the parent's (before the combination) was unchanged at 39.0%, unweighted, and actually *declined* in the weighted sample, from 40.4% to 38.3%. Even for the small sample of mergers in which the acquired company's market value exceeded half that of the parent, the average rise in the debt–market value ratio was small, from 30.0% to 35.4%, unweighted, and from 32.1% to 35.3%, weighted.

CONCLUSIONS

In this chapter, we have examined a sample of 318 mergers and acquisitions that took place over the period 1968–1983. Nearly two-thirds of the mergers were between two manufacturing firms; the average acquiring firm was about ten times the size of the average acquired company.

A substantial fraction of the sample companies entered the mergers with some constraints on their ability to use tax benefits. About a fifth of all mergers in the sample involved cases where one firm faced such a constraint (indicated by the presence of tax credits or losses carried forward), while the other had positive current federal taxes and no such constraints. Such firms may have reduced their combined federal taxes by merging. Our estimates suggest, however, that the magnitude of such gains, though averaging 10.5% of the

acquired firm's market value, exceeded 10% in only a third of the cases, or about 6.5% of the sample. When expressed as a fraction of equity, rather than total market value, gains this large are of a similar order of magnitude as the average stock price premium paid for target firms in successful tender offers (Jensen and Ruback, 1983). Thus, for a small fraction of the mergers, the transfer of tax benefits could have played a significant role.

A second measure of the potential tax gain from merger, associated with the ability to step up the basis of depreciable assets without being subject to capital gains taxes, was generally estimated to be small relative to the acquired firm's market value. Here, however, our measurement technique is limited by the availability of data and may very well have understated the true gains available in cases where assets had greatly appreciated over time.

Finally, we found that the ratio of combined debt to market value for the parent and target firms in our sample increased slightly over the period beginning two years before and ending two years after the merger. The increase of 2.1 percentage points was small, however, given the magnitude of year-to-year changes in aggregate debt-to-value ratios over this period. Even when attention is limited to acquisitions of firms large in size relative to the acquiring companies, increases in leverage are small or absent.

In future work, we hope to extend our analysis by looking at different types of mergers within our sample that have been argued to have a special characteristics (e.g., those in the oil industry). We also plan to use data on firms that did *not* merge to gain a better understanding of the factors, tax-related and otherwise, that lead firms to merge.

APPENDIX

In this appendix, we describe our method for calculating the potential value of the step-up in basis an acquired firm would obtain on its structures.

We begin with the firm's book value of

fixed assets at the end of the last year be-fore the merger. Using data on the firm's gross investment and the capital stock at the end of the earliest year for which it is available for the firm, we use the "perpet-ual inventory" method to estimate the rate of declining-balance depreciation that is consistent with the firm's initial and ter-minal capital stocks. Given this estimate of economic depreciation, we then estimate the current market value of the capital stock by multiplying capital remaining from different vintages by the ratio of the price (represented by the GNP deflator) in the current year to that for the year in which the capital was purchased. We also assume that the initial capital stock was valued correctly on the firm's books. That is, we solve for δ from the equation

$$K_T = (1 - \delta)^T K_0$$
$$+ (1 - \delta)^{T-1} I_1 + \cdots + I_t \quad (19.1)$$

where
K_T is the book capital stock at the end of year T and I_T is fixed investment in year T.

$$K_T^m = (1 - \delta)^T K_0 P_T / P_0 + \cdots + I_t \quad (19.2)$$

We then calculate the market value of the capital stock as We assume that a fraction θ of this market value is structures, where θ measures the fraction of structures for all firms in the same industry (taken from Auerbach, 1983). Note that this will under-state the market value of assets that have increased in nominal value at a rate in ex-cess of the GNP deflator or were worth more than their book value even at time zero.

Since structures are written off at a dif-ferent rate from equipment, they will gen-erally represent a different fraction of the book capital stock than of the market value capital stock. Since structures decay more slowly, the book fraction will be smaller: Inflation has a greater effect on the ratio of current to book value as the time since purchase increases.

If one assumes that the structures' frac-tion of the firm's capital stock at time zero was also θ and that structures are written off at the declining-balance rate ε, it fol-lows that the book value of structures at date T is

$$K_T^S = \theta \left\{ K_0(1 - \epsilon)^T \right.$$
$$+ [K_T^m - K_0(1 + \pi)^T]$$
$$\times \frac{1 - (1 - g + \pi)(1 - \epsilon)}{1 - (1 - g + \pi)^T (1 - \epsilon)^T} \quad (19.3)$$
$$\left. \times \frac{1 - (1 - g)^T (1 - \epsilon)^T}{1 - (1 - g)(1 - \epsilon)} \right\}$$

where π is the average inflation rate over the period from 0 to T and g is the nominal growth rate of investment in structures. These values are easily calculated for each firm. We set $\epsilon = 0.033$, the aggregate value derived in Auerbach and Hines (1986).

Given the market value of the firm's structures capital stock, we estimate the after-tax value of depreciation allowances the firm would receive by multiplying the corporate tax rate by the average present value of depreciation allowances on all structures, estimated by Auerbach and Hines (1986). Somewhat more difficult is to estimate the depreciation allowances the firm would receive if continuing along its previous depreciation schedule, since its capital stock purchase dates are not known. We simply assume that they would get the same present value as is available on new capital per each dollar of remaining basis. Moreover, we assume that recapture will neutralize the additional depreciation allowances received on increases in basis up to the straight-line basis, and that this latter basis equals the actual book value. Thus, the net estimated gain is the present value of depreciation allowances on new structures, multiplied by the corporate tax rate, multiplied by the difference between the market and book values estimated for structures.

NOTES

1. See Auerbach (1983, 1986) for empirical and theoretical analyses of this point.
2. The proposal, prepared by the staff of the Senate Finance Committee, would restrict the

use of losses and credits of an acquired company by a parent by allowing only a certain percentage of them to be used in each year following the merger.

3. See, for example, Butters et al. (1951) and Feld (1982).

4. One that has been suggested to us related to the smoothing of taxable income discussed further later. In reducing the possibility of a tax loss occurring in the future, the firms may make the interest deduction on additional borrowing more valuable.

5. Martin Ginsburg has pointed out to us that many other assets, such as FIFO inventories, may also be written up without recapture. See also Lowenstein (1985).

6. The declining-balance formula specifies that year t's depreciation allowance will be $d(1 - d)^t$, where d is the rate of decline.

7. For further discussion on the economic incentives to turn over assets under a variety of circumstances, see Auerbach (1981) and Auerbach and Kotlikoff (1983).

8. The argument in the text ignores the possibility that firms can, to a certain extent, utilize both approaches simultaneously. We discuss this possibility further in a later section.

9. These provisions are discussed further in U.S. Senate Finance Committee (1985).

10. Testimony of Ronald A. Pearlman, assistant secretary of the Treasury for tax policy, before the Senate Finance Committee, September 30, 1985.

11. The criterion used was that the firm had negative federal taxes, zero investment tax credits, investment tax credits greater than or equal to federal taxes, or a positive, reported, tax-loss carryforward.

12. The average size of the parent companies is somewhat larger, and that of the target companies considerably smaller, than those of the sample of hostile takeovers analyzed by Herman and Lowenstein in Chapter 13 of this volume for a similar sample period. The smaller gap in average sizes for hostile takeovers is not surprising.

13. Experiments suggested that lengthening this time period had a relatively minor quantitative impact on the results.

14. Given the overall fractions of acquired and acquiring companies with unused losses or credits, one would predict fewer than 6, rather than 9, mergers between two firms from this group.

15. We also considered putting the group V firms into group IV. Because there are so few of them, this decision had little aggregate impact.

16. For a small fraction of the sample of target firms, we did not have the data necessary to construct a market value and used the sample mean market value in its place. This substitution would probably tend to understate our results somewhat, since one would expect missing data to be more common among smaller firms. Likewise, there were a smaller number of cases in which the taxable firms did not give a breakdown of total taxes into federal taxes and other taxes. For these firms, we imputed a value of 0.7 times total taxes, based on a regression run on the rest of the sample.

17. This difficulty is likely to be a particular problem in the cases of some oil mergers where large amounts of reserves were transferred.

18. Celebrated examples of this practice led to the restrictions on partial liquidations to corporate shareholders introduced in the Tax Equity and Fiscal Responsibility Act of 1982. Other channels for similar activity may remain.

19. These calculations are based on the Holland-Myers series represented by Taggart.

REFERENCES

Auerbach, A. J. (1981). "Inflation and the Tax Treatment of Firm Behavior." *American Economic Review,* May, 419–423.
——— (1983). *Corporate Taxation in the U.S.* Brookings Papers On Economic Activity, II.
——— (1986). "The Dynamic Effects of Tax Law Asymmetries." *Review of Economic Studies* April, 205–252.
———, and J. R. Hines (1986). *Tax Reform, Investment and the Value of the Firm.* NBER Working Paper No. 1803, January.
———, and L. J. Kotlikoff, (1983). "Investment Versus Savings Incentives: The Size of the Bang for the Buck and the Potential for Self-financing Business Tax Cuts." In *The Economic Consequences of Government Deficits,* ed. L. J. Meyer, 121–149. Hingham, Mass.: Kluwer-Nijhoff.
Butters, J. K., J. Lintner, and W. L. Cary (1951). *Effects of Taxation on Corporate Mergers.* Cambridge, Mass.: Harvard Business School.
Feld, A. (1982). *Tax Policy and Corporate Concentration.* Lexington: D. C. Heath.
Jensen, M. C., and R. S. Ruback (1983). "The Market for Corporate Control." Journal of Financial Economics, **11,** 5–50.
Lowenstein, L. (1985). "Management Buyouts." *Columbia Law Review,* May, 730–784.

Pearlman, R. A. (1985). Testimony before the Senate Finance Committee, Subcommittee on Taxation and Debt Management, September 30.

Taggart, R. A. (1985). "Secular Patterns in the Financing of U.S. Corporations." In *Corporate Capital Structures in the U.S.*, ed. B. Friedman, 13–75. Chicago: NBER, Chicago Press.

U.S. Joint Committee on Taxation (1970). *General Explanation of the Tax Reform Act of 1969*. Washington, D.C.: U.S. Government.

U.S. Senate Finance Committee (1985). *Staff Report on the Subchapter C Revision Act of 1985*. Washington, D.C.: U.S. Government.

20

The Takeover Controversy: Analysis and Evidence

MICHAEL C. JENSEN

The market for corporate control is fundamentally changing the corporate landscape. Transactions in this market in 1985 were at a record level of $180 billion, 47% above the $122 billion in 1984. The purchase prices in 36 of the 3000 deals in 1985 exceeded a billion dollars, compared with 18 in 1984.[1] These transactions involved takeovers, mergers, and leveraged buyouts. Closely associated were corporate restructurings involving divestitures, spinoffs, and large stock repurchases for cash and debt.

The changes associated with these control transactions are causing considerable controversy. Some argue that takeovers are damaging to the morale and productivity of organizations and therefore damaging to the economy. Others argue that takeovers represent productive entrepreneurial activity that improves the control and management of assets and helps move assets to more productive uses.

The controversy has been accompanied by strong pressure on regulators and legislatures to enact restrictions that would curb activity in the market for corporate control. In the spring of 1985 there were over twenty bills under consideration in Congress that proposed new restrictions on takeovers.[2] Within the past several years the legislatures of New York, New Jersey, Maryland, Pennsylvania, Connecticut, Illinois, Kentucky, and Michigan have passed antitakeover laws. The Federal Reserve Board entered the fray early in 1986 when it issued its controversial new interpretation of margin rules, which restricts the use of debt in takeovers.

Through dozens of studies, leading financial economists have accumulated considerable evidence and knowledge on the effects of the takeover market. Since most of the results of the work completed prior to 1984 are well summarized elsewhere,[3] I focus here on current aspects of the controvery and new results. In a nutshell, the previous work tell us the following:

1. Takeovers benefit target shareholders—premiums in hostile offers historically exceed 30%, on average, and in recent times have averaged about 50%.
2. Acquiring-firm shareholders on average earn about 4% in hostile takeovers and roughly zero in mergers.
3. Takeovers do not waste credit or re-

Professor of Business Administration, Harvard Business School, and LaClare Professor of Finance and Business Administration and Director of the Managerial Economics Research Center, William E. Simon Graduate School of Business Administration, University of Rochester. This research was supported by the Division of Research, Harvard Business School, and the Managerial Economics Research Center, University of Rochester. Earlier versions of this paper were presented at the National Bureau of Economic Research Summer Institute, Workshop of Mergers and Acquisitions, July 1985; at the MIT Center for Energy Policy Research Conference on "The World Oil Market: Why Won't It Be Still?" June 1985; and at the William G. Karnes Symposium on Mergers and Acquisitions sponsored by the University of Illinois at the Continental Illinois Bank, Chicago, Illinois, May 1985.

I am grateful for the research assistance of Michael Stevenson and the helpful comments by Sidney Davidson, Harry DeAngelo, Robert Kaplan, Jay Light, Nancy Macmillan, Susan Rose-Ackerman, Richard Ruback, Wolf Weinhold, Toni Wolcott, and especially Armen Alchian.

sources; they generate substantial gains—historically 8.4% of the total value of both companies. Recently, the gains seem to have been even larger.
4. Actions by managers that eliminate or prevent offers or mergers are most suspect as harmful to shareholders.
5. Golden parachutes for top-level managers do not, on average, harm shareholders.
6. The activities of takeover specialists such as Icahn, Posner, Steinberg, and Pickens, on average, benefit shareholders.[4]
7. Takeover gains do not come from the creation of monopoly power.

This chapter analyzes the controversy surrounding takeovers and provides both theory and evidence to explain the central phenomena at issue. The paper is organized as follows: The first section contains basic background analysis of the forces operating in the market for corporate control that provides an understanding of the conflicts and issues surrounding takeovers and the effects of activities in this market. The second section discusses the conflicts between managers and shareholders over the payout of free cash flow and how takeovers represent both a symptom of this conflict and a resolution of the conflict. The third section analyzes the problems the Delaware court is having in dealing with the conflicts that arise over control issues and its confused application of the business judgment rule to these cases. The fourth section provides the summary and conclusions.
The following topics are discussed:

1. The reasons for takeovers and mergers in the petroleum industry and why they increase efficiency and thereby promote the national interest.
2. The role of debt in bonding management's promises to pay out future cash flows, to reduce costs, and to reduce investments in low-return projects.
3. The role of high-yield debt (junk bonds) in helping to eliminate mere size as a takeover deterrent.
4. The effects of takeovers on the equity

markets and the claims that managers are pressured to behave myopically.
5. The effects of antitakeover measures such as poison pills.
6. The misunderstandings of the important role that "golden parachutes" play in reducing the conflicts of interests associated with takeovers and the valuable function they serve in alleviating some of the costs and uncertainty facing managers.
7. The damaging effects of the Delaware court decision in *Unocal v. Mesa* that allowed Unocal to make a self-tender that excluded its largest shareholder (reverse greenmail).
8. The problems the courts are facing in applying the model of the corporation subsumed under the traditional business judgment rule to the conflicts of interest involved in corporate control controversies.
9. The inefficiency introduced into the corporate control market by SEC Schedule 13d disclosure requirements.

THE MARKET FOR CORPORATE CONTROL—BACKGROUND

The Benefits of Takeovers

The market for corporate control is creating large benefits for shareholders and for the economy as a whole. The corporate control market generates these gains by loosening control over vast amounts of resources and enabling them to move more quickly to their highest-valued use. This is a healthy market in operation, on both the takeover side and the divestiture side.

Gains to Target Firms

Total benefits created by the control market have been huge, as reflected in gains of $40 billion to stockholders of acquired firms in 260 tender offers alone in the period January 1981 through May 1985.[5] This figure does not include the gains from other control transactions such as mergers, leveraged buy-outs, or divestitures, nor does it include the gains from reorganizations such as those of Phillips, Unocal, and others that have been motivated by take-over attempts. (The Phillips, Unocal, and ARCO reorganizations alone created gains of an additional $6.6 billion.) Paulus (1986) estimates the total premiums received by shareholders of target firms to be approximately $75 billion in $239 billion of merger and acquisition deals in 1984 and 1985.

Gains to Bidding Firms

The evidence on the returns of bidding firms is mixed. The data indicate that prior to 1980 shareholders of bidding firms earned on average about zero in mergers (which tend to be voluntary) and about 4% of their equity value in tender offers (which tend to be hostile).[6] These differences in returns are associated with the form of payment rather than the form of the offer (tender offers tend to be for cash and mergers tend to be for stock).[7]

There is reason to believe the estimates of gains to bidding firm shareholders are too low. A recent study by Dennis and McConnell (1986) of 90 matched acquiring and acquired firms in mergers in the period 1962–1980 shows that the values of bonds, preferred stock, and other senior securities, as well as the common stock prices of both firms, increase around the merger announcement. The value changes in senior securities are not captured in measures of changes in the value of common stock prices summarized previously. Taking the changes in the value of senior securities into account, Dennis and McConnell find the average change in total dollar value of both bidders and target firms is positive.[8] A study by Eckbo of over 1800 mergers involving Canadian target firms in the period 1964–1983 indicates significantly positive average returns to approximately 1200 bidding firms listed on the Toronto Stock Exchange and negative average returns (in the announcement month) to approximately 500 bidders listed on the New York Stock Exchange.[9] Recent SEC estimates indicate that since 1980 U.S. bidders in tender offers have also earned zero returns on average. Allen and Sirmans (1987) in a study of 38 REIT mergers in the period 1977–1983 find that the bidding firms

earned significantly positive returns of about 9% in the 20 days surrounding the announcement of the offer.[10]

Although measurement problems make it difficult to estimate the returns to bidders as precisely as the returns to targets,[11] the bargaining power of target managers, coupled with competition among potential acquirers, appears to grant much of the acquisition benefits to selling shareholders. In addition, federal and state regulation of tender offers seems to have strengthened the hand of target firms; premiums received by target firm shareholders increased substantially after introduction of such regulation.[12]

Causes of Current Takeover Activity

The current high level of takeover activity seems to be caused by a number of factors, including the following:

- The relaxation of restrictions on mergers imposed by the antitrust laws.
- The withdrawal of resources from industries that are growing more slowly or that must shrink.
- Deregulation in the financial services, oil and gas, transportation, and broadcasting markets that is bringing about a major restructuring of those industries.
- Improvements in takeover technology, including a larger supply of increasingly sophisticated legal and financial advisors, and improvements in financing technology (e.g., the strip financing commonly used in leveraged buy-outs and the original issuance of high-yield noninvestment-grade bonds).

Each of these factors has contributed to the increase in total takeover and reorganization activity in recent times. Moreover, the first three factors (antitrust relaxation, exit, and deregulation) are generally consistent with data showing the intensity of takeover activity by industry. For example, the value of merger and acquisition transactions by industry in the period 1981–1984 given in Table 20.1 indicates that acquisition activity was highest in oil and gas, followed by banking and finance, insurance, food processing, and mining

Table 20.1. Intensity of Industry Takeover Activity as Measured by the Value of Merger and Acquisition Transactions in the Period 1981–84 (as a Percent of Total Takeover Transactions for Which Valuation Data Are Publicly Reported) Compared with Industry Size (as Measured by the Fraction of Overall Corporate Market Value)

Industry Classification of Seller	Percent of Total Takeover Activity[a]	Percent of Total Corporate Market Value[b]
Oil and gas	26.3	13.5
Banking and finance	8.8	6.4
Insurance	5.9	2.9
Food processing	4.6	4.4
Mining and minerals	4.4	1.5
Conglomerate	4.4	3.2
Retail	3.6	5.2
Transportation	2.4	2.7
Leisure and entertainment	2.3	0.9
Broadcasting	2.3	0.7
Other	39.4	58.5

[a]*Source:* Grimm (1984), p. 41.

[b]As of 12/31/84. Total value is measured as the sum of the market value of common equity for 4305 companies, including 1501 companies on the NYSE, 724 companies on the ASE, plus 2080 companies in the over-the-counter market. *Source: The Media General Financial Weekly* (December 31, 1984), p. 17.

and minerals. For comparison purposes, the last column of the table presents data on industry size measured as a fraction of the total value of all firms. All but two of the industries, retail and transportation, represent a larger fraction of total takeover activity than their representation in the economy as a whole.

Many areas of the U.S. economy have been experiencing slowing growth and, in some cases, even retrenchment—a phenomenon that has many causes, including substantially increased competition from foreign firms. This slow growth has increased takeover activity because takeovers play an important role in facilitating exit from an industry or activity. Major changes in energy markets have required a radical restructuring of and retrenchment in that industry, and as discussed in detail later, takeovers have played an important role in accomplishing these changes. Deregulation of the financial services market is consistent with the high ranking in Table 20.1 of banking and finance, and insur-

ance. Deregulation has also been important in the transportation and broadcasting industries. Mining and minerals have been subject to many of the same forces impinging on the energy industry, including the changes in the value of the dollar.

Takeovers and Competition for Top-Level Management Jobs

The market for corporate control is best viewed as a major component of the managerial labor market. It is the arena in which alternative management teams compete for the rights to manage corporate resources.[13] Understanding this point is crucial to understanding much of the rhetoric about the effects of hostile takeovers.

Managers formerly protected from competition for their jobs by antitrust constraints that prevented takeover of the nation's largest corporations are now facing a more demanding environment and a more uncertain future.

The development of innovative financing vehicles, such as high-yield noninvestment-grade bonds (junk bonds), has removed size as a significant impediment to competition in this market. Although they have not been widely used in takeovers yet, these new financing techniques permit small firms to obtain resources for acquisition of much larger firms by issuing claims on the value of the venture (i.e., the target firm's assets) just as in any other corporate investment activity. Not surprisingly, many executives of large corporations would like relief from this new competition for their jobs, but restricting the corporate control market is not the efficient way to handle the problems caused by the increased uncertainty in their contracting environment.

Takeovers and External Control

The internal control mechanisms of corporations, which operate through the board of directors, generally work well. On occasion, however, they break down. One important source of protection for investors in these situations is the takeover market. Other management teams that recognize an opportunity to reorganize or redeploy an organization's assets and thereby create new value can bid for the control rights in the takeover market. To be successful, such bids must be at a premium over current market value. This premium gives investors an opportunity to realize part of the gains from reorganization and redeployment of the assets.

The Market for Corporate Control as an Agent for Change

Takeovers generally occur because changing technology or market conditions require a major restructuring of corporate assets. In some cases, takeovers occur because incumbent managers are incompetent. When the internal processes for change in large corporations are too slow, costly, and clumsy to bring about the required restructuring or change in managers efficiently, the capital markets, through the market for corporate control, are doing so. Thus, the capital markets have recently been responsible for substantial changes in corporate strategy.

Managers often have trouble abandoning strategies they have spent years devising and implementing, even when those strategies no longer contribute to the organization's survival. Such changes can require abandonment of major projects, relocation of facilities, changes in managerial assignments, and closure or sale of facilities or divisions. It is easier for new top-level managers with no ties with current employees or communities to make such changes. Moreover, normal organizational resistance to change commonly lessens significantly early in the reign of new top-level managers. For example, the premium Carl Icahn was able to offer for TWA and his victory over Texas Air for the acquisition of TWA were made possible in part by the willingness of TWA unions to negotiate favorable contract concessions with Icahn—concessions that TWA was unable to win prior to the takeover conflict. Such organizational factors that make change easier for newcomers, coupled with a fresh view of the business, can be a major advantage to new managers after a takeover. On the other hand, lack of detailed knowledge about the firm poses risks for new managers and increases the likelihood of mistakes.

Takeovers are particularly important in bringing about efficiencies when exit from an activity is required. The oil industry is a good example. Changing market conditions mandate a major restructuring of the petroleum industry, which is not the fault of management. Management, however, must adjust to the new energy environment and recognize that many old practices and strategies are no longer viable. Many managers have difficulty dealing with the fact that some firms in the oil industry have to go out of business. Exit is cheaper to accomplish through merger and the orderly liquidation of marginal assets of the combined firms than by a slow death in a competitive struggle in an industry saddled with overcapacity. The end of the competitive struggle often comes in the bankruptcy courts, with high losses and unnecessary destruction of valuable parts of organizations that could be used productively by others.

Summary

In short, the external takeover market serves as a court of last resort that plays an important role in (1) creating organizational change, (2) motivating the efficient use of resources, and (3) protecting shareholders when the corporation's internal controls and board-level control mechanisms are slow and clumsy or break down.

Erroneous Criticism of Divestitures

If assets are to move to their most highly valued use, acquirers must be able to sell off assets to those who can use them more productively. Therefore, divestitures are a critical element in the functioning of the corporate control market, and it is important to avoid inhibiting them. Indeed, over twelve hundred divestitures occurred in 1985, a record level.[14] Labeling divestitures with emotional terms such as *bust-ups* is not a substitute for analysis or evidence.

Moreover, divested plants and assets do not disappear; they are reallocated. Sometimes, they continue to be used in similar ways in the same industry, and in other cases they are used in very different ways and in different industries. But in both cases they are moving to uses that their new owners believe are more productive, which is beneficial to society.

Finally, the takeover and divestiture market provides a private market constraint against bigness for its own sake. The potential gains available to those who correctly perceive that a firm can be purchased for less than the value realizable from the sale of its components provide incentives for entrepreneurs to search out these opportunities and to capitalize on them by reorganizing such firms into smaller entities.

The mere possibility of such takeovers also motivates managers to avoid putting together uneconomic conglomerates and to break up existing ones. This is now happening. Recently, many firms' defenses against takeovers have led to actions similar to those proposed by their potential ac-

quirers. Examples are the reorganizations occurring in the oil and forest products industries, the sale of "crown jewels," and divestitures brought on by the desire to liquidate large debts incurred to buy back stock or make other payments to stockholders. Unfortunately, the basic economic sense of these transactions is often lost in a blur of emotional rhetoric and controversy.

The sale of a firm's crown jewels, for example, benefits shareholders when the price obtained for the division is greater than the present value of the future cash flows to the current owner. A takeover bid motivated by the desire to obtain such an underused division can stimulate current managers to reexamine the economics of the firm's current structure and to sell one or more of its divisions to a third party who is willing to pay even more than the initial offerer. Brunswick's sale of its Sherwood Medical Division to American Home Products after a takeover bid by Whittaker (apparently motivated by a desire to acquire Sherwood) is an example of such a transaction. The total value to Brunswick shareholders of the price received for selling Sherwood to American Home Products plus the remaining value of Brunswick without Sherwood was greater than Whittaker's offer for the entire company.[15]

Managers May Behave Myopically but Markets Do Not

It has been argued that growing institutional equity holdings and the fear of takeover cause managers to behave myopically and therefore to sacrifice long-term benefits to increase short-term profits. The arguments tend to confuse two separate issues: (1) whether *managers* are short-sighted and make decisions that undervalue future cash flows while overvaluing current cash flows (myopic managers), and (2) whether *security markets* are short-sighted and undervalue future cash flows while overvaluing near-term cash flows (myopic markets).

There is little formal evidence on the myopic-managers issue, but I believe this phenomenon does occur. Sometimes it occurs when managers hold little stock in their companies and are compensated in ways that motivate them to take actions to increase accounting earnings rather than the value of the firm. It also occurs when managers make mistakes because they do not understand the forces that determine stock values.

There is much evidence inconsistent with the myopic-markets view and no evidence that indicates it is true:

1. Even casual observation of the equity markets reveals that the market values more than current earnings. It values growth as well. The mere fact that price-earnings ratios differ widely among securities indicates the market is valuing something other than current earnings. Indeed, the essence of a growth stock is one that has large investment projects yielding few short-term cash flows but high future earnings and cash flows.

2. The continuing marketability of new issues for start-up companies with little record of current earnings, the Genentechs of the world, is also inconsistent with the notion that the market does not value future earnings.[16]

3. McConnell and Muscarella (1985) provide evidence that (except in the oil industry) stock prices respond positively to announcements of increased investment expenditures and negatively to reduced expenditures. Their evidence is also inconsistent with the notion that the equity market is myopic.

4. The vast evidence on efficient markets indicating that current stock prices appropriately incorporate all currently available public information is also inconsistent with the myopic-markets hypothesis. Although the evidence is not literally 100% in support of the efficient-market hypothesis, there is no better documented proposition in any of the social sciences.[17]

The evidence indicates, for example, that the market appropriately interprets the implications of corporate accounting changes that increase reported profits but cause no change in corporate cash flows.

Examples are switches from accelerated to straight-line depreciation techniques and adoption of the flow-through method for reporting investment tax credits. Here the evidence indicates that "security prices increase around the date when a firm first announces earnings inflated by an accounting change. The effect appears to be temporary, and, certainly by the subsequent quarterly report, the price has resumed a level appropriate to the true economic status of the firm."[18]

Additional evidence is provided by the 30% increase in ARCO's stock price that occurred when it announced its major restructuring in 1985. This price increase is inconsistent with the notion that the market values only short-term earnings. The market responded positively even though ARCO simultaneously revealed it would have to take a $1.2 billion write-off as a result of the restructuring.

5. Recent versions of the myopic-markets hypothesis emphasize increasing institutional holdings and the pressures they face to generate high returns on a quarter-to-quarter basis. It is argued that these pressures on institutions are a major cause of pressures on corporations to generate high current earnings on a quarter-to-quarter basis. The institutional pressures are said to lead to increased takeovers of firms (because institutions are not loyal shareholders) and to decreased research and development expenditures. It is hypothesized that because R&D expenditures reduce current earnings, firms making them are therefore more likely to be taken over, and reductions in R&D are leading to a fundamental weakening of the corporate sector of the economy.

A recent study of 324 firms by the Office of the Chief Economist of the SEC finds substantial evidence that is inconsistent with this version of the myopic-markets argument.[19] The evidence indicates the following:

• Increased institutional stock holdings are not associated with increased takeovers of firms.

- Increased institutional holdings are not associated with decreases in R&D expenditures.
- Firms with high R&D expenditures are not more vulnerable to takeovers.
- Stock prices respond positively to announcements of increases in R&D expenditures.

Those who make the argument that takeovers are reducing R&D spending also have to come to grips with the aggregate data on such spending, which is inconsistent with the argument. Total spending on R&D in 1984, a year of record acquisition activity, increased by 14% according to *Business Week's* annual survey of 820 companies. (The sample companies account for 95% of total private-sector R&D expenditures.) This represented "the biggest gain since R&D spending began a steady climb in the late 1970's."[20] All industries in the survey increased R&D spending with the exception of steel. Moreover, R&D spending increased from 2% of sales, where it had been for five years, to 2.9%. In 1985, another record year for takeovers, *Business Week's* survey showed that R&D spending again set new records, reaching 3.1% of sales.

An Alternative Hypothesis

There is an alternative hypothesis that explains the current facts, including the criticisms of managers, quite well. Suppose some managers are simply mistaken, i.e., their strategies are wrong, and that the financial markets are telling them they are wrong. If they don't change, their stock prices will remain low. If the managers are indeed wrong, it is desirable for the stockholders and for the economy to remove them to make way for a change in strategy and more efficient use of the resources.

FREE CASH FLOW THEORY OF TAKEOVERS

More than a dozen separate forces drive takeover activity, including such factors as deregulation, synergies, economies of scale and scope, taxes, managerial incompetence, empire building, and increasing globalization of U.S. markets.[21] One major cause of takeover activity, the agency costs associated with conflicts between managers and shareholders over the payout of free cash flow, has received relatively little attention. Yet it has played an important role in acquisitions over the last decade.[22]

Managers are the agents of shareholders, and because both parties are self-interested, there are serious conflicts between them over the choice of the best corporate strategy. Agency costs are the total costs that arise in such cooperative arrangements. They consist of the costs of monitoring managerial behavior (such as the costs of producing audited financial statements and devising and implementing compensation plans that reward managers for actions that increase investors' wealth) and the inevitable costs that are incurred because the conflicts of interest can never be resolved perfectly. Sometimes, these costs can be large, and when they are, takeovers can reduce them.

Free Cash Flow and the Conflict Between Managers and Shareholders

Free cash flow is cash flow in excess of that required to fund all projects that have positive net present values when discounted at the relevant cost of capital. Such free cash flow must be paid out to shareholders if the firm is to be efficient and to maximize value for shareholders.

Payment of cash to shareholders reduces the resources under managers' control, thereby reducing managers' power and potentially subjecting them to the monitoring by the capital markets that occurs when a firm must obtain new capital. Financing projects internally avoids this monitoring and the possibility that funds will be unavailable or available only at high explicit prices.

Managers have incentives to expand their firms beyond the size that maximizes shareholder wealth.[23] Growth increases managers' power by increasing the resources under their control. In addition, changes in management compensation are positively related to growth.[24] The tendency of firms to reward middle managers through promotion rather than year-to-year bonuses also creates an organizational bias toward growth to supply the new positions that such promotion-based reward systems require (see Baker, 1986).

The tendency for managers to overinvest resources is limited by competition in the product and factor markets, which tends to drive prices toward minimum average cost in an activity. Managers must therefore motivate their organizations to be more efficient to improve the probability of survival. Product and factor market disciplinary forces are often weaker in new activities, however, and in activities that involve substantial economic rents or quasi rents.[25] In these cases, monitoring by the firm's internal control system and the market for corporate control are more important. Activities yielding substantial economic rents or quasi rents are the types of activities that generate large amounts of free cash flow.

Conflicts of interest between shareholders and managers over payout policies are especially severe when the organization generates substantial free cash flow. The problem is how to motivate managers to disgorge the cash rather than invest it at below the cost of capital or waste it through organizational inefficiencies.

Myers and Majluf (1984) argue that financial flexibility (unused-debt capacity and internally generated funds) is desirable when a firm's managers have better information about the firm than outside investors. Their arguments assume that managers act in the best interest of shareholders. The arguments offered here imply that such flexibility has costs—financial flexibility in the form of free cash flow, large cash balances, and unused borrowing power provides managers with greater discretion over resources that is often not used in the shareholders' interests.

The theory developed here explains (1) how debt for stock exchanges reduces the organizational inefficiencies fostered by substantial free cash flow, (2) how debt can substitute for dividends, (3) why "diversification" programs are more likely to be associated with losses than are expansion programs in the same line of business, (4) why mergers within an industry and liquidation-motivated takeovers will generally create larger gains than cross-industry mergers, (5) why the factors stimulating takeovers in such diverse businesses as broadcasting, tobacco, cable systems, and oil are essentially identical, and (5) why bidders and some targets tend to show abnormally good performance prior to takeover.

The Role of Debt in Motivating Organizational Efficiency

The agency costs of debt have been widely discussed,[26] but the benefits of debt in motivating managers and their organizations to be efficient have largely been ignored. I call these effects the "control hypothesis" for debt creation.

Managers with substantial free cash flow can increase dividends or repurchase stock and thereby pay out current cash that would otherwise be invested in low-return projects or wasted. This payout leaves managers with control over the use of future free cash flows, but they can also promise to pay out future cash flows by announcing a "permanent" increase in the dividend.[27] Because there is no contractual obligation to make the promised dividend payments, such promises are weak. Dividends can be reduced by managers in the future with little effective recourse available to shareholders. The fact that capital markets punish dividend cuts with large stock price reductions is an interesting equilibrium market response to the agency costs of free cash flow.[28]

Debt creation, without retention of the proceeds of the issue, enables managers effectively to bond their promise to payout future cash flows. Thus, debt can be an effective substitute for dividends, something not generally recognized in the corporate finance literature.[29] By issuing debt in exchange for stock, managers bond their promise to payout future cash flows in a way that simple dividend increases do not. In doing so, they give shareholder-recipients of the debt the right to take the firm into bankruptcy court if they do not keep their promise to make the interest and principal payments.[30] Thus, debt reduces the agency costs of free cash flow by reducing the cash flow available for spending at the discretion of managers. These control effects of debt are a potential determinant of capital structure.

Issuing large amounts of debt to buy back stock sets up organizational incentives to motivate managers to payout free cash flow. In addition, the exchange of debt for stock also helps managers overcome the normal organizational resistance to retrenchment that the payout of free cash flow often requires. The threat of failure to make debt service payments serves as a strong motivating force to make such organizations more efficient. Stock repurchase for debt or cash also has tax advantages. Interest payments are tax-deductible to the corporation, that part of the repurchase proceeds equal to the seller's tax basis in the stock is not taxed at all, and that which is taxed is subject to capital gains rates.

Increased leverage also has costs. As leverage increases, the usual agency costs of debt, including bankruptcy costs, rise. The incentives to take on projects that reduce total firm value but benefit shareholders through a transfer of wealth from bondholders is one source of these costs. These costs put a limit on the desirable level of debt. The optimal debt-equity ratio is the point at which firm value is maximized, the point where the marginal costs of debt just offset the marginal benefits.

The control hypothesis does not imply that debt issues will always have positive control effects. For example, these effects will not be as important for rapidly growing organizations with large and highly profitable investment projects but no free cash flow. Such organizations will have to go regularly to the financial markets to obtain capital. At these times the markets have an opportunity to evaluate the company, its management, and its proposed projects. Investment bankers and analysis play an important role in this monitoring, and the market's assessment is made evident by the price investors pay for the financial claims.

The control function of debt is more important in organizations that generate large cash flows but have low growth prospects, and it is even more important in organizations that must shrink. In these organizations the pressures to waste cash flows by investing them in uneconomic projects are most serious.

Evidence from Financial Transactions

Free cash flow theory helps explain previously puzzling results on the effects of various financial transactions. Smith (1986, Tables 1–3) summarizes more than twenty studies of stock price changes at announcements of transactions that change capital structure as well as various other dividend transactions. These results and those of others are summarized in Table 20.2.

For firms with positive free cash flow, the theory predicts that stock prices will increase with unexpected increases in payouts to shareholders and decrease with unexpected decreases in payouts. It also predicts that unexpected increases in demand for funds from shareholders via new issues will cause stock prices to fall. In addition, the theory predicts stock prices will increase with increasing tightness of the constraints binding the payout of future cash flow to shareholders and decrease with reductions in the tightness of these constraints. These predictions do not apply to those firms with more profitable projects than cash flow to fund them.

The predictions of the agency cost of free cash flow are consistent with all but 3 of the 32 estimated abnormal stock price changes summarized in Table 20.2. Moreover, one of the inconsistencies is explainable by another phenomenon.

Panel A of Table 20.2 shows that stock prices rise by a statistically significant amount with announcements of the initiation of cash dividend payments and increases in dividends and specially designated dividends, and fall by a statistically significant amount with decreases in dividend payments. (All coefficients in the table are significantly different from zero unless noted with an asterisk.)

Panel B of Table 20.2 shows that secu-

Table 20.2. Summary of Two-Day Average Abnormal Stock Returns Associated with the Announcement of Various Dividend and Capital Structure Transactions (Returns are weighted averages, by sample size, of the returns reported by the respective studies; all returns are significantly different from zero unless noted otherwise by *)

Type of Transaction	Security Issued	Security Retired	Average Sample Size	Average Abnormal Two-Day Announcement Period Return	Sign Predicted by Free Cash Flow Theory	Agreement with Free Cash Flow Theory	Agreement with Tax Theory
Panel A Dividend changes that change the cash paid to shareholders							
Dividend initiation[a]			160	3.7%	+	Yes	No
Dividend increase[b]			281	1.0	+	Yes	No
Specially designated dividend[c]			164	2.1	+	Yes	No
Dividend decrease[b]			48	−3.6	−	Yes	No
Panel B Security sales (that raise cash) and retirements (that pay out cash) and simultaneously provide offsetting changes in the constraints bonding future payment of cash flows							
Security sale (industrial)[d]	Debt	None	248	−0.2*	0	Yes	No
Security sale (utility)[e]	Debt	None	140	−0.1*	0	Yes	No
Security sale (industrial)[f]	Preferred	None	28	−0.1*	0	Yes	Yes
Security sale (utility)[g]	Preferred	None	251	−0.1*	0	Yes	Yes
Call[h]	None	Debt	133	−0.1*	0	Yes	No
Panel C Security sales which raise cash and bond future cash payments only minimally							
Security sale (industrial)[d]	Conv. debt	None	74	−2.1	−	Yes	No
Security sale (industrial)[g]	Conv. preferred	None	54	−1.4	−	Yes	No
Security sale (utility)[g]	Conv. preferred	None	9	−1.6	−	Yes	No

Panel D
Security retirements that pay out cash to shareholders.

Self-tender offer[i]	None	Common	147	15.2	+	Yes	Yes
Open-market purchase[j]	None	Common	182	3.3	+	Yes	Yes
Targeted small holdings[k]	None	Common	15	1.1	+	Yes	Yes
Targeted large-block repurchase[l]	None	Common	68	−4.8	+	No[v]	No[v]

Panel E
Security sales or calls that raise cash and do not bond future cash flow payments

Security sale (industrial)[m]	Common	None	215	−3.0	−	Yes	Yes
Security sale (utility)[n]	Common	None	405	−0.6	−	Yes	Yes
Conversion-forcing call[t]	Common	Conv. preferred	57	−0.4*	−	No	Yes
Conversion-forcing call[t]	Common	Conv. debt	113	−2.1	−	Yes	Yes

Panel F
Exchange offers, or designated-use security sales that increase the bonding of future cash flows

Designated-use security sale[o]	Debt	Common	45	21.9	+	Yes	Yes
Exchange offer[p]	Debt	Common	52	14.0	+	Yes	Yes
Exchange offer[p]	preferred	Common	10	8.3	+	Yes	No
Exchange offer[p]	Debt	Preferred	24	3.5	+	Yes	Yes
Exchange offer[q]	Income bonds	Preferred	18	1.6	+	Yes	Yes

Panel G
Transaction with no change in bonding of payout of future cash flows

Exchange offer[r]	Debt	Debt	36	0.6	0	No	No
Designated-use security sale[s]	Debt	Debt	96	0.2*	0	Yes	Yes

Table 20.2 (Continued)

Type of Transaction	Security Issued	Security Retired	Average Sample Size	Average Abnormal Two-Day Announcement Period Return	Sign Predicted by Free Cash Flow Theory	Agreement with Free Cash Flow Theory	Agreement with Tax Theory
Panel H							
Exchange offers, or designated-use security sales that decrease the bonding of payout of future cash flows							
Security sale[s]	Conv. debt	Debt	15	−2.4	—	Yes	Yes
Exchange offer[p]	Common	Preferred	23	−2.6	—	Yes	No
Exchange offer[p]	Preferred	Debt	9	−7.7	—	Yes	Yes
Security sale[s]	Common	Debt	12	−4.2	—	Yes	Yes
Exchange offer[u]	Common	Debt	81	−1.1	—	Yes	Yes

[a]Asquith and Mullins (1983).

[b]Charest (1978) and Aharony and Swary (1980).

[c]From Brickley (1983).

[d]Dann and Mikkelson (1984), Eckbo (1986), and Mikkelson and Partch(1986).

[e]Eckbo (1986).

[f]Linn and Pinegar (1985) and Mikkelson and Partch (1986).

[g]Linn and Pinegar (1985).

[h]Vu (1986).

[i]Dann (1981), Masulis (1980), Vermaelen (1981), and Rosenfeld (1982).

[j]Dann (1980) and Vermaelen (1981).

[k]Bradley and Wakeman (1983).

[l]Calculated by Smith (1986, Table 4) from Dann and DeAngelo (1983), and Bradley and Wakeman (1983).

[m]Asquith and Mullins (1986), Kolodny and Suhler (1985), Masulis and Korwar (1986), and Mikkelson and Partch (1986).

[n]Asquith and Mullins (1986), Masulis and Korwar (1986), and Pettway and Radcliffe (1985).

[o]Offers with more than 50% debt; Masulis (1980).

[p]Masulis (1983). These returns include announcement days of both the original offer and, for about 40% of the sample, a second announcement of specific terms of the exchange.

[q]McConnell and Schlarbaum (1981).

[r]Dietrich (1984).

[s]Eckbo (1986) and Mikkelson and Partch (1986).

[t]Mikkelson (1981).

[u]Rogers and Owers (1985), Peavy and Scott (1985), and Finnerty (1985).

[v]Explained by the fact that these transactions are frequently associated with the termination of an actual or expected control bid. The price decline appears to reflect the loss of an expected control premium.

*Not statistically different from zero.

rity sales and retirements that raise cash or pay out cash and simultaneously provide offsetting changes in the constraints bonding the payout of future cash flow are all associated with returns insignificantly different from zero. The insignificant return on retirement of debt fits the theory because the payout of cash is offset by an equal reduction in the present value of promised future cash payouts. If the debt sales are associated with no changes in the expected investment program, the insignificant return on announcement of the sale of debt and preferred also fits the theory. The acquisition of new funds with debt or preferred is offset exactly by a commitment bonding the future payout of cash flows of equal present value.

Panel C shows that sales of convertible debt and convertible preferred are associated with significantly negative stock price changes. These security sales raise cash and provide little effective bonding of future cash flow payments, because when the stock into which the debt is convertible is worth more than the face value of the debt, management has incentives to call them and force conversion to common.

Panel D shows that, with one exception, security retirements that pay out cash to shareholders increase stock prices. The price decline associated with targeted large-block repurchases (often called greenmail) is highly likely to be due to the reduced probability that a takeover premium will be realized. These transactions are often associated with standstill agreements in which the seller of the stock agrees to refrain from acquiring more stock and from making a takeover offer for some period into the future.[31]

Panel E summarizes the effects of security sales and retirements that raise cash and do not bond future cash flow payments. Consistent with the theory, negative abnormal returns are associated with all such changes. However, the negative returns associated with the sale of common through a conversion-forcing call are statistically insignificant.

Panel F shows that all exchange offers or designated-use security sales that increase the bonding of payout of future cash flows

result in significantly positive increases in common stock prices. These include stock repurchases and exchange of debt or preferred for common, debt for preferred, and income bonds for preferred. The two-day gains range from 21.9% (debt for common) to 2.2% (debt or income bonds for preferred).[32]

Panel G of Table 20.2 shows that the evidence on transactions with no cash flow and no change in the bonding of payout of future cash flows is mixed. The returns associated with exchange offers of debt for debt are significantly positive, and those for designated-use security sales are insignificantly different from zero.

Panel H of Table 20.2 shows that all exchanges or designated-use security sales that have no cash effects but reduce the bonding of payout of future cash flows result, on average, in significant decreases in stock prices. These transactions include the exchange of common for debt or preferred or preferred for debt, or the replacement of debt with convertible debt. The two-day losses range from −9.9% (common for debt) to −2.4% (for designated-use security sale replacing debt with convertible debt).

In summary, the results in Table 20.2 are remarkably consistent with free cash flow theory, which predicts that, except for firms with profitable unfunded investment projects, prices will rise with unexpected increases in payouts to shareholders (or promises to do so) and will fall with reductions in payments or new requests for funds from shareholders (or reductions in promises to make future payments). Moreover, the size of the value changes is positively related to the change in the tightness of the commitment bonding the payment of future cash flows. For example, the effects of debt-for-preferred exchanges are smaller than the effects of debt-for-common exchanges.

Tax effects can explain some of these results but not all—for example, the price increase on exchange of preferred for common or replacement of debt with convertible debt, which have no tax effects. The last column of Table 20.2 denotes whether the individual coefficients are explainable by these pure corporate tax effects. The tax theory hypothesizes that all unexpected changes in capital structure which decrease corporate taxes increase stock prices and vice versa.[33] Therefore, increases in dividend and reductions of debt interest should cause stock prices to fall and vice versa.[34] Fourteen of the 32 coefficients are inconsistent with the corporate-tax hypothesis. Simple signaling effects, where the payout of cash signals the lack of present and future investments that promise returns in excess of the cost of capital, are also inconsistent with the results—for example, the positive stock price changes associated with dividend increases and stock repurchases.

If anything, the results in Table 20.2 seem too good. The returns summarized in the table do not distinguish firms that have free cash flow from those that do not have free cash flow. Yet the theory tells us the returns to firms with no free cash flow will behave differently from those who do. In addition, only unexpected changes in cash payout or the tightness of the commitments bonding the payout of future free cash flows should affect stock prices. The studies summarized in Table 20.2 do not, in general, control for the effects of expectations. If the free cash flow effects are large and if firms on average are in a positive free cash flow position, the predictions of the theory will hold for the simple sample averages. If the effects are this pervasive, the waste due to agency problems in the corporate sector is greater than most scholars have thought. This waste explains the high level of activity in the corporate control market over the past decade. More detailed tests of the propositions that control for growth prospects and expectations will be interesting.

Evidence from Leveraged Buy-Out and Going-Private Transactions

Many of the benefits in going-private and leveraged buy-out transactions seem to be due to the control function of debt. These transactions are creating a new organizational form that competes successfully with the open corporate form because of advantages in controlling the agency costs of free cash flow. In 1984, going-private transactions totaled $10.8 billion and represented 27% of all public acquisitions.[35] The evidence indicates premiums paid averaged over 50%.[36]

Desirable leveraged buy-out candidates are frequently firms or divisions of larger firms that have stable business histories and substantial free cash flow (i.e., low growth prospects and high potential for generating cash flows)—situations where agency costs of free cash flow are likely to be high. Leveraged buy-out transactions are frequently financed with high debt; 10-to-1 ratios of debt to equity are not uncommon. Moreover, the use of strip financing and the allocation of equity in the deals reveal a sensitivity to incentives, conflicts of interest, and bankruptcy costs.

Strip financing, the practice in which risky nonequity securities are held in approximately equal proportions, limits the conflict of interest among such securityholders and therefore limits bankruptcy costs. A somewhat oversimplified example illustrates the point. Consider two firms identical in every respect except financing. Firm A is entirely financed with equity, and Firm B is highly leveraged with senior subordinated debt, convertible debt, and preferred as well as equity. Suppose Firm B securities are sold only in strips, i.e., a buyer purchasing X% of any security must purchase X% of all securities, and the securities are "stapled" together so they cannot be separated later. Securityholders of both firms have identical unlevered claims on the cash flow distribution, but organizationally the two firms are very different. If Firm B managers withhold dividends to invest in value-reducing projets or if they are incompetent, stripholders have recourse to remedial powers not available to the equityholders of Firm A. Each Firm B security specifies the rights its holder has in the event of default on its dividend or coupon payment—for example, the right to take the firm into bankruptcy or to have board representation. As each security above equity goes into default, the stripholder receives new rights to intercede in the organization. As a result, it is quicker and less expensive to replace managers in Firm B.

Moreover, because every securityholder in the highly levered Firm B has the same claim on the firm, there are no conflicts between senior and junior claimants over reorganization of the claims in the event of default; to the stripholder it is a matter of moving funds from one pocket to another. Thus, Firm B need never go into bankruptcy; the reorganization can be accomplished voluntarily, quickly, and with less expense and disruption than through bankruptcy proceedings.

Securities commonly subject to strip practices are often called "mezzanine" financing and include securities with priority superior to common stock yet subordinate to senior debt. This arrangement seems to be sensible. Because of several other factors ignored in our simplified example, strictly proportional holdings of all securities are not desirable. For example, IRS restrictions deny tax deductibility of debt interest in such situations and bank holdings of equity are restricted by regulation. Riskless senior debt need not be in the strip because there are no conflicts with other claimants in the event of reorganization when there is no probability of default on its payments.

It is advantageous to have top-level managers and venture capitalists who promote the transactions hold a larger share of the equity. Top-level managers frequently receive 15% to 20% of the equity, and venture capitalists and the funds they represent generally retain the major share of the remainder. The venture capitalists control the board of directors and monitor managers. Managers and venture capitalists have a strong interest in making the venture successful because their equity interests are subordinate to other claims. Success requires (among other things) implementation of changes to avoid investment in low-return projects to generate the cash for debt service and to increase the value of equity. Finally, when the equity is held primarily by managers or generally by a small number of people, efficiencies in risk bearing are possible by placing more of the risk in the hands of debtholders when

the debt is held in well-diversified institutional portfolios.

Less than a handful of these leveraged buy-out ventures have ended in bankruptcy, although more have gone through private reorganizations. A thorough test of this organizational form requires the passage of time and another recession.

Some have asserted that managers engaging in a buy-out of their firm are insulating themselves from monitoring. The opposite is true in the typical leveraged buy-out. Because the venture capitalists are generally the largest shareholder and control the board of directors, they have both greater ability and incentives to monitor managers effectively than directors representing diffuse public shareholders in the typical public corporation.

Evidence from the Oil Industry

The oil industry is large and visible. It is also an industry in which the importance of takeovers in motivating change and efficiency is particularly clear. Therefore, detailed analysis of it provides an understanding of how the market for corporate control helps motivate more efficient use of resources in the corporate sector.

Mandatory Reorganization of the Industry

Radical changes in the energy market from 1973 to the late 1970s imply that a major restructuring of the petroleum industry had to occur. These changes include the following:

- A tenfold increase in the price of crude oil from 1973 to 1979.
- Reduced annual consumption of oil in the United States.
- Reduced expectations of future increases in the price of oil.
- Increased exploration and development costs.
- Increased real interest rates.

As a result of these changes, the optimal level of refining and distribution capacity and crude reserves fell over this period; and as of the late 1970s, the industry was plagued with excess capacity. Reserves are reduced by reducing the level of exploration and development, and it pays to concentrate these reductions in high-cost areas such as the United States.

Substantial reductions in exploration and development and in refining and distribution capacity meant that some firms had to leave the industry. This is especially true because holding reserves is subject to economies of scale, but exploration and development are subject to diseconomies of scale.

Price increases created large cash flows in the industry. For example, 1984 cash flows of the ten largest oil companies were $48.5 billion, 28% of the total cash flows of the top 200 firms in Dun's Business Month (1985) survey. Consistent with the agency costs of free cash flow, management did not pay out the excess resources to shareholders. Instead, the industry continued to spend heavily on exploration and development even though average returns on these expenditures were below the cost of capital.

Paradoxically, the profitability of oil exploration and drilling activity can decrease even though the price of oil increases if the value of reserves in the ground falls. This decrease can occur when the price increase is associated with reductions in consumption that make marketing newly discovered oil difficult. In the late 1970s the increased holding costs associated with higher real interest rates, reductions in expected future oil price increases, increased exploration and development costs, and reductions in the consumption of oil combined to make many exploration and development projects uneconomic. The industry, however, continued to spend heavily on such projects.

The hypothesis that oil industry exploration and development expenditures were too high during this period is consistent with the findings of a study by McConnell and Muscarella.[37] Their evidence indicates that announcements of increases in exploration and development expenditures by oil companies in the period 1975–1981 were associated with systematic *decreases* in the announcing firm's stock price. Moreover, announcements of decreases in exploration and development expenditures were associated with increases in stock prices. These results are striking in comparison with their evidence that exactly the opposite market reaction occurs with increases and decreases in investment expenditures by industrial firms, and SEC evidence that increases in research and development expenditures are associated with increased stock prices.

Additional evidence of the uneconomic nature of the oil industry's exploration and development expenditures is contained in a study by Bernard Picchi of Salomon Brothers (1985). His study of the rates of return on exploration and development expenditures for 30 large oil firms indicated that on average the industry did not earn "even a 10% return on its pretax outlays" in the period 1982–1984. Estimates of the average ratio of the present value of future net cash flows of discoveries, extensions, and enhanced recovery to expenditures for exploration and development for the industry ranged from less than 0.6 to slightly more than 0.9, depending on the method used and the year. In other words, taking the cost of capital to be only 10% on a pretax basis, the industry was realizing on average only 60¢ to 90¢ on every dollar invested in these activities. Picchi concludes:

For 23 of the companies in our survey, we would recommend *immediate* cuts of perhaps 25%–30% in exploration and production spending. It is clear that much of the money that these firms spent last year on petroleum exploration and development yielded subpar financial returns—even at $30 per barrel, let alone today's $26–$27 per barrel price structure.[38]

The waste associated with excessive exploration and development expenditures explains why buying oil on Wall Street was considerably cheaper than obtaining it by drilling holes in the ground, even after adjustment for differential taxes and regulations on prices of old oil. Wall Street was not undervaluing the oil; it was valuing it correctly, but it was also correctly valuing the wasted expenditures on exploration and development that oil companies were making. When these managerially imposed "taxes" on the reserves were taken into account, the net price of oil on Wall Street was very low. This low price provided incentives for firms to obtain reserves by purchasing other oil companies and reducing expenditures on non-cost-effective exploration.

High Profits Not Usually Associated with Retrenchment

Adjustment by the energy industry to the new environment has been slow for several reasons. First, organizations cannot easily change operating rules and practices that have worked well for long periods in the past, even though they do not fit the new situation. Nevertheless, survival requires that organizations adapt to major changes in their environment.

Second, the past decade has been a particularly puzzling period in the oil business, because at the same time that changes in the environment have required a reduction of capacity, cash flows and profits have been high. This condition is somewhat unusual in that the average productivity of resources in the industry increased while the marginal productivity decreased. The piont is illustrated graphically in Figure 20.1.

As the figure illustrates, profits plus payments to factors of production other than

capital in 1985 were larger than in 1973. Moreover, because of the upward shift and simultaneous twist of the marginal productivity-of-capital schedule from 1973 to 1985, the optimal level of capital devoted to the industry fell from Q_1 to Q_2. Thus, the adjustment signals were confused because the period of necessary retrenchment coincided with substantial increases in value brought about by the tenfold increase in the price of the industry's major asset, its inventory of crude oil reserves.

The large cash flows and profits generated by the increases in oil prices both masked the losses imposed by the product markets on marginal facilities and enabled oil companies to finance major expenditures internally. Thus, the normal disciplinary forces of the product market have been weak and those of the capital markets have been inoperative during the past decade.

Third, the oil companies' large and highly visible profits subjected them to strong political pressures to reinvest the cash flows in exploration and development to alleviate the incorrect, but popular, perception that reserves were too low. Furthermore, while reserves were on average too high, those firms that were substan-

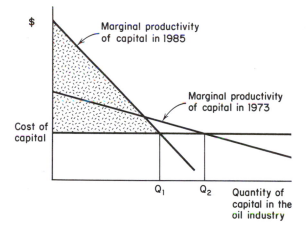

Figure 20.1. Optimal level of capital in the oil industry prior to 1973, Q_1, and in 1985, Q_2. The shaded area represents the profits (plus payments to factors of production other than capital) earned by the industry in 1985. The shift in the marginal-productivity-of-capital schedule raised the average productivity of capital but reduced the marginal productivity to a level below the cost of capital. As a result, profits and cash flow increased, but capital had to leave the industry.

tially short of reserves were spending to replenish them to avoid the organizational consequences associated with reserve deficiencies. The resulting excessive exploration and development expenditures by the industry and the considerable delays in retrenchment of refining and distribution facilities wasted resources.

In sum, the stage was set for retrenchment in the oil industry in the early 1980s. Yet the product and capital markets could not force management to change its strategy because the industry's high internal cash flows insulated them from these pressures.

The fact that oil industry managers tried to invest funds outside the industry is also evidence that they could not find enough profitable projects within the industry to use the huge inflow of resources efficiently. Unfortunately, these efforts failed. The diversification programs involved purchases of companies in retailing (Marcor by Mobil), manufacturing (Reliance Electric by Exxon), office equipment (Vydec by Exxon), and mining (Kennecott by Sohio, Anaconda Minerals by ARCO, Cyprus Mines by Amoco). These acquisitions turned out to be among the least successful of the last decade, partly because of bad luck (e.g., the collapse of the minerals industry) and partly because of a lack of managerial expertise outside the oil industry.

The Effects of Takeovers

Ultimately, the capital markets, through the takeover market, have begun to force managers to respond to the new market conditions. Unfortunately, there is widespread confusion about the important role of takeovers in bringing about the difficult but necessary organizational changes required in the retrenchment.

Managers, quite naturally, want large amounts of resources under their control to insulate them from the uncertainties of markets.[39] Retrenchment requires cancellation or delay of ongoing and planned projects. This adjustment affects the careers of the people involved, and the resulting resistance means such changes frequently do not get made without the major

pressures often associated with a crisis. A takeover attempt can create the crisis that brings about action where none would otherwise occur.

T. Boone Pickens of Mesa Petroleum perceived early that the oil industry must be restructured. Partly as a result of Mesa's efforts, firms in the industry were led to merge, and in the merging process they paid out large amounts of capital to shareholders, reduced excess expenditures on exploration and development, and reduced excess capacity in refining and distribution. The result has been large gains in efficiency. Total gains to the shareholders in the Gulf/Chevron, Getty/Texaco and DuPont/Conoco mergers, for example, were over $17 billion. Much more is possible. Jacobs (1986) estimates total potential gains of approximately $200 billion from eliminating the inefficiencies in 98 petroleum firms as of December 1984.[40]

Recent events indicate that actual takeover is not necessary to induce the required adjustments:

- The Phillips restructuring plan, brought about by the threat of takeover, involved substantial retrenchment and return of resources to shareholders, and the result was a $1.2 billion (20%) gain in Phillips' market value. It repurchased 53% of its stock for $4.5 billion in debt, raised its dividend 25%, cut capital spending, and initiated a program to sell $2 billion of assets.
- Unocal's defense in the Mesa tender offer battle resulted in a $2.2 billion (35%) gain to shareholders from retrenchment and return of resources to shareholders. It paid out 52% of its equity by repurchasing stock with a $4.2 billion debt issue and will reduce costs and capital expenditures.
- The voluntary restructuring announced by ARCO resulted in a $3.2 billion (30%) gain in market value. ARCO's restructuring involves a 35% to 40% cut in exploration and development expenditures, repurchase of 25% of its stock for $4 billion, a 33% increase in its dividend, withdrawal from gasoline marketing and refining east of the Missis-

sippi, and a 13% reduction in its work force.

- The announcement of the Diamond-Shamrock reorganization in July 1985 provides an interesting contrast to the others and further support for the theory because the company's market value *fell* 2% on the announcement day. Because the plan results in an effective increase in exploration and capital expenditures and a reduction in cash payouts to investors, the restructuring does not increase the value of the firm. The plan involved reducing cash dividends by $0.76 per share ($-43\%$), creating a master limited partnership to hold properties accounting for 35% of its North American oil and gas production, paying an annual $0.90-per-share dividend in partnership shares, repurchasing 6% of its shares for $200 million, selling 12% of its master limited partnership to the public, and *increasing* its expenditures on oil and gas exploration by $100 million per year.

Free Cash Flow Theory of Takeovers

Free cash flow is only one of approximately a dozen theories to explain takeovers, all of which are of some relevance in explaining the numerous forces motivating merger and acquisition activity (see Roll, Chapter 14 of this volume). The agency cost of free cash flow is consistent with a wide range of data for which there has been no consistent explanation. Here I sketch some empirical predictions of the free cash flow theory for takeovers and mergers and what I believe are the facts that lend it credence.

The positive market response to debt creation in oil and other takeovers (see Bruner, 1985) is consistent with the agency costs of free cash flow and the control hypothesis of debt. The data is consistent with the notion that additional debt increases efficiency by forcing organizations with large cash flows but few high-return investment projects to pay out cash to investors. The debt helps prevent such firms from wasting resources on low-return projects. Acquisitions are one way managers spend cash instead of paying it out to shareholders. Therefore, free cash flow theory predicts which mergers and takeovers are more likely to destroy, rather than to create, value; it shows how takeovers are both evidence of the conflicts of interest between shareholders and managers and a response to the problem. Therefore, the theory implies that managers of firms with unused borrowing power and large free cash flows are more likely to undertake low-benefit or even value-destroying mergers. Diversification programs generally fit this category, and the theory predicts that they will generate lower total gains. The major benefit of such transactions may be that they involve less waste of resources than if the funds had been invested internally in unprofitable projects.

Acquisitions made with cash or securities other than stock involve payout of resources to (target) shareholders, and this can create net benefits even if the merger creates operating inefficiencies. To illustrate the point, consider an acquiring firm, A, with substantial free cash flow that the market expects will be invested in low-return projects with a negative net present value of $100 million. If Firm A makes an acquisition of Firm B that generates zero synergies but uses up all of Firm A's free cash flow (and thereby prevents its waste), the combined market value of the two firms will *rise* by $100 million. The market value increases because the acquisition eliminates the expenditures on internal investments with negative market value of $100 million. Extending the argument, we see that acquisitions that have *negative* synergies of up to $100 million in current value will still increase the combined market value of the two firms. Such negative-synergy mergers will also increase social welfare and aggregate productivity whenever the market value of the waste that would have occurred with the firms' investment programs in the absence of the merger. The division of the gains between the target and bidding firms depends, of course, on the bargaining power of the two parties. Because the bidding firms are using funds that would otherwise have been spent on low- or negative-return projects, however, the opportunity cost of the funds is lower than their cost of capital. As a result, they will tend to overpay for the acquisition and thereby transfer most, if not all, of the gains to the target firm's shareholders. In extreme cases they may pay so much that the bidding firm's share price falls, in effect giving the target shareholders more than 100% of the gains. These predictions are consistent with the evidence.

Low-return mergers are more likely to occur in industries with large cash flows whose economics dictate retrenchment. Horizontal mergers (where cash or debt is the form of payment) within declining industries will tend to create value because they facilitate exit—the cash or debt payments to shareholders of the target firm cause resources to leave the industry directly. Mergers outside the industry are more likely to have low or even negative returns because managers are likely to know less about managing such firms. Oil fits this description, and so does tobacco. Tobacco firms face declining demand as a result of changing smoking habits but generate large free cash flow and have been involved in major diversifying acquisitions recently—for example, the $5.6 billion purchase of General Foods by Philip Morris. The theory predicts that these acquisition in nonrelated industries are more likely to create negative-productivity effects, although these appear to be outweighed by the reductions in waste from internal expansion. Forest products is another industry with excess capacity and acquisition activity, including the acquisition of St. Regis by Champion International and Crown Zellerbach by Sir James Goldsmith. Horizontal mergers for cash or debt in such an industry generate gains by encouraging exit of resources (through payout) and by substituting existing capacity for investment in new facilities by firms that are short of capacity.

Food industry mergers also appear to reflect the expenditure of free cash flow. The industry apparently generates large cash flows with few growth opportunities. It is therefore a good candidate for leveraged buy-outs, and these are now occurring; the

$6.3 billion Beatrice LBO is the largest ever.

The broadcasting industry generates rents in the form of large cash flows on its licenses and also fits the theory. Regulation limits the overall supply of licenses and the number owned by a single entity. Thus, profitable internal investments are limited, and the industry's free cash flow has been spent on organizational inefficiencies and diversification programs, making these firms takeover targets. The CBS debt-for-stock exchange and restructuring as a defense against the hostile bid by Turner fits the theory, and so does the $3.5 billion purchase of American Broadcasting Company by Capital Cities Communications. Completed cable systems also create agency problems from free cash flows in the form of rents on their franchises and quasi rents on their investment and are likely targets for acquisition and leveraged buy-outs. Large cash flows earned by motion picture companies on their film libraries also represent quasi rents and are likely to generate free cash flow problems. The attempted takeover of Disney and its subsequent reorganization is also consistent with the theory. Drug companies with large cash flows from previous successful discoveries and few potential future prospects are also likely candidates for large agency costs of free cash flow.

The theory predicts that value-increasing takeovers occur in response to breakdowns of internal control processes in firms with substantial free cash flow and organizational policies (including diversification programs) that are wasting resources. It predicts hostile takeovers, large increases in leverage, the dismantling of empires with few economies of scale or scope to give them economic purpose (e.g., conglomerates), and much controversy as current managers object to loss of their jobs or changes in organizational policies forced on them by threat of takeover.

The debt created in a hostile takeover (or takeover defense) of a firm suffering severe agency costs of free cash flow need not be permanent. Indeed, sometimes "over-leveraging" such a firm is desirable. In these situations, levering the firm so highly that it cannot continue to exist in its old form yields benefits. It creates the crisis to motivate cuts in expansion programs and the sale of those divisions that are more valuable outside the firm. The proceeds are used to reduce debt to a more normal or permanent level. This process results in a complete rethinking of the organization's strategy and structure. When it is successful, a much leaner, more efficient, and competitive organization results.

Consistent with the data, free cash flow theory predicts that many acquirers will tend to perform exceptionally well prior to acquisition. This exceptional stock price performance will often be associated with increased free cash flow, which is then used for acquisition programs. The oil industry fits this description. Increased oil prices caused large gains in profits and stock prices in the mid to late 1970s. Empirical evidence from studies of both stock prices and accounting data also indicates exceptionally good performance for acquirers prior to acquisition.[41] Exceptional performance tends to generate the free cash flow for the acquisition.

Targets will be of two kinds: firms with poor management that have done poorly before the merger, and firms that have done exceptionally well and have large free cash flow that they refuse to pay out to shareholders. Both kinds of targets seem to exist, but more careful study is required. Asquith (1983) finds evidence of below-normal stock price performance for 302 target firms in the 400 days before 20 days prior to the takeover bid. Mandelker (1974) finds negative abnormal performance for target firms in the period from 40 months before until 9 months before the outcome of the merger bid is known. Langetieg (1978) reports significant negative returns in the period from 72 months before until 19 months before the outcome date, but positive abnormal returns in the 19 months preceding the merger date.

Ravenscraft and Scherer in Chapter 12 of this volume examine the average accounting return on equity measured by the ratio of operating income (before interest,

extraordinary charges, and income taxes) to book value of equity for 634 small manufacturing firms acquired in 1968, 1971, and 1974. They find average return on equity of 20.2% in the year prior to merger. In the same period, the average return to all manufacturing firms was 10.9%. Because their sample represents small (median premerger asset size of $2.4 million) and mainly private manufacturing firms acquired through an exchange of stock, it is of limited usefulness in making inferences about recent takeovers of large publicly held manufacturing and nonmanufacturing companies (many acquired for cash). As Table 20.1 shows, takeovers are occurring to a large extent in industries outside manufacturing and are much larger—billion-dollar acquisitions are now common [36 were completed in 1985 (Grimm, 1985)]. Valuing this entire Ravenscraft-Scherer sample at the median value of $2.4 million yields an estimate of *total* value of $1.5 billion, which means that even allowing for a positively skewed distribution, its total value is less than $5 billion dollars. Thus, on a pure value basis, their sample deserves weight equal to no more than half that given to the Socal acquisition of Gulf in 1984, which was valued at $13.2 billion and provided total gains to shareholders of both firms of $9 billion. Moreover, the sample contains few if any of the cash offers that are creating so much controversy today.

The theory predicts that takeovers financed with cash and debt will create larger benefits than those accomplished through exchange of stock. Stock acquisitions do nothing to take up the organizations' financial slack and are therefore unlikely to motivate managers to use resources more efficiently. The recent evidence on takeover premiums is consistent with this prediction.[42]

Stock acquisitions tend to be different from debt or cash acquisitions and are more likely to be associated with growth opportunities and a shortage of free cash flow. They therefore represent a fundamentally different phenomenon from the nongrowth- or exit-motivated acquisitions that have been occurring in the 1980s. Thus the growth-oriented and conglomerate mergers and acquisitions of the late 1960s and the early 1970s reflect a different phenomenon than that represented by the exit-motivated mergers and acquisitions of the late 1970s and 1980s.

The Ravenscraft and Scherer (1985 and Chapter 12 of this volume) study of the mergers of the late 1960s and the early 1970s provides evidence of relevance to the free cash flow theory of takeovers. The special characteristics of their sample, however, make it significantly different from the mergers and acquisitions that have taken place since the late 1970s. Ravenscraft and Scherer studied 27 years of merger history, including over five thousand acquisitions by 456 manufacturing corporations prior to 1977. Half of all their mergers were completed before 1967. These acquisitions were small, both in absolute terms and in relation to the size of the acquirer. The targets tended to be privately held; in only 69 of the 5000-plus mergers did the merging firms' assets differ by as much as a factor of two—the study's criterion for a merger of equals. Using line-of-business profit data obtained from the Federal Trade Commission, the authors find that mergers of equals had a positive effect on profits in the line of business they were merged into in 1975, 1976, and 1977, the three years for which they have acquiring-firm profit data. They also find that mergers that were treated for accounting purposes as pooling of interests tended to be positively related to profitability of the line of business in the three test years, although the effects are not always statistically significant.

Ravenscraft and Scherer (Chapter 12) conclude: "The most agnostic view would be that the profitability effects of acquisition ... jump around a fair amount and, averaged over three years of the business cycle, are mildly and insignificantly positive" (p. 203).

Forty-seven percent of the Ravenscraft and Scherer sample of mergers were treated for accounting purposes as purchases. In a purchase, the target's assets are recorded on the acquiring firm's books at their purchase price rather than at book value, as they are under the pooling-of-interests method. The authors' estimates indicate purchase mergers were associated with significantly lower profits in the lines of business into which they were merged. This result is consistent with free cash flow theory because of the Accounting Principles Board rules that restricted the use of pooling for mergers after 1970. After that time, all cash mergers had to be accounted for as a purchase and numerous other specific criteria had to be met to qualify for the use of pooling of interests for noncash transactions. Thus purchase mergers after 1970 are likely to be characterized by high agency costs of free cash flow. Therefore, in these mergers we expect to see declining market share if the new management is reducing the overinvestment. Ravenscraft and Scherer do not test for this decline directly, but they find that changes in market share are a significant explanatory factor in their profits regression. They also find the amount of previous purchase merger activity to be negatively associated with the profits of the line of business in the 1974–1977 period. Part of this negative association results from the negative effects of the higher depreciation of the written-up assets. Controlling for these effects by using cash flow deflated by sales instead of profits indicates the higher depreciation charges are not the whole story, because the cash flow regressions also indicate a negative influence. This result is inconsistent with free cash flow theory if it is true for cash purchases after 1970. Unfortunately, the authors did not control for differences in the accounting treatment of mergers before and after 1970. They also did not control for differences in the method of payment.

Free cash flow theory predicts that mergers in the same line of activity will show larger profits than diversification mergers. Ravenscraft and Scherer find this result to be true for pooling mergers, although they do not test for this effect in purchase mergers. In the pooling mergers that were horizontal or in related businesses (same two-digit industry but no horizontal or vertical connection), the effects on profits were systematically positive. On the other hand,

Elgers and Clark (1980) find shareholders of merging firms gain more from conglomerate than nonconglomerate mergers, and Asquith and Kim (1982) and Wansley et al. (1983) find no differences in returns for conglomerate and nonconglomerate mergers.

Palepu (1986), in the best study to date of the determinants of takeover, finds strong evidence consistent with the free cash flow theory of mergers. He studied a sample of 163 firms that were acquired in the period 1971–1979 and a random sample of 256 firms that were not acquired. Both samples were in mining and manufacturing and were listed on either the New York or American Stock Exchange. He finds that target firms were characterized by significantly lower growth and lower leverage than the nontarget firms, although there was no significant difference in their holdings of liquid assets. He also finds that poor prior performance (measured by the net of market returns in the four years before the acquisition) is significantly related to the probability of takeover and, interestingly, that accounting measures of past performance such as return on equity are unrelated to the probability of takeover. He also finds that firms with a mismatch between growth and resources are more likely to be taken over. These are firms with high growth (measured by average sales growth), low liquidity (measured by the ratio of liquid assets to total assets), and high leverage, and firms with low growth, high liquidity, and low leverage. Finally, Palepu's evidence rejects the hypothesis that takeovers are due to the undervaluation of a firm's assets as measured by the market-to-book ratio.

The McConnell and Muscarella (1985) findings of positive average market response to announcements of increase in capital expenditure programs in all industries except oil is inconsistent with free cash flow theory. The inconsistency between the results reported in Table 20.2 and in this study could occur because firms that announce changes in capital expenditure programs tend not to have free cash flow. Resolution of these issues awaits more explicit tests.

Mueller (1980) presents a series of studies of mergers in seven developed countries. The studies are based almost entirely on accounting data and therefore are of limited use in measuring the effects of mergers. Nevertheless, as Mueller concludes:

In four countries—Belgium, the Federal Republic of Germany, the United Kingdom, and the United States—the merging firms realized a slightly superior performance based on after-tax profits than the size-matched control group companies. . . . In the other three countries—France, Holland, and Sweden—there was evidence of a relative decline in the profitability of the merging firms following the mergers. . . . As in the first four countries, the differences . . . were not large, however, and the levels of significance were generally low. No consistent pattern of either improved or deteriorated profitabilities can therefore be claimed across the seven countries. . . . If a generalization is to be drawn, it would have to be that mergers have but modest effects, up or down, on the profitability of the merging firms in the three to five years following merger. (pp. 304–306)

These results are expected from samples that pool both growth- and exit-motivated mergers.

HIGH-YIELD ("JUNK") BONDS

The past several years have witnessed a major innovation in the financial markets with the establishment of active markets in high-yield bonds. These bonds are rated below investment grade by the bond-rating agencies and are frequently referred to as junk bonds, a disparaging term that bears no relation to their pedigree. They carry interest rates 3 to 5 percentage points higher than the yields on government bonds of comparable maturity. High-yield bonds are best thought of as commercial loans that can be resold in secondary markets. By traditional standards they are more risky than investment-grade bonds and therefore carry higher interest rates. In an early study, Blume and Keim (1984) find that the default rates on these bonds have been low and the realized returns have been disproportionately higher than their risk.

High-yield bonds have been attacked by those who wish to inhibit their use, particularly in the financing of takeover bids. The invention of high-yield bonds has provided methods to finance takeover ventures similar to those that companies use to finance more traditional ventures. Companies commonly raise funds to finance ventures by selling claims to be paid from the proceeds of the venture; this is the essence of debt or stock issues used to finance new ventures. High-yield bonds used in takeovers work similarly. The bonds provide a claim on the proceeds of the venture, using the assets and cash flows of the target plus the equity contributed by the acquirer as collateral. This basic structure is the common way that individuals purchase homes; they use the home plus their down payment as collateral for the mortgage. There is nothing inherently unusual in the structure of this contract, although those who would bar the use of high-yield bonds in takeover ventures would have us believe otherwise.

Some might argue that the risk of high-yield bonds used in takeover attempts is "too high." But high-yield bonds are by definition less risky than common stock claims on the same venture. The claims of common stockholders are subordinate to those of the holders of high-yield bonds. Would these same critics argue that the stock claims are too risky and thus should be barred? The risk argument makes logical sense only as an argument that transactions costs associated with bankruptcy or recontracting are too high in these ventures or that the bonds are priced too high and that investors who purchase them will not earn returns high enough to compensate for the risk they are incurring. This overpricing argument makes little sense because there is vast evidence that investors are capable of pricing risks in all sorts of other markets. That they are peculiarly unable to do so in the high-yield bond market is inconceivable.

In January 1986 the Federal Reserve Board issued a new interpretation of the margin rules that restricts the use of debt in takeovers to 50% or less of the purchase price. This rule reintroduces size as an effective deterrent to takeover. It was apparently motivated by the belief that the use of corporate debt had become abnormally and dangerously high and was threatening the economy. This assessment is not consistent with the facts. Figure 20.2 plots three measures of debt use by nonfinancial corporations in the United States. The debt-equity ratio is measured relative to

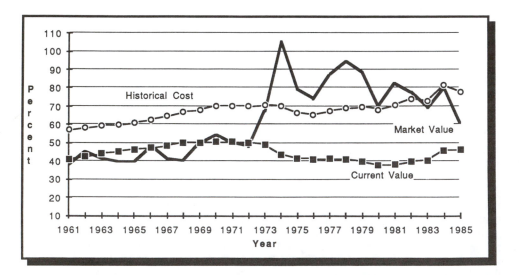

Figure 20.2. Debt-to-equity ratios for nonfinancial corporations in the period 1961–1985. (*Source:* Federal Reserve System, 1986.)

three bases: market value of equity, estimated current asset value of equity, and accounting book value of equity measured at historical cost.

Although debt-equity ratios were higher in 1985 than in 1961, they were not at record levels. The book-value debt-equity ratio reached a high of 81.4% in 1984 but declined to 78% in 1985. The fact that debt-equity ratios measured on an historical-cost basis is relatively high is to be expected, given the previous decade of inflation. Maintenance of the same inflation-adjusted debt-equity ratio in times of inflation implies that the book-value ratio must rise because the current value of assets in the denominator of the inflation-adjusted ratio is rising. The current-value ratio, which takes account of inflation, fell from 50.7% in 1970 to 46.5% in 1985. The market value ratio rose from 54.7% in 1970 to 80.5% in 1984 and plummeted to 60.8% in 1985. The 1985 market value ratio was 45 percentage points below its 1974 peak of 105.2%. Thus, the Federal Reserve System's own data are inconsistent with the reasons given for its restrictions on the use of debt.

High-yield bonds were first used in a takeover bid in early 1984 and have been involved in relatively few bids in total. In 1984, only about 12% of the $14.3 billion of new high-yield debt was associated with mergers and acquisitions. In 1985, 26% of the $14.7 billion of new high-yield debt was used in acquisitions.[43] Some of the acquisitions, however, such as the Unocal and CBS offers (both unsuccessful), have received intense attention by the media, and this publicity has fostered the belief that high-yield bonds are widely used in takeovers. Nevertheless, high-yield bonds are an important innovation in the takeover field because they help eliminate mere size as a deterrent to takeover. They have been particularly influential in helping to bring about reorganizations in the oil industry.

Historical default rates on high-yield bonds have been low, but many of these bonds are so new that the experience could prove to be different in the next downturn. Various opponents have proposed regulations or legislation to restrict the issuance of such securities, to penalize their tax status, and to restrict their holding by thrifts, which can now buy them as substitutes for the issuance of nonmarketable commercial loans. These proposals are premature. Policymakers should be wary of responding to the clamor for restrictions by executives who desire protection from the discipline of the takeover market and by members of the financial community who want to restrict competition from this new financing vehicle.

The holding of high-yield bonds by thrifts is an interesting issue that warrants further analysis. The recent deregulation of the banking and thrift industries presents many opportunities and challenges to the thrifts. Elimination of restrictions on interest paid to depositors has raised the cost of funds to these institutions. Thrifts have also received the right to engage in new activities such as commercial lending. Survival requires these institutions to take advantage of some of these new business opportunities.

The organizational costs of developing commercial lending departments in the 3500 thrifts in the country will be substantial. Thousands of new loan officers will have to be hired and trained. The additional wage and training costs and the bad-debt losses that will be incurred in the learning phase will be substantial. High-yield bonds provide a promising solution to this problem. If part of the commercial lending function can be centralized in the hands of investment bankers who provide commercial loans in the form of marketable high-yield debt, the thrifts can substitute the purchase of this high-yield debt for its own commercial lending and thereby avoid the huge investment in such loan departments.

THE LEGITIMATE CONCERNS OF MANAGERS

Conflicts of Interest and Increased Costs to Managers

The interests of corporate managers are not the same as the interests of corporations as organizations, and these differences in interests become intense when major changes in the organization's strategy are required. Competition causes change, and change creates winners and losers, especially in that branch of the managerial labor market called the takeover market.

Managers' Private Incentives versus Overall Efficiency

The costs of takeovers have fallen as the legal and financial skills of participants in the takeover market have become more sophisticated, as the restrictions on takeovers imposed by antitrust laws have been relaxed, and as financing techniques have improved. Thus, if we exclude new regulatory constraints on the use of debt, the largest of the Fortune 500 companies are now potentially subject to takeover. The abolition of mere size as a deterrent to takeover is desirable because it has made possible the realization of large gains from reallocating larger collections of assets to more productive uses.

This new susceptibility to takeover has created a new contracting environment for top-level managers. Many managers are legitimately anxious, and it will take time for the system to work out an appropriate set of practices and contracts reflecting the risks and rewards of the new environment. Some of the uncertainty of top-level managers formerly insulated from pressures from the financial markets will fade as they learn how their policies affect the market value of their companies.

The Desirability of Golden Parachutes

Unfortunately, a major component of the solution to the conflict of interest between shareholders and managers has been vastly misunderstood. I am referring to severance contracts that compensate managers for the loss of their jobs in the event of a change in control—what have been popularly labeled "golden parachutes."

These contracts are clearly desirable, even when judged solely from the viewpoint of the interests of shareholders, but they are also efficient from a social view-

point. When correctly implemented, they help reduce the conflicts of interest between shareholders and managers at times of takeover and therefore make it more likely that the productive gains stemming from changes in control will be realized. The evidence indicates that stock prices of firms that adopt severance-related compensation contracts for managers on average rise about 3% when adoption of the contracts is announced.[44] There is no easy way to tell how much of this could be due to the market interpreting the announcement as a signal that a takeover bid is more likely and how much is due to the reduction in conflict between managers and shareholders over takeovers.

At times of takeover, shareholders are implicitly asking the top-level managers of their firm to negotiate a deal for them that frequently involves the imposition of large personal costs on the managers and their families. These involve substantial moving costs, the loss of position, power, and prestige, and even the loss of their jobs. Shareholders are asking the very people who are most likely to have invested considerable time and energy (in some cases a life's work) in building a successful organization to negotiate its sale and the possible redirection of its resources.

It is important to confront these conflicts and structure contracts with managers to reduce them. It makes no sense to hire a realtor to sell your house and then penalize your agent for doing so. Yet that is the implication of many of the emotional reactions to control-related severance contracts. The restrictions and tax penalties imposed on these severance payments by the Deficit Reduction Act of 1984 are unwise interferences in the contracting freedoms of shareholders and managers and should be eliminated. Moreover, one must eliminate the misunderstandings about the purpose and effects of these contracts that has been fostered by past rhetoric on the topic so that boards of directors can get on with the job of structuring these contracts.

Golden parachutes can be used to restrict takeovers and to entrench managers at the expense of shareholders. How does one tell whether a particular set of contracts crosses this line?

The key is whether the contracts help solve the conflict-of-interest problem between shareholders and managers that arises over changes in control. Solving this problem requires extending control-related several contracts beyond the chief executive to those members of the top-level management team who must play an important role in negotiating and implementing any transfer of control. Contracts that award severance contracts to substantial numbers of managers beyond this group are unlikely to be in the shareholders' interests. The contracts awarded by Beneficial Corporation to 234 of its managers are unlikely to be justified by analysis as in the shareholders' interests.[45]

Particularly important is the use of severance-related compensation contracts in situations where it is optimal for managers to invest in organization-specific human capital, i.e., in skills and knowledge that have little or no value in other organizations. Managers will not so invest where the likelihood is high that their investment will be eliminated by an unexpected transfer of control and the loss of their jobs. In such situations the firm will have to pay for all costs associated with the creation of such organization-specific human capital, and it will be more costly for the firm to attract and retain highly talented managers when they have better opportunities elsewhere. In addition, contracts that award excessive severance compensation to the appropriate group of managers will tend to motivate managers to sell the firm at too low a price.

No simple rules can be specified that will easily prevent the misuse of golden parachutes because the appropriate solution will depend on many factors that are specific to each situation (e.g., the amount of stock held by the managers, and the optimal amount of investment in organization-specific human capital). In general, contracts that award inappropriately high payments to a group that is excessively large will reduce efficiency and harm shareholders by raising the cost of acquisition and by transferring wealth from shareholders to managers. The generally appropriate solution is to make the control-related severance contracts pay off in a way that is tied to the premium earned by the stockholders. Stock options or restricted stock appreciation rights that pay off only in the event of a change in control are two options that have some of the appropriate properties. In general, policies that encourage increased stockownership by managers and the board of directors will provide incentives that will tend to reduce the conflicts of interests with managers.

TARGETED REPURCHASES

The evidence indicates takeovers create large benefits for shareholders. Yet virtually all proposals I have seen to protect shareholders from asserted difficulties in the control market will harm them by either eliminating or reducing the probability of successful hostile tender offers. These proposals will also stifle the productivity increases that are the source of the gains.

Most proposals to restrict or prohibit targeted repurchases (transactions that are pejoratively labeled *greenmail*) are nothing more than antitakeover proposals in disguise. Greenmail is an appellation that suggests blackmail; yet the only effective weapon possessed by a greenmailer is the right to offer to purchase stock from other shareholders at a substantial premium. The "damage" to shareholders caused by this action is difficult to find. Those who propose to "protect" shareholders hide this fact behind emotional language designed to mislead. Greenmail is actually a targeted repurchase, an offer by *management* to repurchase the shares of a subset of shareholders at a premium, an offer not made to other shareholders.

Greenmail is the Trojan horse of the takeover battle in the legal and political arenas. Antitakeover proposals are commonly disguised as antigreenmail provisions. Management can easily prohibit greenmail without legislation: It needs only to announce a policy that, like Ulysses tying himself to the mast, prohibits the board or management from making such payments.

The ease with which managers can prevent targeted repurchases makes it clear that the problem lies with managers who use targeted repurchases to protect themselves from competition in the market for corporate control. What these managers want is not the elimination of targeted repurchases but the partial or complete elimination of hostile takeovers, and virtually every proposal I have seen to "restrict" greenmail would have this effect. Three excellent studies of these transactions indicate that when measured from the initial toehold purchase to the final repurchase of the shares, the stock price of target firms rises.[46] Therefore, shareholders are benefited, not harmed, by the whole sequence of events. There is some indication, however, that the stock price increases might represent the expectation of future takeover premiums in firms in which the targeted repurchase was not sufficient to prevent ultimate takeover of the firm. If so, then possibly, much as in the final defeat of tender offers found by Bradley et al. (1983),[47] all premiums are lost to shareholders in firms for which the repurchase and associated standstill agreements successfully lock up the firm. The evidence on these issues is not yet sufficient to issue a final judgment either way.

PROBLEMS IN THE DELAWARE COURT

Delaware courts have created over the years a highly productive fabric of corporate law that has benefited the nation. The court is having difficulty, however, sorting out the complex issues it faces in the takeover area. The court's problems in settling conflicts between shareholders and management over control issues reflect a fundamental weakness in its model of the corporation, a model that has heretofore worked quite well. The result has been a confusing set of decisions that, in contrast to much of the court's previous history, appear to make little economic sense.[48]

Altruism and the Business Judgment Rule

The Delaware court's model of the corporation is founded in the business judgment rule—the legal doctrine that holds that unless explicit evidence of fraud or self-dealing exists, the board of directors is presumed to be acting solely in the interests of shareholders. In particular, the board is presumed to act altruistically and never out of incentives to preserve the interests of managers or their own positions as board members.

The altruistic model of the board that is the implicit foundation of the business judgment rule is incorrect as a description of human behavior. In the end, people are self-interested, and board members do not always have incentives to act in the shareholders' interests. The conflicts need not arise solely over monetary considerations. They can arise, for example, over the reluctance of board members to take actions that will harm friends who are members of management. In spite of its falsity, the altruistic model of the board has been sufficiently robust to yield good law for a wide range of cases for many years. Alternative models of the corporation that incorporate conflicts of interest between board members and shareholders are much more complicated. Thus in the past the court could avoid dealing with these complex alternatives when the simple model worked well. The court is now being forced to deal with these complexities, but it is doing so with an inadequate analytical foundation.

The Agency Model of the Corporation

The altruistic model of the board and the model of the corporation it yields are not sufficiently robust to provide proper answers to the conflicts surrounding corporate-control disputes. The court will be forced eventually to come to grips with the problem and to adopt something like the now well-developed agency model of the corporation, in which all individuals are presumed to be acting out of self-interest and their conflicting interests are resolved through a complex set of contractual and market forces, including the market for corporate control.[49]

Managers and boards of directors are the agents of shareholders, who are correctly viewed as the principals in these contracts that are effected through the corporate charter. To illustrate the problem the Delaware court is facing, consider the simple situation in which a principal hires an agent to take some actions on his behalf. To effect this arrangement, the principal delegates to the agent a set of decision rights. On entering the relationship, the principal wants the court to honor (i.e., enforce) the contract delegating decision authority to the agent. That is one of the primary purposes of the business judgment rule, to keep the courts out of the business of second-guessing the agent's decisions and holding the agent liable for damages. Doing so would make it difficult or impossible for principals to hire agents in the first place, which would eliminate the benefits of specialization.

Depending on the circumstances, the principal may want to delegate a wide range of decision rights to the agent. In no event, however, will it be sensible for the principal to delegate the ultimate control rights to the agent. Control rights are the rights to hire, fire, and set the compensation of the agent.[50] If the principal were to delegate the control rights to the agent, the agent could not be fired and would have the right to set his own compensation. In this circumstance the agent would no longer be an agent. He would be the effective owner of the decision rights (although he probably could not alienate them) and could be expected to use them in his own interests.

The simple agency example makes clear why the courts must not apply the business judgment rule to conflicts over control rights between principals and agents. If the business judgment rule is applied to such conflicts, the courts are effectively giving the *agent* the right unilaterally to change the control rights. In the long run, this interpretation of the contract will destroy the possibility of such cooperative arrangements, because it will leave principals with few effective rights.

Recently, the courts have applied the business judgment rule to the conflicts over the issuance of poison pill preferred stock, poison pill rights, and discriminatory targeted repurchases, and have given managers and boards the rights to use these devices.[51] In doing so, the courts are essentially giving the agents (managers and the board) the right to unilaterally change critical control aspects of the contract, in particular, the right to fire the agents. This has major implications for economic activity, productivity, and the health of the corporation. If the trend goes far enough, the corporation as an organizational form will be seriously handicapped.

Poison Pills

Poison pill securities change fundamental aspects of the corporate rules of the game that govern the relationship between shareholders, managers, and the board of directors. They do so when a control-related event, such as a takeover offer or the acquisition of a substantial block of stock or voting rights by an individual or a group, occurs. The Household International version of the poison pill rights issue is particularly interesting because it was a major test case in the area.

When the Household International board of directors issued its complicated right to shareholders, it unilaterally changed the nature of the contractual relationship with Household's shareholders in a fundamental way. The right effectively restricts the alienability of the common stock by prohibiting shareholders from selling their shares, without permission of the board, into a control transaction leading to merger at a price that involves a premium over market value of less than $6 billion. Since Household had a market value of less than $2 billion at the time, this was a premium of over 300%—more than six times the average takeover premium of 50% common in recent times—a premium difficult to justify as in the shareholders' interests.

The November 1985 Delaware court decision upholding the Household International rights issue will significantly restrict hostile takeovers of firms that adopt similar provisions. Before that decision, 37 pills of various forms had been adopted. Over one hundred fifty corporations adopted pills in the seven months following that decision.[52] Unlike most other antitakeover devices, this defense is very difficult for a prospective acquirer to overcome without meeting the board's terms (at least one who desires to complete the second-step closeout merger). An SEC study analyzed the 37 companies introducing pills between June 1983, when Lenox introduced the first one, and December 1985. Eleven of these 37 firms experienced control changes; five experienced a negotiated change in control while the pill was in effect (Revlon, Cluett Peabody, Great Lakes International, Lenox, and Enstar), two were taken over by creeping acquisitions (Crown Zellerbach and William Wright), two were taken over after their pills were declared illegal (AMF and Richardson-Vicks), one (Superior Oil) was acquired after the pill was withdrawn in the face of a lawsuit and proxy fight by its largest holder, and one (Amsted) has proposed a leveraged buy-out (Office of the Chief Economist of the SEC 1986). The study finds that "announcements of [twenty] poison pill plans in the midst of takeover speculation have resulted in on average 2.4 percent net of market price declines for firms adopting the plans." The effects of another 12 plans adopted by firms that were not the subject of takeover speculation were essentially nil.

Sir James Goldsmith recently gained control of Crown Zellerbach, which had implemented a rights issue similar to Household International's. Goldsmith purchased a controlling interest in the open market after Crown's board opposed his tender offer and refused to recall its rights issue. In this situation the acquirer must either tolerate the costs associated with leaving the minority interest outstanding and forsake the benefits of merging the assets of the two organizations or incur the costs posed by the premium required by the rights on execution of the second-step closeout merger. The Crown case revealed a loophole in the Household/Crown version of the pill (which has been closed in newly implemented versions), because although Goldsmith could not complete a second-step merger without paying the high premium required by the rights, he could avoid it by simply liquidating Crown.

Rights issues like Household's and Crown Zellerbach's harm shareholders. They will fundamentally impair the efficiency of corporations that adopt them, and for this reason they will reduce productivity in the economy if widely adopted.

The Malatesta and Walkling (1985) study of the effects of poison pills also indicates that they have a negative effect on stock prices. On average, stock prices fell by a statistically significant 2% in the 2 days around the announcement in the *Wall Street Journal* of adoption of a poison pill for their sample of 14 firms that adopted these securities between December 1982 and February 1985. This price decline, however, was smaller than the average 7.5% increase in price that occurred in the 10 days prior to the adoption of the pill. Firms adopting pills appear to be those in which managers and directors bear a substancially smaller fraction of the wealth consequences of their actions. In all but three of the firms the percentage of common shares owned by officers and directors was substantially below the industry average ownership of shares. The average ownership of firms in the same industry was 16.5%, and for the firms adopting pills it was 7.5%.

A broad interpretation of the business judgment rule is important to the effectiveness of the corporation because a system that puts the courts into the business of making managerial decisions will create great inefficiencies. The court has erred, however, in allowing the Household board, under the business judgment rule, to make the fundamental change in the structure of the organization implied by the rights issue without vote of its shareholders. It is unlikely that the court would allow the board to decide unilaterally to make the organization a closed corporation by denying shareholders the right to sell their shares to anyone at a mutually agreeable price without the permission of the board. The Household International rights issue places such a restriction on the alienability of shares but only with a subset of transactions—the control-related transactions so critical for protecting shareholders when the normal internal board-level control mechanisms break down. Several other poison pill cases have been heard by the courts with similar outcomes, but one New Jersey and two New York courts have recently ruled against poison pills that substantially interfere with the voting rights of large-block shareholders.[53] An Illinois district court recently voided a poison pill (affirmed by the Seventh Circuit Court of Appeals) and two weeks later approved a new pill issued by the same company.[54]

The problem with these special securities and the provisions they contain is not with their appropriateness (some might well be desirable), but with the manner in which they are being adopted, i.e., without approval by shareholders. Boards of directors show little inclination to refer such issues to shareholders.

One solution to the problems caused by the Houseold decision is for shareholders to approve amendments to the certificate of incorporation to restrict the board's power to take such actions without shareholder approval. This task is not easy, however, given the pressure corporate managers are bringing to bear on the managers of their pension funds to vote with management.[55] Even more problematic is the provision in Delaware law that requires certificate amendments to be recommended to shareholders by the board of directors.[56]

Many poison pill preferred issues were made easier by prior shareholder approval of "blank-check" preferred. These are shareholder grants of authority to the board to issue preferred stock whose terms could be set by the board at time of issue. Shareholders concerned about the costs created by issuance of poison pill preferred will be more cautious about authorizing blank-check preferred in the future. This may be a moot point, because most poison pills now seem to take the form of rights issues to subscribe to already authorized securities.

Exclusionary Self-tenders: The *Unocal v. Mesa* Decision

The Delaware Supreme Court surprised the legal, financial, and corporate communities in the spring of 1985 by giving Unocal the right to make a tender offer to 29% of its shares while excluding its largest shareholder, Mesa Partners II, from the offer. This decision enabled the Unocal management and board to avoid loss of control to Mesa. The decision imposed large costs on Unocal shareholders and, if not reversed, threatens major damage to shareholders of all Delaware corporations.[57]

Effects of the Unocal Decision

The Unocal victory over Mesa cost the Unocal shareholders $1.1 billion ($9.48 per postoffer share). This is the amount by which the $9.4 billion Mesa offer exceeded the $8.3 billion value of Unocal's "victory."[58] This loss is 18% of Unocal's pretakeover value of $6.2 billion. The $2.1 billion net increase in value to $8.3 billion resulted from Unocal's $4.2 billion debt issue, which, contrary to assertions, benefits its shareholders. It does so by effectively bonding Unocal to payout a substantial fraction of its huge cash flows to shareholders rather than reinvest them in low-return projects and by reducing taxes on Unocal and its shareholders.

For his services in creating this $2.1 billion gain for Unocal shareholders, T. Boone Pickens has been vilified in the press, and Mesa Partners II has incurred net losses before taxes—obviously a perversion of incentives.

In addition to Mesa's losses, shareholders of all Delaware corporations lose because the court's decision gives management a weapon so powerful it essentially guarantees that no Delaware corporation that uses it will be taken over by a tender offer. A determined board could, in the extreme, pay out all the corporation's assets and leave the acquirer holding a worthless shell. Because of this new power, shareholders are denied the benefits of future actions by Pickens and others to discipline managers whose strategies are wasting resources.

Society also loses. The chilling effect on takeovers means the decision stifles the productivity increases that are the source of the takeover gains and thereby handicaps Delaware corporations in the competition for survival.

Unocal's self-tender for 29% of its shares at $72 per share ($26 over the market price) was designed to defeat Mesa's $54-per-share cash offer for 50.4% of Unocal's shares plus $54 per share in debt securities for the remaining 49.6%. The Unocal offer would have paid 59% of Unocal's pretakeover equity to other shareholders while denying participation to the 13.6% minority holding of Mesa Partners II. This offer would transfer about $248 million from Mesa's holdings to other Unocal stockholders—a classic case of corporate raiding that contrasts with the beneficial effects of the actions of takeover specialists like Pickens, Carl Icahn, and Irwin Jacobs on other shareholders.

Faced with the threat of legalized expropriation of $248 million, Mesa accepted a settlement in which Unocal backed off from the Mesa exclusion. The settlement involved repurchase of part of Mesa's shares at the terms of the tender offer, a 25-year standstill agreement, a promise to vote its shares in the same proportion as other shares are voted, and constraints on Mesa's rights to sell its remaining shares.

The essential characteristics of Unocal's exclusionary repurchase defense are now incorporated in newly popular poison pill plans called back-end plans.[59] These plans give shareholders a right to tender their shares for securities worth more than the market value of their stock when a shareholder exceeds a certain maximum limit of stock ownership that ranges from 30% to 50%. As with Unocal's exclusion of Mesa, the large shareholder is denied the right to similarly tender his shares. This arrange-

ment threatens a shareholder who violates the holding limit with potentially large dilution of his holdings. It thereby limits the existence of large stock holdings.

"Protection" from Two-Tier Tender Offers

The court ruled that the objective of Unocal's offer was to protect its shareholders against "a grossly inadequate and coercive two-tier front-end-loaded tender offer" and greenmail. This assessment of the situation was upside down. Paradoxically, the court's ruling imposed on Unocal shareholders exactly the evil it purported to prevent. Unocal defeated Mesa's $1.1 billion higher offer precisely because Mesa's offer was a level $54 offer and Unocal's offer was an extreme front-end-loaded two-tier offer, $72 for 29% of its shares in the front end with a back-end price of $35 for the remaining 71% of the shares. (The back-end price was implicit but easy to calculate and reported in the press at the time of the offer.) The effective price of the Unocal offer was therefore only $45.73 per preoffer share (the weighted average of the front- and back-end prices).

Comparing the Unocal offer with SEC estimates of average premiums in two-tier tender offers indicates the extreme nature of the Unocal two-tier offer. Historically, the average back-end premium on outside two-tier offers is 45% higher than the stock price measured 20 trading days prior to the offer.[60] This figure contrasts sharply with the *negative* back-end premium on Unocal's self-tender of -25%. That is, the $35 back-end price was 25% below the Unocal market price of $46\frac{3}{8}$ 20 days before the offer.

The negative back-end premium on Unocal's offer means that the holders of 20 million Unocal shares who failed to tender to the first tier of the Unocal offer were particularly hurt. As of the close of the offer, they had suffered total losses of $382 million, $215 million from the loss of $37.12 per share on 29% of their shares,[61] plus a loss of $167 million from being denied the $54 in debt securities they would have received in the back end of the Mesa offer.[62]

Protection from Targeted Repurchases

The court also erred in its concern over greenmail. In ruling to eliminate the threat of greenmail, the court in fact authorized Unocal to make a greenmail transaction that differed from the usual variety only in that it penalized, rather than benefited, the large-block holder (i.e., reverse greenmail). In authorizing this form of targeted repurchase, the court granted large benefits to managers who desire protection from competition but harmed shareholders.

One of the great strengths of the corporation is the long-held principle that holders of a given class of securities are treated identically in transactions with the corporation. The Unocal decision threatens to turn the corporation into a battleground where special-interest groups of shareholders fight over the division of the pie much as special interests in the public sector do. The result will be a much smaller pie.

Responsible boards of directors interested in the welfare of shareholders and the survival of the corporation as an organizational form will implement procedures to ban all targeted repurchases that carry premiums over market value (both greenmail and reverse greenmail).

Implications of the Application of the Business Judgment Rule to Conflicts over Control

The continued application of the business judgment rule to conflicts over control has far-reaching consequences. If the current trend continues, this process will erode the limits to judicial interference in the management of corporations historically provided by the business judgment rule and severely cripple the corporation in the competition for survival. Indeed, the protection afforded managers by the business judgment rule is already eroding.[63] The court seems to be imposing a higher standard on corporations that adopt a poison pill. This erosion of the business judgment rule appears to be motivated by the court's understanding that the pill gives management and the board great power. So the court is brought into the business of sec-ond-guessing managers' business decisions. The court currently seems to be inclined to give this scrutiny only to control transactions.

The erosion of the protection afforded by the business judgment rule is unlikely to continue in its currently limited form. Protected by impenetrable takeover defenses, managers and boards are likely to behave in ways detrimental to shareholders in other areas as well. Self-interested control transactions are only one way managers can harm shareholders and, from their standpoint, probably not the best way. As this process continues, we can expect to see managers who are protected from the disciplinary forces of the control market begin to abuse their obligations to shareholders in decisions outside the control area. The court will probably be drawn into these conflicts, and as they are, the business judgment rule will be further diluted. The end result, if the process continues unchecked, is likely to be the destruction of the corporation as we know it. I believe such destruction is unlikely to happen because the court will recognize the problems with its current approach. The easiest solution to the problem is for the court to deny protection under the business judgment rule to managerial decisions on control issues unless those decisions have been ratified by shareholder vote.

DO WE HAVE TOO FEW TAKEOVERS?

To argue that there is too much takeover activity has become popular. Yet the opposite is most likely true because of free-riding problems caused by the current regulations that require disclosure of holdings and intentions of the purchaser in SEC 13d reports.[64] These reports must be filed within 10 days of acquisition of 5% or more of a company's shares and must disclose the number of shares owned, the identity of the owner, and the purpose of the acquisition. Current rules allow the acquiring firm to buy as many additional shares as it can in the 10-day window between the time the 5% filing barrier is reached and the time of filing. This rule allows buyers to acquire shares that average 7.6% of the target firm.[65]

Since market prices adjust to the expected value of the takeover bid immediately after the 13d announcement, the acquirer's profits are made almost entirely on the difference between the price paid for the shares purchased prior to the filing of the 13d and their value after the acquisition. This drives a wedge, however, between the private benefits earned by the acquirer and the total social benefits of the acquisition; the acquirer pays 100% of the acquisition costs and, on average, captures less than 10% of the benefits. The remaining benefits go to the other shareholders. The activities of Mesa Petroleum, for example, have yielded benefits to the shareholders of companies involved in its transactions that exceed $13 billion dollars. Mesa itself has paid hundreds of millions of dollars in financing, legal, and investment banking fees and borne all the risks of loss. Yet is has earned only about $750 million on these transactions.

Consider an acquisition that promises total expected gains of $100 million. If the acquirer expects to capture only $7.6 million of this amount if the bid is successful (7.6%), the bid will occur only if the legal, investment banking, and other costs (including the required risk premium) are less than $7.6 million. All such acquisitions that are expected to cost more than this will not be made, and shareholders and society are thus denied the benefits of those reorganizations. If the costs, for example, are expected to be $10 million, the bid will not occur and the $90 million benefit will not be realized. The solution to this problem is to abolish the SEC 13d reporting requirements or to increase significantly the trigger point from the current 5% level. Unfortunately, in its proposal to reduce the 10-day window to two days, the SEC is moving in exactly the wrong direction.

CONCLUSION

Although economic analysis and the evidence indicate that the market for corporate control is benefiting shareholders, society, and the corporation as an organizational form, it is also making life more uncomfortable for top-level executives. This discomfort is creating strong pressures at both the state and federal levels for restrictions that will seriously cripple the workings of this market. In 1985 there were 21 bills on this topic in the congressional hopper, all of which proposed various restrictions on the market for corporate control. Some proposed major new restrictions on shareownership and financial instruments. Within the past several years the legislatures of numerous states have passed antitakeover laws. This political activity is another example of special interests using the democratic political system to change the rules of the game to benefit themselves at the expense of society as a whole. In this case the special interests are top-level corporate managers and other groups who stand to lose from competition in the market for corporate control. The result will be a significant weakening of the corporation as an organizational form and a reduction in efficiency.

NOTES

1. W. T. Grimm, *Mergerstat Review* (1985).
2. The bills were as follows: securities bills: H. R. 1480 (Markey), shareholder vote on tender offers; S. 286 (Riegle), greenmail; S. 631 (Chafee), Schedule 13D; tender offer disclosure and approval; S. 706 (Proxmire), approval of hostile stock purchases; S. 860 (Metzenbaum), restrictions on stock ownership, defensive tactics, and greenmail; tax bills: H.R. 1003 (Jones) and S. 420 (Boren), Section 338 election; greenmail tax; denial of interest deduction; H.R. 1100 (Jones) and S. 476 (Boren), greenmail tax and denial of interest deduction on junk bonds; H.R. 1553 (Dorgan), denial of interest deduction on loans in connection with takeovers; S. 414 (Nickles), denial of interest deduction; S. 632 (Chafee), Section 338 election; denial of deduction for greenmail and interest on hostile acquisition indebtedness; judiciary committee bills: H.R. 998 (Edwards) and S. 473 (Nickles), moratorium on hostile takeovers of petroleum companies; investigation; H.R. 1974 (Rodino), Hart-Scott-Rodino waiting period; H.R. 1075 (Rodino), anticompetitive acquisitions; H.R.

1182 (Rose), temporary moratorium on hostile takeovers of petroleum companies; H.R. 1515 (Seiberling), anticompetitive acquisitions; H.R. 1830 (Rodino), record of outside communications; H.R. 1831 (Rodino), moratorium on hostile takeovers; advisory commission on hostile takeovers; H.R. 1832 (Rodino), Office of Competition and Economic Concentration.

3. A detailed summary of this evidence is available in Jensen and Ruback (1983) and Jensen (1984). See also Halpern (1973).

4. See Holderness and Sheehan (1985) and Mikkelson and Ruback (1985).

5. As estimated by the Office of the Chief Economist of the SEC and provided to the author in private communication.

6. See Jensen and Ruback (1983, Tables 1 and 2).

7. See Huang and Walkling (1987).

8. Dennis and McConnell (1896).

9. Eckbo (1985) concludes that the zero returns to U.S. bidding firms is due to difficulties in measuring the gains to bidding firms when the bidder is substantially larger than the target firm. In his sample the average Canadian bidder was approximately the same size as the average target; the average U.S. bidder is approximately eight times the size of the average Canadian target.

10. Allen and Sirmans, (1987).

11. See Jensen and Ruback (1983).

12. See Jarrell and Bradley (1980).

13. See Jensen and Ruback (1983).

14. Grimm (1985).

15. See the analysis in Jensen (1984, p. 119).

16. For a survey of the 100 largest initial public offerings each year, see the April issue of *Venture* magazine.

17. For an introduction to the literature and empirical evidence on the theory of efficient markets, see Elton and Gruber (1984), Chap. 15, and the 167 studies referenced in the bibliography). For some anomalous evidence on market efficiency, see Jensen (1978, pp. 93–330). For recent criticisms of the efficient-market hypothesis, see Shiller (1981a, 1981b). Marsh and Merton (1983, 1986) demonstrate that the Shiller tests depend critically on whether, contrary to generally accepted financial theory and evidence, the future levels of dividends follow a stationary stochastic process. Merton (1985) provides a discussion of the current state of the efficient-market hypothesis and concludes: "In light of the empirical evidence on the nonstationarity issue, a pronouncement at this moment that the rational market theory should be discarded from the economic paradigm, can, at best, be described as 'premature'" (p. 40).

18. Kaplan and Roll (1972, p. 245.) The evidence is not so clear on the effects of switches from FIFO to LIFO inventory valuation techniques. This accounting change reduces reported current income and yet increases cash flows by reducing taxes. Some evidence indicates stock prices of firms that make such switches increase even though reported earnings decline. Moreover, the increases are positively associated with estimates of the value of the tax savings. See Sunder (1975) and Biddle and Lindahl (1982). Ricks (1982) presents evidence that firms adopting LIFO experienced temporary price declines in the year of adoption and that these declines were eliminated within 12 months. Ricks and Biddle (1987) provide evidence that market reactions to LIFO adoptions in 1974 were negative and were related to large, negative, analyst earnings forecast errors for the year. They found that when one controls for analysts' forecast errors, "the results support a positive association between excess returns and the magnitudes of LIFO tax savings" (p. 2).

19. Office of the Chief Economist (1985).

20. "R&D" Scoreboard: Reagan & Foreign Rivalry Light a Fire Under Spending," *Business Week,* July, 8, 1985, pp. 86–87.

21. Roll in Chapter 14 of this volume, discusses a number of these forces.

22. This discussion is based on Jensen (1986).

23. Gordon Donaldson (1984), in a detailed study of 12 large Fortune 500 firms, concludes that managers of these firms were not driven by maximization of the value of the firm, but rather by the maximization of "corporate wealth." He defines corporte wealth as *"the aggregate purchasing power available to management for strategic purposes during any given planning period. . . .* This wealth consists of the stocks and flows of cash and cash equivalents (primarily credit) that management can use at its discretion to implement decisions involving the control of goods and services" (p. 3, emphasis in original). "In practical terms it is cash, credit, and other corporate purchasing power by which management commands goods and services" (p. 22).

24. Where growth is measured by increases in sales. See Murphy (1985). This positive relationship between compensation and sales growth does not imply, although it is consistent with, causality.

25. Rents are returns in excess of the opportunity cost of the resources committed to the activity. Quasi rents are returns in excess of the short-run opportunity cost of the resources to the activity.

26. See Jensen and Meckling (1976), Myers (1977), and Smith and Warner (1979).

27. Interestingly, Graham and Dodd (1951, Chaps. 32, 34, and 36) place great importance on the dividend payout in their famous valuation formula: $V = M(D + 0.33E)$ (p. 454); where V is value, M is the earnings multiplier when the dividend payout rate is a "normal two-thirds of earnings," D is the expected dividend, and E is expected earnings. In their formula, dividends are valued at three times the rate of retained earnings—a proposition that has puzzled many students of modern finance (at least of my vintage). The agency cost of free cash flow that leads to overretention and waste of shareholder resources is consistent with the deep suspicion with which Graham and Dodd viewed the lack of payout. Their discussion (Chap. 34) reflects a belief in the tenuous nature of the future benefits of such retention. Although they do not couch the issues in terms of the conflict between managers and shareholders, the free cash flow theory explicated here implies that their beliefs, sometimes characterized as a preference for "a bird in the hand is worth two in the bush," were perhaps well founded.

28. See Charest (1978) and Aharony and Swary (1980).

29. Literally, principal and interest payments are substitutes for dividends. However, because interest is tax-deductible at the corporate level and dividends are not, dividends and debt are not perfect substitutes.

30. Rozeff (1982) and Easterbrook (1984a) argue that regular dividend payments can be effective in reducing agency costs with managers by ensuring that managers are forced more frequently to subject themselves and their policies to the discipline of the capital markets when they acquire capital.

31. See Bradley and Wakeman (1983), Dann and DeAngelo (1983), and Mikkelson and Ruback (1985, 1986).

32. The two-day returns of exchange offers and self-tenders can be affected by the offer. However, if there are no real effects or tax effects, and if all shares are tendered to a premium offer, then the stock price will be unaffected by the offer and its price effects are equivalent to those of a cash dividend. Thus, when tax effects are zero and all shares are tendered, the two-day returns are appropriate measures of the real effects of the exchange. In other cases the correct returns to be used in these transactions are those covering the period from the day prior to the offer announcement to the day after the close of the offer (taking account of the cash payout).

See, for example, Rosenfeld (1982), whose results for the entire period are also consistent with the theory.

33. See, however, Miller (1977), who argues that allowing for personal tax effects and the equilibrium response of firms implies that no tax effects will be observed.

34. Ignoring potential tax effects due to the 85% exclusion of dividends received by corporations on holdings of preferred stock.

35. By number. See Grimm (1985, Figures 36 and 37).

36. See DeAngelo et al. (1984) and Lowenstein (1985). Lowenstein also mentions incentive effects of debt but argues tax effects play a major role in explaining the value increase.

37. McConnell and Muscarella (1985).

38. Picchi (1985); emphasis in the original.

39. See Donaldson (1984).

40. Jacobs (1986).

41. See Magenheim and Mueller (Chapter 11 of this volume), Bradley and Jarrell (Chapter 15 of this volume), Mandelker (1974), Langtieg (1978), and Asquith (1983).

42. See Wansley et al. (1983, 1986), who find higher returns to targets and to bidders in cash transactions, and Wansley and Fayez (1986).

43. Data from Drexel Burnham Lambert, private correspondence.

44. Lambert and Larcker (1985).

45. Morrison (1982).

46. Holderness and Sheehan (1985); Mikkelson and Ruback (1985, 1986).

47. Bradley et al. (1983).

48. See, e.g., *Moran v. Household International, Inc.,* 490 A.2d 1059 (Del. Ch.1985) aff'd 500 A.2d 1346 (Del. 1985) (upholding the poison pill rights issue); *Smith v. Van Gorkom,* 488 A.2d 858 (holding the board liable for damages in the sale of a firm at substantial premium over market price); *Unocal v. Mesa,* 493 A.2d 946, 954 (Del. 1985) (allowing discriminatiory targeted repurchase that confiscates wealth of the largest shareholder); *Revlon, Inc. v. MacAndrews & Forbes Holdings, Inc.,* 506 A.2nd 173, 180 (Del. 1986) (invalidation of Revlon's lockup sale of a prime division to Forstmann Little at a below-market price).

49. Easterbrook (1984b) and Jensen and Smith (1985) provide summaries of much of the work in the area.

50. See Fama and Jensen (1983a, 1983b, 1985).

51. *Moran v. Household International* and *Unocal v. Mesa.*

52. See Office of the Chief Economist (1986) and Corporate Control Alert (February, March and April, May and June, 1986).

53. *Ministar Acquiring Corporation v. AMF, Inc.,* 621 Fed Sup 1252. (So Dis N.Y., 1985); *Unilever Acquisition Corporation v. Richardson-Vicks, Inc.,* 618 Fed Supp 407. (So Dist. N.Y. 1985); *Asarco, Inc. v. M. R. H. Holmes a Court,* 611 Fed Sup 468. (Dist. Ct. N.J. 1985); *Dynamics Corporation of America v. CTS Corporation.*

54. *Dynamics Corporation of America v. CTS Corp.,* et al., U.S. District Court, Northern District of Illinois, Eastern Division, No. 86 C 1624 (April 17, 1986), affirmed Seventh Circuit Court of Appeals Nos. 86–1601, 86–1608, and *Dynamics Corporation of America v. CTS Corporation,* et al. (May 3, 1986).

55. See Koleman (1985) and Investor Responsibility Research Center (1985).

56. 8 *Del. C.* § 242(c)(1).

57. The discussion in this section is based on Jensen (1985).

58. The $8.3 billion value of Unocal securities held by its shareholders is calculated as $4.1 billion in stock (116 million shares at $34\frac{7}{8}$ on May 24, the first trading day after close of the offer) and $4.2 billion in Unocal debt trading at $73.50.

59. See Office of the Chief Economist (1986).

60. See Comment and Jarrell (1896); an earlier version appeared as Office of the Chief Economist (1984).

61. Calculated as the $72 value of the Unocal debt offered in exchange for 29% of their shares less the $34.875 postoffer closing price of the shares.

62. See M. Bradley and M. Rosensweig, The Law and Economics of Defensive Stock Repurchases and Defensive Self-Tender Offers (unpublished manuscript, University of Michigan, 1985), for a thorough discussion of the issues involved in self-tender offers.

63. See *Revlon, Inc. v. MacAndrews & Forbes Holdings, Inc,* 506 A.2nd 173,180 (Del. 1986), in which the court seems to be reviewing very detailed aspects of the board's decision leading to the invalidation of Revlon's lockup sale of a prime division to Forstmann Little at a below-market price. The Court of Appeals for the Second Circuit in *Hanson Trust v. SCM Corporation* (Nos. 85–7951, 85–7953, 2d Cir. Jan. 6, 1986) (written opinion filed Jan. 6, 1986) enjoined lockups given by SCM defending itself from takeover by Hanson Trust. See also Herzel et al. (1986) for detailed analysis of these cases and lockups in general.

64. Grossman and Hart (1980) present an extensive discussion of the free-riding problem in corporate takeovers.

65. See Mikkelson and Ruback (1985, 1986).

REFERENCES

Aharony, J., and I. Swary (1980). "Quarterly Dividend and Earnings Announcements and Stockholder's Returns: An Empirical Analysis." *Journal of Finance* **35**, 1–12.

Allen, P. R., and C. F. Sirmans (1987). "An Analysis of Gains to Acquiring Firm's Shareholders: The Special Case of REITs." *Journal of Financial Economics* (forthcoming).

Asquith, P. R. (1983). "Merger Bids, Uncertainty, and Stockholder Returns." *Journal of Financial Economics* **11**, 51–83.

Asquith, P. R., and E. H. Kim (1982) "The Impact of Merger Bids on the Participating Firms' Security Holders." *Journal of Finance* **37**, 1209–1228.

———, and D. Mullins (1983). "The Impact of Initiating Dividend Payments on Shareholder Wealth." *Journal of Business* **56**, 77–96.

———, and D. Mullins (1986). "Equity Issues and Offering Dilution." *Journal of Financial Economics* **15**, 61–89.

Baker, G. (1986). Compensation and Hierarchies. Unpublished paper, Harvard Business School, January.

Biddle, G. C., and F. W. Lindahl (1982). "Stock Price Reactions to LIFO Adoptions. II. The Association Between Excess Returns and LIFO Tax Savings." *Journal of Accounting Research* **20**(2), 551, 588.

Blume, M. E., and D. B. Keim (1984). Risk and Return Characteristics of Lower-Grade Bonds. Unpublished paper, The Wharton School, December.

Bradley, M., and M. Rosensweig (1986). "Defensive Stock Repurchases." *Harvard Law Review* **99**(7), 1378–1430.

———, and L. M. Wakeman. (1983). "The Wealth Effects of Targeted Share Repurchases." *Journal of Financial Economics* **11**, 301–328.

———, A. Desai, and E. H. Kim (1983). "The Rationale Behind Interfirm Tender Offers: Information or Synergy?" *Journal of Financial Economics* **11**, 183–206.

Brickley, J. (1983). "Shareholder Wealth, Information Signaling and the Specially Designated Dividend: An Empirical Study." *Journal of Financial Economics* **12**, 187–209.

Bruner, R. F. (1985). The Use of Excess Cash and Debt Capacity as a Motive for Merger. Unpublished paper, Colgate Darden Graduate School of Business, December.

Charest, G. (1978). "Dividend Information, Stock Returns, and Market Efficiency. II," *Journal of Financial Economics* **6**, 297–330.

Comment, R., and G. A. Jarrell (1986). Two-Tier Tender Offers: The Imprisonment of the Free-Riding Shareholder. Unpublished manuscript, March.

Crovitz, G. (1985). Limiting Defensive Tactics in Takeovers By Contract, Not Fiduciary Duty. Unpublished manuscript, Yale Law School, Spring.

Dann, L. (1980). The Effect of Common Stock Repurchase on Stockholder Returns. Unpublished Ph.D. dissertation, University of California, Los Angeles.

——— (1981). "Common Stock Repurchases: An Analysis of Returns to Bondholders and Stockholder." *Journal of Financial Economics* **9**, 113–138.

———, and H. DeAngelo (1983). "Standstill Agreements, Privately Negotiated Stock Repurchases and the Market for Corporate Control." *Journal of Financial Economics* **11**, 275–300.

———, and W. H. Mikkelson (1984). "Convertible Debt Issuance, Capital Structure Change and Financing-Related Information: Some New Evidence." *Journal of Financial Economics* **13**, 157–186.

DeAngelo, H., L. DeAngelo, and E. Rice (1984). "Going Private: Minority Freezeouts and Stockholder Wealth." *Journal of Law and Economics* **27**(2), 367–401.

Dennis, D. K., and J. J. McConnell (1986). "Corporate Mergers and Security Returns." *Journal of Financial Economics* **16**(2), 143–187.

Dietrich, J. R. (1984). "Effects of Early Bond Refundings: An Empirical Investigation of Security Returns." *Journal of Accounting and Economics* **6**, 67–96.

Donaldson, G. (1984). *Managing Corporate Wealth.* New York: Praeger.

Easterbrook, F. H. (1984a). "Two Agency-Cost Explanations of Dividends." *American Economic Review* **74**, 650–659.

——— (1984b). "Managers' Discretion and Investors' Welfare: Theories and Evidence." *Delaware Journal of Corporate Law* **9**(3), 540–571.

Eckbo, B. E. (1985). Do Acquiring Firms Gain From Merger? A Note on Relative Size and Foreign Acquisitions in Canada. Unpublished manuscript, University of British Columbia, September.

——— (1986). "Valuation Effects of Corporate Debt Offerings." *Journal of Financial Economics* **15**(1/2), 119–151.

Elgers, P. T., and J. J. Clark (1980). "Merger Types and Shareholder Returns: Additional Evidence." *Financial Management* **9**(2), 66–72.

Elton, E., and M. Gruber (1984). *Modern Portfolio Theory and Investment Analysis.* New York: Wiley.

Fama, E. F., and M. C. Jensen (1983a). "Separation of Ownership and Control." *Journal of Law and Economics* **26**, 301–325.

———, and M. C. Jensen (1983b). "Agency Problems and Residual Claims." *Journal of Law and Economics* **26**, 327–349.

———, and M. C. Jensen (1985). "Organizational Forms and Investment Decisions." *Journal of Financial Economics* **14**, 101–119.

Finnerty, J. D. (1985). "Stock-for-Debt-Swaps and Shareholder Returns." *Financial Management* **14**(3), 5–17.

Graham, B., and D. L. Dodd (1951). *Security Analysis: Principles and Technique.* New York, McGraw-Hill.

Grossman, S., and O. Hart (1980). "Takeover Bids, the Free-Rider Problem, and the Theory of the Corporation." *Bell Journal of Economics,* Spring, 42–64.

Halpern, P. J. (1973). "Empirical Estimates of the Amount and Distribution of Gains to Companies in Mergers." *Journal of Business* **46**(4), 554–575.

Herzel, L., D. E. Colling, and J. B. Carlson (1986). "Misunderstanding Lockups." *Securities Regulation Law Journal,* September, 150–180.

Holderness, C. G., and D. P. Sheehan (1985). "Raiders or Saviors? The Evidence on Six Controversial Investors." *Journal of Financial Economics* **14**, 555–579.

Huang, Y.-S., and R. A. Walkling (1987). "Abnormal Returns Associated with Acquisition Announcements: Payment, Acquisition Form, and Managerial Resistance Effects." *Journal of Financial Economics* (forthcoming).

Jacobs, E. A. (1986). The Agency Cost of Corporate Control: The Petroleum Industry. Unpublished paper. MIT, March.

Jarrell, G., and M. Bradley (1980). "The Economic Effects of Federal and State Regulation of Cash Tender Offers." *Journal of Law and Economics* **23**, 371–407.

———, A. Poulson, and L. Davidson (1985). Shark Repellents and Stock Prices: The Effects of Antitakeover Amendments Since 1980. Unpublished manuscript, September.

Jensen, M. C., ed. (1978). "Symposium on Some Anomalous Evidence on Market Efficiency." *Journal of Financial Economics* **6**(2-3) 95–101.

——— (1984). "Takeovers: Folklore and Science." *Harvard Business Review,* November–December, 109–121.

——— (1985). "When Unocal Won over Pickens, Shareholders and Society Lost." *Financier* **IX**(11), 50–53.

———— (1986). "Agency Costs of Free Cash Flow, Corporate Finance and Takeovers." *American Economic Review* (forthcoming).

————, and W. H. Meckling (1976). "Theory of the Firm: Managerial Behavior, Agency Costs and Ownership Structure." *Journal of Financial Economics* **3**, 305–360.

————, and R. Ruback (1983). "The Market for Corporate Control: The Scientific Evidence." *Journal of Financial Economics* **11**, 5–50.

————, and C. Smith, Jr. (1985). "Stockholder, Manager, and Creditor Interests: Applications of Agency Theory." In *Recent Advances in Corporate Finance*, ed. E. I. Altman and M. G. Subrahmanyam, 93–131. Homewood, Ill.: Irwin.

Kaplan, R., and R. Roll (1972). "Investor Evaluation of Accounting Information: Some Empirical Evidence." *Journal of Business,* April, 225–257.

Koleman, J. (1985). "The Proxy Pressure on Pension Fund Managers," *Institutional Investor,* July, 145–147.

Kolodny, R. and D. R. Suhler (1985). "Changes in Capital Structure, New Equity Issues, and Scale Effects." *Journal of Financial Research* **8**, 127–136.

Lambert, R., and D. Larcker (1985). "Golden Parachutes, Executive Decision-Making, and Shareholder Wealth." *Journal of Accounting and Economics* **7**, 179–204.

Langetieg, T. C. (1978). "An Application of a Three-Factor Performance Index to Measure Stockholder Gains from Merger." *Journal of Financial Economics* **6**, 365–384.

Linn, S., and J. M. Pinegar (1985). The Effect of Issuing Preferred Stock on Common Stockholder Wealth. Unpublished manuscript, University of Iowa.

Lowenstein, L. (1985). "Management Buyouts." *Columbia Law Review* **85**, 730–784.

McConnell, J. J., and C. J. Muscarella (1985). "Corporate Capital Expenditure Decisions and the Market Value of the Firm." *Journal of Financial Economics* **14**(3), 399–422.

————, and G. Schlarbaum (1981). "Evidence on the Impact of Exchange Offers on Security Prices: The Case of Income Bonds." *Journal of Business* **54**, 65–85.

Malatesta, P. H., and R. A. Walkling (1985). The Impact of Poison Pill Securities on Stockholder Wealth. Unpublished paper, University of Washington, December.

Mandelker, G. (1974). "Risk and Return: The Case of Merging Firms." *Journal of Financial Economics* **1**(4), 303–336.

Marsh, T. and R. C. Merton (1983). *Aggregate Dividend Behavior and Its Implications for Tests of Stock Market Rationality.* Working

Paper No. 1475–83, Sloan School of Management, MIT, September.

————, and R. C. Merton (1986). "Dividend Variability and Variance Bounds Tests for the Rationality of Stock Market Prices." *American Economic Review,* June, 483–498.

Masulis, R. M. (1980). "Stock Repurchase by Tender Offer: An Analysis of the Causes of Common Stock Price Changes." *Journal of Finance* **35**, 305–319.

———— (1983). "The Impact of Capital Structure Change on Firm Value: Some Estimates." *Journal of Finance* **38**, 107–126.

————, and A. Korwar (1986). "Seasoned Equity Offerings: An Empirical Investigation." *Journal of Financial Economics* **15**, 91–118.

Merton, R. C. (1985). *On the Current State of the Stock Market Rationality Hypothesis.* Working Paper No. 1717–85, Sloan School of Management, MIT, October.

Mikkelson, W. (1981). "Convertible Calls and Security Returns." *Journal of Financial Economics* **9**, 237–264.

————, and M. Partch (1986). "Valuation Effects of Security Offerings and the Issuance Process." *Journal of Financial Economics* **15**(1/2), 31–60.

————, and R. S. Ruback (1985). "An Empirical Analysis of the Interfirm Equity Investment Process." *Journal of Financial Economics* **14**, 523–553.

————, and R. S. Ruback (1986). Targeted Repurchases and Common Stock Returns. Unpublished manuscript, June.

Miller, M. (1977). "Debt and Taxes." *Journal of Finance* **32**, 261–276.

Morrison, A. (1982). "Those Executive Bailout Deals." *Fortune,* December 13, 82–87.

Mueller, D. ed. (1980). *The Determinants and Effects of Mergers: An International Comparison.* Cambridge, Mass.: Oelgeschlager, Gunn & Hain.

Murphy, K. J. (1985). "Corporate Performance and Managerial Remuneration: An Empirical Analysis." *Journal of Accounting and Economics* **7**(1–3), 11–42.

Myers, S. C. (1977). "Determinants of Corporate Borrowing." *Journal of Financial Economics* **5**(2), 147–175.

————, and N. S. Majluf (1984). "Corporate Financing and Investment Decisions When Firms Have Information That Investors Do not Have." *Journal of Financial Economics* **13**, 187–221.

Palepu, K. G. (1986). "Predicting Takeover Targets: A Methodological and Empirical Analysis." *Journal of Accounting and Economics* **8**, 3–35.

Paulus, J. D. (1986). *Corporate Restructuring,*

"Junk," and Leverage: Too Much or Too Little?" New York: Morgan Stanley.

Peavy, J. W., III, and J. A. Scott (1985). "The Effect of Stock for Debt Swaps on Security Returns." *Financial Review* 20(4), 303–327.

Pettway, R. H., and R. C. Radcliffe (1985). "Impacts of New Equity Sales upon Electric Utility Share Prices." *Financial Management* 14, 16–25.

Picchi, B. J. (1985). *The Structure of the U.S. Oil Industry: Past and Future.* New York: Salomon Brothers.

Ravenscraft, D., and F. Scherer (1985). "The Profitability of Mergers." Unpublished paper, December.

Ricks, W. (1982). "The Market's Response to the 1974 LIFO Adoptions." *Journal of Accounting Research* 20(2), 367–387.

———, and G. Biddle (1987). "LIFO Adoptions and Stock Price Reactions: Further Evidence and Methodological Considerations." *Journal of Accounting Research* (forthcoming).

Rogers, R. C., and J. E. Owers (1985). "Equity for Debt Exchanges and Stockholder Wealth." *Financial Management* 14(3), 18–26.

Rosenfeld, A. (1982). *Repurchase Offers: Information-Adjusted Premiums and Shareholders' Response.* MERC monograph series MT–82–01, University of Rochester, Rochester, N.Y.

Rozeff, M. (1982). "Growth, Beta and Agency Costs as Determinants of Dividend Payout Ratios." *Journal of Financial Research* 5, 249–259.

Shiller, R. J. (1981a). "Do Stock Prices Move Too Much to Be Justified by Subsequent Changes in Dividends?" *American Economic Review* 421–436.

——— (1981b). "The Use of Volatility Measures in Assessing Market Efficiency." *Journal of Finance* 36, 291–304.

Smith, C. W., Jr. (1986). "Investment Banking and the Capital Acquisition Process." *Journal of Financial Economics* 15(1/2), 3–29.

———, and J. B. Warner (1979). "On Financial Contracting: An Analysis of Bond Covenants." *Journal of Financial Economics* 7, 117–161.

Sunder, S. (1975). "Stock Price and Risk Related to Accounting Changes in Inventory Valuation." *Accounting Review,* April, 305–315.

Vermaelen, T. (1981). "Common Stock Repurchases and Market Signalling." *Journal of Financial Economics* 9, 139–183.

Vu, J. D. (1986). "An Empirical Investigation of

Calls of Nonconvertible Bonds." *Journal of Financial Economics* 16(2), 235–265.

Wansley, J. W., and A. Fayez (1986). Determinants of Return to Security Holders from Mergers. Unpublished manuscript, Louisiana State University, January.

———, W. R. Lane, and H. C. Yang (1983). "Abnormal Returns to Acquired Firms by Type of Acquisitions and Method of Payment." *Financial Management* 12(3), 16–22.

———, W. R. Lane, and H. C. Yang (1987). "Gains to Acquiring Firms in Cash and Securities Transactions." *Financial Review* (forthcoming).

You, V. L., R. E. Caves, J. L. Henry, and M. M. Smith (1987). "Mergers and Bidders' Wealth: Managerial and Strategic Factors." In *The Economics of Corporate Strategy,* ed. L. G. Thomas Lexington, Mass.: Lexington Books (in press).

"Cash Flow: The Top 200" (1985). *Dun's Business Month,* July, 44–50.

Corporate Control Alert (1986). February, March, and April. New York: American Lawyer.

Economic Report of the President (1985). Washington, D.C.: U.S. Gov't. Printing Office, Chap. 6.

Federal Reserve Board (1986). *Balance Sheets, Flow of Funds.* Washington, D.C.: U.S. Gov't. Printing Office.

Grimm, W. T. (1984) *Mergerstat Review 1984.* Chicago, Ill.: Grimm.

——— (1985). *Mergerstat Review 1985.* Chicago, Ill.: Grimm.

Investor Responsibility Research Center, Inc. (1985). Corporate Governance Service: Voting by Institutional Investors on Corporate Governance Questions, 1985 Proxy Season, pp. 19–25. Washington, D.C.: IRRC, Inc.

Media General Financial Weekly (1984). December 31, 17.

Office of the Chief Economist, SEC (1986). The Economics of Poison Pills. Washington, D.C.: Unpublished manuscript, Securities and Exchange Commission.

——— (1985a). Shark Repellents and Stock Prices: The Effects of Antitakeover Amendments Since 1980. Unpublished manuscript, July 24. Washington, D.C.: Securities and Exchange Commission.

——— (1985b). Institutional Ownership, Tender Offers, and Long-Term Investments. Unpublished manuscript, April 19. Washington, D.C.: Securities and Exchange Commission.

——— (1984). "The Economics of Any-or-All, Partial, and Two-Tier Tender Offers. *Federal Register,* June 29, 26, 751–26, 761.

21

Comment

RICHARD S. RUBACK

Empirical studies of takeovers document that substantial economic gains result from mergers and tender offers.[1] These gains accrue to shareholders of the firms involved in the takeover—particularly to the stockholders of the target firm. Knowing that stockholders gain is important information. It tells us, for example, that stockholders of target firms do not need protection from raiding bidders. But knowing that takeovers create value to stockholders doesn't answer all our questions about the benefits of takeovers. To answer these questions, we want to know why takeovers occur and where the gains come from.

Economists have been trying to determine the sources of the gains in takeovers for a long time. In theory, there are many possible sources for the observed gains. The list includes synergy from economies of scale; vertical integration and coordination; managerial efficiencies, inefficiencies, and empire building; monopolization; and taxes. The empirical verification of these hypothesized sources of gains has been elusive, primarily because the type of information required to directly document the gains is unavailable. Generally speaking, the results of this research have *excluded* explanations. For example, one of the most important explanations that has been empirically excluded is monopolization; see Eckbo (1983) and Stillman (1983).

Two of the chapters in this part of the volume examine the tax motive for takeovers. Chapter 18, by Professors Gilson, Scholes, and Wolfson, focuses on the appropriate way to measure the tax benefits of takeovers. The other tax-related chapter, Chapter 19, by Auerbach and Reishus, attempts to measure the tax benefits in a large sample of mergers. The remaining chapter in this part, Chapter 20, by Professor Jensen, focuses on managerial explanations for takeovers and provides an explanation for the recent large takeovers and reorganizations in the petroleum industry.

I will discuss the two tax-related chapters first and then conclude with some thoughts on Professor Jensen's analysis.

Auerbach and Reishus attempt to isolate mergers that generated tax benefits. They also provide a rough estimate of the magnitude of the tax gains. These estimates focus on the *corporate* tax savings. As Gilson, Scholes, and Wolfson point out, the corporate tax benefit is an incomplete measure of the actual tax benefit. The corporate benefit can be offset by tax liabilities at the personal level or by transaction costs. Also, the corporate benefits may have occurred without the merger and therefore are not attributable to the merger. Nevertheless, a significant *corporate* tax benefit seems to be a prerequisite for a total tax benefit. Thus, an appropriate place to begin is with the evidence on the corporate tax benefits to mergers.

Three sources of corporate tax gains are examined by Auerbach and Reishus: (1) gains from the transfer of tax losses and credits; (2) gains from the step-up in basis of the target's assets and the higher depreciation tax shields that result; (3) the gains from interest tax shields that are associated with merger-induced leverage increases. Data on 322 corporate mergers between the years 1968 and 1983 are examined.

Somewhat surprisingly, the evidence indicates that the corporate gain from the step-up in basis and the resulting increase in depreciation tax shields are negligible. Also, there does not appear to be an increase in the long-term leverage of the combined firm, so that the gains from increases in interest tax shields appear to be nil.

In contrast, the transfer of net operating losses and tax credits does appear to generate corporate tax benefits from mergers. To determine which mergers have the potential for creating these gains, Auerbach and Reishus classify firms into two general categories: firms that could use tax losses and credits, and firms with tax losses and credits. Tax benefits can occur when a firm that can use tax benefits acquires a firm with benefits or when a firm with tax benefits acquires a firm that can use them. The search is for mergers between firms in different categories.

Most target and bidding firms in the sample are profitable and pay taxes. The transfer of losses and tax credits does not create corporate tax savings in these mergers because there are no such losses or credits to transfer. There are, however, 40 mergers, or 12% of the sample, in which a bidding firm that could use tax benefits acquires a target with benefits. Also, in 21 mergers, or 7% of the sample, an acquiring firm with tax benefits merged with a target that could use those benefits. Therefore, corporate tax benefits may occur in about 20% of the mergers. Overall, the estimated tax benefits are about 10.5% of the value of the target firm. Note, however, that the benefits are quite small for most mergers with such corporate tax benefits. The benefits exceed 10% of the value of the target firm in only 7% of the mergers.

The existence of *corporate* tax benefits from the transfer of tax losses and tax credits does not mean that there are *total* tax benefits from these mergers. Gilson, Scholes, and Wolfson argue that the appropriate measure of the tax effects of mergers ought to include both the corporate tax effects and the personal tax effects. Furthermore, the tax benefits from mergers should be compared with the next best alternative strategy to realize these tax benefits. The

costs of realizing tax benefits through mergers, such as transaction and organizational costs, should also be included.

Let us apply the Gilson, Scholes, and Wolfson arguments to the transfer of losses and tax credits, which is the one circumstance for which Auerbach and Reishus identified tax corporate benefits from mergers. For the 21 cases in which acquiring firms with tax benefits acquired target firms that could use the benefits, the argument for no net tax benefits from mergers is relatively simple. The corporate tax gain in these mergers occurs by using the income of the target firm to offset the bidding firm's losses and credits. From the bidder's viewpoint, any source of taxable income would suffice. The simplest way to acquire taxable income is by buying a Treasury bill. Such an investment, if financed with equity, will use the tax losses and credits. Furthermore, Treasury bills have none of the complications or premiums that are typically associated with acquiring another firm to provide the taxable income. Thus, the corporate tax benefits that result from mergers between an acquiring firm with tax losses and credits and a target firm with taxable income could be accomplished in other ways. So there are no net tax benefits in these cases. Put differently, the analysis indicates that these mergers were not purely tax-motivated.

Auerbach and Reishus also identify 40 mergers in which an acquiring firm that could use tax benefits merged with a target that had tax losses and credits. As Gilson, Scholes, and Wolfson argue, the case for a *corporate* tax benefit is not clear in these cases. There are restrictions that limit the transfer of the target firm's losses and credits to the acquiring firm. However, even if these restrictions are ignored, the case for a net tax benefit from the merger is suspect. A target firm with tax losses or credits could realize the full value of these tax benefits without merging by, for example, buying Treasury bills. Therefore, the merger doesn't provide a tax benefit that could not be realized in the absence of a merger.

In summary, the empirical analysis presented by Auerbach and Reishus, combined with the theoretical analysis presented by Gilson, Scholes, and Wolfson, suggests that tax benefits are not a primary motive for corporate mergers. Of course, tax benefits may provide large benefits in special circumstances. Furthermore, we still don't understand why some firms let tax benefits expire. But overall, the work presented in these two chapters leads us to exclude tax motives as an explanation for most mergers.

Professor Jensen focuses on the external control features of mergers as the source of the gain in takeovers. The market for corporate control is the arena in which management teams compete for the rights to manage corporate resources. When the management of a firm does not make the best use of the firm's resources, another management team will take over the firm and implement a higher-valued operating strategy. I have difficulty disagreeing with the basic thrust of this theory since the foundation for this approach was presented in a paper that I coauthored with Jensen.

The example used to highlight the theory in Professor Jensen's chapter is the oil industry. Many of the recent large takeovers have involved oil firms as targets. Jensen argues that these mergers occur because the managers of the acquired companies failed to reduce their investment in exploration—an action that Jensen claims was obviously called for after the decline in the expected future prices for oil. Jensen relates this mismanagement to the substantial free cash flow in this industry. If he is correct, the theory predicts that managers who are unable or unwilling to make the cutbacks will be replaced by managers who will institute the higher-valued strategy.

There are, of course, other competing explanations for the recent large oil mergers. One of the most plausible is that the mergers have nothing to do with recent changes in the market for petroleum. Instead, the large oil mergers may have occurred recently simply because such mergers were effectively prohibited by antitrust policy prior to 1980.

While I am not fully convinced that Professor Jensen's explanation of the oil mergers is complete, I am convinced that the basic idea behind his discussion is absolutely correct. Takeovers lead to significant economic improvements. The gains we observe in these transactions do not appear to come from a reduction in taxes or an increase in monopoly power. Instead, these gains appear to be due to higher-valued use of the combined resources of the target and bidding firm.

NOTE

1. See Jensen and Ruback (1983) for a review of this evidence.

REFERENCES

Eckbo, B. E. (1983). "Horizontal Mergers, Collusion, and Stockholder Wealth." *Journal of Financial Economics* **11**, 241–273.
Jensen, M. C. and R. S. Ruback (1983). "The Market for Corporate Control: The Scientific Evidence." *Journal of Financial Economics* **11**, 5–50.
Stillman, R. (1983). "Examining Anti-Trust Policy Toward Horizontal Mergers." *Journal of Financial Economics* **11**, 225–240.

22

Comment

JOHN L. VOGELSTEIN

I am neither a lawyer nor an economist. However, as a professional investor, I have been involved, as a principal, in several takeovers and takeoverlike transactions. Given my background, my comments will be based on experience and practical observation.

My first comment is simple: I can assure you that the stockholders of a target company who wake up one morning to find their shares valued at 50% more than they were worth the night before don't wish to be protected against raiders.

My second comment is more complex and the conclusion less clear: Several participants in this conference have put forth the premise that the buyers, or bidders, in takeovers do not necessarily benefit from the takeovers that they complete. I agree with this position, and I can rattle off several major takeover disasters: Xerox–SDS; Exxon–Reliance Electric; Mobil–Marcor; ARCO–Anaconda; Fluor–St. Joe Minerals, and Bendix–Warner & Swasey are a few that come to mind, without research or even much thought. The total loss of value suffered by the buyers in these transactions is billions of dollars.

Nevertheless, there is virtually a feeding frenzy in mergers, acquisitions, and takeovers. The result is bidding wars and financial maneuvers that would have been unthinkable a decade ago: Norton Simon tries to go private but gets jumped by Esmark, which in turn gets jumped by Beatrice, which, after a brief respite, gets bearhugged by KKR. Stokely-VanCamp tries to go private, gets threatened by Esmark, bid for by Pillsbury, and bought by Quaker

Oats. Hanson bids for SCM. Merrill Lynch, backed by a major insurance company, plays white knight, and a bidding war commences. When I last looked, the bid price had approached $75 per share, almost twice what SCM ever sold at before 1984 and almost 20 times earnings. Ronald Perelman, through Pantry Pride, and Forstmann, Little get into a bidding contest for Revlon.

At various times this contest becomes a management buy-out, a nonmanagement LBO, and a bust-up. Crown-jewel options are created, and bust-up fees of $25 million are agreed to, only to be set aside by the courts. Pantry Pride finally wins, pays $100 million in fees, and then apparently agrees to sell Revlon's cosmetics business to Adler & Shaykin, who originally showed up in the transaction through Forstmann, Little. Philip Morris goes after General Foods and gets it without much of a struggle—and after only one price increase. Perhaps there is a lesson here: If you are prepared to pay twice what a company has ever sold for, and that price is almost 20 times earnings and 3 times book value, you *may* be able to complete a takeover without a contest. Of course, it helps if the total consideration is more than $5 billion, since there are not *yet* a lot of competitors in this league.

These examples came to mind because they are so recent or complex as to merit comment, but they are only a very small sample of what is going on in Wall Street and corporate America. Perhaps the underpinning to this frenzy is that takeovers really are created by magicians. After all, who else can buy an exciting business for a big premium, leverage it to the eyeballs with high-cost money, and end up with a great financial transaction?

There is one overriding characteristic about most takeovers: They happen fast. Among other things, this timing means that the amount of security analysis or due diligence performed by most buyers is limited. In some cases, it must be nonexistent. What has changed? History says that buyers of companies often have been wrong; and now we have entered the era of the megadollar takeover, paid for in cash, and financed with debt carrying double-digit interest rates in a disinflationary economy; all of this often accomplished without benefit of significant study or analysis of the target, let alone access to its internal numbers. Sometimes it seems that deals are done in order to do a deal, rather than because the economics of an acquisition are compelling.

Are all recent takeovers, then, mistakes? Of course not. But have some bad mistakes been made, and will they be made in the future? I am convinced that the answer is yes. And will someone really get his "clock cleaned"? I'll bet on it!

I really believe that the excesses in the takeover game brought about by speculation, ego, and greed cannot go on indefi- nitely. Unfortunately, there are several unanswerable questions posed by this prediction. How bad will the problem be? What will it look like? What should we be doing about it?

Frankly, I don't know how bad the problem will be—so much depends upon what triggers it and what psychological state the financial world is in at the time.

I guess the problem, initially, will look like a big, somewhat unanticipated bankruptcy, conceivably with fraudulent overtones; lots of banks, insurance companies, and other financial institutions and financial market participants will be hurt. Remember Penn Central! Clearly, whether we end up with an isolated event or the beginning of a panic is unpredictable.

Finally, I don't really think that anything can be done to prevent a problem from occurring. First of all, it probably already exists and, like many serious diseases, is slowly growing in some or several ill-conceived transactions. Secondly, short of banning takeovers (which is both impractical and, in a free economic system, undesirable), I don't know how to stem a trend of financial behavior that results from underlying economic imbalances, unless one fixes the economic system, which, obviously, won't be done in a hurry.

23

Comment

ELLIOTT J. WEISS

The three chapters prepared for this part of the volume all contain much that is both original and pertinent to the broad questions with which the Takeover Conference is concerned—Why do takeovers occur, and are takeovers good or bad?

The two chapters dealing explicitly with tax issues identify three techniques for generating "tax benefits" in connection with takeovers: (1) stepping up the basis of acquired assets, so as to generate increased depreciation deductions; (2) operating with a more heavily leveraged capital structure, so as to generate increased interest deductions; and (3) using net operating losses of the acquired entity to shield from tax the income of the acquiring entity. The Gilson-Scholes-Wolfson chapter (18) goes on to make the intriguing argument that comparable sources of tax benefits are available to ongoing, or "target," companies in the absence of takeovers. Therefore, Chapter 18 concludes, virtually none of the premiums typically paid in takeovers can be accounted for by tax gains uniquely available to acquirers.

I share a handicap (or, perhaps, a distinction) with Gilson, Scholes, and Wolfson in that I, too, am not a tax expert. Nonetheless, it seems to me that two more or less technical comments about their conclusions are in order. First, they do not identify all the major sources of tax benefits available in connection with takeovers.[1] For example, a recent report prepared by the staff of the Senate Finance Committee noted that an acquirer can obtain a stepped-up basis in inventory or in

certain depletable or amortizable assets without triggering any recapture or ordinary income at the target corporation level.[2] In addition, an acquirer has considerable scope to allocate to specific assets of a target a lump-sum purchase price paid for the target as a whole, so as to minimize recapture income and maximize the present value of future depreciation deductions.[3]

Second, while in theory an ongoing company can obtain tax benefits comparable to those available to an acquirer, in practice an ongoing company is likely to find it more more difficult to realize such tax benefits. Chapter 18, for example, suggests that a company with net operating losses can as easily acquire a company with taxable earnings as be acquired by such a company.[4] But often that is not so. Trans-Union Corporation, the company involved in the much discussed case of *Smith v. Van Gorkom*,[5] provides one illustration of the difficulties a tax-loss company may face. Trans-Union's principal business generated tax benefits that the company was unable to use. Trans-Union's management had searched, without success, for potential acquisitions that it felt would be attractive. Moreover, several of Trans-Union's past acquisitions, which might have been arranged to take advantage of the company's tax losses, had not worked out well and were slated for disposal. Indeed, Trans-Union's problems in finding attractive acquisitions may help explain its chairman's decision to sell the company and thus to realize for himself and Trans-Union's other shareholders some return from the excess tax benefits that Trans-Union's business generated.[6]

Similarly, an ongoing company may have difficulty leveraging its capital structures to the same extent as can an acquirer. One company involved in a leveraged buyout was able to force the holders of its outstanding convertible debentures to provide so-called "mezzanine-level" financing for a merger that cashed out its public shareholders, where restrictions relating to those debentures would have prevented the company's ongoing shareholders from achieving a similarly leveraged capital structure.[7] In other situations, tax rules treating as dividends certain amounts paid by a company to repurchase its own stock mean that an ongoing company cannot alter dramatically its debt-equity ratio unless it engages in a transaction that either alters the basic character of its business or changes materially the interests held by its major shareholders.[8]

These technical comments, however, do not address the more interesting and more central argument of Chapter 18, which is that opportunities to realize tax gains do not explain takeover premiums, because in most situations target companies can generate tax benefits comparable to those that can be generated by acquiring companies. That argument, evaluated in the context of Professor Jensen's chapter (20) and other chapters presented in this volume, provides us with new and interesting perspectives on the relationship between taxes and takeovers.

Specifically, what becomes clear is that tax-gain transactions of the kinds that Gilson, Scholes, and Wolfson assert are available to ongoing companies typically are transactions that involve consequences which most managers find unpalatable. Consider, for example, a transaction in which a company leverages its own capital structure by shrinking equity and/or taking on more debt. A leveraged capital structure involves a number of consequences that a company's managers probably will consider disadvantageous. Leverage will reduce managers' autonomy by requiring

managers to obtain financing, or the consent of financing sources, before engaging in transactions that they otherwise would have authority to consummate without reference to anyone outside the company's management structure. Leverage also will increase the nondiversifiable risks a company's managers must bear. Thus, despite the tax benefits available from a heavily leveraged capital structure, most managers (absent an imminent takeover threat) will prefer to operate with a capital structure that features a large equity cushion.

Sale-leaseback transactions, by means of which an ongoing company can arrange to obtain tax benefits comparable to those available from stepping up the basis of its operating assets, similarly generate consequences that will make managers uneasy. In this case, those consequences relate not to taxes but to accounting.[9] First, a sale-leaseback will increase a company's reported earnings if the company realizes a "gain" on the sale. This increase may create an expectation, either among investors or within the company, that future earnings will be at least as high. But the company's managers will appreciate that, absent additional opportunities for other transactions that generate similar one-shot boosts to earnings, they will not be able to generate future earnings at the same elevated level. In addition, a sale-leaseback will reduce reported earnings in the future if the "rent" to be paid to the lessor exceeds the depreciation charges that the assets in question generated prior to the sale-leaseback.[10]

Gilson, Scholes, and Wolfson may believe, and an extensive literature may demonstrate convincingly, that stock market prices adjust for accounting maneuvers, at least where those maneuvers are fully disclosed. But I have met almost no corporate executives who share that belief. Managers, in most cases, seem to be almost preoccupied with the earnings that their companies are able to report. This preoccupation may explain why relatively few companies (other than those with pressing short-term needs to generate reported earnings[11]) have engaged in extensive sale-leaseback transactions to obtain the tax benefits they may make available.[12]

In sum, tax benefits are relevant to evaluation of takeovers but not in quite the way they customarily have been considered to be relevant. The best characterization of takeovers which give rise to tax benefits might be that they are takeovers directed at one particular species of agency cost—the failure of target company managements to exploit fully the tax benefits available to those companies by, for example, leveraging their capital structures or obtaining the tax benefits associated with the stepped-up market value of their assets.[13] Note that this characterization was stimulated by, and is entirely consistent with, the analysis of Chapter 18.

The recent spate of corporate restructurings, many of which seem to have been stimulated by the threat of (possibly tax-motivated) takeover bids, supports this characterization of many takeovers. According to a report published by the *Wall Street Journal* in August 1985, 398 of North America's 850 largest companies engaged in some sort of restructuring between January 1984 and mid July 1985.[14] Moreover, more than half these restructurings appear to have involved transactions with the potential to generate tax benefits. The *Journal* classified 346 of these restructurings as voluntary and 52 as forced by threatened takeovers.[15] But given the fact that comparable restructuring transactions were far less common before 1984, I conclude that the motive behind many of the "voluntary" restructurings was managers' fear that, absent such transactions, their companies were likely to become the targets of hostile takeover bids. Thus, one can reasonably conclude not only that many takeovers involve potential tax benefits but that the potential tax benefits available to acquirers has caused managers of ongoing companies to exploit opportunities to realize tax benefits which they previously had abjured.

Professor Jensen's analysis of corporate capital structure and of the role debt plays in motivating managers to be efficient is consistent with my characterization of the relationship between takeovers and taxes.

In addition, while this is not the place to dwell on this point, his argument that managers use high debt to signal their commitment to manage efficiently has considerably more explanatory force than did his earlier suggestion that managers signal that commitment by selecting outside directors who have a strong interest in effectively monitoring the performance of those managers.[16]

But even if my characterization is accepted, where does it leave us in terms of the broader policy questions the conference is asking about the merits of and problems associated with takeovers and contests for corporate control? First, it has some implications with regard to future empirical research. Continuing investigation of what Gilson, Scholes, and Wolfson call "the least powerful claim" with respect to tax gains—the extent to which acquisitions can generate pure tax gains—appears to be quite important, because the prospect of exploiting opportunities for such gains may be motivating many takeover bids and many anticipatory restructuring transactions. However, given the complexity of most takeover transactions, and especially the possibility that acquiring companies regularly manipulate the allocation of purchase prices so as to maximize the tax benefits they realize, the data needed to produce more meaningful studies will probably not be readily available. But scholars working in this area, such as Professors Auerbach and Reishus, should be provided with data that allow them to base their future analyses either on the tax returns of the companies actually involved in takeovers or on the planning documents setting forth the tax and economic assumptions which led potential acquirers to launch their takeover bids.

Turning next to more normative questions, if one assumes that substantial tax benefits are being realized, either as a result of takeovers or as a result of restructurings stimulated by the threat of takeovers, should one be troubled or pleased? A person adopting what might be described as a neoclassical view of corporate law presumably would be pleased. He would argue that takeovers and the threat of takeovers are causing managers to pursue strategies that maximize corporate (and hence shareholder) wealth. The fact that these wealth increases occur at the expense of the public fisc should be of no concern, he presumably would maintain, because the well-being of the public fisc is not a matter of concern to a corporation's managers or to its shareholders, acting in their capacities as such.

A person not holding the neoclassical view might disagree. She would argue that corporations survive within a society and that managers and shareholders must consider how corporate activity affects others in that society, even in the absence of strict legal requirements that they do so.

Which of these perspectives would be supported by a person concerned primarily with issue of tax policy is far from clear. If, as Gilson, Scholes, and Wolfson argue, transactions that generate tax gains also typically generate efficiency gains, one concerned primarily with tax policy might well conclude that the tax laws are accomplishing their stated or implicit objectives.[17] Alternatively, one concerned about tax policy could argue that there may be problems in the relationship of tax considerations to takeovers but that those problems derive not from the existence of takeovers but from certain features of the tax laws—such as the different treatment accorded to equity and debt or the special rules relating to taxation of reorganizations—that must be changed if incentives for elaborate tax avoidance schemes of the kinds involved in takeovers are to be eliminated.[18]

Finally, a person concerned primarily with the long-term health of the corporate sector of the economy might have quite a different reaction. For corporations to compete successfully in world markets, such a person might argue, they must do more than minimize the taxes they pay. They must devote most of their creative energies to such basic business problems as designing better products, producing them more efficiently, and marketing them more effectively.

A number of commentators have observed that companies which have adopted a financially oriented, top-down style of planning and management often have found it difficult to achieve the qualitative successes in product design, production, and marketing that are necessary ingredients of sustained competitive success. As former SEC Chairman Harold M. Williams recently put it:

A management spending its days and nights with lawyers, public relations firms and investment bankers is not spending enough time developing new products, manufacturing more efficiently, or improving its balance sheet. . . . The loss in management effectiveness works against corporate and national productivity, the wages of employees, and returns to stockholders. It undermines our economy and our society.[19]

Put somewhat differently, the managers who are most sensitive to the pressures exerted by the possibility of takeover bids, including the pressure to engage in transactions that exploit tax-saving opportunities, may not be the managers who are best able to compete successfully in product and service markets. Success in one arena may require either a different kind of management talent or a different (and perhaps incompatible) kind of corporate culture than does success in the other.

To the extent that these speculations have merit, they support the view that takeovers may be destructive, in terms of societal wealth, because, directly or indirectly, they tend to undermine at least some corporations' competitive potential. But even if that is so, it does not necessarily follow that managers with the ability to compete successfully in world markets will come to the fore in the absence of the monitoring pressures exerted by the capital markets in general and the threat of takeover bids in particular. In fact, we may find that many restructured corporations are able to compete more successfully than were their predecessors.

The only observation warranting much confidence may be that neither the Congress nor the courts are likely to develop a standard that will allow us to discriminate intelligently between those firms that should be insulated from the threat of hostile (and perhaps tax-motivated) takeovers and those firms that should remain vulnerable to such takeovers. Thus, in the absence of more definitive evidence than has been produced to date, the wisest course may be to avoid recommending substantive changes in the laws that govern takeovers, and to propose that we deal with any special takeover-related problems that involve the tax laws by developing proposals designed to reform those laws and to achieve revenue-related objectives.

NOTES

1. The same comment can be made about the Auerbach-Reishus chapter (19). In addition, Chapter 19 analyzes transactions consummated prior to the enactment of Section 338 of the Internal Revenue Code, 26 U.S.C. Section 338, which was directed at eliminating tax benefits available by selectively stepping up the basis of assets acquired in a merger.

2. Staff Report, *The Subchapter C Revision Action of 1985,* Senate Committee on Finance, S.Prt. 99–47, 99th Congress, lst session 1985, 42–43.

3. Ibid., 43; see also p. 44. Conversations with tax practitioners suggest that the very aggressive allocations, designed to maximize the tax benefits realizable by acquiring companies, have become the norm.

4. Gilson, Scholes, and Wolfson also assume that companies with net operating losses must be operating unprofitably. Because of differences between tax accounting and financial accounting, that frequently is not the case. Moreover, even financial accounting, owing to its conservative bias, often characterizes as unprofitable transactions that an economist would consider to be profitable.

5. 488 A.2d 858 (Del. Supr. 1985).

6. The chairman, who also was a substantial shareholder, was nearing retirement. While he was active in management, it seems likely that the benefits he realized by imposing agency costs on other shareholders were greater than the agency costs he bore in his status as a shareholder. After he retired, however, he would lose the benefits he realized as an agent. He could be confident, however, that his successors would continue to impose comparable agency costs on Trans-Union's shareholders and that, absent a takeover, the price of Trans-Union's stock would continue to be discounted to reflect those costs. He also reasonably could expect those

managers to resist any attempt to take over Trans-Union. In such a situation, we can easily understand why the chairman was interested in selling Trans-Union at a premium and in doing so without involving any other senior executives.

7. See *Gardner and Florence Call Cowles Foundation v. Empire, Inc.,* 589 F. Supp. 669 (S.D.N.Y. 1984), *vacated on other grounds,* 754 F.2d 478 (2d Cir. 1985).

8. See Sections 300–306 of the Internal Revenue Code, 26 U.S.C. Sections 300–306.

9. This discussion assumes that the transaction will be accounted for as a sale and leaseback, rather than as a financing transaction. See Financial Accounting Standards Board, *Financial Accounting Standard No. 15.*

10. Also, if the transaction is a true sale-leaseback, the ongoing company will lose at least some of its interest in the residual value of the assets in question.

11. For example, a bank that needs to bolster its capital so as to avoid a reduction in the legal limit on the amount it is allowed to lend to a single customer.

12. A similar argument can be made about asset sales, which have the effect of reducing diversification and thus exposing managers of the resulting less-diversified firm to additional firm-specific risks.

13. Although the discussion in the text deals with leverage and stepped-up basis, the same observation may be applicable to takeovers which generate tax gains relating to use of net operating losses.

14. "Surge in Restructuring Is Profoundly Altering Much of U.S. Industry," *Wall St. J.,* August 12, 1985.

15. Ibid.

16. Jensen and Meckling, "Theory of the Firm: Managerial Behavior, Agency Costs, and Ownership Structure," 3 *J. Fin. Econ.* 305 (1970). Indeed, after observing the responses of target company managers and boards of directors to hostile takeover bids, Jensen evidences a level of distrust concerning managers and directors that is more typical of the work of the legal scholars who have been preoccupied with the potential for managerial overreaching. See, e.g., Brudney, "The Independent Director—Heavenly City or Potemkin Village?" **95** *Harv. L. Rev.* 597 (1982).

17. Of course, there would remain the question of whether the efficiency gains are commensurate in size with the revenues that are being lost.

18. Whether such simplification is possible is problematic.

19. Williams, "It's Time for a Takeover Moratorium," *Fortune,* July 22, 1985, 135, 136. See also Laffey and Daley, "What They *Do* Teach You at Harvard Biz," *Wall St. J.,* December 16, 1985 (describing how much instruction at Harvard Business School is directed at tax avoidance techniques and commenting, "We might have learned how to be more successful businessmen and wealthy individuals, but certainly not through any creation of wealth.").

24

Comment

MARTIN D. GINSBURG

There is a key notion that may be helpful in assessing what we have learned from the papers presented in this section of the conference. When you think about the various tax categories, categories of tax advantage or potential advantage, that have been exposed in these papers, you find that all fall under one general heading. That heading applies whether you are talking about substituting interest expense for the payment of dividends on equity, or use of net operating losses or other beneficial tax attributes, or a stepped-up basis in wasting assets, assets that can be amortized or depreciated to create deductions inside the target company. Indeed, if I leave the field of corporate acquisitions, the general rubric I have in mind also applies to going private transactions or leveraged buy-out transactions that simply involve venture capitalists coming in and joining with the management to eliminate the public shareholders, or even (and finally) the T. Boone Pickins distribution of royalty trust interests from an oil company.

All of these examples are just one sort of tax planning, different manifestations of one idea. It is the notion that you can improve returns if you can lift, either temporarily or permanently, the burden of the corporate tax from a future income stream that otherwise would be subject to corporate tax. And the notion is true whether it is the target's income stream—e.g., if Penn Central acquires a profitable company and Penn Central uses its unbelievably large net operating loss carryforward to shelter the income of the target hereafter—or whether it is the parent's income stream

you are trying to shelter, by acquiring a corporation whose dominant asset is a large net operating loss, and finding a way to use that loss against the parent's income. Thus we are engaged in three, six, nine, ten—the ingenuity of the tax bar is limitless—a hundred ways of accomplishing the same thing.

To what extent does that observation affect what we are doing today? I think it's useful to break this question in two. First, when is the tax law the sine qua non of the corporate acquisition? That is, how often do we see transactions that would never take place at all if it were not for a perceived gigantic tax benefit? Second, when does the tax law work the other way? When does an acquisition, which as a business matter makes sense, get killed because of perceived tax problems? My own answer, and here my answer is anecdotally based, is rarely, sometimes perhaps, but rarely. Let me give one example from real life, a transaction that took place only because of the tax law. Years ago Cero Corporation suffered a very large expropriation loss. It found itself with about $100 million (when dollars were real) of sudden net operating loss it could not efficiently use. What Cero did was go out and acquire a corporation, Behring Corporation, an OTC company in which one person, strangely enough named Mr. Behring, owned about half the stock and the unwashed public owned all the rest. Behring Corporation was what is called a collapsible corporation. Without spending the delightful three hours needed to explain that more fully, let me just say that a collapsible corporation is a bad thing. If you sell your stock, you don't get long-term capital gain, normally, and so on. There is a way, however, the tax law being 8000 pages of ways to do things, in which you can get all the normal tax benefits of selling out provided you stick the buyer with all kinds of terrible future income. It is a special election. That election ordinarily is not made because buyers say, "Oh no, not us." What Cero realized was that they were a prime candidate for making acquisitions of companies like Behring because Cero with its huge loss could swallow the burden of the election. And that's exactly what they did. Now that's a transaction that would not have taken place in the absence of the configuration I described, and Cero made a conscious decision to go out and take advantage of its tax loss in this fashion. As I say, those transactions seem to me rare. And, of course, you will appreciate that in Cero-Behring the tax law simply was being used to avoid a problem the tax law had created in the first place.

What is, I believe, much more interesting is the extent to which the creation of tax benefits in connection with an acquisition may affect the amount which a rational buyer would be prepared to pay above what the buyer would pay in the absence of the tax benefit. Now that kind of thing, of course, is in the mind of the buyer. But let me take a recent transaction where the tax benefit in the transaction may have affected the price in a serious way.

General Motors acquired Electronic Data Systems last year, paying a purchase price, in cash and paper, of about $2.6 million. If you were to look at the 1984 balance sheet of EDS, you would ask: What assets? You cannot find anything like that amount on the balance sheet. But, in fact, perhaps the principal asset of EDS, other than its personnel and management, was computer software that had been built up on a proprietary basis over 27 years and was being used to service all those customers that EDS had out there. It is my understanding that there were appraisals of that software showing a replacement value of

more than $1 billion, and perhaps as much as $2 billion. Now, let me tell you what happens under the tax law with that kind of thing. GM files for EDS a so-called Section 338 election, the tax basis of the EDS assets is stepped up to reflect the purchase price paid by GM for the EDS stock, and there is very little in the way of recapture tax imposed on EDS with respect to that software. There may be an issue under *Bliss Dairy* whether there is not technical statutory recapture but what is called tax benefit recapture. But even if there may be tax benefit recapture for software and the like, the tax does not even begin to encompass $1 billion, let alone $2 billion. A lot of this software was built up in EDS when the dollar was worth a lot more, and hence a lot fewer dollars were spent by EDS. The expenditure defines the outer limit of recapture. Under 1985 tax law, if there is no recapture, no tax at all is imposed, on EDS or on GM, for the privilege of stepping up the basis of the software. The advantage lies in the tax law's permission to amortize the stepped-up basis over five years. Two billion dollars, over five years. That is $400 million a year of deductions, deductions that will offset income of the entire General Motors Group. In present-value terms, that's worth a lot of money. It would seem to me not impossible that in the decision to pay what seemed a substantial premium, I think it was $46 a share purchase price as against a preannouncement market of $31 or under, net tax benefit had something to do with the thinking of General Motors.

My own experience is that very often there are quantifiable net tax benefits in an acquisition, and at least some of them would not be achievable in a different way. In this part of the volume we have talked about sale and leaseback and various other arrangements, and I think the points made were well taken. But I do not know any way in 1984 you could have done the transaction involving EDS and the tax-free stepping up of its basis in software, in the real world, other than through a purchase of the whole company.

LEGAL RULES,
TAKEOVER STRATEGIES, AND
DEFENSIVE TACTICS

25

The Pressure to Tender: An Analysis and a Proposed Remedy

LUCIAN ARYE BEBCHUK

In the face of a takeover bid, shareholders' tender decisions are subject to substantial distortions. A target's shareholder might well tender his shares even if he views the offered acquisition price as lower than the value of the independent target. The shareholder might tender out of fear that if he does not tender, the bidder might still gain control, in which case the shareholder would be left with low-value minority shares in the acquired target. Consequently, a bidder might succeed in gaining control over a target even if the value-maximizing course of action for the target's shareholders would be to reject the bid.

This distortion of bid outcomes has already received much attention. It has been extensively discussed by many commentators.[1] The SEC Advisory Committee on Tender Offers and the SEC have examined it in their recent examination of takeover law.[2] Courts have considered this distortion, as targets have increasingly used it to justify various defensive tactics from discriminatory self-tender offers to poison pills.[3] In recent years many companies have adopted charter provisions aimed at addressing this problem.[4] And some states

have adopted antitakeover statutes which appear to be at least partly motivated by a similar goal.[5] Although the distortion of bid outcomes has received much attention, the understanding of it has remained deficient. As the analysis of this chapter will show, many common views concerning the nature of this problem—and concerning the best ways for dealing with it—are significantly incomplete or flawed. This chapter seeks therefore to contribute to our understanding of the problem and of how it might be best addressed.[6]

Section I puts forward the objective of "undistorted choice": A target should be acquired if and only if a majority of its shareholders view the offered acquisition price as higher than the independent target's value. It is suggested that ensuring undistorted choice is desirable from the perspectives of both target shareholders and society. This objective should therefore guide public officials in the design of takeover law and should guide practitioners in the design of corporate charters.

Section II provides an account of how current takeover rules and the dynamics of takeover bids lead to "distorted" outcomes, outcomes deviating from the undistorted choice standard. The analysis shows that the nature and scope of this problem are often misunderstood. In particular, in contrast to the perception that commentators, courts, and regulators commonly have, the problem is not limited to (or even especially acute in) partial bids and two-tier bids.

This chapter is also scheduled to appear in 12 *Delaware Journal of Corporate Law* (1987). I should like to thank Scott Edelman, Louis Kaplow, and my two discussants at the conference, Douglas Ginsburg and Marshall Small, for their comments. I also gratefully acknowledge the financial support of the Center for Law and Economic Studies at Columbia Law School, the National Science Foundation (grant No. SES-8708212), and the Harvard Law School Program in Law and Economics.

Section III puts forward an arrangement (indeed, two versions of it) that is capable of ensuring undistorted outcomes. Under one version of the arrangement, tendering shareholders would be able to indicate whether or not they "approve" a takeover; and the bidder would be allowed to purchase a controlling interest only if it attracts the required number of "approving" tenders. Under the other version, which is similar to the arrangement contained in some recent state statutes, a bidder would be allowed to proceed only if its bid gains approval in a prior, separate vote among the target's shareholders. The proposed arrangement could in principle be adopted either through appropriate legal rules or through appropriate charter provisions; and both methods of implementation will be considered.

Finally, Section IV examines five alternative remedies, which have been suggested in the literature or adopted by various corporations. Using the preceding analysis of the distorted choice problem, I shall analyze the effectiveness and costs of each of these arrangements. As will be shown, some of these arrangements are much better than others, but even the best are somewhat inferior to the arrangement put forward in this chapter.

Before proceeding, it should be noted that this chapter is concerned only with acquisitions of targets that prior to the acquisition were not controlled by a single shareholder (or a group of shareholders acting in concert). Acquisitions of targets that were previously controlled by a single shareholder pose a special set of problems and require a separate analysis.

THE UNDISTORTED CHOICE OBJECTIVE

According to the undistorted choice objective, a company should be acquired if and only if a majority of its shareholders view the offered acquisition price as higher than the independent target's value. By a majority of the target's shareholders, I shall throughout mean shareholders holding a majority of the target's shares. As to the independent target's value, this term will refer to the value that the target will have if it remains, at least for the time being, independent; this value of the independent target obviously includes the value of the prospect of receiving higher acquisition offers in the future.

The undistorted choice objective provides a standard for evaluating the outcome of any acquisition attempt—whether by a takeover bid, by a merger proposal, or by open-market and privately negotiated purchases. In this chapter, however, I shall limit my discussion to the outcome of takeover bids.[7]

As explained below, ensuring undistorted choice would not only benefit target shareholders but also produce substantial social gains. Consequently, I suggest, this objective should guide public officials in the design of takeover law.[8] The social desirability of ensuring undistorted choice is based on efficiency considerations. Efficiency requires that corporate assets be put to their most productive uses. While the acquisition of some companies would produce efficiency gains from improved management of "synergy," the assets of other companies are best left under the existing, independent mode of operation. Thus, choosing the mechanism that will determine whether a given company will be acquired presents an important question of social policy.

Consider for a moment the outcome of offers to purchase a sole owner's assets. The law generally conditions the sale of a sole owner's assets on his consent. Consequently, such a sale will take place if and only if the owner views the offered acquisition price as higher than the value to himself or retaining his assets (including the value of the prospect of receiving higher acquisition offers in the future).

It is widely thought that the mechanism of enabling sole owners to accept or reject offers serves efficiency. This mechanism prevents an acquisition whenever the potential buyer is unwilling to pay as much as the value to the owner of retaining his assets. In such cases, efficiency is indeed most likely to be served by having the owner retain his assets. To be sure, this mechanism for allocating sole owners' assets is not perfect. For example, sole owners might make mistakes in estimating the value to themselves of retaining their assets. Yet this mechanism appears to be be best available—the one that would bring us closest to efficient allocation of sole owners' assets.

According to the undistorted choice objective, the mechanism governing corporate acquisitions should parallel the mechanism used in the sole owner context. A target should be acquired if and only if its shareholders view selling their company as their value-maximizing course of action. When the shareholders judge the offered acquisition price to be lower than the independent target's value, then the bid should fail; in such a case, efficiency would likely be served by having the target remain independent. Of course, like the corresponding mechansim in the sole owner context, the proposed undistorted choice mechanism is not perfect. But, again, the undistorted choice mechanism appears to be the best available—the one that would bring us closest to efficient allocation of targets' assets.[9]

Now, while a sole owner obviously has only one view as to whether accepting an offer would be value maximizing, a target's shareholders might well differ in their judgments of how the offered acquisition price compares with the independent target's value. It is thus necessary to specify some fraction of a given target's shareholders who must view accepting an offer as value-maximizing if the offer is to be accepted. The undistorted choice objective suggests that this decisive fraction should be a majority of the shareholders. The reasoning behind this choice of the decisive fraction is that the majority is more likely to be right than the minority in its assessment of the shareholders' value-maximizing course of action.[10]

I shall later in this chapter address two objections that are likely to be raised against my claim that ensuring undistorted choice is socially desirable. First, acquisition offers are usually made at a premium over the prebid market price of the target's shares, and it might be argued that a target's shareholders can never rationally

view the rejection of a premium offer as value-maximizing. As Section II will explain, however, there are good reasons to believe that rejecting a bid would be value maximizing in a significant number of instances. Second, it might be argued that, while ensuring undistorted choice would produce an efficient outcome of bids, it might also entail some significant efficiency costs (e.g., by discouraging the search for takeover targets). As I will explain in Section III, however, ensuring undistorted choice through the arrangement proposed in that section would be unlikely to involve any significant efficiency costs.

Finally, note that ensuring undistorted choice is desirable not only from the perspective of efficiency but also from the perspective of target shareholders. Ensuring undistorted choice would enable target shareholders to follow that course of action which would be most likely to be value maximizing. Therefore, this chapter's analysis of the ways to ensure undistorted choice should be of interest not only to public officials concerned with designing optimal takeover law but also to private parties concerned with designing optimal corporate charters.

THE DISTORTED CHOICE PROBLEM

Under current takeover rules, and in the absence of special charter provisions, the outcome of bids might be "distorted"—i.e., might deviate from the one required by the undistorted choice objective. This problem of distorted choice is rooted in the general presence of a gap between the bid price and the value that minority shares are expected to have in the event of a takeover. I shall first examine this gap, and shall then proceed to analyze the resulting distortions and to discuss their practical significance.

The Post Takeover Value of Minority Shares

As the analysis below shows, the post-takeover value of minority shares is generally lower than the bid price. This analysis is supported by the empirical evidence that, after a successful bid is closed, the market price of minority shares is significantly lower than the bid price.[11]

A successful bidder is usually able to effect a takeout merger between itself and the target—a merger that "freezes out" minority shareholders, requiring them to exchange their shares for either cash or securities of the bidder. Takeovers might be thus divided between those that are expected to be followed by a takeout within a short period and those that are not expected to be followed by such a takeout. Below I explain why the post takeover value of minority shares is usually lower than the bid price in *both* kinds of cases.

Takeovers Accompanied by an Immediate Takeout

Current takeout law allows successful bidders to pay minority shareholders in an immediate takeout a consideration with a value lower than the bid price. Acquirers are constrained only by the appraisal rights of the minority shareholders.[12] Appraisal statutes are not designed to give a target's shareholders any share of the gains from the target's acquisition, for such statutes generally exclude from the required compensation any element of value arising from the accomplishment of a merger.[13] Furthermore, in assessing the target's preacquisition value, the appraisal process draws substantially on past earnings and past stock market prices.[14]

Consequently, although appraisal rights usually ensure that minority shareholders are paid no less than the target's prebid price, they usually do not require a takeout consideration as high as the price of a premium takeover bid. Indeed, in recent immediate takeouts, minority shareholders often received securities with a value substantially lower than the bid price.[15] Challenges to such pricing structures have been rejected by the courts.[16]

Takeovers Unaccompanied by an Immediate Takeout

Many successful bidders do not effect an immediate takeout but, rather, maintain the target for the time being as a partly-owned subsidiary. An acquirer that does not effect an immediate takeout might still be able to take advantage of minority shareholders in two ways. First, the acquirer might operate the target's business in such a fashion so as to divert to itself part of the target's profits.[17] For example, the acquirer might engage in self-dealing (transacting with the target on terms favorable to itself),[18] or it might allocate to itself business opportunities belonging to the target.[19] Although such practices might be unlawful, engaging in them is often possible because of the obvious problems involved in detecting and challenging them.

The second way in which an acquirer that does not effect an immediate takeout might be able to take advantage of minority shareholders is by effecting a takeout later on. Indeed, when an acquirer decides against an immediate takeout, it presumably keeps in mind the possibility of a distant takeout. Postponing the takeout might benefit the acquirer by enabling it to influence the size of the takeout consideration to which minority shareholders are entitled. As the Delaware Supreme Court noted, the timing of a takeout might be controlled by the acquirer "to favor the majority only, based upon the status of the market and the elements of an appraisal."[20] For example, because earnings and market price are common elements of the appraisal formula, the acquirer might time the takeout to occur when earnings are abnormally low or when the market price is substantially below the value suggested by the acquirer's inside information. Moreover, the acquirer might also manage the target so as to further lower the elements of appraisal. For example, the acquirer might depress the target's earnings in the period prior to the takeout; or the acquirer might depress the target's market price in that period by using its control over both the target's dividend policy and its release of information.[21]

Because of the expectations that the acquirer will divert earnings or effect a distant takeout, the post-takeout value of minority shares in takeovers unaccompanied by immediate takeouts is generally lower than the bid price. Indeed, as indicated by the empirical evidence, the post-takeover value of minority shares in such instances is usually even lower than the consideration that would be required in an immediate takeout.[22] This is because an acquirer usually will not decide against an immediate takeout unless it expects that, by diverting earnings or by effecting a distant takeout, it will be able to leave minority shareholders with even less than it would have to pay them in an immediate takeout.

To understand the acquirer's reasoning, suppose that an immediate takeout would require the acquirer to pay $8 per share; and suppose that $X is the per-share value that investors would attach to minority shares if they expected no takeout to occur until at least, say, five years following the takeover. If $X were higher than $8, then the acquirer would likely profit from an immediate takeout—even if the acquirer does not wish to remain the owner of all of the target's shares. For the acquirer could effect an immediate takeout at $8 per share and then resell the acquired minority shares to public investors, committing itself not to effect another takeout within five years. Given this commitment, the acquirer would be able to sell the shares for $X per share and would hence make a profit of $(X − 8) per share (less the relatively small transaction costs involved). Thus, because an immediate takeout would likely be profitable if $X exceeded $8, it follows that the acquirer would decide against an immediate takeout only if $X were likely to be lower than the $8-per-share consideration required in an immediate takeout.

In sum, the expected post-takeover value of minority shares is lower than the bid price not only when the acquirer is expected to effect an immediate takeout but also when the acquirer is not expected to do so. It follows that this will be the case as well when there is uncertainty as to which course of action the bidder will follow upon gaining control.

The Acquisition Price in a Takeover

The concept of the "acquisition price" in a takeover is important in defining the un-distorted choice objective and thus in examining deviations from this objective. It is therefore necessary to clarify this important concept.

In a takeover, the successful bidder usually does not acquire through its bid all of the target's shares. There are two reasons for the common presence of unacquired shares. First, many bids are "partial"—i.e., the bidder does not commit itself to purchase more than a specified fraction of the target's shares; and when a partial bid is oversubscribed, the bidder may, and usually does, refuse to purchase more than the number sought. Second, although a successful bidder, by definition, attracts enough tenders to gain control, it usually does not (nor is it expected to) attract tenders from all of the target's shareholders; as the evidence indicates, there is a significant incidence of nontendering in successful bids of all kinds, i.e., in both partial bids and bids for all shares.[23]

Nonetheless, a takeover is, in an important sense, equivalent to purchasing the target as a whole. To understand this equivalency, consider a bidder that gains control of a 100-share target by purchasing 70 shares for a bid price of $10 a share; and suppose that the post-takeover value of the remaining 30 minority shares is $8 per share. At first blush, it might seem that this takeover does not involve the purchase of the target as a whole but involves only the purchase of 70 shares. This view, however, ignores the consequences of acquiring a controlling interest.

Unlike the acquisition of a non-controlling block, the acquisition of a controlling block clearly changes the position of non-selling shareholders. A share in the acquired target will have a different value (whether higher or lower) than a share in the independent target. In a sense, these two shares are different assets, representing different streams of future earnings. The takeover terminates the asset known as "a share in the independent target" and replaces it with a "minority share in the acquired target."

Therefore, we should not view the takeover in our example as involving only 70 shares. Rather, we should view the bidder as having purchased all 100 shares of the independent target, with each of 70 shares purchased for the bid price of $10, and with each of 30 shares exchanged for a minority share worth $8. We should thus regard the bidder as having acquired the target for a total acquisition price of $(70 \times $10) + (30 \times $8) = 940, or a per-share acquisition price of $9.40.

This characterization of the takeover is clearly accurate from the perspective of the target's shareholders. As a result of the takeover, the shareholders as a group have lost all of their 100 shares in the independent target. Instead, they find themselves with $700 in cash and with 30 minority shares worth $240. This characterization of the takeover is also accurate from the bidder's perspective. The value of the minority shares—30 shares worth $8 each, or $240—represents the part of the target's future earnings that the minority shareholders can expect to capture. The bidder, in turn, can expect to capture all of the acquired target's future earnings less $240. Hence, from the bidder's perspective, the takeover is equivalent to a transaction in which it would purchase all of the target's shares for $940 and then sell to public investors 30 minority shares worth $240.

The Distortion of Outcomes

I now turn to explaining how the outcome of bids might be distorted. For an illustrative example, let us consider a case in which a bidder is offering $10 a share and in which the expected post-takeover value of minority shares is $8 a share; and let us denote the independent target's per-share value by V.

The Distortion

The main reason for distorted outcomes is that shareholders' tender decisions might be distorted.[24] In analyzing these decisions, I shall assume that they are all made at the "moment of truth"—the time just prior to the bid's closing. Although shareholders often tender at earlier stages, early tenders can commonly be withdrawn until the moment of truth and hence become final and

irrevocable only at that moment. Consequently, at the moment of truth, shareholders who made early tenders make a decision (at least implicitly) whether to withdraw their shares—a decision that is equivalent to a tender decision.[25]

In making a tender decision, any given shareholder will realize that his decision is unlikely to determine the bid's outcome. Therefore, the shareholder will take into account the two possible outcomes of the bid—the bidder's gaining control, and the bidder's failure to do so—and he will examine for each of them whether he will be better off tendering or holding out.

Consider first the case in which the bidder succeeds in gaining control. In this case, tendering by the shareholder will lead to his having his shares (or at least some of them) acquired for $10 a share; while holding out will lead to his ending up with minority shares worth $8 a share. Therefore, supposing that the bid is going to succeed, the shareholder will prefer to tender no matter how high his estimate of V. Thus, as long as the bid has some chance of success, the prospect of a takeover will pressure the shareholder to tender his shares. As I shall later emphasize, this pressure exists in all bids (i.e., whether or not the bid is partial and whether or not the bid is a two-tier one).

Consider now the case in which the bid fails and the target remains independent. Assuming that the bidder has retained an option not to purchase shares if the bid fails, the bidder might either return tendered shares or elect to purchase them. If the bidder returns tendered shares, the shareholder's tender decision will of course make no difference. If the failing bidder elects to purchase tendered shares, however, the shareholder's decision will matter: Tendering will lead to his having his shares acquired for the bid price of $10 a share, while holding out will lead to his retaining shares in the independent target. Thus, assuming that the bid is going to fail, the shareholder will prefer to tender if and only if he views V as lower than $10. Thus, whereas the shareholders will always wish to have his shares acquired in the event of a takeover, he might or might not wish to have his shares acquired in the event that the target remains independent.

What, then, will the shareholder elect to do? Consider, first, the case in which the shareholder considers $$V$ to be lower than the $10 bid price. In this case, the shareholder will surely tender. For whether the bid is going to succeed or fail, the shareholder will prefer selling his shares at the bid price to retaining them.[26]

Consider now the case in which the shareholder views $$V$ as exceeding the $10 bid price. The shareholder will wish, as always, to have his shares acquired in the event of a takeover. But he will also wish to retain his shares in the event that the target remains independent. Consequently, he might or might not tender. The greater the probability that he attributes to the bid's success, and the greater the gap between the bid price and the expected post-takeover value of minority shares ($2 in our example), then the greater the likelihood that the shareholders will tender even though he views $$V$ as higher than $10.

It might be asked why a rational shareholder would attribute any positive probability to the possibility of a takeover when he views $$V$ as higher than the $10 bid price. There are two reasons why a rational shareholder might do so. First, the shareholder might be uncertain as to what other shareholders' estimates of $$V$ are and as to what other shareholders' estimates of the likelihood of a takeover are. Second, even assuming that all the shareholders view $$V$ as higher than the $10 bid price and that they are all aware of this fact, a rational shareholder might still attach a significant likelihood to the possibility of a takeover. Because shareholders cannot coordinate their actions, they must make tender decisions without assurance as to how others will act. In such a situation, it might be perfectly rational for some, many, or indeed most shareholders to attach a significant likelihood to the possibility of a takeover. For such initial expectations might be self-fulfilling—they could lead to tenders of a sufficient number for the bidder to

gain control. And since such initial expectations might be self-fulfilling, it might be rational to adopt them in the first place. [27]

The above analysis may be summarized as follows: if the shareholders view $$V$ as lower than the expected per-share acquisition price—i.e., if a takeover is desirable—then the bid will indeed succeed. If the shareholders view $$V$ as higher than the expected per-share acquisition price—i.e., if a takeover is undesirable—then the target might still be acquired: If the shareholders' estimates of $$V$ lie between the expected per-share acquisition price and the bid price, the target will surely be acquired; and even if the shareholders view $$V$ as not only higher than the bid price, the target might still be acquired if enough shareholders attach a sufficiently significant likelihood to the possibility of a takeover.

To be sure, my claim is not that the described distortions are irresistible. Bids are not all bound to succeed, and bids indeed fail every now and then. A bid is likely to fail, however, only if (1) the shareholders' estimates of $$V$ exceed not only the expected per-share acquisition price but also the bid price, and (2) there is a widespread confidence among shareholders that the bid will fail. A bidder, then, can offer a per-share acquisition price significantly below the shareholders' estimates of $$V$ and still enjoy a high likelihood of success. Thus, the distortions are not irresistible, but they are substantial.

The Generality of the Distortion

A widely held belief is that to the extent that any distortions of shareholder choice exist, they result from, and hence are limited to, partial bids and two-tier bids. In particular, this view appears to be held by the SEC and the SEC Advisory Committee on Tender Offers,[28] by many commentators,[29] and by litigants and courts.[36]

That many people have come to hold such a view is quite understandable. As we have seen, the pressure to tender results from the fact that should a takeover occur, the value of minority shares will be lower than the bid price. Consequently, the presence of this pressure is much more apparent in two-tier bids and partial bids: In a two-tier bid, the expected low value of minority shares is very conspicuous; and in a partial bid it is very clear that in the event of a takeover some shareholders would have to end up with minority shares.

As the preceding analysis demonstrates, however, the problem of distorted choice is in no way limited to, or even especially acute in, partial bids and two-tier bids. For nothing in that analysis has depended on the bid's being partial or two-tier.

To verify this point, consider first a bid for all shares. What is special about such a bid is that tendering shareholders are assured of having all of their shares acquired in the event of a takeover. This assurance, however, in no way protects shareholders from the pressure to tender. For this pressure is rooted in the consequences that shareholders might suffer if they do not tender. Clearly, the assurance that shareholders will not end up with any minority shares if they do tender in no way alleviates their fear that they will end up with low-value minority shares if they *do not* tender. As long as the expected value of minority shares is lower than the bid price, this fear introduces a pressure to tender. And this low expected value of minority shares, which arises from the powers that a successful bidder would have upon gaining control, does not depend on whether the bidder's offer is partial or for all shares.

To see that the distorted choice problem is not limited to two-tier bids, consider a bid that is not expected to be followed by an immediate takeout. Again, a pressure to tender will exist, because the expected value of minority shares is lower than the bid price. To be sure, if the bid succeeds, it is expected that minority shareholders will be able to retain their shares. Yet the value of minority shares in such a case would still be lower than the bid price, because of the possibilities of earnings diversion and distant takeout. Indeed, as explained earlier, in takeovers unaccompanied by immediate takeouts, minority shares usually have a value even lower than the consideration which the acquirer would have to pay in an immediate takeout.

In sum, the problem of distorted choice exists in bids of all kinds—i.e., whether the bid is partial or for all shares, and whether or not the bid is expected to be followed by an immediate takeout. The problem, then, is more general than is commonly believed.

Market Trading and the Distortion of Outcomes

The analysis thus far, it might be argued, is flawed because it has paid no attention to the existence of an active market trading throughout the period in which the bid is open. The market price of the target's shares, so the argument goes, will reflect shareholders' estimates of $\$V$, the independent target's per-share value. If most shareholders consider $\$V$ to be higher than the per-share value that tendering shareholders can expect to receive in a takeover, the market price of the target's shares will also exceed this per-share value. Consequently, it is argued, no shareholder will tender, since tendering will clearly be inferior to selling into the market.

This market-trading objection, however, is invalid. My analysis has focused on the time just prior to the bid's expiration—the "moment of truth." No matter how many times the target's shares have changed hands since the bid's announcement, at the moment of truth they are all necessarily owned by someone. At this point in time, the shares' ultimate owners face only two alternatives—tendering their shares, and retaining them beyond the bid's expiration. Thus, the preceding analysis of shareholder choice is perfectly applicable to the decisions that the shares' ultimate owners must make at the moment of truth: They might tender even if they view $\$V$ as higher than the per-share value they expect to receive in a takeover.

Because a bid's outcome is determined by the shareholders' decisions at the moment of truth, showing that these decisions are distorted is sufficient to refute the market-trading objection. Still, it is worth pointing out that, in contrast to what this objection mistakenly assumes, the market price of the target's shares during the bid period might not fully reflect investors' estimates of V.

During the bid period, the market price might be affected by the anticipated distortions of shareholders' decisions at the moment of truth. Investors who buy the target's shares during this period are aware that they (or if they resell the shares, those who will buy the shares from them) will be ultimately subject to the pressure to tender. The price that they will be willing to pay will inevitably reflect this awareness. Indeed, in calculating the price that they are willing to pay, investors usually assume that the bid will likely succeed unless it is superseded by a higher bid or impeded by obstructive defensive tactics. Thus, once a bid is made, the target's market price might fail to reflect fully subsequent revisions in investors' estimates of V. In particular, the market price might be capped by the bid price even if investors' most recent estimates of V exceed the bid price.

The Practical Significance of the Problem

Thus far I have shown that a bid might succeed even if the target's shareholders view rejection of the bid as their value-maximizing course of action. It might be argued, however, that this problem is a purely hypothetical one because shareholders may never hold such a view. Acquisition offers usually include a premium over the prebid market price of the target's shares. This prebid price presumably reflects investors' prebid estimates of the independent target's value. Therefore, so the argument goes, shareholders can never rationally view the rejection of a premium bid as value maximizing.

The above argument, however, ignores the ever-changing nature of investors' estimates and the fact that shareholders' tender decisions are usually made several weeks after their company became a takeover target. Investors' estimates of a given company's value usually vary from month to month; estimates are continuously revised as new information about the company and the world is revealed. In the case

of takeover targets, the flow of new information and the resulting revision of estimates are likely to be especially substantial.

A target's shareholders are likely to receive a great deal of new information between the last prebid trading time and the time of their tender decisions. For example, investors might well draw inferences concerning the target's value from the very making of the bid and from the bid's terms. Investors might also revise their estimates, especially in a hostile bid, in reaction to disclosures by the target's management concerning future plans, proposed structural changes, and previously undisclosed facts. Finally, a bid attracts the investment community's attention, and intensified investigations by market participants are likely to reveal a wealth of new information concerning the target.

Because most of this new information is likely to be "good news," investors are likely to hold, at the time of their tender decisions, an estimate of the independent target's value that exceeds the prebid market price. Consequently, they might judge the independent target's value to be higher than the acquisition price offered by a premium bid. It should be emphasized that, in such a case, investors' estimates at the time of their tender decisions are likely to be superior to the estimate implicit in the target's pre-bid market price. While some shareholders' information might be limited, all shareholders are presumably aware of the prebid price. Therefore, assuming minimal rationality on their part, they will adopt a revised estimate only if, on the basis of new developments and new information, they have a good reason to do so. Therefore, although shareholders' decisions to revise their prebid estimates might sometimes prove mistaken, such decisions would presumably be more often right than wrong.

That rejecting a premium bid might sometimes be value maximizing is also indicated by the empirical evidence. A study by Professors Bradley, Desai, and Kim identified several dozen instances in which shareholders rejected a premium bid.[31] In these instances, rejecting the bid indeed proved to be value maximizing: Once the bid was rejected, the market price of the target's shares was significantly higher than the offered per-share acquisition price.

Among the various reasons that might lead shareholders to rationally view rejecting a premium bid as value maximizing, several are likely to be important and deserve specific mention. First, the target's shareholders might expect that another bidder, who can put the target's assets to a more valuable use than can the present bidder, will come forward later on with a higher offer. Indeed, in the cases of bid rejection studied by Bradley, Desai, and Kim, many of the targets that remained independent were later acquired through a higher bid. To be sure, the Williams Act provides a delay period that often enables competing bidders to come forward before shareholders have to make irrevocable decisions concerning the initial bid.[32] But the prescribed delay might in many instances fall short of the time necessary for a competing bid to materialize.[33]

Second, the shareholders might expect that rejection of the present bid would lead the present bidder to make a higher offer. Indeed, at present, a bidder might often offer less than the competitive price—i.e., the price that other potential buyers would be willing to pay. The threat of competing bids might be insufficient to secure a competitive price because the competition in the market for corporate acquisition is far from perfect. In particular, if other potential buyers view the present bidder as the one that places the highest value on the target, they will not enter a costly bidding contest—which they are bound to lose—even if the present bid is below the competitive price.[34]

Third, the shareholders might believe that the bidder's motive for making the bid was the possession of private information that the target's shares were undervalued by the market, and the shareholders might conclude that the target's accurate value exceeds the offered acquisition price. Although undervaluation might not be the dominant motive for takeovers, it might

well be the motive in a nontrivial number of cases. The recent wave of takeovers of oil companies, for example, was widely regarded as motivated by the undervaluation of these companies' stock.[35]

Fourth, the shareholders might raise their estimates of the independent target's value above the offered acquisition price as a result of plans and proposals that the incumbent management puts forward subsequent to the bid. Management might, for example, put forward a plan for a financial or economic restructuring of the target,[36] and such a plan might lead investors to raise significantly their estimates of the independent target's value.

How often are targets acquired even though the target's shareholders view remaining independent as value maximizing? Although one cannot be certain, there are grounds to believe that there is a substantial number of such instances. Because of the described distortions, at present a target is likely to remain independent only if the independent target's per-share value exceeds the offered per-share acquisition price by a considerable margin; the instances of bid rejection identified by Bradley, Desai, and Kim probably belong to that category. Because bidders wish to pay as little as possible, they presumably attempt to set the acquisition price at or just above the minimal level that, given the existing distortions, would be sufficient for the bid's success. The current instances of bid rejection are thus those in which the bidder undershoots even that minimal level. Thus, there are likely to be many takeovers in which the bidder offers less than the independent target's per-share value—but not by a sufficiently large margin for shareholders to overcome the existing distortions and reject the bid.

A PROPOSED REMEDY

This section puts forward an arrangement (indeed, two versions of it) that would effectively ensure undistorted outcomes. The main idea behind the design of the proposed arrangement is to enable shareholders to express their preferences concerning the bid's success separately from their desire to have their shares acquired in the event of a takeover. As will be explained, the arrangement could in principle be adopted either through appropriate legal rules or through appropriate charter provisions; the latter route, however, will be seen to face some difficulties.

The arrangement should apply to all bids aimed at purchasing a controlling interest. It would thus have to include a specification of the level of ownership that would be assumed to provide a buyer with a "controlling interest." This crucial threshold level should be determined so as to ensure that shareholders holding less than the threshold block would be generally unable to exercise any substantial measure of control. For the sake of concreteness, the following discussion assumes that this threshold level would be specified at 20% ownership.

The Proposed Arrangement

The Scheme of Approving and Disapproving Tenders

One version of the proposed arrangement would enable tendering shareholders to tender either "approvingly" or "disapprovingly"—i.e., to indicate whether or not they "approve" a takeover. Specifically, tendering shareholders would be able to indicate their approval or disapproval by marking an appropriate box on the tender form which accompanies all tendered shares.

As will be explained, under the proposed scheme shareholders would by and large tender their shares, either approvingly or disapprovingly. The bid's success would be determined, however, not by the number of tendered shares, but, rather, by whether or not the bid attracts the required number of approving tenders. Specifically, the bid's success would depend on whether the bidder attracts approving tenders from a majority of the target's shareholders.

If the bidder succeeds in attracting the required majority of approving tenders, then the bidder would be allowed to purchase as many shares as it wishes, and a takeover would take place. To ensure that shareholders' choices between tendering approvingly and disapprovingly would indeed reflect their preferences concerning the bid's success, a successful bidder would be prohibited from penalizing disapproving tenders. That is, in purchasing shares, the successful bidder would have to treat equally all tendering shareholders, whether they tendered approvingly or disapprovingly. In a bid for all shares, the bidder would have to purchase all tendered shares; in a partial bid, the bidder would have to use the same proration ratio for all tendering shareholders.

If the bidder fails to attract the required majority of approving tenders, then the bidder would be prohibited from acquiring a controlling interest, and the target would remain independent. The failing bidder, however, might still be able to use its bid to purchase a non-controlling block. A bidder that wants the option of purchasing a non-controlling block if its bid fails would have to include in its tender form a second question (in addition to the question of whether the tenderer approves a takeover). Tendering shareholders would be asked to indicate, by marking an appropriate box, whether or not they permit the bidder to purchase their shares in the event that the bid fails. Subsequently, if the bid indeed fails, the bidder would be allowed to purchase shares of those tendering shareholders who granted it permission to purchase their shares in such a case.[37]

Effectiveness in Attaining Undistorted Choice

Under the proposed scheme of approving and disapproving tenders, the vast majority of a target's shareholders would tender their shares, either approvingly or disapprovingly. Any particular shareholder who has an opportunity to tender (and has no compelling tax reasons for avoiding a sale of his shares) could only profit by tendering. No matter how high the shareholder's estimate of the independent target's value, holding out would be definitely inferior to tendering disapprovingly (with an indication of unwillingness to sell shares in the event that the bid fails). These two courses of action would produce different results for the shareholder only if a takeover occurs, and in that case holding out will bring clearly inferior results.

Given that shareholders would by and large tender, the important issue becomes how a tendering shareholder would decide between tendering approvingly or disapprovingly. Under the proposed scheme, the shareholder's decision will affect his position only if his decision proves pivotal and determines the bid's outcome. Therefore, the shareholder's decision will be determined by his judgment of whether—assuming his decision is going to be pivotal—he would prefer the bid to succeed or to fail.

If the shareholder's decision is going to be pivotal and he makes an approving tender, then a takeover will occur; and because the vast majority of shareholders are expected to tender, the shareholder will expect that the resulting takeover will leave him with roughly his pro rata share of the acquisition price. On the other hand, if the shareholder's decision is going to be pivotal and he makes a disapproving tender, then he will end up with shares in the independent target.

Thus, assuming that the shareholder's choice is going to be pivotal, he would prefer the bid to succeed—and would hence tender approvingly—if and only if he views the expected acquisition price as higher than the independent target's value. It follows that the proposed scheme would bring us fairly close to ensuring undistorted outcomes.[38]

The Separate-Vote Version

Under the proposed scheme of approving and disapproving tenders, shareholders would be able to express their preferences concerning the bid's success in conjunction with the tendering of shares. An alternative version of the proposed arrangement would enable shareholders to express these preferences in a separate vote. Under this alternative version, a vote would be conducted among the target's shareholders (and the vote's outcome would become known) prior to the bid's closing. The bidder would be allowed to purchase a controlling interest only if its bid obtains a prior majority approval in this vote. This separate-vote scheme is similar to the arrangement contained in the "control share acquisition" statutes that were recently adopted by some states and upheld by the Supreme Court.[39]

The similarity in operation between the two versions of the proposed arrangement should be clear. A voting shareholder's choice between voting in favor of or against a takeover would be determined in a similar way to a tendering shareholder's choice between tendering approvingly and disapprovingly. The voting shareholder's choice will affect his financial position only in the event that his choice will determine the bid's fate. If the shareholder's vote is going to be pivotal, then his voting in favor of a takeover would lead to a takeover and to his ending up with his pro rata share of the acquisition price; his voting against a takeover, on the other hand, would lead in such a case to the bid's failure and to his retaining his shares in the independent target. Consequently, assuming that the shareholder's vote is going to be pivotal, he will prefer a takeover—and hence will vote in favor of it—if and only if he views the offered acquisition price as higher than the independent target's value.

The scheme of approving and disapproving tenders, however, is in my view somewhat preferable to the separate-vote scheme. Under the former scheme, expressing approval or disapproval of a takeover would be done in conjunction with the tendering of shares, and shareholders would thus have to act only once. In contrast, the separate-vote scheme might require shareholders to act twice—once to cast a vote and possibly again to tender their shares. This two-stage process would involve higher transaction costs as well as unnecessary delays in consummating acquisitions.

Adoption of the Arrangement

Adoption Through Charter Provisions.

In principle, companies could adopt the proposed arrangement through appropriate charter provisions. As explained below, however, the policies of the stock exchanges and elements of state corporate law make it difficult for most companies to do so.

The proposed arrangement would restrict the transferability of shares in that it would prohibit bidders from purchasing a controlling interest if they fail to attract the required number of approving tenders. The New York Stock Exchange and the American Stock Exchange, however, generally prohibit listed companies from including in their charters restrictions on share transfer (unless the restrictions are required by some external regulatory body).[40] This policy, of course, makes it difficult for all companies listed on these two exchanges to adopt the proposed arrangement.

Additionally, a company's adoption of the proposed arrangement might be impeded by state law constraints.[41] In particular, significant difficulties might arise from the constraint that state law commonly imposes on the retroactivity of limitations on transfer. Under many state corporation statutes, a charter amendment limiting the transfer of shares is effective only with respect to shares whose holders voted in favor of the amendment.[42] As explained below, this rule makes it difficult for existing companies to adopt a charter amendment imposing the proposed arrangement.

Because of the rule, some shareholders would vote against a provision adopting the proposed arrangement even if they wish that the provision be approved. Because a shareholder will realize that his vote is unlikely to determine whether or not the provision will be approved, he will consider the possibility that the provision is going to be approved regardless of how he votes. In such a case, the shareholder will be able to enjoy the provision's benefits (e.g., higher potential acquisition price) even if he votes against the provision; and, since voting against the provision will make the shareholder's own shares exempt from its reach, it will make these shares more valuable in some circumstances. Thus, because shareholders'

votes might be distorted in this way, the provision might fail to pass even if most shareholders would like it to be adopted.

Because the exchanges' policies and the state law doctrines are directed against limitations on share transfer, companies wishing to adopt the proposed arrangement could try to escape the reach of these policies and doctrines by cleverly formulating the arrangement to hide the limitation on transfer that it involves. In particular, a company might adopt a provision which imposes substantial obligations (say, toward minority shareholders) on any bidder that gains control without attracting a majority of approving tenders. Obviously, if the obligations imposed are substantial enough, the provision would be practically equivalent to one that prohibits a bidder from gaining control without attracting a majority of approving tenders.

Adoption Through Legal Rules.

Of course, the proposed arrangement could also be adopted by law. Indeed, because of the difficulties involved in adoption through charter provisions, provision by law might be the only way to enable many companies to benefit from the arrangement. To be sure, provision by law does not imply that the arrangement will be mandatory. Companies might be allowed to opt out of it—i.e., to adopt charter provisions exempting bids for their shares from the prescribed arrangement.

It is worth noting that, even if there were no impediments whatsoever to charter adoption, there would be still some advantages to providing the proposed arrangement by law. Provision by law (while allowing companies to opt out) has several advantages over adoption through numerous private initiatives: It would enable the design of a uniform, efficient mechanism for ensuring compliance by bidders with the arrangement's requirements, it would save transaction and information costs, and it would reduce uncertainty (thus making planning easier).

Would the Proposed Arrangement Involve any Significant Costs?

I now wish to point out that ensuring undistorted choice through (either version of) the proposed arrangement would be unlikely to involve any significant "costs"— from the perspective of either efficiency or target shareholders. Below I therefore consider the three main ways in which ensuring undistorted choice might be initially thought to harm the interests of efficiency and/or target shareholders.

The Search for Potential Targets

Professors Easterbrook and Fischel have emphasized in their recent writings that for the corporate acquisition markets to operate efficiently, it is necessary to provide prospective buyers with an incentive to search for potential targets.[43] They argued that the need to encourage such search makes it desirable to maximize searchers' returns and hence to minimize the premium that is necessary to acquire a discovered target. On this view, ensuring undistorted choice through the proposed arrangement would be undesirable because it would increase takeover premiums.

The need to encourage search, however, does not warrant opposing the proposed arrangement. As I explained in previous work, curtailing takeover premiums is not at all necessary to induce an adequate level of search: Competitive acquisition prices are consistent with providing searchers with rewards that are substantial relative to search costs.[44] For example, prior to making a bid for an identified target, a searcher can and often does make secret purchases of the target's stock.[45] Whether or not the searcher ultimately acquires the target, the searcher will usually make a substantial profit on its secret prebid purchases.[46]

Moreover, even assuming that an increase in the rewards for search is desirable, such an increase could be accomplished by raising the statutory limit on the amount of the target's shares that a searcher can secretly purchase without being required to disclose its purchases. As long as the searcher is required to stay below the effective control threshold, an increase in the disclosure threshold would be consistent with ensuring undistorted choice through the proposed arrangement. Thus, since the existing disclosure threshold of 5% is far below any reasonable specification of the effective control threshold, the existing substantial rewards for search could be greatly enhanced without sacrificing undistorted choice.

Finally, sacrificing undistorted choice to magnify further searchers' rewards might lead to a socially excessive level of search. Search is beneficial to society only to the extent that searchers look for targets whose acquisition would produce efficiency gains. When shareholder choice is distorted and targets might consequently be acquired for less than the independent target's value, bidders would often go after targets whose acquisition would profit the bidder but would not produce efficiency gains (and perhaps even produce efficiency losses). Thus, since searchers would not limit themselves to looking for potential efficiency gains, they would make socially excessive investments in search.

In sum, the need to reward search does not justify forgoing the substantial benefits that ensuring undistorted choice would produce. Even assuming that existing incentives are inadequate, which is by no means clear, the remedy that should be advocated is that of raising the ceiling on secret prebid purchases. Indeed, sacrificing undistorted choice to increase search further not only would forgo the substantial benefits that undistorted choice would produce, but might also have an undesirable effect on the search activity itself.

Beneficial Acquisitions of Discovered Targets

Having considered the effect of the proposed arrangement on the search for targets, let us now examine whether the arrangement might prevent some desirable acquisitions of identified targets. Professors Easterbrook and Fischel have suggested that the existing pressure to tender might be necessary for bids to succeed.[47] If such pressure did not exist, they warned, shareholders would have a strong incentive not to tender even if they prefer that the bid succeed; thus, Easterbrook and Fischel argued, the existence of a pressure to tender is in the interest of both society and target shareholders.

The analysis of this chapter, however, indicates that the above concern is unwarranted. As we have seen, it is quite possible to eliminate the pressure to tender without creating any undue incentive to hold out. Under the proposed arrangement, the only acquisition attempts that would be prevented from succeeding are those that indeed should fail—those in which a majority of the target's shareholders view the independent target's value as higher than the offered acquisition price.

Partial Acquisitions

Since many people believe that partial acquisitions serve valuable economic functions,[48] it is important to point out that the proposed arrangement would in no way either penalize or discourage partial acquisitions. Under the proposed arrangement, a bidder would be free to set any limit it wishes on the number of shares that it would acquire. The bidder would be only required to attract the specified number of approving tenders (or approving votes), and to enable all the tendering shareholders to have the same fraction of their shares acquired for the bid price. Consequently, the arrangement would not prevent any beneficial partial acquisition. A bidder's attempt to purchase a partial interest would fail only if a majority of the target's shareholders view of the bidder's purchase of such a block as value decreasing. In such a case the bid's failure would indeed be desirable.

Conversely, under the proposed arrangement, bidders would make partial bids whenever a partial acquisition is more efficient than a complete acquisition. When a partial acquisition would be more efficient, the bidder would be able to offer a higher per-share acquisition price in a partial bid than it would be able to offer in a bid for all shares; therefore, since under the proposed arrangement the bidder's

chances of success would be enhanced by an increase in the offered acquisition price, the bidder would elect to make a partial bid.

ALTERNATIVE REMEDIES

Having put forward a remedy to the distorted choice problem, I now wish to examine alternative remedies (most of which have been previously suggested by commentators and regulators or have been recently adopted by various companies). Again, these remedies might be adopted (at least in principle) either through appropriate charter provisions or through appropriate legal rules. For each of the alternative remedies to be considered, I shall examine both its effectiveness in attaining undistorted choice and its costs. As will be shown, these remedies vary greatly in their effectiveness and costs; some of them are much better than others. None of these remedies, however, can perform as well as the arrangement proposed in the preceding section.

Prohibiting Partial Bids

As already noted, many (including the SEC, the SEC Advisory Committee, courts, and commentators) hold the view that any existing distortions of shareholder choice must be rooted in the use of partial bids.[49] This view has naturally led to proposals that such bids be prohibited or at least discouraged.[50]

As the analysis of this chapter has shown, however, the distorted choice problem is not limited to—nor even especially acute in—partial bids; the popular view to that effect rests on a misconception of the problem. The problem of distorted choice is largely rooted in the presence of a gap between the bid price and the expected post-takeover value of minority shares, a gap that is generally present in bids of all kinds. Consequently, the problem is substantially present not only in partial bids but also in bids for all shares. It follows that prohibiting or discouraging partial bids would do very little to ensure undistorted choice.

Requiring that the Consideration in Immediate Takeouts be Equal to the Bid Price

As previously noted, the gap between the bid price and the expected post-takeover value of minority shares is most conspicuous in two-tier bids, and such bids have therefore attracted considerable attention. Professors Brudney and Chirelstein have made a well-known proposal that courts require the consideration in an immediate takeout to equal the bid price.[51] In recent years, many companies have adopted a similar requirement by incorporating "fair price" provisions in their charters,[52] and a significant number of states have added such a requirement to their state corporation statutes.[53]

The SEC's Advisory Committee and the SEC's chief economist have suggested, however, that prohibiting immediate takeouts below the bid price would be counterproductive.[54] They observed that the post-takeover value of minority shares is lower in takeovers unaccompanied by an immediate takeout than in takeovers followed by an immediate takeout below the bid price. Hence, they reasoned, allowing such takeouts benefits minority shareholders and reduces the gap between the value of their shares and the bid price.

Below I explain that, contrary to the views of the Advisory Committee and the SEC's chief economist, requiring the consideration in immediate takeouts to equal the bid price would narrow the gap between the post-takeover value of minority shares and the bid price. I shall then go on to show, however, that such a requirement would not generally eliminate this gap (a showing which by itself indicates that the requirement would not ensure undistorted choice).

The Requirement Would Narrow the Gap

The problem with the analysis of the Advisory Committee and the SEC's chief economist is that they drew an incorrect inference from a valid empirical observa-

tion. To see the flaw in their analysis, consider the choice that a successful bidder faces. The bidder can take advantage of minority shareholders by effecting an immediate takeout below the bid price. Refraining from effecting such an immediate takeout, however, might enable the bidder to take advantage of minority shareholders by diverting earnings or effecting a distant takeover. The bidder will presumably follow the strategy that will enable it to take maximum advantage of minority shareholders.

Thus, those instances in which the acquirer decides against an immediate takeout are exactly the instances in which the acquirer expects that, by diverting earnings or effecting a distant takeover, it will be able to leave minority shareholders with even less than it would have to pay them in an immediate takeout. This explains the empirical evidence on which the Advisory Committee and the SEC's chief economist relied, i.e., the evidence that minority shareholders fare worse in takeovers unaccompanied by an immediate takeout than in takeovers accompanied by an immediate takeout below the bid price. By the same logic, however, those instances in which the acquirer effects an immediate takeout below the bid price are exactly the instances in which the acquirer views such a takeout as the best means of taking advantage of minority shareholders.

It follows that, in instances where immediate takeouts currently occur, requiring that the consideration in such takeouts be equal to the bid price would enhance the post-takeover value of minority shares. And this requirement would clearly have no effect on the post-takeover value of minority shares in those instances where the acquirer currently does not effect an immediate takeout. Hence, the requirement would clearly operate to narrow the average gap between the bid price and the post-takeover value of minority shares.

The Requirement Would Not Eliminate the Gap

Although the requirement would often narrow the gap between the bid price and the post-takeover value of minority shares, it would fall short of eliminating it—because acquirers would still be able to take advantage of minority shareholders in other ways than effecting an immediate takeout. Even at present, when acquirers can effect an immediate takeout below the bid price, there are many instances where they elect not to effect an immediate takeout. As explained earlier, the post-takeover value of minority shares in these instances is generally lower than the bid price because of the possibility that the acquirer will divert earnings or effect a distant takeout. In all these instances, the requirement would, of course, leave intact the existing substantial gap between the bid price and the post-takeover value of minority shares.

Moreover, the requirement would greatly increase the proportion of instances in which an immediate takeout does not occur. Instead of effecting an immediate takeout and paying a consideration equal to the bid price, most bidders would presumably refrain from effecting an immediate takeout and rely instead on the possibilities of diverting earnings and effecting a distant takeout. Thus, the instances in which an immediate takeout does not occur would be likely to constitute the great majority of cases, and the effect of the requirement would thus be much more limited than might be initially thought.

In sum, the requirement would not generally eliminate the gap between the bid price and the post-takeout value of minority shares. It follows that the requirement would not ensure undistorted choice.

Ensuring That Minority Shares Have Value Equal to the Bid Price

While prohibiting immediate takeouts below the bid price would not ensure equality between the bid price and the posttakeover value of minority shares, such an equality could nonetheless be secured by adopting some supplemental or alternative measures. Such an equality could be ensured, for example, by requiring a successful bidder to provide minority shareholders in the aftermath of a takeover

with the option of redeeming their shares at the bid price.[55]

Among the five alternative remedies examined in this section, it appears that the approach under consideration would do the best job. As explained below, however, this approach would still perform imperfectly and, in particular, would not perform as well as the arrangement put forward in Section III. It should be first noted that ensuring the sought equality would all but preclude partial acquisitions. Clearly, providing an option to redeem minority shares at the bid price would have this effect, since most minority shareholders would be likely to use their redemption rights. Similarly, it appears that any alternative measure that would secure equality between the posttakeover value of minority shares and the bid price would also practically preclude partial acquisitions.[56] This prevention of partial acquisitions would be undesirable, because a partial acquisition might sometimes be the most efficient form of a given transaction.

The main problem with the approach under consideration, however, is not that it would preclude partial acquisitions but that it would not ensure undistorted outcomes. Under an arrangement ensuring equality between the value of minority shares and the bid price, the outcome of bids would be systematically distorted against bidders, i.e., in a direction opposite to the existing distortions.

Consider the tender decision of a shareholder whose estimate of the independent target's value is lower than the bid price. According to the undistorted choice objective, the shareholder should tender his shares. Under the considered arrangement, however, the shareholder might hold out his shares. The shareholder will realize that if a takeover occurs, the arrangement will ensure that tendering and holding out will have the same results for him. Therefore, the shareholder will only ask himself what his best course of action will be assuming that the bid is going to fail. Assuming that the bid is going to fail, the shareholder will reason, implies that most shareholders are likely to have estimates of the independent target's value that are higher than his own estimate and perhaps even higher than the bid price. Therefore, to determine his best course of action under the assumption that the bid is going to fail, the shareholder will revise his own estimate upwards; his estimate *conditional* on the bid's failure might thus exceed the bid price, and he might consequently hold out his shares.

In other words, by limiting shareholders' considerations to the scenario in which the bid fails, the arrangement would lead shareholders to focus on the contingency that others' estimates exceed their own and to ignore the contingency that the opposite is true. As a result, all shareholders would bias their estimates upwards to make their tender decisions, and this revision upwards would distort the outcome of bids against bidders.[57]

Finally, it is worth explaining why the above problem would not impair the effectiveness of the arrangement put forward in Section III. Under this arrangement, a shareholder that decides between tendering approvingly and disapprovingly would focus on the scenario in which his decision will be pivotal. Thus, he would focus not on the scenario in which most other shareholders have estimates exceeding his own but, rather, on the scenario in which others' estimates are split above and below his. In focusing on such a case, the shareholder would have little reason to bias his own judgment significantly in either direction.[58]

Giving Veto Power to the Target's Management

At present, applicable legal rules and companies's charters generally leave a target's management free to use some defensive tactics (such as litigation or creation of antitrust obstacles) which prevent the bid (at least temporarily) from reaching the shareholders. Furthermore, in recent years some companies have adopted charter provisions that have the effect of strengthening the incumbents' ability to impede a bidder's quest for control;[59] and some companies have issued "poison pills" that also have such an impeding effect.[60]

Giving the target's management some

degree of veto power over an acquisition might be viewed as a remedy for the distorted choice problem.[61] If shareholders' tender decisions might lead to a distorted outcome, then it might be sometimes desirable to take the decision away from them. Management will use its power to impede or block bids, it might be hoped, in those instances where the independent target's value exceeds the expected acquisition price.

Giving management some or complete veto power, however, is a very costly and inadequate remedy for the problem of distorted choice. Most importantly, managers are not perfectly loyal agents of the shareholders and they might well abuse their veto power. To start with, management might refrain from using its power against an inadequate offer by management's favored acquistion partner—a potential buyer that promises management some attractive job prospects or side payments. Even worse, management might decide to obstruct a bid whose acceptance would be value maximizing; management might choose to do so in order to retain its independence, to extract side payments from the obstructed bidder, or to facilitate an acquisition by a rival bidder offering a lower acquisition price to shareholders but a better deal for the managers.

Thus, giving management the power to impede bids is a very poor remedy to the problem of distorted choice. Not only does it not ensure undistorted outcomes, but it also might distort outcomes that would otherwise conform to the undistorted choice objective.

Increasing the Control Threshold

Increasing the threshold of effective control obviously makes it more difficult for bids to succeed. In recent years, many companies have therefore adopted charter provisions that raise the control threshold ("supermajority provisions").[62]

Increasing the control threshold, however, cannot ensure undistorted outcomes. There is no "optimal" level of the control threshold that could be identified and specified in advance and would subsequently ensure that the outcome of any future bid for the company would not be distorted either in favor of or against the bidder. Thus, supermajority arrangements might fail to prevent an undesirable acquisition and might prevent a desirable acquisition.

To illustrate, consider a supermajority arrangement that increases the control threshold to 70%. To see that the amendment might fail to prevent an undesirable acquisition, consider an offer that is viewed as inadequate by a majority of the shareholders. As Section II has shown, the fact that a majority of the shareholders view the offered acquisition price as inadequate in no way rules out the possibility that, say, 80% (or, indeed, even 100%) of the shareholders will be induced to tender.

To see that the arrangement might prevent a desirable acquisition, consider an offer that is viewed as adequate by shareholders holding between 50% and 70% of the target's shares. Because of the arrangement, the tenders of this group of shareholders alone would be insufficient to ensure the bid's success. And although the pressure to tender might produce a sufficient number of additional tenders, this need not be the case.

Finally, it is important to note the effect that a supermajority arrangement might have when the target's management has a significant stake in the target. In such a case, the increase in the level of the control threshold might give management a veto power. As explained earlier, however, giving management such power would in no way ensure undistorted outcomes, because management might well abuse its veto power and use it in a self-serving way.

CONCLUSION

Shareholder choice in corporate takeovers might be distorted. This chapter has provided a framework for evaluating this problem, has described the nature and operation of the existing distortions, has examined the effectiveness of various proposed remedies, and has put forward an arrangement that would likely address the problem without any significant costs. I hope that this analysis of the problem and its possible remedies will prove useful to practitioners in designing charters and strategies and to courts and regulators in designing takeover rules.

POSTSCRIPT

I would like to respond to the criticism of my analysis that Douglas Ginsburg makes in his comments (Chapter 28 of this volume). Ginsburg argues (1) that the distorted choice problem is of no practical, empirical significance, and (2) that my proposed remedy would involve significant costs.

(1) *Ginsburg's Claim That the Distorted Choice Problem is of No Practical Significance.* While Ginsburg agrees that distorted outcomes are theoretically possible, he claims that the evidence suggests that this problem is of no practical significance. He asserts that "Bebchuk slights the important empirical evidence bearing on this issue," and then proceeds to note three pieces of empirical evidence which in his view support his claim.

(i) "The strongest evidence," Ginsburg argues, can be found in a certain SEC study.[63] This study, he says, "shows that target shareholders benefit very substantially regardless of the structure of the tender offer."

Ginsburg's "strongest evidence," however, gives no support to his claim. The study he cites shows that the average premium over the prebid market price is substantial in bids of all types—any-and-all, partial, and two-tier. Now, as I emphasized in the chapter, I am aware that offered acquisition prices usually contain substantial premiums over the prebid market price. Indeed, I am willing to grant that in the majority of cases accepting the bid is the shareholders' value-maximizing course of action. It is not the case, however, that acceptance of a bid with a substantial premium over the prebid market price is always and necessarily in the interest of the target's shareholders. As I explained, at the moment of truth a target's shareholders might estimate, on the basis of novel information and new developments, that the independent target's value exceeds both the prebid market price and the offered acquisition price.

Finally, as to the fact that there is no pronounced difference between the premiums in bids of different types, this fact is in no way inconsistent with my analysis. Ginsburg presumably perceived an inconsistency because of his belief that the distorted choice problem is much more severe in partial and two-tier bids than it is in bids for all shares. As I explained, however, that is not the case. Thus, the pattern found in the SEC study is not surprising and is fully consistent with the claim that the distorted choice problem is a significant one.

(ii) Ginsburg claims that a study by John Pound[64] shows that premiums are not higher in takeovers of targets with concentrated ownership (where, Ginsburg says, shareholders' ability to coordinate their actions should eliminate any pressure to tender). What Pound reports, however, is only that premiums are not higher in targets whose ownership is concentrated in the hands of institutional investors. That the shares of a target are mainly held by institutions in no way means that they are held by a small number of institutions: The target's shares might be held—indeed, are very likely to be held—by a significant number of different institutions. As long as there is more than a small number of shareholders, and it does not matter whether they are institutions or individuals, they are unlikely to be able to cooperate and they might well be subject to a pressure to tender. It is only when the ownership is concentrated in the hands of a small number of shareholders that the pressure to tender will not exist. And these instances are unlikely to be disproportionately represented in Pound's sample of targets whose ownership is concentrated in the hands of institutions; an institutional investor rarely elects to hold a substantial fraction of a given company's shares.

(iii) Ginsburg claims that if choice were distorted, bidders would make offers with very small premiums, which is not usually

the case. The problem with this claim, however, is that the existence of significant distortions does not imply that low premiums should be generally observed. First, bidders face the threat of competing bids. Although the existing competition among acquirers might be far from perfect, it does move premiums up in the direction of the target's independent value. Second, as I explained, the pressure to tender is substantial but not irresistible; and the greater the margin by which the independent target's value exceeds the offered acquisition price, the smaller the likelihood that the pressure will be effective. Thus, when the independent target's value substantially exceeds the prebid market price, the pressure to tender might well be sufficient for the bidder to pay significantly less than the target's independent value but not sufficient to acquire it without a significant premium over the low prebid price.

Indeed, the fact that low-premium bids are rarely observed suggests that the distorted choice problem should be taken very seriously (rather than the other way around, as Ginsburg believes). The prevalence of high-premium bids indicates that the target's independent value is often substantially higher than the prebid market price (for this is presumably the reason why a high premium is offered). And the distorted choice problem is important in exactly those situations where the independent target's value substantially exceeds the prebid market price.

In sum, none of the evidence brought up by Ginsburg supports his claim that the distorted choice problem is empirically of no practical significance. Therefore, I retain my earlier conclusion that distorted outcomes might occur in a significant number of instances.

(2) *Ginsburg's Claim That the Proposed Remedy's Costs Would Be Significant.* Ginsburg makes two arguments to support his claim.

(i) Ginsburg argues that ensuring undistorted choice would decrease the likelihood of bids. I addressed this issue, however, in the chapter.[65] Ginsburg does not answer or even note the various reasons that I offered for believing that this concern does not appear to warrant an opposition to ensuring undistorted choice.

(ii) Ginsburg says that my approach would lead me to prohibit a failing bidder from acquiring a controlling interest in the open market. He says that such an extension of my remedy would produce an additional cost.

While this extension of the proposed remedy is beyond the scope of this chapter, I discussed it in length in an earlier article.[66] In that article I explained that such an extension, which I support, would not be costly. The only acquisitions that it would prevent would be those where the buyer is unwilling to pay for the target more than the independent target's value in the eyes of a majority of the target's shareholders; and these acquisitions would be indeed undesirable.

NOTES

1. Discussions of the problem by practicing lawyers include Ballotti and Finkelstein, "Coercive Structures in Tender Offers," 15 *Rev. Sec. Reg.* 820 (1982); Finkelstein, "Antitakeover Protection Against Two-Tier and Partial Tender Offers: The Validity of Fair Price, Mandatory Bid, and Flip-over Provisions Under Delaware Law," 11 *Sec. Reg. L.J.* 291 (1984); Greene and Junewicz, "Reappraisal of Current Regulations of Mergers and Acquisitions," 132 *Univ. Pa. L. Rev.* 647, 676–693 (1984); Lipton, "Takeover Bids in the Target's Boardroom" 35 *Bus. L.* 101, 113–114 (1979).

Discussions of the issue by legal academics start with Brudney and Chirelstein, "Fair Shares in Corporate Mergers and Takeovers," 88 *Harv. L. Rev.* 297, 336–340 (1974). Such discussions also include Bebchuck, "The Case for Facilitating Competing Tender Offers," 95 *Harv. L. Rev.* 1028, 1039–1041 (1982) (hereinafter cited as Bebchuk, "Competing Bids"); Bebchuk, "The Case for Facilitating Competing Bids: A Reply and Extension," 35 *Stan. L. Rev.* 23, 45–46, 48–49 (1982) (hereinafter cited as Bebchuk, "Reply and Extension"); Carney, "Shareholder Coordination Costs, Shark Repellents, and Takeout Mergers: The Case Against Fiduciary Duties," *Am. B. Found. Res. J.* 341 (1983); Coffee, "Regulating the Market for Corporate Control: A Critical Assessment of the Tender Offer's Role

in Corporate Governance, 84 *Colum. L. Rev.* 1145, 1183–1195 (1984); Easterbrook and Fischel, "Corporate Control Transactions," 91 *Yale L.J.* 698, 710–711 (1982); Gilson, "A Structural Approach to Corporations: The Case Against Defensive Tactics in Tender Offers," 33 *Stan. L. Rev.* 819, 859–862 (1981); Lowenstein, "Pruning Deadwood in Hostile Takeovers: A Proposal for Legislation," 83 *Colum. L. Rev.* 249, 307–309.

Finally, the issue has also been discussed by economists. See Bradley, "Interfirm Tender Offers and the Market for Corporate Control," 53 *J. Bus.* 345, 352–356 (1980); DeAngelo and Rice, "Antitakeover Charter Amendments and Stockholder Wealth," 11 *J. Fin. Econ.* 329 (1983); Grossman and Hart, "Takeover Bids, the Free-Rider Problem, and the Theory of the Corporation," 11 *Bell J. Econ.* 42, 44–47 (1980); Jarrell, "The Wealth Effects of Litigation by Targets: Do Interests Diverge in a Merger?" 28 *J. L. Econ.* 151, 154–158 (1985); Jensen and Ruback, "The Market for Corporate Control: The Scientific Evidence," 11 *J. Fin. Econ.* 5, 31–32 (1983).

2. See Advisory Committee on Tender Offers, SEC, Report of Recommendations, 24–26 (1982) (hereinafter cited as Advisory Committee Report); Securities Exchange Act Release No. 21079 (1984 decisions), Fed. Sec. L. Rep. (CCH) 83, 637 (June 21, 1984) (hereinafter cited as SEC Release).

3. See *Unocal Corp. v. Mesa Petroleum Co.,* 493 A. 2d 946 (Del. 1985) (discriminatory self-tender offer); *Moran v. Household Int'l., Inc.,* 490 A. 2d 1059 (Del. Ch. 1985) (poison pill). Targets' claims that the distortion of bid outcomes justifies defensive tactics have been endorsed by various commentators. See note 61.

4. See e.g., Carney, note 1.

5. See e.g., Block, Barton and Roth, "State Takeover Statutes: The 'Second Generation,'" 13 *Sec. Reg. L.J.* 332 (1986).

6. This chapter restates, and presents in a more concise and accessible form, the gist of an analysis that I developed in two previous papers. An earlier, highly detailed analysis of the subject was presented in Bebchuk, "Toward Undistorted Choice and Equal Treatment in Corporate Takeovers," 98 *Harv. L. Rev.* 1695 (1985) (hereinafter cited as Bebchuk, "Undistorted Choice and Equal Treatment"); and a mathematical, game-theoretic analysis, formally deriving many of this chapter's points, was presented in Bebchuk, *A Model of the Outcome of Takeover Bids,* Discussion paper No. 11, Program in Law and Economics, Harvard

Law School, November 1985 (hereinafter cited as Bebchuk, "Model of Bids").

7. For a discussion of the legal rules (or charter provisions) that should (in light of the proposed objective) govern other methods of corporate acquisition, see Bebchuk, "Undistorted Choice and Equal Treatment," note 6.

8. Ensuring undistorted choice should not be the only objective guiding public officials in the design of takeover law. Other objectives are discussed in Bebchuk, "Undistorted Choice and Equal Treatment," note 6, at 1706–08, 1780–87, 1792–94. First, on grounds of efficiency, it is desirable not only to ensure undistorted choice by targets but also to ensure undistorted choice by acquirers, and (2) to address the distortions resulting from the existence of private gains (such as gains from tax savings and increased market power) that do not represent net social gains. Second, on grounds of fairness considerations, it is desirable to ensure that the acquisition price in a target's acquisition be distributed prorata among the target's shareholders. As explained in that paper, however, ensuring undistorted choice by target shareholders is perfectly consistent with, if not conducive to, pursuing these other objectives.

9. The two main reasons why the undistorted choice mechanism is not perfect are discussed in Bebchuk, "Undistorted Choice and Equal Treatment," note 6, pp. 1770–1774. First, a target's shareholders might make mistakes in their assessment of how the offered acquisition price compares with the independent target's value. Second, a bidder that values a target's assets by more than the independent target's value might still offer an acquisition price below the independent target's value and consequently fail; and although such a failing bidder might raise its bid, it might also elect not to do so (because of strategic considerations or transaction costs). After examining these problems, I conclude that they are similar in severity to the corresponding problems present in the sole owner context, and that the undistorted choice mechanism appears to be the best we can employ.

10. This reasoning presumably underlies those corporate-law doctrines which follow the majority judgment in matters requiring shareholder vote. (For example, most state corporation statutes use the majority of shareholders as the decisive fraction in a merger vote.) It is important to note, however, that the proposed definition of the decisive fraction is in no way crucial to this chapter's thesis—and that one who would define the decisive fraction differently should find the chapter's analysis wholly relevant. This is because the chapter's analysis will focus on ensuring that shareholders' tender decisions reflect their judgment as to whether the offered acquisition price exceeds the independent target's value. And the desirability of ensuring such undistorted tender decisions does not depend on how the decisive fraction is defined. Thus, for example, the arrangement proposed in Section III could be easily amended to one ensuring that a company will be acquired if and only if a supermajority (rather than a simple majority) views the acquisition as value maximizing.

11. See e.g., Bradley, note 1.

12. Indeed, some legislatures have even permitted the elimination of appraisal rights when there is an active market in the target's stock. See, e.g., Del. Code Ann. tit. 8, Sec. 262(b) (1) (1983); Model Business Corp. Act. Sec. 81 (1977).

13. See e.g., Del. Code Ann. tit. 8 Sec. 262(h) (1983); Model Business Corp. Act Sec. 81 (1972).

14. Courts have traditionally given weight to the target's stock market prices, its current and past earnings, and the sale value of its assets. See, e.g., Chazen, "Fairness from a Financial Point of View in Acquisitions of Public Companies: Is Third-Party Sale Value the Appropriate Standard?" 36 *Bus. L.* 1439 (1981). In the recent case of *Weinberger v. UOP, Inc.,* 457 A. 2d 701 (Del. 1983), however, the Delaware Supreme Court showed a willingness to use a more flexible approach to valuation.

15. See e.g., *Radol v. Thomas,* 556 F. Supp. 586 (S.D. Ohio 1983).

16. For example, in the immediate takeout that followed the takeover of Marathon Oil by U.S. Steel, minority shareholders received a per-share consideration of dozens of dollars below the bid price. See *Wall St. J.,* February 3, 1982.

17. See e.g., Brudney, "Efficient Markets and Fair Shares in Parent Subsidiary Mergers," 4 *J. Corp. L.* 63, 69–70 (1978).

18. See e.g., *Schlick v. Penn-Dixie Cement Corp.,* 507 F. 2d 374 (2d Cir. 1974); *Sinclair Oil Corp. v. Levien,* 280 A. 2d 717 (Del. 1971).

19. See e.g., *Swanson v. American Consumer Indus.,* 415 F. 2d 1326 (7th Cir. 1969); *Greene & Co. v. Dunhill Int'l., Inc.,* 249 A. 2d 427 (Del. 1968).

20. *Roland Int'l Corp. v. Najjar,* 407 A. 2d 1032, 1037 (Del. 1979).

21. Indeed, the prospect of a takeout might by itself depress the market price of minority shares. Even supposing that the informational efficiency of capital markets is perfect, the threat of an impending takeout might lead the market

to price minority shares at a considerable discount. Suppose, for example, that the per-share value of the acquired target's future earnings is $100. Suppose also that investors believe that the acquirer is committed to a strategy of paying no dividend until it will be able to effect a takeout at $50 per share. In this case, the value that investors will rationally attach to minority shares is $50 per share, and this valuation will be immediately reflected in the market price. Of course, different expectations concerning the acquirer's strategy will lead to different discounts (or even to no discount at all).

Finally, it is important to note that postponing a takeout might be also profitable for the acquirer because the acquirer might obtain inside information that will improve its ability to predict whether a takeout will prove profitable. If the inside information suggests that the target's prospects are good, the acquirer will effect a takeout before the information becomes reflected in the market price. And if the inside information is unfavorable, the acquirer will let minority shareholders retain their shares. In this way the acquirer will expose minority shareholders to the downward side of the target's uncertain prospects, while denying them the potential benefits of the upward side.

22. See Office of the Chief Economist, SEC, The Economics of Any-or-All, Partial, and Two-Tier Tender Offers (April 1985).

23. *Id.*

24. A second reason which is worth noting is that a bidder might gain effective control even if it does not attract tenders from a majority of the target's shareholders. In the absence of special antitakeover charter provisions, it is often possible to gain effective control merely by purchasing a substantial plurality of the target's shares.

To see how the possibility of effective control without majority ownership might by itself lead to distorted outcomes, assume for the moment that shareholders will tender their shares if and only if they estimate V, the independent target's per-share value, to be lower than the offered per-share acquisition price; and suppose that 40% of the shareholders view the offered per-share acquisition price as higher than V, while 60% hold the contrary view. According to the undistorted choice objective, the bid should fail. But tendering by the 40% who view the offered per-share acquisition price as higher than V might be sufficient to give the bidder control over the target. See Bebchuk, "Undistorted Choice and Equal Treatment," supra note 6, at 1718–19 (discussion of the effective control problem and how the problem might produce

deviations from the undistorted choice objective).

25. Furthermore, because shareholders can always postpone tendering until the moment of truth, a shareholder will not tender early unless he expects that at the moment of truth he will probably still prefer to tender. Therefore, for our purpose—that of understanding how a bid's outcome is determined—the critical question is what determines shareholders' explicit or implicit tender decisions at the moment of truth.

26. That shareholders will tender if they view V as lower than the $10 bid price implies by itself that their tender decisions might be distorted. According to the undistorted choice objective, shareholders should tender only if they view V as lower than the expected per-share acquisition price. And as explained earlier, the expected per-share acquisition price is generally significantly lower than the bid price in both partial bids and bids for all shares. To use an example, suppose that the $10 bid is for 50% of the target's shares. In this case, V, the expected acquisition price, is $9 a share. Thus, according to the undistorted choice objective, shareholders should tender only if they view V as lower than $9. But, as the analysis has shown, the shareholders will surely tender as long as they judge V to be lower than $10.

27. To be sure, it is also possible that all or most shareholders would adopt initial expectations that the bid will fail, and such initial expectations might also be self-fulfilling. Thus, shareholders' initial expectations can go either way; and because these initial expectations are likely to be self-fulfilling, the bid's outcome can also go either way.

28. In examining the possible existence of a pressure to tender, the SEC Advisory Committee and subsequently the SEC limited their examination to partial and two-tier bids. See Advisory Committee Report, note 2, pp. 24–26; SEC Release, note 2, pp. 86, 914–915. A similar approach was recently taken by Commissioner Grundfest in a speech on the subject. See 19 BNA SRLR 788 (May 29, 1987).

29. See, e.g., Ballotti and Finkelstein, note 1; Finkelstein, note 1; Greene and Junewicz, note 1.

30. See, e.g., cases cited in note 3.

31. See Bradley, Desai, and Kim, "The Rationale Behind Interfirm Tender Offers: Information or Synergy?" 11 *J. Fin. Econ.* 183, 188 (1983).

32. See 15 U.S.C. § 78n (d) (5) (1982).

33. Of course, the prescribed delay period could be extended. But since the resolution of bids should not be delayed unnecessarily,

adopting a long mandatory delay period would be undesirable. Ensuring undistorted choice would provide target shareholders with the necessary flexibility: The mandatory delay period would remain quite limited; but when further delay would seem beneficial, the shareholders would be able to choose freely to remain independent for the time being.

34. See Bebchuk, "Competing Bids," note 1, p. 1036 (note 45).

35. See, e.g., Lowenstein, note 1, p. 277.

36. See, e.g., Hicks, "Zellerbach Rejects Goldsmith's Offer," *N.Y. Times,* April 12, 1985 (Zellerbach's management proposed a major restructuring of the company in response to a tender offer by Sir James Goldsmith).

37. The proposed arrangement for determining a bid's fate is similar to one that the British City Code applies to partial bids. See City Code on Take-overs and Mergers, Rule 27 (City Working Party 1976). The Code prohibits the purchase of any shares through a partial bid unless the bid has been approved by the target's shareholders. Approval is signified by an entry in a separate box on the tender form, where a tendering shareholder can indicate whether or not he approves the partial bid. The limitation of the approval requirement to partial bids is apparently a result of the drafters' belief that partial bids pose different and more serious problems than do bids for all shares (a belief which is, as we have seen, mistaken). In bids for all shares, the Code establishes a different arrangement, which distorts outcomes against bidders. For a detailed discussion of the British arrangements and a comparison of these arrangements with the arrangement proposed in this chapter, see Bebchuk, "Undistorted Choice and Equal Treatment," note 5, pp. 1795–1801.

38. Although the proposed arrangement, as thus far outlined, would bring us close to attaining undistorted choice, it might not do a "perfect" job. As presently explained, the two main reasons for this possible imperfection are the possible presence of nontendering shareholders and of shares held by the bidder. These two problems could be largely addressed by two refinements of the required number of approving tenders. Therefore, although the precise specification of the required number of approving tenders is not central to my thesis, these two refinements are worth describing.

(i) *Nontendering Shareholders.* Although under the arrangement most shareholders would tender their shares (either approvingly or disapprovingly), some shareholders would still hold out either because of lack of an opportunity to tender or because of some special tax circumstances. Note that these nontendering shareholders would not be characterized by especially high estimates of the independent target's value: Under the arrangement, a high estimate of the independent target's value would by itself lead not to holding out but rather to making a disapproving tender. Thus, there is no reason to assume that the distribution of estimates among the nontendering shareholders would be significantly different from the distribution of estimates among the tendering shareholders. It follows that requiring bidders to attract approving tenders from a majority of the target's shareholders (i.e., from more than a majority of the tendering shareholders) would be likely to introduce a slight bias against the bidder (vis-à-vis the benchmark established by the undistorted choice objective). Instead, we should require the bidder to attract approving tenders only from a majority of the *tendering* shareholders.

(ii) *Shares Controlled by the Bidder.* In the preceding analysis of shareholder choice, I have assumed that every shareholder is "disinterested"—in the sense that his preference concerning the bid's success is determined by the effect that a takeover would have on the value of his shareholdings (and thus by his judgment of how the expected acquisition price compares with the independent target's value). In fact, however, some shareholder's preferences concerning a takeover might be shaped by considerations other than the takeover's expected effect on the value of their shareholdings.

In particular, the bidder might own, directly or through subsidiaries, some initial stake in the target. The bidder would presumably prefer the bid to succeed whether or not it views acceptance of the bid as the shareholder's value-maximizing course of action. Counting the approving tenders made by the bidder and its affiliates would clearly distort the outcome, because they would make such approving tenders regardless of whether they view the offered acquisition price as higher than the independent target's value. Therefore, the bidder should be required to attract approving tenders not from a majority of the tendering shareholders but rather from a majority of the *disinterested* tendering shareholders.

39. See CTS Corp. v. Dynamics Corporation of America, 107 S. Ct. 1637 (1987). Control share acquisition statutes typically require acquirers to obtain a vote of approval from the target's shareholders prior to making a "control share acquisition" (usually defined as any acquisition of at least 20% of the target's stock). See, e.g., Ohio Rev. Code Ann. § 1701.831 (Baldwin 1985).

40. As confirmed in telephone conversations between the author and officials of the two exchanges, this prohibition has been the general and consistent policy of the exchanges. The exchanges have made exceptions—for example, in the case of some savings and loan associations—only when the restrictions on transfer were required by some external regulatory body because of the particular nature of the company's business.

41. A good discussion of the possible state law impediments is contained in the comments of Marshall Small (Chapter 29 of this volume). While I agree with most of his analysis, I differ from him in believing that, for the reasons presently discussed, the state law constraint on retroactivity is a serious impediment to adoption through charter provisions.

42. See e.g., Del. Code Ann. tit. 8, § 202 (b); Cal. Corp. Code § 204 (b); Revised Model Bus. Corp. Act § 6.27 (1984).

43. See Easterbrook and Fischel, "The Proper Role of a Target's Management in Responding to a Tender Offer," 94 *Harv. L. Rev.* 1161, 1199–1201 (1981); Easterbrook and Fischel, "Auctions and Sunk Costs in Tender Offers," 35 *Stan. L. Rev.* 1 (1982). The need for incentives to search was also stressed by Grossman and Hart, note 1.

44. See Bebchuk, "Competing Bids," note 1; Bebchuk, "Reply and Extension," note 1.

45. The searcher may purchase 5% of the target's stock without being required by the Williams Act to disclose the purchases. 15 U.S.C. § 78n (d) (1) (1982).

46. If the searcher acquires the target, then its prebid purchases will enable it to save the bid premium on the stock it already owns. If another buyer acquires the target, the searcher will earn on its stock the acquisition premium paid by that buyer. Finally, if the target's shareholders reject all available bids, then the searcher will still make a substantial gain, because in such a case the market price of the independent target's shares will probably be substantially higher than the prebid price for which the searcher bought its shares. The gain that a searcher can make on its prebid purchases often approaches 2% to 3% of the target's value. See Bebchuk, "Competing Bids," note 1, pp. 1035–1036.

In addition to making a profit on prebid purchases, searchers can also gain in other ways. In particular, even in a regime of undistorted choice, a searcher that acquires an identified target would often not have to pay as much as its valuation of the target. Of course, the searcher would have to pay at least the competitive price—i.e., the price that other potential buyers would be willing to pay. The searcher, however, might place a higher value on the target's assets than do other potential buyers: Buyers often vary substantially in the amount of efficiency gains that they can produce by acquiring the target. In such a case, the searcher would usually capture a substantial fraction of those gains from the acquisition that other buyers would be unable to produce. Indeed, the searcher would likely capture the lion's share of these gains: The searcher would have a substantial advantage in the "bargaining" over the division of these gains between itself and the target's shareholders—because in the takeover context, unlike a standard buyer-seller situation, only the bidder can make offers.

Finally, note that search costs do not appear to be all that large. Because prospective buyers often lack appropriate in-house resources, the search is frequently done for them by investment bankers. In such cases, the search costs are a fraction of the investment bankers' total fees. These total fees, in turn, are often less than 1% of the target's value. See Bebchuk, "Competing Bids," note 1, at 1036–1037.

47. See Easterbrook and Fischel, note 1, pp. 705, 710–711. See also Grossman and Hart, note 1 (discussing the extent to which the value of minority shares must be "diluted" for takeovers to be possible).

48. See, e.g., Advisory Committee Report, note 2, pp. 24–25.

49. See notes 28–30 and accompanying text.

50. The SEC Advisory Committee considered a ban on partial bids but decided against recommending such a ban because it believed that partial bids serve valuable economic functions. Instead, the committee recommended encouraging such bids by requiring that they remain open longer than bids for all shares. See Advisory Committee Report, note 2, pp. 24–26. One member of the committee, however, expressed disappointment that the committee did not recommend "anything meaningful" to regulate partial bids (ibid., pp. 144–145; statement of Jeffrey Bartell). Similarly, Greene and Junewicz (note 1, pp. 691–693) criticized the regulatory disincentive proposed by the committee as too weak.

51. See Brudney and Chirelstein, note 1, pp. 336–340; Brudney and Chirelstein, "A Restatement of Corporate Freezeouts," 87 *Yale L. J.* 1354, 1361-1365 (1978).

52. See, e.g., Carney, note 1.

53. See, e.g., Maryland Corporations and Associations Code Ann. Sec. 3–602; Georgia Code Ann. Sec. 14–2–232 (Supp. 1985); Connecticut

Gen. Stat. Sec. 33–366 (1984). For a discussion of these state law provisions, see Block, Barton and Roth, note 5, at 332.

54. See Advisory Committee Report, note 2, pp. 24–25; SEC Release, note 2, pp. 86, 679.

55. Recently, several states adopted a statute requiring successful bidders to give minority shareholders a redemption option. See, e.g., Pa. Cons. Stat. Ann. Sec. 1408, 1409.1, 1910 (Supp 1986). For a discussion of these statutes, see Block et al., note 5. Under these statutes, however, minority shareholders who redeem their shares are entitled not to the bid price but rather to the "fair value" of their holdings as of the date prior to the takeover.

56. Consider, for example, measures aimed at limiting the extent to which an acquirer that does not effect an immediate takeout can, by diverting earnings or by effecting a distant takeout, take advantage of minority shareholders. Because of the nature of the activities regulated, such measures cannot ensure that whenever an immediate takeout does not occur, the value of minority shares will be *exactly* equal to the bid price. Consequently, if the measures are stern enough to ensure that the post-takeover value of minority shares never falls below the bid price, then they will in most circumstances drive that post-takeover value above the bid price. Such a result would force bidders always to commit themselves to effecting an immediate takeout upon gaining control; for if an immediate takeout is not expected, and if minority shares are expected in this case to have a post-takeover value exceeding the bid price, then shareholders might hold out even if they view the bid price as higher than the independent target's per share value.

57. There is another way to demonstrate that the arrangement would not ensure undistorted outcomes—by first assuming that it would, and then showing that this assumption creates a contradiction. Assuming that the arrangement would ensure undistorted outcomes implies that shareholders would hold out only if they view the independent target's per-share value as higher than the bid price. Hence, the target would remain independent only if most shareholders view the independent target's per-share value as higher than the bid price. This proposition in turn implies that, if the bid fails and the target remains independent, the market price of the independent target's shares will be likely to exceed the bid price. But this latter proposition means that a shareholder might well find it in his interest to hold out even if his own estimate of the independent target's per-share value is lower than the bid price. And this

possibility contradicts the initial assumption that shareholders' tender decisions would be undistorted.

58. Having seen that eliminating the gap between the bid price and the post-takeover value of minority shares would distort outcomes against bidders, it might be still suggested that we could attain undistorted outcomes by curtailing this gap to some "low" optimal level. Unfortunately, there is no "optimal" level for the post-takeover value of minority shares (or for the gap between this posttakeover value and the bid price) that could be specified and would ensure that the outcome of future bids would not be distorted either in favor of or against the bidder. To be sure, for any particular situation, there might exist a level of the expected post-takeover value of minority shares that would ensure an undistorted outcome. This level, however, depends on such features of the situation as the height of the effective control threshold and the extent to which the distribution of shareholders' estimates is widespread. Consequently, this level not only is hard to identify for a particular situation but, more importantly, might vary from situation to situation. Therefore, no arrangement that guarantees a certain post-takeover value for minority shares could be designed to ensure an undistorted outcome in future situations—whose particular features are unknown at the time of adopting the arrangement.

59. See, e.g., Gilson, "The Case Against Shark Repellent Amendments: Structural Limitations on the Enabling Concept," 34 *Stan. L. Rev.* 775 (1982).

60. See Note, "Internal Transfers of Control Under Poison Pill Preferred Issuance to Shareholders: Toward a Shareholder Approval Rule," 60 *St. John's L. Rev.* 94 (1984).

61. Several commentators have argued that the possible distortions of shareholder choice justify obstructive tactics. See Greene and Junewicz, note 1; Lipton,, note 1; Lowenstein, note 1. Lipton would allow such tactics subject only to the liberal test of the business judgment rule. Lowenstein would allow such tactics subject to a shareholder vote of approval. Greene and Junewicz would allow such tactics only in partial bids, the bids to which they believed the distorted choice problem is limited. Several other commentators have used the distortion of bid outcomes as a basis for an argument supporting a particular kind of defensive tactics. See, e.g., Bradley and Rosensweig, "Defensive Stock Repurchases," 99 *Harv. L. Rev.* 1377 (1986) (defending self-tenders); Macey and McChesney, "A Theoretical Analysis of Corpo-

rate Greenmail," 95 *Yale L.J.* 13 (1985) (defending greenmail); Note, "Protecting Shareholders Against Partial and Two-Tiered Takeovers: The 'Poison Pill' Preferred," 97 *Harv. L. Rev.* 1964 (1977) (defending poison pills).

62. See Carney, note 1; Gilson, note 59.
63. See Chapter 28, p. 453.
64. See Chapter 28, p. 453.
65. See text accompanying notes 43–46.
66. See Bebchuk, "Undistorted Choice and Equal Treatment," note 6, pp. 1788–1792.

26

Comparative Dimensions of Takeover Regulation

DEBORAH A. DE MOTT

Systems of corporate law and securities regulation differ considerably among jurisdictions; the principal focus of this chapter is differences among rules that pertain to corporate takeovers. However complex its terms, no jurisdiction's regulation of tender offers operates in a legal or economic vacuum. Thus, the chapter begins by examining the institutional and economic factors that define the regulatory and transactional climate for tender offer regulation; as this portion of the chapter argues, these factors in large part explain why hostile takeover transactions occur in significant numbers in only relatively few countries. The chapter then surveys available information describing the takeover environment in four of those countries, namely, the United States, Great Britain, Canada, and Australia. Considered next is the legal context in which takeover regulation is embedded in these countries and the restraints it imposes on bidders and target management; the discussion then narrows to a comparison of these systems' rules that pertain to specific issues in tender offer regulation. The chapter concludes by considering the larger question of whether specific impacts on transactional activity can be traced to particular aspects of these regulatory systems. On each of these matters, in the interests of clarity, the chapter first presents material for the United States, followed by Britain, Canada, and Australia, almost always in that order.

I am grateful to Robert Austin, John C. Coffee, Jr., and Douglas Ginsburg for their comments on an earlier version of the manuscript.

INSTITUTIONAL AND ECONOMIC FACTORS

Comparative writing about legal rules carries its risks, one being the possibility of overemphasizing the differences among jurisdictions' rules at the expense, first, of adequate attention to their similarities and, second, of inadequate attention to other less specifically "legal" aspects of the systems under comparison which may complement if not always explain some of the legal dissimilarities. Of particular importance to understanding the institutional and economic context in which corporate takeovers occur is the structure of stock exchanges in each system and the exchanges' regulatory function; equally important are patterns of corporate ownership and control.

Stock Exchanges

In the United States, there are several stock exchanges and an organized system for over-the-counter trading in securities, all regulated by the federal Securities and Exchange Commission. Among the exchanges, the New York dominates in number and market value of securities listed, with about four times the number of securities listed as the second exchange, the American, and about twenty times the market value of securities listed.[1] Stock exchanges in the United States operate autonomously, not jointly, and do not impose uniform standards for listing. At least traditionally, the nation's largest companies have been listed on the New York Exchange; the fact, coupled with the New York's more exacting requirements for listing, has lent some cachet to an issuer's listing on that exchange. The New York Exchange's listing requirements have often functioned as an important supplement to legally imposed requirements for corporate practice and operation. For example, the exchange has long required corporations to have audit and nominating committees composed of independent directors; and although the exchange's position has recently shifted, by declining to list nonvoting common shares (and voting shares of issuers with nonvoting common shares) and common shared with differential voting rights, the exchange has significantly inhibited the issuance of such securities by the most visible corporate constituency in the United States.

Britain, in contrast, has one stock exchange; although under its guidance a limited over-the-counter market has developed in the past few years, most companies seek a listing on the Stock Exchange if they propose to issue shares to the public. The listing requirements for the Stock Exchange, interpreted and enforced by its Quotations Department, are in some respects more demanding than those imposed on corporate issuers by the Companies Acts.[2] Most significant for our present purposes, however, is the Stock Exchange's participation in the Panel on Take-Overs and Mergers, the self-regulatory body in Britain that administers and periodically revises the City Code on Take-Overs and Mergers. The Stock Exchange, the Bank of England, and other British financial institutions created the panel in 1968 to deal with perceived abuses in corporate takeovers. Sanctions for violations of the code are extralegal and include, potentially, delisting of securities by the Stock Exchange and denial of the use of the facilities of British brokerage houses.

Canada, like the United States, has several stock exchanges,[3] which are regulated by the provinces in which they are situated. Important to all comparisons of corporate regulation between Canada and the United States or Britain is the fact that the Canadian Constitution, unlike that of the United States, does not confer plenary power to regulate interprovincial commerce on the national government; thus although Canada has a national corporations statute, securities regulation—and more specifically, the regulation of stock exchanges—is a provincial matter, and the provinces have not enacted uniform legislation. Nonetheless, the Toronto Stock Exchange dominates the field in number and perceived quality of securities listed,[4] and this institutional fact has given Ontario a bellwether position in securities regulation generally. Like exchanges in the United States, Canadian stock exchanges operate autonomously and have no common set of requirements for listing. There is little over-the-counter trading in Canada.

In Australia, each of the six capital cities[5] has a stock exchange; all are members of the Australian Associated Stock Exchanges Ltd. (the AASE), as are some country exchanges. At present, Melbourne and Sydney operate almost as one exchange, and all exchanges' listing agreements are virtually uniform.[6] The AASE, as noted later, has itself played a substantial regulatory role in connection with corporate takeovers. As in Canada, for constitutional reasons aspects of corporate law and securities regulation are prerogatives of the six states;[7] unlike Canada, Australia now has uniform companies and securities codes as a result of a compact among the states to follow the lead established by federal statutes in these areas. In Australia, as in the United States, administrative responsibility for enforcement of securities legislation is lodged with a federal commission, the National Companies and Securities Commission (the NCSC), but a separate body composed of persons appointed by the state governments, the Ministerial Council, has policy-making and general supervisory functions.[8] There is no developed over-the-counter market in Australia.

Even the simplest comparison of the institutions described here suggests that they differ significantly in their regulatory capacities. The Stock Exchange in London, alone and through the Panel on Take-Overs and Mergers, and the AASE in Australia have achieved uniform listing standards and other rules for the corporate issuers under their aegis, and as shown in detail later, operate as significant regulatory forces in defining acceptable conduct in corporate takeovers. In contrast, stock exchanges in Canada and the United States do not speak with one voice; although one exchange in each country is dominant, and through its listing requirements imposes major constraints on its constituency of issuers, these nations' exchanges as groups appear to play a less forceful regulatory role on issues relevant to takeovers than do the AASE and the London Stock Exchange. In addition, the vigor of over-the-counter trading in the United States means that issuers who seek to raise public capital do not necessarily need to seek listing for the securities on an exchange.[9] This institutional fact also decreases the exchanges' regulatory potential in the United States.

Patterns of Corporate Ownership and Control

The type of takeover bid that elicits the most popular and professional interest is, of course, the hostile offer, a bid unwelcomed by the target's management; in contrast, "friendly" bids can be seen as negotiated corporate acquisitions or amalgamations executed through the technique of an offer made directly to a corporation's shareholders. Whether hostile bids are feasible in any country is in large part a function of patterns of share ownership in that country, of shareholders' ability freely to transfer their shares, and of the voting rights allocated to publicly held shares.

In the United States financial institutions hold a substantial percentage of the shares of the largest publicly traded companies.[10] Relatively few large, publicly traded companies, on the other hand, have one shareholder who owns more than 50% of the shares, amounting to legal control; although more large companies have shareowners whose holdings are large enough to give them effective control, these still amount to less than one-sixth of all large companies.[11] Thus, ownership of large corporations may be significantly in-

stitutional, but it is significantly diffused as well. Furthermore, the norm in public companies in the United States is free transferability of shares, a norm reinforced by the New York Stock Exchange's refusal to list shares that are not freely transferable. Only that exchange, however, declines to list shares with restricted or differential voting rights.

Patterns of shareownership in large companies are strikingly different in Canada: A majority of large, publicly traded Canadian corporations are legally or effectively controlled by an identifiable shareholder or group of shareholders,[12] and aggregate concentration (i.e., percentage of economic activity accounted for by the largest firms) in Canada, although it has decreased from its levels earlier in this century, is currently higher than in the United States.[13] Indeed, economic power in Canada appears to be concentrated in a few family-controlled groups—in 1985 nine families were reported to control 46% of the top 300 companies traded on the Toronto Stock Exchange[14]—which personalizes the concentration of corporate control in striking fashion. In contrast with the New York Exchange, the Toronto Stock Exchange permits issuers to have common shares with restricted or differential voting rights;[15] The Toronto Exchange appears also to list shares of companies with bylaws restricting transfer of shares beyond stated percentages to nonresidents of Canada.[16]

In Britain, financial institutions dominate as shareowners to an even greater extent than in the United States.[17] Although the London Exchange will list nonvoting shares provided they are so designated,[18] fully paid-up shares must be freely transferable.[19] Finally, although the British economy is believed to be more concentrated than that of the United States,[20] large British companies are not thought, like their counterparts in Canada, to be controlled by a small number of identifiable family groups.

Share holdings in Australia are also dominated by institutions, especially life insurance companies. Of course, the dollar volume of trading on the Australian exchanges is much smaller than that on exchanges in the United States: Whereas the estimated volume for the NYSE might be $3.5 billion on one typical day, on all exchanges in Australia the comparable volume would be A$40 million.[21]

Once again, however, one should not overemphasize the importance of the differences among these countries. For they share one trait of supervening importance for the purpose of this chapter: All have active markets in corporate acquisitions in which hostile as well as negotiated transactions occur frequently. The question that immediately comes to mind is why such transactions and in particular hostile ones do not occur with equivalent frequency in any number of other countries with market economies that also have active public trading in securities. The hostile corporate transaction is, indeed, virtually a nonevent in many countries that otherwise are similar to those discussed in this chapter; countries on the European continent, for example, and Japan appear to have few if any hostile corporate takeovers.[22]

Explaining why events do not happen, although frequently more interesting than explaining why events do happen, also tends to be more difficult, and especially so where, as with the nonoccurrence of hostile takeovers in some countries, many different types of explanation are plausible for the nonevents. Nonetheless, one can isolate two features of shareownership patterns that are essential to the development of an active market for corporate acquisitions, including hostile acquisitions: shareholders' ability to transfer shares free of restraints within the unilateral control of the company's management, and public ownership of shares holding voting rights sufficient to constitute legal control. In countries in which hostile acquisitions do not occur, one or both of these elements appear to be missing.

Share Transferability

As noted earlier, stock exchange listing requirements preclude the use of restrictions on share transferability in publicly traded companies in the United States and Britain; indeed, in both countries the restriction on share transfer is typically charac-terized as an earmark of a private company.[23] In other systems, however, restrictions on share transferability are not similarly confined to closely held enterprises by law or practice. Canadian corporation statutes, for example, permit public offerings of shares that restrict transfer to non-Canadian residents when the company needs, for licensing purposes, to maintain a stated percentage of ownership by Canadians,[24] and in some instances permit even broader prohibitions on transfer to non-Canadians.[25] Even though Canada obviously has an active corporate acquisitions market, because its economy historically has attracted substantial amounts of foreign capital investment,[26] imposing a test of Canadian residency on some share transfers may in fact preclude some hostile takeovers that would otherwise occur.

Broad restrictions on share transferability are permitted by corporate statutes in continental Europe, even in publicly held companies. For example, in France the provisions of the Code des Sociétés concerning the Société Anonyme, the business corporation in France most similar to the American corporation, permit the corporation's articles to require that transfers to "a third party whomever he may be" be subject to the corporation's consent;[27] if the corporation does not consent to the transfer, it may, with the seller's consent, repurchase the shares itself, or it may cause the shares to be purchased by a shareholder or a third party.[28] Even more draconian restraints on transfer are possible under Swiss corporate law, which permits a corporation's articles to prohibit transfer of registered shares altogether.[29]

Public Shares' Voting Rights

Other prevalent characteristics of countries without active acquisition markets are widespread corporate cross ownership of shares and restrictions on the voting rights of publicly held shares. Although corporations are known to place blocks of shares in friendly hands to guard against hostile bids even in countries with active acquisition markets, extensive cross ownership tends to preclude hostile bids. The leading example is Japan, in which patterns of corporate cross ownership of shares are common,[30] although centralized mechanisms controlling ownership and credit are much weaker than they were prior to World War II.[31]

A hostile bid will also not be made for a company unless the shares available for sale (typically the public shares) can exercise sufficient voting rights to entitle a new owner to exercise legal control or at least effective control. One possibility available in all systems of corporate law is the issue of separate classes of stock that hold different voting rights.[32] On the European continent, however, corporation statutes authorize an additional technique for restricting the voting rights of publicly held shares, including common stock: the restriction of an owner's and his proxies' voting rights to a stated number or percentage, independent of the number of shares owned. These restrictions originated in response to the common use of bearer shares (as opposed to registered shares); in a corporation with bearer shares, the identity of their owners is not known to management, with the exception of shareholders who appear in person or by proxy at the company's annual meeting. Probably the most extreme position is taken by the Belgian corporation statute, which itself provides that no single shareholder (or proxy holders on his or her behalf) may cast more than one-fifth of the total votes.[33] Belgian authorities view this restriction as an attempt to protect minority shareholders;[34] its operation is partly analogous to mandatory cumulative voting rights in some American states, with the exception, of course, that mandatory cumulative voting simply ensures sizable minorities of representation on the corporation's board of directors, whereas the Belgian rule means that a majority stockowner will not be able to cast a majority of the votes, and that the majority owner's ability to exercise control depends on his or her ability to gain support from other shareholders. Such restrictions on voting rights are also permitted by German corporate law; in recent years German corporations have used them to limit the voting power of petrodollar investors.[35] The use of bearer shares can also lead to a predominance in corporate voting for the banks with whom the shares are deposited for safekeeping. In Germany, although the "bankers' vote" has long been recognized as a significant factor in corporate control,[36] the interests of depository banks may diverge sufficiently to weaken the banks' collective influence on corporate management.[37]

In short, one limit on the occurrence of hostile bids is the availability of shares which, if purchased, will entitle their new owner to exercise voting control over the company. Closely related is the proportion of shares held by the public or by institutions likely to sell in response to an offer at an above-market price, in contrast to the proportion of shares held in "strong hands," i.e., by allies of incumbent management. The experience on the European continent with restrictions on shares' voting power demonstrates that such restrictions can effectively preclude the appearance of hostile bids.

THE TAKEOVER ENVIRONMENT

The United States, Great Britain, Canada, and Australia have all had a high level of corporate acquisition activity in recent years. After a brief discussion of activity in the United States, this section of the chapter presents available information concerning merger, acquisition, and takeover transactions in the other three countries.

In the United States, 1985 was a record-setting year for merger and acquisition activity; the dollar amount of such transactions is estimated to be $180 to $190 billion, topping the record set in 1984 of $122.2 billion.[38] Also distinguishing 1985 was the number of large transactions: 128 transactions valued at more than $100 million apiece occurred, up from 87 transactions of such value in 1984. Many of the 1985 megadeals were negotiated friendly acquisitions, although some of these transactions concluded a series of events that began with a hostile bid or a perceived threat of such a bid. Finally, four of the billion-dollar deals closed in 1985 were leveraged buy-outs. In contrast, from 1969 to

1980, only 12 transactions valued at more than $1 billion took place between U.S. firms; in 1985, U.S. firms agreed to 30 deals worth at least $1 billion.

Great Britain also had a high level of takeover activity in the past year, somewhat more so than in immediately prior years. The annual reports of the Take-Over Panel (based on an April 1 to March 31 reporting year) indicate that 3645 takeover bids—not all of which succeeded—were announced between April 1970 and March 1985.[39] The 1984–1985 total was 202. During the same fifteen-year period, the panel described 442 bids as "failed," and 25 were characterized as "failed" in 1984–1985. The "failure" category does not include bids that were not ultimately made, such as bids withdrawn prior to issuance of the offer document because a higher competing offer was announced. Over the fifteen-year period, 256 bids fell into that category, and 10 bids were so characterized for 1984–1985. Not all of the "failures" were bids resisted by the target company's board. The overall "success" rate for bids in Britain over this period, excluding failed bids and bids that otherwise did not go through, is 81%. Very few of the bids made in Britain were partial bids, i.e., bids for less than any and all of the target's share. Only 31 partial bids were made over the period, and several of these were bids which resulted, or if successful would have resulted, in the offeror holding shares carrying less than 30% of the voting rights of the target.

Some rough contrasts can be drawn with the "failure rate" and "success rate" for bids in the United States over a portion of this period. A survey of 114 unsolicited tender offers from 1976–1980 found that 28% of the targets remained independent, but only 6% were acquired by the offeror at the price initially offered. In 26% of the transactions, the offeror acquired the company at a higher price, and 39% of the targets were acquired by a white knight, a party friendly to its management.[40] If one treats these white knight acquisitions as "failures" from the perspective of the initial unsolicited offeror, such bids then had a "success rate" of 33%, if "success" in-cludes paying more than the original price offered.

Much takeover activity has also occurred in Canada in recent years. The dollar value of mergers in Canada from 1975 to 1979, adjusted for the smaller size of its economy, was five times as large as the value of mergers in the United States. From 1980 to 1985, the value of Canadian mergers was two and a half times as large as the comparable value for the United States.[41] Indeed, the volume of takeover activity has been high enough to significantly reduce the "float" (i.e., the shares outstanding and available for trading not owned by controlling interests) on the Toronto Stock Exchange.[42] Even though some shareholders who receive a cash payment in a takeover transaction invest that cash in other equity securities, and even though new public issues obviously add to the volume of shares available for public investment, the supply of public investment choices represented by the float has shrunk measurably over the past five years.

Canadian transactions, like those in the United States, have been studied to determine the distribution of the gains from the transaction as between the acquiring (or bidding) firm and the acquired (or target) firm, as measured by positive abnormal stock returns as a result of the merger announcement. Studies of merger and acquisition transactions in the United States indicate that, on average, a takeover announcement is associated with large gains to shareholders of the target firm but only small and statistically insignificant abnormal returns to the bidder firm.[43] While this discrepancy might be explained by competition among bidders, which would drive the gains from the transactions to the target shareholders, another plausible explanation is the difference in size in the United States between the typical bidder and target, along with the fact that many bidders are "repeat players" so that part of the gain expected from merger activity would already be anticipated in the bidder's share price. Evidence on these questions from the Canadian market is strikingly different. In Canada, both bidders and targets appear to enjoy statistically significant abnormal returns after takeover and merger announcements.[44] In contrast to the United States, in Canada bidders and targets tend to be of similar asset size, and weak antitrust enforcement leads to a large number of horizontal mergers. Finally, in the Canadian market a substantial portion of merger activity is accounted for by multiple acquisitions by a few relatively active acquirers.

In Australia in recent years, many corporate takeovers have occurred, and as in Canada, much takeover activity appears to be attributable to a small number of active acquirers. The Australian environment for such transactions has several characteristics that, taken together, make it unique. Relatively fewer bids in Australia than in the United States attract competing offers,[45] and a larger proportion of bids fail, even in the absence of competing bids. Furthermore, many more bids in Australia are partial offers—currently 40% of all bids by recent estimates[46]—while target shareholders, on average, appear to receive lower premiums than in the United States.[47] Finally, because until 1986 Australia did not tax capital gains transactions, its level of acquisition activity is driven in part by a tax-related factor not present in the other three countries.[48]

THE LEGAL CONTEXT

The legal regulation of corporate takeovers (apart from its antitrust dimensions, which are beyond the purview of this chapter) is embedded in a context consisting of general corporation statutes, securities regulation, and judicial interpretations of the fiduciary standards applicable to decisions of corporate managers. Each of these bodies of law, along with the interrelationships among them, is important to understanding fully the legal environment in which corporate takeovers occur. This section of the chapter briefly surveys the relevant corporate law and securities regulation for each of the countries under discussion, and discusses at length the differing treatments of corporate managers' fiduciary obligations in each system. As a general matter,

in each system two types of legal rules are significant to the regulation of corporate takeovers: rules that by regulating the offeror and the terms of the offer itself effectively raise the cost of the acquisition to the bidder or shift on to the bidder risks that would otherwise be borne by shareholders of the target company, and rules that define the circumstances under which the target's management—or, for that matter, its shareholders—may engage in behavior or transactions designed to defeat a hostile takeover proposal.

The United States

In the United States, tender offers are regulated by the Williams Act,[49] enacted by Congress in 1968 and applicable to tender offers for securities of companies registered with the SEC under the Securities and Exchange Act of 1934. The Williams Act also grants rule-making authority to the SEC. The statute is enforceable by the SEC in actions for injunctive relief as well as actions brought by private litigants. Many states have also enacted statutes regulating tender offers, in some cases inconsistently with the Williams Act provisions, although the constitutionality of state legislation in this area is frequently challenged under the supremacy and commerce clauses of the U.S. Constitution.

Prior to the enactment of the Williams Act, tender offers inhibited the transactional equivalent of the Hobbesian state of nature: They were, at least to some observers, nasty, brutish, and in most cases short as well, since the offeror was free to structure the offer so that it was of brief duration. Offerors could freely define the terms and conditions of their offers and bind offerees, once the offer was accepted, to an enforceable contract to sell the offeree's shares. Apart from the general antifraud and antimanipulation provisions of the federal securities laws, the legal regime was one of *caveat vendor*. Offerees could thus be presented with a take-it-or-leave-it proposition with a short fuse; by reducing the possibility that any competing offer might emerge—or that the target's management might have time to persuade the shareholders that the company would be worth more than the offer price as an independent firm—such offers increased the risk that offeree shareholders would sell for less than the company would bring in an open auction.

The Williams Act, like the other regulatory systems surveyed by this chapter, altered this situation by prescribing mandatory or minimal terms for some elements of offers, thereby leaving the offeror, at least for those matters so addressed by the statute, no longer the full master of the offer's terms and structure. Offerors now must keep offers open for a specified minimum period,[50] and if the offer is for fewer than all of the target's shares, it may not be made on a "first come, first served" basis, for in the event such an offer is oversubscribed, the offeror is required to accept shares on a prorated basis from those shareholders who have tendered.[51] Under the Williams Act, but not all other systems of takeover rules, shareholders have the right to withdraw shares tendered within specified time limits and to receive any increase in consideration under the offer.[52] The act requires offerors to disclose specified information either prior to or contemporaneous with the announcement of the offer, and the target corporation's management must circulate its views on the offer to its shareholders. The Williams Act also requires that persons who acquire 5% or more of a company's equity securities disclose the acquisition within 10 days after the acquisition is made.[53]

Although the Williams Act introduced regulation of offerors as to transactions that previously had not been subject to particularized federal regulation, and although the effect of the statute is to cause bidders to bear risks that otherwise could be allocated to target shareholders, it is at best a problematic assumption that the Williams Act inhibited the occurrence of hostile bids or, in the view of the President's Council of Economic Advisors, "likely caused a decrease in the number of takeovers and a decrease in the gains resulting from takeover activity."[54] For an additional effect of Congress's enactment of the statute was to jeopardize inhibitive state regulation of tender offers,[55] significantly so because the states' regulatory choices on these transactions tended to be more restrictive than the regulatory posture embodied in the Williams Act. Furthermore, drafters of the Williams Act stated that they desired its effect to be neutral,[56] and implicitly a statutory posture of neutrality toward a type of transaction tends to legitimate it.

A further issue in regulation of offerors is whether to restrict the offeror's discretion to condition its bid. The offeror's ability freely to condition its bid, i.e., to condition its obligation to take and pay for tendered shares on the occurrence or nonoccurrence of any number of possible events, is important to defining the cost and risk the offeror bears in making the bid. Unlimited power to condition the bid is unlimited power to shift to the offeree risks that would otherwise be borne by the offeror. The Williams Act, however, does not restrict the offeror's ability to condition its bid, and offerors in the United States frequently include conditioning language in the offer addressing such matters as the availability of financing for the transaction and the absence of significant litigation challenging the transaction. Nor is there any requirement in the United States that large share acquisitions be made through a general offer to all shareholders.[57] Offerors are, however, prohibited from making purchases other than through the tender offer itself once the offer has been announced.[58] In short, and in contrast with the other regulatory systems discussed later, offerors in the United States have considerable discretion in structuring acquisitions.

Counterposed with offerors' relative freedom in the United States is that of target company management to take steps to discourage hostile offers generally and to frustrate particular unwelcome bids. Courts assess management's decisions in these respects against the fiduciary obligations of care and of loyalty; although, as we shall see, the officers and directors of target corporations are freer in the United States than in some other systems to engage in defensive tactics, that freedom is not unbounded, and the fiduciary norms are of real significance.

The central question in the American cases, explored most fully in Delaware and New York, is the extent to which the court will defer to the decision of the corporation's directors, as an exercise of their discretionary business judgment, to defend against an actual or prospective offer, deploying defenses against a particular offer or antitakeover device with more generalized effect. The line of significant Delaware authority begins in 1964 with *Cheff v. Mathes*, in which the corporation's directors caused it to repurchase, at a premium over market price, the stock held by a shareholder who had demanded a seat on the board and criticized the corporation's method of product distribution.[59] The Delaware Supreme Court held that although the directors had the burden in litigation of justifying the repurchase, the directors' burden could be satisfied by showing good faith and reasonable investigation. As applied to the specific factual context in *Cheff*, this standard was interpreted by the court to require the directors to show reasonable grounds for belief that the shareholder's continued stockownership constituted "a danger to corporate policy and effectiveness," a showing found by the court to have been made by the directors.[60] *Cheff* has been criticized as unduly lenient and as permitting the use of corporate assets to preserve the incumbents' control, as long as they are able to demonstrate in retrospect the existence of a dispute with the challenger over some aspect of corporate policy.[61] Nonetheless, in the same era the Delaware Supreme Court imposed limits on tactics available to management resisting challenges to its control. In *Schnell v. Chris-Craft Industries, Inc.*, a majority of the court held that the corporation's directors had abused their amendment power over the corporation's bylaws by revising them to advance the date of the shareholders' meeting, thereby disrupting the dissidents' proxy fight.[62]

Federal courts have also interpreted Delaware law to embody a "business judgment" standard that insulates the merits of

directors' decisions from judicial scrutiny in the absence of fraud, bad faith, gross overreaching, or abuse of discretion.[63] This federal statement of Delaware law may, nonetheless, be unduly broad in light of more recent Delaware cases; although some recent cases have upheld directors' use of specific defensive tactics, not all have deferred to the directors' decisions. Furthermore, the more recent Delaware cases appear to examine much more closely the fit between the alleged threat to the corporation and each defensive transaction authorized by the directors, rather than regarding the appropriateness or necessity of the transactions as within the unreviewable discretion conferred on directors by the business judgment approach.

In *Unocal Corp. v. Mesa Petroleum Co.*, the Delaware Supreme Court held that the directors of a target corporation properly exercised sound business judgment in responding to a hostile two-tier tender offer with a self-tender by the target for its own shares that excluded the hostile offeror from participation.[64] In *Unocal*, the court emphasized that the directors' actions cannot be motivated solely or primarily by a desire to retain office and must reflect "a good faith concern for the corporation and its stockholders, which in all circumstances must be free of any fraud or other misconduct."[65] Furthermore, the response must be "reasonable in relation to the threat posed;"[66] thus the directors must analyze the nature of the offer and its effect on the corporate enterprise. On both of these questions the initial burden of proof lies with the directors. Later the same year, in *Moran v. Household International, Inc.*, the court upheld a corporation's adoption of a "rights plan" in advance of any actual offer; the intricate plan entitled each shareholder to rights triggered in the event of a tender offer for 30% of the company's stock or the acquisition of 20% of its stock by any single entity or group.[67] If a merger or consolidation occurred after any one acquired 20% of the company's stock, holders of rights would be entitled to buy $200 of the acquirer's common stock for $100. The court held that the business judgment rule, as construed in *Unocal,* applied to the board's adoption of a defensive mechanism designed to ward off future offers;[68] the directors sufficiently established that the plan was adopted in response to the threat of two-tier offers, that they were not grossly negligent in adopting the plan, and that the plan was a reasonable defensive mechanism in light of the perceived threat. No allegation was made that the plan was adopted in bad faith or to entrench the directors in office. Finally, in *Moran,*[69] as in *Unocal,* the court's opinion stresses the enhanced credibility of defensive measures adopted by directors who are independent outsiders.[70]

Nonetheless, to assess fully the significance of *Unocal* and *Moran,* one must take into account two other contemporaneous Delaware cases. In *Smith v. Van Gorkom,* the court held that a gross-negligence standard applied to whether directors had exercised an appropriate degree of care in making decisions related to significant corporate transactions.[71] The court held that the directors' behavior in *Smith* did not meet this standard because they assented to a merger proposal without the benefit of extensive deliberations or an expert's opinion as to the company's value, and because they reached their decision quickly and without inquiry into the basis for the merger price or the consequences and structure of the merger agreement. Finally, in *Revlon, Inc., v. MacAndrews & Forbes Holdings, Inc.,* the Delaware Supreme Court invalidated a target's grant of an option on its most valuable assets to a bidding group proposing a leveraged buy-out that included members of the target's senior management, during a bidding contest with a hostile offeror who had made a series of cash bids for any and all shares and had announced its determination to top any bid made by the management group.[72] The court held that the board's grant of the option demonstrated apparent self-interest because it was motivated at least in part by the directors' wish to alleviate the legal consequences of an earlier defensive transaction by retaining the involvement of the management-allied bidding group, which

had agreed to take steps that would protect the directors against liability arising from the earlier transaction.[73] *Revlon* states that lockup options are not necessarily inherently improper but that the business judgment rule does not protect their adoption when the breakup of the company appears to be inevitable. At that point, the directors' role is limited to the auctioneering function of obtaining the highest price for its assets.

Recent judicial interpretations of New York law have also imposed limits on the directors' ability to defend aggressively against hostile offers under the protective mantle of the business judgment rule. In *Norlin Corp. v. Rooney Pace Inc.,* the target's directors responded to large and unwelcome purchases of the corporation's stock by issuing common and voting preferred stock to a Panamanian subsidiary and a newly created employee stockownership plan, to such an extent that the board effectively ensured itself of continued and irrefrangible voting control over the target.[74] The Federal Second Circuit Court, applying New York law, held that the directors' desire to retain control, indeed to do so at all costs, appeared to be their sole justification for issuing the stock, and further held that the defendants had not established that their actions were "legitimate" or "fair and reasonable." The same court invalidated the defensive use of a lockup option on substantial target assets in *Hanson Trust PLC v. ML SCM Acquisition, Inc.*[75] In *Hanson Trust,* as in *Revlon,* the directors granted the asset option to a bidding group proposing a leveraged buy-out and proposing an equity stake in the enterprise for members of the target's senior management after the consummation of the buy-out.[76] Furthermore, the pricing of the option appeared quite favorable to the bidding group and unfavorable to the issuer. The court held that while the directors' adoption of the option could not be characterized as grossly negligent, plaintiff had made a prima facie showing of a lack of due care, raising sufficient doubts concerning the directors' commitment to protecting shareholder interests that the directors had the burden of justifying the option transaction and its terms. The procedural consequence of this holding was to entitle the plaintiff to a preliminary injunction against the exercise of the option.

Thus, recent cases have interpreted Delaware and New York law to impose substantial limitations on the protection afforded by the business judgment rule to directors' adoption of defenses against hostile tender offers. Defensive transactions are most likely to be vulnerable in litigation if they are adopted in the midst of an active bidding contest, if the decision to adopt the defense does not appear duly deliberative and mindful of its consequences, if the effect of the defense is to terminate the bidding contest, and if the directors' decision has self-interested qualities. In contrast to the British and Australian precedents, however, even these recent American cases do not suggest that directors of a target improperly interfere with the constitutional prerogatives of shareholders in defending against hostile bids.[77]

Great Britain

Most regulation of takeovers in Britain is extralegal. Although, as noted later, the Companies Acts by defining corporations' legal powers limit the defensive transactions available to targets, the rules regulating bidders and targets in bids for public and some private companies are contained in the City Code, the product of the Panel on Take-Overs and Mergers. In some respects the City Code's regulation of bidders is similar to that imposed by the Williams Act. The code, like the Williams Act, requires extensive disclosure by bidders,[78] sets a minimum duration for offers,[79] and requires prorated acceptance for oversubscribed partial bids.[80] The code also grants withdrawal rights to tendering shareholders, although these rights differ somewhat in technical respects from the withdrawal rights granted by the Williams Act.[81] The code, unlike the Williams Act, regulates conditions imposed on offers, disapproving of conditions "depending solely on subjective judgments by the directors of

the offeror or the fulfillment of which is in their hands.[82] But offerors in Britain, unlike those in the United States, are permitted to purchase target shares outside the offer itself even after the offer has been announced.[83]

The code differs more strikingly from the Williams Act in its treatment of partial bids. The panel's consent is required for any partial offer, and it is normally granted for those bids that will not result in the offeror holding shares with 30% or more of the target's voting rights. Consent will not normally be granted for any offer that would give the offeror more than 30% but less than 100% of the target's voting rights if the offeror or its associates have purchased shares in the target during the preceding 12 months.[84] Indeed, the panel's consent is required to purchase any target shares during the 12 months *after* any partial bid; purchases during a partial bid are prohibited.[85] Finally, any partial offer that could give the offeror more than 30% of the target's voting rights must be approved separately by a vote of a majority of the target's voting securities.[86]

The City Code's treatment of partial bids makes them less attractive as a means of acquiring effective control of a target; in particular, the requirement of a separate shareholder plebiscite significantly restricts the offeror's ability to acquire a substantial position by offering a relatively low premium, because it permits shareholders to tender their shares while voting against the transaction itself. Thus, the separate voting requirement reduces the risk that a partial bid at a low premium will succeed simply because shareholders will tender because they fear being left behind, with a new controlling stockholder, if their fellows tender.[87] The restrictions on share purchases before and after partial bids may also make the partial bid itself unattractive, while protecting shareholders against the risk that the offeror will acquire shares at prices higher than the partial-bid price.

The City Code also imposes on offerors, and other persons who acquire a sizable number of shares, an obligation to offer to buy out the target's remaining shareholders that has no counterpart in the Williams Act. Under the code, any person who together with those persons acting in concert with him acquires 30% or more of the voting securities or rights of a target is obliged to make an offer to the target's remaining shareholders (whether their shares are voting or nonvoting) at the highest price paid by the acquiring person or his associates for shares of that class within the preceding 12 months.[88] This buy-out requirement is structured to apply to sizable share acquisitions independent of the acquisition technique used, so that stock market transactions or privately negotiated acquisitions, as well as formal tender offers, all trigger the obligation.

The City Code's imposition of a buy-out requirement accomplishes a number of separate goals. It ensures that all shareholders, noncontrolling as well as controlling, will share equally in any premium paid by a buyer as long as at least 30% of the company's shares are sold. It protects nonselling shareholders against the risk that the new controlling shareholder will exploit its position to their disadvantage.[89] It eliminates the possibility that nonselling shareholders (especially those in the wake of a successful partial bid) will be bought out in a freeze-out merger for a lesser consideration than that of the tender offer.

The position of target management also differs in Britain. The City Code requires that all offers be put in the first instance to the target's board or its advisors,[90] who must obtain "competent independent advice" on the offer and share the substance of that advice with their shareholders.[91] The code also requires that any information given by a target to a preferred offeror be made equally available, on request, to other bona fide offerors or potential offerors.[92] Once an offer has been made or appears to be imminent, the code requires that defensive transactions which could frustrate the offer be tested by a shareholder plebiscite: If the target board (except to fulfill obligations under a prior contract) proposes to issue shares or options on shares, create or issue securities convertible into shares, sell or agree to sell any material amount of assets, or enter into contracts "otherwise than in the ordinary course of business," the shareholders must vote in a general meeting to approve the transaction.[93] The same requirement applies to any redemption or purchase by the target of its own shares (except in pursuance of a prior contract) once an offer has been announced or appears imminent.[94] These rules do not, however, reach transactions that precede the time an offer is announced or reasonably appears to be in the offering. Recently, target managements have mounted advertising campaigns in the popular media to defend against hostile bids—without uniform success, however. The panel responded in 1986 by attempting to ban takeover advertising, due to advertisements that attempted to "denigrate" the opposition or indulged in misleadingly selective use of statistics.[95]

The code's treatment of defensive transactions developed against a legal context that impsoed substantial restrictions on the ability of the target's directors to use their powers to defeat hostile takeover bids. In the leading case, *Hogg v. Cramphorn, Ltd.,* after receiving an unsolicited bid for all of the company's common and preferred shares, the target's board responded by establishing a trust for the benefit of the company's employees, appointing themselves trustees of the trust, and issuing to the trust a large block of authorized but theretofore unissued preferred stock, which was assigned ten votes per share, assuring that over half of the votes were in friendly hands.[96] The court held that this use of the directors' power to allot shares was improper, although, interestingly enough, the court faulted neither the directors' good faith nor their motivation, which was to maintain a management structure they believed to be more advantageous to the shareholders, staff, and company than would be the changes likely to follow the takeover offer if it succeeded. Instead, in the court's view, the directors acted simply to retain their control and improperly interfered with the "constitutional rights" of a potential shareholder majority by preventing the bidder's offer from reaching the shareholders. *Hogg v. Cramphorn* reasons that while directors may choose to pursue many courses, they nonetheless are under an obligation not to use their power to oppress shareholders.[97]

The significance of *Hogg v. Cramphorn, Ltd.,* is not so much in its immediate and practical application in Britain (where the City Code now regulates defensive tactics in bids for most companies) but in its statement of principle to be followed, or at least distinguished, by Commonwealth courts outside Britain. In this respect, as noted later, the force of the principle appears to have been somewhat vitiated by later Commonwealth cases. Even in Britain, in a later case, *Cayne v. Global National Resources P.L.C.,* Vice-Chancellor Megarry took the position that the principle of *Hogg v. Cramphorn* "must not be carried too far"; although in his view directors' actions are improper if they are motivated by a purpose of retaining or preserving "control as such," if other elements are present as well, the motivation of retaining control is not necessarily improper.[98] An example set in the opinion is a defensive allotment of shares by a target to defeat a business competitor's acquisition of shares in the target "with the object of running [the target] down so as to lessen its competition."[99] Thus, even under the British authorities, target directors may be able to justify defensive share allotments (and other transactions as well) on the basis of their full range of motivations as directors for seeking to retain control; the extremity of the example used in *Cayne* leaves open the question of how concrete and palpable the projected injury to the target must be in order to support the directors' use of their powers so as to preserve their control.[100]

The position of directors in British companies is also, of course, defined by provisions in statutory company law. Of particular significance is the fact that company law provides for the removal of directors by ordinary resolution passed by a simple majority of shareholders, without a showing of cause for removal and notwithstanding anything to the contrary in the company's articles or in any agreement

between the company and the director.[101] In contrast, in the United States, the Delaware corporation statute provides that directors whose terms are staggered (so that not all directors' terms expire each year) are only removable *for cause* unless the company's certificate of incorporation states to the contrary.[102] This difference in statutory treatment appears to suggest that the tenure in office of British directors is inevitably more tenuous than that of their Delaware counterparts. But this apparent difference should not be overemphasized: In 1970 the House of Lords held that a provision in a company's articles assigning multiple votes to shares held by a director only in respect of a resolution to remove him from office was valid and was not inconsistent with the statutory prescription of removal by ordinary resolution.[103] To be sure, many British cases since 1970 mention shareholder resolutions to remove directors but do not note the existence of weighted-voting protections for the directors.[104] Whether the nonuse of weighted voting to protect directors against removal reflects more than simple inattention to the possibility is an unanswerable question.

A final point about English company law relevant to takeover transactions is that the Companies Acts, in contrast to corporation statutes in Canada and the United States, but like Australian corporation statutes, do not contain provisions that as readily enable negotiated corporation mergers and acquisitions to be executed in a relatively simple and straightforward fashion, based on the negotiation of an agreement to merge or sell assets, followed by approval by the company's directors and shareholders. Transactions in which a corporation agrees to merge with or to sell all of its assets to another corporation are channeled by the Companies Acts into provisions dealing with voluntary winding-up transactions, which require shareholders' authorization in general meeting, rights of dissent for shareholders, the appointment of a liquidator for the company, and an account of the winding up from the liquidator to the public registrar of companies.[105] The mechanics of the takeover bid, in contrast, may be executed more simply and quickly. In short, an important facet of the transactional climate in Britain—and in Australia as well, for the same reasons—is that at least some transactions that in the United States or Canada would likely be structured as negotiated mergers are executed instead through the mode of takeover bids, due to the complexity and awkwardness of corporate statutory law.

Canada

In general, the aspects of Canadian corporate law and securities regulation pertinent to takeover regulation demonstrate the influence of both the United States and Great Britain. Geographic proximity and historical circumstance make this influence unsurprising. Until recently, Alberta, British Columbia, Manitoba, Saskatchewan, and Ontario were "uniform-act" provinces for securities regulation and had substantially similar statutes; and Quebec, although not formally a uniform-act province, developed compatible legislation. Statutory uniformity indeed seems to be the legal counterpart to the Canadian view that the country has a "genuinely national capital market."[106] Provincial securities legislation began to diverge in 1979 with the enactment of a new securities act in Ontario, the statute now in effect in that province, which contains provisions regulating corporate takeovers that no other province has adopted. In other respects, however, some of the other provincial statutes are compatible with the Ontario statutes; although the discussion that follows focuses primarily on Ontario, statutes and cases from other provinces are noted as well. Ontario's importance in takeover regulation is enhanced by the jurisdictional breadth of provincial securities legislation in Canada. The provincial statutes apply to takeover bids for any company, regardless of the situs of its incorporation, when the bid is made to any shareholder whose last registered address on the target's books is in a particular province.[107] Canada also has a national corporation statute, which includes provisions regulating takeovers, applicable only to corporations incorporated under that statute.

Under the Ontario Securities Act, unless the transaction fits within a stated exemption, any offer to purchase voting securities[108] in the target that would, if accepted, result in the offeror owning more than 20% of the target's voting securities[109] is defined to be a "takeover bid" and may not be made except in compliance with the statute's requirements, which include a general offer to all the corporation's shareholders. The two most notable exemptions cover bids made through the facilities of the Toronto Stock Exchange (TSE), which are regulated separately by the TSE itself, and purchases made privately from 14 or fewer stockholders. As in the United States, partial bids are freely allowed, subject to a proration requirement in the event of oversubscription and, in addition, to separate timing requirements.[110]

In addition to requiring that significant share acquisitions be structured as "all-holders" tender offers at one price, the Ontario statute also requires an acquiring person in some circumstances to offer to buy out the target's remaining stockholders. Under §91(1) of the statute, an offeror who becomes the owner of more than 20% of the target's voting securities through a private agreement with 14 or fewer holders (and thus is exempt from the general offer requirement) is obliged to make a follow-up offer "at least equal in value" to the target's remaining stockholders of the same class within 180 days of the date of the private agreement, if there is a published market for the securities and the value of the consideration paid by the offeror under the private agreement exceeds the market price of that date plus reasonable brokerage fees plus other commissions.[111] "Market price" has been defined by the Ontario Securities Commission as "an amount 15 percent in excess of the simple average of the closing price of securities of that class for each day on which there was a closing price and falling not more than ten business days before the relevant date."[112] Thus, the offeror who pays a premium of less than 15% to offerees in a private transaction is not subject to the statutory buy-out obligation. The Ontario statute also exempts as *de minimis* acquisitions of up to

5% of the target's voting securities by the offeror and its affiliates within a 12-month period, as long as the price paid does not exceed any published market price plus reasonable fees and commissions; the availability of this exemption, however, is limited by the fact that acquisitions made through an exempt TSE bid must be counted against the 5% limit. Acquisitions made through an exempt private agreement or through a general offer to stockholders do not count against the 5%.[113]

The Ontario strictures on bidders are clearly the result of a concern that control premiums should be shared with all stockholders when sufficient shares to constitute effective control are bought from a small number of shareholders.[114] Indeed, the bidder's obligation to buy out the remaining stockholders is triggered only by the "private agreement" transaction and is not triggered by other types of transactions that may also pass effective control, such as a partial bid made to all stockholders or a bid made on the TSE.[115] But the most striking contrast is not among the treatment of various transactions within the Ontario statute but between Ontario and the United States, in which persons buying and selling shares are under no obligation to structure the transaction so as to result in an equal sharing of any control premium among all shareholders. In general, the Ontario approach results in a more integrated treatment of separate transactions that may shift control in the target company because it requires acquisitions that would give the pruchaser a sizable (i.e., 20%) holding to be made through a general all-holders offer; it further achieves equal treatment of target stockholders if the transaction shifting control results from purchases from a few, presumably large stockholders. The buy-out obligation created by the Ontario statute also contrasts with the considerably broader buy-out obligation imposed by the City Code in Britain (discussed earlier), which has a higher trigger point (30% rather than 20%) but is applicable to all acquisitions giving the acquiror 30% voting control.

One possible explanation for the narrower focus of the buy-out obligation in Ontario is the relatively large number of Canadian companies controlled by a small number of family-identified groups, as discussed earlier. Permitting control premiums to be paid to a small number of stockholders may seem especially unfair when, as seems likely in Canada, the vendors are repeat players receiving premiums in many such transactions. Although no other Canadian province has followed Ontario's lead in imposing a buy-out obligation in the context of private sales of control, the Quebec securities legislation regulates such transactions in a style that is consistent with the concern for apparent fairness described previously. Under the Quebec statute, the exemption from the general obligation to make an all-holders bid if the acquirer would thereby obtain more than 20% of a class of voting securities is available only for purchases from five or fewer holders, at a price not in excess of 15% over the average market price.[116] The Quebec solution, then, is to require a general offer to all shareholders if a premium of more than 15% would otherwise be paid to more than 14 vendors.

Industry practice prior to the adoption of the Ontario requirement in 1981 also helps to explain its structure. From the TSE's records, traceable private-agreement transactions were accompanied by an announcement of an offer to buy out the other shareholders in all but one instance. A majority of these offers were identical to the consideration in the private agreement; the remainder offered substantial if not comparable consideration. The one exception—where no offer to the remaining shareholders was made—met with negative reactions in the securities industry and the financial media and is thought to have added impetus for the adoption of the legal buy-out requirement.[117] Thus, the buy-out requirement in Ontario, although narrowly focused, is consistent with the financial community's private mores that preceded it.

Another facet of takeover regulation in Ontario that differs substantially from the United States is the statutory treatment of conditions in bids. Under the Ontario Securities Act, but not the Williams Act, the offeror's ability to condition its bid is limited to three types of conditions specified in the statute: that a minimum number of shares be tendered, that no material change in the target occur other than changes caused by the offeror, and that all required governmental approvals be forthcoming.[118] In contrast, in Britain the City Code, as described earlier, rather than specifying permissible conditions, prohibits those whose fulfillment turns on the offeror itself or its subjective judgment.[119] The Ontario legislation, finally, grants more limited withdrawal rights than does the Williams Act.[120]

The legal position of target management in Canadian corporations also shows the influence of both Britain and the United States. Like the Williams Act in the United States, the Canadian securities statutes, with one exception, do not directly regulate defensive transactions; the constraints on target management as a result stem from statutory company law and common law interpretations of the fiduciary obligations owed to the company by its management. A basic limitation on directors' positions is the same as that established in Britain: Under Canadian corporation statute directors are always removable through a shareholder vote by ordinary resolution, subject to the protection of cumulative voting rights.[121] On the other hand, under the Canadian Business Corporations Act (CBCA), a corporation is not required in its articles to stipulate any authorized capital.[122] Thus directors of CBCA corporations that have not specified an authorized capital are free to allot additional shares unconstrained by the corporation's articles.[123]

The one limitation in Canadian securities regulation that affects defensive transactions concerns the regulation of issuer bids (in the U.S. parlance, "self-tenders") and, specifically, an issuer's ability to make an offer to repurchase its own shares that excludes specified stockholders, in particular, a hostile bidder. In the United States, courts have held that a selective or discriminatory issuer tender offer does not violate the Williams Act[124] and that target directors, having authorized such an offer, may be protected by the business judgment

rule.[125] If the target is able to exclude shares held by a hostile bidder from its offer, the cost of making its self-tender offer is reduced for the target, while the hostile bidder, after the self-tender, holds shares in a target corporation with fewer liquid assets or more debt (incurred in order to finance the self-tender) or both. In contrast, this technique is not available to targets under the Ontario securities statute, which requires that all takeover bids, including issuer bids, "be sent to all holders of the class of securities sought."[126] True, the statute does not expressly require that the offer be *made* to all holders, but the "sending" requirement seems substantially the same.

To be sure, directors of Canadian corporations, like their counterparts in Britain and the United States, hold their powers—including the power to repurchase shares and the power to allot additional shares—subject to the fiduciary obligation to exercise them only in what they bona fide consider to be the company's best interests. In the leading (and widely cited) Canadian case, *Teck Corporation Ltd. v. Millar,* the British Columbia Supreme Court rejected the principal of *Hogg v. Cramphorn,* holding that "the directors ought to be allowed to consider who is seeking control and why. . . . The exercise of their powers to defeat those seeking a majority will not necessarily be categorized as improper" if the directors believe substantial damage to the company's interests would otherwise ensue.[127]

In *Teck Corporation,* the directors of a mining corporation with an unexploited copper property signed an exploitation contract with a major mining company giving it the right to a 30% equity position in the company owning the copper mine; the effect of the prospective share allotment would be to reduce below a legal majority the shareholdings of another mining conglomerate that had, prior to the signing of the exploitation contract, acquired a majority shareholding in the company with the copper property, with the expressed intention of contracting to exploit the mine. The court, believing the target's directors to be motivated by a desire to make the best contract for exploitation that they could for their company, noted that it considered the respective experience and success in the mining industry of the two contestants for control and chose the one it believed most likely to develop the property efficiently and profitably.[128] Indeed, this view of the directors' motivation enabled the court to distinguish *Hogg v. Cramphorn* as applying to facts in which the directors' primary purpose was to frustrate a takeover rather than, as in *Teck Corporation,* to make the best possible deal for their company. *Teck Corporation* also explicitly rejected the position stated in *Hogg v. Cramphorn* that directors' powers may not be used to frustrate an attempt to take control of the corporation on the basis that the limitation on directors' power stated in *Hogg* could not readily be limited to share allotments: The relevant criterion is the directors' purpose and its propriety or impropriety, which "does not depend on the nature of any shareholders' rights that may be affected by the exercise of the directors' powers."[129]

Teck Corporation thus represents a view of target directors' actions that gives primacy to motivation rather than to a conception of shareholders' "constitutional" rights to acquire voting control, on which *Hogg v. Cramphorn* seems to be based. One palpable difference in result between these two approaches is the nature of the task imposed on the court that must apply the test to evaluate the directors' conduct: The test based on motivation adopted in *Teck Corporation* requires extensive review of the factual context surrounding the transactions, an exercise that is unnecessary if a case can be resolved from conceptions of shareholders' rights, as in *Hogg*.[130]

Another possible constraint on target directors of Canadian corporations (albeit one that does not appear to have been used thus far in litigation over takeovers in Canada) stems from the statutory remedies for corporate conduct "that is oppressive or unfairly prejudicial to or that unfairly disregards the interests of any security holder, creditor, director or officer of the corporation."[131] The Ontario corporation statute authorizes the court to make an order to rectify such conduct, including conduct

that "threatens to effect" such a result, and broadly defines the types of orders the court may make.[132]

Awaiting further development in the case law is the distinction, if any, between defensive transactions undertaken for an improper purpose under the test stated in *Teck Corporation* and defensive transactions that under the statute are "oppressive or unfairly prejudicial" or unfairly disregard the interest of a securityholder. A potential point of tension is between the assumption in *Teck Corporation* that directors' duties are owned solely to "the company," and the assumption in statutory oppression remedies that actions undertaken by directors on behalf of "the company" may improperly infringe on obligations owed to shareholders. In any event, a practical constraint on many target and potential target directors is the requirement of the Toronto Stock Exchange that listed companies give it immediate notice of each proposed option or issue of treasury securities; under its bylaws the TSE may require shareholder approval of the transaction as a condition of accepting the notice.[133]

Australia

Australian corporate law and securities regulation, albeit as unique as the country itself in many respects, nonetheless in their treatment of takeover-related issues resemble somewhat other Commonwealth systems and the United States system. Corporate takeovers specifically are regulated by the Companies (Acquisition of Shares) Act of 1980 (CASA), a federal statute adopted by each of the Australian states. CASA, a much lengthier and much more detailed statute than its counterpart legislation in the United States and Canada, confers enforcement authority on the National Companies and Securities Commission (NCSC) and is to be read to make applicable all of the remedial provisions in the Companies Code. CASA also gives the NCSC power to determine that in light of the statute's purposes, parties' acquisitions of shares or other activities are "unacceptable" notwithstanding literal compliance with CASA itself, and to apply to a court for orders appropriate to protect the rights or interests involved.[134] In this respect the NCSC's posture under CASA resembles the stated position of the Take-Over Panel in Britain, which states in the City Code that its "spirit as well as the precise wording . . . must be observed."[135]

CASA, like the Ontario legislation, in essence defines a closed system, with stated exceptions: Under CASA, any acquisition that would give the acquiring person, together with his associates, 20% or more of the target's voting securities must be made either through a general offer to all shareholders or through a regulated stock exchange bid.[136]Nonetheless, the NCSC's powers to compel an offeror to proceed with an offer have been tested in litigation and found wanting, at least in some circumstances.[137]

Significant exceptions for our purposes from the general bid requirement created by CASA are acquisitions of shares in a company that has fewer than 15 shareholders[138] and acquisitions that have been approved at a shareholders' meeting by a majority of the target's shares, excluding from the vote those shares held by the prospective acquirer and its associates.[139] Like the Ontario statute, CASA contemplates the possibility of tender offers made through a stock exchange; but CASA, unlike the Ontario statute, regulates such offers in great detail. CASA restricts in some aspects an offeror's ability to condition its bid.[140] CASA does not require a follow-up bid and regulates partial offers to be made on a proportional basis to shareholders, so that the bid must be structured as an offer to buy the same specified percentage of the holdings of each shareholder.[141] Thus, in contrast to the Williams Act in the United States, but paralleling the Ontario Securities Act, CASA requires that sizable share acquisitions, or at least those giving the acquiring person 20% of the target's voting power, be made through a general offer to all shareholders. In contrast to the Ontario legislation and the City Code in Britain, CASA does not treat such sizable acquisitions as events triggering an obligation on the part of the acquiring shareholder to

offer to buy out the target's remaining shares. In this respect, the operative norm of equity in CASA is an equality of opportunity rather than equality of treatment. Finally, unlike all the other regulatory systems discussed heretofore in this chapter, CASA grants no withdrawal rights to shareholders.[142]

An additional aspect of the corporate legal context in Australia that defines the acquisition environment is the absence, from the Australian corporate statutes, of any provisions explicitly enabling negotiated corporate mergers or amalgamations. Thus, in contrast to Canada[143] and the United States, but like Britain,[144] Australia makes effecting a negotiated merger between two companies difficult to achieve through the mechanisms set forth in the corporation statute itself, a fact that must be relevant to the popularity of the device of the takeover bid.[145]

The powers of target company directors in Australia are, on balance, more significantly limited by aspects of Australian statutory corporate law than is the case for target directors under other corporation statutes reviewed in this chapter. Greater similarity obtains for the fiduciary constraints upon directors' exercise of those powers.

Under the Australian companies Code, a corporation's directors are removable by ordinary resolution "notwithstanding anything in its articles or in any agreement";[146] whether this language is sufficient to exclude the possibility of protecting directors against removal through removal-triggered, weighted-voting shares appears to be an open question under the Australian statute, although, as we have seen, the validity of such voting rights has been upheld in the face of similar language in the British Companies Act.[147] An additional limitation stems from the absolute statutory prohibition on corporate share repurchases, which indeed are a crime in Australia.[148] Until recently, corporate share repurchases were also prohibited in Britain. Australian companies are permitted by statute to lend financial assistance to others purchasing their shares only if three-fourths of the shareholders vote by special resolution to approve the transaction.[149] In contrast, in Britain, although lending financial assistance is prohibited, a company may justify giving such assistance if its primary purpose is incidental to some larger purpose of the company itself. Together, these two aspects of Australian company law preclude defensive share repurchases and issuer tender offers, while subjecting to a shareholder approval—at a high threshold—defensive transactions in which the target enlists the support of a favored bidder by permitting the use of its assets and earnings to repay the favored bidder's financing for its offer. The basic position in Australia, then, would be that the leveraged buy-out transaction (in the American parlance) is not an option.

But Australian securities professionals are easily as adept[150] as their American brothers and sisters, and at least two caveats to this basic position must be noted. First, the statute itself exempts from its strictures "the payment of a dividend by a company in good faith and in the ordinary course of commercial dealing"; this exemption suggests one route through which reserves could be drawn out of the target and into the coffers of an acquiring party.[151] Second, if a bidder initially, from its own financing, buys shares in the target and then sells them to an entity favored by the target's management to become the company's new controlling shareholder, it is not unimaginable that the target's assets might ultimately be used to repay the "moral debt" owed to the initial bidder.

The fiduciary constraints on Australian directors' exercise of their corporate powers developed in the Commonwealth context shared with Britain and Canada. In *Howard Smith v. Ampol Petroleum Ltd.,* an appeal from the Supreme Court of New South Wales to the Judicial Committee,[152] the directors of a target company had issued a large block of shares to a preferred bidder, thereby destroying the majority position of the rival bidder, which had, as it happens, made a bid for the remaining shares in the company that its directors considered too low and that was ultimately topped by a higher bid from the preferred bidder (and recipient of the share allot-

ment).[153] The Judicial Committee held that it was improper for the directors to use their power to allot shares purely for the purpose of destroying an existing majority or creating a new majority, because by doing so the directors "interfered with that element of the company's constitution which is separate from and set against their powers," the individual shareholders' right to dispose of shares at a given price.[154] While *Howard Smith* explicitly rejects the argument that the dispute must be decided in favor of the corporation's directors once it is shown they were not motivated by self-interest,[155] it also rejects the argument that the only proper purpose for which shares could be issued is to raise fresh capital, stating that the power should not be understood to be so narrowly limited.[156]

One curious aspect of the opinion in *Howard Smith* is that after discussing the opinion in *Teck Corporation* and the Canadian court's conclusion that the share allotment in that case was proper because its primary purpose was to obtain the best possible deal for the company, the opinion concludes that *Teck Corporation* "appears to be in line with the English and Australian authorities to which reference has been made."[157] But one English authority to which *Howard Smith* refers is *Hogg v. Cramphorn,* whose rationale was specifically rejected by the British Columbia Supreme Court in *Teck Corporation!*[158] Furthermore, although the transactional contexts in *Teck Corporation* and *Howard Smith* were different (for one thing, the bidding battle in *Teck* was in part over the bidders' respective abilities to develop the target company's copper mine), they are not so utterly dissimilar to make the consistent cases' rationales.[159]

The current strength of the legacy of *Howard Smith* is difficult to assess, for although the case has not been overruled, one recent Australian case appears to depart somewhat from its reasoning. In *Pine Vale Investments Ltd. v. McDonnell and East Ltd. and Anor,*[160] Pine Vale controlled about 26% of the shares in McDonnell and East, and had announced a partial takeover bid for McDonnell but had not made a formal offer when Mcdonnell and East, to finance the acquisition of another business, proposed to issue rights to buy additional McDonell shares to all of its shareholders. The effect of the proposed rights issue on Pine Vale would be to increase its cost in making a takeover offer for McDonnell and East, because more shares would be outstanding if the rights were exercised by other shareholders, but also to increase the value of McDonell's and East's assets. The court rejected Pine Vale's application for an injunction, finding that McDonnell's directors were genuinely convinced their acquisition was in the company's best commercial interests and that the proposed transactions by McDonnell were not disadvantageous to the shareholders as a whole. Although the court thought it relevant that these transactions occurred at the time of Pine Vale's proposed takeover, it held this coincidence was not necessarily fatal to the legal position of the target's directors. In the court's view, the directors' duties were owed to the company as a whole and not to individual shareholders, and no individual shareholder could be shown to be discriminated against by the proposed transactions.

The difference between *Pine Vale* and *Howard Smith* is in part one of emphasis, on the perceived commercial logic of the target's proposed transaction rather than the rights of the shareholders and prospective offeror, and this emphasis in turn suggests a willingness in Australian courts to consider target directors' statements of business justification and purpose in the takeover context for transactions that also have a defensive effect.

CASA and the rules of the AASE also regulate the defensive use of share allotments. CASA itself requires shareholder approval to exempt from the requirement that a general all-holders bid be made any issuance of shares to a party who thereby becomes the holder of 20% or more of the issuer's voting securities.[161] Thus, if a target's directors seek to place a block of shares with a likely ally in the event a hostile offer is made or if they seek to entice a friendly offeror into a bidding contest by issuing it a sizable block of shares, the issuer's shareholders must vote to approve the transaction if the transferee of the shares would, as a result, hold 20% or more of the issuer's voting securities.[162] The rules of Australian stock exchanges also require shareholder approval for any additional allotment of shares other than on a proportional basis to existing shareholders, once directors of the issuer have received notice of an actual or potential offer and for three months thereafter.[163]

The significance of the AASE requirement must, however, be assessed in light of the actual transactional environment in Australia in which many partial bids are made. CASA does not require shareholder approval for allotments of less than 20%, and the AASE rule does not require shareholder approval for the additional allotment if it is made *pari passu* to all present shareholders. Either an allotment of less than 20% or a *pari passu* allotment to present shareholders can severely disrupt the arithmetic of a partial bidder. As an example, the rights issue in *Pine Vale* offered 1.5 million shares to McDonnell's shareholders at $3 per share; the unwelcome bid was for 500,000 shares at $6 each. The court believed it "wholly impossible" that the bidder would persist with its offer.[164]

A few additional legal constraints on Australian targets are noteworthy. CASA permits the supreme court to void agreements for compensation for loss of office entered into by the target with its officers or directors in contemplation of a takeover, unless the agreements are approved by a shareholder vote in general meeting at which the beneficiaries do not vote for the resolution.[165] Finally, the National Companies and Securities Commission has taken the position that its power under CASA to declare conduct unacceptable could embrace declarations concerning defensive transactions, including a target's declaration of an unusual dividend in the course of a takeover bid.[166] Taken together, and in contrast with the Canadian and American settings, all of these provisions do restrict the ability of target directors in Australia to defend against unwelcome takeover bids. Again, however, ingenuity of their advisors is considerable; as an example, convertible notes issued to friendly parties are said by an Australian source to be used with increasing frequency as defensive measures, with indentures structured to include a clause making the notes convertible into common shares during a takeover of the issuer.[167] On the other hand, the securities bar is reported to have had difficulty in developing "shark repellant" language for articles amendments that would be acceptable to an Australian stock exchange.[168]

TECHNICAL ISSUES

This section of the chapter explores three more technical questions about the regulation of takeovers that are currently at issue in some, if not all, of the regulatory systems discussed by the chapter; and it contrasts their resolution in these systems. These issues are transactions prior to, or contemporaneous with, or instead of, a formal takeover bid; the treatment of equity securities with lesser voting rights in takeover transactions; and difficulties in the implementation of mandatory offers.

Nonbid Transactions

One question raised by each of the regulatory systems discussed in this chapter is the extent to which it requires an integrated treatment of a series of separate transactions that cumulatively may have the effect of shifting control of a company. If such integration is not required, a prospective acquirer may move quickly and perhaps anonymously as well through stock exchange and private transactions to accumulate shares at prices not available to shareholders other than the vendors in those transactions. Different dimensions of this underlying question arise in the United States, Ontario, and Australia.

The only current constraint in the United States on offerors in this connection is a prohibition, once a tender offer has been announced, on purchasing shares other than through the offer itself while the offer is outstanding. The offeror otherwise is free to precede or follow a tender offer

with share acquisitions—whether through private purchases or stock exchange transactions—at a price or for a consideration different from that of the general tender offer. Partial offers are not discouraged and, apart from the proration requirement described previously, are not subject to special regulatory treatment. Indeed, a controlling position may be acquired in the United States without making any general offer to stockholders; although federal courts in a few cases have been willing to characterize selective purchasing campaigns that resulted in acquisitions of substantial blocks of shares of "tender offers" to which the Williams Act applied, most cases and all of the relatively recent cases have declined to so interpret the reach of the statute.[169] In effect, current law in the United States takes an atomistic view of formally separate transactions that cumulatively may shift control, as long as a formal tender offer is not made to the target's shareholders.

The atomistic view ascribed to the United States is not shared by the other systems reviewed in this chapter. In Canada and Australia, problems of linking or integrating transactions may arise. For example, under the Ontario statute, although an acquisition of shares that would give the acquiring person control of 20% or more of the target's stock must be made as an all-holders bid, prebid purchases up to the 20% threshold are freely permitted, in theory. Other aspects of the Ontario regulatory system, however, require that this theoretical possibility be modified somewhat. First, the Ontario statute requires a takeout bid to the remaining shareholders if the acquirer attains control of 20% or more of the target's voting rights through a private transaction in which a premium of more than 15% over market was paid. If prebid market purchases are followed by prebid private transactions, the target's shareholders or the Ontario Securities Commission's (OSC) staff may argue that the market purchases raised the market price, so that the price paid in the private transaction exceeded the allowable premium and triggered an obligation to make a follow-up bid.[170] Second, the Ontario Securities Commission has taken the position that if an acquirer offers to purchase all the securities of one owner, any "linked" or "related" takeover bid must be at a price at least as great as that offered in the private agreement.[171] That is, if the all-holders bid is "linked" to the private agreement, even if the private agreement does not trigger a buy-out obligation, the purchaser has an obligation to offer an equal price to all holders of the same class of security. The rationale for this position is the statutory requirement that all holders be offered the same consideration;[172] whether the takeover bid can be shown to be "linked" to private purchase depends on proof of the purchaser's intention at the time of the private purchase. Relatedly, the OSC does not permit private-purchase agreements by offerors during the course of a takeover bid.[173]

The Australian dimension of this problem has arisen because CASA, although it does not impose any obligation to make a follow-up bid, requires acquisitions that will give the purchaser 20% voting control of the target to be made through a bid to all shareholders or through a regulated stock exchange bid. In one case before the NCSC, Company A owned 49.9% of the shares of Company B; another company, C, entered into an agreement to buy 19.5% of the B shares held by a subsidiary of A (A's remaining shares of B were held by another subsidiary). This agreement was conditional on C acquiring 48% of B's shares (or 28.5% beyond those covered by the agreement itself). Company C made an offer to B's remaining shareholders at A$0.75 per share; the shares' market price, which had been in the A$0.80 range, jumped to A$1.01 per share. Company A, however, had an incentive to tender because the aggregate price it would receive through the negotiated transaction and acceptance of the public offer amounted to about A$40 million, or A$1.50 per share. Company A would thus receive considerably more value per share for its holdings of B than B's public shareholders. The NCSC alleged before the Supreme Court of New South Wales that this combination of agreements violated CASA; the court adjourned the proceeding pending a meeting of B's shareholders to approve the sale in which A and its associates were not to vote.[174] The central concern, under CASA as under the Ontario statute, is that related transactions not be deployed to deprive public shareholders of a full share in the benefit of sales of corporate control.

Treatment of Inferior Equity Securities

The extent to which differential treatment of securityholders (based on differences in their securities' voting rights) is tolerated varies greatly in each of these systems. In the United States, the protection of securityholders with lesser voting rights does not seem to have surfaced as a regulatory concern in the takeover context. The situation in Canada is in marked contrast. Although the Ontario Securities Act would permit a takeover bid to be restricted to one class of an issuer's securities, and the act restricts the follow-up obligation to securities of that class, no prospectus has been underwritten since 1981 that did not contain protective provisions giving holders of restricted or special voting shares the benefit of any takeover bid.[175] The same problem has been addressed in Britain through the obligation to make a follow-up offer once 30% voting control is acquired. The City Code requires that the follow-up bid be made to "the holder of any class of equity security whether voting or non-voting."[176] The protection afforded by the City Code, however, is only applicable once 30% voting control is acquired and in this respect is less complete than the protection created by the conventional Canadian underwriting practice. In Australia, protection for holders of inferior-grade equity seems weaker. The stock exchange listing requirements formerly required an offeror who was bidding for all shares in a class to make an offer for shares in other classes.[177] CASA continues this requirement only in vitiated form, by providing that an offeror who acquires 90% of a company's voting shares must give notice to all holders of nonvoting shares and convertible shares,[178] who in turn may require the offeror to purchase their securities.[179]

Mandatory Buy-outs—Problems in Implementation

Two of the jurisdictions surveyed in this chapter, Ontario and Great Britain, under some circumstances require purchasers of shares to offer to buy out the corporation's remaining shareholders. This section of the chapter develops further the difference between the buy-out obligations in Britain and Ontario, focusing primarily on difficulties that have arisen in the implementation of each.

In Britain, the City Code requires a buy-out offer when a person and those acting in concert with her acquire shares or rights over shares which give her 30% of the voting rights, when that person and her associates do not already hold shares carrying 30% or more of the target's voting rights.[180] One practical difficulty with the administration of this requirement stems from the extension of the buy-out obligation to persons "acting in concert" with the acquiring person. The applicability of the requirement to "concert parties" (in the British parlance) means that factual questions can easily arise concerning whether any particular associate of the acquiring person is indeed acting in concert to obtain control of a company,[181] and it means that the buy-out obligation may ultimately apply to persons who argue they were unaware of its applicability to them, including persons who did not themselves acquire any shares.[182] The second problem arises from the code's requirement that the mandatory offer be in cash or that it contain a cash alternative equal to the highest price paid by the offeror or its concert party over the preceding 12 months.[183] The panel's ability to achieve compliance with the buy-out requirement, however, has been frustrated in situations in which the acquiring person lacked the cash resources to implement its bidding obligation,[184] and persons acting in concert with it were, for one reason or another, likewise unable to make a cash bid.[185]

Somewhat different problems of implementation have arisen for the buy-out obligation imposed by the Ontario Securities Act. A buy-out offer is required by that statute if more than 20% of a company's voting securities are acquired in a private purchase from 14 or fewer holders at a price more than 15% above the securities' average market price for the ten business days preceding the private purchase.[186] The buy-out offer must be for consideration "at least equal in value" to that paid in the private purchase.[187] The statute's definition of the circumstances that trigger the buy-out obligation has created two separate administrative problems for the Ontario Securities Commission. First, because the statute permits the mandatory bid to offer "at least equal value," the OSC has devoted many hours of hearing time to valuation questions concerning the comparative merits of different packages of securities.[188] The necessity for administrative consideration of such a question is, in contrast, reduced by the City Code in Britain, which requires that all mandatory offers be for cash or contain a cash alternative. Second, the buy-out obligation in Ontario is triggered by the payment of a price under the private agreement that exceeds average market price by more than 15%, and this definition of the trigger event has led the OSC to scrutinize closely the composition of the reported market price. For example, the OSC appears to be open to the argument that reported market price was artificially high because it anticipated a takeover bid or because it had been manipulated, and thus that the "true" market price was lower than the reported price and the purchaser paid a sufficiently high premium over "true market price" in the private purchase to trigger a buy-out obligation.[189] In contrast, the City Code's buy-out obligation does not employ a trigger premised on market price, and thus the question of credibility of market price does not arise.

The timing of the buy-out offer may also create difficulties. Under the Ontario statute, the offeror has 180 days after the private purchase to make a follow-up bid. The potential lag of six months may make the follow-up bid impracticable, owing to changes in the market for target shares or in the offeror's financial position; the length of the lag time may also call into question whether the target's shareholders are truly being offered equivalent consideration and whether they should be compensated for the delay by a payment of interest.[190] The City Code, in contrast to the Ontario statute, does not contain any bright-line test for timing the follow-up bid. The offeror has an incentive to make the bid promptly because under the code, except with the panel's consent, no nominee of persons obligated to make a follow-up offer may be appointed to the board of the offeree company until the mandatory offer document is posted, nor may the offeror or its concert party exercise votes attaching to any share in the offeree company until the offer document is posted.[191]

The difficulty with the Ontario requirement that legally appears most vexatious is its potential for extraterritorial application. The Ontario statute, including the follow-up obligation, applies as long as one shareholder of the target company has a last address in Ontario on the company's books, even though the target is not incorporated in Ontario and the purchase triggering the follow-up obligation takes place outside Ontario. As no other Canadian jurisdiction has chosen to impose buy-out obligations, Ontario's application of its statute to transactions in shares of companies incorporated in other provinces that are executed outside Ontario is seen, at least in some circles, as an affront to intra-Canadian comity.[192] Problems of this sort are inevitable, however, in federal systems with inconsistent bodies of state law where no supervening federal statute applies to the question and where no unanimously assented-to principle clearly establishes states' relative prerogatives.[193]

THE SIGNIFICANCE OF RULES IN SHAPING TRANSACTIONAL CLIMATES

Thus far, the chapter has discussed differences among takeover environments and among legal (and extralegal) rules regulating takeover transactions in four countries.

Whether these two types of differences are connected is examined next. This section of the chapter identifies four respects in which takeover environments seem to differ markedly and traces them, at least in part, to differences among rules governing transactions and rules determining the availability of particular types of transactions.

Hostile Bidders' Success and Failure

The success of hostile bidders in acquiring control of targets seems to vary among jurisdictions: for example, as the second section, "The Takeover Environment," illustrates, the "failure rate" of bidders appears to be higher in the United States than in Britain. Some of this divergence can be explained by differences among the rules defining the transactional environment in which the bid is made. For example, in the United States target managements are more free than in Britain to participate aggressively in takeover contests and, in particular, are able to ease the entrance of friendly bidders into the contest, subject to the constraints of fiduciary duty. Indeed, in the United States target managers are free to participate in bidding groups proposing to buy out the company's stockholders and finance its operations principally through debt; as noted earlier, company law in Britain and Australia limits the availability of leveraged buy-out transactions. Furthermore, the Williams Act rules in the United States may, on balance, encourage more bidding contests than would otherwise occur by granting target shareholders additional rights to withdraw tendered shares, triggered by the appearance of a competing bid.

Thus, the basic legal framework in the United States may make contested bids more likely, and although this likelihood does not mean that more targets will ultimately remain independent, it does reduce the initial hostile bidder's chance for success. Correspondingly, however, the likelihood of contested bids may also increase the premium received on average by target shareholders. To be sure, factors other than the rules applicable to takeover transactions also affect whether competing bids will be made, including the number of prospective bidders who are active in any given market.

Partial Bids

Another difference among the transactional climates discussed in this chapter that can be partly attributed to differences among rules is the prevalence of partial bids in one country (Australia) and their striking paucity in another (Britain). As noted previously, the City Code in Britain has rules that make partial bids unattractive; the code further requires consent of the Take-Over Panel for such bids. None of the other jurisdictions regulates partial bids so sharply as to discourage them, a fact that explains the relative infrequency with which such bids are made in Britain.

The relative popularity of such bids in Australia is more resistant to explanation in terms of divergent rules, for the rules applicable to partial bids in the United States are not so different from those in Australia as to explain why many more bids in Australia are partial offers. One possible explanation is simply the demographic differences between the two countries. Australia, despite its vast landmass, has less than one-tenth the population of the United States[194] and, correspondingly, much smaller financial markets. Australia also has a few individuals who, through complex holding company structures, own controlling interests in hundreds of Australian companies but do not necessarily own all the shares of those companies.[195] In short, the prevalence of the partial bid in Australia may be explained by the activity of a relatively small number of active bidders, who seek to diversify their holding companies' "portfolios" by making partial bids for more targets rather than any-and-all share bids for fewer targers.

Defensive Transactions

The jurisdictions discussed in this chapter also differ significantly in the role that can be played by target management in contesting a hostile takeover bid. In the United States and Canada, few constraints are placed on management by the rules specifically regulating takeovers; in both systems the propriety of management's action is tested by fiduciary standards, and considerable leeway is available to management. Although recent cases have reduced management's prerogatives under some circumstances in the United States, in both countries the cases regard management as properly playing an agressive defensive role, on behalf of the target and its shareholders, and in both countries many types of defensive transactions are available toward that end. Management's defensive role is more modest in Britain and in Australia. In Britain, the City Code requires that shareholders vote to approve defensive transactions when a takeover bid is outstanding or when such a bid appears to be likely. Target management may, however, attempt to persuade shareholders not to tender and may attempt to lay defensive fortifications in advance of a bid. Target management is similarly constrained in Australia by statute and by judicial interpretations of managers' fiduciary obligations. CASA requires target shareholder approval for defensive share allotments of 20% or more. Furthermore, the defensive buy-out transaction, for the reason explained in the third section, is not available in Australia. Finally, in both countries the basic norm of company law that directors are removable without cause by majority vote of the shareholder further limits target management's defensive options.

Postbid Transaction

These jurisdictions' rules also differ in the limits placed on transactions in the wake of a successful takeover bid. In Britain, and under some circumstances in Ontario, once a defined threshold of shareownership is attained, the person acquiring those shares must offer to buy out the other shareholders on comparable terms. Thus, acquiring effective control under these rules entails an obligation to offer to buy all shares, thereby increasing the cost of acquiring effective control. In contrast, in the

United States and Australia, an offeror who obtains effective control is under no obligation to offer to buy out the remaining shareholders. Indeed, the United States permits a cash bid for a legal majority of the target's shares to be followed by a merger transaction in which the remaining shareholders receive different (noncash) consideration, subject only to an appraisal remedy provided by state law. On the other hand, nothing in the United States would prohibit a corporation's shareholders and directors from adopting charter amendments to require equal treatment of shareholders in the event of a shift in effective control.

CONCLUSION

The comparative analysis of institutions and legal rules in this chapter illustrates two basic points about corporate takeovers: First, that whether hostile takeovers occur in any system depends on patterns of shareownership, control, and voting, which can readily be manipulated to pretermit hostile bids; and second, that the countries in which hostile bids occur with frequency differ greatly in the constraints imposed on bidders and on managements of target firms. Indeed, takeover regulation in each of these countries seems to strike a different balance between the strategic positions of hostile bidders and target management. The United States regulates bidders with a markedly lighter hand than do the other three countries. Bidders are not required to make a general all-holders bid if any particular level of shareownership is sought, nor are they required to make follow-up offers to noncontrolling shareholders after a trigger point of shareownership is passed. Partial bids are not especially discouraged by regulation, and bidders may freely condition their offers. Under these rules, a person may acquire effective control of a corporation without being put to the cost of acquiring noncontrolling shares at a price equivalent to that paid for the shares conferring control. But target management enjoys considerable strategic flexibility as well. Organic corporate law in

the United States does not preclude such transactions as defensive share repurchases, selective issuer tender offers, and leveraged management buy-outs. The protective reach of the "business judgment" approach, to test the fiduciary propriety of the use of defensive tactics, is still extensive, although some recent cases have declined to indulge defensive lockup transactions in which target management's preference for one bidder over another is vulnerable to attack as self-interested or insufficiently considered.

In Britain, the rules of the Take-Over Panel make acquisition of effective control a more expensive proposition for the acquiring party, who must offer to buy out the target's remaining shareholders once the 30% threshold is passed. Partial bids are specifically discouraged, especially those that would give the bidder effective control of the target. The bidder's ability to condition the bid is limited by regulation. Target management, on the other hand, is significantly more inhibited than in the United States in its ability to defend aggressively against hostile bids. The City Code requires target shareholders approval for defensive measures that could terminate the bid, and statutory company law limits the target's ability to use defensive share repurchases and lend financial assistance to preferred bidding groups. The City Code's restrictions on target management are consistent with judicial interpretations in Britain of management's fiduciary duties, which historically have recognized in shareholders a right, external to the directors' powers over the company, to assemble majority positions.

Target managers in Canada are in a position quite close to that of their counterparts south of the U.S. border. Organic corporate law enables managers to deploy a wide range of defensive transactions; their use is tested by a standard that gives primacy to the directors' business motivations. The use of defensive share issuances, however, appears to be more inhibited in Canada owing to the Toronto Stock Exchange's reservation of power to consider whether any such transaction should be tested by a plebiscite of the issuing company's shareholders. The costs associated with acquiring control of a Canadian company vary depending on the provincial regulation applicable to the transaction. Under the Ontario statute, acquisitions over a 20% threshold must be made through an all-holders bid, and exempt private acquisitions of 20% blocks must be followed by an offer to buy out the other shareholders. Although partial bids are permitted, the bidder's ability to condition any offer is limited to types of conditions specified in the statute.

In Australia, bidders are free to make partial offers, but as in Ontario, acquisitions over a 20% threshold must be structured through an all-holders bid. The offeror's use of conditioning language in its bid is regulated by statute only if it seeks to make on-market purchases during the offer, in contrast to the regulation of conditions in Ontario and Britain. On the other hand, target management appears to have fewer defensive resources available to it than in the other three systems. Although the judicial response to defensive transactions appears to have mellowed in recent years, organic company law prohibits share repurchases and subject to a shareholder plebiscite the lending of financial assistance for the purchase of company's shares.

Is one of these systems clearly preferable from the standpoint of shareholders' interests generally? On this point, keep in mind that the two systems that make the acquisition of control most costly for the acquiring person (Britain and Ontario), like the other systems, have seen high levels of acquisition activity in recent years. This observation makes problematic the argument that shareholders as a group are invariably better off with rules that, by permitting bidders to minimize their costs, encourage more rather than fewer bids. The consequences of target management's differing role in these systems are difficult to assess. One possibility in the United States and Canada is that management's more aggressive defense leads, in many instances, to higher premiums to target shareholders, if management can ease the path of bidders willing to offer more. But this outcome does not occur in all instances, and in

many, management's motivations seem sufficiently in doubt that a closer regulation of its defensive capabilities is attractive.

NOTES

1. Securities and Exchange Commission, *Annual Report* (1980), 128. In 1985, 936 issues were listed on the American Stock Exchange and 2332 on the New York Stock Exchange. See *Wall St. J.*, January 2, 1986, 9B, 16B. In dollar value of recent trading volume, the Pacific Stock Exchange outranks the American, however. See Toronto Stock Exchange, *1985 Fact Book*, 53 (hereinafter cited as *TSE Fact Book*).

2. The problem of inconsistent but parallel disclosure requirements was resolved in part in 1985, when the Stock Exchange adopted directives implementing EEC Directives intended to harmonize member states' law and practice for listing on stock exchanges. The effect of the regulations is to suspend the prospectus requirements of the Companies Act 1985 for listed companies. See 1 A. Boyle & R. Sykes, *Gore-Browne on Companies* § 10.1 (44th ed. 1986).

3. The Canadian exchanges are the Alberta Stock Exchange (in Calgary), the Montreal Exchange, the Toronto Stock Exchange, the Vancouver Stock Exchange, and the Winnipeg Stock Exchange. Toronto also has a separate futures exchange.

4. As of June 1985, The Toronto Stock Exchange accounted for 76.8% of the total dollar value of shares traded in Canada. Montreal is in a distant second place with 18.7%. See *TSE Fact Book*, note 1, p. 52. By June 1985, 939 companies and 1402 issues of securities were listed on the Toronto exchange (ibid., 18), and 121 Canadian-based issues were listed both in Toronto and on an exchange in the United States (ibid., 53).

5. The capital cities (and their states) are Melbourne (Victoria), Sydney (New South Wales), Brisbane (Queensland), Adelaide (South Australia), Perth (Western Australia), and Hobart (Tasmania).

6. See R. Baxt, *An Introduction to Company Law* (1982), 328.

7. See, generally, Howard, "The Corporations Power in the Australian Constitution," in *The Corporation and Australian Society* ed. K. Lingren, H. Mason, and B. Gordon (1974), 12.

8. The creation of a national body with substantial regulatory capacity over corporate matters was a political achievement requiring considerable finesse to negotiate and subtlety to execute. See Santow, "U.S. Participation in

Australian Financial Services and Securities Markets," in *Legal Aspects of Doing Business with Australia* ed. E. Solomon, M. Brown, and R. Chambers (1984) 67–68. Some of the Australian states' traditional mistrust of organs of national government was reduced by the compact structure, which permits any state to exit from the scheme by repealing its legislation, making the federal legislation applicable in that state. Furthermore, all states have equal representation on the Ministerial Council, arguably reducing potential domination by the Commonwealth government. Finally, although the NCSC is situated in Melbourne, the Ministerial Council is in Sydney; that neither is in Canberra, Australia's national capital, evidences the pervasive Australian concern with national influence. For a general discussion of Australians' district of Canberra and its bases in Australian history, see Albinski, "Australia and the United States," *Daedalus,* Winter 1985, 395.

9. In 1984, the National Association of Securities Dealers Automated Quotation System (NASDAQ) share volume was two-thirds of the share volume of the NYSE and nearly ten times the AMEX volume. See *NASDAQ 1984 Fact Book* (1985), 11. NASDAQ's dollar volume in 1984 was $153.5 billion; indeed, it is the third largest market in the world in terms of dollar value of trading (ibid., 106). Also, 4723 securities were entered in the NASDAQ system (ibid., 10), which through computer technology enables national trading in the securities included. Although NASDAQ sets criteria for inclusion in its system (ibid., 16), its criteria concern such matters as the company's assets and public float and do not include the "regulatory" aspects of a listing agreement with a stock exchange.

10. By the end of 1980, major institutional investors accounted for 35.4% of all NYSE stock. See New York Stock Exchange, *1983 Fact Book,* 52.

11. The following breakdown was derived, as of February 1983, from the Standard & Poor's Index:

	Number of Companies	Percentage of Companies
Shareholder with legal control (50% or more)	6	1.2
Shareholder with effective control (20%–49.9%)	68	13.16
Widely held shares	426	85.2
Total	500	100%

See Securities Industry Committee on Takeover Bids, *The Regulation of Take-over Bids in Canada: Premium Private Agreement Transactions* (1983), 75, note 89 (hereinafter cited as Securities Industry Committee Report).

12. Ibid., 3. The following breakdown was derived from the companies with shares included in the Toronto Stock Exchange 300 Composite Index (ibid., 69, note 9):

	Number of Companies	Percentage of Companies
Shareholder with legal control (50% of more)	137	48.4
Shareholder with effective control (20%–49.9%)	85	30.0
Widely held shares	61	21.6
Total	283	100%

13. See Royal Commission on Corporate Concentration Report, (1978), 11–12 (hereinafter cited as Canadian Concentration Report).

14. See "Taking Aim at Takeovers," *MacLean's,* April 29, 1985, 36.

15. See Toronto Stock Exchange, "Policy Statement on Restricted Shares," 4 *Canadian Securities Law Reporter* (CCH) ¶ 815–422 (1984). The exchange recommends that a company with nonvoting or restricted-voting common shares make provision for such shares to participate, on a "fair" basis, in any premium offered for the shares with superior rights. The inclusion of such protective provisions has become standard practice since 1981 in Canadian underwritings. See Securities Industry Committee Report, note 11, p. 32.

16. Nothing in the Toronto Stock Exchange's (TSE) listing requirements excludes the use of such qualifications for shareownership, and their use in large Canadian companies has been reported. For example, in 1976 the Canadian company Brascan adopted, at its management's urging, a bylaw prohibiting foreign interests from owning more than 49% of Brascan's share. The company's institutional investors believed the change lowered the price of their shares and perceived it as a management device to perpetuate its control. See Brown, "How Jake Moore Lost Brascan," *Can. Bus.,* November 1979, 131.

17. In 1975 institutions owned 46.8% of all shares listed on the London Stock Exchange. See M. Blume, "The Financial Markets," in *Britain's Economic Performance* (1980). More recent estimates set the percentage at a higher point.

18. See The Stock Exchange, *Admission of Securities to Listing* § 9, Ch. 1, para. II (1986).

19. Ibid., Schedule VII, Part A, ¶ A.2.

20. See Secretary of State for Prices and Consumer Protection, *A Review of Monopolies and Merger Policy: A Consultative Document* (1978), 9.

21. See Santow, note 6, p. 63. At present, about 32% of shares are held in the name of persons, whereas in the early 1950s, 75% of shares were held by persons (ibid.). Trading volume on the Australian exchanges is less than comparable volumes on the Toronto and London exchanges, as well as the New York Exchange.

22. A rare exception was the $1.4 billion bid made in 1985 by Trafalgar Holdings and a British partner for Minebea, a manufacturing conglomerate in Japan. The bid, reportedly the first hostile offer for a Japanese firm made by foreign interests, ended in April 1986 when the offerors sold the shares they had acquired in Minebea. After the offer was announced, Minebea announced that it would merge with another Japanese company on terms that would give it control over 30 million shares of its own stock and would increase to 53% the shares in safe hands unlikely to tender. The offer for Minebea also met with opposition from Japan's Ministry of Finance and other agencies. See *N.Y. Times,* April 12, 1986, 19, col. 1.

23. Changes in the provisions of the English Companies Acts touching on these sorts of restrictions occurred as a result of the United Kingdom's adoption in 1980 of legislation to implement the Second Directive on Company Law adopted by the EEC's Council of Ministers in 1976. See *European Report,* January 23, 1985, 2. Under the 1980 legislation, consistent with the Second Directive, the "private company" became the residual form of corporate organization in Britain, and the "public company" form became available only for those firms meeting the qualifications prescribed by the statute, including a fixed amount of minimum capital and a requirement that one-quarter of the shares be paid up. Prior to the 1980 legislation, in Britain as currently in many American states, the public company was the residual form and the private company, like its American counterpart (under some statutes the "close corporation"), was a classification applicable only to those corporations meeting specific tests set forth in the statute. In particular, Section 28 of the Companies Act of 1948 required that the would-be private company's articles include some restriction on the transferability of its shares. The obligation to include restraints on share transfer to qualify as a "pri-

vate company" was eliminated by the 1980 legislation.

24. See, e.g., Ontario Business Corporations Act, § 42(2) (1982).

25. See Canada Business Corporations Act, § 168(1) (1982) (permitting shares offered to the public to be subject only to constraints against transfer to non-Canadian residents and to constraints necessary for the company to qualify under Canadian law to engage in particular business activities).

26. See Canadian Concentration Report, note 13, p. 4 (observing that Canadian industry has a higher proportion of foreign ownership than any other developed economy).

27. Code des Sociétés, art. 274 (6th ed. Dalloz 1985). One question raised by the language quoted in text is whether such a provision in the company's articles applies to transfers among shareholders, so that the corporation's consent is required for such a transfer. In 1976 the Cour de Cassation (France's highest court of ordinary jurisdiction) held that the reference to "a third party, whomever he may be" in Article 274 did not include shareholders of the corporation, so that a shareholder would be free to transfer his shares to another without having the transfer subject to approval by the company. *Dessalien et Renard* C. Soc. anon. Catel et Farcy, 1977 Dalloz Sirez Jurisprudence 455 (Cassation Commerciale 1976).

28. C. Soc. art. 175 (6th ed. Dalloz 1985). *Dessalien et Renard* also laid to rest some doubts concerning Article 275, which provides that if the corporation does not approve the proposed transferee of the shares, the directors or managers must, within three months after giving notice of their refusal of the transfer, cause the shares either to be purchased by a shareholder or, with the seller's consent, to be repurchased by the corporation as a reduction of its capital. The Court de Cassation held that Article 275 did not oblige shareholders to sell to the corporation, nor did it give the corporation the right to dispossess shareholders of their stock if they decide not to sell to the company. Thus the court interpreted Article 275 to mean that shareholders may renounce their intention to sell if their proposed transactions are not approved by the corporation. See 1977 D. S. Jur., 455–56.

29. See Code of Obligations, Articles 621–622, summarized in *Doing Business in Europe, Common Mkt. Rep.* (CCH) ¶ 29,215. No such restriction may be placed on bearer shares, however.

30. See T. Adams and N. Kobayashi, *The World of Japanese Business* (1969), 53. Cross-ownership patterns persist despite the fact that

the traditional holding companies and financial combines were broken up during the occupation following World War II.

31. See B. Richardson and T. Ueda, *Business and Society in Japan* (1981), 23. Nonetheless, Japanese equity markets continue to grow in attractiveness to foreign investors. Foreigners now own about 6% of shares listed in the Tokyo Stock Exchange, primarily through investment and pension funds, even though Japanese equities have an almost negligible dividend yield. See *Far Eastern Economic Review, 1984 Asia Yearbook,* 194.

32. An additional variation is created by corporate law in the Netherlands, which authorizes the use of "priority shares" in all but the very largest public companies. Priority shares may give binding instructions to the shareholder meeting. See 3 *Common Mkt. Rep.* (CCH) ¶ 26,719 (summarizing Civil Code, Book 2).

33. See *Doing Business in Europe, Common Mkt. Rep.* ¶ 21,256 (summarizing Commercial Companies Code, Article 76).

34. Ibid.

35. Ibid., ¶ 23,213. An appellate court in Germany in 1976 upheld a stockholders' resolution restricting voting rights to a 5% share (ibid.).

36. See R. Schlesinger, *Comparative Law,* 4th ed. (1980), 776–777.

37. See Grossfeld and Ebke, "Controlling the Modern Corporation: A Comparative View of Corporate Power in the United States and Europe," 26 *Am. J. Comp. L.* 397, 415 (1978).

38. See *Wall St. J.,* January 2, 1986, 6B, col. 1.

39. The term *announced takeover bid* includes schemes of arrangement to merge and offers to minority shareholders. Prior to 1981, private companies were not covered by the code.

40. See Reich, "Takeovers: An Outline of Current Practice," in *Conference on the Internationalization of the Capital Markets* (1981).

41. See *N.Y. Times,* April 10, 1986, 34, col. 1 (referring to the study by William Stanbury at the University of British Columbia).

42. The statistics on net float loss on the TSE from 1978 to August 31, 1985 are as follows:

Year	Float Loss Due to Takeovers	New Issues (C$ Billion)	Float Change
1981	6.568	1.500	−5.068
1980	1.575	3.185	+1.610
1979	2.147	1.105	−1.042
1978	2.256	0.720	−1.536

Float is calculated on the market value of shares outstanding on the TSE 300 index after a deduction for shares owned by controlling interests.

See Coleman, "Take-over Bids, Insider Bids and Going-Private Transactions—Recent Developments," in *Special Lectures of the Law Society of Upper Canada: Corporate Law in the 80s* (1982), 155.

43. See, generally, Eckbo, Mergers and the Market for Corporate Control: The Canadian Evidence (unpublished, September 1985), 2.

44. Ibid., 9–10.

45. See Coffee, "Partial Justice: Balancing Fairness and Efficiency in the Context of Partial Takeover Offers," 3 *Co. Sec. L. J.* 216, 232 (1985).

46. Ibid., 216.

47. A study of transactions in the United States, conducted by the SEC's Office of the Chief Economist, examined successful tender offers in calendar years 1981–1983 and covered 91 any-or-all offers, 32 two-tier offers, and 25 partial tender offers. The study found that the average premium for any-or-all offers was 63.4%, that the average blended premium for two-tier offers was 55.1% and that the average premium for partial offers was 31.3%. The study also examined the outcome of multiple-bidder contests over the same period, in which at least one offer was a partial or a two-tier bid. There were 26 such contests over this period, involving a total of 62 bidders. See "Two-Tier Tender Offer Pricing and Non-Tender Offer Purchase Programs," (1984–1985 Transfer Binder) *Fed. Sec. L. Rep.* (CCH) June 21, 1984, 637.

The Australian study was conducted by Professor Peter Dodd for the Companies and Securities Law Review Committee and examined offers made for companies listed on the Sydney Stock Exchange from July 1981 through June 1983. During this period there were 118 "full" offers (those for 100%), 26 partial offers (those for less than 100%), and 15 competing bids. Also, 28 bids were revised with new offer prices and closing dates. The mean premium for partial bids was 26.8% over this period. The study also computed investment returns available to target shareholders under the two strategies available to them after a bid is announced: strategy 1, accept the offer; strategy 2, sell, either when the offer is announced or when it closes. Under strategy 1, the highest return to target shareholders in full bids when the offerors accepted all tendered shares was 39.1; under strategy 2, selling at the announcement produced a mean return of 20.4, and selling at the offer's close produced a mean return of 29.3.

More recent information from Australia is

that the proportion of partial to full bids has increased since 1983.

48. The Australian government, however, imposed a capital gains tax (at ordinary income rates) on sales of assets acquired after September 19, 1985. Homes and some personal property will be exempt, and cost bases will be adjusted for the annual inflation rate. See *Wall St. J.* October 16, 1986, 1, col. 5.

Canada may also develop different taxation rules applicable to these transactions. Its national government has under consideration a proposal to make nondeductible interest paid on acquisition debt. See "Taking Aim at Takeovers," *Maclean's,* April 29, 1985. Interest on acquisition debt (i.e., on funds borrowed to acquire shares in other companies) was not deductible in Canada prior to 1972. The then–minister of finance justified the change to deductibility by arguing that if interest on acquisition debt continued to be nondeductible, Canadian corporations would continue to be "at a disadvantage when competing in takeover bids with foreign corporations, which can deduct such interest in their home country." See Bale, "The Interest Deduction to Acquire Shares in Other Corporations: An Unfortunate Corporate Welfare Tax Subsidy," 3 *Can. Tax.* 189, 1981 (1981). As on a number of other regulatory issues, the Canadian choice seems consistent with a profound commitment to Canadian nationalism, to a "Canada owned by Canadians," even if a highly concentrated economy ultimately results. Or in Professor Gordon Bale's trenchant observation, "The fact that the whale is Canadian does not necessarily make it beneficial to be swallowed" (ibid., 200).

49. The Williams Act added Sections 13(d), 13(e), 14(d), 14(e), and 14(f) to the Securities Exchange Act of 1934. See 15 U.S.C. §§ 78l; 78m(d)–(e), 78n(d)–(f).

50. See 15 U.S.C. § 78n(d) (5).

51. See 15 U.S.C. § 78n(d)(6).

52. See 15 U.S.C. § 78n(d)(5), (d)(7).

53. See 15 U.S.C. § 78m(d).

54. See President's Council of Economic Advisors, *1984 Report* (BNA Special Supplement), S–40 (1984).

55. In *Edgar v. Mite Corp.,* 457 U.S. 624 (1982), the Court held unconstitutional the Illinois Business Take-Over Act. Although a majority of the justices believed the state statute to constitute an impermissible interference with interstate commerce, five justices did not join the portion of the "majority" opinion finding that the Illinois statute was preempted by the Williams Act.

56. See, e.g., S. Rep. No. 550, 90th Cong., 1st Sess. (1967).

57. See text accompanying note 169.

58. 17 C.F.R. § 240.10b–13.

59. 199 A.2d 548 (Del. 1964).

60. Contrast *Condec Corp. v. Lunkenheimer Co.,* 43 Del. Ch. 353, 230 A.2d 769 (Del. Ch. 1967), in which the chancery court held that no showing had been made that the plaintiff represented "a reasonable threat to the continued existence" of the corporation, whose directors had issued a large block of authorized shares to a third party to abort the plaintiff's tender offer for the corporation.

61. See Cary, "Federalism and Corporate Law: Reflections upon Delaware," 83 *Yale L.J.* 663, 674–675 (1984).

62. 285 A.2d 437 (Del. 1971). In *Frantz Mfg. Co. v. EAC Industries,* 501 A.2d 402 (Del. 1985), the Delaware Supreme Court upheld a bylaw amendment, adopted through the statutory shareholder consent procedure after an acquiring person obtained control of 51% of the corporation's voting stock, that required a unanimous vote of all directors to take action, and required the presence of all directors for a quorum at meetings.

63. See *Panter v. Marshall Field & Co.,* 646 F.2d 271 (7th Cir.), *cert. denied,* 454 U.S. 1092 (1981).

64. 493 A.2d 946 (Del. 1985).

65. Ibid., 955.

66. Ibid.

67. 500 A.2d 1346 (Del. 1985).

68. Ibid., 1350.

69. Ibid., 1356.

70. 493 A.2d, 955.

71. 488 A.2d 858 (Del. 1985).

72. 506 A.2d 173 (Del. 1986).

73. The target had previously offered to buy out 10 million shares of its common stock in exchange for subordinated notes and preferred stock. The noteholders threatened to sue after the market price of the notes fell when the target announced its intention to accept the buy-out proposal.

74. 744 F.2d 255 (2d Cir. 1984).

75. [Current] Fed. Sec. L. Rep. (CCH) ¶ 92, 418 (2d Cir. January 6, 1986).

76. In *Hanson Trust,* however, unlike *Revlon,* although the target's board knew some of its officers would obtain equity in the new company, their identity had not been disclosed at the time the buy-out agreement was first approved by the target's directors.

77. One recent Delaware case suggests that the duty owed to stockholders may be different if the directors act to undo the consequences of a successful completed takeover bid. In *Frantz Mfg. Co. v. EAC Industries,* 501 A.2d 401 (Del. 1985), the target board issued a large block of

stock to an Employee Stock Option Plan (ESOP) after the unwelcome acquiring party obtained 51% of its voting stock and submitted shareholder consents to amend the target's by-laws to protect its position. The court held that the board's retrospective defense was not protected by the business judgment rule and constituted inequitable conduct.

78. See Panel on Take-Overs and Mergers, *The City Code on Take-Overs and Mergers, Rule 24* (1985) (hereinafter cited as City Code).

79. Ibid., Rule 31.1.

80. Ibid., Rule 36.7 ("Scaling Down").

81. Under Rule 34 of the City Code, target shareholders must have the right to withdraw shares after 21 days from the first closing date of the initial offer, if that offer has not by that date become or been declared unconditional as to offeree acceptances. Rule 10 requires, for any offer that if successful would result in the offeror holding more than 50% of the voting rights in the target, that the offer provide that it will not be declared unconditional unless the offeror has acquired or receives acceptance giving it over 50% of the voting rights. The net effect of this requirement is that the target stockholder may tender, wait to see whether the bidder acquires the mandatory minimum, and then "detender" the shares and "retender" them to any subsequent bidder, if the bidder fails to achieve the mandatory minimum.

82. City Code, note 78, Rule 13.

83. The offeror is under a duty imposed by Rule 27.1 to include any material change in its shareholdings in its communications with offeree shareholders after the offer is made.

84. City Code, note 78, Rules 36.1 and 36.2.

85. Ibid., Rule 36.3.

86. Ibid., Rule 36.5.

87. See Gonski and Keenan, "Partial Takeovers," 7 *Univ. N.S.W.L.J.* 7, 217 (1984).

88. City Code, note 78, Rule 9.

89. Shareholders in British companies who object to such treatment appear to be in a weaker position than their American counterparts to resolve their problem through litigation. For a full development of this comparison, see D. A. DeMott, "Current Issues in Tender Offer Regulation: Lessons from the British," 58 *N.Y.U. L. Rev.* 945, 992–993 (1983).

90. City Code, note 78, Rule 1.

91. Ibid., Rule 3.1.

92. Ibid., Rule 19.4. The unwelcome offeror must, nonetheless, ask specific questions of the target company and cannot simply ask in general terms for all information provided to its competitor (ibid.).

93. Ibid., Rule 21.

94. Ibid., Rule 37.3(a). If the effect of a share repurchase or redemption is to give the directors and persons acting in concert with them 30% of the company's voting rights, they are obliged to make a follow-up bid to the remaining shareholders, subject to possible waiver by the panel if an independent vote of stockholders occurs and procedures prescribed by the panel for seeking the waiver are followed [Ibid., Rule 37.3 and Appendix A ("Whitewash Guidance Note")].

95. See *Times (London),* March 27, 1986, 21, col. 2. The City Code now restricts to categories specified in the code permissible types of advertising by offerors or offeree companies during a takeover. Some types of advertising require the panel's advance clearance. The panel is strongly of the view that financial advisors are responsible for guiding their clients and public relations advisors in dealings with the media during takeovers. See The Panel on Take-Overs and Mergers, Report on the Year ended 31st March 1986 (1986), 7–8

96. [1967] 1 Ch. 254 (1963).

97. Ibid., 269–270.

98. *Cayne v. Global National Resources P.L.C.,* unreported, Chancery Div., August 12, 1982 (Megarry, V.C.), *aff'd on other grounds,* [1984] 1 All E.R. 225 225 (Ct.Ap. 1982) (denying plaintiff's motion for an interlocutory injunction). Vice-Chancellor Megarry's opinion is noted in 56 *Aust. L.J.* 600 (1982).

99. See 56 *Aust. L.J.* 600.

100. Another question raised in the British literature is whether the principle of *Hogg v. Cramphorn* applies to a target company that is the object or victim of a "dawn raid," i.e., the purchase on the Stock Exchange of up to 29.9% of the company's shares at a premium price in a matter of minutes. See Lazarides, "The Fiduciary Duties of Company Directors," 1983 *City of London L. Rev.* 67, 75 (part 2). Dawn raids, however, have been regulated since 1980 by rules that apply to acquisitions of 10% or more of a target's share within any seven-day period, if the acquiring person will as a result own 15% of the voting rights in the target. These rules require that any such acquisition be made either through a partial offer recommended by the target's board and subject to the rules of the City Code, or through an offer on the Stock Exchange announced at least seven days before the offer closes. See Council for the Securities Industry, *The Rules Governing Substantial Acquisitions of Shares* (1985). Dawn raids were objectionable because they enabled the purchaser to acquire either effective control or a substantial toehold at an inflated price and then to wait for the price of target shares to drop before making an offer (at a lower price) to the remaining shareholders.

If the anti-dawn raid rules effectively reduce the risk that this sequence of transactions will occur, the justification for defensive share allotments by the target's board is weakened accordingly.

101. Companies Act, § 303(1) (1985).

102. Del. Code tit. 8, § 141 (k). A director who has been elected through cumulative voting cannot be removed if the number of shares cast against the resolution to remove would be sufficient to elect, if voted cumulatively.

103. See *Bushell v. Faith*, [1970] A.C. 1099 (H.L.). This result was reached in a majority of the speeches by assuming that Parliament could have prohibited such a use of weighted voting had it chosen to do so. Lord Morris's dissenting speech argued that the outcome thwarted the purpose of § 184 by making a director irremovable and thereby made a mockery of the law. (ibid., 1106). Lord Donovan rejoined that Lord Morris's argument necessarily assumed that Parliament "*intended* to cover every possible case and block up every loophole" (ibid., 1110; emphasis in original). He viewed that assumption as unwarranted:

There may be good reasons why Parliament should leave *some* companies with freedom of manoeuvre in this matter. There are many small companies which are conducted in practice as though they were little more than partnerships, particularly family companies running a family business; and it is, unfortunately, sometimes necessary to provide some safeguard against family quarrels having their repercussions in the boardroom. (ibid., 1110–1111; emphasis added).

The difficulty with this argument is that the majority's position does not limit the use of weighted voting only to *some* companies but enables all to insulate directors against removal through removal-triggered weighted voting. For this device to be effective, however, in a publicly held company, either the directors must own many shares or the weighting factor must be very large.

104. On a not entirely unrelated matter, the Judicial Committee upheld, on an appeal from a New Zealand case, an employment contract with a managing director that entitled him to a lump-sum payment equal to five times his gross annual salary, grossed up for income tax purposes, in the event of a takeover of the company. See *The Taupa Totera Lumber Co., Ltd., v. Rowe*, [1977] 3 All. E.R. 123 (P.C.).

105. Companies Act, §§ 572–605 (1985).

106. See Securities Industry Committee Report, note 11, p. 5.

107. The securities bar in Canada appears to view with dismay the prospect that the Ontario Securities Commission could use its consider-able statutory powers to compel compliance with the Ontario legislation when the issuer involved is listed on the Toronto Stock Exchange but is not incorporated in Ontario, and the vendors and purchasers of securities are not Ontario residents. The use of the TSE listing for this purpose has been pejoratively termed the "sandbox theory." See Coleman, note 42, p. 210.

108. The Ontario statute applies to a transaction if at least one owner of the voting securities covered by the offer has a last address in Ontario on the target's books. Thus, the statute may apply to transactions completed outside Ontario; if no vendor is an Ontario resident, the statute is inapplicable unless shares were transferred to a non-Ontario resident for the purpose of avoiding the statute. See the Securities Act (Ontario) § 88(1)(f) (defining "offeree").

109. The takeover provisions of the Canada Business Corporations Act (CBCA), in contrast, are triggered by acquisition of 10% of the voting securities of a CBCA company. See Canada Business Corporations Act § 187.

110. See The Securities Act (Ontario) § 89(1)8.

111. See The Securities Act (Ontario) § 91(1).

112. Ontario Securities Commission, Securities Act Regulation § 163(3), in 3 *Can. Sec. L. Rep.* (CCH) ¶ 50–540b.

113. See 2 V. Alboini, Securities Law and Practice, at § 19.3.12.

114. See, e.g., Committee to Review the Provisions of the Securities Act (Ontario) Relating to Take-over Bids and Issuer Bids, *Report* (September 23, 1983), 15–16. This report proposed that the obligation to make a follow-up bid be eliminated from the statute and that, in its stead, "private agreements" exempt from the general offer requirement be prohibited if they involved a price in excess of 115% of market price averaged over the 20 preceding days (ibid., 16). The nature of the proposed substitute for the follow-up bid—denying an exemption from the obligation to make an all-holders bid if a premium of more than 15% is paid to 14 or fewer shareholders—makes it apparent that Ontario's narrow buy-out requirement was a response to perceived inequalities surrounding sales of control shares by small numbers of shareholders. The report's recommended substitution found its way into legislation proposed by the Ontario government, [see Bill 159, *An Act to Ammend the Securities Act*, 4th Sess., 32nd Legislature (Ontario), 33 Elizabeth II, 1984] at 5–7, but did not go past its first reading, owing to a change in governments.

115. The current version of the Ontario statute was adopted following a 1973 study of the

law pertinent to mergers. A majority of the study committee supported the retention of the exemption for private agreements from regulation as takeover bids and opposed any mandatory buy-out requirement. A minority of the committee supported the imposition of a buy-out requirement when a person became the owner of 20% of the shares through a private agreement. See *1973 Report on Mergers, Amalgamations and Certain Related Matters by Select Committee on Company Law,* 3rd Sess., 29th Legislature, 22 Elizabeth II, 1973. See, generally, Leclerc, "The Sale of Control and the Ontario Follow-up Offer," 23(1) *Les cahiers de droit* 35 (1982).

116. See The Securities Act, 1982 Qué. Stat. Ch. 48, § 116(1). This section of the statute limits the private purchase exemption to bids made "at a price limited to the margin established by regulation. . . . " The price limit has been set by regulation at 15% over the average closing quotation over the ten trading days preceding the bid. Qué. Sec. Act, Regulations § 187.

117. See Securities Industry Committee Report, note 11, p. 32.

118. See The Securities Act (Ontario) § 89(1)12.

119. See the text accompanying note 82.

120. The Ontario statute permits shareholders to withdraw shares within the first ten days after the bid is made but does not grant additional withdrawal rights if a competing bid is made. See The Securities Act (Ontario) § 89(1)4; 2 V. Alboini, Securities Law and Practice 19–57 (1984).

121. See, e.g., Ontario Business Corporations Act § 122(1). Directors elected exclusively by a class or series of shares are removable only by an ordinary resolution passed by holders of that class or series (ibid.).

One question about removal of directors in Canada is whether directors can be protected against that risk by holding shares with a weighted-voting feature triggered solely by a resolution for removal, a possibility validated under the British Companies Act of 1948 in *Bushell v. Faith;* see note 103. A possible limitation is § 22(3) of the Ontario corporation statute, which provides that where a corporation has only one class of shares, "rights of holders thereof are equal in all respects and include the rights, (a) to vote at all meetings. . . . " The Ontario statute also permits articles to authorize the creation of shares in classes or series and to authorize directors to fix their number, rights, and attendant restrictions [ibid., § 25(1)]. Furthermore, CBCA, § 6(4), specifies that a corporation's articles cannot require a greater number of shareholder votes to remove a director than

would be required for an ordinary resolution. The Canadian literature recommends other techniques for insulating directors against the risk of removal. One Canadian authority mentions corporate cross ownership of shares as a way to protect directors against removal by shareholders. See Iacobucci, "Planning and Implementing Defenses to Take-over Bids: The Directors' Role," 5 *Can. Bus. L.J.* 131, 143 (note 39) (1981). The same authority (p. 149) also mentions the limitation of shareholders to a maximum vote regardless of the number of shares held.

122. See Canada Business Corporations Act, § 6(1)(c).

123. This aspect of the CBCA has been criticized. See Iacobucci, note 121, p. 147.

124. See *Unocal Corp. v. Pickens,* [Current] Fed. Sec. L. Rep. (CCH) ¶ 92,296 (C.D. Cal. May 1, 1985) (denying a motion for a preliminary injunction against the completion of a self-tender offer with exclusionary condition). The SEC, however, has since imposed all-holders requirements on tender offers made by issuers for their own shares and on tender offers made by third parties. See Rule 13e–4(f)(8) (issue tender offer) and Rule 14d–10 (third-party offer).

125. See *Unocal Corp. v. Mesa Petroleum Co.,* 493 A.2d 946 (Del. 1985).

126. The Securities Act (Ontario), § 89(1)1.

127. 33 D.L.R. 3d 288, 315 (1972). If this language recalls that of Vice-Chancellor Megarry in *Cayne v. Global Natural Resources P.L.C.,* (see text accompanying note 98), the connection is that the vice-chancellor's opinion in *Cayne* cites *Teck Corporation* as support for the proposed limitation in *Hogg v. Cramphorn.* To an American reader, a striking feature of this entire body of cases is the endurance of the British Commonwealth in complementary and cross-citing legal authorities, in an era in which the Commonwealth as a trading union has weakened and its perpetuation in formal sovereignty relationships has been vitiated as well.

128. 33 D.L.R., 330–331.

129. Ibid., 312. But see *Coleman v. Myers,* [1977] 2 N.Z. L.R. 298 (suggesting that in circumstances of case directors owe a general fiduciary duty to shareholders).

130. A measurable consequence of this differences is the length of judicial opinions applying the two tests: The court's opinion in *Hogg v. Cramphorn* is 10 pages; in *Teck Corporation* it is 43 pages!

131. See, e.g., Ontario Business Corporations Act, § 247.

132. Ibid., § 247(3). See, generally, Kaufman, "Oppression Remedies: Recent Developments," in *Corporate Structure, Finance and*

Operations, ed. L. Sarna (1984), 67; Beck, "Minority Shareholders Rights in the 1980's," in *Special Lectures of the Law Society of Upper Canada: Corporate Law in the 80s* (1982), 311.

133. Shareholder approval, under the bylaw, may be required if "in the opinion of the Exchange" the proposed transaction may materially affect control of the company, or the transaction has not been negotiated at arm's length, or it "is of such a nature to make shareholder approval desirable, having regard to the interests of the company's shareholders and the investing public." See Toronto Stock Exchange, General By-Law, § 19.06(2). In contrast, in the United States, the New York and American stock exchanges have adopted what amounts to a bright-line test for shareholder approval, triggered by share allotments that would increase the outstanding common shares by 18.5%. See *NYSE Company Manual,* A–283; *AMEX Company Guide,* § 7.3.

134. See Companies (Acquisition of Shares) Act, § 60 (1980) (hereinafter cited as CASA).

135. See City Code, note 78, General Principles, Introduction.

136. See CASA, note 134, § 11. For a discussion of the definitional sections of CASA, see Deutsch, "Takeovers and the Scope of the Companies (Acqusition of Shares) (N.S.W.) Code," 11 *Aust. Bus. L.J.* 205 (1983).

137. In *N.C.S.C. v. Industrial Equity Ltd.,* (1982) 1 A.C.L.C. (Sup. Ct. N.S.W.), the court held that the NCSC lacked statutory power to compel an offeror to proceed with an offer, in very complicated circumstances involving, *inter alia,* an arguable breach of CASA, § 11.

138. See CASA § 13(1). This exception is inapplicable if the exempt acquisition would contravene § 11 with regard to the shares of another company.

139. Ibid., § 12(g).

140. CASA, although it defines (in § 6) a set of conditioning events or "prescribed occurrences" concerning the target, can be read not to *limit* the offeror to those specified conditions. See H. Ford, *Company Law,* 3rd ed. (1982), 520. CASA also forecloses the offeror's ability to make market purchases during the bid if the offer is subject to conditions other than those specified in § 13(4)(b), which are the "prescribed occurrences" for the target, minimum acceptable conditions, and any other conditions approved by the commission. The "prescribed occurrences" include a number of events that would reduce the value of the target's assets or increase the number of target shares outstanding. The NCSC has issued a general policy statement concerning conditions in bids that acknowledges that the scope of § 13(3) & (4) is

limited to circumstances in which the offeror desires to assert additional conditions and buy on the market. See *NCSC Policy Statement: Approval of Conditions,* Release No. 107 (1985).

141. See CASA, § 26. Whether partial bids should be subject to additional or different regulation has been under discussion in Australia, at least in part because 40% of recent offers have been partial bids. The Companies and Securities Law Review Committee recommended to the Ministerial Council that bidders making partial offers be required to make them on a proportional rather than a prorated basis—i.e., for example, that a bidder be allowed only to offer to buy 30% of the holdings of each shareholder rather than, as at present, be allowed to bid for 30% of all shares and then prorate acceptances if the bid is oversubscribed. See Companies and Securities Law Review Committee, *Report to the Ministerial Council on Partial Takeover Bids* (August 1985). The Ministerial Council adopted this proposal and CASA now requires that such bids be made on a proportional basis. See CASA, § 16(2)(a), 16(2)(f)(iii). The statute was further amended in 1986 to permit a company, in its constituent documents (i.e., its articles), to require that any partial bid for its shares be subject to approval or disapproval by a shareholder plebiscite. See CASA, § 31A. But the stock exchanges have threatened to delist companies that adopt these plebiscite provisions, despite statutory language providing for plebiscites "not withstanding anything in the business or listing rules of the exchange." See Potter, "Plebiscite Stance Likely This Week," *Aust. Fin. Rev.,* October 1, 1986, 27. Nonetheless, the exchanges were reported to be unlikely to confront their largest listed company (BHP) over its adoption of a plebiscite requirement for partial bids. See *The Age,* October 1, 1986, 29, col. 4.

142. Whether the absence of withdrawal rights in itself inhibits the appearance of competing bids is an open question. At least some Australian observers believe that their absence means only that shareholders wait until the proverbial last moment in order to tender, awaiting until the very end of any bid's duration the appearance of a competing bid. Other observers differ; see Coffee, note 45, p. 233. A separate and separable question is the significance of additional withdrawal rights specifically triggered by the appearance of a competing bid. Such rights are created in the United States by the SEC's Rule 14d–7(a)(2) under the Williams Act; not only do they permit shareholders to withdraw, they also prolong the contest and enhance the prospect of successive bid topping. Additionally, CASA, § 31, provides that if the offeror

makes purchases outside the bid at a higher price, the terms of the bid shall be deemed to be varied to offer the higher price.

143. For example, the Ontario statute authorizes corporations to amalgamate on the basis of an agreement entered into by each corporation, which must then be submitted to a shareholder meeting by the directors of each corporation and approved by special resolution of the holders of each class or series entitled to vote thereon (§§ 174–175). "Special resolutions" under this statute require a two-thirds majority vote to pass [§ 1(43)].

144. See text accompanying note 105.

145. Under the Australian Companies Code, a "compromise or arrangement" requires court approval, and approval by 75% of the members or class of members if the "arrangement" is with only one class (§ 315). The "compromise or arrangement" section includes reconstructions or amalgamations with another company and requires court approval for all such transactions (§ 317).

146. See Companies Code, § 225 (1981).

147. See text accompanying note 103.

148. See Companies Code, § 129(1)(b) & (5). Until relatively recently, the British Companies Acts contained the same prohibition, apparently grounded in the view that the company's capitalization in common stock represents an ongoing and irreducible representation to its creditors. In Britain, the Companies Act (1981) permitted an issuer to repurchase its own shares if procedures set forth in the statute were followed, subject to shareholder approval of the transaction by ordinary resolution. See Companies Act, §§ 46–49 (1981). The Companies Act of 1985 carries over these provisions. See Companies Act, §§ 162–169 (1985).

149. See Companies Code, § 129(10)(a) (1981). In Britain, under the Companies Act of 1981, companies were likewise prohibited from lending financial assistance for the purchase of their own shares, but transactions were excepted from the prohibition if the company's "principal purpose" in giving the assistance was not to give it for the purpose of the acquisition but as an incidental part of some larger purpose of the company, and if the assistance was given in good faith in the company's interests. [Companies Act, § 42(1), (3) (1981)]. The bar on financial assistance was also not violated by a company's repurchase of its own shares [ibid., § 42(5)(g)]. These rules are now part of the Companies Act, §§ 151–153 (1985).

150. The greater complexity of the relevant Australian statutes suggests, if anything, a higher degree of adeptness.

151. See Companies Code, § 129(8)(a). In-

deed, the Australian literature expressly discusses the dividend route as a way to decrease the acquiring party's costs. See Gonski & Keenan, note 87, p. 232. On the other hand, if the acquisition were made through a partial bid, so that dividend payments must be made to other shareholders in addition to the bidder, the target's assets will be reduced by a greater proportion than the reduction in the offeror's effective costs, a phenomenon termed "leakage" of assets (ibid.).

152. In 1975 Australia abolished the right of appeal to Privy Council from judgments of its High Court; likewise, there is no appeal as of right from judgments of the state supreme courts to the High Court. In consequence, the number of appeals brought to Privy Council from the supreme courts has increased. In effect, since 1975 there have been two courts of ultimate appeal from judgments of the supreme courts, leading in some instances to conflicting precedents binding on a state's supreme court. Some Australian litigants apparently find it cheaper—or for other reasons preferable—to appeal from judgments of single state supreme court judges to Privy Council than to appeal to the full supreme court and then seek special leave to appeal to the High Court, and some litigants institute appeals to Privy Council at the same time as applying for special leave to appeal to the High Court. See Gibbs, "The State of the Judicature," 59 *L. Inst. J.* 968, 970 (1985). Indeed, one Australian judge has observed that "the law of New South Wales is growing relatively more quickly in London than in Canberra" (ibid.). But this situation will not continue indefinitely: Agreement has been reached among the Australian Commonwealth, the states, and British authorities to abolish the remaining right of appeal to Privy Council (ibid.). The current chief justice of Australia, although acknowledging with regret the impending rupture of the tie between British and Australian lawyers, nonetheless emphasizes "the urgency of the need to close this chapter in our judicial history" (ibid.).

153. [1974] A.C. 821 (P.C.).

154. Ibid., 837. In an earlier Australian case, *Mills v. Mills,* (1938) C.L.R. 150, 185–186, the emphasis of the court's analysis is instead on the substantial object the company's directors sought to achieve.

155. [1974] A.C. at 838.

156. Ibid., 836.

157. Ibid., 837.

158. Nonetheless, to state that *Howard Smith* thereby takes the position that *Hogg v. Cramphorn* was wrong may be too strong (see Lazarides, note 100, p. 78), because the treat-

ment of *Teck Corporation* in *Howard Smith* is simply too brief to support such a strong reading.

159. Of some relevance may be that the judgment reviewed by the Judicial Committee in *Howard Smith* contained a specific finding that, assuming the target company to be in need of raising more capital, issuing debentures rather than shares would have been more appropriate for it [(1972) 2 N.S.W.L.R. 85].

160. (1983) 8 A.C.L.R. 19, 1 A.C.L.C. 1294 (Sup. Ct. Queensl.).

161. See CASA, § 12(g).

162. In contrast, the Ontario statute, although it bears certain structural similarities to CASA as noted earlier, does not seem to require that a defensive placement of shares be interpreted as a "takeover bid" to which the requirement of a general all-holders offer would be applicable. Even though § 88(1)(k)(ii) of the Ontario statute defines *takeover bid* to include acceptances of offers to sell, the statute also excepts, in § 88(2)(c), offers to purchase through agreements with fewer than 15 security holders. See also 2 V. Alboini, note 113, § 19.2.11 (1982) (*takeover bid* was interpreted not to encompass the purchase of treasury shares from the issuer), and § 19.1.11 (a general discussion of available defensive tactics, including share allotments to friendly parties).

163. AASE Official List Requirement, § 3R(3).

164. See (1983) 8 A.C.L.R., 208.

165. CASA, § 50.

166. See Ford, note 140, p. 536.

167. See O'Bryan, "New Court Requirements Can Make Takeovers 'Absurdly Complex,'" 59 *L. Inst. J.* 74, 75 (1985).

168. See Gonski and Keenan, note 87, p. 253 (note 43).

169. See, e.g., *Hanson Trust PLC v. SCM Corp.*, 774 F.2d 47 (2d Cir. 1985); *Kennecott Copper Corp. v. Curtis-Wright Corp.*, 449 F.Supp. 951, 961 (S.D.N.Y.), *aff'd* in relevant part, 584 F.2d 1195, 1206–1207 (2d Cir. 1978); *S.E.C. v. Carter Hawley Hale Stores, Inc.*, 760 F.2d 945, 949–953 (9th Cir. 1985).

170. See Coleman, note 42, p. 176.

171. Ontario Securities Commission, Policy 9.3(B)(2) and (3).

172. See Ontario Securities Act, § 91(3).

173. Notice, Consensus on Amendments to Take-Over Bids/Issuer Bid Rules, ¶ 3(b). Market purchases, however, are permitted, subject to an obligation to disclose them daily to the commission and to any exchange on which the target is listed.

174. This incident is described in Coleman, note 42, p. 206.

175. See Securities Industry Committee Report, note 11, p. 33.

176. See City Code, note 78, Rule 9.1.

177. See Gonski and Keenan, note 87, p. 228.

178. CASA, § 43(4).

179. CASA, § 43(6).

180. City Code, note 78, Rule 9.1.

181. "Acting in concert" is defined expansively in the code to "comprise persons who, pursuant to an agreement or understanding (whether formal or informal), actively cooperate, through the acquisition by any of them of shares of a company, to obtain or consolidate control . . . of that company" (ibid., B1). "Control" is defined to mean a holding of 30% or more of a company's voting rights, "irrespective of whether that holding or holdings gives *de facto* control" (ibid., B3). The code also obliges directors of the target who sell their shares to a purchaser who incurs a buy-out obligation to "ensure as a condition of the sale that the purchaser undertakes to fulfill his obligations" to make the mandatory offer. Except with the panel's consent, directors should not resign from office until the offer closes or becomes unconditional as to acceptances (ibid., Rule 9.6). Target directors who sell to a purchaser that fails to fulfill its buy-out obligation nonetheless do not appear under the code to be subject to the buy-out obligation themselves.

182. Ibid., Rule 9.2.

183. Ibid., Rule 9.5.

184. See A. Johnston, *The City Take-Over Code* (1980), 288 (describing a situation in which the purchaser lacked the financial resources to make a mandatory offer).

185. Ibid., 294–295 (a South African member of a concert party was unable to implement his obligation to make a mandatory offer owing to difficulties with the exchange control; the panel released him from obligation but directed him not to buy or sell shares in the target or lend stock to a principal purchaser, nor to frustrate any bid for the target acceptable to shareholders who would have received the mandatory offer).

186. Ontario Securities Act, § 91(1).

187. Ibid.

188. See Securities Industry Committee Report, note 11, p. 8.

189. Ibid.

190. Ibid.

191. City Code, note 78, Rule 9.7.

192. See Coleman, note 42, p. 210 (referring disparagingly to the "sandbox theory" of the OSC).

193. For a discussion of related problems in the American context, see DeMott, "Perspectives on Choice of Law for Corporate Internal

Affairs," 48 *L. Contemp. Prob.* 62 (Summer 1985); Kozyris, "Corporate Wars and Choice of Law," 1985 *Duke L.J.* 1.

194. The current population of Australia is reported to be 15,543,600. See *1986 Information Please Almanac,* 151.

195. For example, the defendant in *NCSC v. Industrial Equity Ltd.* is reported to have direct or indirect control over "some hundreds" of companies; after obtaining a substantial interest in a target through a subsidiary, it negotiates for a seat on the board of directors to gain information so that it may determine whether a takeover bid for more shares would be advisable. See (1982) A.C.L.C. 35, 38 (Sup. Ct. N.S.W. 1981).

The Regulation of Takeovers in Great Britain

PETER FRAZER

This chapter sets out briefly to explain the major aspects of British regulation of takeovers, excluding competition matters, and to fill in some of the background, in particular in areas which might be of interest in the United States at the time of writing (October 1985). It does not begin to be exhaustive.

BACKGROUND DIFFERENCES BETWEEN THE AMERICAN AND BRITISH SYSTEMS

The first point is that there is very little statutory or case law in Britain governing takeovers. We have Companies Act shareholding disclosure requirements[1] and some sections governing schemes of arrangement to merge[2] (old-style get-togethers). There is the Prevention of Fraud (Investments) Act of 1958 which, *inter alia,* governs the distribution of materials offering to acquire shares—in effect, you have to be licensed or exempted under the act to distribute takeover offer documents. Furthermore, there is a statutory instrument setting down some basic requirements for the contents of offering circulars issued by licensed dealers.[3] The Prevention of Fraud (Investments) Act will soon be replaced, but the new act is quite unlikely to make any significant changes in the takeover area.

A further aspect of importance is that we are not a litigious nation. We do not have class actions. Nor do we have contingent fees, and if you read Dickens, you will know that going to law in Britain is expensive and takes a very long time, indeed. Another point is that we do not have the federal problem that you have: Other than the differences between English and Scottish law—long may they survive, I say as a Scot—it is more or less one system.

It is one place too, for the most part, for dealing with takeover matters. The vast proportion of takeover business is done in the City—the London financial community. So the same advisers will be meeting, clashing, or cooperating with each other time and again, and to a certain extent, therefore, pulling a slick trick over an opponent is not the attractive proposition which it might be in a country where there are several major financial centers.

Another factor which has been, and may continue to be, of major significance is that, in England, the concept of an agency *directly* backed by government with great powers of rule making and great discretion in applying its rules, thus permitting a very flexible approach, is rather alien. I believe that our Parliament would be unlikely to allow such an agency great freedom. We go for black and white, and I do not think there is much opportunity to argue that the words in a bill must have been intended to mean XYZ: There is no equivalent to the practices, during a law case, of referring to "the purpose which Congress had in mind when legislating" or of using material pulled out of the congressional debates.

ORIGINS OF THE TAKE-OVER PANEL

These are some of the differences. Let me now examine how the Take-Over Code and the Take-Over Panel came into existence. I have already mentioned that to distribute offer documents, you have to be licensed or exempted under the Prevention of Fraud (Investments) Act: Banks are exempted, and the merchant banks picked up the business of advising in takeover matters when the boom in aggressive takeover bids started in the 1950s. Traditionally, the behavior of banks and bankers had been controlled by a twitch of the finger of the governor of the Bank of England, but as techniques developed, these takeover battles became too complicated for dealing with by just a twitch. There were attempts made by the merchant bankers' association, at the instigation of the governor, to write some club rules as to how a decent chap behaves in a takeover, but these rules failed as the going got tough in any particular case, the reason being that they were not administered.

Press and political criticism by the late 1960s meant that the situation could not go on, and following a particularly difficult case,[4] the then–prime minister gave a speech in which he made it clear that unless the City put its house in order as regards takeovers, it would have to face legislation. I do not think that anyone knew what such legislation might involve: The perceived abuses in takeovers had been about behavior and tactics, not lack of disclosure. Fairness and equality of treatment were some of the major issues, and I believe it is correct to say that U.S. takeover regulation at that time contained relatively little which Britain could have taken as a blueprint for legislation.

For several reasons a further attempt at nonstatutory regulation was chosen, and the governor of the Bank of England, together with the chairman of the Stock Exchange, brought into being the Take-Over Panel to administer a new set of rules based on the earlier club rules but very much stiffened up. Considerable doubts were expressed at the beginning as to whether this system could succeed— "There are no teeth; what we need is an SEC," etc.—but succeed it did, in a rather startling way in the view of some commentators.

I myself do not think it was so startling. The Take-Over Panel is made up of the chairmen or nominees of all the major City associations concerned with takeovers— the merchant bank associations, the clearing banks, the Stock Exchange, and various associations of the major investor institutions such as the National Association of Pension Funds, the Association of British Insurers, etc. Also on the panel are represented the Confederation of British Industry and the Institute of Chartered Accountants. All of these associations committed themselves in their various ways to sponsoring the new system and to making it work. It was in their interest to do so. Thus the major players were not going to flout the system. This left the panel taking a nonstatutory "right" over company directors and persons who sought to gain control of public companies. Why should they have followed the rules? Probably there were two main reasons: First, because of the legal requirements I have already outlined, they had to act through professional advisers, and their advisers were not going to buck the system. Second, if they were financial operators, they had to have creditworthiness and credibility. If somebody who wants to operate on the financial scene is publicly criticized by a jury of experts as being unsuitable, untrustworthy, and so forth, he is not going to be very successful.

The introduction to the code sets the scene:

The Code represents the collective opinion of those professionally involved in the field of take-overs on a range of business standards.... The Code has not, and does not seek to have, the force of law but those who wish to take advantage of the facilities of the securities markets in the United Kingdom should conduct themselves in matters relating to take-overs according to the Code. Those who do not so conduct themselves cannot expect to enjoy those facilities and may find that they are withheld.

Most of the many discussions about the sanctions available or the lack of them are of theoretical rather than practical importance. Or they have been so far. While there have doubtless been some undiscovered breaches—say, the covert acquisition of effective control of some small company—in the big league it would not pay and nor would it work to breach the code in a major way. Most of our fights nowadays are really on rather trifling matters— e.g., dealing with a filibustering argument by an adviser who has allowed his client to make an ambivalent statement and wants to avoid losing face by issuing a panel-required clarification.

What this all means is that although, as I have already stated, there is little law in Britain governing takeovers, there is effectively a very large amount of unchallenged regulation.

MAIN OBJECTIVES OF THE TAKE-OVER CODE

Let me now briefly list the general objectives of the Take-Over Code:

1. Equality of treatment and opportunity for all shareholders in takeover bids.
2. Equality of information for all shareholders.
3. That shareholders should have adequate information to enable them to assess the merits of the offer and also that they should know clearly what the basic structure of the offer is, what time they have, what the offeror can do as regards closing his offer or revising it, etc.
4. That no frustrating action may be taken by a target company board during the offer period without shareholders being allowed to vote on it.
5. Generally, the maintaining of orderly markets and the protection of the reputation of the U.K. financial community.

Besides these main objectives, the code contains a number of general principles and a series of specific rules drawn from them. I examine some of the rules later, but first I should complete the history.

HOW THE BRITISH SYSTEM WORKS

For its first six years the panel was operating in a bull market, and its main tasks were to curb excesses. At the end of 1973 the financial situation altered abruptly, and the emphasis of the work became rather different. Drawn from the equality-of-treatment principle, one of the major objectives of the code is that when control of a company changes (we define control as 30% of the voting rights, which is rough and ready but works reasonably well), there should be a general offer in cash, or accompanied by a cash alternative, to all the shareholders at the highest price paid for shares by the new controlling group during the previous 12 months.[5] That is fairly straightforward when you have one new controlling person but becomes much more difficult, quite obviously, when a group of persons acting in concert has gained control. From 1974 on, the panel has frequently been involved in investigations to establish whether or not there has been concerted action by groups.

The bear period of 1974 led to rather extensive extra rule writing—in my opinion it was overdone—and the code became more complicated. We have recently reordered it in an attempt to bring regulation back to a size and shape in which practitioners can operate with a reasonable degree of certainty—although our system does demand a great deal of prior consultation in the more esoteric areas.

The system works in the following way: Where any aspect of a takeover plan would appear to raise a question under the code, the advisers to the offeror consult the panel staff in advance; similarly, once an offer has been announced, there may well be questions raised by the target company, its advisers, or shareholders. Typical examples might be to establish whether the panel would treat a proposed condition of an offer as being sufficiently objective (the code does not permit the use of conditions which give announced offerors a free choice whether or not to go ahead) or whether a summary rather than a complete copy of a property valuation may be used (where it is contended that full disclosure would be commercially damaging). These consultations are in confidence, and we are very strict about this. The staff will then give a ruling; and either it will be accepted or, if the practitioner finds it unacceptable, he has a right of appeal to the full panel, the tribunal, to explore the case with them. In practice, such appeals are rare. In the year to March 1985 there were only two appeals to the full panel—both, it so happens, unsuccessful. This figure was perhaps exceptionally low, but it is in the ballpark. This situation should be looked at in light of the fact that there are some 400, on average, questions raised with us each week, and 20 or 30 of them will involve significant rulings. Once a significant ruling of general application has been established, it is the practice to amend, or add a clarifying note to, the code.

The full panel would be very reluctant to act on an *ex parte* basis, and therefore the "other side" will have to be able to attend a hearing. On the whole, this question of *ex parte* does not produce problems, although it can be fairly difficult if, for tactical reasons, the aggressor wants to avoid having his offer conditionally out in the open before getting a ruling. I do stress that these are very rare situations; when they arise, the aggressor will tend to rely on guidance from the executive rather than an appeal to the full panel.

When a case goes before the full panel on appeal, the panel will give its ruling, and in all but one instance over the past 17 years, such rulings have been accepted. That is not a bad record. If the staff has a problem so new it does not believe that anything in the code or in precedent gives any clear guidance, it will refer the matter to the full panel—two such references in the year to March 1985. A third variety of panel meeting will be where the staff wishes to take disciplinary action against someone—none in the year ended March 1985. In this third variety of case, following the panel hearing there is a right of appeal to a special Appeal Committee of the panel presided over by a former judge in order to give the appropriate natural justice safety valve.

You may wonder where an appellant would go if he was not satisfied with a final ruling from the panel or its Appeal Committee. The answer is that I do not know. Clearly, there must be the possibility of going to the courts if one can argue that the

panel has taken harmful action wildly unrelated to its rules or has come to a decision on evidence that should have taken no reasonable group of persons to such an end. I can only say that this situation has not happened.

The panel has gone to great lengths to make sure it does not clash with the law, albeit it does impose requirements greater than those imposed by the law. It is, of course, not protected by absolute privilege and indeed has a large libel insurance policy—this has only been at risk in one case,[6] where we won our defense and where, in the circumstances of that case, qualified privilege was successfully established. In a number of cases the courts have recognized that the requirements laid down by the panel are desirable, representing best business practice, and that departure from them can be a perfectly valid reason for action to be taken against, say, directors of a company.

The panel is interventionist. It plays an active role rather than a passive one and is prepared to issue public statements during takeover situations to demand clarity, to criticize, or to do whatever else may be necessary. You are not going to be very successful as a predatory takeover offeror if people are being warned by the panel about your activities during the course of a bid. For example, not many people accepted an offer where the panel had to make a public statement pointing out that the offer document breached the code by failing to include independent confirmation that the necessary funds were available. No one, therefore, is likely intentionally to put himself in a position where such public criticism or comment might occur.

All I have said means that, more or less from the beginning of the Take-Over Code and the panel, the new system wiped out a whole series of abuses that used regularly to be part of the takeover scene. Big premiums to controlling groups, creation of minorities with no chance to get out, cash to insiders and exotic Chinese paper to widows and orphans, special deals for large institutions, overoptimistic profit forecasts, and various defensive techniques such as the issue of new shares to friends were all virtually ended by the first code in 1968. Many tactical ploys that would be unthinkable now were everyday occurrences in the fifties and sixties.

WHY IT HAS WORKED

The practitioners have wanted the system to succeed and on the whole have acted so that it did so. The great merit, of course, apart from the low cost, is speed in settling matters and, if necessary, in changing the rules at short notice (not in the middle of a particular game!). Also there is flexibility; some of the rules are very tough and would be unacceptable if there was no power of dispensation accompanying them. An example may help to illustrate this flexibility. The general rule is that if an offeror has acquired 15% of the votes in the previous 12 months, its offer must include a cash alternative at the highest price paid: If a small part of that 15% was purchased, say, 10 months ago when the sector was priced on a different level and/or the target board is not quarreling with a lower-priced offer, the panel would give a dispensation.

A further advantage is that the panel is staffed largely by seasoned professionals from various parts of the securities industry so that the "we" and "they" feeling, which is a risk with permanent bureaucracies, is not present. There has been a great deal of cooperation with the staff of the Stock Exchange, with the merchant bank associations, and also with the Department of Trade, the branch of government concerned in this area.

There are great changes coming in the City of London. The restrictive practices case against the Stock Exchange has been dropped consequent upon the Stock Exchange agreeing to various changes including the removal of restrictions on membership and the end of the single-capacity system. There are those who think these changes will ultimately mean an end to the success of the panel—"The Yanks are coming" and all that! I do not believe that there is any evidence to suggest that this line of thought is correct. We have found

over the years, in fact, that non-British persons operating in Britain are anxious to be whiter than white and to follow the domestic practices. Perhaps the stresses and strains of internationalization will eventually lead to a legislation program, and if they do, then so be it. My point is simply that we have no reason at the present time to think that these coming changes will be the cause.

I strongly believe that were we to have to turn the rules into law, we would have to throw several of them away as being far too tough or necessarily uncertain to be dealt with on a black-and-white basis. As an example, suppose a few weeks before an offer was announced, the offeror company's chairman has been reported as making some optimistic remarks—words, not clear figures—about the current year's likely profits. We would pick that up, if appropriate, deem it to be effectively a profit forecast, and require the chairman to deny or confirm; and in the latter case reports on the forecast by financial advisers and accountants would be mandatory. I cannot see that sequence as part of a legal system. In fact, a widely held view is that some of the areas that the code attempts to deal with are more or less unlegislatable.

The introduction to the general principles in the code begins: "It is impracticable to devise rules in sufficient detail to cover all circumstances which can arise in takeover or merger transactions." I can certainly confirm this view because, after more than 17 years, the staff still finds a high proportion of the questions raised present new problems of interpretation.

Apart from these difficulties, there would inevitably be a new tactic of litigating to gain time. As an aside, I might perhaps comment that a legislative program could solve another U.K. problem at the present time and that is unemployment—one might perhaps envisage six-month short courses to turn the unemployed into the necessary number of securities lawyers. From U.S. ratios of lawyers to civilians that would, I guess, reduce our unemployment figure by some 3 million persons!

FACTORS RELEVANT TO MAJOR CURRENT PROBLEMS

In the time and space available, I cannot analyze the background to all of the rules in the code. I will therefore just touch on the rules and other factors which have relevance to some of the questions reportedly exercising regulators, practitioners, and shareholders in the United States currently. First, bear in mind that in Britain the offeror and persons acting in concert with him can buy target shares, subject to a large number of requirements and restrictions. Several of these restrictions appear in the following list. I have somewhat simplified this list and I make no excuse for that; it is necessary if the chapter is to have a degree of coherence.

1. Under the Companies Act there is a 5% disclosure requirement within five business days.

2. Under the Substantial Acquisitions Rules (a set of rules contained in the same volume as the Take-Over Code but not precisely part of it) a person holding or moving through 15% of the voting rights of a company may not buy, on or off the market, more than 10% in any seven-day period; there are exceptions in certain circumstances—in particular, one transaction with a single shareholder for a higher figure. Any person already over 15% acquiring more than 1% has to disclose by midday on the following business day. These are the essentials of a rather complicated set of rules.

3. If there are rumors, speculation, or an abnormal price movement in the shares of what is in fact an unannounced target company for a takeover bid, the potential offeror may well be required by the panel to make an announcement of position and intentions.

4. Once a takeover bid has been announced, there has to be disclosure by all interested parties of the number of shares dealt in and the prices paid by midday on the business day after the transactions.

5. Broadly, unless a takeover bid is recommended for acceptance by the board of the target company, the bidder may not go to 30% or more of the voting rights until after the first closing date of its offer; there is a major exception for a purchase from a single shareholder. (I should mention at this point that the period in which a takeover offer is open tends to be longer in Britain than in the United States, up to 60 days.)

6. If an offeror has purchased 15% or more within the previous 12 months, then its offer must be in cash, or be accompanied by a cash alternative, at the highest price paid for shares in that period.

7. A linchpin of the code is that any person who acquires 30% or more of the voting rights of a company, inside or outside the market, must immediately announce that fact and must make a general cash offer at the highest price paid within the previous 12 months; there are virtually no exceptions to this rule. Such offer must not be subject to any conditions except that the offeror achieve a total holding of shares carrying over 50% of the voting rights and that the offer will lapse if the authorities refer the case to the Monopolies and Mergers Commission (antitrust). (If subsequently the takeover is permitted, then the offer has to be renewed.)

8. Partial bids—i.e., bids made to all shareholders but for less than 100% of their share holdings—are very rare in Britain; there is perhaps on average one a year. The panel's consent has to be obtained for such a bid, and it will not usually be given if significant numbers of shares have been purchased in the previous 12 months or if any purchases at all have been made while a partial bid was in contemplation. If a bid were to be made where the offeror would end up with more than 30%, approval, as distinct from acceptance, from 50% of the independent shareholders would be required.

9. As a general policy, the Take-Over Panel attempts to be evenhanded and not tilt the balance in favor of the offeror or of the offeree. What we call "abusive defensive tactics" by management without the approval of shareholders were one of the original targets of the code, and they have largely been removed by its existence. Some people contend that other parts of the code, designed originally to promote fairness to shareholders, may have introduced a degree of imbalance, particularly in the case of hostile offers—e.g., the restriction on a unilateral offeror buying shares for a period at the beginning of the offer at a time when defending directors and their associates are free to buy. I do not think, however, that any imbalance is too marked. Indeed, the comment is probably somewhat superficial; the regulations in themselves may be slightly out of balance but the game is not—after all, offerors prepare for and choose their moment of attack and so start with a huge advantage.

Those are a number of the governing background features. I will now examine some of the subjects about which so much discussion has been taking place over the past few years.

WHAT IS A TAKEOVER OFFER?

Both in the United States and Britain there have at varying times been dilemmas as to what a takeover offer is and, therefore, when the regulations start to work. In Britain we used to differentiate between building a control holding by general market purchasing over a period of time and selective purchases perhaps from insiders. The United States, I believe, has not been able to agree on a definition of "tender offer" and has, as a guide for various cases, SEC comments in releases, proposed rules and the like. I am convinced that this approach creates huge difficulties and that trigger

points, however arbitrary, are a better route. If there are going to be trigger points, they must be clear and not leave room for maneuvering.

TWO-TIER BIDS

I take *two-tier bids* to describe cases where a control stake is obtained by an offeror at $x and the rest of the shares, or a further proportion of them, are then offered for at a value of $x − $y shortly afterward. The possibility of the second stage will have been made public, as I understand it, from the outset.

In Britain the Take-Over Code requires that the same offer be made to all shareholders. Except in the rare cases of partial offers where the offeror will end with 30% or more of the voting rights (in which cases approval of the offer by 50% of the independent shareholders is required), the offeror must obtain 50% of the voting rights to be able to declare its offer unconditional. If you don't get to 50%, you don't get anything under the offer, and you cannot make another offer for 12 months. Once an offer is unconditional as to acceptances, it must remain open for a further 14 days so that all shareholders have the opportunity to accept, having seen that control has passed.

There are two other relevant restrictions. We have a ban the other way round, as it were, so that you cannot, having made an offer for 100% (i.e., a full as distinct from a partial offer) at £x under which you have acquired over 50%, buy further shares at £x + £y during the next six months. There are two arguments for this ban: an extension of the equality-of-treatment principle generally and the prevention of devices to take out the "widows and orphans" cheaply but pay the "real" price to an important shareholder. Furthermore, after a partial offer where the offeror ends with over 30%, no purchases would be permitted for another 12 months.

These various restrictions effectively mean that a two stage takeover is not possible.

ARRANGING DEFENSES BEFORE AN OFFER IS IN EXISTENCE

Under this heading of arranging defenses might fall supermajority voting arrangements, golden parachutes, poison pills, and, a new one which I have only recently come across, lobster traps (I understand this phrase signifies an arrangement whereby there is a convertible the terms of which bar a holder from converting if, thereafter, he or she would own or control 10% or more of the voting rights—the little fish can swim through).

We have relatively little experience of this kind of thing. The Take-Over Code applies to some very small, unlisted companies, and I suppose some of these defenses might be set up in such companies, although I do not recall any instances. In the case of listed companies, Stock Exchange regulations and the attitude of the Investment Protection Committees set up by the major groups of institutional shareholders would, I think, prevent the introduction of most such arrangements.

According to the latest figures published by the Stock Exchange, the proportion of shares in listed companies held by institutions as distinct from private shareholders is just over 70%.[7] It is inconceivable to me that institutions would help vote into existence "exploding" warrants or "poison pill" convertible preference shares. Nor would I expect the Stock Exchange to permit listing of such securities—I should mention that in Britain there is one central Stock Exchange as far as regulation is concerned.

We do in Britain, of course, still have shares with no voting rights or with lower voting rights than another class, but the general view is that persons who invested in such shares knew what they were going into. In fact, the code looks after nonvoting and low-voting shareholders rather better than might be expected by requiring an offer for their shares if control changes and by ensuring that there is not too great a disparity in value between the offer for such a class and the offer for the class where control lies.

DEFENSE TACTICS ONCE THERE HAS BEEN AN ANNOUNCEMENT THAT AN OFFER MAY BE MADE

Let me start by saying that we have a longer period between announcement and distribution of offer documents than is the case in the United States. In order to prevent damage by leaks and reduce the opportunities for insider trading, we attempt to get an announcement made as early as possible, and if necessary, it will simply be of the possibility of a bid as distinct from a firm announcement that a bid will definitely be made. Once there has been an announcement, the "offer period" begins and the Take-Over Code applies.

In the Appendix I have included the rule which covers the restrictions on target company boards from the commencement of the offer period. Poison pills (even if the poison was so mild that under Stock Exchange regulations they would have been possible before the offer period), golden parachutes, issues of further shares, sales of the crown jewels, the Pac Man defenses, etc., can all only happen subject to shareholders' approval.

GREENMAIL

For a company to buy back its own shares has only recently become legally permissible in Britain. To do it, the company must obtain shareholders' approval. That is the law. If a takeover situation exists—i.e., if there is an offer period, or even before that if the board of the target company has reason to believe that a bona fide offer might be imminent—no redemption or purchase by the company of its own shares may, unless there is an earlier contract, be effected without the approval of the shareholders at a general meeting.

Of course the directors of a company or associates could buy out a threatening shareholder themselves—but this is not greenmail—and if they did so, they would, as a group, be controlled by the Take-Over Code; so that if as a result of their purchases the group came to hold 30% or more of the voting rights of the company, they themselves would have to make a general offer at the highest price paid. An awkward shareholder can only be got rid of if arrangements can be made to place his shares at arm's length; in these circumstances he is unlikely to get a premium.

A further deterrent for greenmailers would be the code's requirement that approval be obtained from the panel for the making of a partial bid. One could not, for example, do what Steinberg did, I understand, in the Disney case—buy roughly 11% and threaten to make a partial bid for a further 40%; the second step would not be permitted by the panel in the light of the earlier purchase.

SUMMARY

Essentially, the British system gives shareholders a bigger say than management with regard to defense tactics. Thus there may be at least two areas of increased concern: overemphasis on public relations and management continually looking over its shoulder and possibly tending to concentrate too much on short-term performance. But no doubt these problems are present in many cases under both our systems.

Expressed oversimply, a great deal of the Take-Over Code was written in response to pressure for fairer treatment for shareholders in takeover bids, and the thinking was that it was the innocent individual shareholder away from the big city who needed this protection. Well, we have taxed most of these people out of existence as shareholders! The shareholder now is predominantly the fund manager who, one hopes, will not be overinfluenced by the excesses of public relations experts.

What form, if any, regulation to protect shareholders in takeover target companies will take depends, of course, enormously on the state of the law and the attitude of the government or self-regulatory authorities in the country in question. Considerations other than those of the protection of shareholders and of the reputation of the marketplace seem to me beyond the concern of market regulators. National, employee, and environmental interests are surely matters for government; even the use of junk bonds as takeover currency falls, to my mind, for banking regulators and government to deal with.

The considerations which bring about the need for regulation of takeovers may be a desire for a clean market to encourage the public to invest in shares; a straightforward and respectable wish for fairness for its own sake; what is best for the economic well-being of the society in question and, cynically, the need for governments and authorities to get the press off their backs! I find it hard, however, to think that such regulation, whatever stimulates it, should not include as central concepts those of equality of treatment for all shareholders and the possibility of all of them having a telling vote at a critical time. Fifty percent + 1 should surely rule the day.

NOTES

1. Companies Act, Part VII, § 198–220 (1985).
2. Companies Act, Part XIII, § 425–427 (1985).
3. The Licensed Dealers (Conduct of Business) Rules (1983).
4. Thorn Electrical Industries/Aberdare Holdings/Metal Industries (Summer 1967).
5. Rule 9 of the Take-Over Code contains this requirement and is set forth in the Appendix to this chapter.
6. *Laurence Graff v. Lord Shawcross*, D. C. Macdonald and P. R. Frazer (Autumn 1980).
7. Based on various surveys and on Stock Exchange statistics. The percentage has almost doubled in the past two decades.

APPENDIX

The following pages contain the rules of the Take-Over Code relevant to the following items:

1. The 30% threshold restriction, which, when exceeded, necessitates a general offer on specified terms to all shareholders.

2. Restrictions on actions which may be taken by defending boards without the prior approval of shareholders.
3. Partial offers—i.e., offers for less than 100% of the share capital of a company.
4. Certain aspects of the redemption or purchase by a company of its own voting shares. *Note:* Cross-references to other parts of the code have been omitted.

SECTION F. THE MANDATORY OFFER AND ITS TERMS

RULE 9

9.1 When It Is Required and Who Is Primarily Responsible for Making It

Except with the consent of the Panel, where:

(a) any person acquires, whether by a series of transactions over a period of time or not, shares which (taken together with shares held or acquired by persons acting in concert with him) carry 30% or more of the voting rights of a company, or

(b) any person who, together with persons acting in concert with him, holds not less than 30% but not more than 50% of the voting rights and such person, or any person acting in concert with him, acquires in any period of 12 months additional shares carrying more than 2% of the voting rights,

such person shall extend offers, on the basis set out in Rules 9.3, 9.4 and 9.5, to the holders of any class of equity capital whether voting or non-voting and also to the holders of any class of voting non-equity share capital in which such person or persons acting in concert with him hold shares. Offers for different classes of equity capital must be comparable; the Panel should be consulted in advance in such cases.

NOTES ON RULE 9.1

PERSONS ACTING IN CONCERT
The majority of questions asked of the Panel in the context of Rule 9 relate to persons acting in concert. The definition of "acting in concert" contains a list of persons who are presumed to be acting in concert unless the contrary is established.

. . .

9.2 Obligations of Other Persons

In addition to the person specified in Rule 9.1, each of the principal members of a group of persons acting in concert with him may, according to the circumstances of the case, have the obligation to extend an offer.

NOTE ON RULE 9.2

Prime responsibility

The prime responsibility for making an offer under this Rule normally attaches to the person who makes the acquisition which imposes the obligation to make an offer. If such person is not a principal member of the group acting in concert, then the obligation to make an offer may attach to the principal member or members and, in exceptional circumstances, to other members of the group acting in concert. This could include a member of the group who at the time when the obligation arises does not hold any shares. In this context, the Panel will not regard the underwriter of a mandatory offer, by virtue of his underwriting alone, as being a member of a group acting in concert and, therefore, responsible for making the offer.

An agreement between a shareholder and a banker under which the shareholder borrows money for the acquisition of shares which gives rise to an obligation under the Rule will not of itself fall within the above.

9.3 Conditions and Consents

(a) Offers made under this Rule must be conditional upon the offeror having received acceptances in respect of shares which, together with shares acquired or agreed to be acquired before or during the offer, will result in the offeror and any persons acting in concert with it holding shares carrying more than 50% of the voting rights.

(b) Other than as set out in (a) above, offers under this Rule must be unconditional (but see also Rule 9.4).

(c) Except with the consent of the Panel, no acquisition of shares which would give rise to a requirement for an offer under this Rule may be made if the making or implementation of such offer would or might be dependent on the passing of a resolution at any meeting of shareholders of the offeror or upon any other conditions, consents or arrangements.

NOTES ON RULE 9.3

1. Where more than 50% is held

The offer should normally be unconditional where the offeror and persons acting in concert with it hold shares carrying more than 50% of the voting rights before the offer is made.

2. Convertible securities etc.

3. Governmental clearances

The Panel will not normally consider a request for a dispensation under paragraph (c) of this Rule other than where some governmental, including EEC, clearance is required before the offer document is posted. In such cases the person who has incurred the obligation under Rule 9 must endeavour to obtain clearance with all due diligence. If clearance is obtained, the offer must be posted immediately. If clearance is not obtained, the same consequences will follow as if the merger was prohibited following a reference to the Monopolies and Mergers Commission (see Rule 9.4).

9.4 Monopolies and Mergers Commission

Offers under this Rule must, if appropriate, contain the term as to reference to the Monopolies and Mergers Commission required by Rule 12.

NOTES ON RULE 9.4

1. If an offer is referred

If an offer under Rule 9 lapses on reference to the Monopolies and Mergers Commission, the obligation under the Rule does not lapse and, accordingly, if thereafter the merger is allowed, the offer must be reinstated on the same terms and at not less than the same price as soon as practicable. If the merger is prohibited, the offer cannot be made and the Panel will consider whether, if there is no order to such effect, to require the offeror to reduce its holding to below 30% or to its original level before the obligation to offer was incurred if this was 30% or more. The Panel would normally expect an offeror whose offer has been referred to the Commission to proceed with all due diligence before it. However, if after a reference, with the consent of the Panel, an offeror sells to unconnected parties within a limited period sufficient shares to reduce its holding to below 30%, or to its original level before the obligation to offer was incurred if that was 30% or more, the Panel will regard the obligation as having lapsed.

2. Further acquisitions

While the Commission is considering the reference of a case where an obligation to make an offer under this Rule has been incurred, the offeror or persons acting in concert may not acquire any further shares in the offeree company.

9.5 Consideration to be Offered

(a) Offers made under this Rule must, in respect of each class of share capital involved, be in cash or be accompanied by a cash alternative at not less than the highest price paid by the offeror or any person acting in concert with it for shares of that class within the preceding 12 months. The Panel should be consulted where there is more than one class of share capital involved.

(b) If the offeror considers that the highest price should not apply in a particular case, the offeror should consult the Panel, which has discretion to agree an adjusted price.

NOTES ON RULE 9.5

1. Nature of consideration

Where shares have been acquired for a consideration other than cash, the offer must nevertheless be in cash or be accompanied by a cash alternative of at least equal value, which must be determined by an independent valuation.

Where there have been significant acquisitions in exchange for securities, General Principle 1 may be relevant and such securities may be required to be offered to all shareholders: a cash offer will also be required. The Panel should be consulted in such cases.

2. Calculation of the price

(a) In calculating the price paid, stamp duty and commission should be excluded: in the case of a put-through, the jobber's turn should be included.

(b) If shares have been acquired in exchange for listed securities, the price will normally be established by reference to the middle market price of the listed securities at the time of the acquisition.

(c) If shares have been acquired by the exercise of conversion rights or warrants, the price will normally be established by reference to the middle market price of the shares in question at the close of business on the day on which the relevant notice was submitted.

In addition, if the convertible securities or warrants were acquired in the 12 months before the obligation under this Rule arose, the Panel will take into account the cost of such securities together with any costs of exercise.

The Panel should be consulted in advance in the circumstances described in (b) and (c) above.

3. Dispensation from highest price

Factors which the Panel would take into account when considering an application for an adjusted price include:—

(a) the size and timing of the relevant purchases;

(b) the attitude of the board of the offeree company;

(c) whether shares had been purchased at high prices from "insiders"; and

(d) the number of shares purchased in the preceding 12 months.

9.6 Obligations of Directors Selling Shares

Where directors (and their close relatives and related trusts) sell shares to a purchaser, as a result of which the purchaser is required to make an offer under this Rule, the directors must ensure that as a condition of the sale the purchaser undertakes to fulfil his obligations under the Rule. In addition, except with the consent of the Panel, such directors should not resign from the board until the first closing date of the offer or the date when the offer becomes or is declared unconditional as to acceptances, whichever is the later.

9.7 Restrictions on Exercise of Control by the Offeror

Except with the consent of the Panel, no nominee of the offeror or persons acting in concert with it may be appointed to the board of the offeree company, nor may the offeror and persons acting in concert with it exercise the votes attaching to any shares held in the offeree company, until the offer documented has been posted.

NOTES ON DISPENSATIONS FROM RULE 9

1. Independent vote of shareholders on the issue of new securities ("Whitewash")

When the issue of new securities as consideration for an acquisition or a cash subscription would otherwise result in an obligation to make

a general offer under this Rule, the Panel will normally waive the obligation if there is an independent vote at such meetings as may be convened to approve the issue of the new securities. The requirement for a general offer will also be waived, provided there has been an independent vote of shareholders, in cases involving the underwriting of an issue of shares.

In all such cases the appropriate provisions of the Code apply. Full details of the potential shareholding must be disclosed in the document sent to shareholders relating to the issue of the new securities, which must also include competent independent advice on the proposals the shareholders are being asked to approve together with a statement that the Panel has agreed to waive any consequent obligation under this Rule to make a general offer. The resolution must be made the subject of a poll. The Panel must be consulted and a proof document submitted at an early stage.

Where a person or group of persons acting in concert may, as a result of such arrangements, come to control more than 48% of the voting rights of the company (at over 48% a holder has the freedom to move to 50% or more without incurring an obligation under this Rule), specific and prominent reference to the possibility must be contained in the document and to the fact that the controlling shareholders will be able to exercise their control and increase their overall shareholding without incurring any further obligation under Rule 9 to make a general offer.

Where a waiver has been granted, as described above, in respect of convertible securities or rights to subscribe for shares, details, including the fact of the waiver, should be included in the company's Extel card.

Notwithstanding the fact that the issue of new securities is made conditional upon the prior approval of a majority of the shareholders independent of the transaction at a general meeting of the company:—

(a) the Panel will not normally waive an obligation under this Rule if the person to whom the new securities are to be issued or any persons acting in concert with him have purchased shares in the company in the 12 months prior to the posting to shareholders of the circular relating to the proposals but subsequent to negotiations, discussions or the reaching of understandings or agreements with the directors of the company in relation to the proposed issue of new securities;

(b) a waiver will be invalidated if any purchases are made in the period between the posting of the circular to shareholders and the shareholders' meeting.

In exceptional circumstances, the Panel may consider waiving the requirement for a general offer where the approval of independent shareholders to the transfer of existing shares from one shareholder to another is obtained.

2. Foreclosure on security for a loan

Where a shareholding in a company is pledged as security for a loan and upon foreclosure the lender would otherwise incur an obligation to make a general offer under this Rule, the Panel will normally waive the requirement provided that the security was not given at a time when the lender had reason to believe that foreclosure was likely. In any case where arrangements are to be made which amount to a virtual foreclosure, the Panel will have to be convinced that a foreclosure would otherwise be necessary, taking into account the proviso above. When a lender following foreclosure wishes to sell all or part of his shareholding, the provisions of this Rule apply to the purchaser: Although a receiver or liquidator of a company is not required to make an offer when he takes control of a holding of more than 30% of another company, the provisions of the Rule apply to a purchaser from a receiver or liquidator.

3. Rescue operations

There are occasions when a company is in such a serious financial position that the only way it can be saved is by an urgent rescue operation which involves the issue of new shares without approval by an independent vote of shareholders or the acquisition of existing shares by the rescuer which would otherwise fall within the provisions of this Rule and normally require a general offer. The Panel will, however, consider waiving the requirements of the Rule in such circumstances: particular attention will be paid to the views of the directors and advisers of the potential offeree company.

The requirements of the Rule will not normally be waived in a case where a major shareholder in a company rather than that company itself is in need of rescue. The situation of that shareholder may have little relevance to the position of other shareholders and, therefore, the purchaser from such major shareholder must expect to be obliged to extend an offer under the Rule to all other shareholders.

4. Inadvertent mistake

If, due to an inadvertent mistake, a person incurs an obligation to make an offer under this Rule, the Panel will not normally require an offer if sufficient shares are sold within a limited period to persons unconnected with him.

5. Where 50% will not accept

The Panel will consider waiving the requirement for a general offer under this Rule where the holder or holders of shares carrying 50% or more of the voting rights state in writing that they would not accept such an offer.

6. Enfranchisement of non-voting shares

There is no requirement to make a general offer under this Rule if a holder of non-voting shares becomes upon enfranchisement of those shares a holder of 30% or more of the voting rights of a company, except where shares have been purchased at a time when the purchaser had reason to believe that enfranchisement would take place.

RULE 21. RESTRICTIONS ON FRUSTRATING ACTION

During the course of an offer, or even before the date of the offer if the board of the offeree company has reason to believe that a bona fide offer might be imminent, the board must not, except in pursuance of a contract entered into earlier, without the approval of the shareholders in general meeting:—

(a) issue any authorised but unissued shares;

(b) issue or grant options in respect of any unissued shares;

(c) create or issue or permit the creation or issue of any securities carrying rights of conversion into or subscription for shares;

(d) sell, dispose of or acquire, or agree to sell, dispose of or acquire, assets of material amount; or

(e) enter into contracts otherwise than in the ordinary course of business.

The notice convening such a meeting of shareholders must include information about the offer or anticipated offer.

Where it is felt that an obligation or other special circumstance exists, although a formal contract has not been entered into, the Panel must be consulted and its consent to proceed without a shareholders' meeting obtained.

NOTES ON RULE 21

1. Consent by the offeror

Where the Rule would otherwise apply, it will nonetheless normally be waived by the Panel if this is acceptable to the offeror.

2. "Material amount"

For the purpose of determining whether a disposal or acquisition is of "material amount" the Panel will, in general, have regard to the following:—

(a) the value of the assets to be disposed of or acquired compared with the gross assets of the offeree company;

(b) the aggregate value of the consideration to be received or given compared with the gross assets of the offeree company;

(c) where appropriate, net profits (after deducting all charges except taxation and excluding extraordinary items) attributable to the assets to be disposed of or acquired compared with those of the offeree company.

The Panel will normally consider relative values of 10% or more as being of material amount, although relative values lower than 10% may be considered material if the asset is of particular significance.

If several transactions relevant to this Rule, but not individually material, occur or are intended, the Panel will aggregate such transactions to determine whether the requirement of this Rule are applicable to any of them.

The Panel should be consulted in advance where there may be any doubt as to the application of the above.

3. Interim dividends

The declaration and payment of an interim dividend by the offeree company, otherwise than in the normal course, during an offer period may in certain circumstances be contrary to General Principle 7 and this Rule in that it could effectively frustrate an offer. Offeree companies and their advisers must, therefore, consult the Panel in advance.

4. References to the Monopolies and Mergers Commission

When an offer is referred to the Monopolies and Mergers Commission it must lapse in accor-

dance with Rule 12. The Panel will, however, normally consider that General Principle 7 and Rule 21 apply while the Commission is considering the reference.

5. When there is no need to post

The Panel may allow an offeror not to proceed with its offer if, at any time during the offer period prior to the posting of the offer document, the offeree company:—

(a) passes a resolution in general meeting as envisaged by this Rule; or

(b) announces a transaction which would require such a resolution but for the fact that it is pursuant to a contract entered into earlier or that the Panel has ruled that an obligation or other special circumstance exists.

6. Service contracts

The Panel will regard amending or entering into a service contract with, or creating or varying the terms of employment of, a director as entering into a contract "otherwise than in the ordinary course of business" for the purposes of this Rule if the new or amended contractor or terms constitute an abnormal increase in his emoluments or a significant improvement in his terms of service.

This will not prevent any such increase or improvement which results from a genuine promotion or new appointment, but the Panel should be consulted in advance in such cases.

SECTION O. PARTIAL OFFERS

RULE 36

36.1 Panel's Consent Required

The Panel's consent is required for any partial offer. In the case of an offer which could not result in the offeror holding shares carrying 30% or more of the voting rights of a company, consent will normally be granted.

36.2 Buying Before the Offer

In the case of an offer which could result in the offeror holding shares carrying 30% or more but less than 100% of the voting rights of a company, such consent will not normally be granted if the offeror or persons acting in concert with it have acquired, selectively or in significant numbers, shares in the offeree company during the

12 months preceding the application for consent or if shares have been purchased at any time after the partial offer was reasonably in contemplation.

36.3 Buying During and After the Offer

The offeror and persons acting in concert with it may not purchase shares in the offeree company during the offer period nor, in the case of a successful partial offer, may the offeror or persons acting in concert with it, except with the consent of the Panel, purchase such shares during a period of 12 months after the end of the offer period.

NOTES ON RULE 36.3

1. Discretionary clients

Dealings by discretionary clients of a financial adviser may be relevant (see Rule 7.2).

2. Partial offer resulting in less than 30%

The consent of the Panel will normally be granted for share purchases within 12 months of the end of the offer period, where a partial offer has resulted in a holding of less than 30% of the voting rights of a company.

36.4 Offer for Between 30% and 50%

Where an offer is made which could result in the offeror holding shares carrying not less than 30% and not more than 50% of the voting rights of a company, the precise number of shares offered for must be stated and the offer may not be declared unconditional as to acceptances unless acceptances are received for not less than that number.

36.5 Offer for 30% or More Requires 50% Approval

Any offer which could result in the offeror holding shares carrying 30% or more of the voting rights of a company must normally be conditional, not only on the specified number of acceptances being received, but also on approval of the offer, normally signified by means of a separate box on the Form of Acceptance and Transfer, being given by shareholders holding over 50% of the voting rights not held by the offeror and persons acting in concert with it. This requirement may on occasion be waived if over 50% of the voting rights of the offeree company are held by one shareholder.

36.6 Warning About Control Position

In the case of a partial offer which could result in the offeror holding shares carrying over 48% of the voting rights of the offeree company, the offer document must contain specific and prominent reference to this and to the fact that, if the offer succeeds, the offeror will be free, subject to Rule 36.3, to acquire further shares without incurring any obligation under Rule 9 to make a general offer.

36.7 Scaling Down

Partial offers must be made to all shareholders of the class and arrangements must be made for those shareholders who wish to do so to accept in full for the relevant percentage of their holdings. Shares tendered in excess of this percentage must be accepted by the offeror from each shareholder in the same proportion to the number tendered to the extent necessary to enable it to obtain the total number of shares for which it has offered.

36.8 Comparable Offer

Where an offer is made for a company with more than one class of equity share capital which could result in the offeror holding shares carrying 30% or more of the voting rights, a comparable offer must be made for each class.

SECTION P. REDEMPTION OR PURCHASE BY A COMPANY OF ITS OWN VOTING SHARES

RULE 37

37.1 Directors and Persons Acting in Concert with Them May be Required to Make a General Offer

When a company redeems or purchases its own voting shares, a resulting increase in the percentage voting rights carried by shareholdings of the directors and persons acting in concert with them will be treated as an acquisition for the purposes of Rule 9. Subject to prior consultation, the Panel will normally waive any resulting obligation to make a general offer if there is an independent vote of shareholders and a procedure on the lines of that set out in Appendix 1 is followed.

NOTES ON RULE 37.1

1. Responsibility for making an offer

If an offer obligation under this Rule is incurred and a dispensation is not granted, the prime responsibility for making the offer will attach to the principal member or members of the group of persons who are acting in concert and who, as a result of the redemption or purchase by the company of its own shares, obtain or consolidate control of that company. In certain circumstances, the obligation to make such an offer may attach to other members of that group but no such obligation will attach to the company itself.

2. A shareholder not acting in concert with the directors

A shareholder not acting in concert with the directors will not incur an obligation to make a general offer if, as a result of the redemption or purchase of its own shares by a company, he comes to exceed the limits set out in Rule 9.1.

37.2 Limitations on Subsequent Acquisitions of Shares

Subsequent to the redemption or purchase by a company of its own shares, all shareholders will be subject, in making acquisitions of shares in the company, to the provisions of Rule 9.1.

NOTE ON RULE 37.2

Calculation of limits

The limits referred to in this Rule will be calculated by reference to the outstanding issued voting capital subsequent to the redemption or purchase by the company of its own shares.

37.3 Redemptions or Purchases of Offeree Company Shares

(a) Shareholders' approval

During the course of an offer, or even before the date of the offer if the board of the offeree company has reason to believe that a bona fide offer might be imminent, no redemption or purchase by the offeree company of its own shares may, except in pursuance of a contract entered into earlier, be effected without the approval of the shareholders at a general meeting. The notice

convening the meeting must include information about the offer or anticipated offer. Where it is felt that an obligation or other special circumstance exists, although a formal contract has not been entered into, the Panel must be consulted and its consent to proceed without a shareholders' meeting obtained.

(b) Public disclosure

During an offer period, the offeree company must immediately disclose to The Stock Exchange, the Panel and the press the total number of its own shares which it has redeemed or purchased in the market or otherwise, and the price or prices paid, and it must also disclose the total number of shares of the relevant class remaining in issue following the redemption or purchase.

(c) Disclosure in the offeree board circular

The offeree board circular advising shareholders on an offer must state the number of shares of the offeree company which the offeree company has redeemed or purchased during the period commencing 12 months prior to the offer period and ending with the latest practicable date prior to the posting of the document, and the details of any such redemptions and purchases, including dates and prices.

37.4 Redemptions or Purchases of Offeror Shares

(a) Public disclosure

For the purposes of Rule 8, dealings in relevant securities include the redemption or purchase of, or taking or exercising an option over, any of its own securities by an offeror.

(b) Disclosure in the offer document

The offer document must state (in the case of a securities exchange offer only) the number of shares of the offeror which the offeror has redeemed or purchased during the period commencing 12 months prior to the offer period and ending with the latest practicable date prior to the posting of the offer document and the details of any such redemptions and purchases, including dates and prices.

28

Comment

DOUGLAS H. GINSBURG

COMMENTS ON DE MOTT AND FRAZER

The De Mott and Frazer chapters present general summaries of the regulations governing takeovers in Australia, Canada, Great Britain, and the United States. Both focus on the specific form of the takeover regulations, with less attention to the theoretical or empirical effects of such rules.

There are three points worth noting about the De Mott and Frazer chapters. First, De Mott sets out a useful framework for comparative study of takeover regulations. She separates takeover rules into two categories: rules governing the extent to which the costs of takeover can be raised by shifting risks between bidder and target shareholders (e.g., rules governing equality of treatment and information disclosures) and rules that define the circumstances under which target managements can attempt to defeat hostile tender offers. In her analysis, takeover regulations span a continuum from "least regulated" in the United States to most closely regulated in Great Britain.

Second, the De Mott survey indicates that the United States is the only country whose takeover regulations have been determined, at least in part, by competition among different regulatory regimes (i.e., among states). By contrast, Canada, Great Britain, and Australia have uniform or very nearly uniform regulation of takeovers. To the extent that competition among states results in sets of rules that optimally serve a wide variety of corporate structures and circumstances, some benefits of the U.S. system are underestimated by De Mott. A substitute mechanism for

this competition is hinted at by Frazer, who stresses that the Take-Over Panel's decisions are flexible and would be difficult to codify in one "uniform" set of regulations. Such "flexibility," however, probably produces far greater uncertainty as to outcomes than does varying state court precedent. In addition, corporations appear to have limited mobility out of the Take-Over Panel's jurisdiction through access to appeals courts.

The third, and potentially most interesting, aspect of the De Mott and Frazer studies is the dramatically different balance between De Mott's two types of rules struck in the United States and in Great Britain. While British takeover regulations governing the timing, nature, and information requirements of bids appear to severely raise the costs of initiating hostile tender offers, the British rules governing target management's use of defensive tactics (which essentially require shareholder approval for all significant action) make it more likely that any hostile offers that are mounted will be successful. By contrast, U.S. laws make hostile offers more likely but give sufficient latitude to management under the business judgment rule to make their successful outcome far less certain. Because De Mott's purpose is to compare regulatory systems, I would suggest that she follow up with an evaluation of which of these two environments, on balance, results in greater long-run benefits to shareholders. Presumably, such an evaluation would include a balancing of the costs of defensive tactics and the costs of having fewer hostile tender offers. Perhaps an even more interesting question is whether the optimal set of takeover regulations would combine the "back end" of the British system (i.e., limiting defensive tactics) and the "front end" of the American system, (i.e., relatively few restrictions on offers and their terms).

COMMENTS ON BEBCHUK

Summary

Bebchuk sets forth an "undistorted-choice objective" which he describes as a situation in which shareholders could rationally evaluate a tender proposal free of the "prisoner's dilemma." In such a situation there would be no coercion of shareholders. He also asserts, however, without foundation, that this well-known theoretical construction not only exists empirically but also exists to such a degree that a remedy is required. He proposes a remedy that permits shareholders to tender approvingly or disapprovingly, such that the tender offer is only successful if the number of approving tenders exceeds the number of disapproving tenders. This scheme does, in fact, eliminate the distorted-choice problem he describes. Bebchuk also claims, however, unpersuasively, that the scheme is relatively costless.

The two major problems with Bebchuk's chapter are that (1) the empirical evidence does not indicate that a serious distorted-choice problem exists, and (2) the costs of the proposed remedy may not be trivial.

The Problem with the Distorted-Choice Problem

Bebchuk claims that a company should be acquired if and only if a majority of its shareholders view the offered acquisition price as higher than the value that the target would have if it remained independent, which would include the value of higher acquisition offers in the future.[1] The undistorted-choice objective is nothing more than saying that value maximization by the shareholders should be their choice objective.

The theory of shareholder choice that Bebchuk attempts to lay out is well known.[2] The argument is simply that of the "prisoner's dilemma." Consider a two-tier tender offer. Each shareholder, knowing that his or her vote will not influence the final outcome of the takeover, will tender in order to avoid the second-stage minority freeze-out. By contrast, at the opposite end of the spectrum from perfect coercion by the offerors is complete free riding by the shareholders on the information produced by the offers. In the limit, perfect free riding would prevent all takeovers, and complete appropriation could lead to the exit of shareholders from the capital markets. Bebchuk's concern, however, is apparently more with a perceived fairness issue stemming from the pure transfer between offeror and shareholders than with the efficiency-enhancing operation of the market for corporate control.

In fact, the distorted choice that Bebchuk describes may not even exist. First, if there is a perfectly competitive takeover market, appropriation is impossible. Second, state appraisal rights limit the ability of raiders to freeze out minority shareholders.

Bebchuk slights the important empirical literature bearing on this issue. The strongest evidence that significant appropriation has not occurred can be found in the report by the SEC staff.[3] Basically, this study shows that target shareholders benefit very substantially regardless of the structure of the tender offer.[4] In addition, John Pound of the SEC staff has also shown that premiums are not higher in takeovers for target companies with concentrated ownership.[5] Yet one would expect that shareholders' ability to coordinate their actions and to avoid the alleged distortion would be evident as ownership concentration increases.

In addition, if choice were distorted, one should be able to make successful tender offers with very small premiums, which is far from being the case.

Lacking any new empirical evidence that distorted choice is a significant problem, Bebchuk's analysis becomes one of asserting a problem and offering a remedy.

The Problem with the Proposed Remedy

The proposed remedy is quite simple and directly attacks the issue of distorted choice. Bebchuk presents a scheme to separate the act of tendering from the question of approving the offer by permitting shareholders to tender approvingly or disapprovingly. The bid's success is then determined by whether it attracts the specified number of approving tenders. If successful, the offeror would have to treat approvingly and disapprovingly tendered shares equally. Thus, shareholders could "vote" against the tender offer without making the economically irrational decision not to tender.

The obvious costs of the remedy relate to the general free-riding and freeze-out issues. If offerors are now able to appropriate value from shareholders, the result of the proposal would be an increase in the premium levels of takeover bids and consequently a decrease in the likelihood of takeover activity—the same effect that the Williams Act appears to have had. Indirectly, this result could also lead to an increase in entrenched, inefficient management and a decrease in the profit level necessary in order to shield current management from the threat of a takeover. The costs of the remedy are apparently high, however, only if significant levels of distorted choice exist. If distorted choice is not a problem, then one would expect both limited costs and limited benefits from the proposed solution.

A second category of costs potentially raised by Bebchuk's proposal involves the inability of individual shareholders to sell their stock at a premium. Under Bebchuk's scheme, if the offer is disapproved, those shareholders desiring to sell at a premium may have no outlet. Bebchuk proposes that "if the bidder fails to attract the required majority of approving tenders, then the bidder would be prohibited from acquiring a controlling interest, and the target would remain independent" (p. 381). Not clear under his scheme is whether a rejected bidder would also be prevented from acquiring a controlling interest in the open market. If Bebchuk's intention is to eliminate completely the rejected bidder, then his proposal would appear to be far more expansive than a simple change in tender offer regulations. This proposal apparently imposes costs on society by eliminating an available mechanism, independent of tender offers, by which firms can compete in the market for corporate control.

NOTES

1. "The reasoning behind this choice of the decisive fraction is that the majority is more likely to be right than the minority in its assessment of the shareholders' value-maximizing course of action." One should carry this reasoning further and suggest that the entire market is even better than the majority of shareholders at accurately assessing the value of the target firm.

2. See, e.g., Grossman and Hart, "Takeover Bids, the Free-Rider Problem, and the Theory of the Corporation," 11 *Bell Jour. Econ.* 42 (1980).

3. Office of the Chief Economist, Securities and Exchange Commission, *The Economics of Partial and Two-Tier Tender Offers* (49 Fed. Reg. 26755, 1984).

4. Ibid., 26759.

5. J. Pound, *The Effects of Institutional Investors on Takeover Activity: A Quantitative Analysis* (Washington, D.C.: Investor Responsibility Research Center, 1985).

29

Comment

MARSHALL L. SMALL

A basic right of any shareholder is the right to dispose of his or her shares, subject only to reasonable restraints on transfer. This right has traditionally been recognized by judicial decision[1] and in many state corporation statutes[2] without reference to the more recent phenomenon of unsolicited tender offers. However, the same principle should be applicable—shareholders should be entitled to dispose of their shares to a tender offeror subject only to reasonable restraints on their ability to do so.

What are reasonable restraints on transfer in the context of unsolicited tender offers, and how may such restraints be imposed? These issues should be considered from the perspective of allocation of power between shareholders and directors.

POWER OF SHAREHOLDERS WITH RESPECT TO RESTRAINTS ON TRANSFER

The corporation statutes of many states recognize the ability of corporations to impose reasonable restraints on transfer of shares through provisions in articles of incorporation or bylaws adopted by shareholders.[3]

Restrictions on transfer of shares have typically been fashioned to ensure a cohesive body of shareholders in a closely held corporation, through such devices as limiting ownership to active employees or requiring that a shareholder wishing to dispose of shares first offer the shares to the corporation or other shareholders. Such restrictions may require the shareholder (or his or her heirs) wishing to dispose of shares to sell at an agreed-upon price, at a price determined by formula, such as book value or capitalized earnings per share, or at the price offered by a third party who desires to acquire the shares.

There is no reason to limit the use of restrictions on transfer of shares to closely held corporations. Indeed, the device may be utilized in the context of unsolicited tender offers for shares of publicly held corporations to avoid the distortions of choice described by Professor Bebchuk which occur as the result of bids for only a portion of a target corporation's shares.[4] Shareholders of potential target corporations should be able to regulate the behavior of potential bidders by adopting provisions in the articles of incorporation or bylaws of the potential target corporation which would provide that shares could not be transferred to a bidder unless a specified percentage of the target's shareholders approved the bid. The specified percentage might be greater than a simple 51%, particularly if the restriction were imposed by a vote of shareholders of the target corporation which was at least as large as the percentage of shareholders specified in the charter or bylaw provision as required to approve the takeover bid.[5] Such a charter or bylaw restriction might also give shareholders the right to tender their shares conditionally while voting to oppose an offer, so that if the required percentage of shareholders approved the offer, those shareholders who voted no would be assured that at least a pro rata portion of their shares would be purchased in the offer.

The technique of a charter or bylaw provision restricting transfer of shares might also be used to deal with acquisition of control through open-market accumulation of shares by requiring that after a specified block of shares had been accumulated (say, 20%), the accumulating shareholder could not have any additional shares transferred unless he or she were to make an offer for all remaining shares outstanding. Such a charter or bylaw provision, if adopted, would in effect represent an agreement by those shareholders who adopt the provision that any premium paid for transfer of control would have to be shared pro rata among the general body of shareholders.

Assuming that such charter or bylaw provisions may be justified as a means of minimizing the problems inherent in partial takeover offers, should there be any limitation on the types of provisions which could be approved by shareholders?

There are generally three types of limitations that may be placed on the ability of shareholders to restrict transfer of shares: limitations on retroactivity, limitations on discrimination among shareholders of the same class, and limitations which require that restrictions on transfer be reasonable, or at least not manifestly unreasonable.

The first limitation—on retroactivity—is often found in state corporation statutes which preclude the imposition of limitations on transfer of outstanding shares without the consent of their holders.[6] This limitation should not be viewed as a constitutional inhibition in view of the reserved power in most state corporation statutes to alter shareholder rights by appropriate shareholder vote,[7] and where not precluded by statute, retroactive restrictions on transfer could be imposed by majority vote of the shareholders.[8] However, under many existing state corporation statutes, the limitation on transfer may only be imposed on those shareholders who approve the charter or bylaw provision. Since by definition this approval will be at least 51% of the outstanding shares, the charter or bylaw provision should have an operative effect on a substantial number of the outstanding shares. If the charter or bylaw provision is directed at an existing share-

holder (e.g., by prohibiting an existing 20% shareholder from acquiring more shares unless he or she makes a bid for all shares), it may be said to have an improper retroactive effect where the state corporation statute precludes retroactive operation.

The second limitation—on discrimination among shareholders of the same class—may be expressly precluded by state corporation statute.[9] Where discrimination is not expressly precluded, judicial decisions differ as to the ability of shareholders to approve charter or bylaw provisions which discriminate among shareholders of the same class.[10] By regulating the behavior of bidders so as to restrict transfer of shares to them unless a bid is approved by a stated percentage of the shareholders or requiring a holder of a specified percentage of shares to make an offer for all remaining shares, the charter or bylaw amendment does discriminate against such bidders. However, in this context, such discrimination would not appear to be unreasonable unless precluded by express statutory policy.

The third limitation—that a restriction on transfer not be unreasonable—appears in some form either in state corporation statutes or in judicial decision.[11] In the context of a charter or bylaw provision regulating partial takeover bids or sizable market accumulations of shares, for shareholders to provide that unsolicited bids may not be effected unless a specified percentage of shareholders approve the bid does not seem unreasonable, particularly where the restriction is not retroactively imposed on holders of outstanding shares who did not vote to approve the transfer restriction. Similarly, a charter or bylaw provision requiring the holder of a substantial block of shares to make a bid for all shares before accumulating more shares would seem reasonable as long as the triggering block is not made so small as to unreasonably limit transfer of shares.

Restraints on transfer may also operate in less direct fashion than the technique just discussed. For example, in an effort to encourage long-term shareholdings, a charter provision might stipulate that a shareholder will gain additional voting or other rights by holding shares for a specified period of time. Such a provision may act as some inhibition on the transfer of shares, but it would appear to be a reasonable, albeit discriminatory, provision which shareholders should be able to adopt. Furthermore, such a provision may avoid problems of retroactivity as long as it is framed to operate only in a prospective manner. However, if the provision is framed so as to operate retroactively, it may fall afoul of those state corporation statutes which preclude retroactive imposition of restrictions on transfer of shares. For example, if voting rights are diminished by a transfer of shares, such effect would not appear to be capable of imposition on outstanding shares without the consent of their holders. Such a result may not be achievable by simply reclassifying existing shares into two securities, one consisting of the outstanding shares and the other of a new class or series of shares with voting rights which significantly alter the voting rights of outstanding shares, where the net effect of the reclassification is to replace outstanding shares with a new package of securities with significant restrictions on its transferability.

The purpose of the foregoing analysis is not to attempt to set forth with great specificity the outer limits of shareholder power in changing shareholder rights which affect transferability of shares. Rather, it is to suggest that as a matter of state corporation law, within reasonable limits shareholders should have substantial freedom to frame their rights in charter documents in ways which may have an effect on the behavior of bidders and the response of shareholders of the target in the context of unsolicited tender offers.[12]

POWER OF DIRECTORS WITH RESPECT TO RESTRAINTS ON TRANSFER

While shareholders may be entitled to impose reasonable restraints on transfer of shares within the limits just noted, directors are not entitled to exercise the same power. Under the usual state corporation statute, direct restraints on transfer of shares may only be imposed by vote of the shareholders.[13] However, we see today an increasing resort by directors to devices which have an effect on transfer of shares through issuance of special shares or warrants to purchase special shares as a dividend on outstanding shares. In view of the general right of shareholders to transfer their shares—including transfer to a takeover bidder—the question must be asked as to what circumstances should justify directors' action without shareholder approval in placing limitations on the right of shareholders to accept an offer for their shares. Directors should have that power when they can demonstrate that they must act to protect the corporation from immediate and substantial harm or that their action is in the economic best interests of the shareholders. Absent such circumstances, shareholders should not be inhibited in their ability to transfer and thereby accept an offer for their shares.

Of course, defensive actions directors take in the context of an unsolicited takeover bid could be construed as precluding shareholders from having the opportunity to accept a bid and therefore could be viewed as restraining transfer of their shares.[14] Many of such defensive actions are taken by directors under severe time constraints where the best choice for shareholders may be subject to differing views. Some courts have engaged in motivational analysis in determining whether to hold directors responsible for their actions, by inquiring whether the directors sought to entrench themselves in office.[15] Such an approach offers little guidance to directors and exposes them to potentially large liabilities if a court concludes that their motives were not pure. Some recent decisions have put the burden on directors to at least come forward with proof that their defensive actions are reasonable in relation to the threat posed or are otherwise appropriate.[16] A better procedure is to provide that directors be required to meet the burden of proving that they are acting in the best economic interests of the shareholders when they seek to take defensive action which will preclude shareholders from transferring their shares to accept a takeover bid, if their actions are challenged in an injunction proceeding, but to protect the directors against personal liability in a suit against them for damages unless the party challenging their conduct sustains the burden of proving that they failed to satisfy the requirements of the business judgment rule. In application of the business judgment rule in this context, nonmanagement directors would not be viewed as interested (and therefore disqualified from the protection of the business judgment rule) simply because they might be found to have taken actions which caused them to be retained in office.

NOTES

1. See, e.g., *Allen v. Biltmore Tissue Corp.,* 2 N.Y.2d 534, 141 N.E.2d 812 (1957); 1 Model Bus. Corp. Act. Ann., 428–429 (3rd ed.).

2. See, e.g., Del. Gen. Corp. Law, § 202(b); Cal. Corp. Code, § 204(b).

3. See 1 Model Bus. Corp. Act. Ann. § 6.27, 428–431 (3rd ed.).

4. Bebchuk, Chapter 25 of this volume.

5. Compare Model Bus. Corp. Act, § 6.27(b).

6. See, e.g., Del. Gen. Corp. Law, § 202(b); Cal. Corp. Code, § 204(b).

7. See Revised Model Business Corporation Act, § 10.02(b); Official Comment in 2 Model Bus. Corp. Act. Ann., 1147–1148 (3rd ed.).

8. *See Tu-Vu Drive-In Corp. v. Ashkins,* 61 Cal. 2d 283, 38 Cal. Rptr. 348, 391 P.2d 828 (1964).

9. *See* Cal. Corp. Code, §§ 400(b), 1100.

10. Compare *Providence & Worcester Co. v. Baker,* 328 A.2d 121 (Del. Sup. Ct. 1977), with *Asarco, Incorporated v. M.R.H. Holmes A Court,* 611 F. Supp. 468 (D.N.J. 1985) (construing the New Jersey statute).

11. See 1 Model Bus. Corp. Act. Ann., 424–443 (3rd ed.).

12. This chapter does not address the extent, if any, to which shareholder action permitted by state corporation law may be inhibited by federal regulation of tender offers under § 14(d) and 14(e) of the Securities and Exchange Act of 1934.

The U.S. Supreme Court decision in CTS Corporation v. Dynamics Corporation of America 95 L. Ed. 2d 67 (1987) recognizes that those statutory provisions would not preclude collective shareholder action of the types described in this chapter.

13. See Del. Gen. Corp. Law, § 202(b); Cal. Corp. Code, § 204(b); Rev. Model Bus. Corp. Act., § 6.27(a); 1 Model Bus. Corp. Act. Ann., 427 (3rd ed.).

14. Some recent decisions which have invalidated actions by directors creating special series of shares or warrants without shareholder approval have been based in part on the improper restraint on transfer imposed on shares as a result of the directors' action. See *Unilever Acquisition Corp. v. Richardson-Vicks, Inc.,* 618 F. Supp. 407 (S.D.N.Y. 1985); *Minstar Acquiring Corp. v. AMF, Inc.,* Fed. Sec. L. Rep. (CCH), ¶ 92,066 (S.D.N.Y. 1985).

15. See, e.g., *Treadway Companies, Inc. v. Care Corp.,* 638 F.2d 357, 382 (2d Cir. 1980); *Norlin Corporation v. Rooney, Pace, Inc.,* 744 F.2d 255 (2d Cir. 1984); *Bennett v. Propp,* 41 Del. Ch. 16, 187 A.2d 405, 509 (Del. Sup. Ct. 1962); *Petty v. Penntech Papers, Inc.,* 347 A.2d 140, 143 (Del. Ch. 1975); *Condec Corp. v. Lunkenheimer Co.,* 43 Del. Ch. 353, 230 A.2d 769, 773–774 (1962); *Cheff v. Mathes,* 41 Del. Ch. 494, 199 A.2d 548, 555 (1964); *Minstar Acquiring Corp. v. AMF, Inc.,* Fed. Sec. L. Rep. (CCH), ¶ 92,066 (S.D.N.Y. 1985); *Royal Industries, Inc., v. Monogram Industries, Inc.,* 1976–1977 CCH Fed. Sec. L. Rep., 4 ¶ 95,863 (C.D.Cal. 1976).

16. *See Unocal v. Mesa Petroleum Co.,* 493 A.2d 946, 955 (Del. Sup. Ct. 1985); *Moran v. Household International, Inc.,* 500 A.2d 1346, 1356 (Del. Sup. Ct. 1985); *MacAndrews & Forbes Holdings, Inc. v. Revlon, Inc.,* 501 A.2d 1239 (Del. Ch. 1985), aff'd sub nom., *Revlon, Inc. v. MacAndrews & Forbes Holdings, Inc.,* 506 A.2d 173 (Del. Sup. Ct. 1986); *Minstar Acquiring Corp. v. AMF, Inc.,* Fed. Sec. L. Rep. (CCH), ¶ 92,066 (S.D.N.Y. 1985).

30

Comment

STANLEY SPORKIN

I have been an interested observer of the tender offer process for many years. I was there when Rule 10b-(5) was the only real regulatory tool. I had some role in dealing with two of the early abusive practices. Before the Williams Act there was the secret tender offer where the persons making the offer refused to identify themselves. Then came the side-deal tender offer where the tender offeror, after making a public tender offer, made secret, side cash purchases above the tender offer price for particular blocks of stock. The first Williams Act,[1] was supposed to eliminate all the abusive takeover practices but only succeeded in bringing on Williams Act II (i.e., the 1970 and 1977 amendments to the Williams Act.)[2] New problems seem to arise as quickly as new legislation is enacted, with the very gifted players continuing to create new loopholes which require additional plugging.

What is the answer? Do we give up or go back to square one? Do we enact oppressive legislation that would tip the scales too much in favor of one side or another?

I like our present system. It is exciting and allows for free market forces to reach virtually their maximum potential. I do think, however, changes are clearly called for where the system tends to become exaggerated and overreaching and unfairness sets in. I do not think we should or could restructure the process from scratch. I believe what is required is the establishment of a device that allows for three things:

1. A close monitoring of all changes in corporate control to ensure that the rules in effect are strictly enforced. This monitoring is what I call the umpire concept, and I believe that the SEC is the most appropriate organization to play that role.
2. A constant review of the practices being used for the purpose of promptly imposing new rules to curb excessive and abusive practices at the earliest stage. Here, again, I believe that the SEC is the appropriate body to perform this function.
3. The establishment of a separate adjudicative body to determine disputes between private parties or between the government and a private organization. Here, again, I believe the SEC has a role to play.

This last enumerated item is particularly important for several reasons. First, there is a need for uniformity in the takeover adjudicative process. Second, there is a need to ease the burdens on our court system caused by these preemptive court actions. It seems to me unfair for a tender offer player to go to the head of litigation line and bump a litigant who has been waiting many years to have his or her case heard. We all know how easy it is for a tender offer player to get immediate court action. I think such a priority system is unfair.

As to what reforms are needed at this time, I think there are a number of immediate measures called for. First, reform must consider greenmail, which is one of the most abusive practices. Greenmail occurs when an individual takes a substantial stock position in a public corporation for the purpose of forcing the corporation to buy back those shares at a premium through a threat to the corporation that if it does not accede to his request, the individual will either on his own seek to take over the corporation or make his shares available to a third party who will seek control of the corporation. The practice has been almost universally condemned as being improper. The SEC recently sued B. F. Goodrich Company for violation of the federal securities laws when it failed to disclose that it had acceded to the greenmail demands of an individual.[3] Greenmail can be eliminated in any one of several ways:

1. Preclude the issuer from buying back a newly acquired block of shares without making the same offer to all the shareholders.
2. Bring the practice under the § 16b concept by having the threshold reporting amount reduced to 5% and increasing the holding period to two years, with the commission having the ability to exempt a particular transaction where it meets certain criteria and the commission finds it is in the public interest to do so.
3. Adopt the recent proposal made by the New York State legislature which would require a two-thirds shareholder vote before a company could buy back the shares from any shareholder at a price above the current quoted market.[4]

A second reform measure must deal with junk bond[5] financing, which poses a more difficult problem; but I do believe it can be dealt with through the adoption of credit use restrictive measures.[6] I am not suggesting we have a model that can be used as a basis for formulating this new measure, but I do think one could be formulated in a relatively short period of time.

A third measure involves coercive and quick-strike tender offers, which are offers that are designed to compel shareholders to tender quickly without an opportunity to fully consider the merits of the offer. These offers include, for example, two-tiered bids, which coerce shareholders by promising the prospect of a second-step

merger at a lesser price than is offered in the tender offer, and partial bids, where the offer to purchase extends to only a certain, albeit a controlling, percentage of the target's stock. These bids can be handled by having threshold reporting requirements and longer tender offer announcement periods. In addition, such a proposal could require that all shareholders be treated on the same basis where purchases are made within a certain period of time and in effect emanate out of the same acquisition program.

I also recognize there are a number of abusive defensive tactics, some of which involve the partial or total dismantling of the corporate enterprise or the creation of so much debt that the company cannot meet its debt service without a restructuring of the corporation. A Conference Board study released this past summer[7] discussed some of the problems being faced by targets of takeover attempts in this way:

• Objectivity often is lost in the heat of takeover battles, which frequently become emotional tests of wills and egos.
• Defensive measures designed to defeat takeovers can be extreme, costly, and wasteful.
• Vital decisions must be made in a hurried, high-pressure arena that is not conducive to rational decision making.
• Productive, well-managed companies can be damaged, even when they successfully ward off challengers. Cited as examples are firms that have made unwise purchases or divestitures or seriously weakened themselves financially in their fights for independence.

I think most of the abusive tactics will, of course, be reduced by the program I have outlined here to deal with abusive tactics on the offeror side. There are some that can be handled through the normal state corporate codes and others through the listing requirements of our major securities self-regulatory organizations. In addition, the monitoring concept I have advocated would also be available to deal with the other deleterious practices that emerge in the context of a heated takeover battle. I do think we need a leadership dimension in this area. I believe the Securities Exchange Commission is capable of filling that role. I also think the time for action is now and that we have debated these problems much too long.

NOTES

1. Public Law No. 90-439, 82 Stat. 454 (1968).
2. Public Law No. 91-567, 84 Stat. 1497 (1970), and Public Law No. 95-213, 91 Stat. 1494 (1977).
3. *In re B. F. Goodrich Company,* Exchange Act Release 22792 (January 15, 1986).
4. The New York State bill was vetoed by Governor Cuomo on August 13, 1985. On December 10 the legislature passed another anti-takeover bill which was signed by the governor on December 20. The new law limits greenmail by prohibiting the purchase of 10% or more of a company's stock at a price higher than market value unless the purchase is approved by the corporation's directors and shareholders. The greenmail provisions do not apply to an offer to purchase all shares or to stock which the holder has been the owner of for more than two years. See 17 *Securities Regulation Law and Report* (BNA), No. 33 at 1482 (August 16, 1985) and No. 49 at 2156 (December 13, 1985).
5. Junk bonds are low-grade, high-yield bonds. They have become a popular vehicle for raising funds to finance takeover attempts.
6. On January 8 1985, the Federal Reserve Board, in an action that was unknown to the author, adopted certain credit restrictions aimed primarily at stemming the use of junk bonds in acquisitions. The new rule restricts to 50% the amount of debt a company can use through a shell corporation to finance a takeover. See "Fed Votes 3–2 To Limit Use of Junk Bonds; Volcker Stresses Narrowness of Anti-Hostile Takeover Rule,"*American Banker,* January 9, 1986, 1.
7. See *The Conference Board, The Role of Outside Directors in Major Acquisitions,* Research Bulletin No. 10 (August 1985); discussed in *Daily Report for Executives* (BNA), at A-4 (August 15, 1985).

ONE SHARE, ONE VOTE

31

Stock Exchange Rules Affecting Takeovers and Control Transactions

JOEL SELIGMAN

In his article "Regulating the Market for Corporate Control: A Critical Assessment of the Tender Offers Role in Corporate Governance,"[1] Professor John C. Coffee stated: "At present, the most significant limitation on defensive tactics of target corporations is contained neither in the common law of fiduciaries duties nor the anti-fraud rules adopted by the SEC under the Williams Act, but rather is set forth in the New York Stock Exchange policy that effectively limits the magnitude of any stock lock-up the target's board may issue."[2] Impressed by this limitation, he explored "the potential utility of Stock Exchange listing rules as a self-regulatory technique for the adoption of specific 'bright line' rules which avoid many of the problems that vaguer fiduciary standards inherently involve."[3] Coffee emphasized "the recurring problem of a race to the bottom" and suggested that exercise of SEC authority might be necessary to ensure equal regulation by the exchanges and the National Association of Securities Dealers (NASD). He then suggested, as "obvious candidates for regulation through Stock Exchange rules," shareholder approval of "crown-jewel" asset sales, temporal limitations on standstill agreements, limitations on supermajority provisions, prohibition of disenfranchisement provisions, and shareholder approval of "golden-parachute" employment severence agreements.[4]

I am skeptical that stock exchange listing requirements or counterpart requirements adopted for the over-the-counter market by NASD are a likely source for the voluntary adoption of significant new rules affecting takeover transactions. Coffee himself acknowledged some of the reasons security market self-regulatory organizations (SROs) are improbable vehicles of reform. They are handicapped by the difficulty of imposing meaningful sanctions on rule evaders. As Coffee explained:

> Not only has the sanction of delisting been rarely employed, but the threat may be irrelevant to a target corporation that is seeking a merger with a white knight in preference to a takeover by a hostile bidder. In this recurring context, the target knows that its existence as an independent company is at an end and that the only real question is the identity of the company that will acquire it. As a result, the threat of delisting is academic because the target will shortly cease to exist in any event.[5]

Historically, the securities markets also have had difficulty imposing sanctions on major listed companies or member firms. Witness, for example, the inability of the New York Stock Exchange to enforce its general policy of one common share, one vote against Ford Motor Company in 1956[6] or, more recently, against General Motors when it acquired Electronic Data Systems Corporation.[7] Similarly, the securities markets had problems enforcing their net capital and other rules during the late 1960s "back-office" crisis.[8]

A second reason securities market SROs are unlikely voluntarily to adopt significant new rules concerning takeover and control transactions involves market structure. The stock markets and the NASD currently are involved in an intense competition to retain old and attract new corporations for listing or trading. To the extent that rules affecting takeover and control transactions are material to corporations choosing among securities markets, their self-interest dictates that they select the securities markets with the least onerous rules. This process popularly is referred to as "the race to the bottom."[9]

Viewed in institutional terms, the unlikelihood of meaningful, voluntary, stock market SRO reforms becomes apparent for somewhat different reasons. Who, in fact, governs in a securities market? On issues concerning takeover and control transactions, we may reasonably assume that listed firms will have some influence. They are the same firms that habitually oppose reform legislation at the federal and state levels. There is no obvious reason their political preferences should meaningfully change when canvassed in a securities market.[10]

At the same time, the value of SRO rule enforcement cannot be gainsaid. Self-regulators, at times, can go further than government in enforcing their standards because of the less adversarial environment in which they operate. This less adversarial environment permits the enforcement of more minute or less precisely defined standards than a government effectively can enforce. Stock exchange and the NASD's arbitration procedures, for example, regularly sanction stock brokerage firms for conduct far more vaguely defined than the securities laws, at a fraction of the cost of SEC enforcement.[11] In such instances, the stock exchanges or the NASD, in effect, enforce standards, as SEC chairman William O. Douglas put it in 1937, "beyond the periphery of the law in the realm of ethics and morality."[12]

But this type of self-regulatory organization rule enforcement—aptly termed "the traffic regulations" of the securities industry[13]—is quite different from the stock market or the NASD voluntarily implementing significant new rules concerning a leading issue such as corporate takeover transactions. SRO reform on issues of this magnitude is only likely to occur as a result of outside pressures. When Chairman Douglas referred to the SEC keeping "the shotgun . . . behind the door,"[14] he crudely characterized one type of political force that influences a securities market SRO. There are several others, notably including Congress, state securities administrators, federal and state courts, corporations that potentially may list or delist, and investors. Only when one accurately appreciates the confluence of political forces brought to bear on any issue, can one reasonably estimate the probability of reform. In the area of takeover and control transactions, it is my judgment that this probability is very slight.

To illustrate why I reached this conclusion, I want to analyze two sets of current rules affecting takeover and control transactions: those concerning (1) nonvoting common stock and disproportionate voting rights and (2) shareholder approval of transactions when the issuance of common stock could result in an increase in outstanding common shares greater than a designated percentage. I have limited my research to the three largest securities markets: the New York Stock Exchange (NYSE), the American Stock Exchange (AMEX), and the over-the-counter trading system (NASDAQ).[15]

NONVOTING STOCK AND DISPROPORTIONATE VOTING RIGHTS

Section 3 of the NYSE *Listed Company Manual* details that exchange's qualitative listing standards concerning "corporate responsibility."[16] Paragraph 301.00 introduces this section with the statement that "consistent with the Exchange's long-standing commitment to encourage high standards of corporate democracy, every listed company is expected to follow certain practices aimed at maintaining appropriate standards of corporate responsibility, integrity and accountability to shareholders." Pursuant to this policy, each listed company is required to hold an annual shareholders' meeting.[17] Each domestic company with a listed common stock must have an audit committee.[18] No listed company may have a board of directors divided into more than three classes.[19] The exchange encourages a quorum for shareholder meetings of a majority of the common stock.[20] Each listed company agrees that it will not engage in a partial redemption of securities listed on the exchange otherwise then pro rata or by lot.[21] Shareholder approval must be secured for listed securities to be issued which result in a change in the control of a company,[22] or where the present or potential issuance of common stock or securities convertible into common stock could result in an increase in outstanding common shares of 18½% or more.[23]

The NYSE has several standards regarding voting rights. As is well known, "since 1926, the Exchange has refused to authorize the listing of non-voting stock, however designated, which by its terms is in effect common stock."[24] The exchange also will refuse to list the common voting stock of a company which also has outstanding a nonvoting stock however designated which by its term is in effect a common stock.[25] Similarly, the exchange normally will refuse to list voting trust certificates[26] and will object to transactions where shareholder voting rights have been restricted by a voting trust, irrevocable proxy, or any similar arrangement "to which the company or any of its directors or officers is a party directly or indirectly."[27] Presumably, "similar arrangements" would embrace shareholder pooling agreements[28] and vote buying,[29] at least when the purchase is made by the company, directors, or officers. For good measure, the exchange also reserves the power to refuse to list a class of stock which has unusual voting provisions. A situation in which one class of stock has the right to veto the actions of the common stock is offered as an example.[30] The exchange reviews instances where voting power is divided between the common stock and one or more other classes of stock under normal conditions on a case-by-case basis. As a guide, however, the exchange states that it "is of the view that any

allocation of voting power under normal conditions to classes of stock other than common stock should be in reasonable relationship to the equity interests of such classes."[31] By abnormal conditions, the exchange means circumstances in which another class of stock temporarily acquires voting power as a result of dividend default or similar occurrence. In instances of default upon six consecutive quarterly dividends, the NYSE further recommends that preferred stock, voting as a class, should have the right to elect a minimum of two directors.[32]

The AMEX standards treat many of the same topics as those of the NYSE but usually with less rigorous standards. Like the NYSE, the AMEX requires an annual meeting.[33] The AMEX recommends (but unlike the NYSE, does not require) an audit committee.[34] Similarly, the AMEX recommends a quorum of 33⅓% of the voting stock, in contrast to the NYSE's encouragement of a majority quorum.[35] Parallel to the NYSE requirement of shareholder approval for transactions involving the present or potential issuance of 18½% or more common stock, the AMEX requires shareholder approval of transactions that will or potentially could increase the outstanding common shares by 20% or more.[36] The AMEX rule concerning common stock voting rights is sparse compared with that of the NYSE. Paragraph 122 of the American Stock Exchange's *Company Guide* states in toto: "The Exchange will not approve an application for the listing of a nonvoting common stock issue. The Exchange may approve the listing of a common stock which has the right to elect only a minority of the board of directors."[37] Unlike the NYSE, the AMEX has no rule concerning voting trusts. The AMEX does provide that preferred stock, to be eligible for listing, should accord its holders the right to elect at least two members to the company's board no later than two years after an incurred default in the payment of fixed dividends.[38]

The NASD in July 1985 adopted corporate governance rules requiring a minimum of two independent directors on the board of each firm traded in the NASDAQ computer trading system or on its National Market System (NMS) list.[39] The NASD also requires NASDAQ/NMS issues to maintain an audit committee, hold an annual shareholders meeting, and establish a quorum requirement of at least 50% of the outstanding shares for all shareholder meetings. The NASD does not currently have standards requiring common stock to have a vote or proportional voting or proportional voting rights. In July 1985, however, the NASD sought comments on two alternative proposals dealing with shareholders voting. The first would require all firms in the NASDAQ/NMS to honor a one–common share, one-vote standard. Existing NASDAQ/NMS firms with other common stock voting rights would be allowed to retain them under a "grandfather" clause. The second proposal would require one vote per share unless different voting rights were approved by the holders of two-thirds of the outstanding shares, and these differential voting rights were subject to a "sunset provision" of no more than ten years. The maximum difference in voting rights for different classes of stock would be a ratio of 10 to 1.[40]

The primary event inspiring concern with stock exchange or the NASD common share voting rights was the proposal in January 1985 by the NYSE Subcommittee on Shareholder Participation and Qualitative Listing Standards for Dual-Class Capitalization. The subcommittee recommended that an issuer with securities listed on the New York Stock Exchange should not have those securities delisted because of the adoption of charter provisions creating two classes of common stock having disparate voting rights, under the following conditions:

1. The transaction in which the shares with different voting rights are to be issued has been approved by two-thirds of all shares entitled to vote on the proposition.
2. If the issuer had a majority of independent directors at the time the matter was voted upon, a majority of such directors approved the proposal; if the issuer had less than a majority of such

directors, then all independent directors approved.
3. The ratio of voting differential per share is no more than one to ten.
4. The rights of the holders of the two classes of common stock are substantially the same except for voting power per share.[41]

Under pressure from Senate Securities Subcommittee Chairman Alfonse D'Amato and House Energy and Commerce Chairman John Dingell to negotiate a one-share, one-vote standard or face congressional enactment of one,[42] officials of the New York and American stock exchanges and the NASD began discussions to determine if voluntary compliance with a one-vote-for-each-common-share rule is possible in these three markets.[43] These discussions ultimately failed, leading the NYSE directors in July 1986 to approve a proposal permitting dual class capitalization on the NYSE. The directors' version notably does not limit the voting differential between classes to "no more than one vote to ten," does not require that the rights of the two classes be "substantially the same except for voting power per share," and does not require approval "by two-thirds of all shares entitled to vote on the proposition." Instead, as the NYSE press release tersely states, "[t]he new standards require a company proposing to recapitalize to obtain approval of the plan by a majority of its publicly held shares, as well as a majority of its independent directors." Moreover, the directors' proposal provides a two-year period for companies currently in violation of the standard to comply with the rule.[44]

Historical Background

The historical background of the one–common share, one-vote controversy essentially begins in 1925. State corporate law had long before discarded the rule that each shareholder was entitled to only one vote regardless of the number of shares owned, so that "by the end of the nineteenth century . . . [it was] unusual to find a statutory reference to any formula other than one vote per share."[45] Indeed, at the turn of century, frequently both common and preferred stock had equal voting rights; only during the period after 1903 did the author of a leading 1926 study find that corporate stock issues showed "an increasing tendency to restrict the voting rights of certain classes of shareholders."[46] With the controlling factions in the largest business corporation frequently possessing a minority of stockownership, a number of legal devices developed to maintain control. These legal devices notably included "pyramiding," nonvoting preferred stock, and the voting trust.[47]

Then in 1925, a few leading corporations issued nonvoting common stock. The two best-known examples of this legal device were Dodge Brothers, Inc., and Industrial Rayon Corporation. Dodge Brothers issued to the public bonds, preferred stock, and 1.5 million shares of nonvoting class A common stock. The total value of the public investment was approximately $130 million. Control of Dodge Brothers, in turn, was held by the investment bank of Dillon, Read and Company which invested less than $2.25 million to purchase the 250,001 shares of voting class B common stock. Dodge Brothers, Inc., was listed on the New York Stock Exchange in 1925.[48] Industrial Rayon distributed to the public 598,000 shares of nonvoting class A stock, reserving control for the holders of 2000 shares of voting class B stock.[49] The public reaction to the New York Stock Exchange listing of Dodge Brothers, Inc., at a remove of 60 years, appears astonishing. It effectively began with a comparatively brief October 28, 1925, address by Harvard University professor of political economy William Z. Ripley to the Academy of Political Science, then holding its annual meeting in New York City. Ripley predicted an extension of the powers and activities of bodies such as the Federal Trade Commission, in part because of the assumption of absolute control over business corporations "by intermediaries—most commonly bankers, so-called":

All kinds of private businesses are being bought up by banking houses, and new corporations are being substituted for the old, in order that the purchase price (and more) may be recovered by sale of shares to the general public. But the significant change is that the new stock, thus sold, is entirely bereft of any voting power, except in case of actual or impending bankruptcy. General stockholders, to be sure, have always been inert, delegating most of their powers of election. But at worst they might always be stimulated to assert themselves, and, in any event, they all fared alike as respects profits or losses. Under the new style of corporation such general stockholders are boldly deprived of all rights in this direction and new preferred stocks are sold up to the hilt of the value of the assets, if not beyond.[50]

Ripley then briefly described the Dodge Brothers, Inc., and Industrial Rayon Corporation issues of nonvoting common stock. His entire discussion of the issue was contained in five paragraphs of text which covered barely one-half of one page when republished in the Congressional Record. As Ripley himself later was to write, the "response to but a slight stimulus is perhaps unique in our economic annals."[51] The following day the New York Times published much of Ripley's address in a news story,[52] subsequently publishing editorials echoing Ripley's criticism on November 1 and 14, 1925, and feature articles on November 22, 1925, and February 7, 1926. Major coverage also was devoted to a related Ripley address on February 21, 1926, which was published on the front page of the second section of the Times under the headline "Says Wall Street Must Clean House."[53] Ripley's original October 28 address was republished in the Nation,[54] then expanded and printed in the Atlantic Monthly under the title "From Main Street to Wall Street,"[55] which, in turn, was expanded into Ripley's well-known 1927 book, Main Street and Wall Street. Ultimately, on February 16, 1926, Ripley was invited to the White House to confer with President Calvin Coolidge on the subject of nonvoting stock, news accounts simultaneously reporting that the Justice Department was conducting an inquiry to determine whether interstate commerce laws had been violated.[56]

With emphasis on bankers' control a particularly effective theme in a nation whose last major federal corporate reforms had been preceded by congressional investigation of "The Money Trust"[57] and the Louis Brandeis critique of J. P. Morgan, *Other People's Money,*[58] other votaries soon joined Ripley. In April 1926, Adolf Berle published "Non-Voting Stock and Bankers' Control" in the *Harvard Law Review.*[59] An attorney, with the unlikely name of Seligman, delivered an address to the American Bar Association premised on the daring theme, "The persons who share in the profits and losses (meaning, common stockholders) should share in the same proportion in the control."[60] The Interstate Commerce Commission soon disapproved the Nickel Plate consolidation plan because it involved a voting trust, stating, "We believe it to be self-evident that the public interest requires that the entire body of the stockholders of a railroad ... and not a powerful few, shall be responsible for management."[61] Days later, the New Jersey Public Utility Commission withheld approval of a stock issue of the Delaware and New Jersey Transportation Company on the ground that the great majority of the stock would be nonvoting.[62] At its May 1926 board of governors meeting, the Industrial Securities Committee of the Investment Banking Association reached a carefully hedged conclusion, in part, discouraging the use of nonvoting common stock:

Weighing the above arguments for and against the issue of non-voting common stocks, your committee is of the opinion, first, that unless some method be devised to prevent abuses of the privilege major considerations of public welfare require that non-voting common stocks be not issued; second, that if issued under restrictions that will prevent such abuses, issuing houses should fully realize their responsibilities and live up to them, and third, that before causing non-voting common stocks to be issued issuing houses should give a special attention to the legal aspects of control by common voting stocks where a substantial amount of common stock having no voting privilege is also outstanding.[63]

That nonvoting common stock had become a matter of general public concern perhaps was most effectively suggested by the publication of a satirical poem in the *New York World,* "On Waiting in Vain for the *New Masses* to Denounce Nonvoting Stocks":

Then you who drive the fractious nail,
And you who lay the heavy rail,
And all who bear the dinner pail
     And daily punch the clock—
Shall it be said your hearts are stone?
They are your brethren and they groan!
Oh, drop a tear for those who own
     Nonvoting corporate stock.[64]

It was in these circumstances that the New York Stock Exchange first disapproved an issue of nonvoting common stock on January 18, 1926.[65] There was little public explanation of the initial decision. A New York Stock Exchange public statement on January 27, 1926, cryptically explained:

Without at this time attempting to formulate a definite policy, attention should be drawn to the facts that in future the Committee, in considering applications for the listing of securities, will give careful thought to the matter of voting control.[66]

Eight years later Frank Altschul, chairman of the NYSE Committee on Stock List, slightly elaborated on the reasoning of the Committee on Stock List concerning a January 27, 1926, meeting with NYSE president E. H. H. Simmons. Altschul testified:

You will note a reference to action of the governing committee taken on January 27, 1926, in the matter of the issue of common stock without voting power. This device was being increasingly used to lodge control in small issues of voting stock, leaving ownership of the bulk of the property divorced from any vestige of effective voice in the choice of management.

The committee felt that this tendency ran counter to sound public policy, and accordingly decided to list no more nonvoting common stocks. With this action of the committee, the period of the creation of nonvoting common stocks came to an end.[67]

In retrospect, it seems clear that the primary motivation for the initial New York Stock Exchange decision on nonvoting common stock was concern about public opinion. A 1953 memorandum from Phillip West to NYSE President G. Keith Funston variously stated of the background leading the exchange to reject nonvoting common stock for listing:

The term "banker control" became a political football and fell into disrepute.... Criticism arose because of the frequent disproportionate shares of invested capital represented in the respective classes.... Professor William G. Ripley [sic] of Harvard University was one of the foremost critics of the non-voting common stock set-up.[68]

Initially, there were important exceptions to the NYSE policy. For example, Frank Altschul testified in 1934 that the NYSE did not believe that the voting trust certificate "has any of the same general implications that the nonvoting stock has."[69] And in June and November 1926, two nonvoting common stock issues were listed, each on the ground that listing had been sought before the NYSE's January 27, 1926, statement on nonvoting common stock.[70]

Over time, the NYSE's policy against nonvoting common stock hardened and was further articulated. A key statement was made on May 7, 1940, entitled *Statement of Listing Requirements As to Preferred Stock Voting Rights*. It begins with a sentence still found in the NYSE listing requirements, "Since 1926, the New York Stock Exchange has refused to list non-voting common stock."[71] This statement apparently was "the first formal, published enunciation that the Exchange would refuse to list non-voting common stock."[72] As to why the NYSE held this position, various exchange memoranda have termed voting to be an "inherent right."[73] The NYSE *Company Manual* itself states, "Consistent with the Exchange's longstanding commitment to encourage high standards of corporate democracy, every listed company is expected to follow certain practices aimed at maintaining appropriate standards of corporate responsibility, integrity and accountability to shareholders."[74] Invocation of these and similar statements has been used by the NYSE to deny or withdraw listings on several occasions.[75]

A basic difficulty with the NYSE policy is that it is essentially contentless. At no point publicly has the NYSE defined such key terms as *inherent right, corporate democracy, appropriate standards of corporate responsibility, integrity, and accountability to shareholders*. It is far from obvious what, in fact, these standards mean. Nor has the NYSE based its policy on a principle or theory that could give meaning to the ambiguities in the policy.

The NYSE policy concerning common stock voting appears to have endured primarily for political reasons. Apparently, the exchange has long understood that a significant change in its common stock voting policy likely would inspire federal or state legislative or administrative agency response. At the same time, a policy based essentially on political concerns also is susceptible to countervailing pressures. In 1956, for example, the NYSE was willing to list Ford Motor Company, despite the fact that the Ford family's class B common stock could retain 40% of the company's voting power with only 5.1% of the equity.[76] There is no persuasive logical explanation as to why the 1925 listing of Dodge Brothers with insiders possessing 100% of the voting power on approximately 2% of the equity should be the cause of a new NYSE policy while Ford insiders were permitted to have 40% of the company's voting power on approximately 5% of the equity. The obvious explanation is a political one. In 1956, Ford Motor Company was viewed as so important a new listing that the NYSE was willing to compromise its policy.

For similar reasons the NYSE in June 1984 appointed its Subcommittee on Shareholder Participation and Qualitive Listing Standards. The exchange was faced with a dilemma. If it adhered to a one–common share, one-vote policy, it would lose some current and some potential listings to NASDAQ or the American Stock Exchange, neither of which adhered to that policy. The primary reason the NYSE feared this competition was the increased concern corporate managements had with creating effective takeover defenses. Dual classes of common stock with an insider owning the exclusive voting stock or stock with disproportionate voting rights is a most effective defense. A review of the correspondence forwarded in response to an interrogatory mailed by the Subcommittee on Shareholder Participation and Qualitive Listing Standards indicates that the NYSE's respondents, like officials of the NYSE, understood the twin motivations of the subcommittee's proposals. These motivations unquestionably were the exchange's concern about competition from other securities markets and corporate management's desire for a new takeover defense.[77]

I also emphasize that until recently dual capitalization was not perceived by many corporate managers as a desirable financial structure. At this time, approximately 10 firms listed on the NYSE have a dual-capital structure;[78] according to separate estimates by the AMEX and SEC Chairman John Shad, approximately 60 of 785 companies listed on the American Stock Exchange had two classes of stock (i.e., about 7%)[79] and at least 110 of the 4101 companies traded on NASDAQ had multiple classes of stock (or 2.7%).[80] Only within the past year or two has the number of corporations contemplating dual capitalization been statistically significant. As one American Stock Exchange official put it, if there is no agreement among the securities markets and no legislative or administrative agency decision within the next months barring dual capitalization, then the number of telephone inquiries from NYSE listed firms has persuaded him that "the floodgates will open."[81]

The historical background of the AMEX common stock voting rule is comparatively more recent. In 1972, the AMEX adopted the language found in the current Paragraph 122, which prohibits the listing of a nonvoting common stock issue.[82] Through April 1976, 37 corporations were listed on the AMEX with multiple classes of stock, each presumably having disproportionate voting rights.[83] Through that date, the AMEX did not have a clear policy concerning disproportionate common stock voting rights but approved listings on a case-by-case basis.

Early in 1976, Wang Laboratories, Inc., was informed it would not be listed on the NYSE if its shareholders adopted a proposed capitalization that included both common stock with one vote per share and class B common stock having one-tenth of one vote per share. As ultimately adopted, voting as a class, the class B common stock also was entitled to elect 25% of the board of directors rounded up to the nearest whole number, or two of the seven members of the board in April 1976.[84] The purpose of this capitalization was to retain control of the firm in the Wang family. As of July 31, 1984, the family and family trusts owned 71% of the common stock (now denominated class C common) and 27% of the class B limited voting shares.[85]

The AMEX was willing to list Wang Laboratories on this basis. Significantly, the AMEX subsequently published the essence of the prelisting understandings with Wang Laboratories in the form of a statement of policy. That policy statement, sometimes called the "Wang formula" provides the following:

Disproportionate Voting Establishment of a Two Class Issue

Although AMEX rules prohibit the listing of non-voting common stock issues, an application may be accepted from a company for listing of two classes of common stock possessing unequal voting rights. Examples of companies which fall into this category are Wang Laboratories, Inc., Telephone and Data Systems, Inc., Knoll International, Inc., and Blount, Inc.

In addition to the basic listing criteria, a company contemplating listing on the AMEX which has, or is in the process of creating, a new limited voting common stock issue should consider the following AMEX policies. (These policies also apply to previously listed AMEX companies which are considering a recapitalization to create two classes of unequal-voting common stock.)

(a) The limited voting class of the common must have the ability—voting as a class—to elect not less than 25% of the board of directors.

(b) There may not be a voting ratio greater than 10 to 1 in favor of the "super" voting class on all matters other than the election of directors.

(c) No additional stock (whether designated as

common or preferred) may be created which can in any way diminish voting power granted to the holders of the limited voting class. For example, should a listed company create a "blank check" voting preferred, this issue would not be permitted to vote with the limited voting class, since to do so would diminish the limited voting issue's rights. Instead, the preferred would have to vote with the "super" voting issue.

(d) The Exchange will generally require that the "super" class lose certain of its attributes should the number of such shares fall below a certain percentage of the total capitalization.

(e) While not specifically required, it is strongly recommended that a dividend preference be established for the limited voting issue.

After Wang, 22 firms listed on the AMEX used this formula in the period up to August 15, 1985. In addition, 7 of the 37 AMEX firms which had disproportionate voting rights before April 1976 have recapitalized by employing the Wang formula.[86]

Finally, the recently adopted NASD corporate governance requirements and survey concerning common stock voting rights deserve brief comment. Both initiatives were inspired by a common cause. As NASD President Gordon Macklin wrote to his membership on May 13, 1985: "The Corporate Advisory Board believes that the likelihood of achieving a 'blue sky' exemption for NASDAQ/NMS companies in all 50 states will be greatly improved by the implementation of corporate governance criteria."[87] The basis for this belief similarly has been disclosed. "Numerous state securities administrators," explained the NASD, "have noted the difference in approach to corporate governance by NASDAQ/NMS and certain of the Exchanges."[88] Implicit in the concerns expressed by state securities administrators is the reality that securities listed on the NYSE or the AMEX are exempt from state securities registration requirements in 48 states.[89] In contrast, securities traded in the NASDAQ system or on the NMS list are exempt in only six states.[90] The NASD has made no secret of its desire to achieve the same securities market exemption as the NYSE or the AMEX.[91]

Why Have So Few Corporations to Date Employed Dual Capitalization?

One of the more curious aspects of the controversy concerning dual capitalization is that so few managers to date have employed this legal device to ensure control of their corporations. Firms listed on the AMEX or traded in NASDAQ are free to fashion disproportionate common stock voting shares. Yet available evidence suggests that only approximately 170 of the 4886 corporations traded in these two markets have done so.[92] There appear to be four different explanations for this phenomenon.

Dual Capitalization Is Unnecessary to Ensure Control

For over half of a century, most corporate legal scholars and economists studying the agency problems of the large firm have begun with the assumption of a separation of ownership from control. In the pathbreaking Adolf Berle and Gardiner Means study, "ultimate" control was held by majority owners in only 5% of the 200 largest companies at the beginning of 1930; management control accounted for 44%; control through a legal device, 21%; minority control, 23%; private ownership, 6%; and a receiver was in control in 1% of the instances studied.[93]

Although subsequent studies have made similar findings in more recent periods for the 200 largest firms,[94] there also is evidence that majority or near-majority factions control the board of directors a considerably higher proportion of the time as the focus shifts to firms smaller than the largest 200. For example, Professor Harold Demsetz studied the average ownership interest of corporate directors and managers for selected firms on the 1975 Fortune 500 list during the 1973–1982 period. He found that corporate directors and managers owned 2.1% of the shares in the ten largest firms on the Fortune 500 list, 19.3% of the shares in the middle ten firms on the list, and 20.4% for the last ten firms.[95]

With 6355 common stock issuers listed on the NYSE or AMEX or traded in the NASDAQ,[96] these data may underestimate the percentage of firms in which managers own a majority of voting stock or so near a majority that a takeover attempt is implausible. To test this possibility, I analyzed the most recent available proxy statement or 10–K annual report for three lists of firms: (1) the last ten firms on the 1981 Fortune 1000 list (1981 was the last year *Fortune* published a second 500 list); (2) the first ten firms on the NASDAQ non-national market system list; and (3) the first ten firms on the over-the-counter non-NASDAQ list.[97] The last list provides firms normally below the size of the NASDAQ list but for which there is some public trading. See Tables 31.1, 31.2, and 31.3.

I make no claim that these data constitute large enough samples to be generalizable. They are, however, suggestive of what more systematic surveys might learn. What is most striking is the number of instances in which the directors and officers owned a majority of the voting stock (one instance in the Fortune 1000 list; two instances in the NASDAQ non-NMS list; four instances in the OTC non-NASDAQ list). Similarly, a reasonable assumption is that when the directors and officers own nearly a majority, say 40% to 50% of the voting stock, their ownership interest will normally be so near a majority as to dissuade hostile takeover attempts. A few firms had insider ownership of over 40% (one instance in the Fortune 1000 list; one

instance in the OTC non-NASDAQ list). These data suggest that in a significant percentage of firms below the Fortune 500 list, dual capitalization is unnecessary to ensure control. The voting stock owned by directors and officers alone makes these firms impossible or nearly impossible to acquire through a hostile tender offer.

In some percentage of corporations in which managers do not own a majority or near majority of voting stock, control may be achieved through a voting trust or shareholder vote pooling arrangement. Only the NYSE prohibits voting trusts and similar arrangements.[98]

Outside of the context of takeover transactions, it is clear that dual capitalization is unnecessary to ensure incumbent management control of corporations. During the period 1956–1977, the SEC published data on proxy contests for all firms subject to commission jurisdiction under Section 12 of the Securities Exchange Act.[99] During that period, management retained control at least 99.7% of the time each year. During the last 11 years for which data are available, management retained control at least 99.9% of the time each year.[100]

Dual Capitalization and the Value of Publicly Held Common Stock

The right of common stock to vote in director and fundamental transaction elections has a monetary value. All other rights

Table 31.1. Last Ten Firms: 1981 Fortune 1000 List

1981 Rank and Firm	Date of Proxy Statement or 10–K	Sales (in 1000s)	Percent Stock Owned by Directors and Officers
991 Chatham Manufacturing	4–12–84	125,133	17.8%
992 General Automation	11–7–83	124,891	10.5
993 J. L. Clark Manufacturing	3–1–85	124,466	1.79
994 Walso National	10–12–84	124,394	11.8
995 Goody Products	4–9–84	123,943	17.11
996 Checker Motors	4–1–85	123,146	65.2
997 Trico Industries	3–22–82	123,047	9.09
998 Sigma-Aldrich	3–25–85	123,009	7.9
999 Instrumentation Laboratories	6–15–82	122,534	46.2
1000 L. S. Starrett	9–21–83	122,451	6.5

Table 31.2. First Ten Firms: NASDAQ Non-NMS List

Rank and Firm	Date of Proxy Statement or 10–K	Sales (in 1000s)	Percent Stock Owned by Directors and Officers
1 A. A. Importing	4–16–85	13,829	69.5
2 Advance Ross	6–5–85	4,866	7.3
3 Adventure Lands	3–12–85	9,753	.7
4 Aero Services	9–30–84	43,792	25.4
5 Agnico-Eagle	7–5–85	18,014	1.5
6 AlaTenn Resources	12–31–82; 9–26–84	132,872	6.3
7 Alco Health	6–28–85	766,654	1
8 Alexander Energy	3–31–83	2,804	53.91
9 American Guaranty Financial	12–31–84	3,367	2.46
10 Ameribanc, Inc.	12–31–84	5,328	25.78

being equal, a class of common stock with voting rights will sell at a higher price than a second class of common stock without voting rights. The primary reason voting rights have a value is because of the premium tender offer bidders are willing to pay to buy voting control of a target. One crudely can symbolize the value of common stock voting rights in a given firm by multiplying the probable future premium by the probability of a tender offer being made.[101]

Two recent studies have attempted to estimate the value of voting rights in publicly traded American corporations. In one study, Professors Ronald Lease, John McConnell, and Wayne Mikkelson[102] specified that to be included within their sample,

a corporation must have had outstanding two classes of common stock sometime over the period beginning January 1940 and ending December 1978. The two classes of common stock must have differed only in the voting rights

Table 31.3. First Ten Firms: OTC Non-NASDAQ List

Rank and Firm	Date of Proxy Statement or 10–K	Sales (in 1000s)	Percent Stock Owned by Directors and Officers
1 ACS Enterprises	2–25–83; 3–29–85	4,587	70
2 Adcor Electronics	5–7–84	2,792	24.1
3 Advanced Cellular	12–1–84 2–14–85	12,040 (last six months, 1984)	38.7
4 Advanced Medical Imaging	11–30–84	Developmental stage	51.03
5 Advanced Monitoring Systems	9–30–84	1,200	29.96
6 Advanced NMR Systems, Inc	12–31–84	Developmental stage	66.4
7 Advanced Tobacco Products	6–30–84	60	51.5
8 Aerosonic	6–19–85	10,941	35.06
9 Aim Telephone	2–28–85	8,144	20.5
10 AFP Imaging	11–26–84	14,741	44.6

which they conferred upon their owners. Specifically, ownership of the two classes of stock must have conveyed identical claims to future dividends, including any liquidating dividends, to their owners. Finally, both classes must have been publicly-traded and both must have been traded actively in the same market.

To discover stocks fulfilling these requirements for the years 1940 through 1949 we searched the January issue of the Monthly Stock Guide published by C. J. Lawrence and Sons, Inc. For the years 1950 through 1978 we searched the January issue of the Security Owner's Stock Guide published by Standard and Poor's Corporation. This search yielded 30 companies.[103]

The key finding in this study was that for the 26 firms that had two classes of common stock outstanding, but no voting preferred stock outstanding, the class of common stock with superior voting rights traded at a mean price premium of 5.44% to the other class of common stock.[104]

In 1984, Lease et al. conducted a followup study and found similar premiums in a sample of six closely held firms with two classes of common stock that were differentiated only by voting rights.[105] A third study by Halm Levy[106] found considerably larger premiums (mean relative voting premium of 52.11%) in 18 publicly traded Israeli corporations with disproportionate voting rights ranging from 2:1 to 10:1. A fourth study by Sanjai Bhagat and James A. Brickley[107] found a reduction in share values in corporations that eliminated cumulative voting or had cumulative voting and classified their boards of directors. Since the impact either of eliminating cumulative voting altogether or of reducing its effectiveness by classifying the board is similar to the impact of issuing a class of common stock with inferior voting rights to public shareholders, this study provides useful analogous evidence.

There also is other empirical research that can be used by analogy. A recent *Harvard Law Review* note[108] summarized results of six studies, five of which found price declines ranging from an average of 1.73% to 6.8% in the period immediately following public announcement of "greenmail" repurchase agreement with a putative bidder. Since greenmail repayments

lower the probability of shareholders receiving a tender offer premium, the decline in price may be theorized to reflect the dollar value of the lessened probability of a tender offer multiplied by the probable tender offer premium. In recent years, the average tender offer premium has averaged approximately 50% above the immediately prior stock market price.[109]

This consistent pattern of study results suggests that all other things being equal, corporations with dual-class capitalization will see the class of stock with inferior voting rights selling at a discount compared with corporations with a unitary common stock class. A reasonable assumption is that at least some managers may have avoided dual-class capitalization because of a recognition that more money could be raised from the sale of a single class of common stock with equal voting rights than of a dual-class capitalization.

The Legal Status of Dual-Class Capitalization under State or Federal Law

State Law

With limited exceptions, state corporate law statutes permit the creation of classes or series of stock lacking voting rights, having limited voting rights, or having multiple voting rights.[110] Occasionally, state courts have enjoined an ongoing firm from issuing a new class or series of stock with special voting rights, particularly when it occurs during a contest for control.[111] State corporate law, consistent with its "enabling" tradition, however, generally will permit a corporation to create two or more classes of common stock with different voting rights.

That, however, is only the beginning of analysis. Publicly traded companies also would be reviewed by state securities administrators. The Midwest Securities Commissioners in 1968 and the North American Securities Administrators Association (NASAA) in 1980 adopted a statement of policy declaring the following:

Unless preferential treatment as to dividends and liquidation is provided with respect to the publicly offered securities or the differentiation is otherwise justified, the offering or proposed offering of equity securities of an issuer having more than one class of equity securities authorized or outstanding shall be considered unfair and inequitable to public investors if the class of equity securities offered to the public (a) has no voting rights or (b) has less than equal voting rights, in proportion to the number of shares of each class outstanding, on all matters, including the election of members to the board of directors of the issuer.[112]

Consistent with this policy, 18 states have adopted regulations prohibiting the issuance of common stock with unequal voting rights.[113] The regulations represent the most significant legal restraint on disproportionate common stock voting rights. Although this number is a minority of the states, prohibition in such leading states as California, Florida, and Texas ensure that this blue-sky policy will be obeyed by issuers seeking a national distribution or a major state distribution and otherwise unable to obtain an exemption.

There is an interdependence between the stock exchange and blue-sky rules concerning common stock voting rights. Most states that prohibit unequal voting rights exempt the New York and/or American Stock Exchange from this prohibition.[114] These two exchanges currently do not permit nonvoting stock. When the New York Stock Exchange began considering permitting dual-class capitalization, state securities administrators made it known that they would consider ending the stock exchange registration exemption if the NYSE authorized dual capitalization.[115]

Federal Law

In a similar sense, there is an interdependence between the stock exchange, blue-sky, and federal positions on common stock voting rights. With the exception of the Public Utility Holding Company Act of 1935, the Investment Company Act of 1940, and the current Bankruptcy Act, no federal statute expressly requires equal stock voting rights.[116]

The Securities Exchange Act of 1934, in all probability, empowers the Securities and Exchange Commission to adopt a rule forbidding firms whose stock is traded on a national securities exchange or in the NASDAQ system from issuing common stock with unequal voting rights.

Section 19(c), added as part of the 1975 Securities Acts Amendments, provides the following:

The Commission, by rule, may abrogate, add to and delete from . . . the rules of a self-regulatory organization . . . as the Commission deems necessary or appropriate to insure the fair administration of the self-regulatory organization, to conform its rules to requirements of this title and the rules and regulations thereunder applicable to such organization, or otherwise in furtherance of the purpose of this title.[117]

While this subsection does not appear to authorize the SEC to amend SRO rules for the purpose of establishing a comprehensive federal corporation act, covering such matters as the number of directors or how many shall be outsiders,[118] it equally does appear to authorize SEC actions if the SEC can demonstrate they are necessary "to insure the fair administration" of the SRO or "otherwise in furtherance of the purpose of this title." The legislative history of this subsection underlines that it was intended to give the commission "plenary power over self-regulatory rules."[119] "The SEC would be granted," explains the Senate report, "the power to change the rules of a self-regulatory organization in any respect, not just with respect to certain enumerated areas."[120] The key restriction emphasized in the legislative history, one implicit in the language of the statute, is that SEC actions must be "consistent with the purposes of the Exchange Act."[121]

SEC actions to require the NYSE, the AMEX, and the NASDAQ system to have rules requiring that all common shares have equal voting rights would appear to be "consistent with the purposes of the Exchange Act" on three different grounds. First, Section 11A(a)(2) authorizes the SEC to "designate the securities or classes of securities qualified for trading in the national market system from among securities other than exempted securities."[122] The legislative history emphasizes, "The Commission would be required to assure the equal regulation of all markets for qualified securities."[123] Milton Cohen, I believe persuasively, has argued that in order for a security to be "qualified" as a national market system security, the commission could require that "its issuer must meet specified voting and other corporate governance standards—just as it must meet the disclosure, proxy solicitation, stock repurchase and other requirements of Sections 12, 13, 14 and 16." Cohen recognizes that the issue "is not free from doubt" but urges:

In support of the Commission's power to act in the specific circumstances, I would point out that Sections 6(b)(5) and 15A(b)(6) specify that the rules of an exchange or an association must not be "designed to permit unfair discrimination between . . . issuers." If the present rules of the exchanges and the NASD produce a serious form of discrimination among issuers, such as to result in unfair competition among markets with regard to securities in which there is an actual or probable multiple trading interest, I believe it is at least strongly arguable that the Commission is authorized to adopt its own rule or compel self-regulatory rule changes to accomplish the suggested result.[124]

To make Cohen's unfair-competition point in different terms, a primary purpose of the 1975 Act Amendments was to ensure that competition among securities markets and securities dealers generated the best-priced execution of securities transactions at the lowest transaction costs.[125] Section 11A(c)(4)(A) of the Securities Exchange Act directs the SEC to amend "any . . . rule imposing a burden on competition." The reference to competition clearly meant competition to offer executions at superior prices or with the lowest transaction costs.[126] The SEC could adopt a common stock voting rights requirement under Section 11A(a)(2) to avoid the type of "burden" on competition Section 11A(c)(4)(A) directed the commission to obviate.

Second, as Professor Coffee has urged, the SEC also appears empowered "to mandate revisions of Stock Exchange rules in order to help realize the Williams Act's goal of neutrality between the contestants and protection of investors."[127]

Third, the purpose of the proxy solicitation provision of the Securities Exchange Act, Section 14(a),[128] has been recognized by the Supreme Court to protect "the free exercise of the voting rights of stockholders."[129] Lower federal courts have amplified this point. The third circuit in its 1947 decision *SEC v. Transamerica,*[130] for example, stated, "It was the intent of Congress to require fair opportunity for the operation of corporate suffrage. The control of great corporations by a very few persons was the abuse at which Congress struck in enacting Section 14(a)." Similarly, the District of Columbia Circuit in the *Medical Committee* case declaimed, "It is obvious to the point of banality to restate the proposition that Congress intended by its enactment of the Securities and Exchange Act of 1934 to give true vitality to the concept of corporate democracy."[131]

Conceivably, one could argue that the sole purpose of Section 14(a) was to create informed corporate suffrage by ending secretive practices such as the "blank proxy."[132] But the expansive language of Section 14(a) permitting the SEC to prescribe regulations "as necessary or appropriate in the public interest or for the protection of investors" concerning the solicitation of any proxy militates against so narrow a view. Section 14(a) does not refer to mandatory disclosure requirements, as is done in other sections of the 1933 and 1934 securities laws. Both the language of the section and its legislative history have been recognized by commentators as supporting a rule-making authority broader than that necessary to secure the disclosure of information.[133] The commission also has recognized this interpretation. For example, when the SEC lobbied for enactment of what ultimately was adopted as the 1964 Securities Acts Amendments, it urged extension of Section 14(a) to over-the-counter securities as one means of ensuring annual shareholder elections.[134] By a similar logic, the "Commission power to control the conditions under which proxies may be solicited,"[135] to quote both the House and the Senate reports, may be extended to a requirement of equal common stock voting rights. For the primary purpose of Section 14, both reports state, was "to [prevent] the recurrence of abuses which have frustrated the free exercise of voting rights of shareholders."[136] In 1934, Congress presumably must have viewed nonvoting common stock or common stock with disproportionate voting rights as exactly such an abuse.

Dual-Class Capitalization and Successive Duty of Loyalty Suits

There is a fourth, and weaker, reason why corporate boards of directors, even when permitted by applicable law, may hesitate to adopt a dual-class capitalization. In some instances, dual-class capitalization increases the likelihood that shareholders may successfully challenge transactions undertaken by managers owning the class of stock with superior or exclusive voting rights. The key illustration of this greater legal exposure would be the instance when an outsider paid a premium to buy management's controlling class of stock without simultaneously making an offer for the second class of stock. Alternatively, the outsider might offer a higher price for management's class of stock than it does for the second class.

With rare exceptions, in a corporation with a single class of common stock, management may sell a control block and receive a premium.[137] In contrast, profits received by managers in firms with dual-class capitalization have been more rigorously reviewed by the courts. For example, in *Zahn v. Transamerica*,[138] the third circuit allowed a cause of action by holders of Axton-Fisher class A stock challenging a redemption of their shares before liquidation of the firm, when the board could not assert a persuasive business reason for the transaction. The practical consequence of this decision was that the class A shareholders were allowed to receive $240 per share from their liquidation rights rather than $80.80 from the redemption. The burden placed upon the defendant (the corporation owning virtually all of the class B stock) was quite different from the business judgment rule. The court concluded, "Under the allegations of the complaint there was no reason for the redemption of

the Class A Stock to be followed by the liquidation of Axton-Fisher except to enable the Class B Stock to profit at the expense of the Class A Stock."[139] While Delaware does not now require proof of a business purpose in going-private mergers[140] and presumably would not require such evidence in a controversy involving dual capitalization, its supreme court has cited *Zahn* with approval for the proposition "that close judicial scrutiny be given the actions of management which serve to prejudice the interests of subordinate security holders."[141]

Analysis and Conclusions

To begin with a normative conclusion: Nonvoting or disproportionate voting common stock is the corporate law equivalent to price-fixing.[142] It is one of a comparatively few transactions that must be proscribed in order for a market system to effectively operate. To support this conclusion, let me contrast three models of corporate governance.

First, in a model generally operative on the New York Stock Exchange, each common share must have one vote. In effect, this model gives managers a choice. If they wish to obviate the risk of takeover, they may retain or acquire (assumedly through a leveraged buy-out or in concert with others through a merger with a "white knight") a majority of the common stock of the firm. This choice normally will involve substantial costs to managers. To the extent that the majority stock block involves their own investment, they restrict their ability to diversify their holdings. In many instances, acquisition of a majority block can only be acquired through corporate borrowing. This leveraging of the firm's capital structure will increase the bankruptcy risk of the firm, a risk that may be reduced by the sale of some corporate assets.

The alternative for managers is to surrender control and assume the risk of takeover. This action may increase the managers' ability to diversify their holdings, may reduce bankruptcy risk, and may permit management of a larger firm. On the other hand, surrender of a majority block will require managers to subject themselves to ongoing systems of monitoring and certain bonding costs.[143] The monitoring will include not only the takeover market but, more significantly, a board of directors which, at least in theory, may seek their replacement. Managers also will have to submit proposals for fundamental action (e.g., mergers, corporate charter amendments) without the statistical certainty of shareholder approval. While corporate managers are highly successful in winning board of fundamental elections even when they do not own a majority of voting stock, their lack of statistical control will influence both their behavior and the behavior of outside directors. The lack of managerial statistical control of the corporate stock offers the directors a greater opportunity to behave "independently" than they would possess if the managers possessed statistical control of the firm. Similarly, managerial submission of proposals for action will be influenced by their lack of statistical control. Managers will feel a greater incentive to shape these proposals to comport with the preferences of outside shareholders. Both in terms of their relationship to a more independent board and to shareholders, these systems of monitoring contribute to a heightened sense of managerial accountability. Similarly, this sense of accountability will be reflected in various ways through managerial "bonding." Managers lacking statistical control of a firm will feel a greater obligation not to reduce or significantly alter dividend payout practices than they would in a firm in which they held statistical control.

In an age of hostile takeovers, do executives in such a firm require new protections against unemployment risk? I would argue that they do not. The wage market is fully capable of rewarding them for the increased risk of unemployment. Historically, managers have not had a system of lifetime tenure in American corporations. Noteworthy, however, is how much higher their salaries, on average, have been than those of professors, judges, and others who do have lifetime tenure. In effect, the wage market traditionally has compensated managers for their greater unemployment risk. In recent years, as the risk of hostile takeover has increased, the wage market has evolved "golden parachutes," a new form of takeover-related severance agreement. Both the managers' generally higher levels of remuneration and the newer "golden parachutes" represent an effective market response to the increased risk of takeover.

Let us contrast this model with a second one in which managers may obviate the risk of takeover through the issuance of nonvoting or disproportionate voting common stock. The principal collateral consequences of this model concern the monitoring of corporate executives. Obviously, the takeover market will cease to provide any monitoring. Similarly, when managers have statistical control of the firm, the board of directors' ability to act independently will be reduced. Whatever the limitations of a board when managers have a minority of the corporate stock, a board that knows the executives it "monitors" can cause dismissal of directors either immediately or at the next election will operate with less ability to criticize or alter management policies. Furthermore, management decisions concerning fundamental corporate decisions may be made in the absence of a need to persuade a majority of shareholders of the necessity of approving such transactions. In part, the answer to the question "Who shall watch the guardians?" becomes "They themselves." It is not, however, a complete answer. Even in this model with a reduced system of internal corporate monitors, there will endure outside monitoring through product markets or lenders.

Nonetheless, it is probable there will be a modest diminution in stock prices after the issuance of sufficient nonvoting or disproportionate voting stock to give managers statistical control of a firm. This diminution primarily will occur because the possibility of receiving a takeover premium will be ended. The empirical evidence to date suggests that the immediate market reaction to a publicly traded firm adopting such a common stock structure is of a magnitude of 5% or less. The more interesting question is whether the difference in value of firms with such common stock structures compared with firms with equal–common stock voting rights will widen over time. Unclear, for example, is whether institutional investors, on average, will shift their investment dollars from firms with dual common stock voting classes to firms with a single class. Also unclear is to what extent the reduction of internal corporate monitoring will lead to less efficiently managed firms. In theory, a reduction in efficient management will more likely occur in firms operating in monopolistic or oligopolistic product markets than in more competitive markets. But that said, the empirical evidence with which to quantify long-term efficiency effects currently is not available.

The current debate concerning the one-share, one-vote controversy requires analysis of a third model. In this model, managers are permitted to adopt nonvoting or disproportionate voting common stock structures but only after approval by a majority vote of shareholders and/or with a "sunset" provision limiting the duration of the new structure to a specified number of years. To the extent that the objection to nonvoting or disproportionate voting common stock concerns monitoring costs, at a normative level neither device is a persuasive "saving" provision. In all probability, the economy is better served by compensating managers for the increased risk of takeover through a wage market and preserving the takeover market, the board, and shareholder approval of fundamental transactions as ongoing monitors.

With respect to majority stock approval, one can write in its favor that it does require managers to bargain with stockholders to secure approval and will likely result in compensation to shareholders for probable stock price losses through higher dividends, more stock, or other means. If majority approval means a majority of disinterested stockholders, there is a greater likelihood that the bargaining will

reach a fair approximation of the probable discounted lost stock value. But if the basic economic effect of dual-class voting structures is a loss in management efficiency, a payment to shareholders will not compensate for that economic cost.

A sunset provision, regardless of when it occurs, does not alter this conclusion. Sunset provisions, in practice, will lead to inevitable management renewal of the dual-class voting structure. To begin with, the timing of the renewal vote will be in the hands of the managers. To the extent that there are systematic costs associated with firms having dual voting stock classes, there may be some reduction over time in the percentage of these firms owned by institutional investors. This reduction, in all probability, will reduce the likelihood of opposition to renewal of the dual voting stock classes. If managers had any reason to suspect that the outcome of a renewal vote might be in question, they can "buy" support by offering sweeteners (e.g., higher dividends after renewal). In any event, management has immense funding advantages in such a proxy contest. Not only will their own expenses be borne by the corporate treasury, but opponents of renewal will be obligated to pay their proxy expenses out of their own pocket, with reimbursement only possible if they succeed. Thus, to analogize a sunset provision to periodic political elections seems inappropriate. There is in corporate management no organized opposition that can serve as an ongoing monitor. There is no equality in funding rules. There is a general expectation that managers will win corporate elections. And in the rare instance that the expectation might be called into question, management possesses the power to "buy" corporate elections through the use of sweeteners (or to totally prevent their occurring through a buy-out of public stockholders[144] or merger with another firm).

In fine, dual-class capitalization is both inefficient as a way of managing large business corporations and unfair to public shareholders, whose share prices will be reduced by the loss of potential takeover premiums. The Securities and Exchange

Commission or Congress would be wise to proscribe dual-class capitalization for the largest business corporations, specifically, those subject to Section 12 of the Securities Exchange Act of 1934.[145]

SHAREHOLDER APPROVAL RULES

Derivative of the stock exchange voting rules are NYSE and AMEX shareholder approval rules.

NYSE Paragraph 312.00 provides the following in pertinent part:

Shareholder approval is a prerequisite to listing securities to be issued for or in connection with the following:

1. Options granted to or special remuneration plans for directors, officers or key employees.
2. Actions resulting in a change in the control of a company.
3. The acquisitions direct or indirect, of a business, a company, tangible or intangible assets or property or securities representing any such interests:
   (a) From a director, office or substantial security holder of the company (including its subsidiaries and affiliates) or from any company or party in which one of such persons has a direct or indirect interest:
   (b) Where the present or potential issuance of common stock or securities convertible into common stock could result in an increase in outstanding common shares of 18½% or more: or
   (c) Where the present or potential issuance of common stock and any other consideration has a combined fair value of 18½% or more of the market value of the outstanding common shares and the present or potential issuance of common stock has a fair market value in excess of 5% of the market value of the outstanding common shares.[146]

AMEX Paragraph 712 similarly states:

Approval of shareholders is required (pursuant to a proxy solicitation conforming to S.E.C proxy rules) as a prerequisite to approval of applications to list additional shares to be issued as sole or partial consideration for an acquisition of the stock or assets of another company in the following circumstances:

(a) if any individual director, officer or substantial shareholder of the listed company has a 5% or greater interest (or such persons collectively have a 10% or greater interest), directly or indirectly, in the company or assets to be acquired or in the consideration to be paid in the transaction and the present or potential issuance of common stock, or securities convertible into common stock, could result in an increase in outstanding common shares of 5% or more; or

(b) where the present or potential issuance of common stock, or securities convertible into common stock, could result in an increase in outstanding common shares of 20% or more.

There is less available data concerning the historical background of these rules than of the common stock voting rules. In November 1955, the NYSE Board of Governors adopted amendments to the listing policies to specify that stockholder approval was required for an acquisition when there was to be an increase in outstanding shares of 20% or more. At that time, the NYSE Department of Stock List viewed the amendment as closing a loophole. A memorandum from Phillip West explained, "While stockholder approval is required as a matter of law in the case of mergers, consolidation or recapitalizations, it is not generally required by law in connection with acquisitions, regardless of size."[147] This memorandum conceded that the 20% figure was "necessarily an arbitrary one."[148] The rule was further amended in March 1960 to deal with actions resulting in a change in control.[149] Over time, the approximately 20% shareholder rule evolved into the current 18½% rule.[150]

The initial adoption of the NYSE shareholder approval rule clearly was not a response to lockup transactions. NYSE President Funston stated of the change in control rule when it was adopted in March 1960 that the exchange "has consistently sought to increase the number of corporate matters submitted to shareholders for approval." The new rule is "the latest step in that direction."[151] The *Wall Street Journal* characterized the announcement in 1959 of a statement that the NYSE would consider delisting any company that fails to begin soliciting proxies from stockholders by the end of 1961 as a comparable development.[152] In the late 1950s and early 1960s, the approximately 20% shareholder approval rule could not have been a rule the exchange expected to be employed very often. Circumstantial evidence to this effect appears in an address made by the SEC Chief Accountant Andrew Barr in January 1962.[153] On that occasion, Barr spoke about the purchase versus pooling accounting methods for mergers, which was the leading "takeover" issue of the day. Barr found by reviewing 261 combinations that employed either technique, most of which had occurred in the three previous years, that 204 of these transactions (roughly 78%) involved one corporation with 10% or less of the voting power of the other. The other 57 transactions were categorized either in a 10%-to-40% group (47) or in a more-than-40% group (10). Thus, one cannot be more precise about the percentage of mergers which likely would have involved the issuance of 20% or more stock.[154] Clearly, however, a very substantial proportion of mergers could be achieved by the issuance of less than 20% of stock by the acquiring firm.

In the merger context, furthermore, a key consequence of the NYSE rule was not a tightening of the shareholder vote rules but their loosening. In 1967 Delaware, following the NYSE, ended its historic requirement that all mergers had to be approved by shareholders of both firms, and adopted a rule denying the surviving corporation's stockholders a vote when the surviving corporation issued 20% or less stock and satisfied other conditions in merging with an acquired firm.[155]

Nonetheless, in several recent instances, the shareholder approval rule has been enforced, most notably in cases involving "lockup" stock issuances.[156] The SEC's Advisory Committee on Tender Offers recommended "that the issuance of stock representing more than 15% of the fully diluted shares outstanding after issuance should be approved by shareholders." This recommendation, the advisory committee explained, "extends the basic concept of the New York Stock Exchange rule that re-

quires shareholders approval for the issuance of more than 18.5% of a company's shares where such shares are to be listed."[157] Professor Coffee, to return to the point where I began, concluded, "At present, the most significant limitation on defensive tactics by target corporations is contained neither in the common law of fiduciary duties nor the anti-fraud rules adopted by the SEC under the Williams Act, but rather is set forth in the New York Stock Exchange's policy that effectively limits the magnitude of any stock lock-up the target's board may issue."[158] No one can disagree that the bright-line 18½% rule is a more effective restraint than state corporate law judicial decisions, which usually will review a lockup transaction by employing the business judgment rule.[159] Nor can it be doubted after *Schreiber v. Burlington Northern, Inc.,*[160] that the SEC's power to adopt rules under the Williams Act is a limited one.

But that said, the 18½% shareholder approval rule still is subject to significant limitations. First, the 18½% threshold for activating the vote requirement is a high requirement. Many corporations have been able to achieve effective lockups without a shareholder vote by issuing less than 18½% in new securities.[161] Second, since the rule is not a generic one, it can be circumvented by the use of other defensive techniques. For example, the "poison pill" rights plan in the *Moran v. Household International, Inc.,*[162] case adopted solely by a majority vote of Household's board, eventuated in the NYSE listing the rights distributed to shareholders.[163] Third, the NYSE has ceased delisting firms that fail to comply with the shareholder approval rule during its review of shareholder voting rules.[164] Fourth, in any event, precisely because the shareholder approval rules are enforced solely by the NYSE and the AMEX, a corporation could delist and then subsequently adopt a lockup employing the issuance of greater than 18½% new common stock.[165]

In fine, the NYSE's 18½% rule inadvertently may have evolved to be "the most significant limitation on defensive tactics." But given the institutional context of the

securities markets today, it is highly unlikely that the existence of this rule por-
tends other significant rule initiatives in
the takeover area by these markets unless
they are "jawboned" by members of Congress, the SEC, or the blue-sky administrators. It seems virtually inconceivable that
the exchanges or the NASD will adopt
broad generic rules regulating takeover
bidding or takeover defenses that are likely
to make a significant difference to the takeover market.

NOTES

1. 84 *Colum. L. Rev.* 1145 (1984).
2. Ibid., 1255.
3. Ibid., 1254.
4. Ibid., 1259, 1261–1264.
5. Ibid., 1257. Most of the writing to date on
competitive regulatory regimes and specifically
the "race-to-the-bottom" or "least-common-de-
nominator" problem has concerned state corporate charters. For representative opposing
views on this subject; see, e.g., Cary, "Federalism and Corporate Law: Reflections upon Delaware," 83 *Yale L.J.* 663 (1974); Winter, "State
Law, Shareholder Protection, and the Theory of
the Corporation, 6 *J. Leg. Stud.* 251 (1977).
Judge Winter, usually an opponent of the notion that the deterioration in state law standards
necessitates new federal regulation, has written:

Takeover statutes differ, however, since they, unlike
rules governing management conflict of interest and
so on, regulate the market for management control
rather than the capital market. Where the market for
management control is concerned, monopolization by
state law may be possible since existing management
has little incentive to seek out optimal arrangements
and states must fear reincorporation. More importantly, takeover statutes are extraterritorial in effect
and the competition for charters is actually of little effect since such legislation overrides the corporation
code of the chartering state. The recent wave of takeover statutes is evidence of a need for federal regulation to protect competition in that market. (p. 290)

See also Scott, "The Dual Banking System: A
Model of Competition in Regulation." 30 *Stan.
L. Rev.* 1 (1977) (an analysis of how a different
competitive regulatory system, at the least, ob-
scures clear analytical understanding of the dynamics of the banking system).
6. See, text and notes accompanying note 76.
7. To do so, General Motors issued class E

common stock with one-half vote per share
(General Motors Proxy Statement, September
21, 1984).
8. See, e.g., J. Seligman, *The Transformation
of Wall Street: A History of the Securities and
Exchange Commission and Modern Corporate
Finale* (1982), 450–466.
9. Coffee's discussion of this point appears in
his article cited in note 1, pp. 1257–1258.
10. See, e.g., *Securities Industry Study,* report
of the Subcommittee on Securities, Senate
Committee on Banking, Housing and Urban Affairs, 93rd Cong., 1st Sess., Senate Document
No. 93–13, 1973; 145:

The inherent limitations in allowing an industry to
regulate itself are well known: the natural lack of enthusiasm for regulation on the part of the group to be
regulated, the temptation to use a facade of industry
regulation as a shield to ward off more meaningful regulation, the tendency for businessmen to use collective
action to advance their interests through the imposition of purely anticompetitive restraints as opposed to
those justified by regulatory needs, and a resistance to
changes in the regulatory pattern because of vested
economic interests in its preservation.

11. See, e.g., *NASD Manual,* Art. III, § 1: "A
member, in the conduct of his business, shall
observe high standards of commercial honor
and just and equitable principles of trade." And
see *NASD Manual,* Art. III, § 4:

In "over-the-counter" transactions whether in "unlisted" securities, if a member buys for his own account from his customer, or sells for his own account
to his customer, he shall buy or sell at a price which is
fair, taking into consideration all relevant circumstances, including market conditions with respect to
such security at the time of the transaction, the expense involved, and the fact that he is entitled to a
profit; and if he acts as agent for his customer in any
such transaction, he shall not charge his customer
more than a fair commission or service charge, taking
into consideration all relevant circumstances including market conditions with respect to such security at
the time of the transaction, the expense of executing
the order and the value of any service he may have
rendered by reason of his experience in and knowledge
of such security and the market therefor.

12. Douglas quoted in Seligman, note 8, pp.
185–86.
13. So termed by Investment Banking Code
Committee Chairman B. Howell Griswold and
quoted in Seligman, note 8, pp. 188–189.
14. Ibid., 185.
15. The average daily trading volumes (in
millions of dollars) for the NYSE, AMEX, and
NASDAQ during the first six months of 1985
were as follows:

	Volume	Percent of NYSE
NYSE	$3780.0	
AMEX	107.2	2.8
NASDAQ	889.1	23.5

See McMurray, "Continued Survival of AMEX Is Threatened as Its Listings Decline," *Wall St. J.*, July 2, 1985, at 1, col. 8.

16. New York Stock Exchange, *Listed Company Manual*, § 3. This section was analyzed by the exchange in *Impact of Corporate Takeovers*, hearings before the Subcommittee on Securities, Senate Committee on Securities, Senate Committee on Banking Housing and Urban Affairs, 99th Cong., 1st Sess. 1985, 1110–1163.

17. Ibid., ¶ 302.00.

18. Ibid., ¶ 303.00.

19. Ibid., ¶ 304.00.

20. Ibid., ¶ 310.00(A). The exchange does not encourage any specific quorum for preferred stock [ibid., ¶ 310.00(B)].

21. Ibid., ¶ 311.03. The paragraph reiterates an agreement that appears in the New York Stock Exchange, Listing Agreement, I(9).

22. See New York Stock Exchange, note 16, ¶ 312.00(2).

23. Ibid., ¶ 312(3)(b). Shareholder approval also is required for the present or potential issuance of common stock and any other consideration that has a combined fair value of 18½% or more of the market value of the outstanding common shares and the present or potential issuance of common stock has a fair market value in excess of 5% of the market value of the outstanding common shares [ibid., ¶ 312(3)(c)]. Similarly, shareholder approval is required before listing warrants which could purchase more than 18½% of the outstanding common stock [ibid., ¶ 312(3)].

24. Ibid., ¶ 313.00(A). An exception is recognized for the nonvoting common stock of quasi-governmental corporations whose voting stock is restricted by legislative or judicial mandate.

25. Ibid.

26. Ibid. However, the paragraph notes, "Exception has been made in the case of voting trusts established pursuant to reorganization proceedings under court direction."

27. Ibid., ¶ 313.00(B). The New York Stock Exchange long regarded the voting trust as posing the same type of policy issues as nonvoting stock but only adopted its current proscriptions in 1957. In the preceding five years, 12 firms listed on the NYSE had voting trusts and one firm had an irrevocable proxy. See S. Robbins,

An Evaluation of the New York Stock Exchange Listing Policy on Voting (New York Stock Exchange Study, 1978), 10–11; see, generally, pp. 9–13, 56–56, and 158–163. The NYSE neither endorses nor confirms the findings of the Robbins report. The report is used for reference purposes by the exchange (letter to the author from Mr. J. Paul Wyciskala, managing director, Marketing Division, October 3, 1985).

28. See H. Henn and J. Alexander, Laws of Corporations and Other Business Associations (1983), 534–536.

29. A relatively recent article exhibiting sympathy for some forms of vote buying was published by Clark, "Vote Buying and Corporate Law," 29 *Case West. L. Rev.* 776 (1979). See also the discussion in 17 *Sec. Reg. L. Rep.* (BNA) 1594–1595 (September 13, 1985), regarding "vote rental." A more conventional analysis appears in Sneed, "The Stockholder May Vote as He Pleases: Theory and Fact," 22 *Univ. Pitt. L. Rev.* 23, 45–46 (1960) ("The rule is prevalent in American corporate law that a stockholder cannot, for a private and personal consideration, agree to cast his vote in a certain way. The sale of voting power is said to be against public policy and hence invalid.").

30. New York Stock Exchange, note 16, ¶ 313.00(C).

31. Ibid., ¶ 313.00(D).

32. Ibid., ¶ 313.00(E). This paragraph adds that the right to elect directors should accrue regardless of whether defaulted dividends occurred in consecutive periods and should remain in effect until cumulative dividends have been paid in full or until noncumulative dividends have been paid regularly for at least a year.

33. American Stock Exchange, *Company Guide*, ¶ 704.

34. Ibid., ¶ 121.

35. Ibid., ¶ 123.

36. Ibid., ¶ 712, 713.

37. As will be shown, this paragraph is amplified by a statement of AMEX policy. See the discussion in the text accompanying notes 85–86.

38. American Stock Exchange, note 33, ¶ 124(a). The NYSE provision accords preferred shareholders a vote after default upon six consecutive quarterly dividends. See the text accompanying note 32.

39. The NASDAQ computer system and NMS list are described in Seligman, "The Future of the National Market System," 10 *J. Corp. L.* 79, 95–105 (1984). Gordon Macklin, NASD president, testified on May 22, 1985, before the Subcommittee on Telecommunica-

tions, Consumer Protection, and Finance of the House Committee on Energy and Commerce that there were over eighteen hundred companies now traded in the NASDAQ/NMS. He further asserted "there are some 600 to 700 NASDAQ securities which meet the financial criteria for listing on the New York Stock Exchange and some 1800 which would qualify for listing on the American Stock Exchange."

40. *NASD to Consider Rule on Shareholder Voting Rights for NASDAQ/NMS Companies* undated NASD press release; the substance of this release was printed in 17 *Sec. Reg. L. Rep.* (BNA) 1358–1359 (July 26, 1985).

41. Initial Report of the Subcommittee on Shareholder Participation and Qualitative Listing Standards, Dual-Class Capitalization (Presented to the Public Policy Committee of the board of directors of the New York Stock Exchange, Inc., January 3, 1985), 4–5. The subcommittee intended to make recommendations with respect to issuers which apply for a listing at a later date (ibid., 5).

42. *Wall St. J.* June 13, 1985, at 4, col. 1. On June 18, 1985, Senators D'Amato, Metzenbaum, and Cranston introduced § 1314 which would prohibit common stock "that is part of a class of securities of the issuer which is nonvoting or which carries disproportionate voting rights" to be employed by any security registered on a National Securities Exchange under § 12 of the Securities Exchange Act of 1934 (15 U. S. C. 781) or traded in an automated quotation system operated by a national securities association registered under § 15A of that act (15 U. S. C. 780–783). The same bill was introduced by Congressman Dingell (H.R. 2783, 99th Cong., lst Sess. June 18, 1985.

43. These negotiations failed because of the NASD's insistence that it would support a one-share, one-vote proposal only if the NYSE and AMEX help the NASD persuade state securities regulators to provide the same exemption from blue-sky laws for NASDAQ/NMS securities that generally is provided to NYSE- and AMEX-listed securities. The NYSE and AMEX refused to do so. See 17 *Sec. Reg. L. Rep.* (BNA) 1097 (June 21, 1985), and 1707–1708 (September 27, 1985). In November 1985, the NASD hired University of Chicago law professor Daniel Fischel to prepare a study of dual-class capitalization (*N.Y. Times,* November 7, 1985), at 20, col. 3.

44. New York Stock Exchange, New York Stock Exchange Directors Approve Amendment to Allow Dual Classes of Common Stock for Listed Companies (July 3, 1986); Sterngold, *Big Board Ends Equal Vote Rule, N.Y. Times,* July 4, 1986, at D1, col. 1. The proposal that was

approved in July was formally submitted to the SEC on September 16, 1986. *NYSE's Proposed Rule Changes on Disparate Voting Rights,* 18 Sec. Reg. L. Rep. (BNA) 1389–1392 (September 19, 1986). It cannot go into effect without commission approval. See Exchange Act Release No. 23,724 (October 17, 1986), 51 Fed. Reg. 37,529 (1986).

45. Quoting Ratner, "The Government of Business Corporations: Critical Reflections on the Rule of 'One Share, One Vote,'" 56 *Corn. L. Rev.* 1, 8 (1970); see, generally, pp. 3–11. See also Rohrlich, "Corporate Voting: Majority Control," 7 *St. John's L. Rev.* 218 (1933); Sneed, note 29, pp. 23–24; Henn and Alexander, note 28, p. 493 (note 3). Among other points, Ratner suggested that the election of directors in publicly held corporations might be subject to the Fourteenth Amendment's equal-protection clause in the same spirit that Supreme Court decisions beginning with *Baker v. Carr* [369 U.S. 186 (1961)] had held that states may not elect any public official or legislative body in an election according one group of electors greater weight than that of any other group. See Ratner, pp. 38–44. One second circuit opinion, *Davis v. American Telephone and Telegrpah Co.,* 478 F.2d 1375 (2d Cir. 1973)] subsequently dismissed a complaint that the one-share, one-vote rule violated the equal-protection clause.

46. Stevens, "Stockholders' Voting Rights and the Centralization of Voting Control," 40 *Q.J. Econ.* 353, 355 (1926). See also Stevens, "Voting Rights of Capital Stock and Shareholders," 11 *J. Bus.* 311 (1938).

47. A. Berle and G. Means, *The Modern Corporation and Private Property,* rev. ed. (1968), 69–75. Berle and Means estimated that in 21% of the 200 largest corporations at the beginning of 1930, ultimate control was attributable to a legal device, (ibid., 109).

48. Ibid., 71 (description of the Dodge Brothers, Inc., 1925 stock issue). See also W. Ripley, *Main Street and Wall Street* (1927), 86–87; J. Livingston, *The American Stockholder* (1958), 186–187; Robbins, note 27, pp. 52–53.

49. Ripley, note 48, p. 87; Robbins, note 27, p. 52. Other examples of nonvoting common stock during that period appear in Ripley, pp. 87–88, and Berle and Means, note 47, p. 72.

50. *Congressional Record,* 69th Cong., 1st Sess., April 19, 1926), 7719–7720.

51. Ripley, note 48, pp. 121–122.

52. *N.Y. Times,* October 29, 1925, at 27, col. 1. Ripley's central role in galvanizing opposition to nonvoting common stock was widely recognized. See, e.g., J. Sears, *The New Place of the Stockholder* (1929), 27–28; Livingston, note 48, p. 172; and Loomis and Rubman, "Corpo-

rate Governance in Historical Perspective," **8** *Hofstra L. Rev.* 141, 152–153 (1979). The house history of the NYSE on voting rights similarly observes, "The focus of public attention was drawn to this development [nonvoting common stock] by Professor William Ripley" (Robbins, note 27, p. 57).

53. *N.Y. Times,* November 1, 1925, at III, p. 8, col. 2; November 14, 1925, at 14, col. 3; November 22, 1925, at IX, p. 5, col. 1; February 7, 1926, at VIII, p. 1, col. 1; February 21, 1926, at II, p. 1, col. 6. Related news stories were published on October 30, 1925, at 27, col. 2; November 13, 1925, at 40, col. 4; January 28, 1926, at 25, col. 1; January 29, 1926, at 32, col. 2; February 3, 1926, at 32, col. 3; February 17, 1926, at 1, col. 7.

54. Ripley, "More Power to the Bankers," 121 *Nation* 618 (1925).

55. 87 *Atlantic Monthly* 94 (1926).

56. See, e.g., *N.Y. Times,* February 17, 1926, at 1, col. 7. History does not record this to have been a particularly effective meeting. One anecdotal account, inaccurately dating the meeting in 1927, explained:

Professor William Z. Ripley of Harvard, whose work on business problems and abuses had earned him a reputation as one of the nation's leading business economists, was invited to the White House to discuss his ideas with the President. Coolidge listened carefully to Ripley, apparently recognizing that the Professor's criticisms of corporate practices were sound, that oftentimes businesses operated contrary to the public interest, and that there was an unhealthy concentration of economic power. When Ripley was finished, Coolidge removed his cigar from between his clenched teeth, leaned forward, and asked: "Is there anything we can do down here?" Ripley answered that under existing legislation the President was powerless, and in any case, the problem should be solved through state action. Coolidge leaned back and heaved a sigh of relief.

See R. Sobel, *The Big Board: A History of the New York Stock Exchange* (1965), 236. Ripley himself seems to have been more impressed with an unsolicited invitation to the annual dinner of the Gridiron Club (Ripley, note 48, p. 121).

57. *Regulation of the Stock Exchanges,* hearings before the Senate Committee on Banking and Currency, 63rd Cong., 2d Sess. 1914.

58. L. Brandeis, *Other People's Money* (1913).

59. 39 *Harv. L. Rev.* 673 (1926).

60. Seligman, "Broader Legal Aspects of Customer Stock Ownership," 50 *Rep. Am. B. Assoc.* 851, 853 (1925). In fairness to my namesake, I should observe his remarks were delivered at the 48th annual meeting of the ABA, held in September 1925, some weeks before Ripley's celebrated address.

61. *N.Y. Times,* April 6, 1926, at 43, col 1; Ripley, note 48, p. 120.

62. *N.Y. Times,* April 6, 1926, at 43, col. 1. The commission explained: "The power to control the management of public utility corporations should be in the hands of their stockholders."

63. *N.Y. Times,* May 31, 1926, at 26, col. 1.

64. Reprinted in Ripley, note 48, p. 121. Ripley also refers to "inumerable editorials" and "cartoons" condemning nonvoting common stock (ibid., 118–122).

65. Fox Theatres Corporation had applied to list 800,000 shares of nonvoting class A common stock. All voting rights were to be held by the voting class B common shares owned by the company's president, William Fox. See memorandum to Mr. Keith Funston from Mr. Phillip L. West, re: Non-Voting Common Stock (May 4, 1953), 3 (on file with NYSE); *N.Y. Times,* January 28, 1926, at 25, col. 1; January 29, 1926, at 32, col. 2; February 3, 1926, at 32 col. 3.

66. Statement printed in *N.Y. Times,* January 28, 1926, at 25, col. 1; and Robbins, note 27, p. 180.

67. *Stock Exchange Practices,* Hearings on S. Res. 84, 72nd Cong. and S. Res. 56 and 97, 73rd Cong. Before the Senate Committee on Banking and Currency, 73rd Cong., lst Sess. 1934, 6677 (testimony of Frank Altschul). The circumstances of this meeting are further described in Robbins, note 48, p. 180. On March 23, 1926, exchange President Simmons similarly was quoted as stating:

On January 27 the New York Stock Exchange opposed the abuses which might arise from the relatively new corporate practice of issuing non-voting stock. It is true that the Exchange's statement regarding this matter was couched in general terms only, and that it merely declared its intention to take cognizance of the non-voting feature of common stocks without attempting to formulate a definite policy at once.

As I have pointed out many times the Exchange cannot well expand its specific listing requirements in advance of actual experience, and the issuance of non-voting common stock is a relatively new development in this country. The problem of non-voting stock cannot in actual fact ever be settled on paper merely by logic or dogmatic conviction. It must depend for its ultimate solution upon an open-minded development of precedents based upon concrete circumstances and specific cases.

While the Stock Exchange has made no positive and irrevocable rule against the listing of non-voting common stock, it intends to inquire into such issues when they apply for a listing, and it will refuse to open the facilities of its market to issues wherein an abuse of this practice seems likely to occur.

See *N.Y. Times,* March 24, 1926, at 34, col. 3.

68. West memorandum, note 65, pp. 1–2; see also p. 15. Loomis and Rubman, note 52, p. 153, similarly observed, "The demise of non-voting common resulted from outside pressure and outrage." See also Ripley, note 48, pp. 118–122.

69. *Stock Exchange Practices* hearings, note 67. p. 6680. Altschul offered two fundamental distinctions between nonvoting common stock and voting trust certificates:

In the case of the voting trusts the laws of the various states on voting trusts are set up providing limits of time at the end of which the stockholder again returns to his former status.

The second point is that in a great many cases and in most of these that we have seen in the stock exchange, voting-trust certificates are issued in exchange for the stock and the exchange was made voluntarily by the stockholder, who exchanged his voting right for what he considered to be a good reason, and there are at times good reasons of that sort.

70. Gotham Silk Hosiery Company was listed June 23, 1926, with 150,000 shares of nonvoting common authorized but not issued. See *N.Y. Times,* June 24, 1926, at 31, col. 1. An additional 666,628 shares of nonvoting common at Pan-American Petroleum Transport Company were listed on November 24, 1926. See *N.Y. Times,* November 25, 1926, at 40, col. 2.

71. Quoting Robbins, note 27, p. 183.

72. Ibid.

73. Ibid., 37. The idea of common stock voting rights as inherent rights has been often articulated by others. See, e.g., Stevens, note 46, p. 385 ("Nothing can alter the fact that stock is stock and that the right to vote is one of the inherent rights of a shareholder."); Rohrlich, note 45, p. 219 (quoting court opinions stating, "the right to vote is a 'properly right,' 'a vested interest,' 'a vital right,' 'an inherent right'"). Such assertions alone are question begging. Why is common stock voting an inherent right? The NYSE does not clearly explain but takes refuge in other equally question-begging assertions; e.g., "There is no moral justification for depriving a stockholder of his right to vote" (NYSE memorandum, July 30, 1975, to the American Distilling Company, p. 5; quoted in Robbins, note 27, p. 37).

74. NYSE, *Company Manual,* note 16, ¶ 301.00.

75. In 1947, Cannon Mills distributed one share of nonvoting class B common stock to each holder of a share of common stock. The Cannon Mills common was listed on the NYSE. The NYSE did not succeed in persuading Cannon Mills to recall the nonvoting common stock. See Robbins, note 27, p. 8. Cannon Mills ultimately was delisted in 1962 for failure to comply with the NYSE requirements that all listed firms solicit proxies. See Coffee, note 1, p. 1257 (note 339). In several other instances, the NYSE more effectively proscribed nonvoting common stock. To quote Robbins in his house history, note 27, p. 8:

In a series of cases, the Exchange took a firm stand against the use of non-voting common stock. It required American Cyanamid, for example, to reclassify its common stock into one class of voting common for the purpose of listing. It advised companies such as M. A. Hanna and Talon that if they changed their common stock into voting and non-voting categories, neither issue would be eligible for listing. It warned W. A. Sheaffer Pen Company, whose common stock was then listed, that if the issue were reclassified into a Class A non-voting stock and a Class B voting stock, the former would not be eligible for listing and there were some doubts if the Class B stock would be eligible.

Wang Laboratories, (discussed in the text accompanying notes 84–85) is another example. The board of directors of Carter Products, in 1962 sought to amend its articles of incorporation to create a new class of nonvoting common stock. The NYSE indicated that if this step was taken, it would probably delist Carter's voting common stock. Before the NYSE could act, minority stockholders succeeded in securing an injunction against the issuance of the nonvoting common stock. See *United Funds, Inc., v. Carter Products, Inc.,*1961–64 Fed. Sec. L. Rep. (CCH) ¶ 91,288 (Maryland Cir. Ct. 1963).

76. See Livingston, note 48, pp. 166–177. The NYSE *Listed Company Manual,* note 16, ¶ 313.00(D), takes a case-by-case approach to the issue of "proportionate voting power," stating, in part, "the Exchange is of the view that any allocation of voting power under normal conditions to classes of stock other than common stock should be in reasonable relationship to the equity interests of such classes."

77. Mr. A. A. Sommer, Jr., cochairman of the NYSE Subcommittee on Shareholder Participation and Qualitative Listing Standards, was kind enough to provide me copies of each of 52 letters the NYSE forwarded to him from the 425 letters received by the exchange in response to an August 1984 letter mailed to 3200 listed companies, member firms, major institutional investors, lawyers, academics, and state securities administrators. The 1984 letter posed six inquiries:

• Should the NYSE continue present shareholder participation requirements?
• Should the NYSE modify its policies to per-

mit two classes of stock if approved by shareholders?

- Should approval by independent directors be an acceptable alternative to present restrictions?
- Should the NYSE urge the SEC or Congress to require other markets to adopt shareholder participation measures similar to the NYSE's?
- Should the NYSE impose restrictions on "greenmail," "golden parachutes," etc.?
- Would the possible loss of listings affect the responses to the foregoing inquiries?

Of the 52 letters, 27 were from listed or once listed corporations (Allied, Allied Stores, American Express, AT&T, Baxter Travenol Laboratories, Bell South, Boise Cascade, Coastal, Control Data, Dow-Jones, Ex-Cell-O, Gearhart, General Foods, General Motors, Hershey, Imperial Chemical, Massey-Ferguson, Meredith, Mesa Petroleum, Mobil, Morton Thiokol, Pfizer, Robertshaw, N.V. Koninklijke Nederlandsche Petroleum, Scott, Sterling Drug, and Tenneco); 5 were from institutional investors (Battermarch, John Hancock Mutual Life Insurance, Jennison Associates, New York Life, and TIAA/CREF); 5 were from academics (professors Tamar Frankel, Louis Lowenstein, William Painter, Morris Mendelson, and Donald Schwartz); 4 were from member firms (Alex Brown & Sons, Bartlett & Co., Kidder, Peabody, and Parker/Hunter); 2 were from state securities administrators (California and New Jersey); and 7 were from attorneys (George Makohin, John J. Cole, Herbert B. Cohn, Daniel J. McCauley and Frederick Lipman, John P. Campbell, Mark Grobmyer, and James L. Purcell). There were also letters from the American Society of Corporate Secretaries and an investor named Paul L. Bennett.

While the letters reflect a variety of viewpoints, two themes predominated. First, there was recognition that listing on the NYSE no longer was inevitable for leading firms; NASDAQ and the American Stock Exchange provided acceptable alternatives. See, e.g., American Express letter, p. 2: "In our view listing requirements of the Exchange that go beyond state law run the risk of prompting some companies to forgo listing"; Coastal letter, p. 2: "We are prepared to move from the N.Y.S.E. to NASDAQ, based on the advice of our independent financial advisor that such a move would not have a material adverse effect"; Control Data letter, p. 3: "While listing on the New York Stock Exchange, in view of the rapid development of other markets, is much less important than it was even recently"; General Motors let-

ter, p. 4: "The existence of a truly national over-the-counter market, integrated by a highly sophisticated automated quotation system and providing quality standards through the designation of certain securities as National Market System Securities, has dulled the market imperative for listing on the 'Big Board'"; Morton Thiokol letter, p. 2: "We believe that where listing requirements impede the ability of companies to act in the long-term interests of their stockholders, more and more companies will accept the possibility of being de-listed"; Tamar Frankel letter, p. 1: "The Exchange's relaxation of the [one–common share, one-vote] rule may attract more issues"; Louis Lowenstein letter, p. 2: "The problem obviously is that the Exchange's requirements are self-imposed and do not extend, therefore, to the over-the-counter market"; Mark W. Grobmyer letter, p. 2: "I am afraid as it now exists with a listing on the New York Stock Exchange and the attendant regulatory requirements and burdens that are inherent in Exchange membership such membership is going to become more rare as more and more companies desire to avoid Exchange listing"; Donald Schwartz letter, pp. 4–5: "I believe that the Exchange should adhere to its policies as suggested even if it were known that some companies would forgo listing on the Exchange because of the higher standards. However, if there was a serious threat of the loss of listed companies because of the implementation of these policies, I think the Exchange would have no choice but to seek its own survival."

Second, much emphasized was the belief that NYSE voting rules did not permit adequate defenses to hostile takeovers. For example, the Boise Cascade letter, pp. 1–2, stated: "The Exchange's policies, adopted at a time when changes in corporate control were by negotiated transactions, do not work well in today's era of unilateral takeover bids. In this new environment, boards of directors must act prudently but with dispatch to represent long-term shareholder interests. Exchange policies which impede the adoption of legitimate actions are inappropriate since they place Exchange-listed companies at a serious disadvantage to companies not listed on the Exchange or traded in other markets." Similarly, the Gearhart letter, p. 1, asserted: "Present rules of the N.Y.S.E. serve only to assist the acts of a hostile raider, which just isn't right"; Louis Lowenstein's letter, p. 2: "The pressure to find defenses against takeovers has increased the pressure either for relaxation of the Exchange's policies or to delist"; Daniel J. McCauley and Frederick Lipman letter, p. 1: "By imposing shareholder participation requirements on issuers, quality issuers are discouraged from having their securities listed on the New York Stock Exchange in view of their greater vulnerability to hostile takeovers. The better quality issuers, which the Exchange should attempt to attract, are, in many cases, the more appetizing targets for hostile tender offerors. Too often, a requirement for shareholder democracy merely translates in practical terms into a vulnerability to hostile takeovers."

Similar views were expressed by senior officials of the securities markets who testified before the House of Representatives subcommittees in May and June 1985. John Phelan, chairman of the New York Stock Exchange in testimony to the Subcommittee on Oversight and Investigations of the House Committee on Energy and Commerce, June 17, 1985, p. 5, notably stated:

Philosophically, the Exchange continues to believe in "one share, one vote." All other things being equal, there would probably be little or no reason to consider modifying it. But all other things are far from equal today. The rapidly changing environment of the securities marketplace has made competition for listings every bit as intense as competition for customers' orders, competition among market-makers, and competition among marketplaces. And the fact is that other markets that offer publicly held companies alternative trading arenas for their stocks have less stringent standards that serve as a competitive attraction.

The problem is complicated by a rising number of unnegotiated tender offers that are leading the manager of target and potential target companies to consider steps they deem appropriate to protect their enterprises in the long-term best interests of their shareholders. One such step has involved creating—with shareholder approval—a second class of common stock having more than one vote per share, with the goal of strengthening management's control over the company's destiny.

Such measures are inconsistent with the Exchange's "one share, one vote" policy. So. when a listed company goes that route, the Exchange must consider whether to continue to list the stock. Since none of the other markets with which the NYSE competes for corporate listings requires "one share, one vote," NYSE listed companies, faced with the possibility of delisting, know they will be welcome in those markets.

Arthur Levitt, Jr., chairman of the American Stock Exchange, Inc., testifying before the Subcommittee on Telecommunications, Consumer Protection and Finance of the House Energy and Commerce Committee, May 22, 1985, devoted 11 of 13 pages of prepared testimony discussing "two wholly unrelated phenomena . . . the rash of corporate takeovers . . . [and] the increasing competition among securities marketplaces" in his analysis of the proposed NYSE changes in its common stock voting rules.

Finally, A. A. Sommer, Jr., in his article "Drop the 'One Share, One Vote' Rule" in *N. Y.*

Times, April 7, 1985, Section F, at 2, col. 3, began: "Spurred by the actions of corporate managers intent on repulsing 'hostile' takeover attempts," then noted "intensifying competition for new listings" and that "the New York Stock Exchange, alone among the major markets, has refused to countenance so-called 'disproportionate voting rights,'" as evidence of "an environment very different from that which prompted [the NYSE's equal voting rights policy]."

78. Besides Ford Motor, as of September 30, 1985, Dow-Jones, Hershey Foods, General Motors, General Cinema, Fedders, Coastal, American Family, J. M. Smucker, and Kaufman and Broad were NYSE firms with a common stock class with unequal voting rights. See also Sherrid, "Class Struggle," *Forbes,* February 27, 1984, 73. The American Family and J. M. Smucker plans provide each common share with ten votes per share, but shareholders acquiring stock after the relevant amendment to the articles of incorporation will have one vote per share until the stock has been held for four years. See American Family Corporation Proxy Statement (April 22, 1985), 9–12; J. M. Smucker Company Proxy Statement (July 25, 1985); 10–15.

79. American Stock Exchange Executive Vice President Richard Scribner indicated in a letter to the author, August 15, 1985, that there were then 60 companies listed in the AMEX with multiple classes of stock.

80. The NASDAQ estimate is in the testimony of John S. R. Shad, to the Subcommittee on Oversight and Investigations of the House Committee on Energy and Commerce, June 17, 1985, 2–3.

81. Telephone interview with Richard Scribner, American Stock Exchange Executive Vice President for Legal and Regulatory Affairs, August 9, 1985.

82. Letter to the author from Mr. Richard Scribner, note 79. The full text of ¶ 122 is quoted in the text accompanying note 37.

83. Letter to the author from Mr. Richard Scribner, note 79.

84. Wang Laboratories, Inc., Proxy Statement Special Meeting of Stockholders, March 12, 1976.

85. Wang Laboratories, Inc., Proxy Statement, September 18, 1984.

86. Letter to the author from Mr. Richard Scribner, note 79.

87. Memorandum to all NASDAQ companies from Gordon Macklin, President NASD, re: Survey on Certain Corporate Governance Issues (May 13, 1985).

88. The NASD quoted in 17 *Sec. Reg. L.*

Rep. (BNA) 589 (April 5, 1985). Both the California and New Jersey state securities administrators responded to the NYSE survey concerning dual capitalization by warning the NYSE if it adopted less rigorous common stock voting rights it might lose its blue-sky law exemption. Mr. Franklin Tom, California commissioner of corporations, wrote Mr. Richard A. Grasso, NYSE executive vice president, October 5, 1984:

As you know, California's securities law imposes a form of merit regulation. Several of our merit standards are directed toward assuring a fair form of corporate democracy. Since 1969, California has, by statute, exempted from registration securities listed or approved for listing on the New York Stock Exchange. In effect, California has deferred to the NYSE's listing standards, deeming them to provide sufficient protection to shareholders that it is unnecessary to separately apply California's merit standards. In 1971 this statutory exemption was extended to securities listed or approved for listing on the American Stock Exchange, which has less stringent listing standards than the NYSE. No such blanket exemptive treatment has been afforded to securities traded on any other exchange or over the counter. This exemptive pattern is common to a number of states. It is worth noting that the Registration Exemption Committee of the North American Securities Administrators Association has recently suggested that these exemptions should be reexamined because the states currently have no effective means of correcting problems when exchanges (1) do not rigorously apply their listing criteria, (2) allow themselves to be used as devices to evade state registration requirements, or (3) lower their listing standards. We in California share the same concerns and are currently reviewing our registration exemptions.

Similarly, Mr. James McLelland Smith, New Jersey chief, bureau of securities, wrote Grasso on September 25, 1984: "if standards must be lowered or modified in a 'race to the bottom' to maintain membership, then at some point the Exchange must be willing to give up some or all of the respect and preferred treatment it receives."

89. In references to the blue-sky laws, full citations may be found in *Blue Sky L. Rep.* (CCH). The notes cite the state and section or rule number of the blue-sky law or regulations. In the following states, securities listed on the NYSE and AMEX are exempt from registration: Alabama § 8-6-10(7); Alaska § 45-55-140(a)(10); Arizona § 44-1843(7); Arkansas § 67-1248(a)(7); California § 25100(o); Colorado § 11-51-113(1)(g); Connecticut § 36-490(a)(8); Delaware § 7309(a)(8); Florida § 517.061(17); Georgia § 10-5-8(8); Hawaii § 485-4(8); Idaho § 30-1434(8); Illinois § 137.3(G); Indiana § 23-2-1-2(a)(5); Iowa § 502-202(8); Kentucky § 292.400(8); Louisiana § 51:704(6); Maine §

873(5); Maryland §11-601(8); Massachusetts § 402(a)(8); Michigan § 451-802(a)(7); Minnesota § 80A-15(1)(f); Mississippi § 75-71-201(8); Missouri § 409-402(a)(8); Montana § 30-10-104(13); Nebraska § 8-1110(7); New Hampshire § 421-B:17(I)(f); New Jersey § 49:3-50(a)(8); New Mexico Rules § 2.02B.2; New York § 359-f(1)(k); North Carolina § 78A-16(8); North Dakota § 10-04-05(G)(9) (and other conditions); Ohio § 1707.02(E); Oklahoma § 401(a)(8); Oregon § 59.025(4); Pennsylvania § 202(f); Rhode Island § 7-11-8(d); South Carolina§ 35-1-310(7); South Dakota § 47-31-71; Tennessee § 48-2-103(a)(9); Texas § 6(F); Utah § 61-1-14(1)(g); Vermont § 4203(b); Virginia §13.1-514(a)(8); Washington Rules WAC 460-42A-081; West Virginia § 32-4-402(a)(8); Wisconsin § 551.22(7); Wyoming § 17-4-114(a)(vii).

90. E.g., the following states exempt NASDAQ/NMS or all NASDAQ securities from registration: Delaware Rule 9(a)(13); Georgia § 10-5-8 and Order reprinted in **1A** *Blue Sky L. Rep.* (CCH), ¶ 18,515; New Mexico Rules 2-02B.2; Utah § 61-1-14(1)(g); Virginia Rule 502(5) (with conditions including equal common stock votes).

91. See text accompanying note 87.

92. See text accompanying notes 79-80.

A wide variety of dual-class capitalization (or similar) plans currently are employed as takeover defenses, including the following types of plans.

Stock issuance to existing shareholders. One common type of plan is illustrated by Dow-Jones & Company, Inc., Proxy Statement, March 16, 1984. This plan involved the issuance of one share of class B stock for each two shares of common stock. Each class B share had 10 votes. After the class B was issued, holders of the common stock, voting separately as a class, would be entitled to elect one-third of the corporation's directors. The common stock, together with the class B, will elect the other two-thirds of the directors. The common and class B shares have essentially equal rights to dividends and other distributions. Class B stock, however, may only be transferred to the holder's spouse, certain of the holder's relatives, certain trusts or charitable organizations; or be converted on a share-for-share basis into common stock. As a practical matter, the Dow-Jones type of plan permits a controlling stockholder to retain a majority of the votes while reducing its percentage ownership of the common stock.

The Wang Laboratories 1976 recapitalization essentially employed the same techniques as Dow-Jones. See Proxy Statement, September

17, 1976. Wang paid a dividend of one share of class B stock for each four shares of common stock outstanding. Both common and class B had identical dividend rights except that the class B stock was entitled to a $0.02½ additional dividend per share in any quarter a cash dividend was paid to the common stock. The holders of the class B stock were entitled to elect 25% of the directors, rounded up to the nearest whole number. The remaining directors were to be elected by the common stock. On all other matters, both classes of stock voted together, with class B shares having one-tenth of one vote per share and common stock having one vote. In 1985, Wang added a new wrinkle providing that any merger or consolidation would require both a vote of two-thirds of the class B common stock and the common stock (by then renamed as class C common stock) voting together as well as a majority of each class of stock voting separately. See Proxy Statement, September 16, 1985.

Issuance of a new class of stock with dividend preferences. The most common dual-class capitalization technique in recent years has been to create a dual-class structure with one class possessing superior voting rights and inferior dividend rights. The superior dividend rights of the second class create an incentive for noncontrolling stockholders to exchange their stock for the class with the higher dividends but inferior voting rights.

One illustration of this approach was the 1983 recapitalization of Hechinger Company. See Proxy Statement, August 30, 1983. Hechinger redesignated its common stock as class B and gave each class B share ten votes. A new class of common stock, class A, was authorized with one vote per share. At any time, class B could be converted into class A on a share-for-share basis. The incentives to convert were the dividend preferences enjoyed by class A. These preferences included the possibility of receiving a dividend on class A even if no dividend is paid on class B. In addition, the class A dividend normally would equal the class B dividend plus $0.01 per share. Moreover, the $0.01-per-share class A dividend preference is cumulative so that if a class A dividend is not paid in a given quarter, the $0.01-per-share preference must be paid in a subsequent quarter before class B shares can receive a dividend. Generally, the class A and class B shares vote as a single class.

A similar recapitalization was adopted by Waldbaum, Inc., in 1985. See Proxy Statement, June 13, 1985. Waldbaum's common stock was redesignated class A and a new class B was created. Class A retained one vote per share, and class B was given ten votes per share. Both classes normally voted together. Class A was entitled to a noncumulative cash dividend preference of $0.05 per annum. A "one-time-only" offer was made to the class A holders to exchange their shares on a share-for-share basis for class B.

In 1984 Hershey employed another variant of this plan. See Proxy Statement, August 27, 1984. Its common stock retained one vote per share, and a new class B was given ten votes per share. The common stock, voting separately as a class, was entitled to elect one-sixth of the board. Otherwise, both classes vote together. The common stock would be paid a cash dividend 10% higher than that of the class B. Shareholders were to be given the opportunity to exchange their common stock for class B. Since the plan designers could reasonably expect that not all common stockholders would do so, the plan would result in the controlling stockholder, the Hershey Trust, being able to retain control by exchanging some portion of its common stock for class B.

Issuance of a class of stock with a conversion sweetener. Alternative to a dividend preference is the device of offering holders of the class of stock with superior voting rights a "sweetener" for exchanging their shares for the class with inferior voting rights.

An illustration of this technique was provided by Charter Medical, which in 1981 designated its common stock as class B and created a new class A. See Proxy statement, October 28, 1981. Charter also offered to exchange 1.1 shares of class A for each share of class B. Class A stock could receive a dividend of no more than $0.0625 per share in a quarter without any dividend being paid to class B. Class A stock (together with series C preferred stock) was entitled to elect 25% of the board (rounded up to the nearest whole number). Class B (also voting with the series C preferred) would be entitled to elect the remaining directors.

A similar "sweetener" was used by BDM International Inc. See Proxy Statement, December 13, 1983. Like Charter, BDM adopted a class A–B structure, with class A entitled to elect 25% of the board and class B, 75%. Class A would receive cash dividends equal to 115% of cash dividends paid to class B. Each class B share would be convertible into 1.1 shares of class A.

Temporal voting stock restrictions. J. M. Smucker and American Family in 1985 each employed a different system. See J. M. Smucker Proxy Statement, July 25, 1985; American Family Corporation, April 22, 1985. In both firms, each common share was given ten votes per share as long as the same beneficial owner had held the stock during the four years preceding the record date of a shareholders' meeting. The four-year holding period was intended to discourage "raiders." During the four years, each common share would have only one vote.

Reductions in the voting power of large shareholders. A quite different approach is taken by MCI, which places a "threshold limitation" of 10% of the voting shares of any class of MCI stock. See Proxy Statement, June 5, 1981. Once a person has reached the 10% limit, additional shares are entitled to only one-hundredth of a vote per share. In no event may a shareholder cast more than 15% of the total number of votes. The MCI plan is different in kind from each of the earlier types of plans discussed. Nonetheless, like the earlier plans, the MCI approach also has the fundamental consequence of frustrating outside bidders attempting to put together statistical control of a firm.

Non–takeover-defense-inspired voting restrictions. A different type of dividend preference was used by General Motors (GM) when it issued class E stock to acquire Electronic Data Systems (EDS). In its September 21, 1984, Proxy Statement the GM board explained that it intended to "to adopt a policy that the annual per share dividends on class E stock . . . will equal approximately 25% of the quotient of (i) the Separate Consolidated Net Income of EDS divided by (ii) the greater of 60,000,000 (. . . the number of shares of EDS Common Stock presently outstanding) or the number of shares of class E stock then outstanding." In return for this performance-related dividend, EDS stockholders agreed to accept one-half of a vote per class E share, in contrast to GM common stock, which has one vote per share. A similar approach was employed by GM late in 1985 when it proposed the creation of class H stock to acquire Hughes Aircraft Company. The class H stock, like the earlier class E, would be entitled to a one-half vote per share and performance-related dividends. See Press Release, November 13, 1985. In contrast to the aim of most other dual-class capitalization plans, the purpose of the GM plan is not to create a takeover defense but to provide a form of incentive compensation to the shareholders of an acquired firm. Accordingly, unlike each of the plans discussed in this note, the GM plan could not give rise to a duty of loyalty analysis under existing case law [see *Norlin Corp. v. Rooney Pace, Inc.,* 744 F.2d 255 (2d Cir. 1984)] but would be analyzed like other business decisions under the business judgment rule.

While the GM plan is entitled to a more sympathetic judicial scrutiny, it is equally offensive to the monitoring concept analyzed. Moreover, there is no necessity to restrict the votes per common share to create a performance-related dividend. Even if the law imposes a strict one share for each common share, GM or any other firm could issue stock with performance-related dividends.

93. Berle and Means, note 47, p. 109. Management control was defined to mean that "ownership is so widely distributed that no individual or small group has even a minority interest large enough to dominate the affairs of the company. When the largest single interest amounts to but a fraction of one percent—the case in several of the largest corporations—no stockholder is in the position through his holdings alone to place important pressure upon the management" (ibid., 78). Control through a legal device means control through stock pyramiding, nonvoting stock, common stock with disproportionate voting rights, or a voting trust, (ibid., 69–75). Minority control "may be said to exist when an individual or small group hold a sufficient stock interest to be in a position to dominate a corporation *through their stock interest*" (ibid., 75). An example discussed by Berle and Means was the John D. Rockefeller control of Standard Oil Company of Indiana with 14.9% of the stock (Ibid., 75–78).

94. See, e.g., E. Herman, *Corporate Control, Corporate Power* (1981), 56–59; M. Useem, *The Inner Circle 204,* (1984), note 11 (citations to 14 American studies).

95. Demsetz, "The Structure of Ownership and Theory of the Firms," 26 *J.L. Econ.* 375, 387–389 (1983).

96. Adding to the number of AMEX and NASDAQ firms noted in the text accompanying notes 79–80 were 1469 firms listed on the NYSE as of December 31, 1983. See 50 *Sec. Ann. Rep.* 111 (1984).

97. The list of OTC firms was selected from the *Wall Street Journal,* August 28, 1985. The proxy statement or 10–K studied was the most recent available in the public reference room of the SEC or the Gelman Library, George Washington University. On the NMS list, Aegon was excluded because of foreign ownership; Alden Electronics was excluded because it had dual capitalization.

98. See text accompanying notes 25–29.

99. § 14(a) requires all firms registered pursuant to § 12 of the Securities Exchange Act to obey SEC proxy rules. § 12(a) requires registration of all firms traded on a national securities exchange; § 12(g) requires registration of each

issue with total assets of $1 million or more and a class of equity stock held by 500 or more shareholders. Otherwise, covered issues with assets not exceeding $3 million currently are exempt from § 12(g). See Rule 12g–1, 17 CFR 240.12g–1.

100. Date for proxy elections for boards of directors in the period 1956–1977 are given in the following table. These data were compiled from Securities and Exchange Commission, *Annual Report* (1956–1977), 22–43.

101. Other reasons are noted in Easterbrook and Fischel, "Voting in Corporate Law," 26 *J. L. Econ.* 395, 406–408 (1985) [e.g., their speculation that the premium for voting rights "probably represents the anticipated (and fully diluted) value attributable to the opportunity of those with votes to improve the performance of the corporation"].

102. "The Market Value of Control in Publicly-Traded Corporations," 11 *J. Fin. Econ.* 439 (1983).

103. Ibid., 443. Market price dates for the last trading day of each month (after January 1970) were found in the *Wall Street Journal*, ibid., 450; gives the procedure.

104. Ibid., 469.

105. "The Market Value of Differential Voting Rights in Closely Held Corporations," 57 *J. Bus.* 443 (1984).

106. "Economic Evaluation of Voting Power of Common Stock," 38 *J. Fin.* 79 (1982).

107. "Cumulative Voting: The Value of Minority Shareholder Voting Rights," 27 *J. L. Econ.* 339 (1984).

108. "Greenmail: Targeted Stock Repurchases and the Management-Entrenchment Hypothesis," 98 *Harv. L. Rev.* 1045, 1051–1054 (1985).

109. See, e.g., Bradley, "Interfirm Tender Offers and the Market for Corporate Control," 52 *J. Bus.* 345 (1980).

110. See, e.g., 8 Del. Code Annon. Ch. 1, § 151(a); Henn and Alexander, note 28, pp. 499–501. See also *C.A. Cavendes Soeciedad v. Florida Nat'l Banks of Florida, Inc.*, 556 F. Supp. 254 (M.D. Fla. 1982) (Florida corporation code provides that "each outstanding share, regardless of class, shall be entitled to one vote on each matter submitted to a vote of a meeting of shareholders").

111. See, e.g., *Asarco, Inc., v. MRH Holmes A Court, 1984–1985 Fed. Sec. L. Rep.* (CCH), ¶ 92,220 (D.N.J. 1985), which enjoined the issuance of a series C preferred stock which would have had different voting rights depending upon whether a series C share was held by a 20% holder. The federal district court concluded that while the New Jersey Business Corporation Act permits changes of voting rights between classes

Fiscal Year	Total No. Corporations	Total No. Proxy Contests	Percent Management Unopposed	No. Contests for Representation	No. Contests for Control	No. Managements Lost Control	Percent Management Retained Control
1977	6607	41	99.4	11	30	5	99.9
1976	6807	18	99.7	3	15	2	99.9
1975	6801	25	99.6	5	20	1	99.9
1974	6741	15	99.8	1	14	4	99.9
1973	6744	23	99.7	5	18	10	99.9
1972	6328	23	99.6	7	16	4	99.9
1971	5864	31	99.5	9	22	7	99.9
1970	5095	24	99.5	4	20	5	99.9
1969	4548	25	99.4	5	20	5	99.9
1968	4473	27	99.4	6	21	5	99.9
1967	4370	37	99.2	19	18	5	99.9
1966	3632	37	99.0	13	24	8	99.8
1965	2391	26	98.9	10	16	7	99.7
1964	2274	18	99.2	6	12	1	99.9
1963	2205	27	98.8	9	18	5	99.8
1962	1807	17	99.0	7	10	4	99.8
1961	1680	32	98.1	12	20	5	99.7
1960	1864	25	98.7	9	16	1	99.7
1959	1790	19	99.0	8	11	3	99.9
1958	1780	34	98.1	12	22	6	99.7
1957	1726	20	98.8	9	11	3	99.8
1956	1705	17	99.0	9	8	2	99.9

or series, it does not permit different voting rights to be created *within* a class or series.

A subsequent federal district court opinion extended the reasoning of *Asarco* to hold under New Jersey law that AMF's issuance of poison pill rights was illegal. See *Minstar Acquiring Corp. v. AMF, Inc.,* 1984–1985 Fed. Sec. L. Rep. (CCH), ¶ 92,066 (S.D.N.Y. June 7, 1985). Other jurisdictions have permitted issuance of classes of stock with different voting rights. See *Unocal Corp. v. Mesa Petroleum Co.,* 1984–1985 Fed. Sec. L. Rep. (CCH), ¶ 92,077 (Del. Supr. 1985); *Providence & Worcester Co. v. Baker,* 378 A.2d 121 (Del. Supr. 1977); *Deskins v. Lawrence County Fair & Development Corp.,* 321 S.W. 2d 408 (Ky. Ct. Ap. 1959); *Honigman v. Green Giant Co.,* 309 F.2d 667 (8th Cir. 1962), *cert. den.,* 372 U.S. 941 (1963) (Minnesota law). See also Annot., "Validity of Variations from One Share–One Vote Rule Under Modern Corporate Law," 3 ALR 4th 1204.

112. Statement of Policy on Non-Voting Stock, 1 *Blue Sky L. Rep.* (CCH), ¶ 5319.

113. Alabama Rule 830–X–4–.13 (one class of common stock required if issuer in formative stages); Alaska Rules § 3 AAC 08.210; Arizona Rules § R14–4–105(B) (promotional stock); Arkansas Rule 12.07; California Rule 260.140.1; Florida Rule SE–700.06 (developmental-stage entities); Indiana Rules § 710 1AC 1–2–24; Iowa Rules § 510–50.40 (502); Kansas Rules § 81–7–1(k); Louisiana Rule C–08; Minnesota Rules Part 2875.3080; Missouri Rules § 30–52.110; Nebraska Rules Ch. 8; South Carolina Rule 113–13(2) (preincorporation subscriptions); Tennessee Rule 0780–4–3.06 (4)(i); Texas Rule § 113.3(6); Washington Statement of Policy No. 82–17 (December 21, 1982), reprinted in 3 *Blue Sky L. Rep.* (CCH), ¶ 61.786F; Wisconsin Rules § SEC 3.07; Wyoming Rules § 3(h).

114. See text accompanying notes 89–90.

115. See note 88.

116. Public Utility Holding Company Act §§ 6(e) and 7(c), 15 U.S.C. § 79(c); Investment Company Act § 18, 15 U.S.C. § 80a–18; Federal Bankruptcy Reform Act of 1978, § 1123(a)(6), 11 U.S.C. § 1123(a)(6). See Leary, "Voting Rights in Preferred Stock Issues Under the Public Utility Holding Company Act of 1935," 27 *Tex. L. Rev.* 749 (1949); Note, "Voting Rights of Preferred Stockholders Under the Public Utility Holding Act of 1935," 51 *Yale L.J.* 138 (1941). The 1938 Chandler Bankruptcy Act also forbade nonvoting shares in reorganized firms. See 52 *Stat.* 840, 897 (1938) [§ 216(12)(a)].

117. 15 U.S.C. 78s(c).

118. See "Discussion from the Floor," 31 *Bus. L.* 1091, 1095–1096 (1976). See also

Kripke, "The SEC, Corporate Governance, and the Real Issues," 36 *Bus. L.* 173–174 (1981).

119. S. Rep. No. 94–75, 94th Cong., 1st Sess. 1975, 131. See also Note, "Stock Exchange Listing Agreements as a Vehicle for Corporate Governance," 129 *Univ. Pa. L. Rev.* 1427 (1981).

120. S. Rep. No. 94–75, 94th Cong., 1st Sess. 1975, 131.

121. Quoting *Summary of Principal Provisions of Securities Acts Amendments of 1975,* Senate Committee on Banking, Housing and Urban Affairs, 94th Cong., 1st Sess. (Committee Print), 1975, 8; see, generally, pp. 11 and 16. The same language is used in Senate Report No. 94–75, 94th Cong., 1st Sess. 1975, 31 {"The bill would give the SEC clear authority to amend any self-regulatory organization's rules in any respect consistent with the objectives of the Exchange Act [19(c)]"}.

122. 15 U.S.C. 78K–1(a)(2).

123. S. Rep. No. 94–75, 94th Cong., 1st Sess. 1975, 105. *The Conference Report,* H. Rep. No. 94–229, 94th Cong., 1st Sess. 1975, 93–94, elaborated:

Finally, the Senate bill and the House amendment required the Commission to assure that equal regulation, within the national market system, is achieved. Under the House amendment, the Commission was directed to promulgate rules and regulations applicable to specialists, market makers and certain other dealers who perform similar functions to assure that competition occurs within the context of equal regulatory requirements. Equal regulation was defined in competitive terms and would have been applicable only to dealers.

The Senate bill also defined "equal regulation" in competitive terms, but made it applicable generally to the regulation of the trading markets and the conduct of the securities industry. Equal regulation was applied in broader areas in the Senate bill, directing the Commission to assure equal regulation not only of dealers, but also of all markets for qualified securities, exchange members, and brokers. The Senate provision was agreed upon in conference with a modification to make clear that it is the Commission, subject to appropriate judicial review, that is to decide whether any regulatory disparity is not necessary or appropriate in furtherance of the purposes of the Exchange Act. The conferees expect that Commission will act in these areas in an expeditious manner to remove unjustified disparities in regulation as may result in unfair competitive advantages.

124. Letter to John P. Wheeler III, secretary, Securities and Exchange Commission, from Milton Cohen, re: File No. S7–37–84, Release No. 34–21498 20–21 (February 8, 1985).

125. See Seligman, "The Future of the National Market System," 10 *J. Corp. L.* 79 (1984).

126. 15 U.S.C. 78K–1(c)(4)(A).

127. See Coffee, note 1, pp. 1266–1267; see, generally, pp. 1266–1269.

128. 15 U.S.C. 78n(a).

129. *J. I. Case v. Borak,* 377 U.S. 426, 431–432 (1964). Accord: *Mills v. Electric Auto-Lite Co.,* 396 U.S. 375, 381 (1970). Both the House and Senate committee reports on the Securities Exchange Act of 1934 explicitly state that the purpose of § 14 was to ensure "fair corporate suffrage." In the words of the House Commerce Committee report:

Fair corporate suffrage is an important right that should attach to every equity security bought on a public exchange. Management . . . should not be permitted to perpetuate themselves by the misuse of corporate proxies. . . . Inasmuch as only the exchanges make it possible for securities to be widely distributed among the investing public, it follows as a corollary that the use of the exchanges should involve a corresponding duty of according to shareholders fair suffrage. For this reason the proposed bill gives the . . . Commission power to control the conditions under which proxies may be solicited with a view to preventing the recurrence of abuses which have frustrated the free exercise of the voting rights of shareholders.

H.R. Rep. No. 1383, 73rd Cong., 2d Sess. 1934, 13; Accord, S. Rep. No. 792, 73rd Cong., 2d Sess. 1934, 12, 77.

130. 163 F.2d 511, 518 (3d Cir. 1947), *cert. den.,* 332 U.S. 847 (1948).

131. *Medical Committee for Human Rights v. SEC,* 432 F.2d 659, 676 (D.C. Cir. 1970); *vacated as moot,* 404 U.S. 403 (1971).

132. Management secrecy in soliciting proxies was much emphasized in the legislative history of § 14(a). See, e.g., 14 *Stock Exchange Practices,* hearings before the Senate Committee on Banking and Currency, 73rd Cong., 2d Sess. on S. Res. 84 (72nd Cong.), S. Res. 56, and S. Res. 97 (73rd Cong.), 1934, 6206–6216; *Stock Exchange Regulation,* hearing before the House Committee on Interstate and Foreign Commerce, 73rd Cong., 2d Sess. on H.R. 7852 and H.R. 8720, 1934, 138–142, 925, 937 (testimony and brief of Thomas Corcoran); S. Rep. No. 1455, 73rd Cong., 2d Sess. 1934, 74–77 ("In order that the stockholder may have adequate knowledge as to the manner in which his interests are being served, it is essential that he be enlightened not only as to the financial condition of the corporation, but also as to the major questions of policy, which are decided at stockholders' meetings. Too often proxies are solicited without explanation to the stockholder of the real nature of the matters for which authority to cast his vote is sought."); Accord, S. Rep. No. 792, 73rd Cong., 2d Sess. 1934, 12; H.R. Rep. No. 1383, 1934, 13–14 ("Managements of properties owned by the investing public should not be permitted to perpetuate themselves by the misuse of corporate proxies. Insiders having

little or no substantial interest in the properties they manage have often retained their control without an adequate disclosure of their interest and without an adequate explanation of the management policies they intend to pursue. Insiders have at times solicited proxies without fairly informing the stockholders of the purposes for which the proxies are to be used and have used such proxies to take from the stockholders for their own selfish advantage valuable property rights."). See also Berle and Means, note 47, pp. 149–131 (confirm); Bernstein and Fisher, "The Regulation of the Solicitation of Proxies: Some Reflections on Corporate Democracy," 7 *Univ. Chi. L. Rev.* 226, 228–229 (1940); Friedman, "SEC Regulation of Corporate Proxies," 63 *Harv. L. Rev.* 796 (1950); Orrick, "The Revised Proxy Rules of the Securities and Exchange Commission," 11 *Bus. L.* 32 (1956); Loomis and Rubman, note 52, pp. 154–155.

133. Professor Loss has explained: "The Commission's power under § 14(a) is not necessarily limited to ensuring full disclosure. The statutory language is considerably more general than it is under the specific disclosure philosophy of the 1933 Act." See 2 L. Loss, *Securities Regulation,* 2nd ed. (1961), 868. Armstrong, in "The Role of the Securities and Exchange Commission in Proxy Contests of Listed Companies," 11 *Bus. L.* 110, 111 (1955), has stated: "The breadth of the grant of authority can hardly be questioned, considering the wording of the Exchange Act." Caplin, in "Shareholder Nominations of Directors: A Program for Fair Corporate Suffrage," 39 *Va. L. Rev.* 141, 155 (1953), similarly noted:

The . . . statutory standard, if not precise in its scope, certainly lends itself to the interpretation that Congress intended to grant to the SEC the broadest of authority in the control of proxy solicitation, a grant which would support the adoption by the SEC of any reasonable regulatory provision and not simply provisions devoted to securing the bare disclosure of information."

See also Latcham and Emerson, "Proxy Contest Expenses and Shareholder Democracy," 4 *Wes. Res. L. Rev.* 5, 6–7 (1952).

The commission has recognized its power to prescribe a rule requiring inclusion of shareholder nominees in the corporate proxy by circulating such a rule for comment in 1942. See text of rule and discussion in Caplin, "Proxies, Annual Meetings and Corporate Democracy," 37 *Va. L. Rev.* 653, 682–685 (1951). Note that his doubts about the commission's power were quickly dispelled. See Caplin, "Shareholder Nominations of Directors: A Program for Fair

Corporate Suffrage," 39 *Va. L. Rev.* 141, 154–161 (1953).

134. *SEC Legislation, 1963,* hearings before a subcommittee of the Senate Committee on Banking and Currency, 88th Cong., 1st Sess. on S. 1642, 1963, 402 (statement of the Securities and Exchange Commission), stated:

The New York Stock Exchange now requires issuers of securities listed on that exchange to solicit proxies each year. The American Stock Exchange has embarked on a program to achieve the same purpose. However, similar requirements as to listed or unlisted securities are not imposed by other exchanges or by any other authority. Because evasion of the disclosures required by the proxy rules is made possible by the simple device of not soliciting proxies, many stockholders are deprived of the material information concerning their company which is disclosed in proxy materials. This problem would be accentuated by the extension of the proxy rules to over-the-counter securities where nonsolicitation would occur more frequently because of management's relatively larger holdings. Enactment of this proposal would be a major step in providing shareholders with material information and enabling them to vote upon the basis of a fair presentation of the relevant and material facts.

135. See quotation in note 128.

136. Ibid.

137. There are rare exceptions such as *Perlman v. Feldman,* 219 F.2d 173 (2d Cir. 1955), *cert. den.,* 349 U.S. 952 (1955), in which the sale of control was accompanied by the misappropriation of corporate opportunities.

138. *Zahn v. Transamerica,* 162 F.2d 36 (3d Cir. 1947).

139. Ibid., 46.

140. *Weinberger v. UOP, Inc.,* 457 A.2d 701, 715 (Del. Supr. 1983).

141. *S. A. Judah v. Delaware Trust Co.,* 378 A.2d 624, 628 (Del. Supr. 1977).

142. This normative analysis focuses solely on firms that are publicly traded. It does not analyze close corporations or corporations in a developmental phase, each of which introduces countervailing considerations not addressed in this chapter.

143. The concepts of monitoring and bonding costs are further explored in Jensen and Meckling, "Theory of the Firm: Managerial Behavior, Agency Costs and Ownership Structure," 3 *J. Fin. Econ.* 305 (1976).

144. See Lowenstein, "Management Buyouts," 85 *Colum. L. Rev.* 730 (1985).

145. Under § 12(b) and (g) of the Securities Exchange Act of 1934, 15 U.S.C. 781(b), (g), corporations whose securities are listed on a national securities exchange or held of record by 500 or more shareholders with total assets exceeding $1 million are subject to registration requirements. See also Rule 12g–1, 17 CFR 240, 12g–1, exempting a corporate issuer from registration if it has total assets of less than $3 million.

146. Shareholder approval would also be a prerequisite to listing warrants where the aggregate of common shares purchasable upon exercise of those warrants exceeds 18½% of the outstanding common shares at the time of issuance of such warrants.

147. Memorandum to members of the Advisory Committee from Phillip L. West, re: Stockholder Approval Policy Regarding: 1. Definition of "Substantial"; 2. Definition of "Stockholder Vote" (November 17, 1955) 2 (on file with NYSE).

148. Ibid.

149. See Loss, note 133, p. 806 (note 73); *Report of Special Study of Securities Markets of the Securities and Exchange Commission,* House Document No. 95, 88th Cong., 1st Sess. 1963, 568.

150. For example, in July 1961, the NYSE determined that the proposed acquisition by the Hupp Corporation of the Hercules Motor Corporation required stockholder approval despite the fact that the transaction involved the issuance of only 19.5% of Hupp's outstanding shares. Memorandum to the members of the Advisory Committee from Phillip L. West, re: The Possible Revision of the Exchange's Stockholder Approval Policy (October 13, 1961) (on file with NYSE).

151. *Wall St. J.,* March 29, 1960, at 18, col. 6. See also *N. Y. Times,* March 29, 1960, at 53, col. 5.

152. *Wall St. J.,* March 29, 1960, at 18, col. 6.

153. *Business Combinations and Other Financial Reporting Problems,* hearing before the Controllers Institute of America (January 18, 1962) (on file at SEC).

154. On the pooling versus purchase controversy, see generally, Seligman, note 8, pp. 416–430.

155. See. E. Folk, *The Delaware General Corporation Law* (1972), 318–323. Professor Folk was the reporter of the 1967 Revision to the Delaware General Corporation Law. As the cited pages illustrate, he clearly was aware of the NYSE rules.

156. See, e.g., *Norlin Corp. v. Rooney, Pace Inc.,* 744 F.2d 255 (2d Cir. 1984) (issuance of blocks of stock to a subsidiary and an employee stock option plan was deemed by the NYSE to result in a change of control without shareholder approval; Norlin was suspended from trading on April 16, 1984). See also *Gearhart*

Ind. v. Smith Int'l, Inc., 741 F.2d 707, 724–726 (5th Cir. 1984) (the NYSE announced plans to begin delisting Gearhart for issuing a greater-than-18.5% stock block to Aetna Life and Casualty Company without shareholder approval); *Chris-Craft Ind. Inc. v. Piper Aircraft Corp.,* 480 F.2d 341, 351–352 (2d Cir. 1973), *cert. den.,* 414 U.S. 910 (1973) (the NYSE refused to list a greater-than-18.5% block of Piper stock to be sold to Gruman, absent shareholder approval). See also *Gaynor v. Buckley,* 318 F.2d 432 (9th Cir. 1963) (the NYSE required shareholder approval of an option issued to a corporate officer); *Applied Digital Data Systems v. Milgo Electronic,* 425 F. Supp. 1145, 1149 n. 4 (S.D.N.Y. 1977) (a transaction was restructured to involve less than an 18.5% block consistent with the NYSE rule); *Kaplan v. Goldsamt,* 380 A.2d 556, 561 (Del. Ch. 1977) (the NYSE persuaded the firm to seek shareholder approval of a "greenmail" payment); 1 M. Lipton and E. Steinberger, *Takeovers and Freezeouts* § 4.01[4] (1984); Coffee, note 1, p. 1256 (note 336).

157. SEC Advisory Committee on Tender Offers, *Report of Recommendations* (July 8, 1983), 44.

158. Coffee, note 1, p. 1255.

159. See, e.g., *Buffalo Forge Co. v. Ogden Corp.,* 717 F.2d 757 (2d Cir. 1983); *cert. den.,* 104 S. Ct. 550 (1983); *Whittaker Corp. v. Edgar,* 535 F. Supp. 933. 951 (N.D. Ill. 1982). But see *Condec Corp. v. Lunkenheimer,* 43 Del. Ch. 353, 230 A.2d 769 (Ch. 1967).

160. 105 S. Ct. 2458 (1985). The SEC recently construed its rule-making authority under the Williams Act to permit proposal of rules requiring (i) a tender offer must be extended to all holders of the class of stock which is the subject of the offer; and (ii) all such holders must be paid the highest consideration offered under the tender offer rule. See Sec. Act. Rel. No. 6595, 33 SEC Dock. 762 (1985). The commission, in part, relied on the language and legislative history of § 14(d)(7) as authority for this proposal (ibid., 33 SEC Dock., 764, note 11).

161. See examples of less than 18½% lockups noted in 1 A. Fleischer, *Tender Offers: Defenses, Responses and Planning* (1983), 328 (note 110).

162. 500 A.2d 1346 (Del. Supr. 1985).

163. 490 A.2d 1067.

164. See, e.g., *Wall St. J.,* June 10, 1985, at 5, col. 5, indicating that the NYSE will hold in abeyance during its review of shareholder approval policies its delisting proceedings against Allis-Chalmers for converting $65 million of debt to equity without shareholder approval.

165. For example, the *Datatab* case, involving a firm traded over the counter, concerned an option to purchase shares equal to 200% of the initially outstanding stock. See *Data Probe Acquisition Corp. v. Datatab, Inc.,* 568 F. Supp. 1538, 1542, *rev'd,* 722 F.3d 1 (2d Cir. 1983), *cert. den.,* 104 S. Ct. 1326 (1984).

32

Organized Exchanges and the Regulation of Dual Class Common Stock

DANIEL R. FISCHEL

Entrepreneurs of firms who decide to raise funds from capital markets have considerable discretion in choosing an appropriate capital structure. They must decide, for example, whether to sell common or preferred stock, issue secured or unsecured debt, or undertake some combination of the above.[1] They also must decide what the voting rights of the various classes of investors will be.

One important decision that must be made is under what circumstances, if any, classes of investors other than common stockholders will have the right to vote. Another important decision is what the voting rules will be for common stockholders. Some of the possibilities include one share-one vote, cumulative voting, or multiple classes of common stock with unequal voting rights. Multiple classes of common stock with unequal voting rights are commonly referred to as dual class common stock.

Whatever voting rules are selected, it is possible to alter the rules in the future in light of changed circumstances. Thus cumulative or dual class voting might be eliminated or implemented, notwithstanding the prior rule, if certain previously agreed upon procedures are followed (typically approval of the proposed change by shareholders).

I would like to thank Alan Frankel and David Ross for their invaluable assistance and Geoffrey Miller, Richard Posner, and Alan Sykes for helpful comments.

The laws of many states—including Delaware, the state in which most firms incorporate—impose only the most minimal regulation on the choice of voting rules.[2] Dual class voting, like cumulative voting and virtually all other possible voting schemes, is neither prohibited nor required.[3] The voting rules are considered to be a matter of private contract between the firm and its various types of investors.

The organized exchanges have taken several approaches toward dual class voting. The National Association of Securities Dealers (NASD) has placed no restrictions on the trading of dual classes of common stock on its automated quotation system (NASDAQ). The American Stock Exchange (AMEX) allows the trading of dual classes of common stock, provided that the inferior voting stock has some voting rights.[4] Historically, the New York Stock Exchange (NYSE) is at the opposite extreme from the NASD. Since 1926, the NYSE has prohibited listed firms from issuing any type of dual class common stock.[5]

In recent years, however, there has been considerable debate among member firms on the NYSE whether to retain the prohibition against dual class common stock. In January, 1985, an advisory committee recommended to the Board of Directors of the NYSE that the exchange allow the trading of dual class common stock in certain situations.[6] Although the NYSE decided in June, 1986 to accept the advisory committee's recommendation,[7] the change will not be effective until approved by the Securities and Exchange Commission.

The current controversy concerning dual class common stock also has attracted the attention of Congress. Legislation has been introduced in both houses of Congress that would require the NASD and the AMEX to adopt the historic NYSE prohibition on the trading of dual class common stock. The stated justification for the proposed legislation is that the ability of exchanges to choose different rules regarding the trading of dual class common stock will lead all exchanges to adopt the rule that is most detrimental to investors. By preventing this "race to the bottom" among exchanges and forcing all exchanges to adopt the NYSE's prohibition on trading of dual class common stock, the argument runs, the proposed legislation will protect investors.

The NYSE itself has endorsed this "race to the bottom" argument in explaining the departure from its historic prohibition on the listing of dual class common stock. The NYSE has stated that it would prefer to retain the prohibition, but only if other exchanges adopted the prohibition or were forced to do so by federal regulation.[8]

This chapter analyzes whether exchange rules permitting the trading of dual class common stock are economically beneficial to investors and whether federal regulation is necessary to protect investors from such exchange rules. The first section discusses the role of exchanges and the incentives of exchanges to offer the type of transaction and ancillary services that investors want. The "race to the bottom" thesis is critically analyzed in the next section. The third section discusses the reasons why some firms might choose to have dual class common stock in light of the economic theory of voting; it also summarizes the available empirical evidence. Next, the relationship between dual class common stock and the current debate concerning defensive tactics in response to takeovers is analyzed. The fifth section discusses the effects of a change in the NYSE's historic prohibition on the listing of dual class common stock. The final section is a conclusion.

VOTING RULES AND THE ROLE OF ORGANIZED STOCK EXCHANGES

The Economic Function of Exchanges

Stock exchanges facilitate transactions between buyers and sellers of securities. They do this by providing a centralized location, such as an exchange floor, for trades to take place or by providing an electronic system to perform the same function. As with all marketplaces, the primary benefit of exchanges is that they save traders the cost of independently searching for someone on the other side of the transaction.[9] A competitive broker or arbitrager in the market demands less of a discount when purchasing a security and charges less of a premium when selling a security if, on average, he does not have to hold it in inventory for very long or incur large search costs to find buyers and sellers. The lower costs are reflected in low bid/ask spreads and high liquidity.

A related benefit is that organzied exchanges provide a forum that allows customer orders to be executed with minimum delay. Thus brokers can usually execute a customer's order quickly because the exchange provides swift access to other buyers and sellers. This immediacy is extremely important for purchasers and sellers of securities since prices can move between the time of the order and the time the transaction is consummated. By providing liquidity, exchanges minimize the risk of price fluctuations borne by investors during trading delays.

In addition to providing a centralized location or electronic system to facilitate trades of securities, exchanges provide a set of ancillary services. For example, exchanges police the conduct of member firms to ensure that they are adequately capitalized, do not act fraudulently toward consumers, or otherwise act in ways that harm the reputation of the exchange. Exchanges also may promulgate rules for listed firms governing financial disclosure, annual meetings, or corporate structure.

Exchanges market these transaction and ancillary services by selling access to a trading floor or to an electronic quotation system. The NYSE is run for profit and access to the system is available to members holding one or more of a limited number of seats (and in recent years a small number of nonmembers). The AMEX and regional exchanges are organized along similar lines. The "over-the-counter" NASDAQ trading system, by contrast, is owned by the NASD, a non-profit organization, which places no limits on the number of members and charges members fees depending on the level of services they select from the electronic quotation and trading system.

The value of access to an exchange is a function of the commission income (and trading profits) that can be earned by members. This income is in turn a function of the ability of the exchange to attract listings and facilitate trading of securities of listed companies. The higher the quality of transactional and ancillary services (at a given cost) the more listings will occur and the more investors will be willing to trade. For this reason, exchanges have strong incentives to provide transactional and ancillary services that are in the best interests of investors.

In this sense, exchanges face the same incentives to provide high-quality products (i.e., transactional services) as any other business. Just as a manufacturer of automobiles has strong incentives to make a product that consumers want in order to maximize its profitability, an exchange has incentives to design transactional and ancillary services that investors prefer.[10]

The Incentive of Exchanges to Adopt Voting Rules That Maximize Investors' Welfare

The choice of which, if any, voting rules to implement is one of countless decisions exchanges must make in designing customer services. Exchanges have strong incentives to make these decisions—including those about voting rules—in investors' best interests to maximize their own profitability.[11] In addition to these incentives, certain characteristics of exchanges and voting rules ensure that exchanges will not be able to fool investors into believing they are purchasing high-quality transactional services when they are in fact buying services of poor quality.[12] These characteristics can be summarized as follows:

1. *Observability.* The more observable a particular product characteristic, the less likely consumers will be fooled. It is extremely difficult to deceive consumers with respect to the number of rooms in a house, for example, because consumers can ascertain the truth by counting the rooms themselves. At the other extreme are product characteristics that are very difficult to observe. A representation by an automobile mechanic that a given part should be replaced once the car has been taken in for other work, for example, is notoriously difficult to verify at low cost. As a result, the probability that consumers will be misled in this situation is much higher than in the matter of house size.

In terms of observability, the choice of voting rules is much closer to house size than to the condition of automobile parts. The rules chosen by a particular exchange are a matter of public record and thus completely observable.[13] Accordingly, it is unlikely that exchanges will be able to dupe investors by implementing voting rules that operate to their detriment.

2. *Reputation of the seller.* The greater a seller's stake in maintaining a reputation for honesty and fair dealing, the less likely the seller will engage in deceptive practices. A well-established large department store is less likely to misrepresent product quality than a transient street vendor selling the same product.

Organized exchanges have strong incentives to maintain good reputations. The long-run profitability of an exchange is highly dependent on trading volume, which will fall if consumers doubt the exchange's integrity. It is clearly in the interest of exchanges to promote consumer confidence by policing abuses by members that cause investors to lose money—at least to the extent that policing is economically feasible. Accordingly, it is in the interest of exchanges to choose voting rules that prevent investors from being exploited. If voting rules allowed by an exchange produced systematic exploitation of investors, investors would lose confidence in the exchange and the exchange would lose trading volume as investors took their business elsewhere.

3. *Repeat transactions.* Maintaining a good reputation is most important when repeat transactions are contemplated: the more important future business is, the greater the costs of losing it through damage to reputation. Victims of abusive practices are not likely to be repeat players in the same game. An organized exchange, by definition, is dependent on repeat business for survival; it is thus less likely to abuse investors.

4. *The role of informed investors.* Informed traders or consumers reduce the probability that an exchange or other type of seller will be able to misrepresent product quality. If an exchange adopts voting rules detrimental to investors, informed traders may refuse to transact at all (which may cause the exchange to fail) or only transact on terms that reflect the probability of the abusive practice (which would reduce the exchange's profitability). Because uninformed market participants commonly transact on the same terms as those who are informed, the uninformed will be protected by the monitoring of exchange rules by the informed—including rules governing voting rights.

Therefore, the relevant inquiry in assessing the need for regulatory intervention in the choice of voting rules is not whether *all* investors are informed; rather, it is whether *enough* are informed so that the exchanges act as if all investors are informed.[14] Institutional investors, financial intermediaries, and wealthy individuals are responsible for a high (and increasing) percentage of trading on organized exchanges. The actions of these sophisticated market participants—in deciding what securities to purchase and on what terms—lead exchanges to adopt rules that benefit all investors.

5. *Competition among sellers.* If one exchange were to implement voting rules that harmed investors, other exchanges then would have incentives to correct this mistake to attract listings and volume away from the first exchange. This competitive pressure also creates incentives on the part of exchanges to adopt rules that investors want.[15]

Differences Among Exchanges

That exchanges have incentives to offer transactional and ancillary services that investors demand does not imply that all exchanges will be identical. On the contrary, it is common in most markets for different firms to cater to a particular group of consumers. The different strategies followed by firms imply nothing more than specialization within a market. The decision to manufacture luxury cars, for example, is not inherently superior to the decision to manufacture compact cars. Differences among exchanges can be analyzed along the same lines. Although the NASD, NYSE, and AMEX all provide transactional and ancillary services, there are differences among them. One such difference is the NYSE's historic policy of refusing to list the securities of firms with dual class common stock compared with the opposite policy of the NASD. But this is only one of the many differences. The exchanges also have different listing and delisting standards, as well as different requirements for listed firms.[16]

Probably the most important difference among exchanges is in their trading technologies. The NYSE uses a "specialist system" to match buy and sell orders for each security. The specialists are charged with the responsibility of maintaining an "orderly" market, in addition to acting as transactional intermediaries. In practice this role means they attempt to moderate price changes by buying or selling for their own account.

In contrast to the NYSE, the NASDAQ system maintains competitive "market makers." These are firms committed to announcing at all times prices at which they will buy or sell a minimum number of shares of a stock. Decentralized market forces thus ensure that prices will move quickly and accurately to reflect all available information.

The differences among exchanges, however, are becoming increasingly blurred. For example, while the specialist and competitive market maker system appear to be dramatically different, most large trading on both the NYSE and the NASDAQ is done in a nearly identical manner in the "upstairs" market. A broker dealing in a large block of stock will call other dealers and institutions to find one interested in the other end of the deal. The specialist on the floor of the NYSE, the subject of much attention, actually serves as a market maker only for the residual small blocks and odd lots of stock, as well as a backup broker for floor traders.

The governance rules imposed by exchanges also appear to be moving in the same direction. In July of 1985, for example, the NASD (perhaps in response to regulatory pressure) proposed rules requiring listed firms to have an audit committee and a certain number of independent directors. These requirements are similar to those imposed by the NYSE. In other areas, the NYSE has moved in the direction of the NASD. One example of this development is the abolition of fixed commission rates.[17] Another example is the suspension by the NYSE of its prohibition of the listing of securities of firms with dual class common stock.

Notwithstanding these developments, basic differences among the exchanges remain. The differences in trading technologies, listing requirements and governance rules reflect the different strategies of the exchanges. The NYSE has attempted to attract large, mature firms, while the NASD has tailored its NASDAQ system to the needs of smaller, more entrepreneurial firms. The rules and trading technologies of each exchange reflect the set of conditions best suited for the firms listing on the exchange. Since firms issuing stock differ, the best exchange rules for them will differ as well.

THE "RACE TO THE BOTTOM" THESIS

Critics of competition among exchanges argue that efforts by exchanges to attract listings leads them to adopt promanage-ment rules to the detriment of investors. These critics assume that since corporate managers decide whether and where to list, they will base their decision on which exchange offers them the greatest opportunity to exploit investors. If one exchange relaxes its rules, and allows this exploitation to occur, the argument runs, other exchanges will be forced to follow suit to avoid a drain of their listings to the first exchange. The result is a "race to the bottom" in which all exchanges end up with similar (promanagement, antishareholder) rules.[18]

The argument that competition among lawmaking bodies leads to a "race to the bottom" is not a new one. The identical argument was made in the past to support the replacement of state chartering of corporations by federal chartering. It was in this earlier debate that the phrase "race to the bottom" originated.[19] Under a system of state chartering, it was argued, competition among states to attract incorporations causes states to adopt increasingly promanagement, anti-investor rules. The claim was that only federal chartering of corporations or federal legislation setting minimum standards could protect investors from the adverse consequences of "lax" state corporation laws.

In connection with this proposal for federal chartering of corporations, the "race to the bottom" thesis has been vigorously analyzed and discredited on both a theoretical and an empirical level.[20] The analogous argument that competition among exchanges in their choice of voting rules is harmful to investors is equally without merit.

The Assumptions Underlying the "Race to the Bottom" Thesis

The argument that competition leads exchanges to adopt anti-investor rules to attract listings is based on at least three related misconceptions: (1) that managers prefer exchange rules that allow them to exploit investors; (2) that it is in the interests of exchanges to adopt such rules; and (3) that the absence of regulation is necessarily evidence of a promanagement, anti-investor bias. These three misconceptions are discussed below.

Managers' Incentives

Entrepreneurs or corporate managers who attempt to raise equity capital must convince investors that the securities being sold at the price offered are superior to alternative uses of investment dollars. These alternative uses are almost infinite in number. Investors can purchase equity or debt securities of other firms, put their money in a bank, buy government securities, invest in real estate, purchase gold or other precious metals, and so forth. The greater investors perceive the probability that they will be exploited—that the funds invested will be used to benefit the managers at the expense of investors—the more attractive competing investments will become. Alternatively, investors simply may pay less for securities when they perceive that managers' discretion will be too great.

Thus, in an efficient market it is entrepreneurs who want to raise capital, not investors, who bear the costs of inefficient rules that allow investors to be exploited.[21] The greater the inefficiency, the less willing potential investors will be to invest and the lower the price investors will be willing to pay. This result will increase the entrepreneurs' cost of capital but will not harm investors who discount the inefficiency by paying a lower price.

To decrease their cost of capital, entrepreneurs have strong incentives to adopt rules or governance mechanisms that allay investors' concerns. These rules or governance mechanisms can take a variety of forms, as will be demonstrated later. Managers also have strong incentives to decide where to incorporate based on which set of state laws is suitable for the particular needs of their firm. Similarly, they will decide whether and where to list based on which exchange will further the interests of their investors. Entrepreneurs have every incentive to adopt rules, including the decision of which exchange rules to be governed by, in the best interests of investors in order to lower their cost of capital.

The logical fallacy in the "race to the bottom" thesis is that it assumes that managers will seek exchanges that facilitate the exploitation of investors. This strategy will only work if investors as a class are irrational or completely ignorant. Why else would investors, notwithstanding the virtually infinite number of investment alternatives, continue to entrust their money to managers who seek rules that allow investors to be exploited? The assumption that investors as a class are completely ignorant or irrational, however, is implausible in light of the observability of exchange rules and the increasing dominance of institutional investors and financial intermediaries. Once investors as a class are assumed to be rational, the incentive of managers to choose exchanges that maximize, not minimize, investors' welfare in order to lower their cost of capital is compelling. And competition among exchanges, by providing managers with more choices in choosing an exchange with rules suited to the needs of a particular firm, allows the cost of capital to be lowered further.

The Incentives of Exchanges

Even if we assume that the managers of some firms intend to expropriate the wealth of their stockholders, it still does not follow that it is in the interest of the exchange to allow this expropriation to occur. Exchanges do not compete for listings per se, but rather seek to maximize the volume of trade, which is a function of the number of listings and the amount of trading in listed securities. As we saw above, it is not in the best interest of the exchange to allow exploitation of investors.

If an exchange allows managers of some firms to exploit investors, investors will lose confidence in the exchange, as a whole, causing *all* firms on the exchange to face higher costs of capital. This in turn will decrease the amount of listings in the future and thus also will reduce the amount of trade. Loss of confidence in the exchange also will lead to a decline in the value of currently listed securities. A decline in the value of listed securities, like a decline in the amount of trade, will decrease income from commissions. And any action that decreases commission income will decrease the value of membership on the exchange. Thus, any decrease in the amount of trade or value of securities listed on the exchange reduces the wealth of member firms. Once again, it is clear that the profit-maximizing strategy for an exchange is to promulgate rules that maximize, not minimize, investors' welfare.

The Relationship Between Regulation and Investors' Welfare

A final misconception accompanying the "race to the bottom" thesis is that one can identify the "bottom" by determining which jurisdiction or exchange is the least regulatory. But to equate the level of investor protection with the amount of regulation is a serious error. Consumers or investors do not necessarily benefit from regulation.[22]

For example, few today would argue that the NYSE was alone in protecting investors because it had a policy of fixed commission rates while the other exchanges did not.[23] Nor would many argue that the abolition of this regulation—which was justified in large part as a device to protect investors and which was abandoned as a result of competition from other markets—represented an example of the race to the bottom. Similarly, the fact that one exchange has, for example, stricter disclosure requirements may mean that investors of firms on that exchange must bear costs of regulation that exceed its benefits, costs not borne by investors of firms on other exchanges. If competition in this situation forces the first exchange to drop the regulation, investors benefit.[24]

The inaccuracy of equating regulation with the protection of investors is further demonstrated by two related factors that have special relevance to dual class voting.[25] First, particular regulations can have mixed effects. A prohibition of dual class voting may protect investors in some instances yet harm them in others. Whether a prohibition is desirable depends in large part on a weighing of these costs and benefits. For the reasons discussed above, exchanges have strong incentives to weigh these costs and benefits and strike the appropriate balance.

Second, no reason exists to believe that one type of regulation is optimal for all firms. Some types of firms might benefit

from rules allowing dual class common stock while others might not. Just as we observe successful firms incorporated in jurisdictions with strict state laws and equally successful firms incorporated in jurisdictions with liberal state laws, so too may firms listed on exchanges with one set of governance rules be as successful as firms on exchanges with another set of governance rules. Both types of exchanges may be optimal for the firms choosing to list on them.

The Empirical Evidence

Proponents of the "race to the bottom" thesis assume that managers' decisions to list on exchanges that prohibit dual class common stock (or are more regulatory in other ways) will benefit investors. Analogously, proponents of this thesis in the state chartering debate assume that incorporation in Delaware, the jurisdiction that for decades afforded managers the greatest discretion, will harm investors.

These are testable propositions. If the hypothesis that the rules of enabling jurisdictions such as Delaware are promanagement and anti-investor is correct, then firms that reincorporate in Delaware should experience lower stock prices. The evidence, however, is to the contrary.[26] Similarly, if the NYSE protects investors while other exchanges do not, the decision by firms to switch their listing to the NYSE should be perceived as good news by investors.

Numerous studies have attempted to measure the gains, if any, from listing on the NYSE rather than being traded over the counter or listed on other exchanges.[27] After adjusting for movements in the overall market, these studies generally find that firms newly listed on the NYSE tend to have abnormally favorable performance in the months prior to the announcement to list, normal performance at the time of announcement, abnormally positive performance between the announcement and the eventual listing, and abnormally negative performance after listing.

Overall, this combination of normal, positive, and negative performance for different periods surrounding the listing decision suggests that the evidence does not point unambiguously to any conclusion on the effect of listing on the NYSE on investors' wealth. The absence of a statistically significant positive reaction to the announcement to list on the NYSE,[28] the most direct test of how investors perceive the change in listing, only reinforces this conclusion.

The inconclusive nature of the empirical results has significant implications for the "race to the bottom" thesis. Proponents of the thesis assume that the NYSE is a haven for rules that protect stockholders, and that the other exchanges are the "bottom" because they do not have these protective rules. If this were true, we would expect that rational investors would be willing to pay sigificantly more for a stock that listed on the NYSE. This proposition is not supported by the existing evidence.

Two caveats are in order. First, the evidence must be interpreted with considerable caution because it is impossible to disentangle investors' perceptions of the differences in trading technologies from their perceptions regarding governance rules. Second, the immense success of the NYSE over long periods of time suggests that there must be benefits to listing there for many firms—notwithstanding the inconclusive findings of studies to date. Of course, the identical point can be made in connection with the NASDAQ system, which also has enjoyed spectacular success. Both exchanges appear to be providing transactional and ancillary services that are well suited to the needs of their respective firms.

DUAL CLASS COMMON STOCK AND THE ECONOMICS OF SHAREHOLDER VOTING

In designing a firm's capital structure, managers must choose voting rules. This section discusses the economics of shareholder voting and the criteria that determine whether a rule of one share, one vote or dual class voting is optimal for a particular firm. It also summarizes the empirical evidence regarding the costs and benefits of dual class voting.

Voting as a Monitoring Mechanism

Publicly held corporations are characterized by a separation of the functions of management and risk bearing. This separation enables skilled managers to run businesses—even though they lack the personal wealth to finance all of the firm's investment projects; it also enables those who have wealth to invest it—even though they lack managerial skills. This specialization of function also enables investors to diversify their portfolios, thus reducing risk and making investment more attractive.

While the separation of management and risk bearing allows investors to capture the benefits of specialization of function, it also exposes them to the risk that their funds will be used for managers' personal benefit. Market forces such as competition in product and labor markets limit the ability of managers to engage in behavior that does not maximize the wealth of the firm[29]—although they do not eliminate it entirely. In anticipation of the prospect of such behavior, investors will discount the price they are willing to pay for shares. To minimize the size of this discount, those who raise capital have incentives to establish institutional arrangements whereby the performance of managers is continually monitored.

Voting rules are one type of monitoring mechanism.[30] The right to vote provides shareholders with the opportunity to decide whether their agents have performed well enough to continue in office. Typically, voting rules also force managers to obtain the approval of investors for certain fundamental decisions such as mergers or amendments to the corporate charter. Thus, the right to vote acts as a constraint on the ability of managers to take actions that harm investors.

But voting is a very imperfect monitoring mechanism. Many shareholders are passive investors who hold many different investments. They have little interest in managing the firm and insufficient incentive to learn the details of management. Moreover, any attempt by shareholders to monitor managers is likely to fail because of the serious problems of collective action and free riders. No shareholder can capture the full gains from monitoring a firm's managers. The benefits from such monitoring efforts will accrue to investors according to the size of their holdings, not according to their monitoring efforts. Because other shareholders can take a free ride on the monitoring efforts of any one shareholder, no individual shareholder has much of an incentive to expend resources in monitoring managers. As a result, shareholders routinely vote for incumbent managers and approve management-sponsored initiatives in all but the rarest of cases.

The one important exception where voting does matter is in contests for corporate control—mergers, proxy fights, or tender offers. Contestants in the market for corporte control typically accumulate large blocks of stock; this in turn reduces the free rider problem. Holders of large blocks of shares have a sufficient interest in the firm to participate actively in management decisions and to terminate managers who are behaving inefficiently. The ability to vote, and thereby control who will manage the firm's assets, is fundamental to the incentive to acquire large blocks of shares in battles for corporate control.

Many other forms of monitoring arrangements exist.[31] Examples are the sale of securities through investment bankers, the retention of third-party accountants to verify financial statements, and the use of independent directors. Still another method of monitoring is to tie managerial compensation to firm performance. This arrangement can be accomplished if managers own a large percentage of the outstanding stock or if changes in compensation are linked to the success of the firm.

Rules, whether a product of state law, federal law, or exchange rules, also can minimize divergences of interest between managers and investors. Such rules are beneficial when they economize on the cost of contracting. The economic justification for the rule against fraud, for example, is that it saves the parties the costs of negotiating and drafting contractual provisions to prohibit the practice.

Significantly, all of these monitoring mechanisms impose costs as well as create benefits. Independent directors, for example, are likely to be more impartial but also less competent. In some cases, the costs of less informed and more bureaucratic decision making may exceed the benefits of greater impartiality. Similarly, strict legal or exchange rules may limit self-dealing but in the process stifle a large number of beneficial transactions. Because monitoring mechanisms are costly, no presumption should exist that they are always beneficial or that they will be used by all firms in identical proportions.

Thus, some firms may rely heavily on independent directors; others, on closely linking managerial compensation to the performance of the firm's outstanding securities; and still others, on locating in a jurisdiction with more stringent regulation. Each of these decisions may be optimal for different firms. Similarly, the importance of the market for corporate control as a monitoring mechanism may vary for different firms. The choice between a rule of one share, one vote and dual class common stock depends in large part on the importance of the market for corporate control as a monitoring device for a particular firm.

The Rule of One Share, One Vote

The vast majority of publicly held corporations have limited the right to vote to shareholders (except in situations of financial distress) and have attached one vote to every share. This is true for firms regardless of where they are listed, even though firms listed on the AMEX or the NASDAQ system could have chosen an alternative rule.

Shareholders (rather than, say, employees or creditors) typically have the right to vote becaue they are the group with the best incentives (collective action problems to one side) to maximize the value of the firm. As residual claimants to the firm's income, shareholders receive most of the marginal gains and incur most of the marginal costs from decisions made about how the firm's assets should be deployed. Thus they will be most directly affected by managerial decisions that change the value of the firm. Those with fixed claims such as debtholders, by contrast, are only con-

cerned about the probability of bankruptcy. As a result, debtholders' incentives to maximize the value of the firm
generally will be inferior to those of shareholders.

While shareholders as a class typically
have the best incentives to maximize firm
value, not all shareholders are identical.
Those with a large stake in the venture
have much better incentives than those
with a tiny stake because they reap more of
the gains and bear more of the costs from
abnormally good or bad performance. The
rule of one share, one vote reflects this economic reality by assigning votes, and thus
the ability to monitor the managers, in direct proportion to shareholders' stake in
the venture.

In most cases, the collective action problem faced by dispersed shareholders renders voting relatively ineffective as a
monitoring mechanism. Nevertheless,
managers realize that they are being monitored by those who have the best incentives (that is, the largest stakes), and also
realize that the collective action problem
can be overcome at any time by the accumulation of shares and exercise of the attached votes. Managers' knowledge that
they can be ousted by the exercise of these
votes provides them an incentive to maximize the value of the firm.

Dual Class Common Stock and Economic Incentives

The one share, one vote rule enhances voting as a monitoring mechanism because it
facilitates transfers of control. Dual class
common stock, by contrast, makes hostile
takeovers—one type of transfer of control—more difficult becaue it allows insiders to hold 51% of the votes without holding 51% of the equity. For a given equity
base, then, insiders must commit a smaller
fraction of their own wealth to retain a
controlling interest in the firm.

For this reason, the question why firms
adopt dual class common breaks down
into two questions. First, is it efficient for
insiders in some cases to retain control?
Second, is it ever efficient for insiders to retain control by holding 51% of a superior
voting stock rather than holding 51% of the

entire equity base? These questions are discussed next.

The Value of Control to Insiders

Managers of a particular firm may desire to
retain control for several reasons that are
entirely consistent with the goal of maximizing the shareholders' wealth. First, insiders may simply value control more than
outsiders. This explains why family-run
firms or firms still controlled by the founding entrepreneur often issue dual class
common stock or are reluctant to issue
new equity when doing so would dilute
their own holdings.[32] It is even possible
that the market value of the shares of such
firms would be higher if the family or
founding entrepreneur would relinquish
control. In this event, the family or entrepreneur is paying for its preference for control in the form of a higher cost of capital.
Of course, the opposite can also be true.
The market value of shares in a firm controlled by a family or founding entrepreneur may be higher if, for example, continuity of management is valued by
investors and there exist alternative governance mechanisms to align the interests
of managers and investors.

Second, insider control may increase
managers' incentives to invest in firm-specific human capital.[33] Managers frequently
must invest their own time and resources
to gain knowledge concerning a particular
firm's investment opportunities, personnel, specific practices, and organization.
Once acquired, these skills are specific to
the particular firm. Firm-specific skills, in
turn, make managers who acquire them
more valuable to their particular firm than
to firms generally. Managers' incentive to
acquire these firm-specific skills results
from the expectation that they will continue to be employed by their firm for a
long period and thus obtain a return on
their investment.

Stockholders also benefit from the acquisition of firm-specific skills, since managers who possess them make the firm
more valuable. However, managers always
run the risk that they will be terminated by
shareholders or, more realistically, by a
purchaser of control who might change the

use of the firm's assets. The greater the managers' perceived probability that they may be denied a return on their firm-specific investments, the less willing they will be to make them in the first place. Shareholders and managers will both be worse off in this event because there will be fewer returns on firm-specific investments to share.

One method of assuring managers that their firm-specific investments will not be appropriated is to allow insiders to retain control. This is not the only method. Consider, for example, golden parachutes. The difference between insider control and golden parachutes is that insider control protects managers from transfers of control while golden parachutes compensate them in the event a transfer occurs. Both techniques have costs and benefits as methods of protecting firm-specific investments.

Golden parachutes may be difficult (costly) to negotiate and their enforceability is suspect. They also create a moral hazard. If managers believe they will be compensated when a transfer of control occurs, they may take actions such as running the firm inefficiently to increase the probability of such an event. Insider control, by contrast, denies shareholders the ability to receive control premiums and also denies them the ability to share in the gains created by the transfer of assets to more highly valued uses. Notwithstanding these costs of golden parachutes and insider control, one or both techniques may be beneficial in particular cases to protect firm-specific investments.

The third possible benefit of insider control is that it decreases the need for managers to expend resources to convince potential bidders for control that the current use of the firm's assets is optimal.[34] In situations of asymmetric information—where managers have information that outside investors do not—managers may have to employ costly signaling devices to communicate their private information. Examples of such signaling devices include high debt-equity ratios, dividend changes, and share repurchases.[35] The need to convince outsiders not to attempt a transfer of

control also may affect investment decisions. Managers may choose more "visible" projects rather than more valuable projects whose value is too difficult to communicate. If insiders control the firm, these costs need not be incurred.

Fourth, insider control may allow shareholders of a target corporation to obtain a higher price when a transfer of control does occur. One difficulty that dispersed shareholders face when confronted with a hostile tender offer is that they are unable to act collectively. This inability to coordinate makes it impossible for shareholders to negotiate with the bidder to obtain a better price. Insider control is a device that overcomes this collective action problem among the shareholders. Its effect is to force potential acquirers to deal directly with management, who in turn can negotiate on behalf of all shareholders. Granting insiders what amounts to a veto power over transfers of control is likely to decrease the number of control transactions but increase the price paid per transaction. Such action is likely to reduce the wealth of potential bidders—and perhaps even, shareholders as a class—but may be rational behavior for shareholders of a particular firm.[36]

Dual Class Voting as a Mechanism for Preserving Insider Control

If every share is entitled to one vote, insiders can retain control of a firm by holding 51% of the outstanding equity. Why would insiders eschew this alternative in favor of dual class common stock? One reason is that insiders may simply lack the personal wealth to maintain 51% ownership when the value of the outstanding equity becomes sufficiently large. Indeed, the magnitude of most publicly held corporations greatly exceeds the magnitude of most personal fortunes. Outside equity enables the firm to pursue investment opportunities that have expected returns higher than alternative uses of capital regardless of the size of insiders' wealth.

Even an owner/manager who has sufficient personal wealth to purchase 51% of the outstanding equity may prefer not to do so. Outside investors with access to capital markets can diversify risk more efficiently than insiders who already have a large percentage of their wealth tied up in their firm in the form of their human capital. Diversified investors in effect charge a lower price to bear risk than would a less diversified owner/manager.[37] Allowing these more efficient, outside risk bearers to share the risk lowers the cost of risk to the firm.

This risk sharing arrangement between owner/managers and outside investors benefits managers and stockholders, and also society as a whole. Society benefits because profitable investment opportunities are pursued even if they are risky or will not generate cash flows until sometime in the future. Owner/managers who finance projects with their personal wealth, by contrast, will tend to choose less risky projects—even if they have a lower present value—because of their inability to diversify. Similarly, owner/managers will tend to choose projects that produce returns during their tenure with the firm—even if these projects have a lower present value than projects with more extended payoffs. The tendency of firms financed with equity[38] to choose investment projects under the market value rule—to choose those projects with the highest net present value—increases the production of goods and services in the economy as a whole.

Dual class common stock allows insiders to obtain the benefits of outside equity financing while still retaining control over the firm. This is not to suggest that all firms should employ dual class common stock. The cost of dual class common stock is that the effectiveness of the market for corporate control as a monitoring device is reduced. Whether this substantial cost is outweighed by the benefits of dual class voting is an empirical question that is discussed below.

Other Uses of Dual Class Common Stock

Dual class common stock is employed for reasons other than making transfers of control more difficult. General Motors' new classes of E and H stock are examples of dual class common stock with a completely different purpose. The dividends and other distributions to the holders of these stocks are tied to the performance of acquired divisions and so the price of these stocks reflects the prospects of these divisions rather than the whole of the firm. In addition, holders of these shares have inferior voting rights to those of stockholders in General Motors. Because the value of these stocks is tied to particular divisions of General Motors rather than General Motors as a whole, their holders have less incentive to monitor the management of General Motors. Inferior voting rights reflects this decreased incentive to monitor management relative to other shareholders of General Motors.

Dual Class Common Stock and Corporate Democracy

Some may argue that unequal voting rights is undesirable because it is inconsistent with the principle of "corporate democracy." This argument, however, is fundamentally flawed. All firms, including corporations, consist of contractual relationships freely entered into by economic actors to maximize their joint welfare. Who has the right to vote and how and when the vote can be exercised are rights that are typically allocated by contract. In contrast to voting rules for democratic governments—which are usually designed to serve broader goals than wealth maximization—the optimal voting rules for any particular firm are those that maximize its value.

Two important implications follow from this insight. First, no reason exists to believe that the optimal voting rules for publicly held corporations engaged in the production of goods and services will be identical to the voting rules for representative governments. Indeed, there is little similarity between the voting rules for the two institutions. For example, most corporate actors—employees, bondholders; suppliers, preferred stockholders, and managers—have no votes even though they are all investors in the firm. For common stockholders, the group that does vote, the most common structure is one share, one vote—not one person, one vote as in the political context. Thus votes in the corporate, but not political, context are typically assigned by reference to the extent of property ownership. Just as there is no reason to believe that votes in the political arena should be assigned according to wealth, so there is no reason to believe that principles from political democracy should serve as a model for corporate governance.

The second implication that follows from the economics of voting rules is that the rules for all firms need not be identical. The optimal voting rule depends on which rules will maximize the value of the firm; different rules may be optimal for different types of firms. Participants in general partnerships, for example, typically have equal votes while most participants in limited partnerships have no votes. Similarly, the voting rights of investors in dual class firms differ from those of investors in firms with only one class of common stock. These observed differences in voting rights may reflect differences in optimal voting rules for different firms.

Moreover, differences in nominal voting rights understate differences across firms in effective voting rights.[39] Effective voting rights depend on the concentration of the ownership of votes. For example, the holder of 10% of the outstanding shares of a publicly held corporation that has the rule of one share, one vote may have very powerful voting rights if shares are widely dispersed, but virtually no power if there is another shareholder who owns 51% of the outstanding shares.

Contractual arrangements also may affect voting rights. Cumulative voting, voting trusts, and standstill agreements are all examples of arrangements that, like dual class common stock, have the effect of altering effective voting rights. Holding companies can have a similar effect. For example, consider an investor who owns 50.1% of the votes of a holding company, which in turns owns 50.1% of the votes of another firm. Under a rule of one share, one vote, such an investor has effective control over the subsidiary firm with only about a 25% interest in its cash flows.

In sum, for different types of firms to have different voting rules is not unusual.

Nor is it unusual for effective voting rights to differ across firms all of which nominally have a rule of one share, one vote. All of these arrangements—as well as the rule of one share, one vote itself—are inconsistent with the political model of one person, one vote. Dual class common stock is simply another form of voting arrangement that affects effective voting rights. The misguided analogy to political democracy provides no basis for prohibiting dual class common stock, or any other voting rule, that has the effect of maximizing the value of certain firms.

Dual Class Common Stock: The Evidence

Characteristics of Firms with Dual Class Common Stock.

A small percentage of publicly traded firms employ dual class common stock and that percentage has fluctuated over time but has not grown appreciably larger.[40] The small number of firms that have dual class common stock is significant. The NASD, AMEX, and the laws of most states permit the listing of dual class common stock. Thus the fact that most firms utilize the rule of one share, one vote strongly suggests that dual class common stock is not optimal for the vast majority of publicly held firms. At the same time, the fact that the rule of one share, one vote is desirable for most firms does not mean it is desirable for all firms.

A number of researchers have studied the types of firms that have adopted dual class common stock.[41] These studies reveal that firms that adopt dual class common tend to have certain common and related characteristics. First, managers of dual class firms (defined as corporate officers and their families) tend to own approximately 55% of the voting rights.[42] Indeed, one motivation for recapitalizations appears to be the desire to obtain voting control. Thus management ownership of voting rights is significantly greater after recapitalizations than before.[43] Second, managers of dual class firms own a greater percentage of votes than rights to cash flows. Nevertheless, managers tend to have a significant equity stake in the firm; the median cash flow interest is 24%.[44] Third, dual class firms tend to exhibit highly concentrated ownership of voting rights. For the typical dual class firm, approximately 96% of all stockholders own shares of the inferior voting class.[45]

Fourth, dual class firms are characterized by a significant amount of family control. In many dual class firms, two or more related individuals (by blood or marriage) currently hold top management positions and family members have sometimes held such positions for several generations.[46] Fifth, most dual class firms are conservatively leveraged. The average ratio of long-term debt to total assets for dual class firms is approximately 0.1.[47] Sixth, dual class firms frequently issue new equity within a short time after recapitalizations.[48] Thus managers' desire to issue new equity without diluting their proportionate ownership of voting rights also appears to be a motivation for recapitalizations.

These characteristics of dual class firms are consistent with the theory of insider control discussed previously. Dual class common stock enables managers to control a majority of votes without owning 51% of the outstanding shares. The large family involvement in many dual class firms suggests one reason why insiders value control. Protecting firm-specific investments of human capital and economizing on the costs of communicating information to investors to avoid takeovers may, as discussed previously, be other reasons. The highly concentrated ownership of votes in dual class firms further suggests that such arrangements may overcome collective action problems faced by dispersed shareholders.

The frequency with which newly recapitalized dual class firms issue new equity is also consistent with the analysis of the costs and benefits of control. Constraints based on wealth as well as lack of diversification may make managers reluctant to pursue investment projects if obtaining the necessary financing would dilute their voting rights. Thus, dual class common stock enables insiders who in many cases already have control to finance new projects without fear of loss of control.[49]

Finally, the theory of insider control predicts that the reduced effectiveness of the market for corporate control as a monitoring device would lead dual class firms to rely more heavily on alternative monitoring mechanisms. The evidence seems to support this view. In particular, the family ownership of many dual class firms may act as a substitute for the market for corporate control. The obligation that family members feel to each other may act as a constraint on self-interested behavior that reduces the value of the firm. Similarly, the significant equity interest of managers in dual class firms, even though less in percentage terms than their ownership of votes, tends to align the interests of managers and investors.

Pricing of Dual Class Common Stock

Researchers have studied the relative prices of multiple classes of equity securities with unequal voting rights.[50] The typical procedure is to consider firms for which (1) both classes of stock are publicly traded in the same markets and (2) the two classes differ only with respect to voting rights—that is, each class has identical rights to any cash distributions. The purpose of this procedure is to isolate the value of the vote to the investors.

Lease et al. studied the share prices of thirty companies that had two classes of publicly traded common stock outstanding during the period from 1940 to 1978—classes that had unequal voting rights but were otherwise identical. Twenty-six of these firms had two classes of common stock and no other voting securities. Four of the firms had voting preferred stock in addition to the two classes of common stock.

Month-end prices for the two classes of common stock from the same day of trading were used to calculate the value of voting rights. Specifically, they calculated for each firm the ratio of the superior voting stock's month-end price to the inferior voting stock's price at the end of the same month. They then took the average of these ratios. If investors valued superior and inferior voting shares equally, this average ratio should be one. If the superior voting shares were more highly valued, the average ratio should exceed one and if the superior voting shares were valued less, the average ratio should be less than one.

For the twenty-six firms that had two classes of common stock and no other class of voting securities, Lease et al. found that the average observed ratio of month-end prices was greater than one. The average price premium placed on the shares with superior voting rights relative to the class with inferior voting rights was 5.4%. For the 4 firms with voting preferred in addition to two classes of common stock, however, they found that the average observed ratio of month-end prices was less than one. The average discount of the superior voting class of common stock was 1.25%. Both results are statistically significant.[51]

The existence of these premiums and discounts may seem surprising. The price of a security, like any other asset, should reflect the present value of future cash flows. Since the sample was constructed to include only those securities with guaranteed *identical* rights to future cash flows, finance theory predicts that the prices of the different classes of common stock should be identical—regardless of voting rights.

A possible explanation for the premiums and discounts is that the holders of one class of securities rationally anticipate different net cash flows regardless of the charter provision guaranteeing identical payoffs. Lease et al. examined various possibilities. They found that the corporate charters of the firms studied expressly forbid cash buy backs at premium prices and sales of new securities at discounts that would benefit one class and not the other. Nevertheless, the receipt of different benefits is still possible. For example, those with voting control may anticipate a premium price for their shares in the event of a takeover bid. Alternatively, those with control may be able to benefit by directing the firm's resources to their own gain. A firm, for example, may purchase inputs from (or sell outputs to) another firm owned by the controlling stockholders at above (or below) market prices.

Some direct evidence on these points is provided by DeAngelo and DeAngelo.[52]

They examined corporate takeover payments to both classes of stock for firms that had dual classes outstanding when acquired. Differential compensation was paid in one-third of the cases they studied.[53] These instances of differential payoffs in the event of an acquisition may help explain why investors are willing to pay a premium for the superior voting class. The possibility of a higher payoff when acquisitions occur also may explain why shareholders who exchange voting shares for limited voting shares frequently receive rights to a slightly higher dividend. The higher dividend is compensation for the lower expected payoff in the event of an acquisition.[54]

The Effect of Dual Class Common Stock on Investors' Wealth

Firms may issue limited or nonvoting stock in two circumstances. They might offer such securities when they go public. Alternatively, firms that are already publicly owned may recapitalize by offering such securities to existing shareholders or the general public.

As a theoretical matter, initial public offerings of limited or non-voting stock can never harm investors. The price of a security when a firm goes public reflects the value of that security to investors. Investors only purchase a security when they estimate that the value of whatever rights and cash flows it carries equals or exceeds its price. If investors value voting rights and a firm fails to provide them, then the firm's securities simply sell at a lower price. The organizers of the firm may be worse off, but investors are not.

Recapitalizations pose a different issue. Such recapitalizations may increase investors' wealth if, for example, they protect firm-specific investments of human capital or they signal that the firm has valuable investment opportunities that will be financed by new equity issues. This possibility can be described as the *shareholder interests* explanation of recapitalizations. Alternatively, recapitalizations may reduce investors' wealth by insulating incumbent management from the discipline of the market for corporate control. This possibility can be described as the *management entrenchment* explanation of recapitalizations.

To distinguish between these two explanations for dual class common stock, Megan Partch studied 44 recapitalizations that occurred from 1962 to 1984 in which a publicly traded firm issued a new class of limited voting stock.[55] She found that the average stock price reaction to the announcement of plans to create dual class common stock was positive, and that investors experienced larger positive wealth effects when insiders already owned a large percentage of votes prior to the recapitalization. Thus, the market responds more positively to proposals to issue limited voting stock when the motivation of the recapitalization is to maintain, rather than gain, control.[56] Thus shareholders seem to be voting rationally when they approve recapitalizations creating dual class common stock.

In another study, Gregg Jarrell has found that NYSE listed firms experienced abnormal losses following the announcement of proposals to create dual class common stock.[57] The reason for such losses may be the risk of delisting if dual class common stock is adopted. This observation might explain the negative returns except that it is a puzzle why firms risk delisting (and shareholders approve) if doing so is wealth-reducing. One possibility is the very fact that firms would risk delisting signals the market that the firm has particularly bad prospects. Another possibility is that the market for corporate control is more important as a monitoring device for NYSE firms because they tend to be larger and have lower insider holdings. The proposed recapitalization, under this view, is perceived by investors as a form of managerial entrenchment. Even if this view were correct, however, it would not explain why shareholders approve recapitalizations for NYSE firms.

With the exception of NYSE firms, the evidence suggests that recapitalizations creating dual classes of common stock are consistent with shareholders' interests. This result, however, should be interpreted with some caution because Partch's findings are preliminary and have not yet been replicated by other investigators. In addition, the potential exists for particular recapitalizations to harm stockholders. Nevertheless, the evidence does demonstrate that for an important class of firms, recapitalizations have been beneficial. Based on the current evidence, therefore, no basis exists for the conclusion that investors as a class would benefit from a blanket prohibition of the use of dual classes of common stock.

DUAL CLASS COMMON STOCK AND DEFENSIVE TACTICS IN RESPONSE TO TAKEOVERS

Considerable evidence now exists that shareholders of target companies experience significant increases in wealth as a result of hostile takeovers. On average, a target's shareholders experience an increase in the value of their shares of approximately 30% as a result of a successful takeover attempt.[58] These gains are, on average, lost in their entirety if the target's managers are able to defeat the offer by engaging in defensive tactics and the target is not acquired by another bidder.[59] Moreover, several studies indicate that shareholders of target corporations typically experience a statistically significant decrease in the value of their shares when management engages in defensive tactics.[60]

Overall, the evidence indicates that shareholders of targets benefit from takeovers and are harmed by defensive tactics that make takeovers more difficult. Shareholders of bidding firms and shareholders as a class also are likely losers if defensive tactics cause fewer acquisitions to occur and make those that do occur more expensive. As a result, several commentators have argued that shareholders' wealth would be maximized if managers did not engage in defensive tactics to resist hostile takeovers.[61]

Concern has been expressed that dual class common stock may be another form of defensive tactic that operates to the detriment of investors. Without question, there is some basis for this concern, particularly with respect to the NYSE listed firms that have risked delisting. Nevertheless, to equate dual class common stock with defensive tactics taken in response to perceived takeover threats is misleading for several reasons. First, the claim is not factually accurate. Many firms have had dual classes of common stock for several generations—some from their inception as publicly held firms. DeAngelo and DeAngelo found that the median firm in their sample had a dual class voting structure for about twenty years.[62] Similarly, Partch found that no firms in her sample were the subject of a takeover attempt in the two years prior to the recapitalization.[63] Furthermore, many recapitalizations are better understood as attempts to maintain control of a firm in light of anticipated additional equity financing rather than attempts to prevent outsiders from taking over the firm. Transfers of control in such cases are not at issue; the issue is whether the firm, given that there will not be a transfer of control, will be able to finance new projects with equity. Moreover, as the example of General Motors demonstrates, shares with limited voting rights are sometimes issued for reasons having nothing to do with the prevention of transfers of control.

Second, not all transactions that make hostile takeovers more difficult are necessarily harmful to investors. No one could credibly argue, for example, that the failure to take a firm public is necessarily harmful to investors. Similarly, the evidence suggests that going private is beneficial to investors.[64] The relevant issue is the importance of the market for corporate control as a monitoring mechanism in comparison with other monitoring mechanisms for any particular firm.

A third reason why dual class common stock should not necessarily be equated with defensive tactics to fend off takeovers is that many dual class firms are eventually acquired.[65] The dual class structure may allow management to negotiate more effectively on behalf of investors.[66]

Finally, dual class common stock varies from other defensive tactics adopted in response to takeover threats both in terms of the procedural safeguards involved and in their effect on investors' wealth. Most defensive tactics in response to takeovers tend to be changes that managers can implement quickly and without the approval of shareholders. These types of defensive tactics tend to have a negative effect on shareholders' wealth. Recapitalizations creating dual classes of common stock, by contrast, typically must be approved by shareholders. And, most importantly (with the exception of NYSE listed firms) there is no evidence that the implementation of dual classes of common stock reduces investors' wealth.[67]

A NOTE ON THE NYSE AND THE ONE SHARE, ONE VOTE RULE

The NYSE is now attempting to change its historic policy against listing dual class common stock. The stated reason for this possible change is competitive pressure from the other exchanges. The previous discussion suggests that the competitive effects of a change in rules by the NYSE are more complex than might first appear. To be sure, a change in rules might allow the NYSE to keep listings of firms that want to adopt dual class common stock. The preliminary evidence indicates, however, that recapitalizations for NYSE firms adopting dual class common stock have caused large negative wealth effects. Assuming that these effects are not caused by the threat of delisting, if NYSE rules are changed to permit these large negative wealth effects to occur, listing on the NYSE will be less valuable to investors. All else being equal, the NYSE will lose listings as a result or be forced to charge less for the transactional and ancillary services it provides. Thus, the NYSE appears to face a clear trade-off in deciding whether to change its rule.

Put differently, the NYSE's historic rule can be seen as a means whereby management could make a commitment to stockholders of certain types of firms that takeovers would not be resisted by creating dual classes of common stock. Tough delisting standards made this commitment all the more credible. Under this interpretation, the change in the NYSE rule will allow managers of certain firms to break this commitment. Thus, the proposed change may have certain short-term gains for the NYSE but may also impose long-term losses because a bonding mechanism aligning the interests of managers and investors will no longer be available.

There is, however, another equally plausible interpretation of the effect of the NYSE's proposed change in voting rules. Under this alternative interpretation, the change will increase the flexibility of firms listed on the NYSE. In theory, this increase in flexibility may be beneficial for at least certain firms. The proposed rule change, in other words, might allow NYSE listed firms to obtain the benefits of dual class common stock to the same extent as non-NYSE listed firms.

The existing empirical evidence does not generate unambiguous predictions of what the consequences will be if the NYSE changes its rule. While recapitalizations of firms listed on the NYSE appear to have caused large negative wealth effects, the evidence is meager. And, as discussed above, the negative wealth effects may have been caused by the threat of delisting rather than any problem inherent in dual class stock. The evidence to date is not sufficient to generate a meaningful prediction of what the wealth effects will be of recapitalizations for NYSE firms if these firms do not risk delisting.

Similarly, it is not obvious that a change in the NYSE rule will prevent managers from making credible commitments to shareholders of certain firms not to resist takeovers by creating dual classes of common stock. The same commitment can be made by contract, perhaps in the corporate charter with special provisions defining the rules for amendment. In short, it is simply not possible at this stage to predict what the ultimate effect will be of a change in the NYSE's prohibition on the listing of dual class common stock.

CONCLUSION

Dual class common stock appears to be beneficial for investors of a small minority of firms. Accordingly, the willingness of certain organized exchanges to list the dual classes of common stock of these firms similarly has been beneficial. It does not follow, however, that all exchanges should have the same governance rules. It is impossible to predict whether the proposed change of the NYSE's historic prohibition on the listing of dual class common stock will, if implemented, harm or benefit investors.

NOTES

1. There is an enormous literature, both theoretical and empirical, concerning the relationship between capital structure and firm value. The seminal paper is Franco Modigliani and Merton H. Miller, "The Cost of Capital, Corporation Finance, and the Theory of Investment," 48 *Am. Econ. Rev.* 261 (1958). See also David Cass and Joseph E. Stiglitz, "The Structure of Investor Preferences and Asset Returns, and Separability in Portfolio Allocation: A Contribution to the Pure Theory of Mutual Funds," 2 *J. Econ Theory* 122 (1970; Fischer Black and Myron Scholes, "The Effects of Dividend Yield and Dividend Policy on Common Stock Prices and Returns," 1 *J. Fin. Econ.* 1 (1974); Joseph E. Stiglitz, "On the Irrelevance of Corporate Financial Policy," 64 *Am. Econ. Rev.* 851 (1974); Eugene F. Fama, "The Effects of a Firm's Investment and Financing Decisions on the Welfare of its Security Holders," 68 *Am. Econ. Rev.* 272 (1978).

2. See, e.g., 8 Del Code §§ 151(a), 221 (firms permitted to give shares any number of votes and to give votes to bondholders in addition to, or instead of, shareholders); 8 Del. Code § 214 (cumulative voting optional).

3. See generally Annot., Validity of Variations from One Share-One Vote Rule Under Modern Corporate Law, 3 ALR 4th at 1204 (1981).

4. See American Stock Exchange Company Guide § 122.

5. See NYSE Listed Company Manual § 313.

6. See NYSE Dual Class Capitalization: Initial Report of the Subcommittee on Shareholder Participation and Qualitative Listing Standards (Jan. 3, 1985).

7. See Big Board Agrees to Let Companies List More Than One Class of Common Stock, *Wall St. J.* 2, col. 3 (July 7, 1986).

8. See NYSE News Release (July 3, 1986); Impact of Corporate Takeovers, Testimony of the NYSE to the Securities Subcommittee of the Senate Committee on Banking, Housing, and Urban Affairs, 99th Cong., 1st Sess., p. 1110–1234 (June 12, 1985); Testimony of the NYSE to the Subcommittee on Telecommunications, Consumer Protection and Finance of the House Committee on Energy and Commerce (May 22, 1985).

9. There is little fundamental difference between the economic role of a stock exchange and that of any ordinary shopping center or flea market. All facilitate trading by bringing together buyers and sellers in a known location and thereby reducing search costs.

10. The analogy between exchanges and other types of selling is developed in Daniel R. Fischel and Sanford J. Grossman, "Customer Protection in Futures and Securities Markets," 4 *J. Futures Mark.* 273 (1984).

11. This conclusion does not depend on whether the market for exchanges is competitive. Monopolists, like firms operating in competitive markets, have incentives to offer the level of quality that consumers demand. See Fischell and Grossman, note 10, p. 283.

12. There is now a large literature on what conditions will facilitate informed judgments by consumers or investors as to product quality. See, e.g., Daniel R. Fischel, "Regulatory Conflict and Entry Regulation of New Futures Contracts," 59 *J. Bus* 85 (1986); Frank H. Easterbrook and Daniel R. Fischel, "Mandatory Disclosure and the Protection of Investors," 70 *Va. L. Rev.* 669 (1984); Alan Schwartz and Louis L. Wilde, "Intervening in Markets on the Basis of Imperfect Information: A Legal and Economic Analysis," 127 *Univ. Pa. L. Rev.* 630 (1979); Phillip Nelson, "Advertising as Information," 82 *J. Pol. Econ.* 729 (1974); Michael R. Darby and Edi Karni, "Free Competition and the Optimal Amount of Fraud," 16 *J. L. Econ.* 67 (1973); Richard A. Posner, "Regulation of Advertising by the FTC" (1973).

13. It makes no difference whether all investors are aware of the voting rules of an exchange. As long as a sufficient number of investors are aware of the rule, its effects will be reflected in prices and the exchange will behave as if everyone were informed. See note 14 and accompanying text.

14. For a more general discussion of this point, see Daniel R. Fischel, "Use of Modern Finance Theory in Securities Fraud Cases Involving Actively Traded Securities," 38 *Bus L.* 1 (1982).

15. With improved technology, the exchanges are now much more competitive than they previously were. See Gary C. Sanger and John J. McConnell, "Stock Exchange Listings, Firm Value and Security Market Efficiency: The Impact of NASDAQ," 21 *Fin. Quant. Anal.* 1 (1986); John J. McConnell and Gary C. Sanger, "A Trading Strategy for New Listings on the NSYE," Jan.–Feb. 1984 *Fin. Anal. J.* 34. However, as discussed above at note 11, even a monopolist has strong incentives to offer a level of quality that consumers demand.

16. For example, the NYSE generally requires that listing companies have an annual income of at least $2.5 million and an aggregate market value of stock that is greater than $18 million, with at least 1.1 million public shares held by at least 2000 investors with 100 or more shares. In contrast, NASDAQ requires only that a firm have $2 million in assets, with 100,000 shares held by at least 300 shareholders. See NYSE Fact Book, 35 (1986); NASD, NASDAQ Fact Book, 16 (1984). On delisting requirements, see generally Securities and Exchange Commission, Comparison of Fundamental Qualitative Listing Standards Imposed by the New York Stock Exchange, American Stock Exchange, and National Association of Securities Dealers (mimeo).

17. For a discussion of the deregulation of brokerage commissions, see Gregg A. Jarrell, "Change at the Exchange: The Causes and Effects of Deregulation," 27 *J. L. Econ.* 273 (1984).

18. See note 8 and accompanying text.

19. See William L. Cary, "Federalism and Corporate Law: Reflections Upon Delaware," 83 *Yale L. J.* 663 (1974).

20. See, e.g., Ralph K. Winter, "State Law, Shareholder Protection, and the Theory of the Corporation," 6 *J. Leg. Stud.* 251 (1977); Barry D. Baysinger and Henry N. Butler, "The Role of Corporate Law in the Theory of the Firm," 28 *J. L. Econ.* 179 (1985); Roberta Romano, "Law as a Product: Some Pieces of the Incorporation Puzzle," *J. L. Econ. & Org.* 225 (1985); Peter Dodd and Richard Leftwich, "The Market for Corporate Charters: 'Unhealthy Competition' versus Federal Regulation," 53 *J. Bus.* 259 (1980); Daniel R. Fischel, "The 'Race to the Bottom' Revisited: Reflections on Recent Developments in Delaware's Corporation Law." 76 *Nw. U. L. Rev.* 913 (1982). But see Jonathan R. Macey and Geoffrey P. Miller, "Toward an

Interest Group Theory of Delaware Corporate Law," 65 *Tex. L. Rev.* (forthcoming 1987) which argues that managers have some very limited discretion to act to the detriment of investors in choosing a state of incorporation.

21. Michael C. Jensen and William H. Meckling, "Theory of the Firm: Managerial Behavior, Agency Costs, and Ownership Structure," 3 *J. Fin. Econ.* 305 (1976).

22. Several economists have concluded that the widespread assumption that investors have benefited from securities regulation is not supported by the empirical evidence. See, e.g., Susan M. Phillips and J. Richard Zecher, *The SEC and the Public Interest* (1981); Greg A. Jarrell, The Economic Effects of Federal Regulation of the Market for New Security Issues," 24 *J. L. Econ.* 613 (1981); George J. Benston, "Required Disclosure and the Stock Market: An Evaluation of the Securities Exchange Act of 1934," 63 *Am. Econ. Rev.* 132 (1973); George J. Stigler, "Public Regulation of the Securities Markets," 37 *J. Bus.* 117 (1964). For the opposite perspective, see Irwin Friend, Economic and Equity Aspects of Securities Regulation (Working Paper No. 7-82, Rodney L. White Center for Financial Research, University of Pennsylvania 1982). For a review of this evidence, see Frank H. Easterbrook and Daniel R. Fischel, "Mandatory Disclosure and the Protection of Investors," 70 *Va. L. Rev.* 669 (cited in note 12). On the economics of regulation generally, see Stephen Breyer, *Regulation and Its Reform* (1982).

23. See Jarrell, 27 *J. L. Econ.* p. 276 (cited in note 17).

24. Conversely, competition among exchanges in other situations may force exchanges to adopt regulations.

25. Both of these factors are discussed in greater detail later.

26. See Dodd and Leftwich, 53 J. Bus. p. 261 (cited in note 18); Romano, 1 *J. L. Econ. & Org.* 255 (cited in note 18); Baysinger and Butler, 28 *J. L. Econ.* 188 (cited in note 20).

27. See e.g., Sanger and McConnell, 21 *J. Fin. Quant. Anal.* 1 (cited in note 15); Louis W. Ying, Wilbur G. Lewellen, Gary G. Schlarbaum, and Ronald C. Lease, "Stock Exchange Listings and Securities Returns," 12 *J. Fin. Quant. Anal.* 415 (1977); James C. Van Horne, "New Listings and Their Price Behavior," 25 *J. Fin.* 783 (1970). See also McConnell and Sanger, Jan.–Feb. 1984 *Fin. Anal. J.* 34 (cited in note 15).

28. Sanger and McConnell test whether the effect of listing on the NYSE has changed after the introduction of the NASDAQ system. They find

that price response to the announcement to list on the NYSE is positive before and after the introduction of NASDAQ, but statistically significant only in the pre-NASDAQ period. Sanger and McConnell, 21 *J. Fin. Quant. Anal.* 22 (cited in note 15). They conclude that the superiority of the NYSE in providing transactional services has diminished significantly with the introduction of NASDAQ. Ibid., 22–23.

29. See Eugene F. Fama, "Agency Problems and the Theory of the Firm," 88 *J. Pol. Econ.* 288 (1980).

30. For a more complete discussion of voting as a monitoring mechanism, see Frank H. Easterbrook and Daniel R. Fischel, "Voting in Corporate Law," 26 *J. L. Econ.* 395 (1983).

31. These alternative monitoring arrangements are discussed at length in Daniel R. Fischel and Michael Bradley, "The Role of Liability Rules and the Derivative Suit in Corporate Law: A Theoretical and Empirical Analysis," 71 *Cornell L. Rev.* 261 (1986); Easterbrook and Fischel, 70 *Va. l. Rev.* 669 (cited in note 12).

32. See Harry DeAngelo and Linda DeAngelo, "Managerial Ownership of Voting Rights," 14 *J. Fin. Econ.* 33 (1985).

33. See, e.g., Benjamin Klein, Robert G. Crawford, and Armen A. Alchian, "Vertical Integration, Appropriable Rents, and the Competitive Contracting Process," 21 *J. L. Econ.* 297 (1978); Oliver E. Williamson, "Transaction-Cost Economics: The Governance of Contractual Relations," 22 *J. L. Econ.* 233 (1979).

34. See DeAngelo and DeAngelo, 14 *J. Fin. Econ.* p. 33 (cited in note 32).

35. See, e.g., Ronald W. Masulis, "The Effects of Capital Structure Change on Security Prices: A Study of Exchange Offers," 8 *J. Fin. Econ.* 139 (1980). For a sampling of the large economic literature on signaling, see John G. Riley, "Competitive Signalling," 10 *J. Econ. Theory* 174 (1975); Michael Spence, "Job Market Signaling," 87 *Quart. J. Econ.* 355 (1973); Joseph E. Stiglitz, "The Theory of 'Screening' Education and the Distribution of Income," 65 *Am. Econ. Rev.* 283 (1975).

36. On the tension between which strategy is optimal for a particular firm and which is optimal for shareholders as a whole, see Sanford J. Grossman and Oliver D. Hart, "Takeover Bids, the Free-Rider Problem, and the Theory of the Corporation," 11 *Bell J. Econ.* 42 (1980); Frank H. Easterbrook and Daniel R. Fischel, "Auctions and Sunk Costs in Tender Offers," 35 *Stan. L. Rev.* 1 (1982).

37. Eugene F. Fama and Michael C. Jensen, "Agency Problems and Residual Claims," 26 *J. L. Econ.* 327 (1983); Eugene F. Fama and Mi-

chael C. Jensen, "Organizational Forms and Investment Decisions," 14 *J. Fin. Econ.* 101 (1985).

38. I do not discuss here the costs and benefits of debt financing. For a discussion, see Jensen and Meckling, 3 *J. Fin. Econ.* 305 (cited in note 21).

39. The differences between nominal and effective voting rights are emphasized in DeAngelo and DeAngelo, 14 *J. Fin. Econ.* 33 (cited in note 32).

40. Indeed, there were more dual class firms in 1970 than in 1980 and more still in 1960. The decrease in dual class firms over this period is a result of both acquisitions and expiration of the time period for dual class common stock as stipulated in corporate charters. Recently, however, the use of dual class common has become somewhat popular. Since 1980, at least 37 firms have issued limited voting stock, and 23 of these occurred in 1983 or 1984. See M. Megan Partch,"The Creation of a Class of Limited Voting Common Stock and Shareholder Wealth," *J. Fin. Econ.* (forthcoming 1987) (table 1). As of October 1985, approximately 100 of the slightly over 4000 companies traded on NASDAQ (or about 2.5% had multiple classes of common stock. As of July 1984, approximately 50 of the over 900 firms listed on the American Stock Exchange (or about 6%) has two or more classes of common stock outstanding. A handful of firms listed on the NSYE also have adopted dual capitalization pending resolution of the controversy over listing standards on the NYSE. See DeAngelo and DeAngelo, 14 *J. Fin. Econ.* p. 54 (cited in note 32).

41. The most important studies are DeAngelo and DeAngelo, 14 *J. Fin. Econ.* 33 (cited in note 32); Ronald C. Lease, John J. McConnell, and Wayne H. Mikkelson, "The Market Value of Control in Publicly-Traded Corporations," 11 *J. Fin. Econ.* 439 (1983); and Partch, cited in note 40.

42. See DeAngelo and DeAngelo, 14 *J. Fin. Econ.* p. 45 (cited in note 32).

43. It is also true, however, that managers own a large percentage of the outstanding votes (an average of 48.6%) prior to recapitalizations. See Partch, cited in note 40 (table 3).

44. See DeAngelo and DeAngelo, 14 *J. Fin. Econ.* p. 47 (cited in note 32).

45. Ibid., 41.

46. Ibid., 30.

47. Ibid., 41.

48. Approximately one-third of dual class firms issue new equity within one year after the creation of the limited class voting stock. Partch, *J. Fin. Econ.* (cited in note 40) (section

2.4). This figure should be compared with the results of another study that found that only 17% of a random sample of industrial firms actually completed sales of common stock publicly at least once within an eleven-year period. See Wayne H. Mikkelson and M. Megan Partch, "Valuation Effects of Security Offerings and the Issuance Process," 15 *J. Fin. Econ.* 31, 36 (table 2).

49. The frequency with which newly recapitalized dual class firms issue new equity also acts as a safeguard for investors. Because capital markets penalize inefficient arrangements, when owner/managers go to the capital market frequently, their incentive to adopt voting rules that are harmful to investors is reduced.

50. See Lease et al. 11 *J. Fin. Econ.* 439 (cited in note 41). Haim Levy, "Economic Evaluation of Voting Power of Common Stock," 38 *J. Fin.* 79 (1982), provides evidence for the Israel Stock Exchange that is similar to that discussed in this article. DeAngelo and DeAngelo, 14 *J. Fin. Econ.* 33 (cited in note 32), examined forty-five dual class firms, but focused mainly on other characteristics of these firms.

51. Lease et al. 11 *J. Fin. Econ.* at 469 (cited in note 41).

52. DeAngelo and DeAngelo, 14 *J. Fin. Econ.* 33 (cited in note 32).

53. They discovered 30 such events that occurred between 1960 and 1980. Of these, they found no explicit direct or indirect payments in 12 cases. In 6 cases, they found that different compensation, which was difficult to value, was paid to different classes (an example is the sale of a division at book value to a manager). In 8 cases, both classes received equal compensation per share as a result of the acquisition—even though the inferior class had been entitled to a slightly higher dividend payout. Finally, they identified 4 cases in which the superior class received explicit (and often substantial) premiums per share. See DeAngelo and DeAngelo, 14 *J. Fin. Econ.* p. 57 (cited in note 32).

54. The finding of Lease et al. that superior voting shares sell at a small discount when there is a class of voting preferred outstanding is more of a puzzle. The small sample size (only four firms) suggests that their finding may be an aberration. If it is not, one possible explanation is that the value of control in some situations may be *negative.* If the holders of control gained indirect benefits from control in the past, for example, they may face costly legal claims. If a more complicated ownership structure (such as a structure with two classes of common stock and a class of voting preferred) makes costly

legal claims more likely, this may cause superior voting shares to sell at a discount.

55. Partch, cited in note 40. Specifically, Partch examined the changes in wealth experienced by investors on and between certain "event" dates. The event dates are the date of the board of directors' meeting where the proposal is made, the date of the proxy mailing on which the proposal is made public, and the date of the shareholders' meeting on which the proposal is approved.

On the most important day, the day the recapitalization proposal is announced, investors experience a positive and statistically significant return of 1.2%. Investors also experience a positive and statistically significant return on other event dates. The overall return experienced by investors from the time of announcement to the time of approval is negative, but not statistically significant. The overall return from announcement to approval is a less direct test of the wealth effects of creating limited voting stock than the return on event days. The reason is that the interval between announcement and approval necessarily includes events unrelated to the creation of limited voting stock.

56. Significantly, for the entire sample, Partch found that insiders control an average of 48.6% of the votes at the time of the recapitalization.

57. Gregg A. Jarrell, The Stock Price Effects of NYSE Delisting for Violating Corporate Governance Rules (unpublished manuscript on file with *Chicago L. Rev.,* December 1984).

58. Michael C. Jensen and Richard S. Ruback, "The Market for Corporate Control: The Scientific Evidence," 11 *J. Fin Econ.* 5, 10 (1983) summarizes the results of thirteen studies of takeovers.

59. See Michael Bradley, Anand Desai, and E. Harv Kim, "The Rationale Behind Interfirm Tender Offers: Information or Synergy?," 11 *J. Fin. Econ.* 183, 194 (1983).

60. For example, Dann and DeAngelo studied acquisitions, divestitures, issuances of additional voting stock, and repurchases of voting stock by target firms in response to a hostile takeover attempt. They found a statistically significant abnormal return of 2.33% on average when these changes were announced. Larry Y. Dann and Harry DeAngelo, Corporate Financial Policy and Corporate Control: A Study of Defensive Adjustments in Asset and Ownership Structure (Working Paper No. MERC 86-11, U. Rochester Grad. Sch. Mgmt, August 1986). See also Paul H. Malatesta and Ralph A. Walking, Poison Pill Securities: Stockholder Wealth, Profitability, and Ownership Structure (Working Paper, U. Washington September 1986); Larry Y. Dann and Harry DeAngelo, "Standstill Agreements, Privately Negotiated Stock Repurchases, and the Market for Corporate Control," 11 *J. Fin. Econ.* 275 (1983). Some contrary evidence also exists. See Gregg A. Jarrell, "The Wealth Effects of Litigation by Targets: Do Interests Diverge in a Merge?," 28 *J. L. Econ.* 151 (1985). Jarrell finds that when litigation leads to additional bids from rival acquiring firms, target shareholders earn abnormal positive returns.

61. See e.g., Alan Schwartz, "Search Theory and the Tender Offer Auction," 2 *J. L. Econ. & Org.* 229 (1986); Frank H. Easterbrook and Daniel R. Fischel, "The Proper Role of a Target's Management in Responding to a Tender Offer," 94 *Harv. L. Rev.* 1161 (1981).

62. DeAngelo and DeAngelo, 14 *J. Fin. Econ.* p. 53 (cited in note 32).

63. Partch cited in note 40 (section 2.4).

64. Harry DeAngelo, Linda DeAngelo, and Edward M. Rice, "Going Private: Minority Freezeouts and Stockholder Wealth," 27 *J. L. Econ.* 367 (1984).

65. DeAngelo and DeAngelo 14 *J. Fin. Econ.* p. 57 (cited in note 32).

66. It is not clear, however, that actions by a target's management that maximize the price paid per offer necessarily maximize the welfare of shareholders as a class. See note 36 and accompanying text above.

67. In this sense, there is a similarity between dual class common stock and antitakeover amendments that also must be approved by shareholders and generally do not have significant effects on wealth. Regarding the evidence on the effects of antitakeover amendments on shareholders' wealth, see Scott C. Linn and John J. McConnell, "An Empirical Investigation of the Impact of 'Antitakeover' Amendments on Common Stock Prices," 11 *J. Fin. Econ.* 361 (1983); Harry DeAngelo and Edward M. Rice, "Antitakeover Charter Amendments and Stockholder Wealth," 11 *J. Fin. Econ.* 329 (1983).

33

Comment

ROBERT H. MUNDHEIM

I found Professor Seligman's chapter very useful and agree with the conclusion that self-regulatory organizations acting separately cannot reasonably be expected to solve the problem of disparate voting rights for economically equivalent shares of corporate common stock. If a solution needs to be crafted, it should probably apply without regard to the organized public-trading market on which the shares of a company are traded. The solution should rather depend upon the nature of the company and the circumstances surrounding the creation of the voting disparity.

I would like to turn from the question of who should make the decision and focus my remarks on some observations relevant to the formulation of principles designed to shape a solution. The reason we worry about a capital structure which locks control into the hands of those who own a small percentage of a company's equity capital is not because it allows a departure from notions of political democracy. The problem is management accountability, and the need for that is not only to provide for investor protection but also to ensure optimal allocation of resources. History provides numerous examples of what happens in the absence of adequate accountability mechanisms. The experience of the public utility holding company industry in the United States provides one vivid lesson: You will remember that there was massive stealing in this highly pyramided industry.[1] I think that if the voting stock is sufficiently widely held so that management has not locked itself in, then there should not be much concern about a capital structure with nonvoting or light voting stock. Thus, General Motors' creation of a special common stock in the acquisition of Electronic Data Systems should not cause concern.[2] In the discussion of earlier chapters, one author suggested that in other countries (e.g., Japan) alternative accountability mechanisms (lender control and governmental oversight) flourished. To the extent these or other alternative mechanisms are successfully created in the United States, there may be less need to focus on the voting role of shares of common stock as a major accountability mechanism in this country.

We are used to thinking about the inclusion of nonvoting or limited voting rights for stock in the capital structure of closely held companies. The use of such stock encourages the entrepreneur to raise equity capital without threatening his or her control of the business. In addition, the closely held company typically involves parties who seem to know what they are getting into. Should the same considerations apply to a company going public or a public company (a majority of whose stock is owned by the entrepreneur) wishing to raise additional public funds? This model presents, at least at this time, a situation where each potential investor can decide whether or not the investment on the terms offered makes sense. There is no particular pressure to make the investment. Alternatively, one could take the position that any voluntary entry into the public-trading markets crosses the threshold for legitimate public concern about accountability. If entry into the public market represents a bailout of a portion of the controlling stock rather than an addition to the capital of the company, the balance may tip against allowing that bailout to consist of nonvoting or limited voting stock.

Nonvoting or limited voting common stock may also be created where a company seeks to convert a portion of its previously issued common stock into nonvoting or limited voting common stock. This conversion might be effected by offering the holders of the common stock nonvoting or limited voting stock with enhanced dividend rights, in effect, offering to buy the vote of the common stock. This technique was used by Coastal Corporation when it sought to protect itself against an unfriendly takeover bid by concentrating voting control in the hands of management.[3] The rationale for permitting this technique is not that it enhances the capital resources of the enterprise but that shareholders should be able to decide that a secure management can produce better economic results. The question which comes to mind is, How would a rational stockholder act if confronted with an offer to exchange 500 shares of voting stock for 500 shares of nonvoting stock with an enhanced dividend? If the shareholder thinks that a substantial number of other shareholders will accept the offer, he had better accept the offer too or he will be left with stock without an enhanced dividend and a vote which has no value. Thus, there is a pressure to accept the offer, and there may not be an undistorted choice for the shareholder.

Suppose, however, that the exchange would not occur unless a majority of the shareholders voted for it. (A shareholder vote will be needed if the nonvoting stock has to be authorized.) Would that vote embody an informed and free choice? The answer to that question turns on how intelligently proxies are voted. Professor Seligman has already related his concerns about the voting process. To the extent that proxies are not voted intelligently, a shareholder may continue to be faced with a distorted choice.

The use of nonvoting and light voting stock also focuses attention on the appropriateness of allowing the payment of a premium for the transfer of controlling shares of a corporation. If control is lodged in the holder of 1% of the common stock of a company, a buyer wishing to acquire control will likely pay a substantial premium to the owner of that 1%. The buyer will, of course, have to recapture the premium. The theory is that the buyer would do so by making all the equity shares more valuable. However, where the new controller owns only a small fraction of the company's equity, the task of enhancing the value of every share enough to cover the premium becomes very difficult, and there will be increasing temptation for the control group improperly to divert corporate income and opportunities to itself. In some cases there has been an attempt to meet this problem by providing that the super voting shares lose their super vote when they are transferred. Thus, a buyer will have to buy the super voting stock and a substantial amount of the normal voting stock to acquire control, thus decreasing the temptation to divert disproportionate portions of the corporate earnings stream to itself. Of course, the potential acquirer will have to persuade the holder of super voting shares to sell and will likely pay a substantial premium to that holder to effect the purchase of the company. Because control is lodged in a clearly identifiable segment of the shareholders, this situation dramatizes the much debated question of the fairness of allowing a segment of the shareholders to pocket the premium frequently paid for the transfer of control.

My final observation concerns the growing complexity of corporate capital structures. The introduction of nonvoting and light voting stock into those capital structures makes them more complex and difficult to understand. The modern capital markets appear to delight in increasingly complex financial instruments, but some observers (including myself) worry about this trend because we doubt that investors or companies fully understand the rights and obligations created. The process of education can be expensive and painful.

NOTES

1. See Public Utility Holding Co. Act of 1937 Sec. 1(b)(2) and the investigatory reports referred to in Section 1(b) of the Act.

2. For a description of the special common stock, see Johnson, "The Use of Special Common Stock in Acquisitions," in *Thirteenth Annual University of California Securities Regulation Institute,* Vol. II (January 1986).

3. See Hector, "The Flap Over Super-Shares," *Fortune,* September 16, 1985, 114.

34

Comment

A. A. SOMMER, JR.

Not surprisingly, Professor Seligman has presented a scholarly, well-documented, well-thought-through analysis of a very difficult problem—the place, if any, of multiple classes of common stock in the capital structure of a publicly held company.

As Professor Seligman indicates, the problem is hardly a new one. He traces the history of the New York Stock Exchange's involvement from 1926 when, in response to Professor Ripley's biting criticism of entrenchment, the exchange took its first steps toward the prohibition of such capital arrangements. However, questions of the voting rights of holders of common stock antedate those events considerably. From the earliest days of corporations in England there has been discussion of the extent to which holders of common stock should be permitted to vote.[1] In the early days of the republic Alexander Hamilton, in reporting on a proposal for a national bank, stated the problems with both one-share, one-vote and one-shareholder, one-vote arrangements:

A vote for each share renders a combination between a few principal stockholders, to monopolize the powers and benefits of the bank, too easy. An equal vote to each stockholder . . . allows not that degree of weight to large stockholders which it is reasonable they should have, and which, perhaps, their security, and that of the bank, require. A prudent mean is to be preferred.[2]

The solution to his dilemma was a provision, commonly adopted in those days, placing a maximum on the number of votes a shareholder could cast regardless of the number of shares held or, in the alternative, "scaling" the vote—e.g., one vote per share up to 10, one per 2 shares up to 20, one per 10 up to 50, and no votes for shares held over 50.[3]

The *ultimate* foundation of the notion that Professor Seligman expresses that holders of common stock should have one vote for each share held is obscure. There is some suggestion that the root lies in the political axiom that each voter in a political election has one vote regardless of whatever other characteristics he may have—wealth, position, inheritance. There is no necessary nexus between this proposition and the idea of one share, one vote; in fact, a stronger case using this analogy could be made for the idea of one shareholder, one vote.

Moreover, it clearly does not lie in the belief that the *investors* in a corporation should per se have the ultimate control. Bondholders are investors in an enterprise, and they are rarely given a vote.[4] Moving to the equity part of the ledger, usually preferred shareholders whose holdings often differ from common stock only in dividend and liquidation preference are not given a vote, and no voice is raised in protest. Exactly *why* another class of stock often distinguishable only because of the absence of a liquidation preference should be entitled to a vote is obscure. Is it because of the residual nature of the common, the fact that it is only entitled to a distribution in liquidation after all creditors' and preferred holders' claims are satisfied? Is it because the common stockholders are the ultimate risk takers in the enterprise? What of a preferred that is entitled to a preference in liquidation, after which it is entitled to participate with the common in the residue?

Apart from these puzzlers, the issue has broader implications that bring into the spotlight smoldering controversies and problems. While popular lore has it that the Civil War was over the continuation of slavery in the United States, historians recognize that the broader issues were the nature of the political union that bound the states together, the extent of state sovereignty, and even more profoundly, what it means to be a human being.

So in this case the issue of one share, one vote poses a host of other issues, and how one thinks it should be dealt with depends to some extent upon the beliefs one has with regard to these deeper issues. Among those issues are the following:

1. To what extent should the federal government and to what extent should the state governments have the final authority over such matters as the capitalization and more particularly the allocation of power in publicly held companies?
2. What is the proper role of securities exchanges (and quotation systems) at the present time?
3. What is the proper role of the SEC with respect to corporate governance?
4. Are hostile struggles for corporate control desirable for the economy and society? (A subsidiary question, What should be the proper role of directors and management in such contests? is largely answered by the position one takes on the larger question.)

There are a host of other questions which might be addressed, but let's focus on these four.

The first question involves the capital structure of corporations and the allocation of power among constituencies in the corporation, which historically have been a matter of state law. Notwithstanding proposals for federal incorporation of corporations (with varying degrees of size suggested as the threshold for requiring such) that date back to the constitutional convention,[5] with the exception of a few corporations incorporated under a specific act of Congress,[6] every corporation is incorporated under state law. Every effort to mandate federal incorporation has been opposed as an infringement on states' prerogatives and an inappropriate intrusion into the internal affairs of corporations.[7] Virtually every state incorporation law permits variations on the one-share one-vote pattern, and the courts in interpreting these statutes have afforded corporations broad latitude in designing voting structures.[8]

Thus, many see any action by the federal government—either directly by legislative mandate, as proposed by Senator D'Amato[9] and Congressman Dingell,[10] or by the SEC under the authority discussed by Professor Seligman, or indirectly by the SEC through its authority over self-regulatory organizations—as a contradiction of hallowed and historic doctrines. Many would regard such a federal intervention as the "camel's nose under the tent" which would culminate in federal incorporation.

Interestingly, the SEC's Advisory Committee on Tender Offers justified a number of intrusions into areas historically the responsibility of the states on the grounds that takeovers "take place in a national securities market."[11] This rationale could, of course, justify a good deal of federal legislation or regulation of matters now thought to lie within the domains of the states, including, one would guess, prohibiting the trading in any market, *or perhaps in any way as long as jurisdictional means were used,* of any common share having less than equal voting rights with other common stock.

A second broad question is the role of the organized markets today. Do they have a role in regulating and disciplining the issuers whose securities are traded on them? In 1926 when the New York Stock Exchange first wrestled with the voting problem, the exchange was "the only game in town." It was the preeminent market, and no company aspiring to prestige and reputation would want for a moment to be traded elsewhere. The only alternatives were the New York Curb Exchange, only lately physically removed from the curb, a few little regionals, and virtually no over-the-counter market. Thus when, as Professor Seligman describes it, the public demanded action to stop the abuses of nonvoting common stock, the exchange was the only force capable of stopping it. The exchange at that time was the only institutional means of enforcing standards on publicly held corporations: State corporation laws were increasingly permissive; state securities regulators were a nullity; there was no federal agency or officer with power over the general course of corporate conduct; and shareholders consisted almost entirely of ill-informed individuals who had no effective means of banding together to effect changes in management or the conduct of the corporation's affairs.

But all of those circumstances that demanded that the exchange act to defuse the popular clamor are changed or nullified: There is federal legislation and a federal agency that effectively mandate that shareholders be informed when they are asked to vote; blue-sky regulators are increasingly a force to be reckoned with in the area of corporate governance;[12] shareholdings are increasingly concentrated in the hands of institutions which are ever more sensitive to the protection of shareholder rights. Is there then any need for the exchanges to seek through listing requirements to impose governance mandates on corporations? As a matter of fact, many of the historical requirements of the exchanges have been superseded by federal mandate, e.g., the furnishing of an annual report to shareholders.

When the exchange's Subcommittee on Shareholder Participation and Qualitative Listing Standards put the question of whether the exchange should continue to impose requirements on listed companies to ensure shareholder participation to listed companies, member firms, corporate attorneys, legal educators, institutional investors, and blue-sky administrators, 58% of the respondents answered no, with 68% of the listed companies so answering.[13]

Exchanges arose as convenient, efficient, and economical means of trading securities. Only gradually did they impose standards on the companies whose securities were traded on them, and these standards appear to have been the default by-products of a combination of public demand for responsible conduct by corporations and the absence of any public authority willing and able to respond to the demand, plus a fear in the financial and corporate community that failure to respond would lead to an expansion of governmental interference in business. Many believe that with the circumstances that occasioned their involvement in corporate governance the province of other effective agencies, they now should revert to their original role—and no more.

If markets are regarded as continuing to have a role in corporate governance, the question then is posed: Where and how should the limits of their activity be drawn? It is as logical to say that the NYSE should ban from the exchange companies which adopt "poison pills" as it is to say they should bar companies with two classes of common. It is a small step to say listed companies should not be permitted to pay "greenmail" or provide "golden parachutes" without shareholder approval. In 1968 the exchange took note with alarm of the onset of supermajority and similar charter provisions to protect against hostile takeovers and intimated it would consider listing requirements aimed at such practices. This was met with such protest from listed companies that the exchange beat a hasty retreat, and nothing more was heard of the suggestion.[14]

The difficulties of drawing a line delineating the sort of additional corporate defensive practices that should be prohibited will probably never be encountered, since there appears to be no disposition on the part of either the exchange or its listed companies to extend the exchange's listing standards in that direction.[15]

The third question is the role of the SEC in corporate governance. Commonly accepted is that the commission's role is limited to mandating disclosures that bear upon corporate governance and only pe- ripherally beyond that. Through commis- sioner jawboning, imaginative settlements mandating corporate reform,[16] and threats that it might seek a broader legislative mandate,[17] the commission has unques- tionably had a great influence on the way corporations conduct themselves. Is there a power and opportunity for the commis- sion to go further?

Many, fearing that the one-share, one- vote controversy is a harbinger of compe- tition among markets that will steadily erode listing standards, urge that the com- mission forestall such a course by using its powers, particularly those under Section 19(c) of the Securities Exchange Act of 1934, which gives the commission the power to compel any self-regulatory orga- nization to adopt any rule the commission mandates as long as it is "in furtherance of the purposes of this title." Whether this section, or the others cited by Professor Se- ligman, would support an exercise of com- mission authority to impose a one-share, one-vote listing standard is not free of doubt. At a symposium in 1975 soon after the 1975 amendments to the 1934 act were enacted, the following dialogue occurred between Lee Pickard, then director of the SEC's Division of Market Regulation, and Stephen Paradise, then the assistant coun- sel to the Senate Banking, Housing and Urban Affairs Committee which had had jurisdiction over the amendments:

Mr. Pickard: Section 19(c) of the 1934 Act, as recently amended, gives the Commission the authority, by rule, to supplement, abrogate or modify the rules of self-regulatory bodies re- garding their exchange activities, and also I think regarding NASDAQ, as would be in the public interest and for the protection of investors.

It is that sort of jurisdictional nexis to which I am alluding in suggesting this analysis. I am not trying to interpret the law today. I want to disclaim that immediately. I am just trying to pursue this matter from a different direction.

Stephen Paradise, Washington, D.C.: In drafting these new sections of the law which give the SEC power over exchange rules, I can tell you there never was any intent to go into this area. The Congress would look at it as a grave breach of Congressional intent, and that is all I intend to say on that.[18]

Apart from its power, what properly should be the role of the commission in this situation? Clearly, Chairman Shad be- lieves it is a problem which the market and SROs should solve,[19] and he has urged the SROs strongly to do so, thus far without success. Should the commission seek to go further? The answer depends upon how broadly one conceives the commission's mandate in the area of corporate gover- nance. The commission has clearly used its disclosure mandate aggressively to require the most fulsome and self-abnegating dis- closure by issuers proposing to authorize and issue common stock with inferior vot- ing rights.[20] Should it seek to go further? Has it a responsibility to thwart the "race to the bottom," if such there may be, among the markets to gain and retain listings?

Finally, there is the broad question of one's attitude toward tender offers in gen- eral. If one believes that the hostile tender offers are for the most part bred in hell and are inflicting grievous harm on the body politic and economic, and if one is exas- perated at the seeming unwillingness of the Congress and the commission to take ac- tion to stem them, leaving beleaguered managements to fend for themselves, then certainly a recapitalization that vests vot- ing control in management is seen as a means of accomplishing a social good—the frustration of efforts to take over control of the company. On the other hand, of course, those like Professor Dan Fischel, SEC Chief Economist Gregg Jarrell, and Judge Frank Easterbrook, who see in tender offers a lubricant to assist in the most effective allocation of resources, be- lieve that anything which hinders tender of- fers is the enemy of such an allocation.

A few brief concluding remarks. Often lost sight of is the fact that no dual-class common stock configuration is adopted without approval of shareholders, and in most recent cases the nonmanagement shareholders have voted overwhelmingly for the necessary charter amendments.[21] As mentioned, the SEC requires that full information about the proposal must be furnished to the shareholders.[22] Why, one may ask, if the shareholders wish to abdicate their voting rights, should anyone thwart them? There is a peculiar anomaly here: The defenders of the exchange's present standards uphold the importance of shareholders' voting rights but contend they should not have the right to vote to give away or reduce the significance of that vote. If one denigrates the significance of the shareholder vote with the dismissal, "Shareholders always vote with management" or "Shareholders don't know what they're doing," then the anomaly is even more startling, for all this talk of defending the shareholders' right to vote would appear to be an effort to preserve to them something they don't know how to use anyway! If they don't know how to use it to protect something as seemingly precious as the right to vote, why should there be so much concern with preserving it?

Finally, Professor Seligman relies heavily upon a number of studies to establish that the prices of the securities of companies with two classes of common suffer from this circumstance. First, many of the studies that conclude there is a differential in the pricing of the lesser voting and the full voting common adverse to the former analyze cases where the *only* difference between the classes is in voting rights.[23] In most recent instances where companies have recapitalized, the lesser voting stock receives a higher dividend than the other voting stock. This result undoubtedly accounts for the fact that several other studies indicate that the two classes generally trade at a parity.[24] Second, analyses purporting to show the price at which a stock would sell were circumstance A not present are in my estimation oversimplifications. Innumerable variables effect the price of a stock, and as yet, no one seems to have found a foolproof way of filtering out a single variable and relating it to price.

The problem of one share, one vote will in all probability not subside quickly. The broader questions discussed here will be around even longer, of that we may be sure.

NOTES

1. Ratner, "The Government of Business Corporations: Critical Reflections on the Rule of 'One Share, One Vote,'" 56 *Cornell L. Rev.* 1, 3 (1970).
2. Quoted in 2 Davis, *Essays in the Earlier History of American Corporations,* (1917), 323.
3. See *Campbell and Voss v. Poultney, Ellicott & Co.,* 6 Md Ct. App. 94 (1834); Act of June 16, 1834, No. 194, ¶ 3 [1835–1836] Pa. Laws 800.
4. See McDaniel, "Bondholders and Corporate Governance," 41 *Bus. L.* 413, 439 (February 1986).
5. Schwartz, "Federal Chartering of Corporations: A Proposal," 61 *Georgetown L. J.* 89, 125 (1972).
6. R. Nader, M. Green, and J. Seligman, *Taming the Giant Corporation* (1976), 65.
7. Schwartz, "Federal Chartering of Corporations: Constitutional Challenges," 61 *Georgetown L. J.* 123, 128 (1972).
8. See, e.g.,, *Providence & Worcester Co. v. Baker,* 378 A.2d 121 (Del. 1977).
9. S. 1314, 99th Cong., 1st Sess. 1985.
10. H.R. 2783, 99th Cong., 1st Sess. 1985.
11. SEC Advisory Committee on Tender Offers, *Report of Recommendations* (1983), 15.
12. The North American Securities Administrators have expressed themselves recently with respect to a number of governance issues, including one share, one vote and the NASD proposals on corporate governance for issuers of National Market System securities. 18 BNA Sec. Reg. & L. Rep. 9 (January 3, 1986).
13. *Initial Report of the Subcommittee on Shareholder Participation and Qualitative Listing Standards—Dual Class Capitalization* (January 3, 1985).
14. Memorandum, re: New York Stock Exchange Policies Regarding Corporate Responsibility for Legal Advisory Committee (1984).
15. *Initial Report,* note 13, p. 12.
16. See M. I. Steinberg, *Corporate Internal Affairs* (1983), 13.
17. *Staff Report on Corporate Accountability,* SEC Division of Corporation Finance, (1980), K–23.
18. 31 *Bus. L.* 1096 (1976).
19. *Impact of Corporate Takeovers,* hearings before the Subcommittee on Securities of the Senate Committee on Banking, Housing and Urban Affairs, 99th Cong., 1st Sess. 1985, 234; Klott, "A Fight over Unequal Stock," *N.Y. Times,* October 22, 1985.
20. Sec. Ex. Act Rel. No. 15230 (October 13, 1978).

21. For example, the recapitalization of Dow Jones & Co., Inc., to provide for two classes of common stock was approved by more than 70% of the shares not held by members of the Bancroft family, which held more than 50% of the outstanding common stock. Coastal Corporation submitted to its shareholders a proposal to authorize two classes of common stock having a voting differential of 100 to 1; 13,280,648 of the shares voting approved the proposal. (Management held 16.6% of the outstanding stock.)

22. *Impact of Corporate Takeovers,* note 19.

23. See Seligman chapter in this volume (note 103).

24. Unpublished studies by investment bankers.

Index

Directors
  in agency model of corporations, 343
  Australian law on, 415–17
  British courts on, 409–10
  business judgment rule of, 342
  Canadian courts on, 413–14
  Delaware courts on, 406–7, 428–29*n*
  economic theory on relationship between
    management and, 45
  Jensen on, 362, 364*n*
  management control over, 214
  nonshareholders compensated by, 111, 132*n*
  outside, 86, 123*n*
  removal of, 410
  transfer powers of, 457–58
Discriminatory self-tenders, SEC rule on, 93, 124*n*
Disequilibrium contracting, 166
Disproportionate voting stocks, 466–82
Diversification
  free cash flow theory of takeovers on, 333
  in petroleum industry, 332
  as takeover motive, 247
Divestitures, 97
  criticisms of, 319
  deconglomeration as, 165
  profitability of sold-off units, 199–201
  in reconfiguring assets, 144
Dividends
  Australian law on, 416
  cash flow and, 322
  default of, 467
  free cash flow theory of takeovers on, 333
  from nonvoting common stock, 522
  stock market prices and, 328
  used to avoid takeovers, 87
Dodd, Peter, 191*n*, 244, 246
  Australian study by, 427*n*
  on postmerger performance, 189–90
  on takeover effects on shareholders, 186–87
Dodge Brothers, Inc., 469, 471
Donaldson, Gordon, 84, 120*n*, 127*n*, 349*n*
  on goals of businesses, 148
  on implicit contracts, 132*n*
Double-auction markets, 35
Douglas, William O., 466
Dow Jones & Company, Inc., 491*n*, 529*n*
Drexel Burnham Lambert Inc.
  junk bonds created by, 10–11
  junk bonds underwritten by, 117*n*
  secondary market for junk bonds by, 124–25*n*
Drucker, Peter, 95
Dual class common stock
  corporate control and, 473–76
  federal laws on, 477–79
  Fischel on stock exchange regulation of, 499–516
  history of, 468–73
  Sommer's comment on, 527–28
  state laws on, 476–77
  Washington Post's, 14
Dubey, P., 39–40, 43

Earnings, excessive retention of, 84
Earnings-price ratio, market fads and, 59, 66*n*
Easterbrook, Frank H., 86–87, 119*n*, 350*n*, 527
  on implicit contracts, 131*n*, 132*n*
  on managerial passivity, 114, 134*n*

  on pressure to tender shares, 384–85
  on stock market prices, 213
Eckbo, B. E., 244, 316, 394*n*, 355
Economic Recovery Tax Act (ERTA; U.S., 1981),
    237–38*n*, 275, 303
Economic rents, 322, 349*n*
Economic surplus, 138–39. *See also* Value creation
Economic theory. *See also* Equilibrium theory
  agency theory and nonsymmetric information, 43–
    44
  based on contracts, 110
  civil law and, 32, 33
  on corporations, 159–62
  efficient-markets hypothesis in, 71, 73*n*
  on gains from takeovers, 253
  of general equilibrium, 34–41
  on government, 106
  on hostile takeovers, 80
  implicit contracts in, 156–57
  Keynes on acceptance of, 260–61
  limitations upon, 44–49
  market fads and fashions in, 58
  portfolio theory, 41–42
  shareholders' interests in takeovers in, 79
  shareholder sovereignty in, 107
  on takeovers, 81–100
  of value creation, 137–40
Edelman, Asher, 116*n*
Edwards, Franklin R., 5, 69–70
Efficiency
  of conglomerates, 89
  in corporate acquisition markets, 384
  debt in motivation for, 322–23
  of hostile takeovers, 211–35
  manager's conflicts of interest and, 340
  in markets, 42–43, 71, 73*n*
  Pareto, 133–34*n*
  in tax implications, 284–85, 293
  in tender offer choices, 372–73
Efficient-markets hypothesis, 71, 73*n*, 260, 320, 349*n*
Eger, C. E., 247, 248
Eisenberg, Melvin, A., 5
  on golden parachutes, 155–58
Ekern, S., 38
Electronic Data Systems (EDS), 145–46, 367, 465,
    521
Elgers, P. T., 337
Ellert, J. C., 183
Employees
  effect of junk bonds on, 151
  impact of corporate risk upon, 105–6
  impact of takeovers on, 262
  implicit contracts between management and, 156–
    58
  renegotiating contracts with, 143
  risks to, in takeovers, 123*n*
  severance compensation for, 109–10
  in TWA takeover, 112
Employee stock ownership plans (ESOPs), 108, 112,
    130*n*, 133*n*
England. *See* Britain
Equilibrium theory, 34–36
  competitive, 50
  efficient markets in, 43
  limitations of, 48–49
  noncooperative, 50–51

Litigation. *See also* Legal issues
  "Clean-up" tender offers to avoid, 246
"Lobster traps," 443
Local communities, 106, 129*n*
Lockup options, 407
London Stock Exchange, 399, 400, 440, 443
Long, J., 38, 219
Loomis, Carol, 236*n*
Lorenzo, Frank, 143, 146
Lorsch, J. W., 148
Loss, L., 496*n*
Losses
  for acquiring firms, 255–56
  profits simultaneous with, 364*n*
  tax benefits in mergers of, 356
  tax carryovers of, 286–93, 304, 366
  tax credits and, 306–8
  in tax hypothesis of takeovers, 247
Lowenstein, Louis, 6, 45, 46
  Bradley and Jarrell's comment on, 257
  discussion comments of, 265, 268
  on efficiency effects of hostile takeovers, 211–35
  on hostile takeovers and junk bond financing, 16, 18–21, 23, 24, 26, 27
  on incentive effects of debt, 350*n*
  Law's comment on, 260–62
  legislative proposal of, 48
  on monitoring of institutional investors, 127*n*
Lubatkin, Michael, 141

McConnell, John J., 247
  on effects of NYSE listing, 518*n*
  on gains for bidding firms, 316
  on myopic-markets hypothesis, 320
  on petroleum industry exploration, 330
  on stock market price response to capital expenditures, 337
  on stock market price response to takeover activity, 241–43
  on synergy hypothesis, 246
  on value of stock voting rights, 475–76
McEachern, W., 121*n*
Mackay, C., 57
Macklin, Gordon, 473
Magenheim, Ellen B., 6, 73*n*, 217
  Bradley and Jarrell's comment on, 254–56
  Jensen's discussion comment on, 265
  Law's comment on, 261
  on shareholders in acquiring firms, 171–90
Majluf, N. S., 322
Malatesta, P. H., 187, 189–90, 344
Malkiel, B. G., 57, 121*n*
Management
  "Abusive defensive tactics" by, 442
  accountability of, 46
  acting on inside information by, 72
  control of corporations by, 493*n*
  corporate restructuring not initiated by, 69
  directors acting in interest of, 342
  discretion of, 159–60, 162
  economic theory on relationship between directors and, 45
  hubris of, 249–50, 267
  in implicit contracts, 110
  in inefficient-management hypothesis, 246

  in managerialist model of firms, 87–88
  market value and, 47
  moral hazard problem for, 101–2
  responsibilities of, 138
  retained in takeovers, 237*n*
  risk imposed upon, by shareholders, 152
  shareholders represented by, 232
  shareholders' voting to monitor, 506–7
  stock repurchases by, 341
  stock voting rights and, 479–80
  takeovers to replace, 213
  of target firms, veto power given to, 388
  value-creation responsibilities of, 139–40
  management self-interest hypothesis, 248–49
Managerialism, 160
  model of firms in, 87–88
Managers
  in agency model of corporations, 343
  aspiration levels and risks taken by, 102–3
  cash flow and conflicts between shareholders and, 321–22
  conflicts of interest in, 339–40
  conflicts between interests of shareholders and, 78–83, 150, 155, 213–14
  corporations controlled by, 473–74
  divestiture decisions made by, 98–99
  employment of, after takeovers, 78
  fiduciary duty versus implicit contracting of, 110–12
  firm-specific human capital of, 508–9
  firms with dual class common stock controlled by, 511–12
  future corporate relationships of, 112–13
  golden parachutes for, 130–31*n*, 153, 155–58, 340–41
  high corporate debt used by, 362
  "hostile" and "friendly" takeovers defined by, 147
  in hubris hypothesis, 249
  impact of corporate risk upon, 105–6
  labor market for, 107–10, 236*n*, 261, 317
  layoffs of, 117–18*n*
  in management self-interest hypothesis, 248
  in managerialist model of firms, 87–88
  market discipline on, 87
  mergers and performance of, 194–209
  movement between firms of, 91
  nonproductive use of, 363
  in "race to the bottom" thesis, 504
  reductions in, 151
  risks to, 159–66
  short-sighted behavior of, 319–21
  status of, in hostile takeovers, 106–7
  strip financing and, 329
  takeovers to discipline, 253–54
Mandatory buy-outs, 420–21
  in Britain, 438, 441, 445–48
Mandelker, G., 183–86, 191*n*, 335
Manne, Henry G.
  on interests of managers, 236*n*
  on managerial compensation, 121*n*
  on market for corporate control, 231
  on mergers to increase efficiency, 195, 215
  on stock market prices as measurement of efficiency, 212–13
  on takeovers to discipline managers, 253